Enterprise and Small Business

Principles, Practice and Policy

PEARSON

At Pearson, we take learning personally. Our courses and resources are available as books, online and via multi-lingual packages, helping people learn whatever, wherever and however they choose.

We work with leading authors to develop the strongest learning experiences, bringing cutting-edge thinking and best learning practice to a global market. We craft our print and digital resources to do more to help learners not only understand their content, but to see it in action and apply what they learn, whether studying or at work.

Pearson is the world's leading learning company. Our portfolio includes Penguin, Dorling Kindersley, the Financial Times and our educational business, Pearson International. We are also a leading provider of electronic learning programmes and of test development, processing and scoring services to educational institutions, corporations and professional bodies around the world.

Every day our work helps learning flourish, and wherever learning flourishes, so do people.

To learn more please visit us at: www.pearson.com/uk

Enterprise and Small Business

Principles, Practice and Policy

Third Edition

Edited by
Sara Carter and Dylan Jones-Evans

Harlow, England • London • New York • Boston • San Francisco • Toronto • Sydney • Auckland • Singapore • Hong Kong
Tokyo • Seoul • Taipei • New Delhi • Cape Town • São Paulo • Mexico City • Madrid • Amsterdam • Munich • Paris • Milan

Pearson Education Limited
Edinburgh Gate
Harlow
Essex CM20 2JE
England

and Associated Companies throughout the world

Visit us on the World Wide Web at:
www.pearson.com/uk

First published 2000
Second edition published 2006
Third edition published 2012

© Pearson Education Limited 2000, 2012

ISBN 978-0-273-72610-4

British Library Cataloguing-in-Publication Data
A catalogue record for this book is available from the British Library

Library of Congress Cataloguing-in-Publication Data
A catalog record for this book is available from the Library of Congress

10 9 8 7 6 5 4 3 2 1
16 15 14 13 12

Typeset in 10/12pt Sabon by 35
Printed in Great Britain by Henry Ling Ltd, at the Dorset Press, Dorchester, Dorset

Contents

List of contributors   xiii
Publisher's acknowledgements   xvi

1 Introduction   1
Sara Carter and Dylan Jones-Evans

    1.1 Background   1
    1.2 The purpose of this book   2
    1.3 Structure of this book   5

Part 1 ENTREPRENEURSHIP   7

2 The evolution of entrepreneurship theory   9
Luke Pittaway

    2.1 Introduction   9
    2.2 Learning objectives   10
    2.3 Economic perspectives   10
    2.4 Early psychological and sociological perspectives   16
    2.5 Contemporary thought   18
    2.6 Chapter summary   25
    Questions   26
    Weblinks   26

3 Entrepreneurship and economic development   27
Robert Huggins and Nick Williams

    3.1 Introduction   27
    3.2 Learning objectives   27
    3.3 Entrepreneurship and economic development   28
    3.4 Regional and local perspectives   31
    3.5 Entrepreneurship and endogenous development   34
    3.6 Knowledge spillovers and entrepreneurship   36
    3.7 Culture, social capital and entrepreneurial places   38
    3.8 Entrepreneurship policy   41
    3.9 Chapter summary   44
    Questions   45
    Weblinks   45

4 Government and small businesses   46
Robert J. Bennett

4.1	Introduction	46
4.2	Learning objectives	46
4.3	The role of government	46
4.4	The case for government action for SMEs	49
4.5	Finding a niche for government action	53
4.6	Limitations on government action	55
4.7	Possibilities for targeting	56
4.8	Forms of government action for small businesses	58
4.9	National policy	59
4.10	Sector policy	66
4.11	Local policy	67
4.12	A case study of SME advice and support: Business Link and LEPs	72
4.13	Chapter summary	76
	Questions	77
	Weblinks	77

5 The real world of the entrepreneur   78
Friederike Welter

5.1	Introduction	78
5.2	Learning objectives	78
5.3	The concept of context	79
5.4	Theorising (about) context	80
5.5	The social world: moving from networks towards families and households	83
5.6	The sociospatial world: a bridge between the social and the societal contexts	85
5.7	The institutional world: between laws, societal values and unwritten codes of conduct	87
5.8	Outlook	90
5.9	Chapter summary	91
	Questions	91
	Weblinks	91

Part 2 THE ENTREPRENEURIAL PROCESS   93

6 The entrepreneurial process   95
Per Davidsson

6.1	Introduction	95
6.2	Learning objectives	95
6.3	Some steps in the entrepreneurial process	96
6.4	The discovery process	99
6.5	The exploitation process	102

6.6   The relationship between discovery and exploitation   106
6.7   The effectuation process: an alternative entrepreneurial logic?   111
6.8   Which process is better?   113
6.9   Chapter summary   117
Questions   118
Weblinks   119

7   Entrepreneurial opportunities   120
Dimo Dimov

7.1   Introduction   120
7.2   Learning objectives   121
7.3   Different levels of thinking about opportunities   121
7.4   Typologies of opportunities   124
7.5   The person behind an opportunity   125
7.6   The process of opportunity recognition   127
7.7   Contextual and social influences on idea generation   131
7.8   Chapter summary   133
Questions   134
Weblinks   134

8   Effectuation and entrepreneurship   135
Saras Sarasvathy

8.1   Introduction   135
8.2   Learning objectives   135
8.3   Entrepreneurial expertise   136
8.4   Non-predictive control: the overall logic of effectuation   137
8.5   The five principles of effectuation   138
8.6   The dynamics of effectuation in the start-up process   144
8.7   The implications of effectuation for the performance of
       firm and entrepreneur   147
8.8   Chapter summary   150
Questions   151
Weblinks   151

9   The psychology of the entrepreneur   152
Frédéric Delmar and Frédérik C. Witte

9.1   Introduction   152
9.2   Learning objectives   152
9.3   The challenges of a psychological approach   153
9.4   Development of the research field: from traits to cognition   154
9.5   Individual characteristics of entrepreneurs and
       entrepreneurial behaviour   164
9.6   Cognitive models of entrepreneurial behaviour   170
9.7   Chapter summary   178

| | Questions | 179 |
| | Weblinks | 179 |

10   Entrepreneurial failure · 180
James E. Dever

10.1	Introduction	180
10.2	Learning objectives	180
10.3	What is business failure?	181
10.4	Antecedents and perceptions of business failure	186
10.5	Entrepreneurial risk	187
10.6	Liquidation or bankruptcy	189
10.7	Fear of failure or comparative optimism	191
10.8	Exit strategies	191
10.9	Chapter summary	193
	Questions	194
	Weblinks	195

Part 3 TYPES OF ENTREPRENEURSHIP · · · · · · · · · · · · · · 197

11   Ethnicity and entrepreneurship · · · · · · · · · · · · · · · · 199
Monder Ram, Giles Barrett and Trevor Jones

11.1	Introduction	199
11.2	Learning objectives	199
11.3	Ethnicity and enterprise	199
11.4	Ethnic minority enterprises: an international perspective	200
11.5	Ethnic minority business activity: the British experience	204
11.6	The business entry decision	206
11.7	Family and co-ethnic labour	208
11.8	Restricted spatial markets	210
11.9	Funding ethnic minority enterprises	211
11.10	Ethnic minority businesses and enterprise support	213
11.11	Millennial shifts	214
11.12	Chapter summary	215
	Questions	217
	Weblinks	217

12   Gender and entrepreneurship · · · · · · · · · · · · · · · · · 218
Sara Carter, Susan Marlow and Dinah Bennett

12.1	Introduction	218
12.2	Learning objectives	218
12.3	Gender and enterprise	219
12.4	The growth of female entrepreneurship	220
12.5	The characteristics and experiences of female entrepreneurs	221
12.6	The management and financing of female-owned businesses	224

12.7   The performance of female-owned firms   227
12.8   Looking to the future: addressing neglect and advancing debate   229
12.9   Chapter summary   230
Questions   231
Weblinks   231

13   Family businesses   232

Carole Howorth and Eleanor Hamilton

13.1   Introduction   232
13.2   Learning objectives   232
13.3   Family businesses   233
13.4   Family firms throughout the world   236
13.5   Theories of family firms   237
13.6   Gender relations in family businesses   245
13.7   Entrepreneurship and innovation in family businesses   246
13.8   Succession   248
13.9   Chapter summary   249
Questions   250
Weblinks   251

14   Habitual entrepreneurs   252

Mike Wright, Paul Westhead and Deniz Ucbasaran

14.1   Introduction   252
14.2   Learning objectives   253
14.3   Defining habitual entrepreneurship   253
14.4   The habitual entrepreneur phenomenon   255
14.5   Resources and capabilities   258
14.6   Performance and strategy   261
14.7   Policy and practitioner implications   263
14.8   Unresolved issues   264
14.9   Chapter summary   266
Questions   267
Weblinks   267

15   Technical entrepreneurship   268

Niall G. MacKenzie and Dylan Jones-Evans

15.1   Introduction   268
15.2   Learning objectives   269
15.3   Defining technical entrepreneurship   269
15.4   Previous literature   270
15.5   Methodologies for analysis   271
15.6   The development of technical entrepreneurship   273
15.7   A typology of technical entrepreneurship by background
       and experience   279

15.8   Examples of technical entrepreneurs   282
15.9   Policy and technical entrepreneurship   285
15.10   Chapter summary   287
Questions   288
Weblinks   288

16 Social entrepreneurship

Dominic Chalmers and Simon Fraser

289

16.1   Introduction   289
16.2   Learning objectives   289
16.3   The emergence of social entrepreneurship   290
16.4   Defining social entrepreneurship   291
16.5   Defining the social element   292
16.6   Defining the entrepreneurial element   293
16.7   Hybridity in social enterprise   294
16.8   Competing logics and multiple identities   295
16.9   Antecedents of social entrepreneurship   295
16.10   Drivers of contemporary social entrepreneurship:
        a UK perspective   296
16.11   Social entrepreneurship: an international perspective   299
16.12   Social entrepreneurship: a critical approach   299
16.13   Chapter summary   300
Questions   301
Weblinks   301

17 Community entrepreneurship

Ingebjørg Vestrum, Gry Agnete Alsos and Elisabet Ljunggren

303

17.1   Introduction   303
17.2   Learning objectives   303
17.3   The role of community entrepreneurship   304
17.4   What is community entrepreneurship?   305
17.5   Community ventures   308
17.6   Community entrepreneurship actors   311
17.7   The process of community entrepreneurship   313
17.8   Chapter summary   315
Questions   316
Weblinks   316

Part 4 ENTREPRENEURIAL MANAGEMENT

317

18 Entrepreneurial marketing

Eleanor Shaw

319

18.1   Introduction   319
18.2   Learning objectives   320

18.3   The characteristics of small firms: implications for marketing   320
18.4   Entrepreneurial marketing: theory and practice   327
18.5   The process and tools of entrepreneurial marketing   330
18.6   Future research   336
18.7   Chapter summary   336
Questions   337
Weblinks   337

19   Entrepreneurial networks and the small business   338
Steve Conway and Oswald Jones

19.1   Introduction   338
19.2   Learning objectives   339
19.3   Alternative foci of network research in entrepreneurship   340
19.4   An overview of the social network perspective   341
19.5   Retelling the Dyson story from a social network perspective   345
19.6   What has research told us about entrepreneurial networks?   351
19.7   Chapter summary   359
Questions   360
Weblinks   361

20   Finance and the small business   362
Robin Jarvis and Emmanouil Schizas

20.1   Introduction   362
20.2   Learning objectives   362
20.3   Finance and the small firm   363
20.4   The finance gap   364
20.5   Sources of finance   369
20.6   The capital structure decision   381
20.7   Financial reporting considerations   383
20.8   Chapter summary   384
Questions   385
Weblinks   385

21   Strategy and the small firm   386
Colm O'Gorman

21.1   Introduction   386
21.2   Learning objectives   387
21.3   What is strategy?   387
21.4   Strategymaking in small businesses   389
21.5   Success strategies in small firms   393
21.6   The strategic problems of small businesses   399
21.7   Chapter summary   402
Questions   403
Weblinks   403

22 Growth and development in the small firm — 404
David Smallbone and Peter Wyer

22.1 Introduction — 404
22.2 Learning objectives — 405
22.3 Growth and development in the small firm — 405
22.4 Explaining growth in small firms — 407
22.5 Barriers and growth constraints – the external operating context — 416
22.6 Barriers and growth constraints – the internal operating context — 418
22.7 Managing growth — 421
22.8 Chapter summary — 428
Questions — 429
Weblinks — 429

23 Internationalisation and entrepreneurial businesses — 430
Kevin Ibeh

23.1 Introduction — 430
23.2 Learning objectives — 430
23.3 Internationalisation and entrepreneurial SMEs — 431
23.4 Internationalisation and entrepreneurial SMEs: concepts, context and extent — 432
23.5 Explaining SME internationalisation — 434
23.6 Stimulating international entrepreneurship — 439
23.7 Barriers to SME internationalisation — 443
23.8 Policy and institutional support for SME internationalisation — 445
23.9 Chapter summary — 446
Questions — 449
Weblinks — 449

References and further reading — 450
Index — 520

List of contributors

Gry Agnete Alsos is Associate Professor of Entrepreneurship at Bodø Graduate Business School, University of Nordland, Norway.

Giles Barrett is a Senior Lecturer in the School of Humanities and Social Science and Director of the Centre for the Study of Crime, Criminalisation and Social Exclusion at Liverpool John Moores University, UK.

Dinah Bennett is Director of the International Centre for Entrepreneurship and Enterprise, Durham, UK.

Robert J. Bennett is Emeritus Professor in the Department of Geography at the University of Cambridge, UK.

Sara Carter is Professor of Entrepreneurship at the Hunter Centre for Entrepreneurship, University of Strathclyde Business School, and visiting professor at the Nordland Research Institute, Norway.

Dominic Chalmers is a Lecturer in entrepreneurship at the Hunter Centre for Entrepreneurship, University of Strathclyde Business School, Scotland.

Steve Conway is Senior Lecturer in Operations and Supply Management at the University of Bath School of Management, UK.

Per Davidsson is Director of the Australian Centre for Entrepreneurship Research (ACE) and Professor in Entrepreneurship, Queensland University of Technology, Australia.

Frédéric Delmar is Professor of Entrepreneurship in the Department of Strategy and Organisation at EM Lyon, France.

James E. Dever is Associate in Entrepreneurship and Entrepreneur in Residence at the Jim Moran Institute for Global Entrepreneurship, Florida State University, USA.

Dimo Dimov is Professor of Entrepreneurship and Director of Doctoral Programmes at Newcastle University Business School, University of Newcastle upon Tyne, UK.

Simon Fraser is a Lecturer in entrepreneurship, based at Aberdeen Business School's Centre for Entrepreneurship, at Robert Gordon University, Scotland.

Eleanor Hamilton is at the Institute for Entrepreneurship & Enterprise Development, and Associate Dean for Undergraduate Studies at Lancaster University Management School, UK.

Carole Howorth is Professor of Entrepreneurship and Family Business at the Institute for Entrepreneurship and Enterprise Development, Lancaster University Management School, UK.

Robert Huggins is Professor and Director of the Centre for International Competitiveness, Cardiff School of Management, University of Wales Institute, UK.

Kevin Ibeh is Professor of Marketing and International Business and Head of the Department of Marketing, University of Strathclyde Business School, Scotland.

Robin Jarvis is Head of SME Affairs at the ACCA and Professor of Accounting at Brunel University, UK.

Oswald Jones is Professor of Entrepreneurship at the University of Liverpool Management School, UK.

Trevor Jones is Visiting Professor at the Centre for Research in Ethnic Minority Entrepreneurship (CREME), De Montfort University, Leicester, UK.

Dylan Jones-Evans is Professor and Director of Enterprise and Innovation at the University of Wales, UK.

Elisabet Ljunggren (PhD) is Senior Researcher at Nordland Research Institute, Bodø, Norway.

Susan Marlow is Professor of Entrepreneurship at Birmingham Business School, University of Birmingham, UK.

Niall G. MacKenzie is Head of the Institute for Innovation Studies at the University of Wales, UK.

Colm O'Gorman is Professor of Entrepreneurship at the Business School, Dublin City University, Ireland.

Luke Pittaway is the William A. Freeman Distinguished Chair in Free Enterprise and Director of the Center for Entrepreneurial Learning and Leadership, College of Business Administration, Georgia Southern University, USA.

Monder Ram is Professor of Small Business and Director of CREME at Leicester Business School, De Montfort University, Leicester, UK.

Saras Sarasvathy is Isadore Horween Research Associate Professor at The Darden School, University of Virginia, USA.

Emmanouil Schizas is a Senior Policy Adviser at the ACCA, London, UK.

Eleanor Shaw is Professor of Marketing at the Department of Marketing, University of Strathclyde Business School, Scotland.

David Smallbone is Professor of Small Business and Entrepreneurship and Associate Director of the Small Business Centre at Kingston University, UK.

Deniz Ucbasaran is Professor of Entrepreneurship at Warwick Business School, UK.

Ingebjørg Vestrum is a Researcher at the Nordland Research Institute, Bodø, Norway

Friederike Welter is Professor of Entrepreneurship at Jönköping International Business School, Sweden.

Paul Westhead is Professor of Entrepreneurship at University of Durham Business School and a Visiting Professor at the University of Nordland, Norway.

Nick Williams is a Lecturer in entrepreneurship at the University of Sheffield, UK.

Frédérik C. Witte is a PhD student at EM Lyon, France.

Mike Wright is Professor of Entrepreneurship at Imperial College Business School, Director of the Centre for Management Buyout Research and a visiting professor at the University of Ghent, Erasmus University and Lancaster University.

Peter Wyer is Director of Small Business Development at Strategic Foresight UK.

Publisher's acknowledgements

We are grateful to the following for permission to reproduce copyright material:

Figures

Figure 6.2 from Jonathan T. Eckhardt, An Update to the individual-opportunity nexus, *Springer eBook* (2010), With kind permission from Springer Science and Business Media; Figure 13.1 from Bivalent attributes of the family firm, *Family Business Review*, June, pp. 199–208 (Tagiuri, R. and Davis, J. A. 1996), First published 1982, reprinted 1996, Copyright © 1992,1996 by SAGE Publications. Reprinted by permission of SAGE Publications; Figure 13.2 from *Generation to Generation: Life Cycles of the Family Business*, Harvard Business School Press (Gersick, K. E., Davis, J., Hampton, M. M. and Lansberg, I. 1997). Reprinted by permission of Harvard Business School Press. Copyright (c) 1997 by the Harvard Business School Publishing Corporation; all rights reserved; Figure 13.3 from 'Types' of private family firms: an exploratory conceptual and empirical analysis, *Entrepreneurship and Regional Development*, Vol. 19, Iss. 5, pp. 405–31 (Westhead, P. and Howorth, C. 2007), reprinted by permission of the publisher (Taylor & Francis Ltd, http://www.tandf.co.uk/journals); Figure 18.1 adapted from *Marketing and Entrepreneurship in SMEs: An Innovative Approach*, 1st ed., Prentice Hall International (Carson, D., Cromie, S., McGowan, P., and Hill, J. 1995) (c) 1996. Reprinted and electronically reproduced by permission of Pearson Education, Inc., Upper Saddle River, New Jersey; Figure 18.3 from Putting entrepreneurship into marketing: the processes of entrepreneurial marketing, *Journal of Research in Marketing and Entrepreneurship*, Vol. 2, No. 1, pp. 1–16 (Stokes, D. 2000), © Emerald Group Publishing Limited all rights reserved; Figure 22.1 adapted from *Understanding the Small Business Sector*, Routledge, New York (Storey, D. J. 1994) Copyright (c) 1994 Cengage Learning. Reproduced by permission of Cengage Learning EMEA Ltd.

Tables

Table 10.1 adapted from American Bankruptcy Institute, http://www.abiworld.org/AM/AMTemplate.cfm?Section=Home&CONTENTID=60229&TEMPLATE=/CM/ContentDisplay.cfm. Reprinted with permission from the American Bankruptcy Institute (www.abiworld.org); Table 10.2 adapted from http://www.insolvency.gov.uk/otherinformation/statistics/historicdata/HDmenu.htm (c) Crown copyright 2006; Table 20.1 from Collis, J. (2008) Directors' Views on Accounting and Auditing Requirements for SMEs, London: BERR. Available from: http://www.berr.gov.uk/whatwedo/businesslaw/corp-gov-research/current-research-proj/page18121.html, Contains public sector information licensed under the Open Government Licence v1.0.

Text

Extract on page 106 from Creating something from nothing: Resource construction through entrepreneurial bricolage, *Administrative Science Quarterly*, 50 (3), p. 329 (Baker, T., and Nelson, R. E. 2005), Copyright © 2005 by SAGE Publications. Reprinted by permission of SAGE Publications; Box 13.3 from The F-PEC Scale of Family Influence: A proposal for solving the family business definition problem, *Family Business Review*, March, pp. 45–58 (Astrachan, J. H., Klein, S. B. and Smyrnios, K. X. 2002), Copyright © 2002 by SAGE Publications. Reprinted by permission of SAGE Publications.

In some instances we have been unable to trace the owners of copyright material, and we would appreciate any information that would enable us to do so.

CHAPTER 1

Introduction

Sara Carter and Dylan Jones-Evans

1.1 Background

Attitudes towards entrepreneurship have changed considerably in the past 30 years. The days when an entrepreneur would be viewed as a 'deviant' individual on the margins of society are long gone. Today, people such as James Dyson, Richard Branson, Steve Jobs, Bill Gates and Mark Zuckerberg are world-renowned for their entrepreneurial prowess and revered as role models that many would wish to emulate.

In the same way that entrepreneurs have become an accepted part of everyday life, the influence of the small firm has also grown considerably. While this has been driven by various factors, such as the decline of large businesses, the development of an 'enterprise culture', market fragmentation and technological development, the increasing regard for small firms has been fuelled by a widespread recognition of their crucial economic and social roles. Indeed, new growing sectors, such as social media and networking, have been created and developed by new entrepreneurial businesses – Google, Facebook, Twitter and YouTube, for example – all of which have emerged in recent years to have profound effects on the ways we live and communicate.

Small firms are, perhaps, most valued for their contribution to employment creation. At a time when the global economy is struggling to recover from the worst recession since the 1920s, the role of small firms in creating jobs and wealth cannot be overestimated. While research shows that the ability of an individual small firm to create a large number of jobs is restricted to very few high-growth 'gazelles', the sheer number of smaller enterprises ensures their collective contribution to employment generation is substantial. For example, in the European Union, large firms have experienced employment losses in nearly every member state, while employment by small firms has grown considerably. In addition to creating employment, small firms also play a variety of other roles. While the economies of scale in production and distribution enable large firms to make a significant contribution to the economy, many of them could not survive without the existence of small companies, which sell most of the products made by large manufacturers direct as well as providing them with many of the services and supplies they require to run a competitive business. Small firms have also introduced many products and services to the consumer, especially in specialised markets that are too small for larger companies to consider worthwhile. Finally, small businesses provide an outlet for entrepreneurial individuals, many of whom would have found it almost impossible to work for a large organisation. Therefore, an understanding of both the entrepreneur and the business they lead is of vital importance to those creating the policies that will reinvigorate the world economy. In that respect, we hope this book can make a contribution to the process.

1.2 The purpose of this book

The increased importance of entrepreneurship and the small firm sector has led to considerable growth in interest in entrepreneurs and the companies they establish and grow. As Chapter 2 explains, the study of entrepreneurship originated in the work of eighteenth-century economists such as Richard Cantillon, but the field has grown considerably during the past 30 years to encompass disciplines as varied as sociology, psychology, management studies and organisational studies. Indeed, the chapters within this book draw on various approaches to explain broad issues relating to the enterprise environment, entrepreneurial processes and individuals, as well as small business management and growth. The field of entrepreneurship and small business studies has always been diverse, and this book is intended to both reflect this diversity and present an overview of each of the key themes relating to enterprise and small businesses.

Contemporary interest in entrepreneurship essentially dates from the 1970s and 1980s, when a number of critical events saw both a loss of confidence in large-scale industry and growing popular and governmental interest in small businesses. Even before this period, however, there had been research analysing the small firms sector from historical, geographical and socio-economic perspectives. What has changed in recent years is both the volume of research undertaken and its direct role in influencing national economic policy. Accompanying these changes has been a shift in emphasis away from a focus upon small firms and towards entrepreneurship, plus the emergence of entrepreneurship as a subject domain with its own distinctive approaches, paradigms and methodologies.

The domain of entrepreneurship may be one of the newest management subjects, but it is fast maturing. Scholars (Wiklund, Davidsson, Audretsch and Karlsson, 2011: 1) described the entrepreneurship domain as:

> one of the most vital, dynamic, and relevant in management, economics, regional science, and other social sciences. The Entrepreneurship Division of the Academy of Management increased its membership by 230 per cent – more than any other established division – and with over 2,700 members, it now ranks among the largest in the Academy of Management. Entrepreneurship research has gained considerable prominence in leading disciplinary and mainstream management journals. As a case in point, the best-cited – by far – article of the decade in the *Academy of Management Review* was the agenda-setting (and debated) piece by Shane and Venkataraman (2000). At the same time, the number of dedicated entrepreneurship journals listed by the Social Science Citation Index increased from one to more than half a dozen, the leading among them achieving impact factors in the same range as highly respected management and social science journals. Most importantly, entrepreneurship research has become more theory driven and coalesced around a central core of themes, issues, methodologies, and debates.

While there have been significant developments in entrepreneurship research, there have been equally important developments with regard to the teaching of entrepreneurship, evidenced by the growing number of university-based entrepreneurship centres. Many of these centres have developed courses in entrepreneurship for undergraduate and postgraduate students, either as an integral element of business and management courses or as degrees in their own right. While the USA was an early leader in entrepreneurship education, business schools in Europe, Asia and Australasia have followed in developing courses in entrepreneurship and small business studies.

To explain the popularity of entrepreneurship education, one has to look at emerging and future graduate employment trends. University graduates are more likely than ever to start their own businesses and work within small- and medium-sized enterprises (SMEs). The current economic conditions will lead increasing numbers of people towards self-employment and business start-up. Even graduates whose first career step is within the corporate sector are increasingly expected to work in project-based corporate venture teams. For new graduates entering the labour market, enterprising skills are essential for career success. Unlike their parents' generation, new graduates are likely to experience a portfolio-based working life, working for several employers combined with periods of self-employment or freelance work. Today's graduate has to adopt a more self-reliant ethos, and this much looser connection with employers means that the option of starting their own business through choice or necessity becomes much greater. Increasingly, universities want their graduates to start their business careers well-prepared and with a full understanding of what entrepreneurship entails.

While the rationale for teaching entrepreneurship at university level is strong, many people remain unconvinced that entrepreneurship can be taught. Entrepreneurship is still popularly viewed as an innate talent and entrepreneurs are seen as being different from the rest of us – born with a gift for it. In fact, entrepreneurship is not the only new subject where its 'teachability' has been questioned. Neither is it unusual for new subjects to be viewed more as an individual's innate gift or talent than a discrete set of knowledge and skills that can be deconstructed into component elements and communicated within the classroom. Each time a new subject domain has been introduced to the university curriculum, the same 'teachability' question has been posed. Some 50 years ago, the new subject introduced into the management curriculum was marketing and the same question was debated at great length. Around 50 years before that, the new subject being debated was psychology and, a century before then, the new subject was medicine. It is worth remembering that, in pre-industrial societies, medicine was regarded as the domain of individuals with an innate gift for healing. Just as we no longer question the legitimacy and professionalisation of these well-established subjects, we no longer question whether or not they can be taught.

The analogy with marketing is especially useful for understanding how entrepreneurship has developed as a subject domain and is emerging as a core element of management education. It was commonly believed 50 years ago that marketing could not be taught. Marketing was regarded merely as an individual's ability to sell and this was seen as an innate skill – confined to those born with the 'gift of the gab'. Nowadays, marketing courses exist in almost every university and college, and there is widespread and unquestioned appreciation of marketing as an essential and multi-dimensional business skill required within all organisations. We no longer question that marketing and selling can be taught – these subjects have been central to the management education curriculum for decades. Over time, this will also be the case for entrepreneurship.

Entrepreneurship education focuses on the new venture creation process and its constituent elements:

■ opportunity identification

■ resource acquisition and mobilisation

■ new venture start-up

■ subsequent business growth.

Of course, some of this may be learned 'on the job', but trial and error is time-consuming, expensive and produces poor results.

University entrepreneurship courses tend to use a range of teaching and learning methods to teach entrepreneurship. Formal lectures are complemented by interactive activities, class discussions, tutorials, case studies and interaction with entrepreneurs in the classroom and through field interviews, team exercises, workshops and student placements in high-growth entrepreneurial ventures. This book is designed to accompany such courses by providing students with an overview of the entire subject domain, its history and development and current research debates.

This book addresses the need for a single reference point for the growing number of students undertaking courses in small business and entrepreneurial studies. In determining the themes to be included in this book, guidance was taken from the syllabi of several university and college courses. Many of the initial small business courses taught in universities were designed to encourage and enable students to actually start an enterprise, but courses are now designed to provide a more comprehensive insight into the entrepreneurship process. This reflects both the broad policy imperative to encourage students to start in business for themselves and the future careers of graduates, who are increasingly likely to be employed within the small business sector or in occupations that directly or indirectly support the sector.

As each of the contributions in this volume demonstrates, research undertaken over the past 30 years has led to substantial theoretical and methodological advances. The field is far from exhausted, however. Each chapter within this volume demonstrates the extent – and also the incompleteness – of our understanding of many issues surrounding entrepreneurship and new firms.

This book contains 23 chapters from 38 contributors. Each contributing author was asked to present an overview of a specific body of work and explain how the field had developed over time. Even in such a large volume as this, not all issues can be explained in the depth that may be required. However, we believe that each chapter amply fulfils the criteria of providing a strong starting point for students. One of the advantages of an edited collection of work is the ability to draw on acknowledged subject experts to provide specialised accounts of their specific research areas.

We would like to thank each contributor for not only their chapter contributions but also giving their time and enthusiasm so freely. This book represents a substantial body of knowledge that we hope will provide an excellent reference point for students, researchers and teachers alike.

1.3 Structure of this book

The book is divided into four parts that essentially reflect the four areas that concern the small firm today.

Part 1 introduces the subject of entrepreneurship, the history of entrepreneurship theory and the environment surrounding small business ownership. Part 2 explores the entrepreneurial process. Perhaps the most significant research developments in more recent years have focused on understanding the process entrepreneurs go through, from the very inception of an idea onwards, while a growing body of knowledge is emerging that tries to uncover the experience and consequences of business failure. Part 3 examines some of the main 'types' of individuals who start and subsequently manage ventures. Finally, Part 4 of the book examines the various management functions and activities of new and growing firms. As you will see when reading the various chapters, there are often no distinct boundaries between the issues discussed within the various chapters and, where possible, we have linked the relevant sections to other chapters within the book.

As mentioned, Part 1 introduces the subject of entrepreneurship, beginning with Chapter 2, which presents and explains the development of entrepreneurship theory over time, focusing on the way in which the definition of entrepreneurship has varied for different theories and thinkers. Building on this, Chapter 3 examines the role of entrepreneurship in stimulating economic development and growth, at national, regional and local levels. Chapter 4 then examines, in detail, the role of government in supporting and influencing entrepreneurs and the small firm sector. The final chapter in this section looks at the 'real world of the entrepreneur', focusing on the influence of context and the external environment on entrepreneurial behaviour.

Part 2 focuses on the process of entrepreneurship within the small firm. One of the defining characteristics of entrepreneurs is their ability to recognise and develop opportunities. This theme is examined in Per Davidsson's Chapter 6, which introduces the entrepreneurial process and, more specifically, by Dimo Dimov in Chapter 7 in his account of entrepreneurial opportunities. The next two chapters look specifically at influences upon the entrepreneur. Chapter 8 presents an introduction to effectuation – one of the most compelling developments in our understanding of the entrepreneurial process – by exploring the key elements of entrepreneurial expertise with a view to identifying, understanding and evaluating particular decisions, actions, strategies and mechanisms. Chapter 9, by Frédéric Delmar and Frédérik C. Witte, explores the various approaches to the psychology of the entrepreneur. Part 2 is concluded by a discussion in Chapter 10 of an issue that is rarely found in textbooks on small businesses – namely, entrepreneurial failure.

Part 3 contains seven chapters, each examining a distinctive type of entrepreneur. The first three chapters in this section explore the influence of ethnicity, gender and family on the experience of entrepreneurship. These are followed by chapters exploring habitual, technical, social and community entrepreneurship – each group demonstrating specific characteristics and influences that differentiate them from other types of owner-managers.

Part 4 focuses on the specific management functions within small businesses. Mainstream management subjects such as strategy, HRM, finance and marketing are discussed from the specific viewpoint of the small firm and its stakeholders, alongside key areas such as growth, networking and internationalisation – all of which are critical to the development of such businesses.

At the end of each chapter, there is a series of questions designed to provoke classroom-based discussion and reinforce your understanding of the main points, plus links to relevant websites.

PART 1

Entrepreneurship

CHAPTER 2

The evolution of entrepreneurship theory

Luke Pittaway

2.1 Introduction

This chapter presents and explains the development of entrepreneurship theory over time. Although the subject of entrepreneurship is often considered to be relatively new, the historical roots can be linked back to the early economic thinkers of the eighteenth century (Bygrave, 1989). The chapter starts by explaining these economic roots, exploring some of the early thinking and the different ways in which entrepreneurship was considered to be important. It then begins to introduce theories from the middle of the twentieth century that moved away from the function of entrepreneurship in the economy to consider more psychological, sociological and behavioural issues. Finally, the chapter explores contemporary theories and thinking and, in this part, maps out the different forms theory has taken (a timeline is presented in Figure 2.1).

Figure 2.1 Timeline of entrepreneurship thought

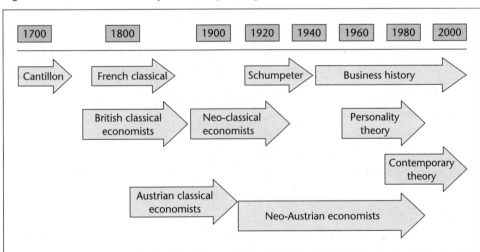

As you progress through this chapter, it is worth noting the different ways in which entrepreneurship has been defined. The common contemporary view is that entrepreneurship is synonymous with 'venture creation' or 'fast-growing companies'. In historical thinking, however, the way in which entrepreneurship has been defined has varied with different theories and thinkers. These different definitions and views are presented throughout this chapter and the logic underpinning these differences will be highlighted.

2.2 Learning objectives

There are three learning objectives for this chapter:

1 to understand the historical nature of the subject of entrepreneurship
2 to appreciate the broad sweep of entrepreneurship thought when relating one theory to another
3 to gain awareness of the differences in entrepreneurship thought and how this impacts how entrepreneurs are defined and understood.

Key concepts

- entrepreneurship theory - history of thought - economic theory

2.3 Economic perspectives

Economic perspectives contribute significantly to the field of entrepreneurship. In most cases when economists seek to understand 'entrepreneurship' they are usually interested in the function that entrepreneurship plays in the economic system.

The economic perspectives can be classified in several ways:

- chronologically (Hébert and Link, 1988; Binks and Vale, 1990)
- in schools of thought (Chell, Haworth and Brearley, 1991)
- by the function the economist has given to the entrepreneur within the economic system (Barreto, 1989).

This chapter presents the different economic thinkers in schools of thought. There are several different schools of thought usually highlighted. These include the:

- French classical school
- British classical school
- microeconomics and the neoclassical school
- Austrian and neo-Austrian school
- Schumpeterian school.

2.3.1 French classical school

Most readers will notice that the word 'entrepreneur' has a French origin. Hoselitz (1960: 237) suggests that it originated during the Middle Ages when the term entrepreneur was applied to 'the man in charge of the great architectural works: castles and fortifications, public buildings, abbeys and cathedrals.' Remains of this interpretation can be found inscribed on the older public buildings in France. Given the origins of the word, it should not be surprising that the early thinkers were French economists.

In most entrepreneurship texts, Cantillon is recognised as the first to use the term 'entrepreneurship' in an economic context (Hébert and Link, 1988; Binks and Vale, 1990). His *Essai Sur la Nature du Commerce en Général* was published in 1732. Cantillon introduced an economic system based on classes of actors – entrepreneurs being one of the three classes. There are 'landowners', who are financially independent aristocracy, while 'hirelings' and 'entrepreneurs' were viewed to be financially dependent on others. Hirelings earned fixed incomes, but entrepreneurs were 'set up with a capital to conduct their enterprise, or are undertakers of their own labour without capital, and they may be regarded as living off uncertainty' (Cantillon, 1732/1931: 55). For Cantillon, individuals who purchased a good at a certain price, used that good to produce a product and then sold the product at an uncertain price could be considered 'entrepreneurs'. Risk and uncertainty play central parts in his theory of the economic system. Successful entrepreneurs were those individuals who made better judgments about changes in the market and who coped with risk and uncertainty better than their counterparts.

Other French economists following Cantillon took up, considered and reconsidered the role of the entrepreneur in economic systems. Quesnay, for example, took a step away from Cantillon's ideas about uncertainty and risk by offering up the first mathematical general equilibrium system in the *Tableau Économique* (Kuczynski and Meek, 1972). Turgot made an additional distinction to Cantillon's ideas by identifying that the ownership of capital and the act of entrepreneurship could be two separate functions of entrepreneurial endeavour. Finally, Say, who became the first professor of economics in Europe (the chair of industrial economy at the Conservatoire des Arts et Métiers, founded in 1819) (Binks and Vale, 1990), further enhanced and built on Cantillon's ideas in two books published in the 1800s: *A Catechism of Political Economy* (1821) and *A Treatise on Political Economy* (1802). Jean-Baptiste Say, as well as being a professor, was a businessperson, founding a cotton-spinning mill in Auchy, Pas de Calais. Perhaps because of his business experience, Say made the entrepreneur the central point, around which his views about the economic system turned (see Figure 2.2).

Say's theory of production and distribution was constructed on three major agents of production:

■ human industry

■ capital – both physical capital, in the form of machines, and money

■ land – including other natural resources.

Say recognised that both land and capital were indispensible to production. He, however, argued the 'key' to production was human industry (Barreto, 1989). Say then proceeded to make a tri-partite division of human industry into 'effort, knowledge and the applications of the entrepreneur' (Koolman, 1971: 271). The entrepreneur was viewed by Say as the coordinator of the system, acting as an intermediary between all

Figure 2.2 Say's theory of production and distribution

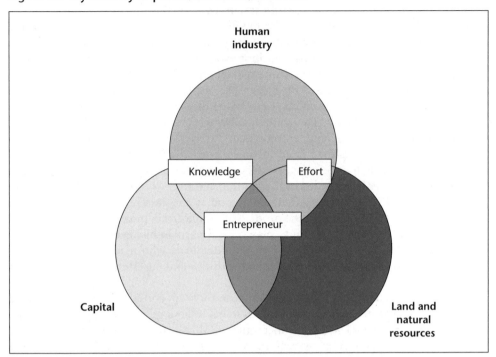

of the other agents of production and taking on the uncertainty and risk. The profit the entrepreneur gained was the reward for the risk undertaken. Successful entrepreneurship needed significant qualities. The most important was judgment or the ability to assess the needs of the market and understand how these needs could be met.

2.3.2 British classical school

Unlike the French classical school, the British classical school did not start with a strong appreciation of entrepreneurship (Ricketts, 1987; Chell et al., 1991). The British school is usually considered to include early Scottish, English and Welsh political economists – for example, Adam Smith's (1904) *The Wealth of Nations* and John Stuart Mill's (1909) *Principles of Political Economy*.

Although several of the key authors in this school of thought are likely to have been familiar with the term 'entrepreneur', particularly Ricardo who corresponded with Say, they never used it in their writing or introduced an equivalent Anglo-Saxon version. A number of reasons have been put forward for this. First, Say suggested that there was no direct parallel for the French word 'entrepreneur' in English (although the word 'undertaker' was used it did not have exactly the same meaning, which might explain why this French word is in common use in the English language). Second, the laws in England and France at the time were different. In France, there was a clear distinction between the ownership of capital or land and the ownership of property and business, whereas in England a capitalist was not only a creditor receiving interest on the capital but also an active partner, sharing in the gains and losses of a business (Tuttle, 1927). Third, it has been suggested that the two groups of theorists used different conceptual apparatus. French political economy was more interested in microeconomic connections and British political economy was more interested in macroeconomic ones (Koolman, 1971). Whatever the reason, the failure of British economic thought to consider the role of the entrepreneur in the economy was unfortunate and may ultimately have led to the neglect of the subject in modern-day economics (Barreto, 1989).

2.3.3 Microeconomics and the neoclassical school

This school of thought includes many economists who use neoclassical approaches to explain how the production and consumption system operates. Notable theorists include Leon Walras, Alfred Marshall, John Bates Clark, Maurice Dobb and Charles Tuttle (Barreto, 1989). Like the British classical school, this group of thinkers has been criticised more for their neglect of the entrepreneurial function than their contributions to understanding entrepreneurship (Kirzner, 1980). This neglect, though, is important to understand as it also helps to explain why entrepreneurship as a subject grew out of and effectively left the economics discipline. A detailed rationale and explanation is provided in Barreto's (1989) book *The Entrepreneur in Micro-economic Theory: Disappearance and explanation*. In this he concludes that there were several reasons for the decline of the entrepreneur in mainstream economic thought.

1 he observed that the decline of the entrepreneurial concept coincided with the rise of the theory of the firm

2 he suggested that the theory of the firm contained three fundamental assumptions (the production function, rational choice and perfect information) that prevented the introduction of the entrepreneurial concept

3 he concluded the desire for consistency in the theoretical structure of the theory of the firm rested on a 'mechanistic' philosophy of the social world that was anathema to the concept of 'human action' implied in entrepreneurial activity.

2.3.4 Austrian and neo-Austrian school

While mainstream economics began to develop theories that tended to exclude entrepreneurship, other economists began to revive the concept. Several such strands of thought have been categorised under the title Austrian or neo-Austrian school (even though, strictly speaking, they should not *all* be so categorised). The theorists in this category regard uncertainty and risk as important features of economic systems that allow entrepreneurs the opportunity to make profit. In this respect, they build on the thinking of the early French political economists.

Much of the Austrian school's ideas can be traced back to the work of von Mangoldt (1855). The first work that makes substantive contributions to understanding entrepreneurship, however, is Knight's (1921) *Risk, Uncertainty and Profit*. Rather than try to develop economic theory that portrays an ideal state of affairs, Knight tried to explain the real market system as it actually operates (Ricketts, 1987) and this sets him apart from the neoclassical school of the time. Knight argued against much of mainstream economics and explained that supply and demand cannot be in equilibrium because, in reality, other forces change the conditions of the market. In this situation of 'disequilibrium', Knight points out, a market must be in a constant state of uncertainty and entrepreneurship becomes the skilful interpretation of market changes and the bearing of responsibility for the successful or otherwise interpretation of market change. In this theory Knight makes some important distinctions between 'risk' and 'uncertainty' that go beyond the work of some of the earlier thinkers. If, on the one hand, change is calculable and predictable, then it is a 'risk' and a person can predict with a certain degree of probability that it will occur. It can then be insured against or incorporated into the costs of doing business. If, on the other hand, change cannot be predicted, then it is unknown and, therefore, uncertain. He argues that entrepreneurship, rather than being a function, a role or a class of people, as in earlier theories, is in fact a type of decision that requires action in the face of unknown future events.

The other Austrian and neo-Austrian economists (von Mangoldt, 1855; Mises, 1949; Menger, 1950; Kirzner, 1973; Hayek, 1990) take a similar stance. Uncertainty, in their approaches, remains important, as does disequilibrium, and they focus more on the entrepreneurial opportunities created from uncertainties in the market.

Most widely cited of these economists is Kirzner (1973, 1980, 1982, 1990), whose 'entrepreneurs' – or, more precisely, 'entrepreneurial decisions' – are considered to be the driving force behind the market. He goes a step further than Knight by arguing that there is a crucial element in all human action that can be described as 'entrepreneurial'; individuals in the market do not always make logical decisions and these are often based on irrationality or subjective preferences. Again, the personal judgment of entrepreneurs is important, as is uncertainty and risk, but it is not only guided by logical choices and decisions but also the individual's propensity to be alert to opportunities. It is this alertness to opportunity that defines the 'entrepreneurial' element of decisionmaking and, in many ways, this view brings economic thinking into the realm of recognising the role of personal characteristics and particularly cognition.

'Entrepreneurship' is not only the propensity to pursue goals efficiently, when the ends and means of those goals have been identified, but also the drive and alertness required to identify which goals to pursue in the first place. It is the acquisition of market information and knowledge, from market participation, that helps provide this alertness to opportunity, but also an individual capacity to 'envisage' future opportunities as it makes 'correct' perception of the market possible. 'Entrepreneurial' ability is dependent on perceiving future market conditions and setting about a course of action that results in a sequence of decisions directed at achieving the outcome anticipated.

In his early work, which he later modifies, Kirzner (1979: 38, his emphasis) defines this 'pure entrepreneur' as a 'decision-maker whose *entire* role arises out of his alertness to hitherto unnoticed opportunities.' The entrepreneur is, therefore, a decisionmaker who begins without any means other than an ability to predict, 'successfully', changes in market conditions.

Another more recent contribution with a similar stance is the work of Casson (1982), who focuses on such information asymmetries and explores the role that information, information exchange and information markets have on an entrepreneur's alertness to opportunity.

2.3.5 Schumpeterian school

While the role of the entrepreneur in economic systems had been considered in economic thought before the 1920s, many contemporary researchers trace the origins of modern thought in entrepreneurship back to Joseph Schumpeter's work (1934, 1963).

Schumpeter's theories of the economic system and the role of entrepreneurship within it have been widely discussed (MacDonald, 1971; Shionoya, 1992, 1997). His principal contribution can be found in his book *The Theory of Economic Development* (1934) and an article 'The fundamental phenomenon of economic development' (1971).

Schumpeter introduced a concept of entrepreneurship that is quite different from the others discussed so far. His theory is focused on economic development and the role of the entrepreneur in the development process. Schumpeter argues, somewhat contrary to the established thought of the time, that the important question in capitalism is not how it supports existing structures and markets, but how it creates and destroys them. In contemporary thought, 'creative destruction' is now seen as one of the crucial functions of entrepreneurial activity within an economy.

The function of the entrepreneur in this new theory is that of innovating or making 'new combinations' of production possible. The concept of 'new combinations' covers five potential cases:

- the introduction of a new good or a new quality of a good
- the introduction of a new method of production
- the opening of a new market
- the development of a new source of supply or raw materials or half-manufactured goods
- the carrying out of a new organisation of any industry (Kilby, 1971).

In Schumpeter's theory, the new combinations he presents *can* happen in existing businesses but, by their very nature, they typically occur in new firms that begin producing beside older firms. He (Schumpeter, in Kilby, 1971: 54) explains his definition of the concepts by arguing:

> These concepts are at once broader and narrower than usual. Broader, because in the first place we call entrepreneurs not only those 'independent' businessmen . . . but all who actually fulfil the function . . . even if they are . . . 'dependent' employees of a company, like managers, members of boards of directors . . . On the other hand, our concept is narrower than the traditional one in that it does not include all heads of firms or managers or industrialists who merely operate an established business, but only those who actually perform that function.

The concept, therefore, includes new businesses that are innovative or forming new combinations of resources (e.g. Facebook) and existing businesses that are doing new innovative things (e.g., Apple). Individuals and businesses are only being 'entrepreneurial', though, when they carry out the new combinations described. They revert back to normal economic activity once their innovative role has been completed.

Schumpeter concludes his theory by pointing out that individuals who are entrepreneurial may need special characteristics and skills. On the one hand, a person who works in a relatively static and unchanging situation can become accustomed to his or her own abilities and experience. On the other hand, somebody working in a dynamic and ever-changing situation must cope with uncertainties in their environment and must seek to shape these uncertainties. He concludes that these are very different things: 'Carrying out a new plan and acting according to a customary one are things as different as making a road and walking along it' (Schumpeter, in Kilby, 1971: 55).

Schumpeter closes by pointing out that this aspect raises important implications for individual psychology, cognition and behaviour. If there are individual differences in people's ability to cope with ambiguity, uncertainty, change and risk, what drives these differences? Understanding what drives the differences could help explain why some people are more entrepreneurial than others.

2.4 Early psychological and sociological perspectives

With quite different theories, both Kirzner and Schumpeter end by pointing out the potential individual differences that might occur in entrepreneurial capability. Schumpeter does not specify these characteristics, while Kirzner focuses on cognitive skills. Both, however, identify a need for theories to explore the individual aspects of entrepreneurial activity. Schumpeter also takes his argument a step further by suggesting that the best way to understand entrepreneurial activity and behaviour is to place it in its context. In so arguing, he highlights the role of historical analysis and provides the basis for taking an historical approach to understanding entrepreneurship – a rationale that many business historians have applied subsequently when studying the subject (Rose, 2000). As a consequence, from the beginning of the 1960s on, entrepreneurship theorising shifts away from economics to focus more on psychological, social psychological and sociological explanations (although a few economists, such as Kirzner and Casson, continued to focus on the economic role of the entrepreneur). (Chapters 6 and 9, for example, explain more about the entrepreneurial process and the psychological theories.) In the remainder of this chapter, theories will be explained in terms of how they fit into the broad history of entrepreneurship thought. Most of these theories span the period 1960 to the early 1980s.

2.4.1 Personality theory

Personality theory began to make contributions to the subject of entrepreneurship in the early 1960s. It is considered to have started with the work of McClelland (1955), who used the concept of the 'achievement motive' to describe the behaviour of entrepreneurs.

Most early personality theory is described as single-trait theory because theorists sought to identify a single-trait and link it to a greater propensity to be a successful entrepreneur. Further single-trait theories followed, including locus of control (Rotter, 1966) and risk-taking propensity (Brockhaus, 1982). Each of these theories encountered difficulty proving a predictive capability.

Partly as a consequence of the lack of predictive success, theorists by the 1970s had begun to move away from single-trait explanations of the entrepreneurial personality. Instead, they offered multi-trait approaches that presented profiles of entrepreneurial characteristics they felt could help predict a person's entrepreneurial potential. These profiles often used standardised personality tests (for example, the behavioural event questionnaire).

As time progressed, these studies began to use ever-wider sets of characteristics to measure entrepreneurial potential or success. Studies exploring traits often used varied samples, so somewhat struggled to define the entrepreneur in a common way and found it difficult to justify the criteria they used to define 'entrepreneurial success' (Gartner, 1989a). The predictive value of these personality measures remained elusive and contentious.

By the late 1980s, a series of researchers questioned the validity of these theories from a philosophical and a methodological stance and argued for a more behavioural or social psychological approach (Gartner, 1989a; Chell et al., 1991; Shaver and Scott, 1991).

2.4.2 Psycho-sociological theory

There were a number of theories and approaches that were on the margins of thinking during the dominance of personality theory and the search for the 'correct' constellation of entrepreneurial traits. For want of a better term, these have been categorised here as psycho-sociological. They include two different forms of displacement theory (Shapero 1975; Kets De Vries, 1977) and a social marginality theory (Scase and Goffee, 1980).

The basic premise of these approaches is that entrepreneurs are displaced people or socially marginal people who have been supplanted from their familiar way of life and have somehow been forced into an entrepreneurial way of life due to their circumstances. Displacement includes many categories of people – for example, political refugees, immigrants, ethnic minorities and other marginalised groups in society. In contemporary research, there is evidence in national business formation statistics that supports this idea of certain groups contributing in an above average way to entrepreneurial activity. Indeed, these areas of research in more recent years have become specific subjects in their own right.

In Shapero's (1975) approach, displacement came about through both positive and negative forces, although the majority were perceived to derive from negative forces. The forces were typically external and societal, which were beyond the power of the individual to influence.

Kets De Vries (1977), in contrast, used Freudian psychology and sought out a psychological explanation for why entrepreneurs feel displaced. He viewed displacement as both psychological and sociological, with a rebellion against existing norms and structures being one of a few reasons for psychological displacement. De Vries (1977) linked much of his thinking on entrepreneurial behaviour back to a person's family life and their early family relationships. Although not explicitly linked, it seems likely more recent research about entrepreneurship that draws on ethnicity, gender and family issues in entrepreneurship (as demonstrated in Chapters 11, 12 and 13) may owe its roots to this earlier thought. Displacement and marginalisation as concepts seem to remain embedded in some of these areas of study, although theories about entrepreneurship based *wholly* on these approaches does not seem to factor in much mainstream thought today.

2.4.3 Sociological perspectives

Although the personality perspective mostly dominated thought in entrepreneurship research during the 1970s and early 1980s, there were a number of significant theories being developed at the time that came to play an important role later. The two most notable were sociological work on organisations that applied a population ecology perspective to the birth and death of firms (Aldrich 1979; Aldrich and Zimmer, 1986; Carroll, 1988) and Greiner's (1972) paper in the *Harvard Business Review* that laid the foundations for research on the growth stages of entrepreneurial businesses.

In the former, Aldrich and Carroll explored how the sociological characteristics of particular markets could help explain business success and failure and, in the latter, Greiner put forward a theory that helped explain how entrepreneurial firms might need to evolve and change as they develop and grow.

Alongside these developments in theory there were ongoing shifts in the industrial and political landscape that were to propel entrepreneurship thought into a new phase.

2.5 Contemporary thought

There is no question that theory and research on entrepreneurship exploded from the early 1970s to the present day. Although the roots, as described earlier, remain, the subject has become increasingly diverse and is now a significant discipline in its own right. For example, in 1999 in the USA, Katz (2003) counted over 2200 entrepreneurship courses, in over 1600 schools, 277 endowed professorships, 44 English-language journals and over 100 research centres. Undoubtedly these numbers have grown considerably in the years that have passed since then and there has been substantial growth in the subject outside the USA since the 1990s. There are many causes of this growth.

1 There were significant changes during the 1970s and 1980s, for many developed economies, away from an industrial landscape based on a few large (often publically backed) organisations towards an economy based on smaller businesses. This key shift in the industrial landscape has led to a point today where the majority of net new jobs are created by entrepreneurial businesses (the Kauffman Foundation's research takes this further and shows that, between 1980 and 2005, virtually all net new jobs created in the USA were by firms that were five years old or less).

2 Alongside this shift in the industrial make-up of advanced economies was a policy shift in government that began to recognise, support and promote entrepreneurship. In the UK, this began with the 1971 Bolton Report and culminated with both Conservative (1979–1997) and Labour (1997–2010) governments introducing policies that supported entrepreneurship and, in the later period, specifically supporting entrepreneurship education.

3 As these contextual changes took place, cultural attitudes towards enterprise and entrepreneurs also changed. Particularly from 2000 to 2010, the number of positive media portrayals of entrepreneurs grew (e.g., *Dragon's Den* and *The Apprentice*) and can be contrasted with the somewhat more negative portrayals in the early 1980s (e.g., Del Boy in *Only Fools and Horses*).

All of these contextual changes point towards a general shift in society towards more acceptance of the role of entrepreneurship and the academy has mirrored and sometimes supported this change. As a consequence, when tracking the growth and diversity of entrepreneurship theory from the 1970s onwards, one has to acknowledge the growth of political interest, funding and, of course, the number of courses offered and professors employed to teach them. All these new professors need to be active researchers and publish and, as a consequence, contemporary thinking has expanded exponentially (see Figure 2.3). In the USA, we must also acknowledge the role and growth of philanthropy – successful entrepreneurs often giving back to their colleges and creating endowed professorships, which have also supported the development of the subject.

2.5.1 Small business or entrepreneurship?

The first disjuncture in thought that appears to have occurred in contemporary thinking and created diversity is between those theorists who focus on 'small businesses' and others who are more interested in 'entrepreneurship'. While the distinction between the two is inherently unclear – for example, researchers have difficulty explaining the difference between an entrepreneur and a small business owner (Carland et al., 1984) – there are definitely differences in focus.

The root cause of this disjuncture can be traced back to Schumpeter's thoughts on the subject. Small business researchers typically explore routine business experience (i.e., running a small business), while entrepreneurship researchers focus more on contexts where innovative effort is required (i.e., the start-up process). In general, 'entrepreneurship' tends to be applied to multiple entrepreneurial contexts – e.g., 'new venture creation', 'high-growth ventures' or 'corporate ventures' – while 'small business' focuses on established small firms that may be in none of those categories. Researchers and professors still use the terms interchangeably, which can often lead to confusion.

This split in thought can be charted through the names applied to journals (*International Small Business Journal* versus *Entrepreneurship Theory and Practice*) and the courses offered to students (small business management versus entrepreneurship). There also seems to be some geographic diversity, with Europeans more likely to focus on generic issues, such as small business and 'enterprise', while North Americans tend towards a greater focus on entrepreneurship.

In terms of theory, due to the lack of clarity in many studies, there is much overlap in the terminology applied and students can even feel this overlap in undergraduate courses. In general, though, small business researchers tend to focus on the firm as their unit of analysis (as opposed to the individual) or on the policy context supporting small firms. This leads to studies that focus on some key aspect of managerial practice inside a small firm (e.g., marketing, e-commerce or human resource management) or explore key contextual issues that may impact and/or concern small firms (e.g., government policy, training, finance). This category would also include research that builds further on Greiner's small business growth stages (Scott and Bruce, 1987), which tries to explain the different managerial practices required during different stages of growth.

In more recent years, further diversification has occurred within the small business research field, to cover particular forms of small businesses and their particular needs.

Figure 2.3 Diversification in contemporary thought

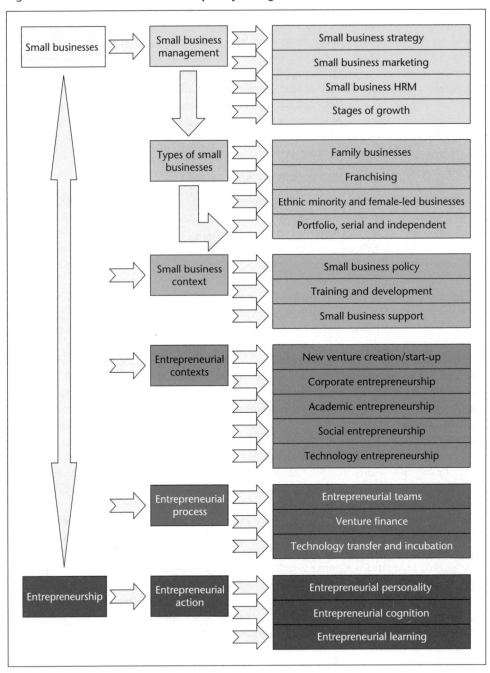

This shift was first illustrated by a move towards typologies – in other words, the ways in which researchers have categorised small business owners (e.g., portfolio versus individual or serial business owners).

The best example of this general shift has been a growing and separate focus on family businesses, which has since become a subject in its own right with its own journal (*Family Business Review*), and has a host of specific issues (e.g., family conflict, succession planning, the role of the spouse). Another clear example of this general trend is a growing emphasis on franchising, which crosses several areas of management research, including small business management, and focuses on issues such as franchisee–franchisor relationships, franchise failure rates and the role of a franchise in business growth. Further examples of this diversification in small business research include a growing focus on ethnic minority and immigrant-led small businesses and female-led small businesses.

While small business research and theory has diversified, research that is focused on entrepreneurship has also diversified significantly; the next section explains these developments.

2.5.2 Diversification and expansion

The second shift that appears to have created much diversity in entrepreneurship theory is a dissatisfaction with the dominant personality approach at the end of 1970s and early 1980s. During this period, the dissatisfaction manifested itself in a number of contexts, at slightly different times and in different ways.

It was best articulated in two seminal papers by Gartner (1989a, b), in which he argued for research to stop exploring *who* entrepreneurs were and explore *what* they did. Much of contemporary thought has since been driven by a desire to explain *what* entrepreneurs do and how they do it. In some respects, this period might be described as a paradigm shift, with many researchers directing their efforts in new directions. Although there are still researchers who explore entrepreneurial psychology, they do so from a different philosophical stance and fewer researchers than before focus on the entrepreneurial personality. Theory in entrepreneurship has, consequently, spun off in several directions.

First, a focus on what entrepreneurs do and how they do it enabled researchers to begin to look more at the context of entrepreneurial endeavour, the issues encountered and the behaviours used. Initially, the entrepreneurial context was narrowly defined as purely about 'new venture creation' (Gartner, 1989a, b), but, as time has passed, this shift enabled researchers to consider the multiple contexts within which entrepreneurial action occurs.

During the 1990s and 2000s, a plethora of other contexts for entrepreneurial action began to grow from this behavioural stance. For example, it is not unusual for researchers to now consider specific entrepreneurial contexts such as high-tech entrepreneurship, corporate entrepreneurship, social entrepreneurship and academic entrepreneurship. What these approaches hold in common is, at their root, a Schumpeterian assumption that entrepreneurship is an innovative process or 'the making of the road' as opposed to 'the travelling along it'. They do, however, agree that the process can occur in different ways in different contexts. For example, creating a new start-up is not entirely the same as creating a new business inside an established organisation or spinning out a technology-led venture from a university. They are *all* forms of entrepreneurship, but the processes involved are quite different from those used in managing established businesses.

Second, while there was a shift in theory that enabled researchers to explore what entrepreneurs do and how they do it, this behavioural focus opened up a criticism of entrepreneurial thought inherited from the 1960s, which was its focus on the individual. The assumption was that entrepreneurship is essentially led by individuals acting alone – it was argued that this 'heroic individual' myth underlies most entrepreneurship theory (Ogbor, 2000). When taking a behavioural stance, though, researchers discovered there was a large variety of contextual factors and a host of other actors that have an impact on entrepreneurial processes. A second branch of theory consequently blossomed from this acknowledgement and began to open up further research avenues, such as work on entrepreneurial teams, venture capital, business angels, banks, technology transfer offices, incubators and business support professionals. The milieu in which entrepreneurial activity occurs became a focus for study and this development is best illustrated by the foundation of some specific journals supporting such work (e.g., *Venture Capital* and *Entrepreneurship and Regional Development*).

Third, while many researchers shifted towards a more behavioural, organisational or even sociological explanation of entrepreneurial activity, not all researchers were willing to give up trying to understand entrepreneurs and the contribution they make to the entrepreneurial process (Carland, Hoy and Carland, 1988). These theorists split four ways.

- The first group continued to develop, expand and build upon personality theory (Johnson, 1990; Shaver and Scott, 1991) and tried to link the entrepreneurial personality to the context and process in which it is applied.

- The second group, taking a leaf from Kirzner's work, began to explore the role of cognition and sought to understand the entrepreneur's capacity to be 'alert' to new opportunities (Bird 1988, 1992; Bird and West, 1997). They developed concepts to explain particular entrepreneurial decisions (e.g., opportunity recognition, intentionality and self-efficacy), which helped to explain how decisions to start businesses might occur (Schwartz, Teach and Birch, 2005).

- The third group took a different philosophical stance to entrepreneurial personality (Chell, 1985; Chell, Haworth and Brearley, 1991) and viewed personality as a social construction. In this approach, entrepreneurial behaviour is an archetype created within society to describe how we expect people acting in entrepreneurial ways to behave. Such work opened up more study of different cultural perspectives as they relate to the ways in which entrepreneurship is perceived within different societies and acknowledged that the concept of the 'individual entrepreneur' is largely of Anglo-Saxon origin.

- The final group began to develop concepts to understand how entrepreneurs learn and become more effective as they engage in the entrepreneurial process (Gibb, 2002; Cope, 2003, 2005). This work recognises the somewhat deterministic stance of prior theory, which assumes little change in the way entrepreneurs are and how they behave, and takes a more voluntaristic stance, which assumes entrepreneurs and their activities emerge as a consequence of a process through which they live. This group applies the thinking that 'entrepreneurs change as they learn and engage and businesses perform better as entrepreneurs learn'.

Finally, as researchers have begun to appreciate the behavioural nuances of entrepreneurship and as the subject has grown, research has begun to focus on entrepreneurship education itself (Pittaway and Cope, 2007). Entrepreneurship education research is now also quite diverse, including many subjects and themes – e.g., teaching methods, higher education policy and, institutional support for student entrepreneurs. The behavioural focus that developed in the mid to late 1980s also led to greater recognition that entrepreneurial activity could be learnt, which provided more justification for exploring how to improve educational practices and this led to a growth in educational research within the subject of entrepreneurship.

Up to the present day, most of the contemporary approaches described here continued to be developed by entrepreneurship researchers and the contemporary academic journals in the field – the undergraduate textbooks and courses all demonstrate this diversity in theory and thought. Such diversity, however, has led to much confusion and debate about the nature of academic inquiry in entrepreneurship. In addition, in more recent years, entrepreneurship research has expanded its domain into public policy and practice via applied research, such as the Global Entrepreneurship Monitor (GEM). The increasing interest of policymakers in understanding how to harness entrepreneurial activity for the good of an economy has led to these debates about theory taking on new significance. Indeed, current changes and shifts in developed countries towards an entrepreneurial economy have also allowed many of the older economic theories (such as Schumpeter's) to develop a more visible prominence in economic decisionmaking.

The final part of this chapter explores what researchers think about this diversity and how they suggest it should be addressed.

2.5.3 Inquiry in entrepreneurship research

One of the first considerations about entrepreneurship inquiry that causes concern is its multidisciplinary nature (see Figure 2.4). The description of the subject's history given in this chapter illustrates that it draws from many different economic theories, different perspectives in psychology, social psychology and sociology and also management theory. This diversity is both an advantage and a disadvantage. It provides for an interesting mix of ideas and topics that can be fascinating and lead to new ideas, but it can also lead to lack of complementarity of theories.

Despite the historical nature of the subject outlined in this chapter and due partly to its growth from the 1980s onwards, many researchers consider it to be a relatively young subject (Davidsson, Low and Wright, 2001). During the 1980s, in particular, it was considered to be dominated by exploratory studies lacking empirical strength and theoretical depth, which led to calls for new methods for analysing data (Bygrave, 1989).

While the subject developed during the 1980s and offered better, more effective empirical research, it remained somewhat underdeveloped in terms of theory (Shane

Figure 2.4 **The disciplinary basis of entrepreneurship research**

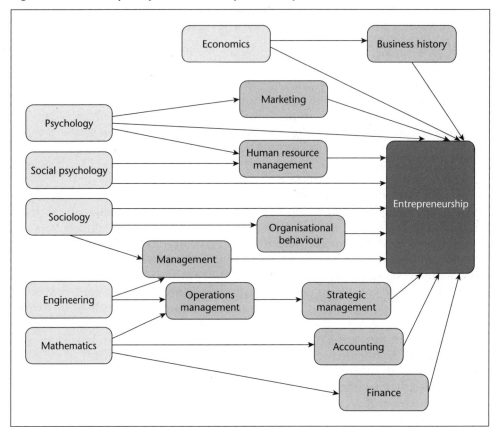

and Venkataraman, 2000). Increases in empirical work followed Bygrave's (1989) call, but methodological sophistication was not necessarily founded on the development of sound theory (Schwartz and Teach, 2000).

During the 1990s, the subject's theoretical foundations are considered to have advanced (Gartner, 2001), but it has been generally accepted that this enhancement of theory has led to further fragmentation, diversity and complexity (Brazeal and Herbert, 1999).

As the volume of work increased, more empirical and conceptual studies have been carried out that are broadly in the domain of entrepreneurship. The expansion of effort from the 1980s onwards has led to an abundance of new theories, the use of many different units of analysis (e.g., the individual, the firm, the network of firms), the use of many different disciplines and some incompatibility in the methods used to conduct research (Chandler and Lyon, 2001).

Different groups of researchers have different solutions to what many see as a common problem of fragmentation in the subject.

■ The first group typifies a 'normal science' perspective, whereby 'general theories' are sought to integrate the subject into a conceptual whole (Shane and Venkataraman, 2000). Views here occupy two trajectories: those seeking expansive theories (Shane and Venkataraman, 2000) that incorporate much thinking into a coherent whole and those seeking to draw the boundaries around the subject more tightly (Low, 2001), thereby excluding certain types of study from the subject. In both views entrepreneurship research involves the representation and analysis of phenomena, such as opportunities and ventures, as they occur via observation.

■ The second group prefer a 'pragmatic science' perspective, whereby communities of scholars are encouraged to build research agendas around discrete themes within a general 'political' definition of entrepreneurship in which many perspectives are located (Gartner, 2001; Ucbasaran, Westhead and Wright, 2001). These views remain embedded within the 'scientific' view of knowledge creation, whereby study should build theory and test it empirically.

■ The third type can be described as the 'interpretive' perspective, whereby differing philosophical traditions underpin theorising, leading to very different forms of knowledge construction that are regarded as equally acceptable (Grant and Perren, 2002; Pittaway, 2005).

In summary, the response seems to be to either consolidate and/or exclude types of research, defining the subject of entrepreneurship more narrowly, or, as an alternative, accept diversity in thinking as a positive outcome for entrepreneurship theory. The different approaches of the groups explained illustrate a community of scholars grappling with a diverse, growing and complicated subject. While it has a long history and deep roots, this is, in some respects, a discipline or subject in the making, so it is a good time to be a student of entrepreneurship.

2.6 Chapter summary

This chapter explored the history of entrepreneurship thought. It started with the early economic theorists and highlighted the different schools of thought and showed how the economic thinkers sought to understand the function of entrepreneurship in the economy, discussing the different theories. In the economic thinking there were some clear differences. The early French economists began the process of considering the subject of entrepreneurs and thought that they played an important function in the economy. British classical and neoclassical economists largely ignored the role of entrepreneurship and the disappearance of the entrepreneur in contemporary economics can be explained by the dominance of their theories in economics today. The Austrians and neo-Austrians took up the challenge from the French and identified key aspects ßof entrepreneurial activity – e.g., making decisions about the allocation of resources and identifying opportunities when faced with uncertainty. Schumpeter put forward a new interpretation and this view guided much of contemporary thought – i.e., the idea that entrepreneurship is about innovation or 'doing new things'.

Towards the end of the chapter, early theories in psychology, social psychology and sociology were introduced. It was explained that the economic focus on entrepreneurship closed with a recommendation to examine individuals. Personality theory became the dominant form from this point, but, in the late 1980s, researchers began to question its value and approach, which led to a diversification in thought from then onwards.

In the final part of the chapter, contemporary thinking about entrepreneurship theory was discussed and several branches were explained, each leading to greater diversity in the subject (see Figure 2.3).

Overall, the chapter shows that thinking in entrepreneurship has a long history. It is rooted in the very beginning of economics as a discipline and early economists considered it to be an important function within the economic system. Over the years, entrepreneurship as a subject has gone through several phases and perhaps gone in and out of fashion as economies have gone through periods of change. From the 1980s onwards, though, the modern subject blossomed and there is now a wide host of topics and themes in the field; you will learn more about some of these in the chapters that follow.

Questions

1 What are the main theories in economics that discuss the entrepreneur? In one of the theories identified, explain the role of the entrepreneur in the economy.

2 Kirzner's theory of entrepreneurship revolves around the concept of 'alertness to opportunity'. Describe and explain the concept and illustrate the idea as applied to entrepreneurs today.

3 Schumpeter's theory of economic development presents the entrepreneur as an innovator. Using examples of contemporary businesses, explain the five forms of innovation and explain why they might be considered entrepreneurial.

4 'Contemporary theory in entrepreneurship has become fragmented.' Consider this statement critically, assessing the strengths and weaknesses of this diversity in thinking.

Weblinks

http://gemconsortium.org
The Global Entrepreneurship Monitor consortium provides country-by-country analysis of entrepreneurship.

www.kauffman.org/Section.aspx?id=Research_And_Policy
The Kauffman Foundation research and policy site provides recent articles on entrepreneurship and the economy.

www.oecd.org/topic/
From the topics' tab, choose 'Industry and entrepreneurship' and the OECD will provide you with studies on entrepreneurship across the OECD countries.

CHAPTER 3

Entrepreneurship and economic development

Robert Huggins and Nick Williams

3.1 Introduction

This chapter reviews and examines the role of entrepreneurship in stimulating economic development and growth. It highlights the resurgence of interest in entrepreneurship among economic theorists and the increased importance given to entrepreneurship by policymakers with a responsibility for economic development.

Although such development is often considered from a national perspective, the chapter shows how entrepreneurship is in many ways a local or regional phenomenon, with entrepreneurs shaped by the geographic boundaries and context within which they operate. In particular, entrepreneurship forms a part of endogenous modes of economic development, consisting of activities, investment and systems arising and nurtured within a region or locality, as opposed to being attracted from elsewhere. As part of these modes, the capability of entrepreneurs to influence economic development is related to their capacity to access and exploit knowledge and generate innovation. It is shown that the cultural traits of places, especially in terms of social capital, may influence entrepreneurial capacity, with policymakers seeking to develop such traits in order to improve entrepreneurial potential. Alongside policies related to cultural development, policymakers have sought to stimulate entrepreneurship through policies targeted at both the economic and social barriers, plus opportunities mediating entrepreneurial activity.

3.2 Learning objectives

This chapter has four key learning objectives:

1 to understand how entrepreneurship facilitates economic development and growth
2 to appreciate how entrepreneurship is linked to related factors underpinning economic development
3 to consider the role of geography in influencing patterns of entrepreneurship
4 to understand the role of government and public policy in supporting and facilitating entrepreneurship.

Key concepts

- entrepreneurship ■ economic development ■ economic growth
- regions and localities ■ endogenous development ■ knowledge spillovers
- social capital ■ public policy

3.3 Entrepreneurship and economic development

Entrepreneurship is increasingly recognised as a crucial element in fostering economic development and growth (Audretsch, Keilbach and Lehmann, 2006; Carree and Thurik, 2006; Romer, 2007). Romer (2007: 128) emphasises the role of entrepreneurship by stating that 'economic growth occurs whenever people take resources and rearrange them in ways that are valuable . . . [It] springs from better recipes, not just more cooking'. The process of entrepreneurship is widely considered to stimulate competition, drive innovation, create employment, generate positive externalities, increase productivity by introducing technological change and provide a route out of poverty (Audretsch and Thurik, 2001; Acs, 2002, 2006; Powell, 2007).

Across major industrialised economies, levels of entrepreneurial activity are positively correlated with levels of per capita gross domestic product (GDP) and the rate of GDP growth (Acs, 2006; Audretsch and Thurik, 2001; Reynolds et al., 2000, 2001, 2002; OECD, 2003). Government intervention within the field of entrepreneurship, therefore, is inspired by the view that the entrepreneur is one of the solutions to weak economic performance and poor levels of job creation (Holtz-Eakin, 2000; Gilbert, Audretsch and McDougall 2004; Audretsch, Grilo and Thurik 2007; Henrekson, 2007).

In the past, the prevailing view of economists was that large-scale enterprises were the key to economic development, while small firms were viewed as relatively inefficient and less involved in innovative activity (Bridge, O'Neill and Cromie, 2003; Audretsch et al., 2006). The notion that economic growth was possible without the innovations of individual entrepreneurs gained support (Galbraith, 1956; Chandler, 1977), with small firms and entrepreneurship viewed as a luxury rather than a necessity (Audretsch et al., 2006; Volkmann et al., 2009). The route to economic growth was seen as being a combination of large-scale production and collectivist ideologies (Acs and Audretsch, 2001), and stability, continuity and homogeneity became the cornerstones of 'managed' economies (Verheul et al., 2001). However, the domination of 'big-firm capitalism' has gradually diminished (Storey, 1994) and centrally planned economies – built around economic concentration and scale economies – have began to wither and ultimately disappear, typified by the fall of the Berlin Wall (Verheul et al., 2001; Audretsch et al., 2006).

Overall, the role and importance of the entrepreneur has witnessed a resurgence in both economic theory and public policymaking (Audretsch, 2003). In the past, entrepreneurship policies were often developed as a temporary solution, to absorb workers displaced by industrial restructuring and downsizing (Storey, 1991), but in more recent years such policies are seen as an essential instrument for encouraging economic growth (Gilbert et al., 2004). However, the notion of the entrepreneur and the contribution of entrepreneurship to economic growth have been interpreted in widely different ways (Hébert and Link, 1989) and, as such, there exists no generally accepted definition (Verheul et al., 2001). Sautet and Kirzner (2006) argue that the concept of entrepreneurship is notoriously difficult to pin down, with economists and policymakers often entirely overlooking it or gravely misunderstanding it.

Schumpeter (1942) describes economic development as being a process of creative destruction, which combines a positive side, whereby new enterprises are introduced and expanded, with a negative one, whereby enterprises exit or contract. Entrepreneurs are crucial in this process, as they start firms in order to commercialise innovations and, by doing so, challenge established structures and drive the course of creative destruction through innovation (Johansson, 2007). As a consequence of this driving nature, the Schumpeterian entrepreneur is a heroic figure, demonstrating boldness and leadership (Schumpeter, 1934).

Kirzner also emphasises a requirement for human action in entrepreneurship and finds that boldness, imagination and creativity are important aspects (Schumpeter, 1942; Kirzner, 1973, 2009). However, Schumpeter and Kirzner differ in their interpretation of entrepreneurial opportunity, with Kirzner stating that entrepreneurship does not necessarily require innovation (Kirzner, 1973, 2009). While the Schumpeterian entrepreneur causes dramatic changes in markets and industries, the Kirznerian entrepreneur engages in arbitrage by being alert to profit opportunities in existing circumstances (Kirzner, 1973, 2009).

A further key theory is that of Baumol, who states that the structure of pay-offs drives the allocation of entrepreneurial activity between productive, unproductive and destructive entrepreneurship (Baumol, 1990). Where there is an absence of productive entrepreneurship, individuals have found better ways of utilising their time and resources (Greene, Mole and Storey, 2007).

Entrepreneurship has been used to define types of individuals (Say, 1880), types of decisions (Knight, 1921) and forms of behaviour (Schumpeter, 1934). As a discrete concept, entrepreneurship has its origin in the work of Cantillon (1732/1931) and has developed through the neoclassical school's emphasis on equilibrium, which found no place for the entrepreneur as a cause of economic activity (Bridge et al., 2003), to the Austrian school's theoretical challenge that entrepreneurship is crucial to understanding economic growth, leading to Schumpeter's (1934: 74) statement that 'the carrying out of new combinations (of means of production) we call "enterprise"; and the individuals whose function it is to carry them out we call "entrepreneurs"'.

The neoclassical model, which links stocks of capital and labour to growth, dominated growth theory (Solow, 1956; Audretsch, 2007). However, entrepreneurship did not fit into this model because, first, the neoclassical axiom of perfect competition implies that there are no profit opportunities for entrepreneurs left to exploit and, second, models of general equilibrium do not take into account the dynamics of innovating entrepreneurship (Wennekers and Thurik, 1999; Huerta de Soto, 2008).

Entrepreneurs drive the market forward towards efficient outcomes by exploiting profit opportunities and moving economies towards equilibrium (Kirzner, 1973). Entrepreneurs also contribute to the market's process of 'creative destruction', with new innovations replacing old technologies (Schumpeter, 1934; Sobel, Clark and Lee, 2007). Entrepreneurship, therefore, involves the nexus of entrepreneurial opportunities and enterprising individuals, and the ability to identify opportunities as a key part of the entrepreneurial process (Shane, 2003; Olson, 2007). Enterprise and entrepreneurship are now commonly viewed as the process of establishing and growing a business (Bridge et al., 2003). However, this can be seen as a narrow view of enterprise and entrepreneurship and disregards Schumpeter's (1934) contention that entrepreneurship is a function of change in society, occuring in a variety of circumstances (Pittaway, 2005). While the creation of a new business is an accurate description of one of the many outcomes of entrepreneurial activity, entrepreneurship encompasses far more than business start-ups and derives from the creative power of the human mind (Sautet and Kirzner, 2006), described as a behavioural characteristic of individuals expressed through innovative attributes, flexibility and adaptability to change (Wennekers and Thurik, 1999; Swedberg, 2000; Bridge et al., 2003).

In general, economic theory holds explicit implications for government intervention to promote entrepreneurship. Schumpeter (1934) views the entrepreneur's role as causing disequilibrium, while Kirzner (1973) emphasises the role of moving the economy towards equilibrium by being alert to new opportunities in existing circumstances. Both views are important in terms of policy intervention as, if government can influence levels and types of entrepreneurship, it is a lever by which to harness economic development. Baumol (1990) proposes that the supply of entrepreneurship is constant, but its distribution across productive, unproductive and destructive activities is affected by institutional arrangements and the social pay-off structure.

Baumol's (1990) theory has further implications for government intervention as policymaking has the possibility of promoting all three activities. A key issue is that policy may promote unproductive activities through incentivised 'rent seeking' based on acquiring government grants, resulting in entrepreneurs moving away from previously productive activities that satisfied consumer desires and led to economic growth. Nevertheless, policies geared towards enhancing entrepreneurship and stimulating enterprise development have become increasingly prevalent across advanced economies (Bridge et al., 2003; Gilbert et al., 2004; Audretsch et al., 2007). Reflecting the raised importance of entrepreneurship over the last two decades, economic development policies have shifted away from trying to attract large manufacturing firms and inward investment and, instead, towards fostering entrepreneurship (Verheul et al., 2001; Kreft and Sobel, 2005; Sobel et al., 2007).

The Global Entrepreneurship Monitor (GEM) aims to explore the links between entrepreneurship and economic growth at national level (Reynolds et al., 2000, 2001, 2002; Bosma and Harding, 2006; Bosma et al., 2008; Harding, 2008; Levie and Autio, 2008; Bosma and Levie, 2009). GEM links the complementary processes through which individuals perceive opportunities and are thereby prompted to create new business activity, which in turn is proposed to impact on economic growth (Bosma et al., 2008; Levie and Autio, 2008). In so doing, the research follows theorists of entrepreneurship in the Austrian tradition, including Schumpeter and Kirzner, as well as other economists who have recognised the role of entrepreneurship in economic development, such as Baumol (Levie and Autio, 2008).

In order to explore these links, GEM has developed a conceptual model that summarises the mechanisms affecting national economies (see Figure 3.1). The model illustrates that the context for entrepreneurship includes a wide range of economic, social and cultural factors and shows national economic growth is a function of

Figure 3.1 **The Global Entrepreneurship Monitor (GEM) conceptual model**

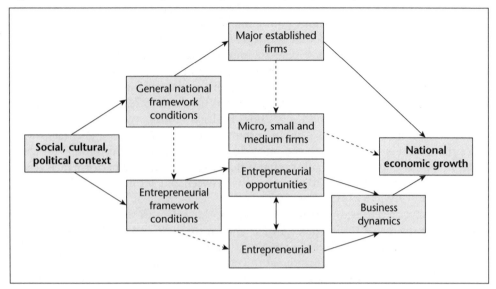

Source: Derived from Reynolds et al. (2000, Figures 1 and 2)

interrelated activities – those associated with major established firms and those related directly to the entrepreneurial process (Reynolds et al., 2000; Hart, 2003b). As such, the entrepreneurial process accounts for a significant proportion of the differences in economic prosperity between countries (Reynolds et al., 2000; Bridge et al., 2003).

The GEM study has found a statistically significant relationship between entrepreneurial activity and national economic growth, although the strength of the association tends to vary depending on the countries included and the nature of entrepreneurial activity considered (Reynolds et al., 2001). GEM makes a distinction between 'necessity entrepreneurship', defined as people who view entrepreneurship as the best option available and not necessarily the preferred option, and 'opportunity entrepreneurship', defined as those who engage in entrepreneurship out of choice (Acs, 2006; Bosma et al., 2008; Hechavarria and Reynolds, 2009). The prevalence rate of necessity entrepreneurship is positively associated with national economic growth and is strongest when countries highly dependent on international trade are excluded. While there may be uncertainty regarding causation, it is clear that entrepreneurship is an important component in economic growth (Wennekers and Thurik, 1999; Reynolds et al., 2000, 2001, 2002; Harding, 2008). Indeed, while 'economic models may not be able to prove that entrepreneurship creates economic growth . . . you won't get growth without [it]' (Harding, 2008: 7).

3.4 Regional and local perspectives

With increasing globalisation, it can be argued that subnational spatial levels have become more important than nations in the development of economic growth (Storper,

1997; Porter, 2000; Camagni, 2002; Scott and Storper, 2003; Krugman, 2005), particularly in terms of firm entry, competition and learning (Fritsch and Schmude, 2006). The reason some locations gain competitive advantage and grow more than others and some once successful locations have failed to change in step with changes in the economy is a matter of keen debate in economics (Westlund and Bolton, 2003; Kitson, Martin and Tyler, 2004). However, regions and cities are considered important sources of economic development, entrepreneurship and competitive advantage within the increasingly globalised economy (Scott, 1995; Cooke, 1997; Amin, 1999; Werker and Athreye, 2004; Steyaert and Katz, 2004; Malecki, 2007).

The subnational level is also an important dimension for entrepreneurship and, while the nation is often used as the unit of analysis in studies of economic development, it is clear that there are substantial differences in economic performance across regions *within* nations (Porter, 2003), as well as between and within cities (Glaeser et al., 1992; Porter, 1995, 1997; Glaeser, 2007).

When competitiveness of regions is discussed, this refers to the presence of conditions that enable firms to compete in their chosen markets and the value these firms generate being captured within their regions (Begg, 1999; Huggins, 2003). Regional competitiveness, therefore, is considered to consist of the capability of an economy to attract and maintain firms with stable or rising market shares in an activity, while maintaining stable or increasing standards of living for those who participate in it (Storper, 1997). The definition of competitiveness equates with the 'high road of regional competition', where regions compete by achieving high levels of innovation, upgrading and growth, rather than the 'low road of competition' associated with promoting the lower costs of labour, land or capital (Malecki, 2004). Competitiveness varies across geographic space and regions develop at different rates depending on the drivers of growth (Audretsch and Keilbach, 2004). Regional development concerns the upgrading of the economic, institutional and social base, with entrepreneurship able to unlock wealth as the prime source of development (Amin, 1999). Consequently, entrepreneurship is considered central to regional economic growth (Audretsch and Keilbach, 2004; Malecki, 2007).

At the local level, rates of entrepreneurship often vary greatly (Glaeser, 2007). Localities that foster entrepreneurial dynamism harness economic growth, with a critical mass of businesses providing opportunities for employment, competition and knowledge generation (Porter, 1995; Anderson, 2005). Furthermore, successful cities will attract migrants from elsewhere who are alert to entrepreneurial opportunities or opportunities to sell their labour in a specific market where pay may be advantageous (Anderson, 2005). As Seabright (2004: 111) states, 'the most innovative people have always been footloose, restlessly seeking out opportunities over time and space'.

A city with a million people potentially offers more than ten times the opportunities for discovery than a town of 100,000 and can attract more people from outside areas (Ikeda, 2008). When this takes place, cities can become 'incubators of new ideas', providing opportunities for entrepreneurship to take place and discovering valuable new knowledge (Glaeser, 2002; Ikeda, 2008). Within cities, successful neighbourhoods need at first to 'feel safe' in order to harness entrepreneurship (Jacobs, 1961). Neighbourhoods that encourage informal contact at all hours of the day and night harness the self-monitoring 'eyes on the street' necessary for feeling safe and the

Figure 3.2 VAT registrations and GVA per head for UK regions

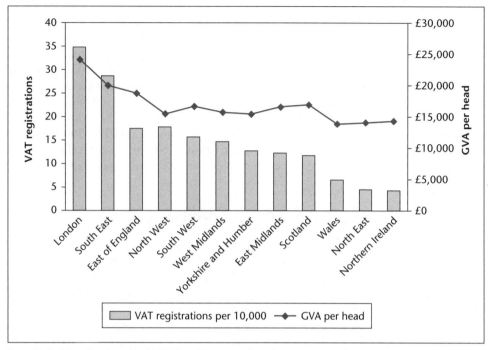

Source: Derived from Huggins and Izushi (2008) and Department for Business, Enterprise and Regulatory Reform (2007b)

emergence of informal networks of trust (Glaeser and Sacerdote, 2000). This informal contact allows for the potential coordination of individuals and assists in harnessing entrepreneurship (Ikeda, 2008).

In order for regions and locations to foster entrepreneurship they must also harness competition, as there is an intrinsic link between entrepreneurship and competition (Kirzner, 1973; Sautet and Kirzner, 2006). Indeed, 'entrepreneurship and competition are two sides of the same coin' (Sautet and Kirzner, 2006: 10). Figure 3.2 highlights the correlation between entrepreneurship (expressed as VAT-registered businesses) and gross value added (GVA) per capital in the regions of the UK. The top three-ranked competitive regions all have the highest levels of VAT registrations and levels of GVA, while, conversely, the less competitive, lagging regions have low levels of registrations and low levels of GVA. In competitiveness terms, London, the South East and the East of England are the only regions to have performed above the UK average since 1997 and the disparities between the leading and lagging nations are persistent (Huggins and Thompson, 2010).

In an environment that allows free entry into the market, entrepreneurs can take advantage of new profit opportunities and create new entrepreneurial possibilities that others can act upon (Minniti, 2005). As such, entrepreneurship creates an environment that makes even *more* entrepreneurship possible (Holcombe, 2007). Therefore, in a competitive environment, entrepreneurs will be alert to opportunities and contribute to regional economic growth (Audretsch and Keilbach, 2004).

In competitive situations where locations compete for investment by companies and governments, one place or a few places are chosen while others are not (Malecki, 2004, 2007). Yet, with the emergence of the knowledge economy, such 'smokestack chasing' is no longer sufficient (Acs and Szerb, 2007). To compete and grow, places must develop infrastructure, specialised services and a quality of place that facilitates the recruitment of skilled and mobile professionals (Florida, 2002). Developing quality of place is an ongoing dynamic process built on authenticity, diversity and interaction, that generates a 'buzz' (Storper and Venables, 2002; Bathelt, Malmberg and Maskell, 2004; Malecki, 2007). This, in turn, attracts creative people to a place, who then stimulate the economy by introducing new ideas, technology and content (Florida, 2002; Acs and Megyesi, 2009). In this sense, creativity is to the twenty-first century what the ability to push a plough was to the eighteenth century (Glaeser, 2005; Acs and Megyesi, 2009).

3.5 Entrepreneurship and endogenous development

Alongside the role of entrepreneurship, economic development is increasingly considered to be based on the complementary roles that knowledge and innovation play within and across economies. The concept of the knowledge-based economy has emerged from an increasing recognition of the requirement for the production, distribution and use of knowledge within modern economies (Harris, 2001). Endogenous growth theory has placed knowledge at the centre of economic development (Romer, 1986; Lucas, 1988; Romer, 1990). Knowledge is viewed as not only the key to the competitiveness of a production unit, i.e. a firm (Nonaka and Takeuchi, 1995), but also regions (Huggins and Izushi, 2007).

Whilst endogenous regional growth can be considered the desired outcome of knowledge-based development and innovation, it is the process of endogenous *development* that underpins the growth trajectories of regions (Maillat, 1998; Garofoli, 2002; Vázquez-Barquero, 2007).

The principles of the endogenous development school of regions are rooted in the role that collective learning and cooperative behaviour plays in the establishment of the innovative milieu – or what some have referred to as 'technopoles' (Castells and Hall, 1994), 'industrial districts' (Capello, 1999), or 'clusters' (Porter, 1998b) – facilitating knowledge flow and new knowledge creation. Implicit is the contention that regional development and growth are best promoted through bottom-up activity focused on the enhancement of local production systems rather than top-down processes of exogenous development focused on seeking to redistribute resources from elsewhere (Maillat, 1998; Garofoli, 2002).

The endogenous school of thought has proved to be of particular relevance in more peripheral and emerging regional environments, which, as a prerequisite for any form of development, need to maximise the effectiveness of particular industrial strengths. Many of these strengths are related to relatively traditional areas of economic activity, requiring transformation, reproduction and innovation if they are to remain competitive and sustainable within the globalising world (Capello, 1999; Lawson and Lorenz, 1999). As Garofoli (2002) argues, endogenous development primarily concerns the capacity to innovate and produce 'collective intelligence' in a localised environment, which explicitly recognises the relevance of diffusing, accumulating, creating and internalising knowledge. In this sense, the region itself acts as an organisational form of coordination, facilitating a sustainable competitive advantage.

Urban settings are increasingly considered to be key territorial units within which endogenous forms of development flourish through their innovative milieu. However, in less-favoured metropolitan settings, regional innovation support policy is seen to be of crucial importance, especially focusing on issues relating to knowledge transfer and functional linkages (Morgan and Nauwelaers, 2003; Cornett, 2009). Asheim and Isaksen (2003) argue that endogenous regional development is unlikely to occur holistically without public intervention to stimulate, for example, cluster creation and network formation. Nauwelaers and Wintjes (2003) classify regional innovation policies according to two core types:

1 firm-orientated – principally access to human capital (e.g., business support and advice), financial capital (e.g., risk capital, loans or subsidies) or physical capital (e.g., incubators, research and technology centres)

2 system-orientated (regional) – principally network-building and brokering, cluster development, innovation system development, building an innovation culture, cooperation and mobility.

However, they recognise that both types may operate in tandem, with a need for co-ordination across policies (Nauwelaers and Wintjes, 2003).

Figure 3.3 summarises some of the key contemporary modes through which endogenous modes of economic development are conceptualised and policy has subsequently been established. Cooke (2004), for instance, suggests that regional innovation systems consisting of interacting knowledge generation and exploitation subsystems are a vital component of regional economic development and competitiveness, while others have focused on the notion of clusters as the key focus of regional economic theory and policy, with the underlying tenet being that competitiveness is determined by the strength of key concentrations of specific industries (Porter, 1998b).

Clusters can be defined as geographically proximate firms in vertical and horizontal relationships involving a localised enterprise support infrastructure with a shared developmental vision for business growth based on competition and cooperation in a specific market field (Cooke and Huggins, 2003). Clusters are considered as offering a means for creating higher value-added by tapping into and distributing the potential of local strengths as a whole rather than as a series of fragmented firms (Roelandt and den Hertog, 1998; Huggins, 2008).

Similarly, public policy intervention in more recent years has drawn on the triple helix model of economic development, which seeks to promote increased interaction across three broad institutional spheres – namely, government, business/industry and higher education (Etzkowitz and Leydesdorff, 2000; Etzkowitz, 2003). Most prominence has been given to the triple helix regime, which is based on overlapping spheres of state, industry and academia through the establishment of hybrid organisations such as intermediaries, innovation and incubation centres and science parks, allowing each sphere to undertake activities from which they were previously excluded. Such overlapping triple helix forms are manifested by industrial policies that seek to develop an industrial structure based on firm engagement in interorganisational alliances and

Figure 3.3 **Modes of endogenous regional development**

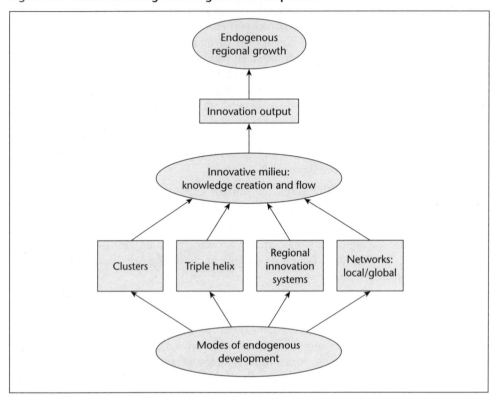

networks with universities. Furthermore, the triple helix approach has been promoted by its conceptual originators as a policy instrument of relevance to lagging regional environments where, due to the relative lack of knowledge-creating enterprises, universities are, by default, key 'knowledge actors'.

3.6 Knowledge spillovers and entrepreneurship

Knowledge is often considered to be a public good that frequently 'spills over' to other firms and individuals, allowing them to reap where they have not necessarily sown (Acs et al., 2009).

Knowledge spillovers can be defined as the continuum between pure knowledge spillovers, which are uncharged, unintended and not mediated by any market mechanism, and rent spillovers, consisting of externalities that are at least partially paid for (Andersson and Ejermo, 2005). While endogenous growth theory assumes that the spillover process is automatic, it is, in fact, driven by economic agents, i.e. entrepreneurs (Audretsch and Keilbach, 2004; Braunerhjelm et al., 2009). Entrepreneurs convert freely available knowledge into economic knowledge (Braunerhjelm et al., 2009) and, by doing so, guide the market, driving the selection process, creating a diversity of knowledge and fostering a market process (Schumpeter, 1942; Kirzner, 1973; Sautet and Kirzner, 2006). The start-up of new firms contributes to diversity by commercialising knowledge (Acs and Plummer, 2005) and, the greater the level of entrepreneurship, the greater the diversity and resultant growth (Audretsch and Keilbach, 2004).

Knowledge spillovers may occur through the flow of skills, expertise, technology, R&D and the like across interorganisational and interpersonal networks (Andersson and Karlsson, 2007). The spillover effects of knowledge can take place through time and across space. A key dimension of spillovers is geographic distance, with the general argument being that knowledge spills over more easily locally than at a distance. A study by Jaffe, Trajtenberg and Henderson (1993) discovered that citations to domestic patents were more likely to be domestic in origin, as well as being more likely to stem from the same region and locality as the cited patents. They also found that the localisation of patent citations was significant, even when the existing concentration of related research activity was taken into account. This suggests that local firms are often embedded in knowledge networks (Breschi and Malerba, 2001).

Also, ready access to local public or private research institutes and universities is another route through which knowledge flows. Such knowledge spillovers are especially important in highly knowledge-intensive entrepreneurship focused on knowledge at the frontier of innovation. A study conducted by Audretsch and Feldman (1996) shows that innovative activity tends to cluster geographically more in knowledge-intensive industries where knowledge spillovers play a decisive role. Although such industries tend to exhibit a geographic concentration of production activity, clustering of their innovation activities tends to be even greater. However, knowledge spillovers do also take place internationally, but usually through more selective routes.

Cutting-edge technology constantly changes, resulting in new, better products and processes. Unless local networks keep abreast of different technological options emerging outside, they run the risk of becoming rigid and outdated (Camagni, 1991; Izushi, 1997; Bathelt et al., 2004). In particular, the success of entrepreneurial endeavours – those taking the risk of starting up new ventures and tapping into new areas outside established technologies and markets – will depend on the entrepreneur's ability to access major markets from other localities and regions (Bresnahan et al., 2001). While firms benefit from local knowledge spillovers as an undirected and spontaneous 'buzz', they may also need to consciously build non-local 'pipelines' to tap into knowledge from outside (Bathelt et al., 2004).

Clearly, knowledge spillovers will not be uniform across all firms and places. For instance, smaller firms in a region may benefit from spillovers of university knowledge as they have fewer resources with which to generate their own knowledge (Acs et al., 1994). Also, regional high-tech firms may tend to benefit from university knowledge (Audretsch, Lehmann and Warning, 2005), with there being a significant correlation between the concentration of high-tech industries and university research in high-tech fields within a region (Nagle, 2007; Huggins, Johnston and Steffenson, 2008).

More generally, the study of entrepreneurship has increasingly reflected the general agreement that entrepreneurs and new firms must engage in networks to survive. Also, it is accepted that the socio-economic climate in which entrepreneurs operate will vary their ability 'to capture the benefits of economic efficiency' that networks facilitate (Szarka, 1990; Jack, 2005; Lechner, Dowling and Welpe, 2006; Bowey and Easton, 2007). Research on the networking behaviour of entrepreneurs has tended to focus on personal, social and professional networks as contributing to the success potential of a venture (Birley, 1985; Aldrich and Zimmer, 1986; Huggins, 2000b). Entrepreneurship models of networking have mainly incorporated social network and resource-dependence theories, as well as a resource-based view of the entrepreneur (Ostgaard and Birley, 1996). Network perspectives are seen as contributing to explaining patterns of entrepreneurship where it is the social role and embedded social context that facilitates or inhibits the activities of entrepreneurs (Aldrich and Zimmer, 1986; Huggins, 2000b, 2010). Networks matter to entrepreneurs because they create efficiencies in assembling the resources necessary in the entrepreneurial process (Thorpe et al., 2005).

3.7 Culture, social capital and entrepreneurial places

At the core of entrepreneurship lies culture, which can be defined as a set of shared values, beliefs and expected behaviours (Hayton, George and Zahra, 2002; Hechavarria and Reynolds, 2009; Huggins and Williams, 2009). Culture shapes what individuals perceive as opportunities and, therefore, entrepreneurial alertness is linked to judgment, creativity and interpretation (Hofstede, 1991; Lavoie, 1991; Sautet and Kirzner, 2006; Hechavarria and Reynolds, 2009). Effective institutions and a culture supportive of entrepreneurship make it possible for economic actors to take advantage of perceived opportunities (Sautet and Kirzner, 2006). Places – cities, regions or smaller communities – with an entrepreneurially conducive culture may increase their competitive advantage by attracting investment, skills and talent (Turok, 2004). Places with strong entrepreneurial traditions have a competitive advantage if they are able to perpetuate it over time and generations (Audretsch and Fritsch, 2002; Parker, 2004; Mueller, 2006). Entrepreneurship capital – i.e., the capacity of a society to generate entrepreneurial activity – is built up and has a positive impact on regional economic performance (Audretsch and Keilbach, 2005).

Entrepreneurship can be considered self-reinforcing in nature and can concentrate geographically because of the social environment, as individuals follow societal clues and are influenced by what others have chosen to do (Feldman, 2001; Minniti, 2005). Thus, entrepreneurial activity can create its own feedback cycle, slowly moving society to a more entrepreneurial culture, with a high density of successful new venture creation by local entrepreneurs offering role models people can conform to (Verheul et al., 2001). Places, therefore, can influence entrepreneurial activities via a shared culture or set of formal and informal rules (Werker and Athreye, 2004). In places where entrepreneurship is seen as providing valuable rewards and entrepreneurs are seen as role models, a sustaining entrepreneurial culture can be formed (Saxenian, 1996).

In a competitive environment, entrepreneurs will be alert to opportunities and contribute to economic development (Audretsch and Keilbach, 2004). However, changes in levels of entrepreneurship and contributions to economic development will take time to emerge and, as such, any impacts may only be seen in the long term (Huggins and Johnston, 2009; Huggins and Williams, 2009). Alternatively, places can be uncompetitive and lack entrepreneurial dynamism because they lack the key strengths that make leading regions prosper and develop (Huggins and Johnston, 2009).

A key cultural trait of places is their social capital, consisting of the economic significance of social relations facilitated through personal contacts, networks and norms of behaviour (Granovetter, 1973, 1983, 1985; Coleman, 1990, 2000; Westlund and Bolton, 2003; Liao and Welsch, 2005; Meadowcroft and Pennington, 2009). Spatial approaches to entrepreneurship and economic development are often built on theories of social capital (Jacobs, 1961; Putnam, 1995; Glaeser and Sacerdote, 2000; North and Syrett, 2008), which can be defined as 'the ability of individuals to secure benefits as a result of membership in social networks or other social structures' (World Bank, 2000: 128). In this sense, social capital is linked to, but distinct from, human capital, which can be defined as individual-related resources (Becker, 1996; Lee and Jones, 2008).

In many ways, social capital can be seen as a *community characteristic* that facilitates or inhibits the kind of innovative, risk-taking behaviour that is part and parcel of entrepreneurship and, in this respect, it acts as part of the *resource endowment* that can be either favourable or unfavourable (Westlund and Bolton, 2003). In drawing upon social resources, an individual's behaviour is affected, influenced and directed by social structures (Storr, 2008). In a way, social capital can be considered as a 'social pressure' that can have positive or negative effects (Becker and Murphy, 2000; Ikeda, 2008). For example, social pressure can increase an individual's utility as a result of a teenager's peers reinforcing the norm of gaining an education or decrease utility by pressuring the teenager to take illegal drugs (Becker and Murphy, 2000).

While social capital is typically considered to generate *positive* externalities, a member of a network could also potentially 'free ride' or act opportunistically so that calculation displaces trust and reciprocity (Portes, 1998). As Adler and Kwon (2002) state, in tight-knit communities, strong norms may dictate the sharing of resources among extended family members, which may, in turn, reduce the incentives for entrepreneurial activity and slow the accumulation of capital. However, individual actors in a social setting cannot be wholly calculating and opportunistic as no one would trade with them; yet neither can they be entirely reciprocating and trusting as they may then open themselves up to exploitation (Axelrod, 1985; Seabright, 2004).

To illustrate how social capital operates positively, Coleman (2000) uses the example of the diamond market in New York where pre-existing social relations enable economic actors to achieve outcomes that would otherwise be unobtainable. While negotiating a sale, diamond traders routinely give other merchants a bag of valuable diamonds to examine in private without any formal guarantee that the buyers will not replace any of the stones in an effort to get a better deal. The arrangement benefits the smooth operation of the diamond wholesale market and is only possible because merchants belong to 'essentially a closed community', sharing ethnic, religious, family and community ties (Coleman, 2000: 17).

As is clear in Coleman's example, networks and trust are important aspects of social capital within a community. Together they form a value-creating phenomenon because they complement other factors, such as labour and technical knowledge, in the production of outputs (Ikeda, 2008) and can be described as civic participation (Putnam, 1995; Fukuyama, 1996) or entrepreneurial creativity (Jacobs, 1961). Social capital can be 'bonding' (i.e., the relationships involved between homogeneous groups) or 'bridging' (i.e., the relations involved between socially heterogeneous groups; Putnam, 1995; Adler and Kwon, 2002; Welter, Trettin and Neumann, 2008; Meadowcroft and Pennington, 2009). Furthermore, the community may consist of either a tight kinship group or a collection of relative strangers and, thus, the relations that constitute social capital are essentially a set of expectations held by most or all members of the community (Ikeda, 2008).

Within local communities, social capital is essentially tacit knowledge (Polanyi, 1962; Ikeda, 2008). It is either knowledge in the form of rules or norms, the meaning of which is impossible to fully articulate, or knowledge the meaning of which is clear only in context, in a particular time or place. Individuals can take advantage of 'strong ties' with family and friends and, thus, create strong trust, and 'weak ties' with acquaintances, customers, suppliers or colleagues (Granovetter, 1973; Burt, 1992; Meadowcroft and Pennington, 2009). Strong ties share the same knowledge and contacts as the individuals themselves, while weak ties are outside the individual's immediate circle of contact and are therefore a diverse and large source of advice and information (Brüderl and Preisendörfer, 1998). Through reciprocity, goodwill can be built up and utilised as a valuable resource (Adler and Kwon, 2002), enabling communities with stocks of social capital to benefit from economic development.

Social capital affects entrepreneurship through its influence on supply costs (not only directly but also indirectly via human capital) and entrepreneurship influences innovative ability, revenues and producer surplus. At all stages there is strong feedback that has impacts on future activity (Westlund and Bolton, 2003; Minniti, 2005). As a result of interaction, social capital makes it easier for agents to rely on strangers in face-to-face encounters and the impersonal market process (Ikeda, 2008). Through this social coordination, entrepreneurial activity can emerge and existing entrepreneurs can adapt to changes in the market (Seabright, 2004).

More recently, the concept of *network capital* has been introduced to complement the notion of social capital (Huggins, 2010). Network capital consists of investments in calculated relations by firms and their entrepreneurs, via which they gain access to knowledge to enhance expected economic returns. Network capital concerns the form of more calculated and strategic networks designed specifically to facilitate knowledge flow and accrue advantage for firms.

Differentiating between network capital and social capital suggests that entrepreneurs must better distinguish the types of relational assets in which their firms invest. Entrepreneurs also need to consider the complexity of interactions, which may be a mix of formal, informal, personal and organisational in terms of their characteristics.

While network capital should *benefit* firms, there are potential downsides for firms highly reliant on social capital. Firms may create or deplete network capital as its interests and requirements change. The stickiness of social capital means that speedy creation may not be possible. A network capital approach to external relationship management allows the adoption of strategies that explicitly seek to make the most effective use of ties, relationships and interactions and ensure these are a firm-level, rather than an individual-level, resource (Huggins, 2010).

3.8 Entrepreneurship policy

Across the world, governments have established policies to promote entrepreneurship (Bridge et al., 2003; Audretsch et al., 2007; Michael and Pearce, 2009). The Organisation for Economic Cooperation and Development (OECD) has a Directorate for Financial, Fiscal and Enterprise Affairs, with the objective of promoting the efficient functioning of markets and enterprises and promoting enterprise development.

In the USA, policies have shifted from attempting to harness the market power of large corporations through a range of measures including regulation, antitrust and government ownership and towards the downsizing of public agencies and government-owned enterprises and the encouragement of entrepreneurial activity (Gilbert et al., 2004).

In Europe, politicians have identified the importance of entrepreneurship and have recognised the importance of enterprise as the engine for growth and a route for closing the productivity gap with the USA (European Commission, 2000; Thurik et al., 2002). In 2000, the European Council of Ministers' Lisbon Conclusions identified a need to stimulate entrepreneurship by creating a 'friendly environment' for starting up and developing innovative businesses (Atherton, 2006).

Implicit in the European approach is a desire to shift towards a European economy that is more like the USA's (Kitson et al., 2004; Atherton, 2006). European policy, therefore, aims to promote entrepreneurship 'consistent with the view that the Anglo-Saxon economies, with their emphasis on individualism and economic liberalism, are providing a more competitive economic environment for entrepreneurial activity' (Parker, 2004: 242). Chapter 4 looks at the role of government in supporting enterprise and small businesses in more detail.

The domain of entrepreneurship policy is large and encompasses activity at several levels of government, from local to national to supranational (Bridge et al., 2003; Huggins and Williams, 2009). As a result of the vast array of policy interventions, it is important to understand what motivates governments to intervene and what the intended benefits of intervention are. This, in turn, informs analysis of which interventions are successful in terms of harnessing higher levels of productive entrepreneurship and which are not.

Despite the traditional emphasis on SMEs and market failure, enterprise policies have developed to become much more pervasive (Huggins and Williams, 2009). While enterprise policies have often been based on SMEs and the notion of correcting market failures, increasing interest in promoting entrepreneurship in its broader context (i.e., not simply in terms of business start-ups or small business growth) has meant that there is less interest than in the past in imperfections in the market, specific firms or 'picking winners' and more in individuals rather than businesses and long-term measures such as enterprise education (Lundstrom and Stevenson, 2001; Audretsch et al., 2007). Lundstrom and Stevenson (2001) have compiled a summary of the key differences between SME and entrepreneurship policies (Table 3.1).

The development of enterprise policies from a focus on business start-ups to a wider conceptual approach has given policymakers a broad-ranging remit in attempting to promote entrepreneurship. To summarise the broad policy approach taken to promote

Table 3.1 Differences between SME and enterprise policies

Feature	SME policies	Entrepreneurship policies
Objective	Firm growth, productivity	Motivate more new entrepreneurs
Target	Existing firms, businesses	Nascent entrepreneurs/new business starters, individuals (people)
Targeting	'Pick winners' (i.e., growth sectors, firms)	General population/subsets (i.e., women, youth)
Client group	Easy to identify 'existing'	Difficult to identify 'nascent'
Levers	Direct financial incentives (tax credits, loans, guarantees)	Non-financial, business support (networks, education, counselling)
Focus	Favourable business environment (i.e., tax regime, reduce red tape)	Entrepreneurial culture/climate (i.e., promote entrepreneurship)
Delivery system	Well-established	Lots of new players (need orientation)
Approach	Generally passive	Proactive outreach
Results orientation	More immediate (results in less than 4 years)	More long-term (results can take longer)
Consultation	SME associations	Forums do not generally exist

Source: Lundstrom and Stevenson (2001: Table 3.1)

entrepreneurship, Verheul et al. (2001) state that there are five main types of policy measures used by governments:

■ G1 – government intervention on the demand side of entrepreneurship; influencing the number and type of entrepreneurial opportunities

■ G2 – government intervention on the supply side of entrepreneurship; influencing the number and types of potential entrepreneurs

■ G3 – government policies aimed at influencing the availability of resources, skills and knowledge of individuals, which generally deal with the input factors of entrepreneurship, i.e., labour, finance and information

■ G4 – government policies aimed at influencing the preferences, i.e., values and attitudes, of individuals

■ G5 – government policies (directly) aimed at the decisionmaking process of individuals (given certain opportunities and individual characteristics, this type of government intervention directly influences the risk–reward profile of entrepreneurship).

A further typology of policy areas related to entrepreneurship policy is shown by Figure 3.4. It illustrates the interplay between the relevant economic and social variables influencing economic development and highlights the central role of culture in fostering entrepreneurship. Economic policy drivers are usually targeted at improving levels of business growth by encouraging new business start-ups, providing appropriate

Figure 3.4 A framework for analysing entrepreneurship policy

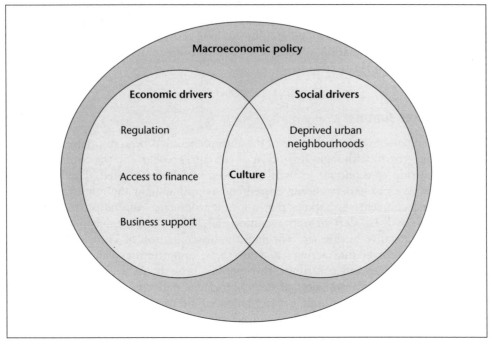

Source: Huggins and Williams (2009)

business support, improving access to finance, supporting specific industries (clusters) that are deemed to be of regional significance, encouraging innovation and investment and ensuring an appropriate regulatory framework.

Social drivers are more commonly associated with 'bottom-up' activities seeking to evolve societal values and norms within particular communities. They are targeted at improving enterprise rates in disadvantaged areas with low rates of entrepreneurship, groups that are underrepresented in terms of business ownership and, more generally, represent key aspects of policies aimed at enhancing social inclusion through entrepreneurship. Furthermore, a framework that seeks to analyse contemporary entrepreneurship policy must also take account of long-term aspects such as culture, particularly as a growing body of research suggests that background conditions are critical to explaining differences in levels of entrepreneurship and economic development (Baumol, 1990; Hart, 2003a).

A key challenge in examining what works with regard to modern entrepreneurship policy is the long-term nature of interventions (Lundstrom and Stevenson, 2001; Bridge et al., 2003; Cumming, 2007; Minniti, 2008). While many studies have sought hard data in order to measure the impacts of policies over time (Greene et al., 2004, 2007), their long-term objective makes such assessment of the impacts difficult, if not impossible (Bridge et al., 2003). As a result of this complexity, research often favours assessing 'intermediate conditions' for entrepreneurship, rather than those influencing 'background conditions' over a decade or more (Hart, 2003a). Yet, it is the background institutional conditions, including economic, social and political incentives, that will determine the pay-offs of productive, unproductive and destructive entrepreneurship and are of critical relevance to policymakers (Baumol, 1990; Minniti, 2008; Sobel, 2008). By overlooking background conditions, long-term policies, such as those introduced through the education system or in deprived areas, remain under-researched (Bridge et al., 2003; Hart, 2003a).

3.9 Chapter summary

This chapter has shown how the role of the entrepreneur has been resurgent in theories of economic growth, although the notion of the entrepreneur and the contribution of entrepreneurship to economic growth have been widely interpreted. The theoretical approaches taken to understanding entrepreneurship highlight the importance of the dynamic and competitive markets that allow it to emerge. In competitive markets, entrepreneurs will be alert to opportunities that lead to the establishment of new, potentially innovative businesses. Through the dissemination of knowledge via spillovers from entrepreneurial activity and alertness, opportunities can be turned into economic knowledge and contribute to economic growth. As geographical location is important for the transmission of tacit knowledge and innovation, so the role of space is important in determining entrepreneurial alertness and the coordination of markets. Entrepreneurship has a pronounced subnational dimension, with differences in regional and local business start-up rates, the success of start-ups and entrepreneurial attitudes all indicating the role of space, place and the local environment in fostering entrepreneurship.

Through a well-functioning knowledge base, regional and local economies can create and innovate new ideas, thoughts, processes and products and translate these into economic value and wealth. The diffusion of knowledge through a collective learning process within an innovative milieu is characterised by openness, personal networks and the proximity of work, social and cultural relationships. This milieu allows social capital to be built, which consists of existing and potential resources inherent within and available through networking relations, enabling individuals to take advantage of entrepreneurial opportunities. As such, social capital plays a central role in the entrepreneurial market process.

Overall, it is clear that there are substantial differences in economic development both across and within nations. Entrepreneurship has potentially short-, medium- and long-term consequences for such development, including the creation of employment and wealth. Efficient firms grow and survive, while inefficient firms decline and fall and the total effect can therefore be either positive or negative. The ability of places to gain from the positive effects of entrepreneurship will depend on their institutional arrangements and the social pay-off structure, plus their ability to turn knowledge into growth through the creation and diffusion of knowledge.

Questions

1 What role does entrepreneurship play in stimulating economic development?

2 Why do levels of entrepreneurship – expressed as new business start-ups – differ between nations, regions and localities?

3 What role do the concepts of 'space' and 'place' play in the analysis of entrepreneurship and economic development?

4 How does culture harness or hold back entrepreneurship?

5 How can higher levels of entrepreneurship be encouraged through public policy?

Weblinks

http://gemconsortium.org
The Global Entrepreneurship Monitor (GEM) consortium provides country-by-country analysis of entrepreneurship.

http://ecorner.stanford.edu
Stanford University's Entrepreneurship Corner offers 2000 free videos and podcasts, featuring entrepreneurship and innovation thought leaders.

www.isbe.org.uk
The Institute for Small Business and Entrepreneurship (ISBE) is a network for people and organisations involved in small business and entrepreneurship research, policy, education, support and advice.

www.triplehelixconference.org/
The annual Triple Helix international conference website.

CHAPTER 4

Government and small businesses

Robert J. Bennett

4.1 Introduction

This chapter introduces how government and small businesses interrelate. How can government act most effectively to help small firms, in particular, and the economy as a whole? Where can government best focus its attention? What are its limitations and how have recent small business policies developed.

4.2 Learning objectives

There are four learning objectives in this chapter:

1 to introduce the case for government action to help small businesses

2 to understand the limitations on government actions to help small businesses

3 to appreciate the different aims, methods and forms that government actions may take

4 to become acquainted with the main examples of government help to small businesses in Britain and their strengths and weaknesses.

Key concepts

■ business support ■ targeting ■ advice and consultancy ■ market failure
■ regulation ■ bureaucratic failure

4.3 The role of government

The first point on which it is important to be clear is that entrepreneurs and managers develop small businesses, not governments. Government, however, can have a profound effect on how all firms, particularly small firms, operate and their opportunities to grow. Indeed, government policy and its influence on the 'institutional environment' and social capital has become a key focus of efforts to help improve how small firms develop and how economies compete – countries, regions and localities. As a result, almost all countries and localities now have an active policy for improving competitiveness, within which is a strong element focused on SMEs. There are three main dimensions to the government role:

- government as regulator
- government as economic agent
- government as strategic planner and promoter.

4.3.1 Government as regulator

Government and legal rules determine how trade rules operate (nationally and internationally), the legal forms of companies, the extent of legal limits on company liabilities and the strength of antitrust, restrictive practices and antimonopoly regulations. Government also influences regulations on conditions at work, consumer protection, food, health, safety, environmental and planning regulation and licensing.

4.3.2 Government as economic agent

Government taxes, charges fees, raises debts and spends. The way in which this operates has a profound effect on business finance and risktaking.

- Taxation and fee levels affect entrepreneurial incentives and market entry; government debt levels severely affect the economic climate.
- Spending influences the competitive environment and procurement rules for government contracts influence markets; the growth of government services influences the factor inputs for SMEs (particularly education, health and transport services).
- As a significant employer, government rates of pay and employment conditions impact local and national pay bargaining, the role of trade unions and employment conditions.
- Government redistribution policies and social engineering influence work incentives and the labour market.

4.3.3 Government as strategic planner and promoter

Government finance can be used to offer grants, subsidies, loans or information and advisory support to SMEs and can seek to improve the infrastructure of business factor inputs. Notable examples are:

- education and skills
- research and development
- marketing and productivity initiatives
- international trade protection or incentives.

4.3.4 Evolution of government support

Over time, the consensus on the extent and form of government policy in each of these areas has changed radically. Up to the early nineteenth century, government sanctioned large monopolistic companies (chartered companies such as the East India Company). Few other limited liability companies could exist and, hence, most businesses were very small traders or partnerships that had limited scope to grow. The creation of laws to allow the establishment of limited liability companies (in Britain, in 1844 and 1856) were critical to providing a means of establishing larger firms on a more general basis. These were initially fairly limited in number, but grew rapidly at the end of the nineteenth century. As time progressed, there was also a consolidation of economic power into larger concerns. Thus, by 1910, 16 per cent of British manufacturing output was generated by the 100 largest companies, but, by 1970, the 100 largest companies accounted for 47 per cent of output and covered 36 per cent of employment (Hannah, 1976; Prais, 1976).

The dominance of the economy by large firms was thus a phenomenon of the mid- and late twentieth century. It was facilitated by company legislation, but was actively encouraged by government in several ways. First, planning of supply during both the First and Second World Wars led to considerable consolidation. Second, until the 1960s, governments encouraged price cartels and collusion between firms, which frequently led to amalgamations and takeovers. The scope for SMEs was limited by these behemoths. Third, and at the same time, the growth of socialism and the Labour Party led to an ideological decision to nationalise many strategic industries, to provide them with large subsidies and control politically the means of production through extensive economic committees. By 1960, 13 per cent of GDP was produced by nationalised industries and they employed 10 per cent of the workforce, on top of which were the dockyards, munitions factories, military and public sector itself (Pryke, 1981). Inevitably the scope for SMEs was limited by the dominance of large firms, nationalised industries and a large public sector. At the micro level, large firms and government policy limited scope for market entry and to compete; at macro level, the public sector squeezed out the scope for entrepreneurship.

The result was a significant long-term decline in the number of businesses up to the 1960s, with major waves of mergers occurring in the 1920s and 1930s, then, in the 1950s and 1960s (Hannah 1976: Table A.1). This evolution is reflected in Figure 4.1, which also shows the relatively limited development of self-employment (single-person businesses) during this time.

The apogee of this period was the establishment in 1962 of the National Economic Development Council (NEDC), which was to be a means for government 'to seek agreement on ways of improving economic performance, competitive power, and efficiency' (Selwyn Lloyd, Chancellor of the Exchequer, 1962, quoted in Middlemas, 1983: ix). This led to a network of tripartite committees – trade unions, government and businesses (generally represented by the CBI) – to inform negotiations on pay and economic policy, plus develop strategies for each sector. This was modelled on the French Commissariate du Plan and the Japanese MITI, though both had mixed successes and failures.

Having planned wars by committee, the government tried to run the economy by committee. At their peak, in the 1960s and 1970s, these committees covered 60 per cent of all manufacturing industry. The collapse of the committee-driven approach was inevitable – as one industry after another suffered increased international competition, its management was unable to respond, its sales collapsed and, as its profits fell,

Figure 4.1 Numbers of self-employed and establishments, 1930–2010

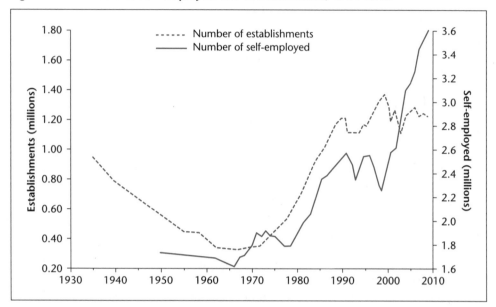

subsidies increasingly became necessary. Government committees interfered with rational economic decisions and based decisions more on political than economic needs. In Middlemas' words (1983: 66), this national process of economic planning was 'too close to government, too dependent on what government did or did not do, too subject to the (political) pendulum'. Most importantly it could not cope with rapid change, increased global competition and it ignored small firms.

In the late 1960s, significant and rapid changes began to occur: the Restrictive Practices Act prevented cartels and price fixing; joining the European Community in 1973 restricted State aids to industry; privatisation of former nationalised industries after 1979 reduced government control radically; new technologies increased the scope for innovative management by small and innovative businesses and their ability to compete with large businesses. Market entry became easier and a rapid growth in small firms resulted. As shown in Figure 4.1, by 2010, SMEs in Britain had grown to nearly four times the number in the 1960s and the number of self-employed sole traders had more than doubled.

4.4 The case for government action for SMEs

In general, government action for SMEs has been justified by three main arguments. These are that:

- market failures exist and these inhibit small firm development
- there is a special public interest in SMEs because of their capacity to create jobs

■ government can develop and act on a strategic vision for the economy, which individual SMEs cannot.

The market failure argument suggests that small firms will not invest or develop some fields and, therefore, government should assist. The main basis of this argument is that, because SMEs are small, they lack control of the markets in which they operate and will, therefore, underinvest. An example might be training, where SMEs may be discouraged from training their personnel because they are concerned about other firms 'poaching' them at higher salaries – particularly larger firms. This is a so-called 'free rider' problem where the non-training firm gains cost advantage over the firm that trains. Similar examples may apply to the implementation of environmental control and research and development, where those firms that do invest may not be able to gain the full benefits because of undercutting, poaching or pirating by others. Smaller firms are less able to protect themselves from these challenges.

These arguments suggest a possible role for government as a regulator (to impose an obligation on *all* firms – e.g., to train, conform to regulations, etc.) or as a supplier (to provide government-financed training or subsidise private provision).

A further component of the market failure argument has claimed that small firms are less aware of advice, information or other business services that are available, are more sceptical about their value and can be more unwilling to seek external support than larger firms (Gibb and Dyson, 1984; Storey, 1994). This argument is frequently used to justify government advice and information initiatives. Whilst there may have been reluctance by small firms in the 1970s, there is little evidence to suggest that it is true today. Extensive surveys of the take-up by small firms of external advice, consultancy, training and other services suggests that they are usually more likely to use them than other firms, with the possible exception of the start-up and those in the very early stages of growth (Bennett and Robson, 1999a; Ramsden and Bennett, 2006).

The most important aspect of possible market failures for small firms is that they suffer specific barriers or unequal treatment that, on grounds of equity, government should help to remove. This was a fundamental plank of the argument in the report of the Bolton Committee (1971), which suggested that a level of government action was justified to help SMEs because they were disadvantaged compared to larger firms. In the market, larger firms will gain advantage of economies of scale in a number of ways (e.g., purchase of inputs at lower unit costs because of bulk purchasing discounts or economics of administration arising from having specialist skills available in personnel, financial, managerial and other fields).

Ironically, however, one of the strongest arguments for government action is that government itself creates disadvantages for small firms because the costs of compliance with its regulatory and administrative requirements tend to have severe diseconomies of scale. For example, studies of the costs of compliance with government procedures suggest that they are two to ten times higher for small firms as costs per employee, on cost per £ of turnover, than they are for large firms (Bannock and Peacock, 1989; Sandford, 1995; Cressy, 2000; Poutziouris, Chittenden and Michaelas, 2001; Poutziouris, Chittenden, Watts and Soufani, 2003; Hansford, Hasseldine and Haworth, 2003). This disadvantage is particularly strong for the smallest businesses (with fewer than 10 employees) and tends to diminish with size – diseconomies are of little consequence for firms with over 200 employees. There are also variations between different regulatory streams. Taxation, employment legislation and health and safety at work were usually the most burdensome over the whole 1990s and 2000s (SERT, 2008). In terms of costs, compliance with labour market directives tend to be more costly than taxation requirements, which are, in turn, more costly than licensing processes. For some businesses, health and safety requirements – in terms of both the costs and the form of regulatory monitoring and inspection and scope for vexatious litigation through regulators or industrial tribunals – can be so costly as to close the business.

A summary of some of the main market and policy gaps is as follows (Bolton Committee, 1971; Bannock, 1990; Storey, 1994; Curran and Blackburn, 1994; Department of Employment, 1989; DTI, 2003; Small Business Service, 2002b, 2004a, 2004b; Small Business Council, 2004a).

- *Taxation* distorts incentives and the capital market and places proportionately higher burdens of compliance costs on small firms.

- *Regulation and bureaucracy* highly regressive with firm size (i.e., proportionately much harder on small firms).

- *Purchasing* large firms and public-sector purchasing is heavily biased towards other large firms and public-sector suppliers.

- *Competition policy* a largely discretionary aspect of government activity in the UK and generally has to reach high levels of abuse before government acts. It, thus, tends to weaken the possibilities of entry by small firms and their chances of success.

- *Education and research* has tended to have little focus on business and enterprise, particularly for small firms. Instead, it has been biased towards either management or employee status rather than entrepreneurship and pure research rather than applied technological innovation and development.

- *Social legislation* as with other regulatory impacts, the effects on incentives to individuals, costs to businesses (especially labour costs) and regarding working hours, redundancy, contracted and forms of employment (part-time, full-time) are regressive for small firms.

These arguments have been used as a basis for a range of special policies to help small business, ranging from subsidies, exemptions or reductions in regulatory requirements to grants and specialised provision of advice and information. The range of initiatives that has resulted is very considerable in almost all countries. A survey of EU countries is contained in the European SMEs Observatory reports (1994, 1995, 1996). A survey of the main market gaps in policies to meet them is shown in Table 4.1.

The second argument for government action for small businesses is that they have become major contributors to the economy. Hence, specific policies for small business are a way to encourage the growth of the economy as a whole. This has been viewed as particularly important since small businesses can create a major growth in jobs.

This argument gained considerable popularity in the 1970s and 1980s, which was a period in which large firms – mainly in the manufacturing sector – were rapidly shedding jobs. An influential study by Birch (1979) suggested that two thirds of the increase in employment in the USA between 1969 and 1976 was in firms employing

Table 4.1 Market imperfections, their causes and areas of policy action required (developed from Bolton Committee, 1971; Bannock and Peacock, 1989)

Market gap	Cause of market gap	Policy action needed
Supply of entrepreneurs	Social and economic bias in favour of employment and unemployment rather than self-employment	Welfare system, education and tax system, 'culture' of social capital
Supply of innovations	Inadequate R&D, misallocated R&D expenditure	Education and research policy, tax system
Supply of capital	Distortions in capital markets	Tax system, subsidised lending, monopoly policy, labour relations policy
Supply of premises	Imperfections in property markets	Planning regulations, infrastructure investment, tax system
Bureaucracy and compliance costs	Growth of government	Simplification, exemptions, tax reform, reorganisation of central and local bureaucracy
Purchasing	Imperfections in supplier markets, government 'crowding out' business and small firms	Monopoly policy, tax system
Marketing	Imperfections in seller markets	Promotional activities, international exporting credits and advice

fewer than 20 workers. Although these findings are disputed, there is no doubt that all governments in Western economies see job creation as one of the major motives for SME policies.

The third argument – that government can develop and act on a strategic vision for the economy which small firms cannot – overlaps with the objective of job generation. With global shifts that limit the scope for governments to act as protectionist sources of support to their economies, they have, instead, sought to take on a role of trying to boost economic growth – so-called supply-side policies. This role is often framed in terms of increasing a nation's competitiveness and has been summarised in a range of competitiveness white papers (e.g., DTI, 2003) and found its way into specific small business policies (e.g., Small Business Service, 2002b, 2004a, 2004b; DTI, 2007; Department for Business, Enterprise and Regulatory Reform, 2007c).

An individual firm is unlikely to be able to see the whole economic picture, even if it is a large firm, so government has a role in taking the larger strategic view and seeking to plug gaps or stimulate what would not otherwise occur. This has led to a burgeoning in the number of reports produced on how countries should fill their skills gaps, infrastructure gaps, research gaps, financing gaps, etc. For example, the British government has argued that 'it is government's role to offer support to business to increase productivity and invest in innovation. Government investment in training should particularly address areas of market failure, by supporting employers in training their low-skilled workers' (Department for Education and Skills, 2003a: 22–3).

A fourth argument, advanced by Storey (2003), is that government policies for small firms can be justified on a welfare basis – i.e., they help to take individuals out of unemployment. It is certainly true that many unemployed people do seek a future for themselves by developing small firms, but it is very contentious whether government policy can be justified on this basis. Welfare policies have strong social justifications, but their linkage to small firm policies is unclear and suffers the danger of distorting decisions by entrepreneurs and government.

A statement of the main political objectives underlying modern small business policy is that by the European Commission (2003, 2004), which, in a green paper, has sought to identify the problems holding back EU business development and offered possible policy solutions.

The perceived European problem is that people prefer employee over self-employed status, with a resulting lower business birth rate in the EU than many other countries, a less dynamic business sector as a whole and, hence, higher unemployment levels. The chief policies advocated are reduction of the barriers to starting a business, trying to reduce risk and increase reward levels, fostering capacity and skills, and broadening the accountability of businesses across society. Specific policy actions are in the fields of education, better regulation, reducing financial gaps and improving cultural support. In a Small Business Act (European Commission, 2008), the Commission sought to lead European countries towards implementing a range of legislative changes. The Commission itself has no authority in these fields, so it hoped that the changes called on in the Act would encourage implementation by national governments.

Despite all this more recent enthusiasm, however, government actions for small firms are much more difficult to implement as specific and effective actions than they are for a policy designer to dream up. Even in the words of one of the economists who is most widely drawn on to justify government intervention, effective actions are very constrained: 'The important thing for government is not to do things which individuals are doing already' (Keynes, 1926: 47). Keynes also felt that actions should be restricted to the aggregate level – the economy as a whole – and small firms had too great an 'animal' behaviour to be capable of being included in government policy.

We analyse below the difficulties of government action for SMEs.

4.5 Finding a niche for government action

It is difficult to evidence that there is a *general* phenomenon of market failure or need for major government action for small firms. Taking the normal definitions, SMEs are 90 to 99 per cent of all businesses, account for nearly 60 per cent of GNP and over 60 per cent of employees and have grown from 2.3 million in 1979 to 4.8 million in

Britain in 2009. SMEs are, therefore, a successful sector of the economy. It is not obvious that they need government help. Of course, it is possible that they could be even more successful, but, if we take evidence of the features that hold back SME development from previous research and surveys of SMEs themselves, there is little evidence of generalised market failure.

Most surveys find that small firms want government to stabilise the economic environment or improve its own regulatory regime (e.g., Storey, 1994; Curran and Blackburn, 1994; Cosh and Hughes, 2003). The NatWest quarterly surveys of small business consistently show economic climate and government regulation as the first and second main concerns of small firms since the 1990s, although in the earlier 1990s and over 2008/2009, cash flow and payments were also important concerns (e.g., SERT, 2008). The concern with regulation is reinforced in the large-scale surveys, such as Your Business Matters (Institute of Directors, 1996; Better Regulation Task Force, 2000), which show that what matters to small firms is chiefly the interface with government itself (legal requirements, VAT, availability of grants, etc.). Only in training is government seen as a major source of support, then the preference is for it to be a supporter rather than a provider. These conclusions are further reinforced by the Bank of England's well-balanced assessment (e.g., Bank of England, 1996), which emphasises the role of market agents in overcoming small firm deficiencies and questions the effectiveness of most policy areas.

The implications of these results are as follows.

- The main needs that businesses have are maintaining and developing their products, markets and internal processes.
- Businesses chiefly want government to maintain a strong and stable economic environment and a *transparent* and *stable* regulatory environment in which compliance costs are low, risks can be assessed reliably, and long-term strategies developed.
- There is no overwhelming demand for government to do things for specific firms or sectors (unless firms are already dependent on support that they do not wish to lose).
- There is no *general* evidence of a market failure, where business needs are not being met by the private sector business services that are available. Where so-called needs have been identified, they relate to areas where well-developed markets already exist – e.g., venture capital, technology transfer, marketing, advice and consultancy, information, skills and training, credit and bad debt collection. Management consultants, lawyers, accountants and other advisers exist in large numbers to meet these needs. It is unclear how governments can do things better than these existing markets.
- Where needs are identified that are generic to many firms or to all or most sectors, they chiefly concern the quality of factor inputs, such as education and skills or transport infrastructure. This suggests that government action needs to be focused primarily not on provision of specific supports to individual firms but, instead, on:
  - the form of regulatory framework influencing market provision
  - the quality of public-sector services influencing factor inputs.
- In cases where individual firms can be benefited by specific support, this is usually related to certain business needs that government is unlikely to be able to meet itself (e.g., product development, design and marketing).

- In some cases, specific needs relate to local problems – e.g., the absence of suitable sites, premises or scope for expansion, gaps in transport and infrastructure, skills shortages and the influence of the local 'business climate'. Many of these firm-specific needs chiefly relate to the role of local and central government in its planning and local services – e.g., speed of planning decisions, willingness to develop new infrastructure, quality of public services, pro-business climate, etc.

These findings do not suggest that large-scale support for SMEs should be high priorities for government policies and, where support is provided, it requires very careful design to avoid market distortions and other adverse side-effects.

4.6 Limitations on government action

The difficulties of finding a niche for government action are increased by the difficulties of doing so effectively once a cause for intervention is found. The existence of a market failure or 'need', in itself, does not justify government action. Not only are there other non-market approaches as alternatives to government but also, most importantly, attempts to overcome market failure may result in actions that do more harm than good. Government and bureaucratic failure is a large and often greater danger than many supposed market failures (Le Grand, 1991). Moreover, the result of government failures is that small firms can be harmed, reducing the welfare of society by diverting resources, deflecting or impeding businesses. As a result, the costs often exceed the benefits of intervention and far exceed the costs of accepting the market failure that existed in the first place. Market failures and 'needs', therefore, do not necessarily always have effective government policy solutions. The world is not a perfect place. Indeed, small firms thrive on exploiting market imperfections by spotting new opportunities.

In general, the difficulties of government action cover each stage, from problem identification to policy execution. At the design stage, how is it that government and its officers, who are not themselves running a business, are likely to be better than a small business at identifying options and designing a solution for business?

The constraints on government action are:

- lack of appropriate and up-to-date information
- lack of technical business skills and understanding
- adoption of targets for public policy rather than business policy
- difficulty of policy termination (admitting that mistakes have been made and making changes)
- difficulty of providing help that adds to *total* net output, rather than helping one firm and, thus, displacing another (achieving, instead, *additionality* of policy)
- difficulty of aligning and coordinating policies so that they do not conflict with each other
- multiple layers of complex decisionmaking, with many and conflicting targets that are slow to change.

As noted by Peacock (in Bannock and Peacock, 1989: 6):

> Too often it is assumed that a case for public production . . . is the sole answer to so-called 'market failure' . . . [but] when consumers have only an indirect control over what is produced and how it is produced, the checks operating on bureaucratic efficiency are weak.

Bannock and Peacock go on to identify four specific weaknesses:

1 consensus views are usually necessary in policy implementation, which means that the aims are deliberately obfuscated to keep everyone happy and this suits bureaucrats and politicians since it is then less easy to identify when the policy fails.

2 there are no real costs or risks to policymakers when things go wrong, especially if the aims are unclear in the first place, so the quality of the design is not incentivised and correction of error is slow.

3 proliferation of specific schemes fosters clients who defend pet schemes, so, instead of the small firms focusing on business development, they put extra resources into bargaining and lobbying with government; this is distortionary, undermines efficiency and creates dependency and clientalism.

4 the costs and benefits of alternatives are rarely assessed and there is no civil service career to be made from not spending allocated public finance and, therefore, reducing tax burdens and improving general economic conditions; as a result, improvement in government policies is usually, at best, slow.

Indeed, a review of HM Treasury (2002: 153) admitted that 'a variant of Gresham's Law might operate, in that bad services drive out good'. A grass-roots view from the engineering sector has stated that most government SME programmes are ineffectual, overly bureaucratic and inaccessible (Jim Hewitt, Engineering Alliance, quoted in *Financial Times*, 7 May 2003).

Commenting on claims to improve government regulations, one prominent entrepreneur states, 'it begs the question of why regulations were there in the first place and why they cannot be removed immediately', that, rather than 'tinker' with taxpayers' money in support and loans, it would be 'better if business retained their money in the first place. Less government means enterprise can get on with running successful businesses' (Roger Dudding, letter in the Institute of Directors' *Director Magazine*, February 2009: 27).

4.7 Possibilities for targeting

This discussion has shown that there are usually rather limited possibilities for policies for small businesses and, when pursued, they should concentrate on the general economic environment. Despite this, there has been a strong tendency for government to pursue micro-targets. For example, a number of initiatives target growth businesses, attempting to distinguish them from those that cannot or are unwilling to grow (which are usually termed 'lifestyle' businesses). The focus on growth companies is strongly built into most government and EU objectives. The argument is that usually targeting:

■ will benefit businesses to the greatest extent, in terms of assistance (a 'need' measure)

- will yield the greatest policy benefit ('leverage' or 'value for money' measures)
- while trying to avoid displacement or what would have happened anyway ('additionality' measures).

The potential benefits of the targeting of policy are obvious:

- it can reduce the range of expenditure
- it may focus resources where they are 'needed'
- it is easier to market.

In the UK, a focus on *growth businesses*, for example, yields a target market of approximately 200,000 businesses (taking the definitions of growth businesses as those with 10 to 200 employees, used by DTI, 1992). A focus on *exporting businesses* yields a target market of about 100,000 businesses (Institute of Export, 1995, quoted in Bank of England, 1996). A focus on *innovation or high-tech businesses* is a fuzzier concept, but yields a target of perhaps 100,000 businesses. If it is possible to distinguish SMEs within these groups, the proportion will be even smaller (Smallbone, 1997). Targeting is, thus, very attractive as a public policy approach, whether viewed from a perspective of 'need', 'leverage' or additionality.

There are great dangers in attempting to target the market in this way, however, and these derive from the variety within the market decided on, regardless of how much it is narrowed. First, the starting point for any change in business activity, as argued at the outset, must be the entrepreneur's own marginal appraisal of the costs and benefits of the change, judged by the characteristics of its suppliers, customers and trading environment and its internal capacities and structures. Any decisions have to be market-driven in two senses – only the business itself can make the decisions and it must judge its decisions on the criteria of its own capacity to continue to meet its customer's needs. Any policy targeting can, therefore, be only of the crudest kind, in the sense of identifying firms that will possibly take it up rather than a specific group, all of which will need to respond. In addition, the target group is not stable. Those businesses that are growth, export or innovation businesses in one period may not have the same characteristics in another period. Although we know that there is a strong correlation between each of these business characteristics over time (i.e., a growth business tends to continue to be a growth business and is also often an innovator and an exporter), there is no prior set of conditions strongly allowing identification of the positively improving performers until they are already growth businesses. After all, if it were easy to spot the high-performance businesses, everyone would be already investing in them! Hence, it is not easy, or feasible, for government to define a stable or exclusive group as potential targets for government action.

There is also a rather strange conflict built into a government policy that seeks to give greater support to these businesses that are already growing and, hence, are successful. There are also particular dangers in trying to distinguish between growth and lifestyle businesses. Any good business is good business! Maintaining a business in a competitive world is itself a major success and the lifestyle business of today may well be the growth business of tomorrow. The gateway to accessing government policy benefits must, therefore, be a flexible one, for both entry and exit. This, in turn, has implications for the management and design of policy contact networks, databases and marketing.

The safest policy of all is *not* to target and, instead, leave open the choice of policy supports used to those best able to assess them – the small businesses themselves.

4.8 Forms of government action for small businesses

There is a variety of ways in which government can seek to help small businesses. It is possible to distinguish these in terms of the underlying policy:

- aims
- methods
- targeting.

The underlying *aims* of government support can be distinguished on the basis of three broad approaches.

- *Cost reduction* – the use of grants, subsidies or reduced-rate loans to lower the cost of inputs into the business. These can be targeted (e.g., a grant to a specific business) or general (e.g., to reduce energy costs, tax or labour costs by, e.g., government financing education and training).
- *Risk reduction* – the use of macroeconomic policies (e.g., tax, interest rates and other instruments) to stabilise the economy and reduce oscillations and uncertainties. Government's regulatory environment itself is a key contribution to the level of risk small businesses experience.
- *Increase the flow of information* – to make more readily available information on international trends in markets, national and local issues and government policies that affect small businesses. This can be via targeted support (and information services) or general publicity.

The *methods* of government support cover four broad fields:

- finance (grants and subsidies; cost effects of tax and compliance)
- providing information
- providing specialist advice
- helping with training and development.

Targeting can focus on:

- stages of business development:
  - idea formation/entrepreneurship
  - start-up
  - early growth
  - development and expansion
- types of businesses:
  - by firm size
  - exporters/non-exporters

- by sector
- by location (e.g., rural, inner-city, community-based, ethnic minority)

- factor inputs and resources:
  - capital
  - land and premises
  - personnel and skills
  - innovation/technology transfer

- general business climate:
  - culture of entrepreneurism and workplace ethics
  - regulatory environment
  - macroeconomic environment.

These are only examples of a large, complex and overlapping field of possible instruments that government can implement in its desire to help small businesses. To understand how these instruments have developed in practice, the next sections summarise the main initiatives in policy in the UK at three levels – national, sector and local.

4.9 National policy

4.9.1 Better regulation

UK governments have attempted to respond to criticisms of the regulatory burdens that undermine small firms' development through better regulation initiatives. An important step was the establishment in 1994 of a Deregulation Task Force. After 1997, this became the Better Regulation Executive and, in 2009, was complemented by an independent Regulatory Policy Commission (RPC).

Demonstrating the breadth and difficulty of the problem of controlling government regulation, these bodies have operated outside of the main government departments and had independent chairs, reporting to a Cabinet committee. This approach has been prominent in attempting to change the way in which government departments work, so as to encourage greater sensitivity in the design of legislation and its implementation or enforcement. SMEs have been a particular concern, in order to reduce compliance costs.

The principles of good practice sought are proportionality, accountability, consistency, transparency and targeting. The chief efforts have been as follows:

- all departmental proposals with an impact on businesses must carry out a compliance cost assessment, risk assessment and regulatory impact assessment (RIA), personally approved by the minister responsible

- a quarterly report from all departments must be produced on what secondary legislation has been introduced and its compliance costs to businesses

- a streamlined procedure for primary legislation to be amended or repealed for deregulation purposes, as well as improving fairness, transparency and consistency of enforcement procedures

- simplification and improved information on relevant business licences and regulatory requirements with an alignment of registration and notification for start-up businesses (with a single point of contact for all tax, social security and VAT matters being developed)

- reduction in the burden of completing government surveys for businesses with fewer than ten employees, plus reduced compliance costs for other surveys

- simplification of many official forms, including Intrastat (recording imports and exports between EU countries)

- attempts at improved and more business-friendly enforcement procedures with clearer appeals mechanisms

- attempts to reduce compliance burdens for *all* businesses with respect to health and safety, building regulations and so on to ensure that regulations apply only to relevant businesses

- setting up 'one-stop-shops' by local government, called Local Better Regulation Offices (at county level), which are arms of central government's Better Regulation Executive (BRE) – these provide a single point of contact for health and safety regulations, etc.

The enforcement of change has been sought through the RIAs (Deregulation Task Force, 1996; Cabinet Office, 1996a; Better Regulation Task Force, 2000, 2004; Regulatory Policy Commission, 2010; National Audit Office, 2011).

Some specific examples of changes have been proposals to change the Consumer Credit Act, following the recommendations by the Office of Fair Trading that small businesses should be excluded from the scope of the Act. Also, the statutory audit requirement for small firms with a turnover of less than £90,000 was abolished from 1996 and extended to all companies with less than £350,000 turnover from April 1997, then raised to £6.5m in 2008. Various attempts have been made to modify the rules for corporate insolvency for small businesses and late payment legislation. Progress in many areas has been limited, however.

Despite some developments, the chairs of the task forces have been critical (e.g., Deregulation Task Force, 1996): 'the culture of Whitehall needs to change more. Regulation is a form of government spending . . . But whereas there are stringent controls that inhibit the growth of conventional public spending, no comparable constraints exist for new regulation'.

It has been doubted that RIAs carry enough weight to inhibit the growth of the regulatory burden. Indeed, one task force member threatened to resign in 1997 because there 'was not enough support from ministers who are too willing to accept new regulations from Brussels'. In the case of new European fire regulations, for example, there was 'an absolutely clear-cut example where there are no benefits and absolutely enormous costs' (Fisher, 1996). Similar conclusions were drawn regarding employment regulations (Small Business Council, 2004b). The Better Regulation Task Force (2004) came to a similar conclusion: 'It is time we did something more to reduce the burden, to achieve deregulation as well as better regulation – a spring clean of existing stock' (Graham, 2004a). The Bank of England (1996) has commented that too much attention has been given to reducing the number of regulations rather than ameliorating the negative impacts of new legislation. The first report of the Regulatory Policy Commission (2010: 16–17), covering the last six months of the Labour government in 2010, found that many RIAs 'lacked analytical rigour' and appeared 'to be produced as an afterthought . . . to obtain approval'. Too much weight was placed on preferred policy options, with insufficient assessment of the alternatives of 'doing nothing' or 'doing the minimum', with poor assessments of costs and benefits. From a sample of 107 RIAs, 21 per cent had serious defects. Of these, 91 per cent had defects on at least 3 of the 6 indicators assessed and half had 4 or more defects. The National Audit Office (2011) confirms the same conclusion, that the majority of RIAs have been perfunctory and the majority of businesses think that government does not understand them well enough to regulate. The British Chambers of Commerce (Ambler, Chittenden and Miccini, 2010: 17–18) stated that 'much of the claimed overall benefit of regulation is no more than "bread and circuses"; giving attractive rewards to citizens and penalising productivity in the process'.

The Small Business Council (SBC) was established in 2000, 'to act as the voice of small business across government'. Although slow to develop real teeth, it also became a prominent critic of the growth of regulation, its 2004 report (Small Business Council, 2004a: 3–4) stating that 'it is time that the cost of being governed should start to reduce year on year . . . The cost of regulation should be reduced. The appraisal process by civil servants should be changed . . . to provide incentives for officials not to introduce new regulations'. Despite these comments, progress was slow and the SBC fell into abeyance in 2008.

The constraints on all these 'better regulation' initiatives is that they work outside of the main departmental decisionmaking process that creates the regulations in the first place. What is required is for the designers of regulations to be far more sensitive to the needs of those who have to comply with them in business. The criticism has been that, rather than simplifying, civil servants do not know what they are doing or overdesign or 'gold-plate' regulations with needless detail and complexity (Better Regulation Task Force, 2004). Overcoming this requires a culture change in Whitehall. Rather than RIAs, which shut the door after the horse has bolted, the civil service needs improved recruitment and major retraining.

4.9.2 Financial assistance to SMEs

The major national governmental financial package available to small businesses has been the Small Firm Loan Guarantee Scheme (SFLGS). This provides a government guarantee for loans by approved lenders (chiefly the major banks). The loans are intended to be for businesses or individuals who cannot obtain commercial finance because they lack security or a proven track record.

The guarantees generally cover 75 per cent of the loan and are available to businesses that are over a couple of years old. Most loans are for less than £70,000 for periods of 2 to 7 years. The minimum is £5000 and maximum £250,000.

The scheme has run since 1983, but became more significant in terms of the number of loans granted and their total value in the 1990s and, again, in the late 2000s (see Table 4.2). It provided £360 million in 2009. EU funding elements are important in these programmes, but their complexity and inflexibility are criticised.

Table 4.2 **The Small Firm Loan Guarantee Scheme**

Financial year	1989–1990	1991–1992	1994–1995	1996–1997
Number	3124	2917	6207	5081
Total value (£m)	94.0	68.7	245.9	201.3
Average loan size (£)	30,103	23,579	39,630	39,626
Financial year	1998–1999	2000–2001	2002–2003	2005–2006
Number	4482	4312	3916	5957
Total value (£m)	188.8	240.5	269.5	422
Average loan size (£)	42,124	55,765	68,870	14,116

Source: Small Business Service

During the 2008/2009 recession, a much larger scheme of up to £10 billion was initiated – the Enterprise Finance Guarantee – but its take-up has been low because it is overly bureaucratic and offers few long-term benefits. It was supposed to encourage expansion and replace some bank lending.

The SFLGS has continued to fill an important gap, but adequate lending by banks to SMEs continues to be criticised. For start-up assistance, central government grants to small firms ran from 1982 to 1994. These were replaced by neighbourhood and urban regeneration schemes and Business Link (see Section 4.12.2).

To help people move from unemployment to self employment, an Enterprise Allowance Scheme and a Business Start-up Scheme were set up in the 1980s. These had a major impact on stimulating self-employment. The schemes evolved into new forms of grant and start-up assistance for the unemployed after 2000.

Other sources of small grants and loans are via Scottish, Welsh and Northern Ireland development bodies and, between 2001–2011, from English Regional Development Agencies and Business Link.

Larger grants of £10,000–100,000 may be available in Assisted Areas (relating to EU Structural Funds regions) through Regional Selective Assistance (renamed Selective Finance for Investment in 2004), provided that they create new jobs or safeguard old ones. Since 2011, Selective Assistance has become part of a Regional Growth Fund, which is focused on stimulating investments in job creation. This gives discretionary grants related to inward investment, relocations or expansions. In addition, there are smaller grants for Innovation Projects in eligible locations and other special initiatives for deprived areas.

Important tax incentives for small firm investments were introduced in 1995, which were subsequently extended for enterprise investment schemes, venture capital trusts and business angels, to encourage equity participation in small firms, as well as participation in management development by angels. In addition, the alternative investment market (AIM) aspect of the Stock Exchange has had significant success in improving equity flows into larger SMEs; the European market 'EASDAQ' has further enhanced this development. It should be noted that, as well as government initiatives,

Britain has one of the best-developed venture capital markets in Europe – the largest agent being 3i – although it does not rival that in the USA.

For small firm management training, there have been Small Firms Training Loans available from government, administered by the major banks. There have also been Career Development Loans to individuals for education or training (Marshall, Alderman, Wong and Thwaites 1993). For the unemployed, a number of other special assistance schemes exist.

The main framework between 2003 and 2011 was Learn Direct, a directory of training providers and financial supports. This directed small firms, their employees or the unemployed to work-based learning provision for adults or New Deal to get people into employment through training. Since 2011, this has become the Work Programme. There is also the Prince's Youth Business Trust and Livewire for those aged 16 to 25, which are sponsored initiatives by major companies.

In addition, since 1994, the government, with the Bank of England, has sought to stimulate, debate and improve the relations between SMEs and banks and other financial institutions. Banks are the largest source of funds for SMEs and dwarf all government schemes. Significant changes have been:

■ a lower and more transparent pattern of bank charges for small businesses – a previously much-criticised area

■ a shift of resources by the banks towards the mid-corporate sector (in excess of approximately £500,000 turnover) – to which they devote more time and advice, conversely turning services to micro firms into a more basic service at lower cost

■ most significant, a shift away from overdrafts to term loans, accounting for about 75 per cent of bank lending to SMEs in 2003 – an increase from 50 per cent in 1992 – which now comes close to that of many other European countries – e.g., in Germany it is over 80 per cent.

This has important implications – it encourages longer-term thinking by small firms and working more closely with their bankers. Some of these relationships unravelled during the 2007–2010 banking crisis, however, and pressure on banks has resulted in renewed calls to reform bank charges and transparency.

4.9.3 Exporting and importing

Only about 1 per cent of all SMEs are exporters. It has been a major concern of policy to try and increase this proportion, particularly since most SMEs that *do* export are chiefly concerned with European and not wider world markets.

The chief aspects of UK export support are the Export Credit Guarantee Scheme (which insures against non-payment for exports) and a range of government services (marketed through Trade Partners UK). These services were enhanced in the late 1990s by the reorganisation of foreign staff positions in embassies so that they give a higher priority to trade issues and the establishment of a more focused approach by the Department of Trade and Industry's (DTI's) staff in this area. Further efforts to continue this adaptation continued in 2010/2011, but, historically, have met with significant resistance from embassy staff, who often prefer to focus on diplomacy. Their main activities are trade fairs, outward missions, overseas seminars, overseas promotions, inward missions and funds to facilitate development in specific overseas markets.

4.9.4 Research and innovation

The emphasis on support for small firms' R&D and technological innovation in the UK has historically been low, with a preference for development of pure research in universities and institutes and an implicit bias towards larger firms. Some attempt to change has occurred through the innovation and technology counsellors in Business Links, greater pressure on research councils, universities and research institutes to be more involved with applied R&D, particularly in SMEs, and various innovation and research tax credits.

Much of this development is slow or uncertain. The applied R&D spend is still low in the UK and connections weaker between research and business than in many other countries, particularly the USA, Korea or Germany. Most initiatives are small and localised rather than diffusing to the whole network of SMEs or research bodies. European programmes are often disproportionately significant as a result, although their economic output is often unclear.

Important research-funding initiatives are EUREKA, Regional Technology Centres, Teaching Company Scheme, Shell Technology Enterprise Programme and Innovation Research and Development Grants. Some local university initiatives, such as science parks, have been particularly successful (e.g., in Cambridge, Heriot Watt, Warwick), though the success elsewhere has been patchy. Shifts in university funding regimes since 2000 have sought to emphasise technology transfer and innovative research spin-offs through so-called 'third stream funding' (which is additional to teaching and general research income).

4.9.5 Education and training

It has long been recognised that one of Britain's chief competitive weaknesses has been a poor general level of education and training. This has been reflected not so much at the most senior levels of management, but, rather, chiefly in the semi-skilled and unskilled employees categories and, it has been argued, this leads Britain into a so-called 'low-skill equilibrium' (Finegold and Soskice, 1988).

As recently as 1981, only 50 per cent of workers in Britain had recognised qualifications and only 13 per cent of the population went into higher education. By 1989, 45 per cent of children left school at 16 with no qualification or only 1 pass at GCSE level. The pattern has improved significantly, but there is still a long way to go, particularly at the level of basic and vocational skills. For example, in 2003, 40 per cent of the adult population aged 16 to 65 were classed as functionally innumerate; 14.9 million adults had numeracy skills below that expected of 11-year-olds and 5.2 million adults had literacy skills below that level (Department for Education and Skills, 2003b).

The deficiency in basic school achievements confirms that, whilst Britain is continuing to produce a very good level of output in terms of highly qualified people, at the basic and vocational levels, there is still a major deficiency, which has severe impacts on small firms. This focuses attention on the earlier years of basic schooling (ages 5–14) as well as the more vocational years of 14–19. For example, in the first ever national test statistics for 11-year-olds in England published in March 1997, 25 per cent of pupils failed to achieve level 4 or above (the required standard) in English, maths and science. In 2010, the proportions had not improved and may have deteriorated, though the measures have changed, making comparisons difficult. These deficiencies have profound implications for SME workforces and for policies on school management and teacher training, which are only beginning to be tackled.

Poor education and training skills are arguably two of the most crucial constraints on small firm growth in Britain. SMEs rely to a greater extent than larger firms on the general quality of the labour market, especially on government-financed basic education and skills, because they can least afford training and are more subject to labour poaching, because they have a less dominant market position and can be outbid in terms of pay. A more formal training system, such as that in Germany, has many advantages for SMEs in overcoming these problems. Deficient education also undermines the more general scope for entrepreneurism, the culture of enterprise and spirit of risktaking.

There have been various attempts to improve SMEs' workforce training. For example, in the 1990s, a Small Business Initiative gave a 1 per cent reduction in the overdraft interest rate or £150 reduction in bank charges per year for 3 years in exchange for a pattern of management training agreed with a bank. Also the Skills for Small Business scheme involved firms with fewer that 50 employees identifying a key worker who was then given subsidised training and assessment skills to develop a company's training programme.

Since 2000, much of this effort has devolved to training providers, industry lead bodies and Sector Skills Councils, including the Small Firms Lead Body, to develop specific qualifications and standards for small firms. In addition, apprenticeships targeted on higher vocational skills have been used to improve training standards assessment and badging of companies to accredited training levels.

Whilst there has been a lot of activity to develop the education and training system in Britain since the 1980s, it is still far from clear that the right mix of programmes and incentives exists to encourage smaller firms. Indeed, it is increasingly being recognised, as noted above, that the most important investments needed for business developments as a whole, but small firms in particular, are in the most basic skill areas of literacy and numeracy.

4.9.6 Information and advice

Failures in the supply of information are a recognised problem for small firms, which interrelates with their relatively low level of market power. In Britain, until the mid-1980s, the main government-supported information service was the Small Firms Service, which was set up at a regional level largely in response to the 1971 Bolton Committee's report. The DTI also acted as a direct supplier of information, as did other departments in relation to the specific industrial sectors with which they were concerned.

From about 1990, this system began to change to a greater emphasis being placed on local delivery and access points. From 1993, a system of Business Links was used as the main delivery mechanism (see Section 4.12.2). However, as well as direct government-supported providers of information and advice, there are many private providers and business associations (nationally, sectorally and locally). With limitations on government spending and expertise being more realistically recognised since 2011, more effort has been made to encourage these producers to fill recognised market deficiencies through signposting and referrals across the public and private sectors rather than using central or local government as providers.

4.10 Sector policy

Up until the 1960s, sector policy and sector committees were a key part of government national economic planning, as discussed in the introduction, but this was abolished in 1979. However, following an initiative launched by the CBI in 1993, a number of government attempts have been made to focus on the development of business sectors. An early change was the reorganisation of the DTI (later called the Department of Business Innovation and Skills) itself into 'Sponsoring Divisions' from 1994. The aim was for the government to help each sector develop competitiveness. Inevitably some of this development has focused on SMEs, but probably there has still been a bias towards larger companies.

Potentially more important for SMEs have been attempts to encourage the role of trade associations and training organisations. These are voluntary bodies in Britain, but they receive recognition from government and some funding to support training and business development initiatives. They suffer from a variable membership take-up by businesses, but many trade associations are important sources of service to SMEs. Indeed, most surveys of businesses show trade associations to be the first and main point of call for services, after banks, accountants, lawyers and other professionals, along with local chambers of commerce, and well ahead of any government-backed agencies (Bennett, 2008).

The main services provided by trade associations are bringing about improvements in government legislation, providing information and advice, conferences, networking and benchmarking. Standard setting, legal and arbitration services are more common in professional associations and bodies serving the smallest firms of the self-employed and owner managers. As it is a voluntary system, as noted, take-up of membership is variable, but density of membership is generally much higher for sector bodies than other UK business associations (Bennett, 1997, 1999) – on average, market penetration is 62 per cent for trade associations and 50 per cent for professional associations. Hence, sector associations are important interfaces with and suppliers of services to SMEs that should be used by government in policy initiatives.

In the middle 1990s, attempts were made by government to help trade associations improve. In 1993, a Benchmarking Challenge initiative provided modest DTI funds to help trade associations set up 'clubs' to help their members create benchmarks in terms of competitiveness. In 1995, an Export Challenge invited trade associations to propose methods to help their members promote exporting. In 1996, a Network Challenge sought innovative proposals from trade associations in their use of IT (Cabinet Office, 1996b; Berry, 1997). Most significant, however, was the promotion from 1996 of a 'model' trade association with criteria and targets of best practice (DTI, 1996; Bennett, 1997).

This aimed to encourage trade associations to benchmark in relation to each other and guide government departments towards those associations that met 'model' criteria. This was thus a source of 'recognition' of trade associations by government. Generally, the 'model' trade association was well received, and was very widely disseminated. After 1997 this initiative was taken over and managed by the CBI through a Trade Association Forum.

From 2001, a key role of sector associations has been to work with government through Sector Skills Councils. These seek to help government develop and promote vocational training standards, apprenticeships and the diffusion of take-up of training by companies. They support government training provision but have tended to direct attention to the issues of low skills and the unemployed. Since 2011, there has been some improved flexibility to emphasise the sector's, rather than government's, goals.

4.11 Local policy

For most small firms, the local context is far more important than it is for larger firms. Small firms depend to a great extent on the local labour market, local financial services and any sources of information and advice available locally. Because of lower levels of absolute resources, thresholds for entry and them having less market power, small firms usually have much less time for search and evaluation, so the local context of what is readily available can be crucial to them. As a result, the general skill level, general role of banks, general level of information and general availability of advice are usually the most significant supports for small firms. This means, ironically, that local support often depends mostly on national policy, even if its effects are consumed by businesses chiefly through the local level.

At a local level, national and sectoral issues come together and are reinforced by the specific local conditions that determine how fertile the local environment is, both for new firm formation and for development. Some geographical areas have a more positive supporting environment for market development than others. A good deal of analysis has gone into assessing what underlies the differences in local business conditions and what improves them. In general, it has been found that the extent of existing entrepreneurism and growth of small firms in an area is a strong stimulus to enterprise, along with occupational structures related to commerce, services (rather than manufacturing) and to management and the professions. High rates of job loss can be strong 'push' factors, whilst long-term unemployment and high levels of employment in branch plants are usually impediments. More general factors – e.g., high levels of educational attainment, availability of skills, premises, local capital and general business climate – are also important in encouraging small firms to develop. Indeed, one of the strongest forces that can promote or impede small firms is the general institutional structure and capacity of an area (Moyes and Westhead, 1990; Bennett and McCoshan 1993).

Various initiatives in Britain have sought to improve the local environment for small firms. Mainly, these have been seen as supply-side approaches to overcome the market gaps outlined earlier. An early approach was the setting up of local Enterprise Agencies. Beginning in 1975, these grew to a network of 400 agencies in 1994 across Britain, chiefly concerned with advising small business start-ups and their immediate aftercare. They were initially the result of initiatives by local large firms and chambers of commerce, but, once government funding was used to stimulate them from 1983, their focus shifted to engaging the unemployed and the voluntary input ebbed. They were subsumed within Business Link and, subsequently, RDAs (Bennett and Payne, 2000).

Local government since the 1980s has also become a major agent for SME support, chiefly as a provider of information, sites and physical regeneration initiatives. Central government limits on local government running companies restricted activities, but new local government initiatives continue to be announced and this has been given added support since 2001 by new local development powers, which were further widened in 2011. The period 2001–2010 saw local government expand its services unrealistically, just like central government. More realistic finances since 2010 have encouraged local government to cooperate more closely with private providers to give support to SMEs.

Many local government SME initiatives have been made in partnership with other agents. Over the 1990s and 2000s, this was primarily with other public agencies. Since 2011, there has been greater effort to use private business associations and cooperation with individual firms, particularly local chambers of commerce.

As a voluntary system, unlike the compulsory systems in France, Germany, Italy or Spain, membership of chambers of commerce in Britain varies. Membership is about 8 per cent of the total UK business population, but much higher in the main cities (at 20–30 per cent). It averages about 23 per cent for established SMEs of 20–200 employees.

The chambers were major providers of government-financed SME schemes over 1990–2010. They offer business representation and provide business skilling and advice, export/import documentation, advice, foreign trade fairs and missions (for which they are an agent of the Department for Business Innovation and Skills), management training and employee training. They, together with other business organisations and local government, have become a key means for taking forward more localised and private sector-led support since 2011.

Supplementing local actions, special purpose urban development bodies have been used to stimulate focused development in inner-city areas since the 1980s. In England, the Rural Development Commission was important in rural areas. In Scotland, Wales and Northern Ireland, development agencies were established in the 1970s and 1980s and continue to play a major role. These bodies have been the main agents for administering the grants and other types of financial support discussed earlier. They have also been important in land preparation and provision of premises, environment improvements and advice for SMEs (particularly for minorities, ethnic and women's groups, etc.).

The scene changed after 1990 with the establishment of local Training and Enterprise Councils in England and Wales and Local Enterprise Companies in Scotland. These were general-purpose bodies that took over the administration of many government SME grants and advice schemes. They were also the chief local agent of central government for financing vocational training for the unemployed. There were 85 of these bodies in England and Wales and 22 in Scotland.

In the period between their launch in 1990 until their abolition in 2001, the Training and Enterprise Councils developed a wide range of small business activities. The most prominent were counselling and training, with a major emphasis on consultancy support and specific advice to start-ups. Much of this was delivered through other agents under contract (Bennett, Wicks and McCoshan, 1994). Surveys showed the full range of activities to be very extensive, but often they were too broad and ill focused to have a major local impact. Partly as a result of these criticisms, the government launched a new initiative in 1993, which became Business Link (see Section 4.12.2).

The scene changed radically again in 2001 with the launch of Regional Development Agencies (RDAs) in England. Also, greater powers were devolved to the Scottish Parliament and the Welsh and Northern Ireland Assemblies, resulting in a strengthening of their development bodies and increases in their budgets. Business Link and most business development initiatives were devolved to these bodies, with the result that different 'business support' strategies operated in each English region, Scotland, Wales and Northern Ireland.

The overall result was that it became rather fragmented. Various assessments of it in England have referred to a 'patchwork quilt', 'chaos', 'labyrinth of initiatives', a 'muddle' (Audit Commission, 1999; HM Treasury, 2002; DTI, 2007). The Better Regulation Task Force (2004) 'struggled with the justification for so many bodies active on the ground . . . Our stakeholders struggled too . . . it will take more than protocols or pieces of paper to ensure close working'. In Scotland, Wales and Northern Ireland, there has been more coherence to the direction of their devolved governments, but there have been criticisms of political interference and dominance by bureaucratic over economic objectives.

Figure 4.2 summarises the range of government departments and agents discussed above and their relative expenditures on business support, mostly for smaller businesses. The total expenditure was estimated at £10.3billion in 2002, of which central government and agricultural support to firms were the largest elements. Whilst in opposition, the Conservatives commissioned a report that suggested expenditure was actually about £12billion after taking account of Scottish, Welsh and Northern Ireland and other supports (Richard, 2007, 2008). This report estimated that about 33.5 per cent of this funding was lost in administration within the complex set of agencies involved. Inefficiencies were further exacerbated by fragmentation into about 3000 different programmes (a figure quoted by the Labour government; see also DTI, 2007), each with its own funding 'silo' and targets.

Using rather simplified statistics, Richard (2007) also demonstrated that there was no correlation between government expenditure increases on support for SMEs and indicators of economic improvement – e.g., growth in entrepreneurship, self-employment, number of businesses, business survival, profitability (see also Bennett, 2008). Whilst clearly supporting one political party, Richard's report (2008) nevertheless echoed the conclusion of most other research, that most government policy supports were achieving very little: they were mostly dead weights, distortionary, had low additionality and were expensive.

Figure 4.2 Expenditure on small firms by government bodies

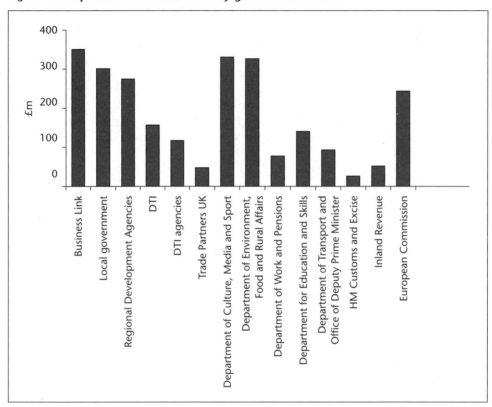

Source: HM Treasury.

Following the conclusions of the Richard report (2008), the Coalition government since 2010 has sought to reduce government funding, increase local flexibility and revive market and voluntary inputs to SMEs. The RDAs in England were abolished (with transition, effective from 2012) and replaced by Local Enterprise Partnerships (LEPs). The LEPs have been formed across groups of local authorities, in most cases, with varying structures. Within the first 24 LEPs, chambers of commerce are leading members in about 40 per cent. The LEPs, local government or chambers directly have taken over most responsibility for SME programmes (as well as other economic development activities; see Department for Business Innovation and Skills, 2010).

An overview of the different organisational structures is given in Figure 4.3, covering the situation in 2011. The names and position of the different local and regional agents for the early periods are also shown, demonstrating the instability of the structures over the period since the 1980s. The figure brings out the different central and regional governments' departmental roles (near the top of the figure), separated for England, Scotland and Wales, from which flow different funding programmes that are supposed to be coordinated at regional level (via the RDAs, Scottish Executive, Highlands and Islands and Welsh Assembly/Welsh Executive). In turn, at local level, specific delivery agents (e.g., Business Link and LEPs) are supposed to coordinate the different

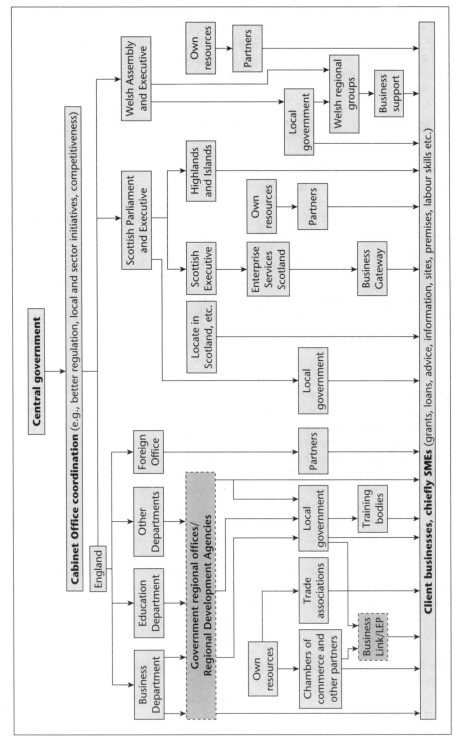

Figure 4.3 Organisation of finance and departmental responsibilities for central government, its agents, local government and small businesses

programmes, working with local partners (chiefly local government) and other agents (such as chambers of commerce, trade associations, etc.). These agents also use their own resources to support SMEs. With a reduced level of government support since 2011, a greater emphasis on delivery by partners has developed (chiefly chambers of commerce, local government and technology transfer bodies, including universities).

4.12 A case study of SME advice and support: Business Link and LEPs

In most countries, government initiatives for small businesses in more recent years have focused on providing advice and support to firms at various stages, from start-up, through early growth, to later innovation and strategic change processes. This is seen as one of the best ways of overcoming areas of market failure (e.g., unequal access to information) with least distortion to markets. This has been the main approach of the US Small Business Administration and is also now followed by most EU countries (European SMEs Observatory, 1996) as well as in most other parts of the world.

Within Britain, the provision of advice over 1993–2011 has been through a range of local agencies – initially called Business Link in England, Business Gateway in Scotland, and Business Connect in Wales. A case study of Business Link is instructive since it provides a good example of the potential for government support to small business, as well as its limitations.

4.12.1 From Bolton to 1993

Before the 1970s there was no government advisory service for small firms in Britain. Instead, the focus, as we have seen, was on national policies, sector support, larger firms and nationalised industries. The Bolton Committee's report in 1971, however, suggested the establishment of a single information and advice telephone helpline for SMEs. This became the Small Firms Service, which operated from 1973 to 1993.

The Small Firms Service was a centralised, telephone-based helpline, with civil service staff who referred callers to other specialist suppliers in the private and public sectors. All small firms were eligible. High volumes of enquiries were dealt with (250,000 per year) and high levels of satisfaction were achieved (95 per cent of customers). In addition, a more specialist Business Development Service responded to 20,000 requests a year for low-cost counselling, which was often provided by secondees from larger businesses on a semi-voluntary basis. The service was supplemented from 1988 to 1993 by the Enterprise Initiative, which provided higher levels of government grant support for consultancy and staffing. Again, high take-up and satisfaction levels were achieved.

4.12.2 Decentralisation, 1993–2001

From 1993, this limited, but successful, approach was abolished and replaced by Business Link. This decentralised the management to local partnerships in 85 areas, with a further 200 local satellites. The aim was to use these local delivery points as a means of integrating a wide range of central government small business services and integrate delivery. The full range of services is summarised in Table 4.3.

Table 4.3 Services provided by Business Link by personal business advisers (PBAs), as well as by referrals, networking and co-location with other partners

Information and advice

Provide high-quality information and advice on:	
■ grants and support schemes	■ technology and innovation
■ finance	■ training
■ late payment	■ marketing
■ VAT, tax and uniform business rates	■ design
■ licensing requirements	■ product sourcing
■ legislation (health and safety, planning, etc.)	■ environmental issues, including
■ standards, including BS5750/BS7850 and TQM	BS7750
■ BSI services	■ application of IT*
■ information (including new legislation)	■ property*
■ business start-up	■ patents, trademarks and copyright*
	■ education/business partnerships*

Personal business advisers (PBAs), who maintain regular contact with a portfolio of companies and construct an integrated package of services to meet their ends

Counselling/consultancy

Provide access to:	
■ diagnostic health check services	■ investors in people
■ start-up counselling	■ other subsidised consultancy schemes
■ general business counselling	■ commercial consultancy
■ survival counselling	■ business consultancy

Business skills and awareness

Provides access to:	
■ business skills seminars (including business planning, quality, marketing, purchasing, etc.)	■ business start-up schemes

Note: *indicates that a service is desirable, but not essential

Source: Department of Trade and Industry, 1992, Prospectus, Annex 2; Bennett et al., 1994, Table 9.15; see also www.businesslink.gov.uk

There were many service targets, of which a major one was to support 10–200-employee firms 'with growth potential'. There were also management incentives to provide intensive consultancy and advice services through a new group of employees called 'personal business advisers' (PBAs). There were financial targets for fee income (initially 25 per cent of the total budget), with the intention that the Business Link would have an ongoing relationship with the small firm being advised and be partially self-financing.

Business Link achieved take-up of advice and more intensive counselling levels similar to those of the earlier Small Firms Service, but with much lower satisfaction levels (60 per cent on average) and great variability between areas (from 20 to 90 per cent). Hardly a success and it cost approximately ten times more than the Small Firms Service.

4.12.3 Regionalisation, 2001–2010

From 2001, the system was reformed through a reduction in the number of geographical areas covered to 45 (based mainly on counties), removal of fee incentives, management through regional agencies and changed contracting structures. In the period 2001–2003, take-up reduced as Business Link managers restructured and refocused, but satisfaction eventually increased to about 85 per cent, although variability between areas remained.

After 2005, direct control of Business Link passed from central government to the English RDAs. Each followed different paths. In the South East, which had limited government resources and little support from the EU since it has fewer economic problems, SME support was chiefly focused on signposting and referral to private-sector advisers, with a limited group of businesses with growth potential selected for high levels of adviser and financial support. At the other extreme, in the North East and North West regions, large amounts of public funding was available, derived from multiple British and EU initiatives. In those regions, attempts were made to integrate small business support with urban regeneration, neighbourhood renewal and industrial restructuring initiatives, as well as confused social welfare agendas. Less referral and signposting was attempted and more small firms, in targeted areas, were able to gain grants or subsidies.

4.12.4 Localism and the market, since 2010

After the abolition of RDAs, the responsibility for local support for SMEs was passed to LEPs (Department for Business Innovation and Skills, 2010). Instead of a central design for defined services with specific government targets for each service, the market of business advisers and consultants, as well as local partners, have been used to a greater extent. This is allowing synergies with partners' own services for SMEs and the direct use of existing market and partner skills and resources. It provides greater scope for bringing initiatives together at a fraction of the cost of Business Link, but its most important change has been to recognise that managers of local support programmes to SMEs have to be free from external targets and, instead, focus on business' direct needs.

4.12.5 The lessons of British experiments, 1970–2011

The evolution of Business Link and early experience of subsequent LEPs provide a major internationally relevant case study of lessons in how government should, and should not, seek to support small businesses. There has been extensive monitoring and assessment. You can read these assessments in Bennett (2008), Bennett and Robson (1999b, 2000, 2003, 2004), Priest (1999), Richard (2007, 2008). The role of the adviser (PBA) has been given detailed assessment by Tann and Laforet (1998) and Mole (2002a, 2002b; Mole, Hart, Roper and Saal, 2008). You can see the current service offers at www.businesslink.gov.uk. The following summarises the main lessons learnt.

First, the quality of advice, overall effectiveness and levels of client satisfaction were significantly higher in Business Link franchises that were managed by partners with private sector expertise – either chambers of commerce or the one private company involved – than for the others. Business Link franchises that were established solely to run the public contract were rated lowest on all criteria. This has been a critical lesson and the subsequent LEPs have, thus, been given greater flexibility and freedom to work with the market of business advisers.

Second, the integration of central and local government services, which was a major aim of the decentralisation to local agencies, only partially occurred. Government departments, local government and other 'partners' retained independent funding 'silos' and programme targets and remained jealous of their own areas, with 'turf wars' occurring. There was little rationalisation of the huge number of government-financed agencies or programmes operating locally (summarised in DTI, 2007) – policy termination remained rare. Business Link became, in many cases, just another agency. The LEPs have generally provided much greater integration as a result of cuts of funding to government bodies that competed with the private sector, but, up to 2011, there remained confusion about different government programme brands.

Third, and interrelated with the 'turf wars', referral to market suppliers of services, chambers of commerce and other non-public agents was very limited. Referral made up perhaps 5 per cent of Business Link's actions up to 2001, whilst under the Small Firms Service in the 1980s it stood at over 90 per cent. Referrals improved a little after 2001, but declined again when RDAs took over the contracts. The LEPs build more directly on partners and, thus, offer built-in cross-referrals, but this has yet to be fully evaluated.

Fourth, the model of intensive support through PBA consultancy proved elusive. Most demand for government support is, in fact, for simple information and advice or for very intensive specialisms. The hope of creating long-term relationships with small firms ignored the market for advice, which is generally for one-offs with different specialists (Riddle, 1986; Hill and Nealey, 1991; Clark, 1995). Encouraging small firms to come into long-term relationships also risked 'moral hazard', in that they would take unwarranted risks and become dependent on public support. This also proved to be a significant problem with those regional agencies that were heavily funded, such as those in Northern Ireland, Scotland, Wales, the North West and North East England. It also introduced a gender bias into initiatives that had not previously existed – perversely, disfavouring female-headed businesses, which it was supposed to single out for support (Bennett, 2008).

Fifth, the target of raising fee income proved both unrealistic ('Who wants to pay for government services?') and severely distorted manager and adviser behaviour. This, more than any other factor, made referrals less likely, as advisers held on to small business enquirers in order to sell them a service and charge a fee (whether or not they wanted or needed it). This, in turn, increased dissatisfaction levels.

Sixth, the concept of government targets for SME growth – e.g., those laid down by the Small Business Service (2004a, 2004b) and the Department for Business, Enterprise and Regulatory Reform (2007c) – have been almost entirely ineffective. This is because of principal–agent problems: government and its agencies are not the bodies that can achieve the targets they were set; only small business themselves can do this and only they are the ones that can define the appropriate targets.

Finally, the decentralisation to a wide range of local areas proved difficult to quality assure. Whilst the aim of bringing advisers and administrators closer to the small firm was laudable, in practice it proved difficult to recruit PBAs of high enough quality to make the system effective. Typical comments regarding advisers were that they were 'poor quality', 'unprofessional', 'too bureaucratic', had 'poor skill levels' (Ramsden and Bennett, 2006). In effect, the policy was overly complex, producing a model for support that few businesses wanted and was difficult to implement. High levels of variability between areas resulted, which was the inevitable outcome of differences in the management capacity of different local Business Link franchises and differences in adviser competence within each area. Evaluations of the intensive support showed that some of it was effective (Mole, Hart, Roper and Saal, 2008) but the benefits of increased employment in aided SMEs never came close to matching the very high total costs of the whole administrative edifice and the effect of Business Link on increasing business turnover (sales volume) was very small or insignificant.

4.13 Chapter summary

This chapter has explored how governments have sought to help small businesses – focusing, in the last sections, on the example of British government schemes and the particular case of Business Link and LEPs.

A key conclusion is that, whilst there is some scope for government to help small businesses, much of this effort is most effective when focused on general public services rather than specific and targeted schemes. This is because government has little technical capacity to be able to segment its strategies in an effective way, has little expertise in business disciplines and suffers from a lack of clear aims to direct programmes, especially for clients such as small firms that are so numerous and varied. In the end, it has proved difficult to mount defensible arguments for why some businesses should be helped and not others.

These experiences suggest that government action is most effective where it improves the generic environment for entrepreneurship and business growth (through maintaining economic stability, and improving education, skills training, infrastructure) rather than seeking specific, targeted and highly intensive initiatives. Moreover, the actions of government in its own areas – as regulator, economic agent, service provider and planner/promoter – remain the key areas where it needs to become more effective. Too often, government initiatives disadvantage small businesses because of the diseconomies of scale that they experience in trying to comply with government procedures. Hence, better regulation and improvement of government services are usually the main actions that government can take to help small firms.

This conclusion is not surprising since each small business is trading in a unique business environment of suppliers and customers with its own specific internal staff, product and management characteristics. Whilst there are many generic features of SMEs, and these are often focused on in targeting policies, the practical demand from small firms is for investment and actions that are specific to their market niches and opportunities. These aspects of the market for SMEs' products and services are *highly segmented* in ways that are difficult for a public administration to target. Thus, an appropriate policy intervention or support for small firms usually has to be a general one, allowing them to adapt what is on offer to their different trading environments.

It should not be surprising, therefore, that there are no simple solutions to designing SME policy. Even when looking at a single field of activity – e.g., training, advice, exporting or better regulation – it is difficult for government to design programmes that are likely to fit a firm's specific needs. As noted by the Bank of England (1996), there is no one solution that will bring about a sudden or dramatic improvement. As a result, there have been many different policy initiatives, with a 'patchwork quilt' of programmes, few of which have been truly effective. This outcome seems to be inevitable, as a result of funding silos and political pressures to target so-called 'needs'. It is as true in Europe as it is in Britain. Our discussion here suggests that government policy support should normally focus on generic and supply-side issues and curtail attempts at specialised targeting.

Questions

1 Which main form of government action is most likely to help small businesses?

2 Assess the arguments for segmenting policy to target parts of the small business market.

3 Has the provision of small business support in Britain since 1990 provided a coherent and effective package for small firms?

4 Using the experience of Business Link to illustrate your argument, which strategies have been most effective for providing government advice to small firms.

Weblinks

http://bis.gov.uk/bre
The Better Regulation Executive (BRE) is part of the Department for Business Innovation and Skills (BIS) and leads the regulatory reform agenda across the UK government.

www.businesslink.gov.uk
Business Link is the UK government's online resource for business.

www.sba.gov
The Small Business Administration in the USA was established to maintain and strengthen the economy by aiding, counselling, assisting and protecting the interests of small businesses.

http://ec.europa.eu/enterprise/index_en.htm
The European Commission's Directorate General Enterprise and Industry website where you can explore policy documents and so on on a range of issues related to entrepreneurship and small businesses at a European level.

CHAPTER 5

The real world of the entrepreneur

Friederike Welter

5.1 Introduction

For a long time, entrepreneurship studies tended to underestimate the influence of the external environment on entrepreneurial behaviour. Nowadays, there is growing recognition that entrepreneurship can be better understood within its context(s) – that it neither happens in a vacuum nor is it solely the business context which influences the nature and extent of entrepreneurship and entrepreneurial behaviour. However, too often, context is taken for granted or controlled away (Johns, 2006), although it offers deeper insights into how individuals interact with situations and how situations influence individuals.

This chapter focuses on the different 'non-business' contexts in which entrepreneurship takes place. It emphasises the 'real world of the entrepreneur', proposing that context is important for understanding when and where entrepreneurship happens and it also influences who becomes involved. This is a much-needed step towards 'understanding the nature, richness and dynamics' of entrepreneurship (Zahra, 2007: 451).

5.2 Learning objectives

There are three learning objectives in this chapter:

1 to become familiar with key theoretical concepts that could be applied when contextualising entrepreneurship

2 to understand the diversity of contexts that may have an impact on the nature and extent of entrepreneurship and the ways in which entrepreneurs may influence their various contexts

3 to understand the challenges involved in contextualising entrepreneurship.

Key concepts
■ context ■ embeddedness ■ household ■ community ■ institutions

5.3 The concept of context

Context relates to circumstances, conditions, situations or environments that are external to a phenomenon. For example, Cappelli and Sherer (1991) understand context as surroundings of specific phenomena that help to illustrate them. Mowday and Sutton (1993) emphasise that context is also stimuli existing in the external environment. Johns (2006) sees context as situational opportunities and constraints on behaviour, furthermore distinguishing between 'omnibus' and 'discrete' contexts. Table 5.1 sets out this distinction in relation to entrepreneurship, the first and second columns illustrating the various types of contexts in which entrepreneurship takes place (i.e., the omnibus contexts), while the third column shows the respective contextual variables related to each context type (discrete contexts). Types of context refer to the social and spatial world of the entrepreneur that simultaneously provide enterprising individuals with opportunities and/or set boundaries for their actions. Also, history and time are important contexts, as indicated by Baumol (1990: 899), who drew attention to the fact that the rules for entrepreneurship '*do* change dramatically from one time and place to another.'

Surprisingly, however, the real world of the entrepreneur still remains somewhat of a 'black box'. Most entrepreneurship research tends to stick to contexts that are easy to operationalise and observe and fit the model of the enterprising individual. Specifically, entrepreneurship research tends to focus on the business context – in particular, the influence of 'money' and 'market', which are two elements of what Bates et al. (2007) consider the traditional '3Ms' required for entrepreneurship: management, money and market. By money is meant the availability of and access to

Table 5.1 Contexts for entrepreneurship

Types of contexts		Contextual variables (examples)
Business	Industry and markets	Stage of lifecycle of industries and markets, number and characteristics of competitors
Social	Networks	Density, frequency of network relations
	Household and family	Roles of household/family in relation to entrepreneurship
Spatial	Regions Neighbourhoods Local communities	Characteristics of physical location of business, support infrastructure, characteristics of local communities, neighbourhoods and regions
Institutional	Culture and society	Societal attitudes and norms
	Political and economic systems	Legal and regulatory regulations Policy and support measures

Source: Adapted from Welter (2011)

financial capital, while market reflects access to business markets and, when setting up a new business, access to opportunities. However, for example, self-perception and ambitions that are influenced by norms, values, beliefs (or, in other words, by the societal and social contexts) have been shown to affect the willingness of entrepreneurs to choose from different possibilities in order to pursue an idea or grow a business (Gatewood, Shaver and Gartner, 1995). This does suggest that entrepreneurial behaviour is likely to be closely linked to the social and family context of the enterprising individual.

Therefore, incorporating context can provide deeper insights into entrepreneurship. This can be illustrated with regard to the nature of opportunities, which are, in one way or another, a function of the environment. Some entrepreneurship scholars understand opportunities as 'objective' elements of environments – they are 'out there', just awaiting an entrepreneur to pick them up (McMullen, Plummer and Acs, 2007) – but they are also created, in the sense of being 'enacted' and socially constructed (Fletcher, 2006). This does not imply that there is no objective reality regarding opportunities, since an 'objective' opportunity may also be considered to be 'subjective' because opportunities emerge as individuals make sense of information and their actions, thus retrospectively discovering and recognising opportunities.

Plummer et al. (2007) attempt to reconcile both perspectives and emphasise that an 'objective' opportunity is something new for all individuals, thus understanding opportunity as a fact of the environment that requires subjective assessments of its value in order for the opportunity to be discovered and exploited. In this regard, entrepreneurs are influenced by the real world 'out there' where, for example, beliefs and values of a society shape their individual interpretations of what constitutes an opportunity. In turn, the scope of their individual actions also has an impact on the real world, pointing to recursive links that exist between individual perceptions, actions and contexts.

5.4 Theorising (about) context

Theorising (about) context requires concepts that allow us to consider the diversity and multiplicity of context together with its two sides – namely, context as asset and context as liability. There is also the fact that not only does context impact on entrepreneurs but also entrepreneurs can have an impact on context.

5.4.1 Context and embeddedness

The real world of the entrepreneur incorporates environments at micro and macro levels or, in other words, the real world covers both proximate and distal contexts (Mowday and Sutton, 1993). Networks, families and households, the local neighbourhood and business environment constitute the proximate contexts (i.e., the real world at micro level), while overall societal rules and culture, regional environments and the political and economic system constitute the distal context, which operates at macro level. Thus, theories that acknowledge context, ideally, would cover different levels of analysis.

The concept of embeddedness, which has been introduced by Polanyi (1957) and built on by Granovetter (1985), allows us to theorise context across levels of analysis.

Granovetter (1992a) stressed the embeddedness of economic goals and activities in socially orientated goals and structures. An important part of Granovetter's focus is the social construction of institutions, emphasising the contingencies associated with factors such as historical background and social structure and the constraints imposed by existing institutions. As Granovetter points out, traditional development theory is critical of economic activity that is embedded in non-economic obligations, which are seen as preventing economically efficient operation. However, he also indicates that where such embeddedness is absent, efficient operation can be prevented by a lack of interpersonal trust, although he alludes to the other side of trust by pointing out the demand for favours that may be placed on a business by members of a family, friends or community.

Zukin and DiMaggio (1990) distinguish four forms of embeddedness – namely, political, cultural, social structure and cognitive. Political and cultural embeddedness put the emphasis on the wider institutional environment of economic actors. This refers to the question of how institutions structure, constrain or foster individual actions and behaviour. Political embeddedness reflects formal institutions as political and economic boundaries for individual action – in this case, for entrepreneurship – while cultural embeddedness refers to informal institutions, which contain the collective understanding of a society as the basis for economic behaviour. Cultural embeddedness is closely linked to both social and cognitive embeddedness. The former refers to 'the contextualization of economic exchange in patterns of ongoing interpersonal relations' (Zukin and DiMaggio, 1990: 18). The latter refers to 'ways in which the structured regularities of mental processes limit the exercise of economic reasoning' (Zukin and DiMaggio, 1990: 15–16).

Context simultaneously provides individuals with entrepreneurial opportunities and sets boundaries for their actions – in other words, individuals may experience it as asset and liability. Related to the local environment, Julien (2007) identifies five types of proximity – namely, cognitive, organisational, sociocultural, institutional and geographical – all of which have positive and negative aspects for entrepreneurs and entrepreneurship development. For example, cognitive proximity allows entrepreneurs to share knowledge and know-how, as well as partake in technological advancements, but it simultaneously could result in conformity and collusion, thus hindering individual business development. Institutional proximity will result in reputation and legitimacy for the entrepreneur and allows the emergence of rules, but it also could foster corruption in those cases where rules leave too much room for discretionary decisions. Organisational and geographical proximity facilitate transactions, interpersonal relations and the knowledge that resources are available within a region, but both factors also might contribute to a lack of openness to the outside and, instead, result in lock-in effects.

Several authors highlighted that the concept of embeddedness need not be static, but could encompass also dynamic elements. For example, discussing the extent to which economic actions are embedded in social relations, Granovetter (1985) draws attention to their constant interplay and changes over time. Aldrich (2009) points out time and space as important factors for the development of organisations, while Emirbayer (1997) highlights the socially negotiated, dynamic nature of social action and moves the idea of embeddedness forward by bringing in a spatial and temporal dimension to supplement relational aspects. Similarly, and from the perspective of economic geography, Bathelt and Glückler (2003) identify contextuality, path dependency and contingency as major elements that determine spatial, temporal and social embeddedness. The concept of path dependency links temporal and historical contexts, explaining how current individual behaviour is influenced by past events and decisions because norms and values governing our behaviour persist over time, as has been illustrated for the example of entrepreneurs in postsocialist environments (Welter and Smallbone, 2011b). Berg (1997) brings in the notion of 'place', which encapsulates social relations within a particular location as a supportive or constraining element of spatial embeddedness. In relation to spatial embeddedness, Hess (2004: 174) also points out the risk of 'overterritorialisation'. In the broader meaning of 'overcontextualisation', however, this might be considered a general danger inherent in any effort made to try and conceptualise and capture the manifold contexts for entrepreneurship.

5.4.2 Context and agency

Entrepreneurs and their behaviour also impact context. For example, in relation to regional development, Feldman, Francis and Bercovitz (2005) analyse the role entrepreneurship plays in triggering the emergence of high-tech agglomerations. With regard to the institutional environment, Henrekson and Sanandaji (2010) suggest abiding, evading and altering as behavioural mechanisms through which entrepreneurs can influence institutions. Welter (2011) uses the example of a young woman entrepreneur in rural Uzbekistan who took up a traditional craft after her father's death to indicate the two-way-relationship between entrepreneurs and their contexts. Traditional Uzbek society forced this entrepreneur into a traditional business activity because this activity could be conducted from home. The entrepreneur and her two sisters, who also set up traditional home-based businesses, started training unemployed girls in their regions, thus acting as role models and mentors. Over time, this could foster changes in the societal and household contexts for women entrepreneurs in rural, traditional Uzbekistan.

Therefore, when theorising context, we need to find approaches that allow us to consider both top-down effects of context on entrepreneurship and bottom-up processes which impact context. A multilayered embeddedness perspective has to be combined with an individual perspective that takes into account the adaptability and learning behaviour of entrepreneurs, thus drawing attention to the process dimension of entrepreneurship where individual action impacts context and contributes to changing a context.

With regard to institutional environments, the concept of institutional entrepreneurship has been put forward as a theoretical approach to considering the impact of agency (Battilana, Leca and Boxenbaum, 2009). For agents to qualify as institutional entrepreneurs they would have to initiate changes that break with the existing institutional framework and actively participate in implementing those, although entrepreneurs might not be successful in implementing institutional changes and institutional entrepreneurship could be a by-product of other (entrepreneurial) actions (Battilana, Leca and Boxenbaum, 2009). So far, however, its application in entrepreneurship research is not without critics as the concept does not appear to capture the complexities of the interplay between institutions and agents, nor does it suggest an adequate conceptual underpinning for exploring agency (Aldrich, 2010).

The concept of mixed embeddedness, which has been developed in relation to analyses of ethnic minority entrepreneurship (Kloosterman, van der Leun and Rath, 1999; Kloosterman, 2010), contains characteristics that make it potentially useful as an overarching conceptual framework. The concept embraces the interplay between social, spatial and institutional contexts, as well as between structure and agency.

The opportunity structure is a key element in mixed embeddedness. Business opportunities are understood as being shaped by a combination of market trends and conditions, which themselves are embedded in a broader institutional framework. Decisions about going into business can also be influenced by the wider structure of alternative opportunities for earning a living. Unlike approaches that narrowly focus on agency and/or cultural values, a mixed embeddedness perspective recognises the diversity and complexity of the different context levels of human agency. Moreover, the emphasis on an interaction between structure and agency, together with the broader spatial and societal context, makes this concept particularly relevant to analysing entrepreneurship within its diverse contexts as well as the impact of entrepreneurs on contexts.

The next sections review the social, sociospatial and institutional contexts in more detail.

5.5 The social world: moving from networks towards families and households

5.5.1 Networks and social capital

Where entrepreneurship scholars have studied other contexts beyond the business world, this mainly refers to the social world of enterprising individuals – in particular, networks and network ties. The 'nature, depth, and extent of an individual's ties into the environment' (Jack and Anderson, 2002: 468) is the main application of a 'non-business' context in entrepreneurship studies. Networks and network ties refer to social capital that is needed for identifying opportunities and accessing the resources required for exploiting those opportunities. Support from network contacts could include financial capital, information, access to potential employees or clients, but also the emotional understanding, encouragement and support that, in particular, strong ties within a network (normally family and friends) are able to offer (Jack, Dodd and Anderson, 2004).

Several studies have confirmed the general importance of social capital for starting and running a business (Brüderl and Preisendörfer, 1998; Davidsson and Honig, 2003). Combining (implicitly) social and institutional contexts, other studies have looked into the role social capital plays for entrepreneurship in difficult environments (Manev, Gyoshev and Manolova, 2005; Smallbone and Welter, 2009) where networking contacts frequently are substituting for weakly specified legal regulations and inadequate law enforcement. Also, social capital can be important for opportunity recognition and exploitation. De Koning (2003) introduces a sociocognitive perspective on opportunity recognition, drawing attention to its social and societal embeddedness, while Jack and Anderson (2002: 484) illustrate the embeddedness of opportunity recognition and exploitation in social networks: 'Embedding is a way of joining the structure; by joining the structure one enacts it . . . the opportunities exist within the structure and only become manifest by the action of entrepreneurial agency'.

Access to resources may be restricted for specific social groups, such as ethnic minorities, young entrepreneurs or women entrepreneurs (Bates, Jackson III and Johnson, 2007). In this regard, several studies have highlighted the importance that social capital may play for the entrepreneurial activities of ethnic minorities (Kloosterman, van der Leun and Rath, 1999; Ram, Theodorakopoulos and Jones, 2008). In these situations, it is particularly social capital from within ethnic groups that allows the access to the resources needed to set up and develop a business. However, the impact of social capital on women entrepreneurs is less clear. Allen (2000) refers to women's networks including fewer entrepreneurs than male's networks, which might restrict their outreach and usefulness for a female entrepreneur. Other studies report generally more homogeneous and less outreaching networks for women entrepreneurs, compared with men, as well as less frequent network activities (Caputo and Dolinsky, 1998). Renzulli, Aldrich and Moody (2000) found out that women tend to rely more on homogeneous networks with a larger share of relatives than those of men, indicating it is less gender than kinship that creates disadvantages in starting a venture.

5.5.2 Households and families

Another means of accessing resources and identifying business opportunities is to look at the household and family contexts. In entrepreneurship research, these have only recently gained importance as contexts for entrepreneurial activities. Discussion of them (implicitly) draws on the concept of socio-economic hybrid systems from agricultural economies – the so-called household–enterprise system (Tschajanow, 1923). Such systems are characterised as small socio-economic units with household and market production, a predominant household and family work constitution and interdependent consumer and investment decisions. This has been taken into account in studies on portfolio entrepreneurship and pluriactivity in the context of farm households (Carter, 1998a) and in the work of Carter (2011), who pointed out the interplay between households and business in relation to financial rewards. Suggesting a family embeddedness perspective on entrepreneurship, Aldrich and Cliff (2003) show how, in general, the wider family can influence opportunity emergence and recognition, the decision to set up a new venture and access to resources.

In the family business field, researchers have only recently started discussing the 'family' side of family businesses – e.g., as a systems perspective on family businesses (Chrisman, Chua and Litz, 2003) or as the influence of 'familiness' (Pearson, Carr and Shaw, 2008). Not surprisingly, entrepreneurship research applying a family embeddedness perspective often emphasises gender issues. Jennings and McDougald (2007) look into work–life balance issues and Baines and Wheelock (1998) study the impact of households and gender on business survival and growth. Other studies focus on the link between entrepreneurship, households and social inclusion (Oughton, Wheelock and Baines, 2003; Wheelock, Oughton and Baines, 2003), also in connection with rural entrepreneurship (Bock, 2004), thus linking social and spatial contexts.

However, a family embeddedness perspective also raises methodological issues that have not yet been solved satisfactorily. Families and households would need to be conceptualised in a way that allows their variety to be captured, which has consequences for empirical research, as emphasised by Aldrich and Cliff (2003: 547): 'The family embeddedness perspective on entrepreneurship implies that researchers need to include family dimensions in their conceptualizing and modelling, their sampling and analyzing, and their interpretations and implications.' Referring to microenterprises, Wheelock and Oughton (1996) point out the implications for the unit of analysis. They argue that for consumption as well as labour supply decisions, the crucial unit is not the individual but the household, thereby emphasising the social setting, as well as the need to recognise the contributions of different members of a household. Furthermore, Carter and Ram (2003: 377) indicate that such a perspective, while recognising the importance of the resources of the family/household and, thus, reflecting the factors influencing strategies and objectives within the enterprise, 'may fail to address issues beyond the family domain'.

All these points highlight the conceptual and methodological challenges as well as the complexity of extending the social context to household and families.

5.6 The sociospatial world: a bridge between the social and the societal contexts

During the last few decades, more and more research has focused on spatial aspects of entrepreneurial activities. While research into the regional context and characteristics fostering or hindering entrepreneurship is an area where considerable progress has been achieved (Davidsson and Wiklund, 2001), the sociospatial world in which entrepreneurs operate on a daily basis has received – and still receives – limited attention. For example, a recent review of spatially orientated entrepreneurship research indicates that the overall interest of the research community in the local spatial context remains moderate (Trettin and Welter, 2011).

A variety of local factors influence an individual's decision to act entrepreneurially – amongst them the local neighbourhood, institutional set-up and support available within the region, as well as family and friends living close by, thus emphasising that any business activity is simultaneously a socio-economic and a spatial phenomenon (Johannisson, Ramirez-Pasillas and Karlsson, 2002). This section thus focuses on the specific impact of local communities, beyond that of determining the location of businesses, and sometimes specific nature of entrepreneurial activities in local communities. Thornton and Flynn (2005) draw attention to the social boundaries of local neighbourhoods and communities. The spatial world is determined by the physical attributes of a specific location, but also by a shared cognitive understanding of those living within that region. In this understanding, the spatial context bridges between the social and the societal (institutional) worlds of the entrepreneur.

5.6.1 Local communities: asset or liability?

Where business and social spheres are heavily intertwined, they foster a local, place-specific identity, as illustrated by Wigren (2003) for the 'spirit of Gnosjö' – the local identity within a Swedish industrial district. The concept of 'institutional thickness' highlights these particular linkages between regional cultures and local (physical) settings (Amin and Thrift, 1992). With their study on returnee entrepreneurs within a particular Swedish region, Gaddefors and Cronsell (2009) also bring in temporal aspects of the spatial world. Their study shows how, over time, entrepreneurs and local stakeholders jointly co-produce an 'entrepreneurial region', thus fostering local development.

Other studies have analysed local neighbourhoods in relation to specific groups of entrepreneurs, such as ethnic minorities or women. For example, Frederking (2004) analyses two ethnic communities (Punjabi and Gujarati) in three neighbourhoods (two in London, one in Chicago) and across two national contexts (the UK and USA), arguing for the relevance of social norms and relationships in entrepreneurial activities. In studying the links between location, ethnic culture and the country framework, the author demonstrates how the sociospatial context can be a liability, an asset or, as in the case of Chicago, irrelevant. A shared cultural understanding assists in building relations that help start-ups with information or develop contacts with suppliers and clients.

Nonetheless, cultural attachment may also limit opportunities to expand the customer base and make business-related decisions in situations where a system of informal hierarchies and social obligations dominates. For example, research on women entrepreneurs in the former Soviet Union highlights how the local context influences women entrepreneurs, oftentimes restricting their scope of action, whilst, at the same time, these entrepreneurs contribute to changes within and of this context.

In the post-Soviet period, the government merged former village soviets with local neighbourhood committees (*mahallas*) that control women socially (Kamp, 2004). Together with a resurgence of traditional and Islamic values in the post-Soviet period, this had an enormous impact on women's scope for action (Welter and Smallbone, 2008, 2011a). Some women entrepreneurs who set up their business in a local neighbourhood experienced envy from neighbours or were hassled by local representatives; other women entrepreneurs supported their community by training local girls, setting up businesses in response to local needs or problems (one example is a kindergarten for paralysed children) and/or offering reduced prices for local community members.

These instances demonstrate a recognition of social responsibility by these women entrepreneurs that extends beyond their businesses, while local norms of reciprocity allowed them to access social capital at the community level. Thus, spatial embeddedness may facilitate entry into entrepreneurship, access to resources and opportunities, while, simultaneously, force some groups to break out of 'place' norms (Berg, 1997). In the long run, this behaviour may contribute to changes of local norms within these places.

5.6.2 Local context and the nature of entrepreneurship

Sociospatial embeddedness, however, could also influence the nature of entrepreneurship, as reflected in, for example, the discussion around community entrepreneurship

(Johannisson, 1990; Dupuis and de Bruin, 2003; Johnstone and Lionais, 2004), 'heritage entrepreneurship', which refers to communities safeguarding their heritage, or 'tribal entrepreneurship' as a specific form of ethnic community undertaking (de Bruin and Mataira, 2003).

These concepts understand entrepreneurship as a collective event in a particular spatial context, where community-based enterprises are rooted in local culture and local social capital, 'transforming the community into an entrepreneur and an enterprise' (Peredo and Chrisman, 2006: 310). They also put the emphasis on social commitment, non-profit goals and benefits for the wider community as (additional) drivers for entrepreneurship. Entrepreneurship could be the leverage for social change and sustainable local development, as, for example, shown by Johnstone and Lionais (2004), who demonstrated that community businesses can foster economic and social development in 'depleted' communities. Again, this also reflects the recursive links between sociospatial contexts and entrepreneurship, where community businesses are a result of the specific local culture, while, at the same time, contributing to local development.

However, when considering the sociospatial worlds of an entrepreneur, we also need to pay attention to its possible negative effects – as, for example, reflected in the above-mentioned studies on women entrepreneurs and ethnic minorities. There has been a tendency in entrepreneurship research to focus on the positive effects of spatial contexts – such as the fact that spatial proximity facilitates the emergence of social networks and, in particular, strong ties – but spatial proximity also has reverse effects, because strong ties within a region could also restrict social change.

5.7 The institutional world: between laws, societal values and unwritten codes of conduct

5.7.1 Institutions and entrepreneurship

The previous sections have pointed out the close links between the institutional world of the entrepreneur and his or her sociospatial contexts. The institutional context has an impact on the nature, pace of development, extent of entrepreneurship and the ways in which entrepreneurs behave. In this regard, Douglass C. North's (1990) concept – which is frequently applied in entrepreneurship research in order to study the institutional environment – distinguishes between formal institutions (constitutions, laws, rules, regulations, property rights) and informal institutions (norms, values, traditions, codes of conduct).

Entrepreneurship-related formal institutions are rules governing the policies and economic structure of a country or region. Examples of formal institutions that impact entrepreneurship include regulations for market entry and exit, such as bankruptcy laws, private property regulations, laws governing commercial transactions, tax policies and the financial system. Formal institutions can create or restrict opportunity fields for entrepreneurship. Fundamental rules of a society, such as the constitution or private ownership rights, can be a major influence on the existence of entrepreneurship and the forms that it takes, whilst the legal framework determines the nature and extent to which productive entrepreneurship develops.

The impact of formal institutions on the extent and, to a degree, also on the nature of entrepreneurship has been well researched. Related studies prefer a macro-level research design and frequently draw on large-scale databases at national or international level, such as the Global Entrepreneurship Monitor or the 'Doing Business' database of the World Bank. The results of these studies generally confirm the link between entrepreneurship and institutions, also pointing to the influence of either a set of institutions or single ones on the nature of entrepreneurship (Henrekson, 2007; Harbi and Anderson, 2010).

Informal institutions are those deeply ingrained structures within a society that guide individual behaviour through unwritten codes of conduct, values and norms. Such informal institutions exert an indirect influence on entrepreneurship as they may have an impact on opportunity recognition and exploitation as well as access to resources. Examples of entrepreneurship-related informal institutions include the value society generally puts on entrepreneurship or the roles of women in society. At the level of society, norms and values shape attitudes towards entrepreneurship and, at the level of communities, they relate to, for example, kinship values or attitudes of ethnic groups.

At macro level, a growing body of studies have focused on the influence of informal institutions on entrepreneurship, although the results are mixed, partly because of differences in the ways in which informal institutions are measured. Research has studied variations in entrepreneurial cognitions across different cultures (Busenitz and Lau, 1996) or the impact of culture and/or nationality on local environments on entrepreneurial behaviour (George and Zahra, 2002). Some research was focused specifically on religion and entrepreneurship (Carswell and Rolland, 2004; Drakopoulou Dodd and Gotsis, 2007). Some authors have studied the interplay of formal and informal institutions in determining the nature of entrepreneurship. For example, based on GEM data, Bowen and De Clercq (2008) show that country-specific institutions could influence the allocation of entrepreneurship to productive activities defined as high-growth entrepreneurial efforts by the authors.

Other popular themes in research into the institutional worlds of entrepreneurs are entrepreneurship in emerging market economies (Smallbone and Welter, 2001; Manolova, Eunni and Gyoshev, 2008) and the interplay of gender, institutions and entrepreneurship, since both formal and informal institutions shape the role of women in a society. Examples of gender-specific formal institutions are the constitution, which may seek to ensure equal opportunities for women and men, labour market rules giving equal access to employment positions and family policies and property rights allowing for female ownership of land. For example, based on GEM data, Elam and Terjesen (2010) show how labour market institutions influence the decision to start a business indirectly, through perceptions, while Welter and Smallbone (2011a) explore the impact of institutional change on women entrepreneurs in the emerging economies of Central and Eastern Europe and Central Asia, where it typically had a negative impact on women, because of the effect of a change in family policies on the subsidies for State enterprise kindergartens.

5.7.2 Institutions and entrepreneurial behaviour

Of particular interest is the impact of institutions on entrepreneurial behaviour, as this reflects the interplay of formal and informal institutions and their changes over time, although this is difficult to operationalise and measure. As a result of this difficulty, little research has been carried out into institutions and entrepreneurial behaviour. Some studies have focused on the role of so-called 'institutional voids' or 'institutional holes', which occur in situations where formal and informal institutions clash.

Informal entrepreneurship is one possible way for entrepreneurs to cope with a deficient institutional environment. In hostile and turbulent environments, informal activities can be a 'stepping stone' towards more substantial businesses, because they allow entrepreneurs to build up their ventures over time and adapt and cope with an uncertain environment. In these circumstances, informal entrepreneurship includes a risk-minimisation strategy in the start-up phase, as has been illustrated for entrepreneurs in developing and emerging market economies (Bennett and Estrin, 2007; Welter and Smallbone, 2009). 'Informal work' (Williams, 2005) can also be a 'getting by' strategy for more established businesses. Evading taxes, paying 'envelope wages', diversifying into unrelated business activities or reverting to illegal cross-border trade are but some of the strategies entrepreneurs apply to cope with institutional voids (Welter and Smallbone, 2011b). For example, a study on informal activities in the Ukraine shows that 85 per cent of those small-scale entrepreneurs formally registered alluded to conducting part of their business informally, while another 90 per cent stated that they had started their venture on 'a cash-in-hand basis', thus progressing from illegal to legal business once their venture became more established (Williams; Round and Rodgers, 2007).

Institutional voids also can result in new opportunities for entrepreneurship, however, at least temporarily. Smallbone et al. (2010) illustrate this for the case of small business service providers in the Ukraine in the late 1990s when some of the most successful and innovative consultancy firms offered a package of business advice together with 'contacts' in local administrations, which were needed to acquire the necessary licences and permits. New opportunities arose in these cases because institutional change malfunctioned or was not properly implemented, although the specific nature of the opportunities was perhaps transient. Also, entrepreneurs exploiting institutional voids can contribute to institutional change, at least over time, which once more draws attention to the recursive links between contexts and entrepreneurship. Mair and Martì (2009) use the example of a non-governmental organisation handing out micro-credits to the very poor in rural Bangladesh, illustrating how this actor contributes to crafting new institutional arrangements that are more supportive of income-generating activities of the rural poor than traditional forms of finance.

Finally, a closer look at entrepreneurial behaviour draws attention to the everyday nature of entrepreneurship, highlighting an important facet of its societal embeddedness. For a specific political and country context – the Soviet Union – Rehn and Taalas (2004) show entrepreneurship flourishing in the daily lives of individuals who searched for ways to cope with the material shortages of the Soviet system. The authors suggest that the Soviet Union 'forced all its citizens to become microentrepreneurs, enacting entrepreneurship in even the most mundane facets of everyday life' (Rehn and Taalas, 2004: 237). In this regard, Holmquist (2003: 79) emphasises that there is a need to consider entrepreneurship 'as a phenomenon to society rather than to the more restricted context of business creation', while Steyaert and Katz (2004: 181) question the wisdom of 'planting' entrepreneurship 'so strongly in the middle of economic life'.

Consequently, if we acknowledge that entrepreneurship is embedded in the everyday life of the entrepreneur, this brings its contribution to society to the foreground. Entrepreneurship, from this perspective, no longer is a purely individual undertaking, but its outcomes are 'socialised', as in the case of community-based enterprises or social entrepreneurship. This once more emphasises the usefulness of studying the different 'non-business'-related facets of the real world of entrepreneurs.

5.8 Outlook

This chapter thus argues for entrepreneurship research to consider the 'real world' of the entrepreneur, acknowledging the embeddedness of entrepreneurial activities in household and family structures, spatial and institutional environments – all of which have an impact on the nature and extent of entrepreneurship. They can serve as assets or liabilities for the entrepreneurial activity, but they also can be influenced by the entrepreneur him- or herself. Such a perspective assists in explaining why some entrepreneurs might recognise opportunities and others do not and why the outcomes of entrepreneurial activities might vary across different countries, regions and institutional environments (Baker, Gedajlovic and Lubatkin, 2005). However, researching the real world of the entrepreneur poses challenges because the 'true measure of entrepreneurship in a society as a whole needs to sample across multiple sectors, domains and spaces' (Steyaert and Katz, 2004: 193).

A context perspective on entrepreneurship questions theories that assume a one-way relationship between context and entrepreneurship, instead asking for theoretical concepts which allow us to theorise top-down and bottom-up links between context and entrepreneurship and incorporate dynamic aspects such as time and history. It questions the unit of analysis. Should it be the entrepreneur? The household and/or family? The community? The process? The activity? It also questions the current dominant application of context in entrepreneurship research, forcing us to go beyond the business context and simple context descriptions (e.g., the country context of a particular study) and, instead, consider the real world, which is messy and difficult to measure.

Also, entrepreneurship researchers need to acknowledge that the field itself needs to be put into context – they bring their own contexts to the research site and entrepreneurship research takes place in specific contexts and communities (Gartner, Davidsson and Zahra, 2006), each with its own history and traditions. In this regard, Zahra (2007) argues for greater care and creativity in contextualising the field as such, which applies especially to theories imported from other disciplines.

Finally, contextualisation entrepreneurship poses a challenge for entrepreneurship policies, asking for a different policy understanding. In other words, if we accept the real world of the entrepreneur as one important influence on the nature and extent of entrepreneurship, we need to rethink the current rationales for support and policy delivery and content.

5.9 Chapter summary

The chapter discussed the real world(s) of the entrepreneur, outlining different contexts in which entrepreneurship takes place and giving particular importance to the diversity and impact of contexts on entrepreneurship. It started with a short introduction to the concept of context before introducing embeddedness as a key theory that could be applied to theorising the impact of contexts on entrepreneurship, the two sides of context – it being a liability and/or an asset – and the influence of entrepreneurs on their contexts.

The chapter proceeded to explore some of the real worlds of the entrepreneur. Where contexts have been studied in entrepreneurship research, these have mainly been business and regional environments, plus social ones of networks and networking.

This chapter argues for a broader context perspective, however. Reviewing the current state of our knowledge of contexts illustrates that entrepreneurs are embedded beyond the business – for example, families and households may influence the decision to start a business or its growth options and the local neighbourhood may have an impact on the desirability of entrepreneurship, as well as access to resources, while society also shapes the nature and extent of entrepreneurship.

The chapter concluded by summarising some of the main challenges to contextualising entrepreneurship.

Questions

1 Discuss whether or not the importance of the various contexts introduced in this chapter may differ depending on the characteristics of the respective entrepreneur and/or his or her venture (e.g., size and age of business, sector).

2 The chapter suggests embeddedness – in particular, the concept of mixed embeddedness – as a conceptual background in order to study the real world of the entrepreneur. Research and discuss possible alternative conceptual approaches.

3 Compile a list of methodological challenges and problems that entrepreneurship researchers face when empirically researching the different contexts outlined in this chapter and discuss possible solutions.

4 Discuss your own context and the ways in which this could influence your own research project.

Weblinks

http://princes-trust.org.uk
The Prince's Trust supports young people starting in business.

www.cbs.network.org.uk
There are quite a few community business websites, but this one – Community Business Scotland Network – is an example of support provided to community-owned enterprises.

PART 2

The entrepreneurial process

CHAPTER 6

The entrepreneurial process

Per Davidsson

6.1 Introduction

This chapter revolves around research-based insights into the entrepreneurial process. By that is meant the process of setting up a new business activity resulting in a new market offer. This new offer may be made by a new or an existing firm, although the main focus here is on the start-up of new, independent firms. Further, the new offer may be innovative, bringing to the market something that was not offered before or imitative, i.e., a new competitor enters the market with products or services very similar to what other firms are already offering. Although the latter type of process may be less complex and also have less market impact, it still entails most of the steps that typically have to be taken in order to get a business up and running. If successful, it also shares, at least to some degree, the consequences that signify entrepreneurial processes:

- it gives consumers new choice alternatives
- it gives incumbent firms reason to shape up
- it attracts additional followers to enter the market, further reinforcing the first two effects (Davidsson, 2004).

Besides, imitative start-ups outnumber by far innovative ones (Reynolds et al., 2003; Samuelsson and Davidsson, 2009).

6.2 Learning objectives

There are four learning objectives for this chapter:

1 to understand the process nature of entrepreneurship
2 to recognise the existence, core contents and interrelatedness of two entrepreneurial subprocesses: *discovery* and *exploitation*
3 to appreciate the non-existence of a universally best approach to exploiting venture ideas
4 to understand under what conditions a systematic, planned and linear process may be suitable and when a more iterative and flexible process is appropriate.

Key concepts

■ process ■ discovery ■ exploitation ■ business planning ■ effectuation
■ uncertainty ■ venture idea ■ individual ■ environment

6.3 Some steps in the entrepreneurial process

6.3.1 The tension between order and chaos in business creation

It is worth emphasising that the start-up of a new business activity is a process, not an event. Different types of research have shown that this process entails quite a number of behaviours or activities, which can take anything from a couple of months to several years to complete. Further, business start-ups do not all follow *one and the same* process. On the contrary, it has been shown that any sequence of events is possible, including having sales before thinking of starting a business (Carter, Gartner and Reynolds, 1996; Reynolds and Miller, 1992; Liao, Welsch and Tan, 2005). Neither is it likely that one particular permutation of the process is universally the *right* way to go. Being emergent and inherently uncertain phenomena, business start-ups typically involve a wrestling or tension between the planned, systematic, (pre)determined and rational(istic) on the one hand and the serendipitous, creative, experimental and flexible on the other. This is a theme that will be returned to throughout this chapter.

It is possible, however, to bring some order to this chaos. One way of doing so is to conceptually distinguish between – and discuss separately – two subprocesses of the entrepreneurial process: *discovery* and *exploitation* (Shane and Venkataraman, 2000).

'Discovery' refers to the conceptual and cognitive side of business creation – i.e., coming up with an initial business idea and the subsequent elaboration, adaptation and honing of it. 'Exploitation' refers to the actual behaviours and activities undertaken to realise this idea – e.g., marshalling and combining resources and convincing would-be customers. Another way to bring some order is to analyse under what circumstances what type of process is likely to work better. As shall be seen, certain characteristics of the *business idea*, the *environment*, the *individuals* involved and the *stage of development* of the venture are suggestive in this regard.

6.3.2 Elements of the business creation process

What, more precisely, is it that one has to do in order to get a business up and going? Gartner and Carter (2003) list no less than 28 'gestation behaviours' that have been investigated in empirical research, ranging from saving money by listing a separate phone for the company to having paid taxes on revenue from the firm. Davidsson and Honig (2003) have a similar list but with 46 possible steps to be taken, although not even that list is an exhaustive account of what founders can, and sometimes have to, do in order to get a business up and running, but such a detailed level will not be dwelled on here. A more fruitful categorisation for our purposes here may be the eight 'cornerstones' of business development that Klofsten (1994; Davidsson and Klofsten, 2003) arrived at after having studied a number of start-up processes close-up. In the listing below, other influential entrepreneurship researchers' support for the centrality of these cornerstones has been added:

- *The business idea* A clear idea should be developed concerning what the firm will offer the market, how and for whom this creates value and how enough of that value can be appropriated so the venture becomes profitable. The critical importance of the value-creation and appropriation mechanisms is emphasised also by many other researchers (Amit and Zott, 2001; McGrath, 2002; Alvarez and Barney, 2004).

- *The product* A functional product or service has to be developed. Obviously the emerging business needs something attractive to sell and, consequently, the provision of new or 'future' products and services is, as Shane and Venkataraman (2000) point out, the essence of entrepreneurship.

- *The market* The target market must be defined in geographical and/or demographic terms. Other scholars emphasise that when the product or service is innovative, the market may need to be created before it can be defined (Sarasvathy, 2001).

- *The organisation* An organisation must be created to coordinate the purchasing, production, marketing, financing, controlling and distribution activities that are needed in order to serve the market in a legal and profitable manner. The pre-eminence of organisation creation as the core outcome of the entrepreneurial process has been especially advocated by Bill Gartner (1989a; Gartner and Carter, 2003).

- *Core group expertise* The competencies most crucial for the business' success must be hired into or developed in the management team. Scott Shane has used both in-depth and broadly based data to provide compelling evidence for the importance of the founders' prior knowledge (Shane, 2000; Delmar and Shane, 2006).

- *Core group drive/motivation* The key individuals must have sufficient commitment to the start-up. In support of this notion, Baum and Locke (2004) demonstrated the importance of passion and tenacity for the long-term success of the new venture.

- *Customer relations* In order to achieve first sales, trustful relationships with some prospective customers have to be developed. For example, Bhave (1994) observes that most of the entrepreneurs he studied had their initial customers lined up well before they created any products.

- *Other relations* Other key relations must also be developed – e.g., with suppliers, investors or government agencies. One of the most important insights from systematic entrepreneurship research is that it is much more a social game than merely an individual one. For example, Davidsson and Honig (2003) showed that social capital (developing one's business network) is very important for making progress in the start-up process.

Klofsten (1994) emphasises the importance of reaching at least a minimum acceptable level for all of these cornerstones; excelling at a few may not help if others are severely underdeveloped. He does not, however, point out a particular sequence in which to develop the cornerstones. Other researchers have found that no particular sequence seems to dominate when studying random samples of start-ups over time. In fact, there are so few common patterns that Liao, Welsch and Tan (2005) found reason to conclude that firm gestation is 'a complex process that includes more than simple, unitary progressive paths' (2005: 15) and 'a process where developmental stages are hardly identifiable' (2005: 13). This does not preclude the possibility that some process sequences are *better* than others with respect to attaining desired results. Based on interviews with 'expert entrepreneurs', Delmar and Shane (2003b) suggest the following sequence of start-up behaviours is advisable.

1 Write a business plan.
2 Gather information about customers.
3 Talk to customers.
4 Make financial projections.
5 Establish a legal entity (i.e., register a sole proprietorship, partnership or limited liability company).
6 Obtain permits and licences (as needed).
7 Secure intellectual property (as much as possible, i.e., patents, trademarks, industrial design protection, copyright, etc.).
8 Seek finance.
9 Initiate marketing.
10 Acquire inputs.

One aspect particularly worth noting about this sequence is that it progresses from activities that require no or small financial commitment to those that are more demanding in this regard.

6.3.3 Business planning

The idea that start-ups should be frugal with spending early in the process is widely embraced among entrepreneurship scholars. Far more controversial is the priority Delmar and Shane's (2003b) list gives to the written business plan. The pros and cons of business planning are very complex and the fact is that researchers using the very same data arrive at different conclusions (Honig and Karlsson, 2001; Delmar and Shane, 2003a; Samuelsson and Davidsson, 2009).

Delmar and Shane's (2003a) research suggests that advance planning is beneficial. However, this does not necessarily mean that *sticking* to the plan is a good strategy. The business plan has several potential roles or uses.

■ It can be an *analysis tool*, used internally to go through the strengths and weaknesses of the venture as well as the threats and opportunities potential customers, competitors and other environmental conditions present.

■ It can be a *communication tool* to explain the logic and goals of the business to other parties, such as banks, venture capital firms and the government agencies that issue required licences and permits.

■ Writing a plan may increase the entrepreneur(s) own *commitment* to the realisation of the project (Cialdini, 1988) and, as noted above, Klofsten (1994) points to commitment as being one of the eight cornerstones of business development in the form of core group drive/motivation.

■ Finally, the plan can be used as a blueprint, a detailed *guide to action.* First you plan, and then you do what the plan says.

It is widely acknowledged that a written business plan makes it easier to get investors to accept the business concept than when there isn't one and it is hard to find a reason to believe that the analysis and communication uses of business plans would be harmful in and of themselves. However, there are possible negatives as well. First, the time used for planning is not used for doing – i.e., for realising the new venture. Second, focusing on a set plan may blindfold the founders to new opportunities (and threats) that emerge along the way. Third, while commitment is good for making things happen, it sometimes amounts to what psychologists call *escalation of commitment* (DeTienne, Shepherd and De Castro, 2008) – i.e., becoming locked into a path that leads founders to throw good money after bad in a 'doomed' venture start-up, which would be better terminated sooner rather than later.

In the light of extant research, the most questionable part of the planning emphasis is perhaps (blind) use of the plan as a guide to action. When something new is launched on the market, the customers' and competitors' reactions are very difficult to predict. The business environment is uncertain and rapidly changing. Under such conditions, sticking to the plan is relatively more likely to prevent entrepreneurs from not only possible and necessary adaptations that can save the future of the venture but also positive deviations from the plan – e.g., the possibility of much bigger sales and profits being attainable than those originally predicted.

Overall, the research evidence suggests that the effects of business planning are mildly positive on average for small firms, but less so for new ventures than established ones (Brinckmann, Grichnik, and Kapsa, 2010). This would seem to reflect the greater uncertainty that surrounds new ventures.

To sum up, it can be noted that a range of activities needs to be carried out after a business idea is first conceived of and before the business is steadily up and running. Some researchers, such as Klofsten, emphasise the importance of not neglecting any critical dimension. Others, such as Delmar and Shane, suggest that a certain sequence of activities leads to better results. Either way, it is clear that starting a business is a process; there is no way all the necessary activities could be conducted at once. The next section takes a closer look at the discovery part of this process.

6.4 The discovery process

6.4.1 Systematic search v. fortuitous discovery

As pointed out at the beginning of this chapter, 'discovery' is used for the ideas side of business development as opposed to the realisation side, which is called 'exploitation'.

It is important to point out that 'discovery', as used here, does not imply that business opportunities somehow exist objectively in the environment, ready to be discovered, before anybody has thought about them. Neither does it imply that the start-up will be successful. As conceived of here, discovery is about developing business ideas and these ideas are the creations of individuals' minds. They may or may not reflect external conditions that make them viable. If someone is working on a business start-up in vain because it is based on a completely incorrect conjecture, the idea development side of the start-up is still an example of a discovery process, eventually leading to the more or less costly insight that the idea will not work (Davidsson, 2003, 2004).

Further, research has revealed that the discovery part of the story is also a process in its own right (Bhave, 1994; de Koning, 2003; Van der Veen and Wakkee, 2004). You start with a rough idea. Before the idea is converted into an up-and-running business, it is likely to have been changed, refined and elaborated. As a case in point, Nathan Furr (2009) notes in his award-winning doctoral dissertation that many emerging ventures and young firms, including present-day giants such as Apple, Google, Microsoft, PayPal and Symantec, underwent significant and sometimes numerous transmutations before they found the form that made them successful in the marketplace.

A hotly debated issue is whether or not it is possible to apply systematic searches for entrepreneurial discoveries – i.e., for new business ideas. The theoretical argument against is, in short, the question (Kirzner, 1973) how can you search for something when you don't know what it is? According to this view, entrepreneurial discovery always carries an element of surprise and all aspiring entrepreneurs can do is to subject themselves to a greater flow of information in general (through extensive networking and media use) in the hope that *something* valuable will turn up, although there is no way they can know in advance *what*, specifically, they are looking for.

Although there was some early support for successful entrepreneurs behaving in this way (Kaish and Gilad, 1991), common sense and later research suggest that it is possible to apply more directed searches (Fiet, 2002). For example, about half of Bhave's (1994) cases were people who had more or less stumbled over a business opportunity without having a strong prior intention to go into business themselves. Consequently, they did not search for or consider multiple business ideas; they encountered one and decided to go for it. The other half, however, first made their minds up they wanted to become independent businesspeople and then started looking more or less systematically for opportunities until they eventually decided they had found one that was promising enough.

Research on a large, representative sample has since shown that these two discovery processes are about equally common (Gartner and Carter, 2003). Researching emerging internal ventures in small, owner-managed firms, Chandler, Dahlqvist and Davidsson (2003) could confirm that business ideas were the result of three different search processes:

- *proactive search* actively looking for new opportunities because you want to
- *reactive search* ditto, but because you have to in order to make up for, for example, lost market share for existing products or unemployment in the case of independent start-ups
- *fortuitous discovery* i.e., stumbling on an unsought for opportunity.

So, the systematic search for viable business ideas is possible. Research strongly suggests that aspiring entrepreneurs do not search randomly or even for the idea with the biggest world market, but for ideas in a domain where they have relevant prior knowledge – e.g., because of work experience or a hobby (Vesper, 1991; Shane, 2000; Fiet, 2002). It is in these areas that aspiring business founders are likely to have or be able to develop the *expertise* and *drive/motivation* that Klofsten (above) points out as being cornerstones in new business development. Research further suggests using existing networks to find and hone business ideas (Kaish and Gilad, 1991; de Koning, 2003).

6.4.2 Examples of discovery processes

In order to illustrate the possibility of making a systematic ideas search, as well as excelling in using networks, consider the following example.

> The entrepreneur in this vignette was already the founder of many companies based on his sophisticated technological knowledge. He travels frequently and, during the trips, he often arranges evenings out with management consultants he knows. While he is quite happy to pick up the bill for an evening's entertainment, he will press the consultants to tell him about some problem that their clients are struggling with and requires a technical solution. One such problem had a robot as its logical answer. However, the work environment was such that contemporary robots did not like it any more than humans did. The entrepreneur then turned to his second network, consisting of university professors in engineering, to find out if something like a 'robust robot' was technologically feasible. Having learnt that this was indeed the case, he again turned to his management consultant network in order to get in touch with the end users. He made these pay the development costs (which also ensured demand for the finished product) incurred by the company he set up together with his academic experts. In the end, he cashed in a handsome profit – without having invested any significant means of his own in the project (McGrath, undated).

As Bhave (1994: 230) observes, the starting point for businesses that are not the result of a systematic search is often that 'the prospective entrepreneurs experienced, or were introduced to, needs that could not be easily fulfilled through available vendors or means.' The non-existence of both entrepreneurial intention and current supply, however, does not mean that this is the realm solely for relatively insignificant products or firms. Here are some examples.

> Carin Lindahl, the inventor of the sports bra – now a worldwide product – was a somewhat bosomy workout enthusiast who had painful personal experience of the insufficient support and inconvenience offered by the bras available at the time, as well as taping and bandaging. Years later, she stumbled on a fabric that expanded in one direction while being completely stiff in the other. This gave her the obvious solution to the problem, so she bought a few yards of the fabric and sewed some bras for herself. She also tried to make manufacturers adopt the product, but to no avail. She then decided to start her own firm to provide the market with sports bras (Lindahl and Skagegård, 1998; Davidsson, 2000).

> In the late 1970s, Bert-Inge Hogsved was the CEO of a medium-sized company. He also had some computing skills in his background. His wife was a chartered accountant. For serendipitous reasons, they were among the first owners of a PC in Sweden. Bert-Inge decided to use his new toy to write some software that would unfetter his wife from some of the most repetitive and tedious number-crunching aspects of her work. Of course, not only she but also her colleagues loved what they saw and they soon wanted to get a copy of the software. When demand had increased to a critical level, the Hogsveds had to decide whether or not to go

into business for themselves wholeheartedly. The result was to become the Hogia Group – the biggest business software company group in Sweden, presently employing 500 people in over 20 semi-independent firms that have diversified into related areas (Hogsved, 1996; www2.hogia.se/website3/1.0.3.0/149/2/index.php).

Tom Scott was 23 in 1988 when he started what was to become Nantucket Nectars – valued at around $100 million in 2002. However, at that time he had no intention of making it big, nor becoming a juice producer. It all started with a business called Allserve, which involved going boat to boat in Nantucket Harbour, selling muffins and newspapers, taking away rubbish, doing laundry. In Tom's words, it was 'like a floating 7-Eleven'. The second summer, his partner Tom First joined in, but, while the business became legitimate and grew, it was decidedly a lifestyle enterprise. The following winter, they stayed on the island. They made making dinner for one another a competition and, one night, in Tom Scott's words, 'Tom made this juice for dinner, peach juice made fresh in the blender. Within five minutes we were saying, "Let's sell this off the boat next summer. We'll call it Nantucket Nectars"' (Scott, 1998; *Food & Drink Weekly*, 2002).

Clearly, in these cases, the fact that these business ideas were not systematically searched for and nobody else had seized these opportunities were not indications that they were in any sense small. Equally clearly, the discovery process was not completed in the moment these entrepreneurs first saw what they were already doing as a business idea. Innumerable steps remained beyond the ends of the vignettes as described above and the fully worked out business models these three firms serve their markets with today. This leads to the question, when does the discovery process end? The only defensible answer is that it *never* does. There is every reason to continue to adapt and expand one's business idea, even long after its initial commercialisation. When founder-owners of a business believe that they do not need to re-examine their business ideas, they are setting the seeds for their demise.

6.5 The exploitation process

6.5.1 Elements of the exploitation process

Except, perhaps, when the exploitation of the business idea consists of a one-off, out-right sale to another organisation, it, like discovery, is a process – it evolves over time. As used here, the concept of exploitation carries none of the negative connotations it has in some other contexts. Neither does it necessarily imply success. What is being referred to here is simply the attempted realisation of the value-creation and appropriation potentials of the business idea.

Obviously, no entrepreneurial process is complete without exploitation. No matter how smart or revolutionary the ideas, no value is going to be created until someone acts upon them. Exploitation activities make the start-up effort tangible (Carter, Gartner and Reynolds, 1996) and stakeholders committed to it (Van der Veen and Wakkee, 2004). In fact, one of the most stunning early findings in research on business start-up processes was that the founders who had managed to achieve their first sale in the 12-month period between a couple of rounds of interviewing had spent a whopping *18 times* more hours on setting up business operations (e.g., purchasing materials, hiring employees, producing the product/service, distributing the product) – i.e., on what is arguably the core of exploitation activities, as the term is used here – than did those who had not achieved a sale within that time. In Table 6.1 the cornerstones and process steps discussed above have been listed and commented upon with regard to how they, respectively, relate to discovery and exploitation. There are many ways one can, on this basis, summarise what exploitation entails. One way to make sense of the entries in the table is to emphasise the following partly overlapping categories:

Table 6.1 Steps in the entrepreneurial process that are related to discovery and exploitation

Klofsten's cornerstones		Shane and Delmar's process steps	
Business idea	**Discovery** conceiving, elaborating and refining a business idea is the core of the discovery process	*Write a business plan*	**Discovery** developing a business plan is essentially the same as developing an elaborate business idea. Communicating the plan is part of *exploitation*, as is doing what the plan promises
Product	**Discovery and exploitation** conceiving of a product/service is an important part of the business idea. Developing a working prototype is part of exploitation	*Gather information about customers*	**Discovery** although behavioural rather than cognitive, this activity largely affects the business idea rather than being part of its implementation
Market	**Discovery and exploitation** defining the market is an important part of the business idea. Actually approaching that market is exploitation	*Talk to customers*	**Discovery and exploitation** talking to customers provides inputs for idea development, but is also a step towards convincing them to buy
Organisation	**Discovery and exploitation** an organisational plan is an important part of the business idea. Hiring people, distributing tasks and imple-menting routines are parts of the exploitation process	*Make financial projections*	**Discovery** this exercise may lead to adaptations of the business idea but does, in itself, not take the emerging venture any closer to market exchange
Core group expertise	**Discovery and exploitation** matching the business idea with existing expertise is part of discovery. Cultivating or hiring management team expertise are aspects of exploitation of the idea	*Establish a legal entity*	**Exploitation** this is a necessary step in the implementation of a business idea. However, learning about particularities of the regulations for different legal forms may in some cases feed back into the business idea (i.e., discovery) *continued*

103

Table 6.1 *continued*

Klofsten's cornerstones		Shane and Delmar's process steps	
Core group drive/ motivation	This cornerstone is not part of either process. It can be an important input to either or a result of good matching of the business idea and the people, as well as the existence of an attractive plan for exploitation	Obtain permits and licences	**Exploitation** this is, for some businesses, a necessary step in implementation. However, learning about aspects of the regulations for the particular type of business may in some cases feed back into the business idea (i.e., discovery)
Customer relations	**Exploitation** developing customer relations is an indispensable aspect of the exploitation process. This exchange can, however, feed back into the discovery process	Secure intellectual property	**Exploitation** this is, for some businesses, a critical factor in value appropriation. Learning about the possibilities may feed back into the business idea (i.e., discovery)
Other relations	**Exploitation** developing relations with other stakeholders is an important aspect of the exploitation process. Again, this can feed back into discovery	Seek finance	**Exploitation** having money is not necessary for dreaming up ideas, but often is for their implementation. Again, this activity can feed back into discovery
		Initiate marketing	**Exploitation** the core of exploitation is to get customers to buy. The more interactive aspects of customer relations have been covered above
		Acquire inputs	**Exploitation** acquiring the resources is necessary for realising the value-creating potential of the business idea

- efforts to *legitimise* the start-up, such as creating a legal entity, obtaining permits and licences, developing a working prototype of the product and developing relations with various stakeholders
- efforts to *acquire resources* – e.g., core group expertise, financial capital, intellectual property and other inputs
- efforts to *combine and coordinate* these resources through the creation of a functional organisation
- efforts to *generate demand* through marketing and the development of customer relations.

While all of the above are important, it may be argued that, for the long-term success of an independent start-up, the most critical aspect of the exploitation process is to obtain resources and resource combinations that are *valuable*, *rare* and *imperfectly imitable* (Barney, 1997), thus providing some 'isolating mechanism' (Rumelt, 1984).

6.5.2 Bootstrapping and bricolage

The implementation of the above elements of the exploitation process seems rational and textbook-like enough. Often it is, such as when the founder is an experienced, habitual entrepreneur, setting up yet another venture in a mature industry (e.g., a new upmarket restaurant) and/or when the start-up is backed by formal venture capital and the external control that follows from that. In other cases, however, the execution of these exploitation behaviours does not look textbook-like at all. That is not necessarily a bad thing, however, as start-ups are often resource-starved so they need to find smart and frugal ways to get ahead. Here are a couple of examples of this point.

> In order to reach her target group, Carin Lindahl, the inventor of the sports bra we met earlier, used an annual all-women running event that attracted some 15,000 participants. Early in the morning, Carin and her friends broke into (without damaging, of course) all the mobile toilets that were set up for the event and stuck up posters advertising the product on the insides of the cubicle doors. After the runners reached the finish line (although not immediately at it, where only official, paying sponsors could operate), they were handed a leaflet with further information. In order to get stores to carry the product, Carin would visit them and show the product's functionality through a very intense and unforgettable workout session in front of the astonished shopkeepers. She would also send family and friends to the stores to ask for the product. If they carried it, they would ask for a different colour. When she needed a (thin) product catalogue, she used herself and friends – among them, a personal friend who happened to also be one of Sweden's most famous female singers – as models and endorsers. In addition, she shot many of the pictures herself. In order to expand her product assortment, she needed to cultivate other relationships within the industry. The way she did this was to invest most of the first year's profits (which were short of £1000 anyway) in a high-quality coffee machine and offer free coffee to fellow exhibitors at trade fairs (this was before the global coffee revolution and really good coffee was a rare find at this type of event). As a result, she got to know 'everyone important' in the industry (Lindahl, personal communication; Lindahl and Skagegård, 1998).

> With Nantucket Nectars, in Tom Scott's own words, 'We started making it fresh and sold it off our boat and out of a little storefront we'd opened. We figured out a way to get the product into recycled wine bottles. Through this period we made money off everything but our boat business. We were doing anything else on the side: painting houses, bartending. Sometimes I lived in my car; other times I lived in a group house where the heat was never turned on. In terms of making the business work financially, what we did was pay our bills slowly, collect our receivables as fast as possible, and pay ourselves nothing. That's how you finance a business . . . We found that being young was an advantage, too: no wives, no kids, no mortgages, no responsibilities. If we wanted to work 14 hours a day, we did; if we didn't have money for clothes, it was OK – we didn't need clothes. We didn't need a car. Also, when we went into the factories, when we met with distributors, there was definitely a sense that, "Hey, here's a couple of young kids – give 'em a break"'(Scott, 1998).

The frugal techniques the entrepreneurs in these examples used are referred to as *financial bootstrapping* (Winborg and Landström, 2001) or *bricolage* (Garud and Karnoe,

2003; Baker and Nelson, 2005). These terms refer to all the more or less smart ways entrepreneurs can find to get ahead without making significant financial outlays. As a bonus, these approaches are often impossible for large, established competitors to copy. According to Baker and Nelson, bricolage consists of three elements:

- *making do* – seeking workable rather than perfect solutions by using resources at hand
- *using resources at hand* – sometimes this involves seeing as a 'resource' something that others would not see as such – e.g., ice, snow, coldness, darkness and remoteness in the case of the highly successful Ice Hotel (http://icehotel.com)
- *recombining resources for new purposes.*

Baker and Nelson (2005: 341–2) also provide the following wonderful example of a serial entrepreneur's application of bricolage principles:

> Tim Grayson was a farmer whose land was crisscrossed by abandoned coal mines [*resource at hand, not necessarily seen as such by others*]. He knew that the tunnels – a nuisance to farmers because of their tendency to collapse, causing mammoth sinkholes in fields – also contained large quantities of methane. Methane is another nuisance, a toxic greenhouse gas that poisons miners and persists in abandoned mines for generations [*resource at hand, not necessarily seen as such by others*]. Grayson and a partner drilled a hole from Grayson's property to an abandoned mine shaft, then acquired a used diesel generator from a local factory and crudely retrofitted it to burn methane [*making do; recombining resources for new purposes*]. During the conversion process, Grayson was repeatedly blown off his feet when the odorless, colorless gas exploded. His bricolage produced electricity, most of which he sold to the local utility, using scavenged switchgear [*making do*]. Because Grayson's generator also produced considerable waste heat [*resource at hand, not necessarily seen as such by others*], he built a greenhouse for hydroponic tomatoes, which he heated with water from the generator's cooling system [*recombining resources for new purposes*]. He also used electricity generated during off-peak hours to power special lamps to speed plant growth. With the availability of a greenhouse full of trenches of nutrient-rich water, heated 'for free', Grayson realized he might be able to raise tilapia, a tropical delicacy increasingly popular in the U.S. He introduced the fish to the waters that bathed the tomato roots and used the fish waste as fertilizer [*making do; recombining resources for new purposes*]. Finally, with abundant methane still at hand, Tim began selling excess methane to a natural gas company.

However, a word of caution is needed here. While these techniques may seem clever, Baker and Nelson also point out that, if overused, the bricolage approach may well become a hindrance to the further development of the business. As is often the case, the trick is to find the right balance.

6.6 The relationship between discovery and exploitation

6.6.1 Interplay of discovery and exploitation

Above it was noted that just because an idea originates with independent individual(s), it does not have to be exploited as an independent start-up and just because an idea emerges in a corporate context, it need not stay there forever. In this regard, then, the discovery and exploitation process are separable. An examination of Table 6.1, however, suggests that they are intricately entwined. If what is being referred to is the *entire* discovery and exploitation process, the latter is the truer image in most cases. Importantly, it is usually *not* the case that ideas (or 'opportunities' as they are often called) are first discovered (i.e., conceptually completed) and then exploited (Bhave, 1994; de Koning, 2003; Van der Veen and Wakkee, 2004).

In an attempt to restore some order, it has been suggested that the entrepreneurial process, while not linear, is at least directional – that the *existence* of an opportunity is a precondition for *discovery*, which is a precondition for its *exploitation* (Shane, 2003; Shane and Eckhardt, 2003). Not even that holds up empirically, however. People develop and hone ideas that do not reflect objectively existing external opportunities and some ideas become viable because of external events that occur *after* the idea was developed. In other cases, they acquire and combine resources that de facto help exploit a business idea they have not yet conceived of or else they successfully exploit a different opportunity than the one they thought they were pursuing because, for example, it was a hit with completely different buyers and/or for uses other than the founders had imagined (Davidsson, 2003).

Figure 6.1 portrays the interrelationships between discovery and exploitation. For example, an entrepreneurial process may start with an individual perceiving what she thinks is an opportunity for a profitable business (discovery). In her efforts to make this business happen, contacts with resource providers and prospective customers (exploitation) could make it clear that the business as initially conceived will not be viable (feeds back into discovery). She changes the business concept accordingly (discovery) and continues her efforts to marshal and coordinate the resources needed for the realisation of the revised business concept (exploitation) (Davidsson, 2004).

Importantly, considerable success is unlikely if either process is severely under-emphasised. Regardless of the degree of temporal separation or integration of these two subprocesses, it is important that *both* receive adequate attention. The perils of lack of balance can be described as follows.

■ Where there is too much emphasis on discovery, no value will ever be created or appropriated. For example, certain kinds of engineer-led high-tech firms are notorious for being eternal playgrounds for the development of the 'perfect' product rather than one for which a significant number of customers are willing to pay a price above its production costs. Also in this vein, Carter et al. (1996) obtained

Figure 6.1 The interrelationships between discovery and exploitation

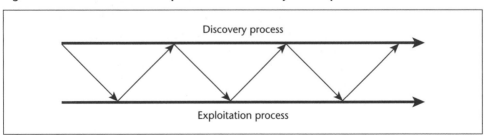

results suggesting that those who did not do enough tangible exploitation activities were less likely to get the business up and running than those who did (Gatewood, Shaver and Gartner, 1995). Further, as observed by Singh (2001), failure is not necessarily evidence that the idea is wrong. It may have been the case that a faulty exploitation effort ruined an otherwise sound idea.

- Where there is too much emphasis on exploitation, there is the risk that not enough value is being created because the founders have not tuned in carefully enough to the customers' real needs and preferences.

- Another type of overly strong emphasis on exploitation is when the founders try to appropriate (close to) *all* the value created by their product or service (or more), rather than sharing the benefits with the customers. The customers will then have incentives to look for other solutions instead. When the founders are unwilling to share the value created with external investors, they may end up being sole owners of a very insignificant operation rather than substantial part-owners of a multi-million pound business.

- Finally, when entrepreneurs try to appropriate value without creating value on the societal level, their activities are socially destructive rather than constructive (Baumol, 1990) and will be looked down upon and/or be subjected to legal counter-action. Examples here might include business activities that are typical for mafia organisations, but there are other examples as well. One real example is a graffiti removal business whose founder-owners used night time (and spray paint) to generate demand for their daytime business activity! While such activities can be profitable in the short term, they are often detrimental in the longer term and/or for entrepreneurs collectively.

6.6.2 Organisational contexts of discovery and exploitation

In many cases, however, capturing and sustaining a strong position in the market is a very difficult task for a new firm lacking resources and a track record (Aldrich and Auster, 1986). Such firms encounter challenges in both input and output markets. Potential financiers and employees may question their stability and their ability to deliver on their promises. Potential customers may, in turn, question the quality of their products/services, if they even get to learn about their existence. More generally, regardless of where they originate, some business ideas are better exploited by existing organisations. This highlights the importance of the *mode of exploitation* (Shane and Venkataraman, 2001).

Combining the possibilities of discovery and exploitation by independent start-ups and existing corporations yields the four cases outlined in Figure 6.2. Although Shane and Eckhardt (2003) emphasise that sufficient research-based knowledge about the prevalence and success rates of these cases does not yet exist, it is possible to exercise informed speculation about the fit between type of idea and exploitation mode. The four cases are as follows.

First there is discovery as well as exploitation by independent start-ups – the *independent start-up mode*. Certain structural characteristics of small or emergent organisations give them discovery advantages (Barker and Gump, 1964; Arrow, 1983;

Figure 6.2 The locus of discovery and locus of exploitation

| | **Exploitation** | |
	Independent	Corporate
Discovery context — Independent	Independent start-up	Acquisition
Discovery context — Corporate	Spin-off	Corporate venturing

Source: Shane and Eckhardt (2003)

Acs and Audretsch, 1990), but that does not necessarily make them the best vehicles for the exploitation of those discoveries as well. It is likely that business ideas originating outside of corporate contexts can also be successfully exploited as independent start-ups when development costs are not prohibitive and small-scale production is economically feasible, the potential market is not large enough to attract large actors, existing firms cannot use their present resource base to exploit the idea in a superior manner, the new firm can successfully develop resources and resource combinations that are difficult to copy, i.e., create sustainable competitive advantage (Barney, 1991, 1997) and/or the new firm is able to stay ahead of the competition through continuous innovation. The latter may be a risky gamble, however. At least one major study suggests those early movers who achieve continued success are not those that try to sustain innovative leadership but those which manage to develop a cost advantage (Durand and Coeurderoy, 2001).

Second there is both discovery and exploitation within a corporate context – the *corporate venturing mode*. This mode includes incremental innovations that leverage an established firm's existing knowledge base, production technology and distribution networks. This is known as *competence-enhancing* (as opposed to competence-destroying) *innovation* (Aldrich and Martinez, 2001). It is also a possibility for radical innovations that require substantial development costs (Arrow, 1983; Acs and Audretsch, 1990) and/or a combination of several highly specialised competencies that already exist in the firm and/or its network.

Third there is discovery within an existing corporation and exploitation by an independent start-up – the *spin-off mode*. This is likely when the new business idea, although it originated within the firm, does not make good use of the firms' existing resources and capabilities. As observed by Kogut and Zander (1992), when firms depart from their knowledge base, their probability of success approaches that of an independent start-up. In fact, for radical innovations, the existing knowledge base and organisational routines can be a *liability* relative to an independent start-up (Anderson and Tushman, 1990; Henderson and Clark, 1990). Another reason in favour of this mode is that the new initiative addresses a small market niche (Christensen and Bower, 1996).

Fourth there is discovery by an independent start-up followed by exploitation by an established corporation – the *acquisition mode* of exploitation. As a mirror image of the independent start-up case, this is the likely path when development and/or small-scale production costs are prohibitive for a small firm, the potential market is large and incumbent firms can use their existing resource bases to exploit the idea. The relation to intellectual property is not clear cut. Without such, the originators would not have much to sell and might just as well try to go it alone. So, it is, rather, when they are in possession of intellectual property that they have an incentive to make the transfer happen. On the other hand, when the concept is promising and not protected, the large actor can easily outmanoeuvre the small actor, with or without acquisition. The independent discoverer thus faces the 'prospector's paradox' (Alvarez and Barney, 2004) and may have to develop some other basis for sustainable competitive advantage – or give up.

A final reason for making a transfer from an independent to a corporate context would be that the individual(s) involved do(es) not feel motivated or able to exploit the idea. For example, academic researchers whose research has commercial potential may not want to switch to a business career, yet, through licensing or an outright sale, they may still reap some of the financial benefits of their discoveries.

In order to further illustrate the mode of exploitation issue, consider the following cases.

The Solar Mower – a solar-powered robotic lawnmower that uses random walk computer software and magnetic cord demarcations to walk and cut the grass little by little, like a modern sheep – was dreamed up by an independent Belgian inventor who happened to have special competence in both of the two main technologies concerned. It was a radical innovation, unlikely to have originated in an existing lawnmower manufacturing company (and, reputedly, a doomed one in the UK because it does not produce straight stripes!). Think of the enormous hurdles this innovator would face in development costs, acquiring or ascertaining reliable production capacity for this new combination of technologies, building awareness about the product and confidence in the new brand and getting into the available distribution channels without prior connections or proof of profitable demand, etc.

Wisely, the inventor decided to sell the idea to Husqvarna, an internationally established lawnmower manufacturer and, as the technology was new to them, the company wisely decided to employ the inventor. However, the product never took off in a big way – presumably because it did not make much use of Husqvarna's capabilities, other than its brand name and distribution network. Apparently, in an effort to bring it closer to the family, the Solar Mower became the Automower, without solar cells but with an ability to find its way back to the recharging pit when needed.

Another problem remained, though – the risk of cannibalisation of Husqvarna's other lawnmower lines if the product achieved great success. Presumably, in an effort to overcome this problem, the Automower was transferred to the Electrolux brand (within the same corporation), where it enjoys similar benefits of strong brand name and distribution, but without in-house competition with other technologies. As a bonus, Electrolux got a cousin to its robotic vacuum cleaner, which was developed on the basis of a very similar idea and with some technological overlap as well (Davidsson, 1994; Bjenning and Bjärsvik, 1999).

When you think of it, the sports bra could very well have originated within an existing underwear or sportswear manufacturer. You could even argue that it should have done, but they failed to see this opportunity before Carin Lindahl did. Not only that, some established firms got the chance but refused to take it when Carin suggested this to them.

Once she had proven the viability of the concept, however, it was very difficult for Carin to establish a sustainable competitive advantage. The manufacturer of the fabric had no reason to give her exclusive rights – the idea was not patentable and industrial design protection would have been very easy to circumvent. Consequently, the big actors marched in and captured most of the world market.

Through emphases on quality, differentiation and brand extension, Carin was able to build and sustain a healthy small business (called Stay In Place), but most of the value her idea created has been appropriated by other actors (Lindahl, personal communication; Lindahl and Skagegård, 1998).

These examples do not exclude the possibility that independent start-ups can successfully exploit opportunities and grow large in their own right. IKEA, McDonald's and Starbucks are spectacular examples of ideas that did not seem (initially) very difficult to copy, yet they managed to both create and appropriate enormous value out of seemingly simple ideas. Over time they have, of course, built brand equity, tacit knowledge, industry secrets and super-efficient business systems that now make them very difficult for an imitator to challenge.

6.7 The effectuation process: an alternative entrepreneurial logic?

A recurrent theme in this chapter has been the tension between the structured, planned and systematic on the one hand and the emerging, iterative and somewhat chaotic on the other. Entrepreneurship researchers have long observed that what business founders do often has little in common with the conventional analysis–planning–implementation–control rationality of normative management textbooks. They have also suspected that, since this is often true also for highly successful entrepreneurs, the deviations from prescribed conventional rationality may, in fact, be well-founded.

Sarasvathy (2001, 2008) has suggested an *alternative* entrepreneurial logic, which she calls 'effectuation' (see Chapter 8). She bases the notion of effectuation on conceptual forerunners, as well as empirical observations of highly successful entrepreneurs. She defines causation and effectuation processes in the following way: 'Causation processes take a particular effect as given and focus on selecting between means to create that effect. Effectuation processes take a set of means as given and focus on selecting between possible effects that can be created with that set of means' (Sarasvathy, 2001: 245).

Causation and effectuation can work towards similar generalised goals. Sarasvathy (2001, 2008) takes 'making dinner' as an illustrative non-business example: either you start from a menu and then get the required ingredients (causation) or you rummage through the cupboards and create a dinner from whatever you find there (effectuation). To further expand on Sarasvathy's (2001) own examples, it can be observed that either process could start with the same generalised goal ('I need to make a living for myself/I want to be my own boss/I want to get rich and control my own destiny') and arrive at the same result (e.g., an Indian fast food franchising chain called 'Curry in a Hurry'). However, the processes would have very different origins and histories. In the causation case, it might start with any business-minded people perceiving a possible gap in the market. The business concept, the target market in terms of location and clientele, the menus, décor, etc., would be carefully worked out before a heavily advertised launch of the initial Curry in a Hurry outlets was made in locations that were selected after careful strategic consideration. The expansion of the chain would follow a set plan based on market-related criteria.

The effectuation process Sarasvathy describes would likely start from a person knowing how to cook Indian food. This person might try it out by starting a small lunch catering service in the lunchrooms of friends' employers, move on to a fast food corner in an established restaurant, then upgrade to a first independent outlet, eventually expand into second and third units run by relatives in the towns where they happen to live and only thereafter, if ever, the business would start to conform to a normal franchised fast food chain. Importantly, however, in the same way that Nantucket Allserve took off in a completely different direction when the founders stumbled on the juice opportunity, Sarasvathy emphasises that her imaginary lunch caterer could, depending on the market response and after a series on incremental steps, end up building a business as a travel agent, motivational consultant or just about anything else instead.

The effectuation process typically starts with the individual's given means (Who am I? What do I know? Whom do I know?) and works incrementally and iteratively towards any of the effects that can be created with these means (and the secondary resources that the initial means allow one to acquire). According to Sarasvathy (2001), the effectuation process is also characterised by the following principles.

- *Affordable loss rather than expected return* By taking incremental steps and avoiding financial commitments whenever possible, the entrepreneur(s) make sure that the worst case scenario does not lead to disastrous consequences. This implies the testable prediction that when they fail, effectuation-based start-ups fail smaller than causation-based counterparts. The affordable loss principle fits well with the bootstrapping or bricolage behaviour that was discussed and illustrated above, but implies that income is forgone in cases when market acceptance of the concept is high. Thus, an effectuation-based start-up may capture the market at a slower pace or obtain a smaller market share than a successful start-up based on causation logic.

- *Strategic alliances rather than competitive analysis* An effectuation strategy emphasises circumventing competition and building strength through alliances (e.g., Curry in a Hurry as a fast food corner of an existing restaurant) rather than building one's own muscles and trying to undo competitors' leads (e.g., raising large amounts of venture capital and launching heavily advertised outlets neighbouring those of competitors).

- *Exploitation of contingencies rather than exploitation of pre-existing knowledge* In an effectuation process, the actors stay open to influences rather than work towards firmly predefined goals. They can therefore exploit contingencies that arise unexpectedly as the process evolves – as Carin Lindahl did when she happened to come across the right fabric or Tim and Tim when they thought others might appreciate fresh juice as much as they did or, later, when they sought expansion finance from one of the yacht owners they had been acquainted with through Nantucket Allserve and who also happened to be a major risk capitalist.

■ *Controlling an unpredictable future rather than predicting an uncertain one* The logic of causation is that if the future can be predicted, one can control it. By contrast, the effectuation logic is that if one can control the future, one does not need to predict it. Thus, effectuation seems to apply well in situations where human action counts when it is very difficult to predict what will happen in the future. Think, for example, of a game of chess. No doubt, the player's skill and strategies count, but, at the same time, chess is a complex game and, it has turned out, it is impossible for even high-powered computers to win the game by using their superior ability to analyse the consequences of possible future moves. Arguably, it makes a strong case for effectuation that, although chess is a very complex and sophisticated game, there is but one opponent who can only choose from a finite number of next moves. In business, there are innumerable other actors with innumerable options. To control one's future by predicting their moves may be too big a challenge to take on.

Sarasvathy's (2008) theorising builds on empirical inputs from successful entrepreneurs. It is also consistent with observations made by other entrepreneurship researchers, as well as some existing theories of organisation and strategy (Sarasvathy, 2001: 254–7). However, the theory has so far not been systematically tested by independent researchers and on representative samples of start-ups. Consequently, Sarasvathy (2001: 246) is careful to point out that effectuation is suggested as a viable and descriptively valid alternative, not as a normatively superior one.

Arguably, there is little doubt that both more and less successful entrepreneurs' behaviour often deviates from conventional, textbook rationality. At the very least, effectuation theory offers a systematic and logically coherent description of such an alternative approach to establishing new business activity. Interestingly, Sarasvathy's reasoning gives us cause to question the first entry in both Klofsten's and Delmar and Shane's respective first steps, as given in Table 6.1. The questions it raises are 'How early should the business idea really be carved in stone?' and 'To what extent can one really plan in a game much more complex than chess?' Regrettably, there are no easy answers. In the next section, however, the analysis of when different approaches are likely to fit better or not so well deepens.

6.8 Which process is better?

So, which is preferable – the planned and systematic or the experimental and flexible?

There is some evidence that a directed and systematic search is possible and, on average, leads to more successful outcomes (Fiet, 2002; Chandler et al., 2003; Dahlqvist, Chandler and Davidsson, 2004). It is not difficult, however, to find examples of spectacular successes based on serendipity and fortuitous discovery.

Delmar and Shane (2003a; 2003b) have obtained results supporting the idea that planning and following the 'right' sequence leads to better performance. However, these results were obtained from a sample dominated by imitative start-ups. Arguably, such start-ups should be characterised by less uncertainty and, thus, it should be possible to successfully organise them with a more analytical approach (Gustafsson, 2006). Samuelsson and Davidsson (2009) have demonstrated that the start-up processes are different for imitative and innovative start-ups, respectively.

One advantage of the less systematic 'effectuation' (Sarasvathy, 2001, 2008) and 'internally stimulated' (Bhave, 1994) processes is that they almost guarantee a high degree of *fit* between the founders and the business idea, as they start from one's own means and/or problems. That fit has been strongly emphasised as a success factor by influential scholars (Vesper, 1991; Shane, 2003).

Another advantage of effectuation was mentioned above: if the venture fails, it fails affordably. In addition, the above-mentioned study by Furr (2009) found that changing the original business concept was positively associated with new venture performance. However, he found big changes had a more positive effect (with some delay), whereas effectuation was more consistent with a series of small changes through iterative incrementalism.

So, the evidence is, at best, inconclusive. In all likelihood, it depends. The question is just on what, more precisely, does it depend? At least four prime suspects can be identified as reasons for the differential effectiveness of the various approaches to discovery and exploitation of new business activity:

- the characteristics of the *venture idea*
- the characteristics of the *environment*
- the *stage of development* of the venture
- who you are – i.e., the characteristics of the *individual(s)*.

In the following subsections, the discussion of each of these sources of contingency effects is expanded on.

6.8.1 The characteristics of the venture idea

To some extent, the discussion above has covered the issue of how the *cost–value structure* of the intended product or service is related to what type of organisation can effectively exploit it. Figure 6.3 helps us take a somewhat different look at this problem, particularly the idea's potential for incremental and experimental exploitation.

Quadrant I represents the situation in which it is costly to produce a short series and when each unit has a high value for the buyer. This type of idea arguably requires more of a causation process as no incremental process governed by concerns for affordable loss would lead to this result and no commercial actor would be willing to experiment haphazardly without knowing what solution there is demand for, backed by willingness and ability to pay. In this situation, one would have to know where one was heading (with the possible positive exception of government-funded basic research at universities and the negative exception of the worst excesses of the dot.com boom and similar speculation bubbles). The high value to the customer, however, implies a potential for strategic alliances and this, in turn, reveals that, despite the costs, a small actor may play a key role. This is, in fact, precisely what the 'robust robot' case illustrates.

Figure 6.3 The cost–value structures of different venture ideas

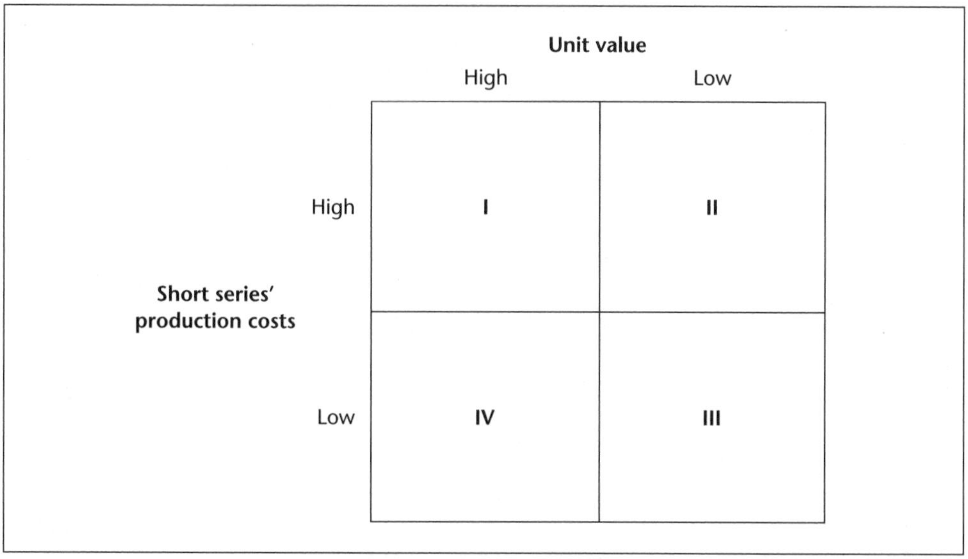

Quadrant II illustrates the case that is the most difficult to exploit with small funds and an incremental strategy. Here, costs are substantial before a single unit has been delivered, yet the value per customer is low. Examples here are Federal Express and the freesheet Metro, which, after its birth in Stockholm in 1995, has been launched (or copied) in many major cities of the world. It is not possible to build this type of business gradually from a very mundane start. New concepts of this kind have to be introduced with a lot of fanfare to reach the volumes required to cover development costs and/or achieve economically viable unit costs for their production. They therefore require pre-launch investments of a size that only large organisations or venture capital consortia can come up with.

Quadrant III, where short series are economical and the value per unit is also low, is perhaps the best option for independent start-ups using an incremental strategy. Here, both producers and customers can afford to experiment without much risk, which makes it easier for new actors to get established. Nantucket Nectars, Curry in a Hurry (if started as a lunch catering operation) and Stay in Place (Carin Lindahl's sports bra) are cases that are in this category.

Quadrant IV is also characterised by low cost for a short series, which makes room for incremental strategies. This would be true for used car dealers, but examples also range from on-site construction of houses to high-value services-based specialist knowledge, such as being one of the few knowing how to repair a machine that has a critical role in a process industry. However, the high value to the customer will make it difficult for new and small actors to enter the market because a trusted existing pro-vider will likely be preferred to an unknown newcomer, even if the new actor claims some advantages in price or product performance. Likewise, as illustrated by the sports bra case (quadrant III), a small actor that approaches the market incrementally will easily be outrun by larger later entrants if the total market holds the promise of being big enough to attract their attention. This may be even truer in quadrant IV, to the extent that the high value to the customer implies potential for high margins.

Another important aspect of the characteristics of the venture idea is its *degree of uncertainty*. Sarasvathy, Dew, Velamuri and Venkataraman (2003) discuss three types of venture ideas (or what they call 'business opportunities') as being related to their degree of uncertainty (note that 'discovery' is here used more restrictively than earlier in the chapter).

- *Opportunity recognition*, which has a low level of uncertainty because the sources of both supply and demand exist rather obviously. An example would be the opening of a new outlet for an existing franchising chain.

- *Opportunity discovery*, which has a medium level of uncertainty because only one side of the demand or supply obviously exists. The authors mention cures for diseases (demand with unknown supply) and applications for new technologies (supply with unknown demand) as examples.

- *Opportunity creation*, which has the highest level of uncertainty because neither demand nor supply exists in an obvious manner. The examples here are radical innovations that create new markets and new behavioural patterns.

Along this uncertainty dimension there is reason to believe that the higher the inherent level of uncertainty about the idea, the more questionable is Klofsten's (1994) emphasis on a clearly worked out business idea and Delmar and Shane's (2003b) placing of the writing of a business plan first in the process – at least if this is interpreted as suggestions for what needs to be done *before* any market-related action is taken.

When the uncertainty surrounding the idea is high, experimentation may be the *only* way to find out what will work or not and, hence, the only way to funnel in on a viable business idea or obtain useful input for a business plan. Further, based on cognitive psychological research on expertise, which suggests that analytical rationality works best in low uncertainty situations, Gustafsson (2006) was able to show that the more uncertain the situation, the less expert entrepreneurs rely on analysis when making their decisions.

6.8.2 The characteristics of the environment

Continuing the uncertainty argument, it may be assumed that causation processes, planning and the early carving out of a narrowly defined business idea are relatively more questionable practices in dynamic and uncertain environments. In line with this, praise of improvisation, learning by doing, etc., is quite frequent in the literature on dynamic capabilities and organisational learning (Zahra, Sapienza and Davidsson, 2006).

6.8.3 The stage of development

It is not only the industry's stage of development but also the stage of development of the venture itself that may affect the viability of different approaches to discovery and exploitation. This also follows the uncertainty argument – as the venture matures, its managers' task environment typically becomes less uncertain. Consequently, the reasoning is that, while effectuation strategies may work or even be superior in very early stages of a venture's life, a causation mode may have to be adopted later in order to secure continued success. Sarasvathy et al. (2003) uses the Starbucks case to illustrate the development from high uncertainty to low uncertainty for the same venture over time, accompanied by a switch from effectuation to causation approaches.

6.8.4 The characteristics of the individual

Finally, and importantly, who you are also matters. It has been noted above that Klofsten (1994) made commitment and drive of the key actors one of his cornerstones of successful business development. It has also been noted that many other researchers emphasise the fit between the entrepreneur(s) and the business idea or, in more general, psychological language, between the individual(s) and the task.

It cannot be ruled out that fit between person and type of process is equally important. To some extent, people can put a straightjacket on themselves, control their impulses and do what the situation requires, even when their real preferences point in a different direction. For example, Gustafsson (2006) was able to show that expert entrepreneurs are able to adapt their decisionmaking style to the characteristics of the task. To some extent, however, it may be necessary for individuals to use the approach they prefer and make that work regardless of what the situation 'objectively' calls for. Thus, those who prefer a systematic, planning-based approach may be better off applying such also in high uncertainty situations and vice versa for people who thrive on chaos, rather than adopting an approach they do not feel comfortable with.

Even better ways to handle this matching problem may be to go for ideas that are a good match with the preferred type of process or have a diverse founder team, where different members' abilities and preferences complement each other in this respect.

6.9 Chapter summary

This chapter has promulgated a process view of entrepreneurship, because entrepreneurship consists of an array of behaviours that cannot be completed all at once. More and less detailed examples of such concrete behaviours were given, such as the development of Klofsten's eight cornerstones. The two subprocesses of discovery and exploitation were distinguished. *Discovery* refers to the cognitive side of starting a new venture – i.e., the conception and further development of a venture idea. The literature shows that, although some real-world entrepreneurs arrive at venture ideas as a result of systematic searches, it is also common for them to more or less stumble on an idea without any prior intention of starting a new firm. Further, such fortuitous discoveries can lead to quite substantial businesses. However, there is no empirically based evidence for the assertion that a systematic search would be futile. The important thing appears to be that prospective entrepreneurs direct their searches at domains where they have particular knowledge and interests.

The *exploitation* process consists of the concrete behaviours that are needed to realise venture ideas. This includes acquiring and combining resources, but also efforts to generate demand and make the business legitimate in the eyes of others. A subsection was set aside for a discussion of the question under what circumstances is an independent start-up a feasible mode of exploiting a venture idea? It was concluded that successful exploitation in that mode is difficult when development costs are high, the potential market large and existing organisations can benefit from their existing knowledge base and resources. The independent start-up is in a good position when the idea makes incumbents' knowledge and resources obsolete and hard-to-copy competitive advantages can be created.

The following subsection discussed the interrelatedness of the discovery and exploitation subprocesses (see further elaboration by Dimov in Chapter 7). Usually these processes are, in part, parallel rather than sequential. Feedback from the exploitation efforts lead to changes in the venture idea and these adaptations, in turn, affect how it can best be exploited. Further, it was emphasised that a balance is needed between the two processes. Excellent exploitation efforts of underdeveloped ideas often lead to failure, as does the poor implementation of excellent ideas.

A central theme in the chapter has been that the behaviour of real-world entrepreneurs often deviates from the planned, systematic and linear process that is typical for normative management textbooks. The fact that this is true also for highly successful entrepreneurs leads to the suspicion such deviations may, under certain conditions, reflect a sound strategy.

Sarasvathy's (2001, 2008) identification of an alternative entrepreneurial logic – the *effectuation* approach – was discussed at some length (see further elaboration by Sarasvathy in Chapter 8).

The final section of the chapter analysed under what conditions a more iterative, incremental and flexible strategy like that used in effectuation may be more successful than its opposite – the textbook-like *causation* approach. It was concluded that the higher the inherent uncertainty of the venture idea and the environment, the less likely it is that all relevant information can be collected and viable long-term strategies can be worked out as a desk assignment prior to market launch. It was further shown that the cost–value structure of the venture idea has a bearing upon what type of process is suitable. Finally, the fit between individual(s) and type of process should also be considered.

Questions

1 Why should the start-up of a new venture be thought of as a process?

2 What characterises the discovery and exploitation subprocesses respectively?

3 What are the different possible uses of a business plan and for which of these uses is there a risk of detrimental performance effects?

4 What types of venture idea are more likely to be successfully exploited by an independent start-up?

5 What characterises causation- and effectuation-driven processes, respectively?

6 Under what conditions can an effectuation-based process be more successful than a causation-based process?

Weblinks

http://effectuation.org
This website gives additional information and references regarding Sarasvathy's effectuation theory.

www.kauffman.org
A website with rich resources for entrepreneurs and others interested in entrepreneurship and innovation, including research-based resources.

CHAPTER 7

Entrepreneurial opportunities

Dimo Dimov

7.1 Introduction

This chapter focuses on research into entrepreneurial opportunities. The topic has generated both excitement among entrepreneurship scholars and vigorous debates about what opportunities are and how they can be studied. Underlying this debate is a diversity of viewpoints that scholars employ in understanding opportunities and assumptions about the entrepreneurs behind them. Therefore, engaging in this debate requires careful consideration of the premises on which different arguments are based. This chapter aims to help navigate the debate by outlining the main viewpoints on the issue and the arguments that stem from them.

The notion of 'opportunity' occupies a central place in entrepreneurship research. When thinking about entrepreneurship, there is a strong, intuitive feeling and wide-spread agreement among scholars that somewhere early in the entrepreneurial process, there is an encounter between individuals and opportunities and this encounter is a distinct and defining feature of the process (Vesper, 1979; Timmons, Muzyka, Stevenson and Bygrave, 1987; Stevenson and Jarillo, 1990; Bygrave and Hofer, 1991; Venkataramen, 1997; Shane and Venkataramen, 2000). The accumulating evidence on nascent entrepreneurs – i.e. people committing time and resources to founding new firms – suggests that thinking seriously about a potential business is among the very first events to occur as these individuals enter the entrepreneurial process (Reynolds and White, 1997; Gartner and Carter, 2003). Understanding the origin of the business idea – i.e. the recognition of an opportunity – is, thus, a major milestone in entrepreneurship research. The challenge for researchers, however, is that the original business idea is both ephemeral and fragile in nature, easily distorted by the subsequent unfolding of events and people's post hoc rationalisation of them.

As a central construct in entrepreneurship research, 'opportunity' captures the possibility for entrepreneurial action (Venkataraman, 1997; McMullen and Shepherd, 2006). Indeed, entrepreneurial success can be easily attributed, at least partially, to the presence of opportunity, while entrepreneurial failure can be attributed to the lack thereof. For this reason, entrepreneurship can be seen as a nexus of individual and opportunity, wherein individuals discover, evaluate and exploit certain opportunities (Venkataraman, 1997; Shane and Venkataraman, 2000).

120

'Opportunity' has been defined as a chance to profitably introduce new goods, services, raw materials, markets and organisational methods (Casson, 1982; Shane and Venkataraman, 2000; Eckhardt and Shane, 2003), but, while such chance is easily seen when writing the history of a successful entrepreneurial endeavour, one is overcome by doubt in deciding whether a current endeavour – one that has not yet unfolded sufficiently to be judged as success or failure – represents such a chance.

It is at this junction that different scholars may disagree on how to proceed. Such disagreements reflect what scholars consider important and worthwhile to study. After all, any business situation invites multiple viewpoints and contains multiple business problems, each to be understood in its own right. In this regard, an opportunity can be seen as both retrospectively significant and prospectively interesting. In other words, it can be conceptualised as an outcome or as an unfolding process. The former invites a desire to explain; the latter invites a need to describe and understand. Each poses distinct questions, engages different relevant concepts and relationships and reaches different generalisations. The point is to strive for totality in understanding rather than for superiority of perspective.

This chapter is organised as follows. It opens with a discussion of the basic perspectives from which an opportunity can be examined, as well as typologies of opportunity. It then looks in greater detail at the person behind an opportunity, the process of opportunity recognition and the contextual and social influences involved.

7.2 Learning objectives

There are five learning objectives in this chapter:

1 to understand the nature of entrepreneurial opportunities as seen from different levels of analysis
2 to appreciate the tension between ex ante foresight and ex post insight in calling something an 'opportunity'
3 to recognise differences between the opportunities pursued by different entrepreneurs
4 to understand the individual factors involved in the generation of venture ideas
5 to understand the different processes involved in the generation and development of venture ideas.

Key concepts

■ entrepreneurship ■ opportunity ■ creativity ■ cognition ■ learning
■ knowledge ■ alertness

7.3 Different levels of thinking about opportunities

There are two levels at which one can think about opportunities: a systemic (bird's-eye) level and an individual (ground) level.

At the systemic level, one is concerned with the role of opportunities in an economic system and examines this role from an economic perspective. From this perspective, opportunities can be seen as an artefact of the constant tendency of the economic system towards equilibrium as it absorbs both endogenous and exogenous shocks.

At the individual level, one is concerned with the substantive reality of opportunities for the particular individuals who pursue them and seeks to understand this from a social–psychological perspective. From this perspective, opportunities can be seen as an artefact of the knowledge and beliefs of individual actors about possible future states.

7.3.1 Systemic level

The main thrust of economic theory has been to explain the organisation of economic activity and the drivers of economic development. Such systemic thinking has been dominated by the notion of equilibrium as an optimal allocation of resources towards which an economic system tends. In this process, an entrepreneur plays a central role as he or she introduces innovations (Schumpeter, 1934; Drucker, 1985b), bears uncertainty (Knight, 1921; Mises, 1949) and corrects market inefficiencies (Kirzner, 1979).

In an extensive overview of the evolution of economic thought, Hébert and Link (1988) identify two fundamental premises about entrepreneurship in economic analysis:

- it is placed in the context of equilibrium and change
- it is regarded in functional terms.

Thus, although an entrepreneur is viewed as a person (Casson, 1982; Hébert and Link, 1988), it is essentially a depersonalised agent who destroys or restores equilibrium.

In this context, the notion of opportunity has been put forth as a central impetus for entrepreneurial action (Venkataraman, 1997; Shane and Venkataraman, 2000). It is essentially ascribed an auxiliary role for connecting action and consequences. Building upon the ideas of Austrian economists, Shane and Venkataraman argue that disequilibrium is a natural state. It is in this sense that 'opportunities themselves are objective phenomena that are not known to all parties at all times' (2000: 220). Eckhardt and Shane (2003) further develop this idea to clarify that opportunities exist because prices are imperfect reflections of value; they are linked to perceptions of new means–ends frameworks. Davidsson (2003), similarly, argues that opportunities can exist as uncountable, propped by a configuration of technological possibilities, knowledge, unfulfilled human needs and purchasing power. As Klein (2008) elaborates, however, these arguments should not be taken as ontological claims about the nature of opportunities, but, rather, an opportunity should simply be viewed as a metaphor, used to describe what entrepreneurs do. It represents the possibility for entrepreneurial action, to be undertaken by some alert entrepreneur (Kirzner, 1979, 2009). In short, at a systemic level, it is sufficient simply to claim that opportunities exist without having to identify and describe specific opportunities.

7.3.2 Individual level

At the level of specific individual endeavours, the systemic notion of opportunity is inoperable as it requires one to make a judgment about whether or not specific instances represent opportunities. At this level, the concept of opportunity is elusive, in that it brings to the fore the tension between ex post insight and ex ante foresight. In other words, it is easy to label something as an opportunity once we know that it has been successfully implemented, but difficult to do the same for something that is yet to be implemented. This is why the traditional definition of opportunity as a chance to profitably introduce new goods, services, raw materials, markets and organisational methods (Casson, 1982; Shane and Venkataraman, 2000; Eckhardt and Shane, 2003) has been challenged for its inapplicability to individual cases because it places emphasis on the objective existence of something that prospectively can only be discussed as a speculative idea and that can be fully articulated and explained only retrospectively.

Another difficulty emerges from the need to conceptually separate the content of the opportunity (i.e., as verbalised in an idea) from its implementation, for the purposes of making attributions of success or failure. A seemingly good idea can be executed badly and result in unsuccessful outcomes. Similarly, a seemingly bad idea can be executed with great discipline and skill and result in, perhaps, moderately successful outcomes. We can, however, never go back to try the same idea with a different implementation or the same implementation with a different idea. As a result, when someone claims to have recognised an opportunity and someone else disagrees, it is one person's word against the other. Simply arguing is futile; the proof lies in the actions undertaken and their consequences.

Various premises have been offered to adapt the notion of opportunity to the realm and worldview of individual entrepreneurs:

- opportunities are created by the actions of entrepreneurs (Alvarez and Barney, 2007; Dimov, 2010a)
- an opportunity represents a stream of continuously developed and modified ideas (Davidsson, 2003; Dimov, 2007a)
- an opportunity cannot be separated from the individual (Sarason, Dean and Dillard, 2006; Companys and McMullen, 2007; Dimov, 2007b)
- an opportunity is intertwined with individual beliefs (McMullen and Shepherd, 2006; Shepherd, McMullen and Jennings, 2007)
- an opportunity exists only in the entrepreneur's imagination (Shackle, 1955; Klein, 2008)
- an opportunity constitutes an organising vision (Lichtenstein, Dooley and Lumpkin, 2006).

At the individual level, thinking about opportunities is related to depicting and understanding the empirical reality of aspiring and acting entrepreneurs. Substantively, every single entrepreneur offers a fascinating story, interweaving personal aspirations and social context. If we were to talk to an aspiring or nascent entrepreneur, we would hear visions of a desirable and anticipated future and verbal descriptions of intended or undertaken actions aimed at achieving that vision. Therefore, the empirical substance of opportunity is what people enthusiastically claim to be an opportunity and energetically pursue it. Even if seemingly speculative, such momentarily perceived opportunities are legitimate, even if they are ultimately proven to be wrong or misguided. At the moment that they are annunciated, there is no 'objective' basis for ruling whether aspiring towards a particular vision of the future constitutes an opportunity or not.

Therefore, from an individual perspective, opportunities sojourn in the minds of aspiring entrepreneurs as venture ideas, propped by perceptions and beliefs formed from the interpretations of tangible evidence (Davidsson, 2003; Dimov, 2007b, 2010b). The content of these ideas pertains to the initiation and perpetuation of market relationships – i.e., selling a product or service to someone. These ideas inspire entrepreneurs to act (McMullen and Shepherd, 2006) and such action breeds new ideas (i.e., new or modified possibilities) and impetus for new action (or inaction) as initial assumptions and intuition about future possibilities are gradually replaced by experiential facts and juxtaposition of circumstances. In other words, in substantive terms, an opportunity comprises the perpetuation of a cycle of venture ideas and actions orientated towards the formation and sustenance of market relationships (Dimov, 2011).

7.4 Typologies of opportunities

In addition to seeking to understand what opportunities are, scholars have also sought to distinguish different types of opportunities. There have been different typologies proposed, from both systemic and individual levels.

At the systemic level, Drucker (1985a) proposes a classification on the basis of the sources of opportunities. He distinguishes between sources *within* and *outside* the domain of activity in question. The sources within include the unexpected, the incongruity, process need, and changes in the industry or market structure. The outside sources include changes in demographics, perceptions and new scientific knowledge. Drucker's analysis suggests that change is a fundamental condition for the emergence of opportunities.

More recently, Eckhardt and Shane (2003) propose a more comprehensive opportunity classification framework that also captures aspects of the change process and has three dimensions: locus of changes, sources of opportunities, and initiator of the change. The locus of changes dimension reflects the elements of the value chain identified by Schumpeter (1934) as objects of innovation: products or services, markets, raw materials, methods of production and ways of organising. With regard to the sources of opportunities, Eckhardt and Shane identify the following opportunity types: information asymmetries versus exogenous shocks, supply versus demand-side changes and productivity-enhancing versus rent-seeking. Finally, opportunities are classified on the basis of the actors initiating the change – non-commercial entities, existing commercial entities and new commercial entities.

At the individual level, classifications of opportunities have focused on the knowledge and beliefs of entrepreneurs. Sarasvathy, Dew, Velamuri and Venkataraman (2002) divide human beliefs about the future into three categories: predictable, unpredictable but driven by an independent environment and unpredictable but driven by human agency. They further argue that each of these beliefs would be associated with a pursuit of opportunities associated with more or less clear sources of demand and supply. So, under beliefs about the predictability of the future, entrepreneurs would pursue opportunities involving clear sources of supply and demand. Under beliefs in an unpredictable future resulting from an independent environment, entrepreneurs would pursue opportunities involving a clear source of either demand or supply. Finally, under beliefs in an unpredictable future resulting from human agency, entrepreneurs would pursue opportunities with no clear sources of demand and supply. Using a similar logic of demand and supply knowledge, Ardichvili, Cardozo and Ray (2003) present a typology of opportunities based on their origin (value sought) and degree of development (value-creation capability). They categorise value sought as unidentified and identified and value-creation capability as undefined and defined. Their main argument in relation to this typology is that the more established the value sought and value-creation capability, the higher the likelihood that a venture pursuing this opportunity will succeed.

Finally, Dimov (2010a) develops a typology of opportunities based on the information context in which they emerge. 'Information context' pertains to the situational ambiguity prospective entrepreneurs have to deal with in terms of 'filling in' the information and reasoning gaps with regard to possible products or customers. To the extent that product or customer information may be either available or lacking and one needs information on at least one of these elements in order to anchor a possible opportunity, Dimov outlines three types of context in which opportunity ideas emerge. The first, 'demand-driven', pertains to available information about possible customer demand and lack of information about possible products that can meet such demand; the second, 'supply-driven', pertains to available information about possible products and lack of information about possible demand that such products can satisfy; the third, 'replication-driven', pertains to available information about both possible customer demand and possible products. The theoretical value of this classification lies in that, based on the context, 'filling in' the missing information requires a qualitatively different insight (Finke, 1995) on the part of the individual.

7.5 The person behind an opportunity

The generation of venture ideas is essentially a creative process. As such, it can be affected by various individual characteristics. The literature on creativity has identified four such characteristics: personality, intrinsic motivation, knowledge and cognitive skills and abilities (Amabile, 1988; Woodman and Schoenfeldt, 1989, 1990). These factors are also well established in entrepreneurship research.

7.5.1 Personality

The quest for understanding how entrepreneurs differ from the general population in terms of various personality characteristics is one of the oldest research traditions in entrepreneurship and mirrors similar infatuations with the personality of great creative persons (Simonton, 1986) or great leaders (Yukl, 1989; see also Chapter 9). Despite criticisms of this trait paradigm (Gartner, 1989a), it is now well accepted that personality remains an important general predictor of entrepreneurial behaviour, once specific mediating factors are considered (Rauch and Frese, 2000; Baum, Locke and Smith, 2001).

There are several factors that have been of great interest to researchers: need for achievement, locus of control, risk propensity and tolerance of ambiguity (McClelland, 1961; Brockhaus, 1982; Begley and Boyd, 1987; Shaver and Scott, 1991), as well as, more recently, self-efficacy and the 'Big 5' personality factors (Krueger, Reilly and Carsrud, 2000; Markman, Balkin and Baron, 2002; Ciavarella, Buchholtz, Riordan, Gatewood and Stokes, 2004). In the context of mixed results, methodological issues, and diverse samples, recent meta-analyses and reflections on this work have emphasised the need to separate the emergence and success of entrepreneurs, search for more proximate or mediating predictors of specific behaviours, take into consideration situational demands and acknowledge the inherent diversity of entrepreneurs (Rauch and Frese, 2000; Stewart Jr and Roth, 2001).

7.5.2 Intrinsic motivation

Intrinsic motivation is fundamental to achieving creative outcomes. Similarly, it is inconceivable to think that people will recognise opportunities if they do not value entrepreneurship as a career option.

Studies of the motivations of both nascent and accomplished entrepreneurs suggest that intrinsic motivation – desire for independence, innovation, personal achievement – is a significant factor in explaining people's entry into the entrepreneurship process (Utsch, Rauch, Rothfuss and Frese, 1999; Rauch and Frese, 2000; Carter, Gartner, Shaver and Gatewood, 2003). Nevertheless, the main premise of economic theories of entrepreneurship is that economic incentives (availability of profit opportunities) spur entrepreneurial discoveries (Kirzner, 1985). Yet, while there is evidence that the promise of financial reward induces a higher number of ideas (Shepherd and DeTienne, 2005), the evidence for it leading to more creative ideas has been mixed at best.

In Shepherd and DeTienne's (2005) experiment, the promise of financial reward exerted different effects on the innovativeness of one's ideas depending on one's prior knowledge – the effect was positive for those with minimal prior knowledge, but negative for those with considerable prior knowledge. In a different experimental setting, posing a difficult problem and for which prior knowledge was not particularly relevant, financial incentives had no effect on the finding of creative solutions (Demmert and Klein, 2003; Kitzmann and Schiereck, 2005). This suggests that the effect of incentives may be contingent upon one's intrinsic motivation or upon the specific situation in which one acts and thinks.

7.5.3 Knowledge

One of the central tenets in creativity research is the positive relationship between (domain) knowledge and creativity (Amabile, 1988). This notion has also been taken up in entrepreneurship research, linking prior knowledge to the construct of alertness (Kirzner, 1979, 1985). Indeed, several empirical studies have provided support for a positive relationship between prior knowledge and opportunity recognition (Shane, 2000; Shepherd and DeTienne, 2005; Ko and Butler, 2006; Corbett, 2007). Nevertheless, in line with the idea that too much domain knowledge may, in fact, impede one's ability to come up with unusual, outside-the-box solutions (Frensch and

Sternberg, 1989), there is evidence that the link between knowledge and opportunities is contingent upon one's mode of learning or thinking (Ko and Butler, 2006; Corbett, 2007; Dimov, 2010b). This suggests that knowledge may be a necessary but not sufficient condition for the recognition of opportunities; rather, it is intertwined with the way in which it is applied and extended in particular situations (Weisberg, 1999) – i.e., it cannot be dissociated from one's cognition or from the situation in which one uses it.

7.5.4 Cognitive skills and abilities

The idea that creative outcomes are associated with distinct cognitive skills and abilities has found fertile ground in entrepreneurship research. Indeed, studies have shown that entrepreneurs use more heuristics than managers (Busenitz and Barney, 1997, but see also Allinson, Chell and Hayes, 2000) and cognitive biases are essential factors in risk perception and the decision to start a venture (Simon, Houghton and Aquino, 2000; Keh, Foo and Lim, 2002). In addition, there are arguments that the recognition of opportunities can be associated with abilities such as higher-level learning that, through the application of mental schemas, heightens one's alertness by inducing higher sensitivity to market disequilibrium signals (Gaglio, 1997; Gaglio and Katz, 2001) and mental simulations and counterfactual thinking, which pertain to reflection on past and future events (Baron, 1999; Gaglio, 2004). Finally, entrepreneurs' different learning and thinking skills help them absorb and process information differently, which may make them sensitive to some opportunities but not others (Ko and Butler, 2006; Corbett, 2007; Dimov, 2010b).

7.6 The process of opportunity recognition

Another way to understand opportunity recognition is by looking at the process through which it unfolds. Several subprocesses can be further distinguished. The first looks at opportunity recognition as a creative process. The second examines the role of active information searches in opportunity recognition. A third approach deals with the cognitive processes associated with opportunity recognition or alertness to new opportunities. The final, fourth, approach focuses on opportunity recognition as a learning process.

7.6.1 Creative process

Because of the significant links between opportunity conception and creativity, there have been several attempts to apply a creativity process framework to opportunity recognition.

Long and McMullan (1984) applied the seminal creativity process framework proposed by Wallas (1926) to the process of opportunity recognition and sought to determine whether or not entrepreneurs indeed followed the five stages of the process – preparation, incubation, insight, evaluation and elaboration. They used a small-scale exploratory study to provide support for and propose a four-stage model, including pre-vision, point of vision, opportunity elaboration and decision to proceed.

This, as well as subsequent studies that have applied the same framework (Hills, Shrader and Lumpkin, 1999), essentially uses a design that relies on the recollection and self-reporting of entrepreneurs on the origin and elements of the opportunity recognition process. For example, Hills et al. (1999) asked 187 businessowners/ entrepreneurs about the degree to which they agreed with 31 statements about the opportunity recognition process.

Using a factor analysis, they showed that there was good consistency with the model proposed by Wallas (1926) and also extended that model by suggesting that the creative process was a staged one, involving feedback loops between the stages of preparation, incubation and insight.

A further refinement of the model has elaborated on the feedback loops between the stages (Lumpkin, Lichtenstein and Shrader, 2003) and has received empirical support (Hansen, Lumpkin and Hills, 2011).

7.6.2 Information search

The study of how prospective entrepreneurs decide to search for opportunities has essentially built on the ideas of Cyert and March (1963) regarding problemistic searches – i.e., searches driven by the perception that particular expectations have not been met.

The motivated search model proposed by Heron and Sapienza (1992) applies the problemistic search idea to the context of entrepreneurship by specifying the conditions that propel individuals towards searching for business opportunities. Specifically, they suggest that individuals engage in problemistic searches when their current performance is below their aspiration level. In an empirical setting, consistent with the above predictions, Sine and David (2003) showed that environmental jolts shook the institutional logics of incumbent organisations and induced searches for new logics that represented an environment of increased opportunity.

Motivated searches, however, are one of several possible ways in which the initiation of opportunity recognition can occur. Bhave (1994) proposed a model for the venture-creation process that suggested two separate paths lead to opportunity recognition. In the first path, the process initiates with a decision to start a business, while, in the second, it starts with a recognised need to which a solution is developed.

Another distinction made between search processes is between directed searches and chance occurrences. For example, Long and McMullan (1984) found that the path to seeing an opportunity could stem from either a deliberate search or be the result of serendipity.

This distinction between searches and serendipity is also reflected in other early work on this subject (Koller, 1988). More recently, there has been active interest in developing more formal classifications of search processes. Chandler, Dahlqvist and Davidsson (2002) develop a taxonomy of opportunity recognition processes by examining the emerging business initiatives of 136 Swedish ventures.

They identify three distinct processes: proactive search, reactive search and fortuitous discovery. A proactive search is exploratory in nature and capitalises on unique knowledge, a reactive search is triggered by poor performance, consistent with Heron and Sapienza's model above, while a fortuitous discovery pertains to unexpected events involving no searches.

Similarly, Chandler, DeTienne and Lyon (2003) developed a typology of the opportunity detection/development process based on a survey of accomplished entrepreneurs. They identified three distinct processes: opportunity as a solution to a specific personal problem, opportunity as a solution to a market problem and opportunity as created. Although all three processes involved active searches and fortuitous discovery, they were distinct in the ways in which the process of opportunity recognition was triggered.

Overall, where studies have sought to examine the relative prevalence of these search approaches, the empirical results show that there is no dominance of one approach over the other (Kaish and Gilad, 1991; Hills and Shrader, 1998; Zietsma, 1999).

In addition to the types of searches employed by entrepreneurs, researchers have also examined the intensity of the searches, determining the amount of information sought. Cooper, Folta and Woo (1995) found that the intensity of the searches was negatively related to prior entrepreneurial experience, domain differences and confidence.

Finally, several studies have looked directly at the sources of opportunities that entrepreneurs have employed. Vesper (1979) argued that all sources are, in one way or another, related to entrepreneurs' prior experience and actions they have undertaken. This argument is consistent with the findings of Long and Graham (1988), that, most often, opportunities originate from the founders. In a survey of 483 small businesses, Peterson (1988) found that spontaneous thoughts had the highest frequency (24 per cent), followed by competitor imitation (18 per cent) and scanning of business periodicals (11 per cent). In a more systematic study, Cooper et al. (1995) distinguished between professional and personal sources of information and related their usage to the prior experiences of the entrepreneurs. They found that the use of professional sources was positively related to domain similarity, while the use of personal sources was negatively related to prior entrepreneurial experience and domain similarity, but positively related to domain differences.

7.6.3 Cognitive processes

The focus on cognitive processes stems from the idea that entrepreneurs form unique mental representations of the world (Shaver and Scott, 1991; Mitchell et al., 2002a; Baron, 2004). The notion of entrepreneurial cognition pertains to 'the knowledge structures that people use to make assessments, judgments, or decisions involving opportunity evaluation, venture creation, and growth' and research into entrepreneurial cognition is 'about understanding how entrepreneurs use simplifying mental models to piece together previously unconnected information that helps them to identify and invent new products or services, and to assemble the necessary resources to start and grow businesses' (Mitchell et al., 2002a: 97).

Ucbasaran, Wright, Westhead and Busenitz (2002) define strong entrepreneurial cognition as using heuristics, higher-level learning and offline evaluation.

In terms of the usage of heuristics (experiential learning), empirical studies have drawn from the findings of the cognitive psychology literature on decisionmaking, pioneered by Kahneman and Tversky (Kahneman, Slovic and Tversky, 1982), on representativeness, heuristics, framing and overconfidence. They have shown that entrepreneurs use more heuristics than managers (Busenitz and Barney, 1997; Simon, Houghton and Aquino, 2000). In expanding on this work, Alvarez and Busenitz (2001) argue that it is this heuristic-based thinking that gives entrepreneurs the distinct capability to discover opportunities.

Higher-level learning pertains to the achievement of new understandings and inter-pretations (Ucbasaran, Wright, Westhead and Busenitz, 2002). One way in which this process has been conceptualised is by using mental schemas, representing an individual's understanding of how the external world works (Gaglio, 1997). In this context, entrepreneurial alertness is conceptualised as a particular schema that has a higher complexity and flexibility and involves a heightened sensitivity to market disequilibrium signals (Gaglio and Katz, 2001).

Finally, offline evaluation is related to the concepts of mental simulations and counterfactual thinking, which pertain to reflection on past and future events (Baron, 1999; Gaglio, 2004). Such reflection is proposed as a distinctive feature of opportunity finders (Gaglio, 2004). Summarising this perspective, Baron (2004) argues that percep-tion, schemas and the self-regulation of behaviour all provide valuable insights into the opportunity recognition process. To this end, Baron and Ensley (2006) argue that pattern recognition plays an important role. More specifically, experience can provide individuals with cognitive frameworks (prototypes) that they can use to identify pat-terns – i.e., 'connect the dots' – amidst seemingly incomprehensible complexity. They compared the business opportunities prototypes of novice and repeat entrepreneurs and found that the latter have prototypes that are more clearly defined, richer in content and more relevant to starting a new venture than those of the former.

More recent work stresses the role of creative cognition – specifically, the usage of conceptual combination, analogies and initial problem formulation in conceiving of opportunities (Ward, 2004). In a very insightful study, Gregoire, Barr and Shepherd (2010) portray opportunity recognition as a process of cognitive alignment of the structural features of a technology and the potential market in which it can be applied. Their study involved an in-depth look at the reasoning employed by nine senior executives when identifying opportunities in response to two presented technology scenarios. Their results indicate that, in recognising opportunities, the participants looked for similarities between the information about the presented technology and the contexts in which this information might be useful.

7.6.4 Learning process

As a series of successively elaborated ideas, opportunity recognition is essentially a learning process whereby new information is used to modify the premises on which a venture idea is based (Dimov, 2007b). Whereas the continuous shaping of an idea is propelled by an individual's sustained belief in the commercial potential of the idea, the belief itself is dependent upon the interpretation and meaning with which the individual envelops the idea. Indeed, it is the diversity of meanings (or different means–ends configurations) that help generate ideas (Kirzner, 1985; Mir and Watson, 2000). As meaning emerges from one's prior experiences (Weick, 1979), opportunity develop-ment is inherently linked to the dynamics of those experiences and is, thus, a learning process (Minniti and Bygrave, 2001; Cope, 2005; Dutta and Crossan, 2005; Ravasi and Turati, 2005).

The 4I organisational learning framework highlights three psychosocial processes taking place at the individual and group levels that may capture this early gestation and transition of opportunities (Crossan, Lane and White, 1999; Dutta and Crossan, 2005).

The first process is that of individuals engaging in *intuiting*, which generates ideas with perceived potential. *Intuiting* is 'the preconscious recognition of the pattern and/ or possibilities inherent in a personal stream of experience' (Weick, 1995: 25). This is an individual process that triggers the learning associated with opportunity development. The essence of this process is one's becoming aware of a business idea that one perceives as holding some potential to meet current or emerging customer needs (Dutta and Crossan, 2005). Individuals emerge from this process with an 'inexplicable', preverbal sense of what is possible (Crossan, Lane and White, 1999). Their initial interpretation of this sense makes it communicable by giving it verbal shape and meaning. The intention to communicate this to others then depends on whether the self-derived meaning reinforces or discredits the initial intuitive sense of possibility.

In the next step, individuals trigger a process of *interpreting* as they try to clarify those ideas by themselves and by engaging third parties in further refining and gaining support for the ideas.

Through these social interactions, a shared understanding of the opportunity idea begins to emerge and, thus, the overall learning process enters the next, *integrating* phase. This is the stage at which a more formal nascent entrepreneurial team may be formed as the idea shows continuing merit and induces an even more intensive pursuit of it.

As this gathers further momentum and results in the emergence of a viable business organisation, its practices gradually become *institutionalised*.

Intuiting and interpreting occur at an individual level, whereas interpreting and integrating occur at a group level – i.e., they involve the (potential) entrepreneur and people from his or her immediate social or business circle. In this regard, there likely are contextual influences that affect the former and social influences that affect the latter.

7.7 Contextual and social influences on idea generation

When individuals engage in intuiting and early interpretation, they are likely situated in a particular context – e.g., executing a particular task, performing a regular job, walking leisurely in the park. The contextual influences that affect both the intuiting and early interpretation of an idea pertain to the characteristics of the immediate task environment as well as the information and attention it affords the individual.

Some contexts exert particular pressures – emotional, time, fatigue – thereby inducing different ways of thinking (Baron, 1998). In addition, particular characteristics of the immediate task environment of the individual – levels of autonomy, positive or negative affect, the nature of the task, the nature and availability of feedback, etc. – affect their propensity to generate ideas (Amabile, 1988; Oldham and Cummings,

1996). These same characteristics then affect the interpretative response (positive or negative) to ideas, so an individual's reaction to a particular idea will likely be different in different situations.

Perhaps more importantly, the information to which an individual is exposed has a considerable effect on the ideas that he or she generates. Indeed, as Drucker (1985a) suggests, innovative ideas come from a variety of sources and are, thus, potentially available to many people. Not all individuals will react to the same information in the same way, however, just as the same individual would not react to different pieces of information in the same way. On one hand, as the opportunistic assimilation hypothesis suggests, new information may interact with problems that have been encoded in a person's long-term memory and, thus, induce an insight – prima facie serendipitously – which helps solve them (Seifert et al., 1995). On the other hand, individuals have different absorptive or learning capacities for assimilating and extending the available information (Corbett, 2007; Dimov, 2010b), thereby generating different meanings from it (Daft and Huber, 1987; Crossan, Lane and White, 1999). These individual learning and interpretation differences stem from the individuals' prior experience (Kolb, 1984; Walsh, 1995). More generally, an individual's ideas and action in a given situation depend not only on what one knows, but also on how he or she applies and extends that knowledge in the situation (Weisberg, 1999; Bontis, Crossan and Hulland, 2002). The context is thus unique in the way it engages a particular individual in the generation and early shaping of ideas.

Interpreting is 'the explaining, through words and/or actions, of an insight or idea to one's self and to others' (Crossan, et al., 1999: 525). In this process, potential entrepreneurs engage in explaining and defending the 'fuzzy' images of their insights. They thus interact not only with their immediate social network – family, friends, classmates, colleagues, teachers – but also some potentially more instrumental stakeholders in the development of the idea – partners, informal and formal investors, consultants, accountants, customers, suppliers, employees (Greve and Salaff, 2003). Depending on the selected conversants, the idea may take different shapes and proportions or be abandoned quickly. The social context not only provides established meanings but also allows for new meanings to be generated (Aldrich and Fiol, 1994).

The social influences on the opportunity development process pertain to the interpretation and integration inputs that the potential entrepreneurs receive from the social audience with which they engage, discussing, selling or defending their ideas. There are several such inputs that this social interaction provides. First, given that market information is dispersed, others can provide valuable insights – to the benefit or detriment of the initial idea – that one does not currently possess. Indeed, as the economic sociology literature suggests, one's social network may provide many information benefits, such as access to diverse or novel information (Burt, 1992), referrals (Shane and Cable, 2002) and timeliness (Gargiulo and Benassi, 2000), which may, in turn, be instrumental in the development of opportunities (Singh, 2000).

In addition, given the larger knowledge base to which one has access in this way, there is a wider set of interpretations of the idea that can be accessed. These interpretations emerge as conversants serve as sounding boards for the initial idea, bringing in suggestions or different evaluation angles. Even more importantly, these social contacts may give the potential entrepreneur access to various resources – financial, technical, marketing, legitimacy – that could potentially increase or shrink the scope of the initial idea (Dubini and Aldrich, 1991; Stuart, Hoang and Hybels, 1999; Shane and Cable, 2002).

Finally, one's social circle, through its imposition of social roles, identities and cultural norms – or, more generally, through affecting one's cognition – may be instrumental in motivating (or demotivating) the individual to further pursue or shape the idea (Krueger, 2000; De Carolis and Saparito, 2006).

7.8 Chapter summary

This chapter has provided an overview of research into entrepreneurial opportunities, focusing on the ongoing debates in the field with regard to the nature of entrepreneurial opportunities and the various perspectives from which opportunities can be studied. Different views about the nature of opportunities were discussed in the context of two levels of analysis – systemic and individual. At the systemic level, opportunities are essentially metaphors for entrepreneurial actions, used to describe what entrepreneurs do. At the individual level, opportunities are situated expressions of prospective entrepreneurs' motivation, knowledge and cognitive and learning abilities.

In addition to these levels of analysis, opportunities can be further distinguished based on their sources and consequences, as well as the nature of available information that prospective entrepreneurs use to generate their venture ideas.

There are various types of research question that can be asked when studying entrepreneurial opportunities. The first pertain to the individuals behind them and seek to understand why certain individuals are more likely to recognise opportunities or generate venture ideas than others. The possible explanations involve personality, motivation, knowledge and cognitive abilities.

The second type pertain to the process involved in opportunities recognition. Again, there are different facets to the process that are of interest to scholars. They include the creative process that culminates with the generation of venture ideas, the process by means of which prospective entrepreneurs search for or are exposed to relevant information, the cognitive process involved in the generation of an opportunity insight and the learning process where initial ideas become shaped and developed through actions and interactions with others.

Finally, the third set of questions pertain to the contextual and social influences that affect opportunity recognition. These influences are an inseparable feature of the process and it is in this sense that opportunities are seen as situated individual expressions.

Questions

1 Why are opportunities difficult to define and study?

2 What are the different levels at which opportunities can be studied? How and why would one choose the level at which to conduct one's research?

3 What are the individual characteristics that can prove instrumental in the recognition of opportunities? Are any of these characteristics necessary or sufficient for one to recognise an opportunity?

4 What are the different processes that are relevant for understanding how opportunities are recognised and developed?

5 What makes particular situations or social circles unconducive to the recognition of opportunities?

Weblinks

http://mises.org
A site devoted to the works of Ludwig von Mises and Austrian economists whose writing has greatly influenced current thinking about entrepreneurial opportunities. A full copy of Mises' classic work, *Human Action*, is also available at this site.

www.kauffman.org
A site devoted to the promotion of entrepreneurship with many resources for researchers, educators and practitioners.

CHAPTER 8

Effectuation and entrepreneurship

Saras Sarasvathy

8.1 Introduction

This chapter summarises the five key elements of entrepreneurial expertise.

For a long time, entrepreneurship had been studied as either a set of personality traits that separate entrepreneurs from non-entrepreneurs and successful entrepreneurs from unsuccessful ones or a set of success factors largely consisting of elements of the environment, such as technological and regulatory changes or sociopolitical institutions, such as property rights.

More recently, researchers began to look into the black box of what entrepreneurs actually do, with a view to identifying, understanding and evaluating particular decisions, actions, strategies and mechanisms. One line of research has focused especially on what constitutes *expertise* in entrepreneurship. In other words, it asks, if you have been an entrepreneur for ten years or longer and have undergone all possible entrepreneurial experiences – from starting multiple ventures, including successes and failures, to taking at least one company public – what are the things you have learned that can also be learned by novice entrepreneurs just starting out on their first venture?

In response to this question, the research has unearthed at least five principles that logically hang together in a way of thinking called effectuation or effectual logic.

8.2 Learning objectives

There are three learning objectives in this chapter:

1 to understand the five principles of effectuation
2 to understand the dynamics of the five principles within the effectual entrepreneurial process
3 to understand how the five principles of effectuation are related to venture performance and the career of the entrepreneur.

Key concepts

- entrepreneurial expertise ■ effectuation ■ effectual logic ■ affordable loss
- self-selected stakeholders ■ non-predictive control

8.3 Entrepreneurial expertise

Are entrepreneurs born or made? If the latter, how exactly do we make them?

For several decades, entrepreneurship researchers tried to isolate the personality traits and characteristics of entrepreneurs, especially successful entrepreneurs. While there was some evidence that entrepreneurs scored higher in self-efficacy – that is, they believed in their own ability to accomplish things – they also scored high in over-confidence – an excessive, mostly unjustified, belief in being able to beat the odds. As for other traits, such as a higher propensity to take risks, the evidence was even more muddled. Different studies found evidence for different levels of risk-taking – high, medium and low. Moreover, it appeared that people with very different personality types were able to start and even successfully run different kinds of companies.

So, researchers began turning their attention to what entrepreneurs actually do, rather than focusing exclusively on who they are. This second avenue proved more useful and, over the last two decades, we have slowly begun to accumulate evidence about how entrepreneurs approach difficult decisions in the start-up process. It turns out that, over a long career of founding and running companies, entrepreneurs learn a distinctive style and logic of decisionmaking that is called 'effectual logic' or 'effectuation' for short.

When a group of 27 *expert* entrepreneurs were asked to talk aloud continuously as they solved exactly the same ten typical decision problems in starting a new venture, they consistently used five distinct principles. 'Entrepreneurial expertise', in the study, was defined as more than ten years of founding experience in multiple firms, including at least one company taken public. These expert entrepreneurs had built companies ranging in size from $200 million to $6.5 billion in several different industries, including software, biotechnology, retail, manufacturing and personal services.

In later studies, the expert entrepreneurs were compared with novices, expert corporate managers and private equity investors. Thereafter, as you will see throughout this chapter, a series of in-depth case studies of the early histories of entrepreneurial ventures confirmed the use of effectual principles in several industries, geographies and across time.

Note: The claim here is neither that expert entrepreneurs use effectual logic to the exclusion of all other approaches, nor that using effectual logic will instantly make you an expert. Instead, the studies show that the more experienced an entrepreneur is, the more likely he or she is to use effectual logic in the start-up phase of a new venture. In other words, whereas entrepreneurs might use a variety of different approaches to decisionmaking depending on their own proclivities, as well as contextual factors such as the stage of the venture they are building, they have learned, through their experiences, that effectual logic is particularly useful in the start-up phase. Moreover, the principles of effectuation are both learnable and teachable and have specific consequences for both the performance of the venture and the overall development of expertise over several successful and unsuccessful ventures. Additionally, histories of enduring companies show how effectual logic has helped shape not only their products and business models but also their markets and even their larger environments. Finally, the five principles that constitute effectual logic are logically consistent with each other, as explained below.

8.4 Non-predictive control: the overall logic of effectuation

In general, expert entrepreneurs do not believe in trying to predict the future. Instead, they prefer to co-create it to the extent possible with people who self-select into the process by making specific commitments to the project at hand. In other words, expert entrepreneurs invert standard beliefs about the relationship between prediction and control.

Most of us invest in efforts to predict the future because of the belief that, to the extent we can predict the future, we can control it. Expert entrepreneurs turn this maxim on its head to make the point that, to the extent you can control the future, you do not need to predict it.

So, the interesting question for the study of entrepreneurial expertise becomes how do you control a future you cannot predict? To put it another way, how do you make decisions without using predictive information?

8.4.1 Three types of uncertainty

It is interesting to note, as early as 1921, the renowned economist Frank Knight had argued that the unpredictability of the future was at the heart of entrepreneurship. In his doctoral thesis, entitled 'Risk, uncertainty and profit', he distinguished between three kinds of uncertainty:

- a known distribution with an unknown draw
- an unknown distribution with an unknown draw
- an unknowable distribution.

To develop a mental model of these three kinds of uncertainty, imagine three urns from which you are allowed to draw objects one at a time. The first contains 50 red balls and 50 green balls, the second contains an unknown number of different-coloured balls and the third contains all kinds of random objects, some of which may or may not be balls. Next, imagine that you are asked to guess the object and its colour as it is drawn. You can quickly see that the first one is the easiest to tackle, the second one could be tackled if you were allowed to make repeated draws, returning the balls back to the urn after each draw, and the third one is impossible, even if you keep drawing and returning the items.

It is this third kind of unpredictability that expert entrepreneurs seem to have learned how to tackle. Through their experience, they have learned a variety of techniques that do not involve prediction. Simply put, in the third kind of uncertainty, since it is impossible to *predict* the future, expert entrepreneurs have figured out ways to *create* it from readily available means at hand – or, more accurately, *co-create* it with other people, each of whom dips into their respective set of readily available means to draw out and invest only what he or she can afford to lose.

In the following sections, we will look at each of the five principles that constitute this co-creation process. You will see that each implements control without the use of prediction.

8.5 The five principles of effectuation

The customary way to think about the entrepreneurial process is as follows. The entrepreneur spots or discovers a great opportunity – maybe a new product or service that addresses a gap in the marketplace or the application of a new technology to solve a problem cheaper, faster or more efficiently. Then he or she sets out to prove this concept by doing extensive market research, including competitive analysis, that leads to the choice of target market and positioning strategies. Thereafter, the entrepreneur calculates estimated revenues, costs and margins that are fed into financial models to be encapsulated in a business plan. The plan is pitched to potential investors before or after putting together a dream team, proceeding to execution once funded.

As is obvious here, each step calls for the best efforts of the entrepreneur to try and predict possible future scenarios, then pick from among them based on risk-adjusted expected return. To paraphrase Canada's hero Wayne Gretzky's famous words, it's about skating to where the puck *will* be, rather than where it currently is.

8.5.1 The bird-in-the-hand principle

Effectual entrepreneurs invert the above logic every step of the way.

Instead of beginning with some vision of a great opportunity, they simply begin with their own means – who they are, what they know and whom they know. They may or may not be trying to bridge a big gap in the market or even trying to do something entirely new. They may start with something mundane, but something they can do with what they already have and that they find worth doing for some reason of their own. The venture could be yet another restaurant or a piece of software or a service that they find they can provide in their local community. It is not that they *cannot* start with the vision of a great opportunity or an acute market need, it is just that they do not *have to*.

The history of entrepreneurship is filled with stories of companies that started with rather mundane ideas. Think about Google – the sixty-fifth search engine – or Sears. A train conductor found himself with a consignment of watches that the person who ordered them did not want and so he began selling the watches up and down his railway route. Then there is the Institute for One World Health that turns unused pharmaceuticals, such as those with expired patents and R&D products cancelled due to lack of profitable markets, into healthcare for the poor. What about companies such as Freitag bags and Agilyx that transform waste into saleable products.

Each of the entrepreneurs who founded these ventures began with means readily available to them – things already within their control. They did what they knew and worked with people they knew to create valuable new products, services, business models and even new markets. Their market research consisted of actually building the product and/or selling it even before they had the product made. They did not wait to find funding before they built the venture. Instead, the actual building of the venture led them to fertile funding sources that often came to them uninvited.

In fact, effectual entrepreneurs are focused on doing the doable. They are more concerned with what they *can* do than with what they *ought* to do. They begin by asking themselves, 'What can I do with what I have?' and then again, 'What else can

I do with what I have?' By starting with means already within your control, you are freed from the necessity of coming up with a brilliant idea, as well as the need to find funding. You can get started right away. You don't even have to leave your job to it. Highly profitable companies such as eBay were started by people who did not quit their full-time jobs until their ventures had grown to the point where they could not deny their compelling potential.

8.5.2 The affordable loss principle

So, let us say you begin with who you are, what you know and whom you know and then come up with things you can do – ventures you can build with what you already have. How do you then decide which one of those ventures to actually build?

The conventional answer to this question, of course, is to pick the venture with the best expected return. You try to size the market in terms of revenue and profit potential after accounting for possible risks, including competitive threats – maybe even predict future cash flows and calculate their net present value.

Effectual entrepreneurs do not spend much time trying to do that. Instead they think through the downside potential and ask themselves whether or not they can live with that and if they would want to do the venture even if their investments may be lost. In other words expert entrepreneurs invest only what they can afford to lose.

What a person can afford to lose is a very subjective calculation and does not call for much predictive information about things outside the person's control. Affordable loss calculations include things like how much time, effort and money am I willing to spend on building this venture? Would I do this venture even if I could lose everything I put into it? Note that it is not about trying to estimate how much money or other resources will be required to build this venture. It is, rather, about asking how much can I *afford* to lose and how much am I *willing* to lose, both of which are dependent on things within your control.

What difference does it make whether we use *affordable loss* or *expected return* as our criteria for choosing between different ventures that we can start? Besides the fact that we are not trying to predict the future nor make decisions involving things outside our control, the affordable loss principle does two important things:

- it allows us to get started immediately without waiting for investments or the perfect timing for the venture
- it forces us to think through non-economic benefits as a key driver of our choice of venture.

The canonical example of the application of the affordable loss principle lies in what is usually called the 'plunge' decision – namely, the decision of an employed person to leave his or her job to start a venture. The usual way to model that decision is in terms of a comparative analysis between the net present value of expected earnings as an entrepreneur and the opportunity cost consisting in the net present value of the earnings from the current job that the entrepreneur is considering quitting. When people use the affordable loss principle to make this decision, however, the choice need not be either/or. They can simply choose to work nights and weekends or take a leave of absence or resign with the determination to get back into the job market after a specific period of time, such as six months or a year if things don't work out. In this case, they are precommitting to the level of loss they are willing to absorb. The plunge decision here is no longer a 'plunge' at all.

As mentioned in the previous section, eBay was started by people who initially kept their day jobs. Let us consider another company in more detail here – the founding of waste management giant Browning Ferris (BFI).

The founder, Tom Fatjo, was an accountant working for a prestigious accounting firm and living in a well-to-do suburb of Houston. At several homeowners' meetings, the troubles with the collection of waste in the development kept coming up, until Fatjo decided to buy a truck and pick up his neighbours' rubbish himself. He did not leave his accounting job until a year later – he simply woke up very early every morning to collect the rubbish, returned home to take a shower and then went off to work.

During that first year, Fatjo learned everything about the waste management business from the ground up. At the end of that year there came a day when his opportunity cost of *not* starting the waste venture appeared to have exceeded any value he could derive from his white-collar accounting job.

Fatjo and other expert entrepreneurs – e.g., Greg Gianforte who founded Rightnow Technologies with a capital outlay of $5000 and grew it to a $30 million business within five years – have, through their experiences, become evangelists for bootstrapping as the primary funding strategy for starting new ventures. Affordable loss is an important enhancement of the notion of bootstrapping.

Examples of the affordable loss principle abound in the history of actual entrepreneurs and their ventures. When Richard Branson decided to start Virgin Atlantic, he did not leverage his assets in Virgin Records to buy a fleet of planes. Instead, he negotiated with Boeing to lease a used plane that he would return in a year if his new airline venture did not take off. Phil Knight was selling shoes out of the boot of his car in the early stages of building Nike. Such stories are endless.

Consider that about two-thirds of the founders of Inc. 500 list of companies never took money from outside investors. Consider also that about three-quarters of all IPOs in the USA did not take money from venture capitalists. So, how did these entrepreneurs fund their ventures?

Part of the answer to the above question lies in the bird-in-the-hand principle – i.e., they only used what was readily available to them, things within their control. Another part lies in the crazy quilt principle that we will examine next.

8.5.3 The crazy quilt principle

Understanding the market is considered key to every good business plan. It is customary for investors or other people assessing a business plan to ask questions such as, 'Who are your likely customers? Who are your likely competitors? How will you sell to your potential customers – what channels will you use? How will you price your product, especially relative to your competition? What differentiates you from your competitors? How are they likely to react to your entry into the market and how will you respond to their reactions?'

Note that, for the most part, all these questions assume the market is an external force to be mapped out and, hopefully, conquered. It is something 'out there' – a space in which you need to position your product or an arena in which you have to wrestle your competition to the ground. To tackle the enemy and gain your ground, you need to be able to strategise ahead of time – anticipate competitors' moves, predict inevitable trends and, as a back-up plan, be nimble and ready to move quickly as changes in the marketplace happen.

Expert entrepreneurs have acquired a very different view of the market. First of all, they shy away from the notion of *the* market. Instead, they begin to imagine ways to *make* a market – *any* market – by allowing a variety of stakeholders to *self-select into* the venture-building process. We will look at this process of self-selection in more detail in Section 8.6. For now, let us examine the contrast between taking 'the market' as given or latent in some way exogenous to the entrepreneurs' actions and the notion of *making* a market through stakeholder partnerships.

Remember that effectual entrepreneurs do not tie themselves to a predetermined vision of an opportunity – be it their own or something derived from market research. Since they simply begin with their means and do the doable, they do not know which particular market or markets they will end up in or end up creating. Since they do not know for sure which market they will be in, it does not make sense to invest too much time and energy in doing elaborate and formal market research such as surveys, nor does it make sense for them to undertake in-depth competitive analyses. Instead, they focus on forging as many partnerships as possible. Depending on who comes on board and what they commit to the venture, the growing network of partnerships determines which markets they end up in or end up creating – or not. Put simply, in the case of the effectual entrepreneur, preset goals or visions do not determine which stakeholder to pursue. Instead, whoever comes on board helps shape the opportunity and, together, they co-create the venture and maybe even new markets for that venture.

Take the case of Virgin Atlantic, mentioned in the previous section. It seems odd that a company which started as a record shop and grew into a recording studio with its own labels would start an airline. Yet, as Richard Branson explained to the BBC, it was a deal with Boeing that made it happen.

As is usual with most accomplished entrepreneurs, Branson saw and imagined opportunities everywhere. One of his ideas was to build a more efficient airline, so he called up Boeing and asked them to lease him a used airplane for a year in order that he could try his idea out. Boeing had never heard of him, but decided to make the deal for reasons of their own. Note here that this deal was an 'affordable loss' for both parties. If Branson did not do well, Boeing would get their airplane back and would have been compensated for the year's wear and tear. Branson also would have lost nothing more than the lease money and some other variable expenses that he could afford since Virgin Records was doing very well at the time. In fact, if he had wanted to really back up his vision, Branson could very well have leveraged his assets and experience from the record company to buy a small fleet of airplanes straight away. Branson has such a reputation for risktaking, it comes as a surprise that he would take the trouble to wrangle with Boeing for a used plane to get Virgin Atlantic off the ground, yet the stories of such 'deals' appear everywhere in the histories of innovative and enduring firms.

Here is another story – about Ted Turner, founder of CNN. One version of how he got started in the television industry – the one told by one of his biographers, Christian

Williams – suggests that Turner took a great risk by buying a rather run-down television station called WJRJ in Atlanta in 1969. As Malcolm Gladwell (2010) points out, however, 'Williams writes that Turner "was attracted to the risk" of the deal, but it seems just as plausible to say that he was attracted by the deal's lack of risk.' The price was really low precisely because of the run-down condition of the channel, but Turner did not pay even that. Instead, he made a stock swap that did not require him to put *anything* down and, at the same time, it also allowed him to get a tax break from its losses to offset the profits from his existing billboard business. Furthermore, the deal allowed him to use the slack from his billboard business (billboards lay blank about 15 per cent of the time anyway) to advertise his new television channel. Also, since he was already in the ad business, he knew how to drum up ads for his new channel as well. You can see from this example how bird-in-the-hand, affordable loss and crazy quilt dealmaking can be used together to create a rather mundane, but flourishing new business that can then be leveraged into something as spectacular and enduring as CNN.

8.5.4 The lemonade principle

'When life gives you lemons, make lemonade' is an American saying that signifies the possibility of surprises, even bad surprises, being transformed into better things with the right approach. Entrepreneurs who choose to follow the effectual method are likely to encounter surprises, even seek them out. In any case, they have to learn to include contingencies as inputs into their means set as they build their new ventures.

The normal course that is urged by conventional wisdom to most educated individuals, including potential entrepreneurs, is to carefully select clear goals, make detailed plans, use proven techniques to achieve those goals and then seek to avoid surprises which might upset those plans.

When you start with flexible goals and are focused on doing the doable, contingencies become resources to be leveraged rather than distractions to be avoided. On the flipside of this argument, consider the fact that contingencies occur even when there are well thought out plans in place. By having an open attitude of welcome rather than a defensive stance of avoidance, you can see new positive possibilities in most contingencies, including negative ones – possibilities that you are likely to miss if you have the attitude that all unanticipated occurrences are distractions from your chosen path.

Take the case of Steve Marriotti, a New York entrepreneur who was assaulted and mugged by youths in a poor neighborhood. Not surprisingly, the incident traumatised Marriotti, yet his response to the event was transformative – not only for him personally but also for inner-city youth everywhere, even outside the USA.

Marriotti decided to seek therapy for his trauma by becoming a substitute teacher in an inner-city school. After trying conventional teaching methods that failed to make a dent in the chaos in his classroom, he began telling his students about starting and running a business. The students responded with surprising gusto and Marriotti realised that entrepreneurship could be a way to teach not only business skills but also other important subjects, such as mathematics, science and even civic and social studies. That insight became the basis of a venture that has helped over 350,000 students from low-income communities across the USA and around the world.

If stories of successful ventures often seem serendipitous, it is because they are. However, it is not the unanticipated contingencies themselves that make those successes happen – it is how the entrepreneurs to whom they happen react to those contingencies. The ones who see surprises as distractions to be avoided or obstacles to be overcome miss out on the opportunities they can engender if they approached those surprises as resources or inputs to be leveraged and transformed into new sources of value in the evolving venture. In other words, if you have ever wondered whether entrepreneurial success is a matter of luck or skill, consider this. Good and bad luck happens to everyone, even if it is in differing ways at different times. So, good luck is always good to have on one's side and may, indeed, explain some of the entrepreneurial successes we see in the world, but skills matter more, especially the skill to transform luck into something useful and valuable. Given the same luck, good or bad, some people learn to transform it into resources or at least into a learning experience that helps strengthen their relationships with others, while others simply quit. Certain types of luck might be entirely outside of your control, but how you respond to the unexpected is always within your control – and with the help of strong stakeholder relationships, you should be able to transform even failures into eventual achievements of some value.

8.5.5 The pilot in the plane principle

An active and optimistic entrepreneur is required for surprises to be seized upon and molded into opportunities. So it is for each of the effectual principles to be put to work in the creation of new ventures and markets. Effectuation, however, puts human action front and centre in the entrepreneurial process in a more important way. Effectuators see human beings not as small cogs in the large machine of socio-economic evolution, but, rather, as prime movers capable of consciously co-creating their future, grappling with choices at more macro levels – choices involving complex collaborations with multiple stakeholders.

Effectuators do not, therefore, take any trend as inevitable or entirely outside the control of human endeavour. Yet, their stance is not one of social engineering. They do not seek to rebuild systems wholesale from scratch. They are not utopians seeking the best of all possible worlds. Instead, they have no problem striving for stable partial orders that can be rearranged and transformed periodically into better configurations – 'better' being defined and arrived at through the very process of reconfiguration.

Consider, for example, the problem of climate change. One answer for it is to encourage individual genius in the invention of renewable energy sources and solutions. Another is collective action at the level of the government or international NGOs.

The effectual entrepreneurs' answer is to bring together inventors and other stake-holders (perhaps including regulators and social movements) to create ventures that can commercialise and broadly disseminate new products and services using renewable energy, preferably in ways that make the ventures financially as well as environmentally sustainable. Of course, not all of these will succeed, but, together, a variety of successful and failed attempts will lead to better answers, especially if the failures can be kept small and young and successes can be cumulated and enlarged through stakeholder affiliations.

Effectuators realise that, on the one hand, invention and individual genius, while necessary, are far from sufficient to solve problems such as climate change. On the other hand, they also realise that it is neither necessary to wait for the lumbering machinery of governmental regulation, nor is it desirable, in most cases, to bring to bear such a behemoth on tasks better left to the nimbler and more creative coordination of the entrepreneurial process.

8.6 The dynamics of effectuation in the start-up process

To recap, effectual entrepreneurs start with who they are, what they know and whom they know and begin doing the doable. They invest only what they can afford to lose and choose those projects that are worth doing even in the worst case scenario. These effectual entrepreneurs are not afraid of unexpected contingencies. In fact, they embrace surprises as useful inputs to be transformed into new sources of value for themselves and their stakeholders and, hopefully, for the societies they live in. Also, since they do not believe in inevitable trends, they seek to co-create the future with stakeholders who self-select themselves into the entrepreneurial process.

The dynamics of such stakeholder self-selection may be worth some special attention. At their core, these dynamics raise issues such as which stakeholders should be approached? Which should be accepted or rejected or actively pursued? How should deals be structured, in terms of reshaping the vision and goals, while executing previous goals and allowing for equitable participation in outcomes?

Effectual entrepreneurs begin with the people they know. They ask open-ended questions with a view to obtaining advice and emotional participation rather than target-specific stakeholders for specific resources. Practical wisdom from experienced entrepreneurs suggests that you are more likely to get money when you ask for advice than get good advice or anything at all when targeting investment. Effectual entrepreneurs talk about their ventures to people they know and also to people they happen to meet serendipitously – at airports and networking events, for example.

Whether approaching someone strategically with a view to obtaining particular resources or effectually with a view to offering them an opportunity to self-select, almost always, these interactions with other people will lead to suggestions to change the product features or aspects of the business model that you are engaged in building. What do you do when a potential stakeholder asks you to change something in your venture?

Figure 8.1 organises your possible responses to this question along the two dimensions of prediction and control, which research has shown to be at the core of entrepreneurial expertise.

If you believe in your ability to predict the future as well as control it, you would be a *visionary entrepreneur*, someone who is unwilling to change his or her vision based on inputs from others. Your only option, then, is to persist with your own vision until you find those who think and believe like you and are willing to follow your vision.

Expert entrepreneurs do learn persistence in the face of negative feedback, but the persistence here is not tied to their preset goals or personal vision. Rather it is simply to keep at the process until the vision comes together through execution and

Figure 8.1 What to do in the face of an uncertain future

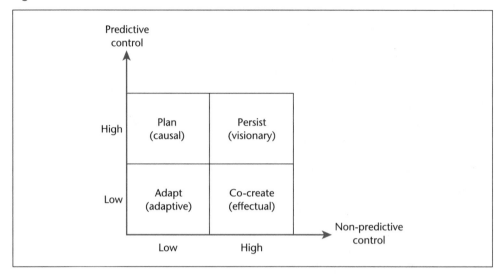

co-creation with others. So, the effectual entrepreneur is visionary in a very different way from the visionary entrepreneur. Effectual entrepreneurs are good at synthesising their visions through the process, rather than setting out with a clear vision that they hold on to at any cost.

An alternative to the visionary entrepreneur is the *adaptive one*, someone who quickly seizes and acts upon the advice of potential stakeholders. Adaptive entrepreneurs believe neither in the predictability nor in the controllability of the future – they simply seek to keep pace with changes and make the most of the opportunities that come their way.

Again, expert entrepreneurs do learn to be nimble and adaptive when necessary, but their preference is to be more proactive than adaptive. They believe they can not only adapt to the environment but also shape it and transform it in ways that matter to themselves and to their self-selected stakeholders.

A third alternative to visionary and adaptive approaches to stakeholder acquisition consists in analysis and planning – a more causal than an effectual approach. The *causal entrepreneur* seeks to map out the entire landscape as clearly as possible based on specific goals that he or she has set. Since such entrepreneurs have a clear vision, but do not believe they have control over the elements required to achieve their vision, they seek to find the best possible fit with the market environment through strategically important stakeholders, pursuing them in a systematic fashion. Whether they are engaged in identifying the best customers to target or the most accomplished employees to hire or the richest investors to woo, they seek to analyse multiple alternatives and find the optimal.

This approach is one that expert entrepreneurs eschew the most for they have learned through experience that the future is not predictable and/or, to the extent it is, it may be better left to established organisations to tackle. The start-up entrepreneur, they have learned, is better off treating the future as unpredictable.

145

Yet, the unpredictability of the future is not cause to give up on the possibility of control – whether over one's own outcomes or even in terms of shaping and creating it, especially when there are others who are willing to come on board with actual commitments that help create it.

Effectual entrepreneurs continually work with things within their control and seek to work with stakeholders who are willing to do the same. The touchstone for their stakeholder choice is 'actual commitment' – not predicted or promised commitments. Effectual entrepreneurs are open to letting stakeholders shape the vision and strategies of the venture *to the extent of the actual commitment each stakeholder makes.* For example, if a stakeholder is willing to underwrite a prototype, they will make the prototype the stakeholder wants, even if that may be somewhat different from their own original vision of the product. If the stakeholder is only willing to call a couple of important potential customers (and not actually underwrite the prototype), then the effectual entrepreneur will co-create the pitch with them and move towards the prototype only after one of the potential customers actually underwrites it.

Effectual entrepreneurs approach potential stakeholders not only with an open mind regarding the *extent* of their commitment but also the *type* of commitment and *role* they might want to play. In other words, you might approach someone thinking he or she might be a potential customer, but you want to talk to them in such a way that if they have the unanticipated potential to be an investor or a supplier or even an employee or lobbyist for you, they would be able to offer on their own. Hence, effectuators advocate a more open-ended approach, seeking advice and psychological or emotional ownership in shaping the venture and its future rather than a well thought out specific pitch requesting particular resources and inputs. The latter is useful only after stakeholders have agreed to make a commitment. Even then, negotiating and co-constructing the terms of the deal within certain preset bounds may be preferable to rigid pitches for specific terms conjured up ahead of time.

It is in exchange for the shaping and co-creation of the future that people make specific commitments to your venture. You allow them to shape and co-create only to the extent that they commit. For a visual illustration of this iterative stakeholder self-selection process, let us go to Figure 8.2. Here we can see that every effectual commitment results in new resources becoming available to the venture, even as new constraints begin to accumulate on the vision and structure of the artefacts being created through the deal – be they products, business models, ventures or markets. In other words, the set of means increases to include the identities, reputations, preferences, abilities, knowledge and networks of the entire group of committed stakeholders at any given point in time. Concurrently, the opportunity, the business model and even elements of the market begin to solidify through particular commitments – in particular, deals that are struck with each self-selected stakeholder.

Eventually, through several iterations of these interactions between the original founder(s) and the evolving network of stakeholders, the effectual process converges into new ventures and sometimes even into new markets. If for some reason the process aborts or fails to converge, any losses that occur are kept to a minimum because they are spread over several stakeholders, each of whom invests only what he or she can afford to lose.

Figure 8.2 Iterative dynamics of self-selected stakeholders in the effectual process

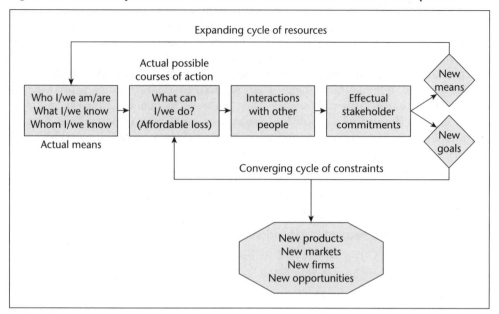

Examining Figure 8.2 closely and working your way through it carefully, you can see very clearly at least two logical consequences of effectuation for new venture performance:

1 the effectual process is likely to lead to a novel outcome

2 the effectual process is likely to reduce the *costs* of failure of the new venture, irrespective of the probability of failure.

Next, we will examine these and other implications for performance in more detail.

8.7 The implications of effectuation for the performance of firm and entrepreneur

It is easy to confuse the success or failure of the venture with the success or failure of the entrepreneur. Even if we limit ourselves to the performance of the venture, it is not easy to define success or failure in the entrepreneurial setting. For example, if a venture returns about 15 per cent on its investment year after year, but is never able to recover the actual investment itself, is it a success or a failure? What if a venture has enough fixed assets on its balance sheet to equal its original investment and has earned its founders enough of a return so they earn approximately the same as their market value in terms of level of pay (including retirement benefits), but it cannot really be sold to someone else and is simply closed on the founder(s) retirement?

As we imagine different scenarios under which ventures may exit or close down, we see that success and failure, even at the venture level, cannot clearly be defined through any one construct or measure. Now, if we begin thinking about the success or failure of an *entrepreneur*, who may start more than one venture during a lifetime, performance gets really complicated and difficult to define.

So, in developing the implications of an effectual process for performance, we have to proceed in hierarchical stages. First, we need to separate the performance of a *venture* from that of an *entrepreneur*. Then we need to define venture success and failure not as a simple 0–1 variable but, rather, as a continuum of possibilities ranging from bankruptcy (involuntary closure with money owed to creditors) to an IPO that endures over decades.

Here is a comprehensive, but perhaps incomplete, list:

- involuntary closure with money owed to creditors (bankruptcy)
- voluntary closure with no debts on the books
- business left to the heirs of the founders
- sale of assets
- sale of the company at a market value higher than the value of its assets
- sale of shares through merger
- sale of shares through a private placement
- initial public offering
- sale or bequeathal of founders' shares after decades of being a public company.

As mentioned in the previous section, bankruptcy is an unlikely outcome when you use the effectual process, as each person in the process invests only what he or she can afford to lose. However, when the venture has been built and established and becomes a larger organisation that calls for more of a mixture of causal and effectual processes, it is possible the venture may take on debt or expand in ways that negatively impact its cashflows, to the extent it might have to declare bankruptcy. When we limit our analysis to the start-up phase, however – say, to the first five years or so of an effectual venture – bankruptcy is a highly unlikely outcome.

Effectuation generally limits the downside, but what about the upside? Are effectual entrepreneurs more likely to build larger and/or more enduring ventures than the other kinds of entrepreneurs?

The implications for this side of the performance spectrum are not as clear. The upside potential of the effectual process may vary depending on at least the following:

- the entrepreneurs' own aspirations
- how these aspirations change as the entrepreneurs' ventures and careers evolve
- how these aspirations are impacted by the stakeholders that the entrepreneurs end up building the strongest relationships with
- the unpredictable events that come their way over time.

There are, however, at least two broad categories within which we can analyse that upside potential:

- the lifecycles of the firm(s) that the entrepreneurs build
- the portfolios of the firms they build over their careers.

Figure 8.2 lays out a framework for analysing these two categories.

We know from empirical facts that most large firms are more causal than effectual in the ways in which they form and implement strategies. We also know that when we look at the early histories of even large firms, we find that the process that led to them being founded was more effectual than causal. This suggests that most enduring firms are created through an effectual process and, somewhere over the course of their lifecycles, they start to become more causal and, by the time they come to our attention as very large public firms, they are mostly causal in the way they operate. Figure 8.3 captures this evolution in the bottom curve (shown as a dotted line).

Now, if we examine the careers of entrepreneurs, we find that novices may start anywhere on the causal–effectual spectrum. Some may have a natural tendency to use causal or effectual strategies. Others may simply be forced to effectuate due to lack of resources – or at least use some version of the bird-in-the-hand and affordable loss principles. In general, though, the more resources they have available to them at the beginning of their entrepreneurial careers, the more causal their strategies are likely to be. Irrespective of whether they started out causally or effectually, they are likely to move to the middle – i.e., begin using both causal and effectual logics as they build their second or third firms. However, if they continue building ventures and gathering entrepreneurial expertise, they become more and more likely to prefer effectual strategies in the early stages of their venture creation.

Figure 8.3 Implications of effectual logic for the performance of firms and entrepreneurs

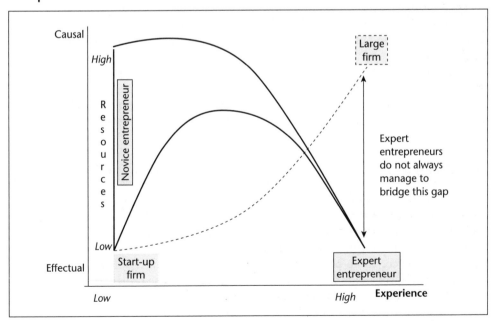

Remember that when entrepreneurs build more than one firm, they are likely to encounter both successes and failures of various kinds. Assuming that they have not taken courses in effectual entrepreneurship – i.e., when they learn from experience alone – each venture they start and the experiences they encounter through those venture-creation processes teaches them the uses and misuses of different kinds of logic in making particular decisions. So, entrepreneurs might be forced to bootstrap their first venture and bring in key stakeholders in return for resources to grow the company. After their first successful exit, they might reason that they now know the 'right' way to start a successful venture and therefore decide to do it 'their' way the next time around. This time, since they have more resources and, perhaps, the illusion that they know how to do it right, they might become causal – follow their vision, invest more than they might have done otherwise and not take on early partners, wanting to do it on their own. There is a good chance that they will fail this time around, irrespective of how they match causal and effectual strategies. It is then that they might begin thinking through the positive effects of investing only what they can afford to lose or bringing in partners early on.

If they survive their first failure and decide not to quit after that, entrepreneurs will be able to learn in more discerning ways from their next ventures than if they had only experienced success and no failures. Eventually, as they experience both successes *and* failures within their ventures, as well as through exits from ventures, they begin to see the merit of not only partnering, but partnering the crazy quilt way – namely, allowing stakeholders to self-select themselves into the process based on real commitments, even if that entails reshaping their own visions for the venture. In Figure 8.3, this learning process that occurs during the setting up of several firms is captured by the two upper curved lines, which converge to form the highly effectual entrepreneurship that we observe in experts who have started multiple ventures over long periods of time.

Note that not all experienced entrepreneurs manage to bridge the gap between the effectual needs of starting enduring firms and the causal needs of managing an established firm. Some simply sell the company after it grows to a certain extent and start more new ventures. Others may stay with the growing company but move out of the CEO position to new business development or internal corporate venturing or simply become chairman of the Board and play a strategic and advisory role. Very few entrepreneurs become the kind of expert entrepreneurs who were part of the in-depth study that led to the discovery of effectual logic – namely, ones who not only start but actually stay and manage several ventures, some of which grow into large firms.

8.8 Chapter summary

In sum, five principles of effectuation were extracted from a study of 27 expert entrepreneurs that required them to think aloud as they solved typical decisionmaking problems all entrepreneurs face while starting a new venture. The study was then replicated with novices and expert corporate managers who had little or no entrepreneurial experience. Some performance implications of a subset of the five principles were also tested using data from private equity investors. The principles were then also matched to techniques found in the early histories of a wide variety of enduring firms, across industries, geographies and time. The five principles are the following:

1 *bird-in-the-hand* use readily available means, such as who you are, what you know and whom you know

2 *affordable loss* invest only what you can afford to lose

3 *crazy quilt* create an expanding network of self-selected stakeholders

4 *lemonade* embrace and leverage surprises as new inputs into your venture

5 *pilot in the plane* co-create the future without worrying about predicting it.

Each of the five principles embodies a logic of non-predictive control. In general, efforts to predict the future are based on the logic that prediction leads to control. Effectual logic inverts this to show that control is achievable without the need to predict. Furthermore, as more stakeholders self-select themselves into the process, they bring new means to the venture, even as each invests only what he or she can afford to lose. Both the commitments and surprises that the effectual process engenders become new resources that can be leveraged to co-create the future. The new markets, new ventures, new products and new opportunities that may be co-created through the effectual process may not even have been envisioned by the self-selected stakeholders actively engaged in the process. As a result, not only does innovation become more probable but also the innovations resulting from the effectual process are more likely to be concurrently low-cost and valuable. Even when failure occurs in the effectual approach to venturebuilding, it is likely to be lower and happen earlier than in other approaches, since each stakeholder in the process invests only what he or she can afford to lose. Moreover, the effectual entrepreneur does not fail alone and so is more likely to get up and get going again after falling down.

So, what are you waiting for? Look around you for your means and get started doing the doable to build doorways your stakeholders can begin to walk through. Happy venturing!

Questions

1 Given that expert entrepreneurs prefer the use of effectual logic in building ventures, what is the role of business plans in the start-up process?

2 What is the difference between adapting to an environment and co-creating it?

3 What are three decisions that an entrepreneur might face in the start-up situation and how would an effectuator make those decisions?

4 What are the most difficult lessons for a novice entrepreneur to learn from effectuation? Why? How can they overcome the difficulties in learning those lessons?

Weblinks

http://effectuation.org
This website gives additional information and references regarding Sarasvathy's effectuation theory.

CHAPTER 9

The psychology of the entrepreneur

Frédéric Delmar and Frédérik C. Witte

9.1 Introduction

It is often believed that entrepreneurs are psychologically different from ordinary people. In this chapter, we review the research on the psychology of the entrepreneur to examine the validity of this belief.

We start by explaining what the kinds of problems that can be addressed by a psychological perspective on entrepreneurship. Next, we describe the historical development of this field, concentrating on different problems and criticisms related to the subject. Thereafter, entrepreneurial traits are reviewed, such as the need for achievement, locus of control and risk-taking propensity. The chapter then continues with an overview of current research into entrepreneurial behaviour, with a focus on cognitive (how people process information) models, which have the ability to address individual differences in entrepreneurial behaviour and performance. This chapter also addresses the training and education of potential entrepreneurs.

9.2 Learning objectives

There are four learning objectives in this chapter:

1 to understand how entrepreneurship can be promoted from a psychological perspective
2 to explore the historical development of the field
3 to understand the strengths and limits of cognitive models
4 to learn how to understand the challenges of developing knowledge about the psychology of entrepreneurs.

Key concepts

■ personality characteristics   ■ proximal and distal processes   ■ cognition
■ motivation   ■ entrepreneurial behaviour

9.3 The challenges of a psychological approach

Figure 9.1 shows the challenges we face when we try to explain why some people, such as Richard Branson or Coco Chanel, tend to excel as entrepreneurs. We here chose throwing darts to illustrate how you can understand differences in human behaviour and performance. Not everyone plays darts and those who do differ in how well they play. It is the same for entrepreneurship. Not everyone recognises a good opportunity, even fewer engage in entrepreneurship and only small minority of them excel at this task, but the outcome is not random.

From a psychological point of view, differences in behaviour and performance in tasks such as darts and entrepreneurship have two sources of explanation:

- individual differences
- contextual differences.

A key challenge for people interested in understanding psychological differences in entrepreneurship is to find out how these two sources affect the entrepreneurial process and what their respective weights are.

When we consider individual differences, we are likely to think that some people have a psychological make-up that makes them more suited to dealing with certain tasks than others. For example, some people are more talented dart throwers, chess

Figure 9.1 **Three stages of entrepreneurship and two sources of exploitation**

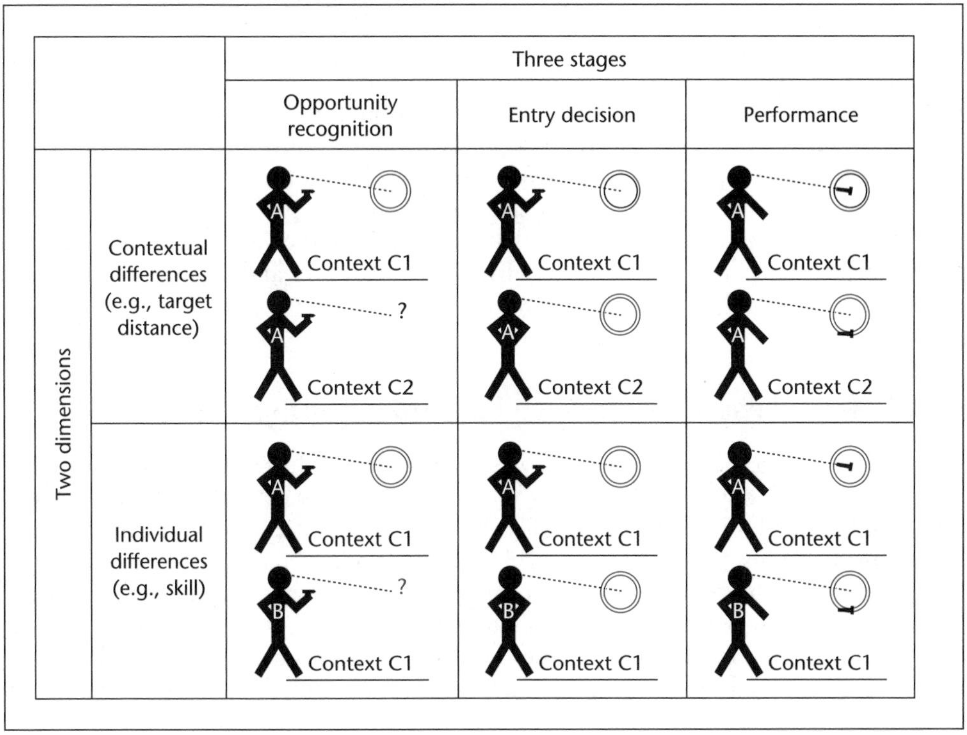

153

players or violin players than others, despite having received the same training and practice as others. Here differences can be attributed to individual characteristics such as skills or personality. They can be innate or learned differences.

When we consider contextual differences, we will probably think that people perform better at certain tasks because they have been exposed to situations fostering such behaviour. For example, it is difficult to become a good skier if you have never had access to snow and mountains. Hence, one would expect people living in the Alps to be better skiers than people living in the UK or the Netherlands. Equally, you would expect someone who has a dart board and darts at home and plays regularly to throw better than somebody who doesn't have these facilities and doesn't play on a regular basis. Here, access to reinforcing or shaping behaviour is central.

Now, you will probably recognise that entrepreneurship is a little bit more complex than throwing darts, so trying to find explanations as to why some of us behave entrepreneurially and excel in it is also a little more complex because we are looking at a social process. Moreover, it is not obvious if and how entrepreneurship can be attributed to innate or learned differences, exposure to specific situations or a combination of them. However, the quest is the same: is it individual differences or contextual differences that lead people to engage and excel in entrepreneurship or a mix of the two? This chapter is our introduction to how the knowledge we have about the psychology of entrepreneurs has developed.

We see entrepreneurs as decisionmakers who actively change their environment (McClelland, 1961; Frese, 2007). From a psychological perspective, entrepreneurial actions are determined by the individual's background, environment, goals, values and motivations. Entrepreneurial ventures are made of men and women and there is a need to understand how they behave.

Gaining knowledge about entrepreneurial behaviour is essential, because it often represents the only available source of information for various stakeholders. For instance, early stage investors have to decide whether or not to invest based on entrepreneurs' past and expected future performance, which is a function of their entrepreneurial behaviour. To make well-informed decisions, those parties need to understand the characteristics of entrepreneurial behaviour and how they are related to entrepreneurial performance (Shepherd, 1999; Hisrich, Langan-Fox and Grant, 2007; Rauch and Frese, 2007).

9.4 Development of the research field: from traits to cognition

The field of entrepreneurial behaviour has seen several shifts in the last few decades, depending on the 'maturity' of the research questions. This section describes this evolution based on the four research questions shown in Figure 9.2. Hopefully, by studying these four questions, you will understand this evolution.

We show how the field has evolved from only examining personality traits to studying the interaction between the entrepreneur's perception, intention and ability, in combination with characteristics of the situation (Rauch and Frese, 2007). Research today focuses on malleable cognitive functions, instead of discussing sets of traits that never change (Busenitz, 2007).

Figure 9.2 The field of applied psychology in entrepreneurship

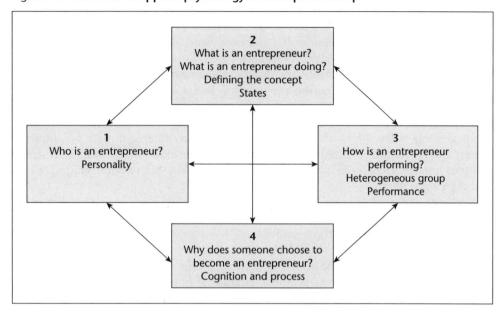

Figure 9.2 illustrates the complexity and inherent problems associated with the psychological perspective. The four boxes each contain a basic question related to the research field and are numbered from one to four. The numbers represent the approximate historical evolution of the field. In short, research started first by trying to find a personality profile for entrepreneurs and answer a question as old as entrepreneurship: are entrepreneurs born or made? It became clear that more conceptual work was needed to define who entrepreneurs are and what they do, hence the second box. This conceptual work increased awareness of how entrepreneurs act at different stages of the entrepreneurial process. Research then refocused to relate different personality traits to performance, so we have the question in the third box. However, traits theories delivered no viable explanations of entrepreneurial behaviour, so cognitive motivation models were adopted instead – shown in the fourth box. It is worth noting that current thinking assumes the boxes to be interrelated and one question cannot be answered without taking the other questions into consideration.

Early research attempted to identify a general personality profile for successful entrepreneurs. Research was based on the simplistic assumption that entrepreneurs belong to an homogenous group and possess distinctive characteristics. This research approach was designed to answer the question 'Who is an entrepreneur?' (in Box 1). Personality characteristics were examined mainly by concentrating on differences between entrepreneurs and other reference groups, such as managers or the general public (Low and MacMillan, 1988). An example is the study by Scheré (1982), who found that entrepreneurs were more tolerant of ambiguity than managers.

Researchers soon discovered that more conceptual work was needed to define entrepreneurial action. The basic realisation was that the category 'entrepreneur' could be associated with many different *states*, such as self-employment, being a small businessowner and manager, starting a business or expanding one. The assumption that these states were similar just did not hold. Two research questions guided this second approach to entrepreneurial personality and behaviour: 'What is an entrepreneur?' and 'What is the entrepreneur doing?' (in Box 2).

One of the first studies that distinguishes between discernable groups of entrepreneurs and extends the basic notion presented in Box 1 is the work by Smith (1967). He differentiated between groups of entrepreneurs and assumed that action and performance were affected by the entrepreneur's personality. However, it was not until the beginning of the 1990s that this thinking had considerable impact on empirical research. The models evolved from simple trait–state models (of Box 1) to more complex models that took into account the individual's behavioural characteristics and their state (Box 2).

Yet, both approaches relied on simple characteristics to explain and predict entrepreneurial actions. Researchers soon conceded the impossibility of characterising entrepreneurs using simple traits and states. Even controlling for one single state, variation in performance is important. As a result, research then focused on how individual differences could be linked to entrepreneurial performance (see Box 3).

This research created a primary understanding of how entrepreneurs become who they are and extended existing concepts to better educate potential entrepreneurs (for a detailed discussion of Box 3, see the next section on personality traits). Therefore, scholars developed more complex models, treated entrepreneurs as a heterogeneous group and tried to explain the actions of specific entrepreneurs. At the level of the firm, researchers examined the link between different personality characteristics of entrepreneurs and related contingency variables such as the firm's age, industry affiliation and organisational structure (Miller and Toulouse, 1986; Miller, 1987). This conceptual development led to a framework where entrepreneurs are active decisionmakers at different stages in the venture-creation process and thereby affect performance.

Today, the approach of uncovering stable traits to determine 'Who is an entrepreneur?' is again under consideration (Mitchell et al., 2002a). For a long time the personality traits approach was deemed infeasible, but more systematic research has emerged (Zhao and Seibert, 2006; Rauch and Frese, 2007).

Cognitive theories dominate current explanations of entrepreneurial behaviour (see Box 4). This completes the shift from searching for stable traits to the view of entrepreneurial behaviour as a process where each stage is characterised by its specific challenges (Baron and Markman, 2005; Johnson and Delmar, 2010). Box 4 describes the current dominant research approach, based on cognitive theories that make it possible to understand the interaction between contextual and behavioural characteristics. These models allow for a better explanation as to why some people are more likely to become entrepreneurs than others, which is because of greater sensitivity as a result of learned individual differences, greater exposure to entrepreneurship-friendly environments or a mix of both. Researchers are discovering more and more changeable cognitive processes that are involved in how entrepreneurs make decisions that lead to success (Haynie, Shepherd and Patzelt, 2011). Hence, it can be concluded that cognitive models have several advantages compared to previous trait-based models. For a detailed discussion of Box 4, see section 9.6.

9.4.1 Question 1 'Who is an entrepreneur?' and the personality traits approach

Now that you have reflected a bit on what is shown in Figure 9.1, you are likely to think that the success of various entrepreneurs can be explained as being a mix of both contextual and individual differences. However, had we asked you straight away why Bill Gates, Mark Zuckerberg or Anita Roddick (or her daughter, Sam Roddick) are successful entrepreneurs, you would likely have answered that it depended on their unique personality.

Students and practitioners often perceive the personality of the entrepreneur to be the most fascinating topic in the field of entrepreneurship because of a general tendency to explain the behaviour of others as being a consequence of their personalities rather than what the situation has to offer or down to pure chance. This bias is referred to as the 'fundamental attribution error' as personality traits can only explain a minor share of entrepreneurial behaviour and differences in business performance.

'Personality' is often loosely defined as a psychological system that mediates the relationship of the individual with the environment in terms of regularities in actions, feelings and thoughts (Snyder and Cantor, 1998; Caprara and Cervone, 2000). Research in entrepreneurship concentrated exclusively on personality traits for a long time, hoping to discover stable individual characteristics – *personality traits* – by relating a trait to the state of being an entrepreneur or the performance of the entrepreneurial venture. Traits are innate, so this would indicate that entrepreneurs are born, not made.

The underlying assumption was that there exists an individual trait, stable across situations and time, that determines the successful outcome of the entrepreneurial venture. The hope was to find an entrepreneurial personality profile so as to better understand which characteristics lead to success or failure. The promise it held was that then we would have an attractive explanation of direct practical relevance. For example, if a stable personality trait could be identified that had a direct relationship with successful entrepreneurial performance, investors could devise a selection instrument to identify 'success-type' entrepreneurs and limit their financial risk exposure (Shepherd, 1999). Furthermore, it would then be possible to encourage those with this 'success-type' personality and discourage those without it to engage in an entrepreneurial career. Psychology cannot offer (at the present time) such a test, but enterprises today are made of men and women and there is still a need to understand how they behave.

The disappointing results of the above approach can be explained by the theoretical as well as methodological problems characterising it (Sexton and Bowman, 1985; Gartner, 1989a; Carsrud and Johnson, 1989; Chell, Haworth and Brearley, 1991; Herron and Robinson, 1993; Delmar, 1996). The empirical search of trait research for the 'holy grail' of entrepreneurial personality stumbled upon several problems and we discuss six of these below. The inability to solve the problems has led researchers to abandon the traits approach in the field of entrepreneurial personality and behaviour until recently (Zhao and Seibert, 2006; Rauch and Frese, 2007; Shane, Nicolaou, Cherkas and Spector, 2010). They have developed more sophisticated models where cognition and motivation are given as the explanatory factors behind entrepreneurial behaviour instead of personality traits (Baum, Locke and Kirkpatrick, 1998; Baron, 2004; Baum and Locke, 2004).

Problem 1: Inconsistency and multiplicity of traits

The first problem with trait research is the inconsistency of trait definitions and their sheer abundance. Hornaday (1982) identified more than 40 traits associated with entrepreneurship – e.g., a need for achievement, internal locus of control, risktaking propensity, being overly optimistic and the need for autonomy (which we will review later on).

Based on the assumption that entrepreneurial traits are both time- and context-invariant, researchers did not reach consensus on the relevance, significance or malleability of individual characteristics. It was difficult to agree a common frame of reference because of the large number of characteristics and their corresponding inconsistencies.

Problem 2: Personality traits as distal factors

When modelling behaviour and subsequent performance, psychologists make a difference between distal and proximal factors influencing behaviour (Ackerman and Humphreys, 1990).

A *distal factor* can explain general behaviours (e.g., eating, sex drive and sleeping), but has little ability to explain how individuals act in a specific situation. For example, individuals have the need to accumulate money because they have to supply themselves with the means to survive.

However, the explanation that behaviour is driven by such needs will not explain why someone will prefer entrepreneurship instead of other alternatives. Actual entrepreneurial behaviour is better explained by *proximal factors* (i.e., task characteristics) than distal factors (i.e., traits and needs). We will come back to this issue several times during the course of this chapter.

Problem 3: The static nature of traits

Another problem is the static nature of entrepreneurial traits and characteristics. The assumption that they are static limits the explanatory force of entrepreneurial traits because entrepreneurs act in changing environments. A major problem is that the traits approach to entrepreneurial psychology has neglected the ties of behavioural actions to their particular contexts (Aldrich and Wiedenmayer, 1993). As a result, traits alone have little ability to explain entrepreneurial behaviour.

Problem 4: Obsolescence of theory

A methodological problem is the obsolescence of trait theories and methods compared to modern psychological research. The concept of personality is not one-dimensional (i.e., quantifiable by only one trait), but multidimensional. Psychologists now measure an individual's personality in five broad dimensions called the 'Big Five' (Hogan, 1991; Goldberg, 1993; Hogan, Hogan and Roberts, 1996). Hence, when measuring personality in an entrepreneurship context, the measures should include at least these five dimensions of personality evaluation.

The 'Big Five' dimensions are:

■ extraversion
■ emotional stability

- agreeableness
- conscientiousness
- openness to experience.

Indeed, more recent findings in entrepreneurship research show that entrepreneurs' conscientiousness is positively related to long-term venture survival (Judge and Bono, 2001; Ciavarella et al., 2004). The entrepreneur's openness is relatively associated to venture survival and the other three measures are not related. 'Venture survival' is operationally defined as the ability to maintain the venture's operations for a minimum of eight years. Zhao and Seibert (2006) found that entrepreneurs differ on four out the five personality dimensions. They are more conscious and open to experience, but less agreeable and neurotic.

Problem 5: Causality

When discussing the role of entrepreneurial characteristics the question of causality arises.

The fact that entrepreneurs exhibit certain characteristics does not necessarily mean that they had them from the very beginning. The characteristics might have developed as an outcome of being entrepreneurs rather than be the cause. Correlation does not mean causality. It is therefore difficult to clearly state whether the characteristics exhibited by entrepreneurs ex-post caused them to become or are the result of being an entrepreneur (Shane, 2000).

Problem 6: Cultural dependence

Another methodological problem relates to the cultural dependence of dominant research findings. Trait research is mainly based on US samples and is likely lacking predictive power for other cultures (Spence, 1985). It has been argued that many of the characteristics mentioned – especially 'need for achievement' – are culturally dependent. Research findings about entrepreneurs' attitudes in different countries give some support to this argument (Mitchell et al., 2002b). Indeed, the cultural dependence of current research designs distorts results, especially when theories based on US samples are translated to fit settings in Asian countries (Stimpson et al., 1990).

9.4.2 Question 2 'What is an entrepreneur?' – defining the concept

The entrepreneurial personality and behaviour field of research is an interdisciplinary one that incorporates relevant concepts from psychology into entrepreneurship. Due to its eclectic nature, entrepreneurship research experiences problems of consistency that arise when researchers translate concepts from one discipline to another. First and foremost of these is the lack of consistency for definitions and concepts.

Whilst defining entrepreneurship or entrepreneur is beyond the scope of this chapter, we want to stress the diversity of definitions and operationalisations and the lack of a general agreement about who is and who is not considered to be an entrepreneur.

The attempt of the personality traits approach to link the general state 'entrepreneur' to specific personality traits is problematic because it assumes that entrepreneurs are homogenous. This assumption does not hold. Current research has to assume heterogeneity and include the differences between various types of entrepreneurs and states of entrepreneurship in their theories. For example, an entrepreneur can be defined as someone who is self-employed, the owner-manager of a small business, starting a new venture or expanding one. These are very different states. Therefore, it is a serious flaw of research for it to not acknowledge that entrepreneurs have different goals for their entrepreneurial ventures and there exist important differences between the various states.

Research has become more aware of the problem of defining entrepreneurship and is paying more attention to existing conceptual problems. Especially challenging today is the conceptualisation of entrepreneurial behaviour at different stages during the entrepreneurial process – stages often identified as opportunity recognition, opportunity commitment or entry into entrepreneurship and the performance of the entrepreneurial venture (survival, growth and profits).

9.4.3 Question 3 'How is an entrepreneur performing?' – the heterogeneity of entrepreneurship

The previous two sections described the development of the field from a simple assumption that entrepreneurs are all alike (but different from other people) to a more complex picture where entrepreneurship can be studied at various stages of a firm's development and entrepreneurs are considered a heterogeneous group.

However, performances differ substantially over the entrepreneurial process and across contexts. Consequently, research has moved towards trying to explain the performance of the firm by examining the link between different personality characteristics of the entrepreneur and contingency variables, such as the age of the firm, industry affiliation and organisational structure (Miller and Toulouse, 1986; Miller, 1987).

Even if we assume that the models evolved from simple trait–states models (as described previously) to more complex models taking into account the characteristics of the firm as well as the characteristics of the entrepreneur, however, the results were still weak. Two main explanations of this phenomenon can be identified – namely, the definition of performance and the linking of personality characteristics, entrepreneurial behaviour and business performance. What is meant by entrepreneurial performance? Four different measures are most often associated with the concept of performance in entrepreneurship literature.

- getting start-ups off the ground – what factors influence the decision and the ability to achieve progress?
- survival of the firm – what factors influence the long-term survival of the firm?
- firm growth – what factors affect the expansion of the firm?
- firm profitability – what factors influence the firm's ability to generate profits?

These performance measures can be operationalised in a number of ways, thus adding to the confusion (Murphy, Trailer and Hill, 1996; Delmar, 1997). A stringent definition of entrepreneurial performance is necessary as research tries to link entrepreneurial behaviour and its origins to entrepreneurial performance. However, this is not the

160

main problem – researchers still need to link traits to behaviour and then link behaviour to business performance.

When modelling behaviour and subsequent performance, psychologists tend, as mentioned earlier, to differentiate between distal and proximal factors affecting behaviour (Ackerman and Humphreys, 1990). To recap, a distal factor is one that may explain general behaviours (e.g., eating, sex drive and sleeping), but which has little ability to explain how individuals act in a specific situation. For example, individuals have the need to eat and the explanation is that they have to refuel energy supplies in order to survive. However, the explanation that behaviour is driven by needs will not explain why someone might have a preference for eating a hamburger over an à la carte meal in a restaurant.

A proximal explanation looks at factors defining the situation in which individuals find themselves – in the above case, choosing somewhere to eat. For example, it may be Friday night, it's pay day and the person wants to impress someone. Therefore, this time, the fancy restaurant will be chosen instead of the hamburger option.

Behaviour is, then, better explained by proximal factors (task characteristics) than by distal factors (traits and needs). Traits are, in general, distal factors and they therefore have little ability to explain actual behaviour, even less business performance.

Furthermore, the entrepreneurial venture can be characterised as highly complex – i.e., the demands on an individual undertaking simple tasks, such as playing pinball, are very different from those of starting and maintaining a business. Campbell (1988) suggests that business venturing is an example of an activity with one of the highest degrees of complexity and such so-called 'fuzzy tasks' – characterised by the presence of both multiple desired end-states and multiple ways of attaining each of the desired outcomes – are also characterised by uncertainty and conflicting interdependence. In such a case, the relationship between behaviour and performance is weakened by the interactive effects that occur between motivational processes, cognitive abilities and environmental factors. Not acknowledging this lack of correspondence between behaviour and performance has serious consequences for understanding the effects of the former on the latter. For example, while motivation can yield high levels of cognitive effort, if misdirected, this will then lead to a failure in performance (Kanfer, 1991).

Research examining the different traits or other psychological factors characterising the entrepreneur needs to take into account the complexity of this situation. That is because traits theories are not sophisticated enough to account for the complexity of entrepreneurial behaviour. Therefore, research in this area has evolved towards more proximal explanations, entrepreneurial behaviour and business performance being explained by more proximal psychological theories and the effect of the situation is better controlled for.

9.4.4 Question 4, 'Why does someone choose to become an entrepreneur?' – cognition and process

As noted, the trait approach has yet to yield great insights. Trying to relate a trait to the state of being an entrepreneur or the performance of the firm is too simplistic. Entrepreneurs are not that different from people in general. However, this does not explain why certain individuals still choose to undertake an entrepreneurial career. It is probably simply the case that different people, depending on their previous experiences, perceive the same situation differently. Alternatively, people do not differ, but are subjected to situations where stimuli to start a business differ in strength. Simple trait theories cannot account for that and, thus, research is developing theories explaining how people perceive and understand the world, how it affects their behaviour and how entrepreneurial reinforcing situations affect us.

Theories that try to explain the behaviour of individuals who perceive and interpret the information around them in this way are called cognitive theories. Paralleling the development of social psychology, entrepreneurship research has moved from simple trait theories towards cognitive ones that are more able to explain the complexity inherent in entrepreneurial behaviour.

Cognitive theories assume that individuals possess limited knowledge of the world because there is simply too much information out there to handle. Consequently, we have to select information and interpret it, so, as this is based on our previous experiences, we each tend to see and know the world differently (Taylor, 1998). For example, one person sees a viable business opportunity, while another regards the same situation as an impossible problem. In short, individuals are actively involved in the construction of their own realities.

Cognitive theories enable a better understanding of why people engage in entrepreneurial behaviour. A basic argument is that the same situation is perceived differently by different people depending on their previous experiences (Shane, 2000; Baron and Ensley, 2006). The contribution these theories make to this field is the possibility of better understanding the interaction between the characteristics of the situation and characteristics of the entrepreneur. In other words, they have led to a movement away from studying the personality of the entrepreneur and towards studying the situations that lead to entrepreneurial behaviour (Carsrud and Johnson, 1989; Shaver and Scott, 1991; Baron, 1998; Baron, 2007; Busenitz, 2007; Rauch and Frese, 2007). Behaviour is heavily based on how we perceive the situation or the environment and how it is presented to us.

Because we lack perfect knowledge, we have limited attention, limited capacity to process all relevant information and we differ in terms of motivation (Mitchell et al., 2007), we see and interpret the world differently (Taylor, 1998). We select information and make sense of it – a process based on our previous experience. We are actively involved in the construction of our own realities (Alvarez and Barney, 2010).

Behaviour is the product of two psychological processes. The first process operates through the selection of environments and the second through the production of environments. When people have, over time, established certain preferences and standards of behaviour, they tend to choose activities and individuals who share the same set of preferences, thereby mutually reinforcing pre-existing personal inclinations and fixed courses of action (Bandura, 1982; Deci, 1992a, 1992b). More precisely, the individual characteristics leading to an entrepreneurial career are only activated when exposed to a favourable socialisation process where an entrepreneurial career is seen as a viable possibility among others. Thus, the social environment is of primary importance for fostering future entrepreneurs. In general, individual characteristics are precursor traits and, in the context of a given 'cafeteria of experiences', they help to determine how experiences are both weighted or attended to and how the individual reacts to them. That is, individuals only activate their entrepreneurial potential if they have:

■ a certain specific ability and sensitivity
■ environmental possibilities available
■ social support.

These three prerequisites must be fulfilled if someone is to take the actions required to become an entrepreneur. For example, there is consistent evidence that children of parents who are entrepreneurs are more likely to become entrepreneurs themselves. Thus, the social environment is of importance in fostering entrepreneurs (Lim, Morse, Mitchell and Seawright, 2010).

The relation between willingness to act in a certain direction, the current situation and experience form the basis for better understanding human and, of course, entrepreneurial behaviour (see Chapter 6 for further elaboration of the entrepreneurial process). The interaction between ability, environmental possibilities and social support likely leads to a positive reinforcing spiral – the entrepreneur finding support and, therefore, can further develop his or her abilities.

Two questions arise from this section and the previous one on the characteristics of the entrepreneurial situation.

■ How do people come to choose an entrepreneurial career?
■ What does the entrepreneur need to do in order to perform satisfactorily or successfully?

These are questions that cannot easily be answered without taking into account the complexity of human nature based on previous experience, abilities and intentions to act. The research field of entrepreneurial behaviour has, consequently, come to rely increasingly on complex cognitive models where process is central. Cognitive motivation models dominate, but also pure decision models, based on how experts think about entrepreneurship, have emerged. The idea behind the first group of models is to explain why people engage in entrepreneurship. The idea behind the latter group is to understand how successful entrepreneurs process information, create decision rules and develop new opportunities and expertise in exploiting them (Baron and Ensley, 2006; Gustafsson, 2006; Sarasvathy, 2001; Baron, 2010). The hope is to use this knowledge to train potential entrepreneurs to develop an entrepreneurial mindset and thereby increase their chance for success (Read, Sarasvathy, Dew and Wiltbank, 2011). This is an exciting development, because the use of more sophisticated psychological models enables the research to better integrate findings from other fields of entrepreneurship.

Motivation theories allow us to understand the choices made by entrepreneurs and why they persist in doing what they are doing. They are easy to use and have proven validity. Thus, we have reliable knowledge of what motivates entrepreneurs. However, it is still problematic to understand the link between the intention to do something and the actual behaviour because motivational theories tend to focus on volitional behaviour, but a large part of entrepreneurial behaviour is dependent on available resources, the co-operation of others and skill. The interaction between motivation and the development of cognitive abilities represents an important avenue for future entrepreneurship research (Ackerman, Kanfer and Goff, 1995; Ackerman and Heggestad, 1997; Sternberg, 2004). This interaction affects both creativity (Fong, 2006) and the development of new cognitive abilities, such as successful intelligence (Collins, Hanges and Locke, 2004).

9.4.5 Summarising the development of research in entrepreneurial behaviour

We have seen that this research area has been dominated by four different basic research questions.

- Who is an entrepreneur (personality)?
- What is an entrepreneur (states)?
- How is an entrepreneur performing (performance)?
- Why does someone choose to become an entrepreneur (cognition and process)?

We suggested that the elaborations on these four questions could explain the development of the research field from its start as a simple quest to try and link single traits to entrepreneurship to complex cognitive models taking into account the heterogeneity of entrepreneurial behaviour. In other words, the field has developed from examining personality traits in isolation to examining the interactions between the entrepreneur's perceptions, intentions, abilities and the characteristics of the situation. Thus, the research field in general does not offer an easy answer to the question 'Who is an entrepreneur?' Instead, it has evolved towards acknowledging that entrepreneurship is a process created by entrepreneurs in co-operation with others. In short, entrepreneurial behaviour should be regarded as the consequence of person–situation interactions.

9.5 Individual characteristics of entrepreneurs and entrepreneurial behaviour

Based on the historical development of the field, scholars developed complex models of entrepreneurial behaviour. Entrepreneurs are understood as a heterogeneous group and active decisionmakers at different stages in the venture-creation process. Today, researchers are especially interested in examining the link between different characteristics of entrepreneurs and venture performance. This section describes five characteristics or traits that affect entrepreneurial behaviour and performance:

- desire for autonomy
- risktaking propensity
- need for achievement
- over-optimism
- locus of control.

Desire for autonomy is consistently found to predict entrepreneurship entry (Rauch and Frese, 2007) and the other four concepts are closely related to entrepreneurial decisionmaking under risk and achievement and are central to entrepreneurship theory (Mellers, Schwartz and Cooke, 1998; Dew, Read, Sarasvathy and Wiltbank, 2009).

Following a discussion of these concepts, we will examine the darker sides of entrepreneurship, where entrepreneurship is not necessarily emerging from positive experiences.

9.5.1 Desire for autonomy

There are consistent findings in the field of entrepreneurial personality and behaviour that entrepreneurs have a high need for autonomy (Sexton and Bowman, 1985), as well as a fear of external control (Smith, 1967). Entrepreneurs value freedom and individualism more than their management peers. Individualism is defined as the possibility of making a difference for oneself. One study found that autonomy and freedom are the most important reasons for becoming an entrepreneur (Rindova, Barry and Ketchen, 2009). This correlation holds true even if those values imply some inequalities in society (McGrath, MacMillan and Scheinberg, 1992; Fagenson, 1993).

The desire to manage one's own business is a central feature of entrepreneurship and the driving force in the entrepreneurship entry decision. However, it is difficult to establish a clear causal order of desire and entry. Put differently, do individuals with a high desire for autonomy start a venture because they want autonomy or do they want autonomy because they do not want others to take control of what they have created? As the causal mechanism remains unclear, we can only conclude that desire for autonomy can result in venture creation but it can also be a result of having created a business.

9.5.2 Risktaking propensity

According to economic theory, entrepreneurship is a function by which growth is achieved (Stevenson and Jarillo, 1990). That is why economists usually focus on the results of entrepreneurial action. They see the entrepreneur primarily as a risktaker or riskbearer within the economic system (Knight, 1921; Buchanan and Di Pierro, 1980). Can we therefore assume that entrepreneurs take more risks than managers?

No, a number of studies have found consistent evidence that there are no significant differences between entrepreneurs and managers in terms of their risktaking propensity (Brockhaus Sr, 1980; Peacock, 1986; Bellu, 1988; Masters and Meier, 1988; Stewart Jr and Roth, 2001). However, this is still debated (Miner, Raju, Stewart and Roth, 2004).

Whilst many past studies assume that risk attitude is independent of the situation, it has been found that risktaking largely depends on two situational factors. First, is the individual's perception of the situation (Hogarth, 1987; Mellers, Schwartz and Cooke, 1998). Depending on how a situation is presented, we can either seek or avoid risk. Second, whether individuals perceive themselves as experts or not in the decision environment is important (Heath and Tversky, 1991; Shane, 2000; Smith, Mitchell and Mitchell, 2009). For instance, Heath and Tversky (1991) demonstrated that individuals take considerably more risks in situations in which they feel competent. Further, entrepreneurship studies have developed a good understanding of which factors influence the risktaking of entrepreneurs – e.g., the entrepreneur's age, motivation, business experience, tenure and education (Schwer and Yucelt, 1984).

Dickson and Giglierano (1986) proposed another perspective on entrepreneurial risktaking. They argued that the concept of risk can be divided into two separate components – namely, the likelihood of committing to a bad opportunity (and failing) and the likelihood of missing a good opportunity. The latter element is conceptually close to exploratory behaviour and the entrepreneur's search for new opportunities. According to this study, research has mainly focused on the likelihood of a new venture failing and not on the threat of missing an opportunity.

Organisation research shows that entrepreneurs are less inclined to identify threats than opportunities, compared to their management peers (Gregoire, Barr and Shepherd, 2010). However, it is not clear whether entrepreneurs judge the likelihood of missing out on a strategic opportunity higher than the likelihood of a new venture failing. Mullins and Forlani (2005) tested this hypothesis based on a sample of 75 CEOs from fast-growing public firms in the USA. They found that entrepreneurs overall preferred risk-averse choices. For example, when asked to choose between two ventures with different associated levels of risk, they preferred the venture with the lowest probability of incurring losses. Furthermore, the entrepreneurs in their sample would rather miss out on a strategic opportunity than jeopardise their existing ventures.

Research results on the risktaking propensity of entrepreneurs are mixed, but it is evident that the perceived context, in terms of knowledge and situational characteristics, is a more important determinant of risktaking than the personality characteristics (Rauch and Frese, 2007; Shane, 2000). For example, differences in risk perception affect the individual's opportunity evaluation and, thus, determine the entrepreneur's risktaking (Keh, Foo and Lim, 2002).

9.5.3 Need for achievement

One of the most popular characteristics associated with entrepreneurs is McClelland's need for achievement (1961, 1969). This concept is closely related to risktaking as it accounts for perceived risk of the situation, as well as the perceived level of competence. According to McClelland, entrepreneurs experience high need for achievement, making them especially suited to creating ventures. Collins, Hanges and Locke (2004) found evidence supporting this hypothesis.

In general, McClelland's theory illustrates that individuals high in need for achievement prefer situations stimulating their achievement motivation. Those situations are characterised by:

■ individual responsibility of the decisionmaker

■ moderate level of risktaking as a function of skill

■ knowledge of decisionmaking results

■ novel instrumental activity

■ anticipation of future possibilities.

Researchers now understand that it is the prospect of achievement satisfaction and not money that drives the entrepreneur (Lee, Wong, Foo and Leung, 2011). Money is important primarily as a measure of how well one is doing in business. McClelland's theory has received consistent empirical support, suggesting that there is a relationship between entrepreneurship and achievement motivation (McClelland, 1961; Perry, MacArthur, Meredith and Cunnington, 1986; Begley and Boyd, 1987; Bellu, 1988; Davidsson, 1989b; Johnson, 1990; Collins, Hanges and Locke, 2004; Delmar, 1996a).

In 1994, Miner and his associates extended McClelland's achievement motivation theory, by developing five motive patterns that replaced the previous single achievement motive. They are:

- self-achievement
- risktaking
- feedback of results
- personal innovation
- planning for the future.

Miner's approach suggested that it is not possible to predict behaviour or performance based on a *single* value, which was the case with McClelland's need for achievement model (1961, 1969). Entrepreneurial behaviour and performance can only be predicted by a complex *set* of values or motive patterns (Miner, Smith and Bracker, 1994).

Miner's five motive patterns form an overall index of task motivation. Results showed that 'Miner scales' have consistent validity. Of particular note is that the total score, combining all the 'Miner scales', correlated significantly with entrepreneurial performance and especially growth (Miner, Smith and Bracker, 1992; Bellu, 1993; Miner, Crane and Vandenberg, 1994; Miner, Smith and Bracker, 1994; Bellu and Sherman, 1995).

9.5.4 Over-optimism

Closely related to risk propensity is the concept of over-optimism – and both are related to the expectations of success. Cooper, Dunkelberg and Woo (1986) studied the entrepreneurs' perceived chances of success shortly after new venture creation and responses were compared to the actual success rate in their respective industries. When asked about the survival probability of a business resembling their own venture, most of the entrepreneurs were optimistic (78 per cent considered the chances of survival as 50:50 or higher). When asked about the survival probability of their own venture the entrepreneurs tended to be extremely optimistic (81 per cent considered the chances of survival to be 70:30 or higher). Egge (1987) also found supporting evidence that a majority of entrepreneurs were over-optimistic about their success rates.

These studies can be compared to the research on personal and general risk perception. Personal risk is measured through ratings that quantify the respondents' perceived risk as pertaining to oneself. General risk is appraised by ratings of risks that pertain to people in general.

Research finds that individuals tend to rate personal risk lower than general risk, exhibiting the people's tendency to understate their personal risk. In other words, people believe that the risk, such as being hit by a car, is larger for others than for themselves.

The difference between personal and general risk perception is related to the previous discussion about perceived control (Sjöberg, 1993). Ray (1986, 1994) found that entrepreneurs are able to give up job security and take specific risks because they have the confidence that they will succeed. Trevelyan (2008) supported this result and distinguished between two elements of confidence – optimism and overconfidence – arguing that both are beneficial when deciding to become an entrepreneur, but overconfidence is harmful when making decisions in response to negative feedback.

In conclusion, over-optimism is related to the expectancy of success and turns our attention towards cognitive biases that lead individual entrepreneurs to misjudge their own venture's survival probability. Cognitive biases have to be discussed not only in the general management setting, but also in the entrepreneurship literature (Simon, Houghton and Aquino, 2000).

9.5.5 Locus of control

Locus of control – a concept illustrating why and how individuals engage in situations with the risk of failure – can be traced back to Rotter's social learning theory (1966), which clarifies how perception of control affects the behaviour of individuals. People are inclined to either think of themselves as being in control or being controlled by the situation, of a potential goal being attained through their own actions or it following from uncontrolled external factors. Someone believes in internal control if they believe that achievement of a specific goal is dependent on personal behaviour or individual characteristics. If, on the other hand, someone believes that an achievement is the result of luck or other external factors, this person believes in external control. In short, locus of control is conceived as one determinant of performance expectancy (Weiner, 1992; Gatewood, Shaver, Powers and Gartner, 2002).

To date, researchers have found mixed results. Some studies report a slight positive correlation between internal control and entrepreneurs, as well as a weak tendency that internal orientation is associated with better performance (Brockhaus Sr, 1982; Miller and Tonlonse, 1986; Chen, Greene and Crick, 1998). A considerable number of studies report no significant differences in locus of control between entrepreneurs and managers (Sexton and Bowman, 1985). The concept and measurement of locus of control has been heavily criticised, especially in the field of psychology (Furnham and Steele, 1993). Therefore, this concept has been abandoned in favour of attribution theory, which has a more complex view on causality orientation (Anderson and Striegel, 1981; Weiner, 1985), as well as self-efficacy, discussed later in this chapter.

In sum, locus of control is a situation-independent concept that is related to the achievement context model of perceived self-efficacy. Due to its distal nature, there are grave methodological concerns, which allow for the conclusion that locus of control should probably not be included in future empirical research on entrepreneurial behaviour.

9.5.6 The dark side of entrepreneurship

As well as the positive characteristics of entrepreneurs, some research has focused on their more negative characteristics.

Any review of the psychological approach to entrepreneurship would be incomplete without mentioning the work of Kets De Vries (1977) on the dark side of entrepreneurship. Despite the fact that the study was conducted more than 30 years ago, we include it in this chapter because of his psychoanalytical approach.

Contrary to most researchers, Kets De Vries argues that entrepreneurship is caused by negative characteristics and drives. Consequently, entrepreneurship and its financial benefits rarely lead to personal satisfaction and happiness. In his own words, the entrepreneur is 'an anxious individual, a non-conformist poorly organized and not a stranger to self-destructive behaviour' (Kets De Vries, 1977: 41).

Kets De Vries suggests that the financial success of the entrepreneurial venture is often followed by a personal crisis and even poverty – what goes up must come down. The behavioural pattern of entrepreneurs is explained by experiences related to a troublesome and very disturbed childhood where the father is often absent. As a consequence, the entrepreneur becomes a person exhibiting low self-esteem and lacks critical self-reflection.

All entrepreneurial actions are driven by the idea of becoming a person in total control and independent of everything and everyone. Kets De Vries' (1977) theory is able to explain why entrepreneurs engage in high-risk situations and choose to create their own organisation instead of working within an established one. The 2007 film *There Will Be Blood* by Paul Thomas Anderson reflects this perspective.

There are many doubts about this line of research. No study so far has found consistent evidence that entrepreneurs are more troubled than anyone else. Also, there is substantial evidence that entrepreneurs come from financially and emotionally stable families. For example, many studies have pointed out that positive role models, especially parents, are of central importance in fostering future entrepreneurs (Scherer, Brodzinski and Wiebe, 1991; Mathews and Moser, 1995; Matthews and Moser, 1996; Aldrich, Renzulli and Laughton, 1997; Krueger, Reilly and Carsrud, 2000; Athayde, 2009).

These results are obviously in conflict with Kets De Vries' study. His main contribution is the acknowledgement that entrepreneurs are not some kind of superhuman heroes. They are people like the rest of us, with faults and merits, and entrepreneurship can be explained by more or less noble goals. He also points to the fact that entrepreneurs encounter problems they cannot solve and the entrepreneurial venture may therefore fail (see Chapter 10 for an overview of research on entrepreneurial failure). Today, it is clear that the psychological perspective has been far too interested in entrepreneurial success, with behaviour in crisis and failure situations being an underresearched field (Shepherd and Cardon, 2009; Shepherd, Wiklund and Haynie, 2009).

9.5.7 Summarising the individual characteristics of entrepreneurs

A large number of characteristics have been proposed to describe entrepreneurs. With the exception of the 'need for achievement' concept, the results have, in general, been poor and it remains difficult to link a set of specific characteristics to entrepreneurship. Nonetheless, recent research advancements allow for more optimism. Better knowledge of when sets of personality characteristics are likely to have an effect on entrepreneurial behaviour, as well as updated and new theories, provide a promising foundation to find some basic relationships between entrepreneurial behaviour and performance.

9.6 Cognitive models of entrepreneurial behaviour

As we have seen, people differ in how they perceive a situation and in what situations they encounter. For example, what one person sees as a business opportunity, another may see as an intractable problem, even if they are both in the same situation. Perceptual differences stem from individual experiences that make them understand the situation differently (Baron and Ensley, 2006; Keh, Foo and Lim, 2002; Gregoire, Barr and Shepherd, 2010). To explain this phenomenon, researchers rely on cognitive models of entrepreneurial behaviour.

Depending on their focus, these models can be divided into three groups. As they are models of human behaviour, they tend to overlap, but focus on different theoretical explanations of human behaviour.

The first group is mainly interested in how our attitudes to entrepreneurship (i.e., starting a business or expanding a business) shape our behaviour. This group is labelled attitude-based models. The second group is concerned with motivation in achievement contexts – i.e., why do individuals engage with and behave in situations where they have to compete with others and therefore risk failure. This group is labelled achievement context models. A third group is related to intellectual ability. While not very developed yet, this is an interesting way to understand how different forms of intelligence shape the entrepreneurial process. This group is labelled ability models.

9.6.1 Attitude-based models

Attitude is a central concept in motivation theory. An attitude is an evaluation of an object or concept and the extent to which it is judged as good or bad (Eagly and Chaiken, 1993). People carefully assess the information they have about a given situation and use this knowledge to form beliefs. They then try to choose actions that are in accordance with their formed beliefs or attitudes. Attitudes are proximal and important determinants of specific behaviour (Bagozzi and Warshaw, 1992; Ajzen, 1995).

Attitudes are interesting for entrepreneurship research because of the field's applied relevance. Attitudes impact behaviour and they can change. Researchers expect individuals with a positive attitude towards entrepreneurship to act in accordance with their attitudes. It is therefore interesting to understand how attitudes are formed and changed. Consequently, the impact of attitudes on entrepreneurial behaviour is worthy of closer examination because they are supposed to have a directive influence on behaviour and are much easier to change than personality and other more distal traits or characteristics. This would mean that if the attitudes characterising entrepreneurs starting a new business were known, other people could be influenced to adopt these attitudes and, as a result, increase the number of people starting a business.

Drawbacks are how well attitudes actually predict behaviours and explain when or why a specific action is engaged in. The importance of attitudes in predicting behaviour is debated, but research shows that they can do so when certain conditions are met (Bagozzi and Warshaw, 1992; Doll and Ajzen, 1992; Kim and Hunter, 1993).

Attitudes are tendencies or dispositions to behave in a generally favourable or unfavourable way towards the object of the attitude. However, even if we know that, for example, someone has a positive attitude towards starting a business, it is difficult to say whether or not he or she will set up a business him- or herself. It is only known that this person will act in a way that is in accordance with his or her attitudes. In this example, the person will behave favourably towards everything that is connected with business start-ups, such as encouraging a friend or relative to start a business, finance a start-up effort or even establish his or her own business.

A shortcoming of attitude theories is the lack of information about how attitudes are translated into action and outcomes. Differently stated, attitude theories help us understand how choices are made and why, but they give little guidance about the chosen level of effort and persistence (Locke, 1991). The link between intentions and actual behaviour is still a black box (Thompson, 2009). However, empirical evidence suggests that stable attitudes and beliefs are strong indicators of realised firm growth (Delmar and Wiklund, 2008). Moreover, the theory of planned behaviour is based on preferences, rather than emotions. This approach neglects that human behaviour is dependent on moods and feelings (Baron, 2008).

Nevertheless, the advantages override the disadvantages. The possibility of closely examining attitudes towards different facets of entrepreneurship, the ability to influence attitudes and the ease of communicating the results to a wider audience (such as policymakers) are strong arguments. Furthermore, even if attitudes are not perfect predictors of behaviours, they still are much better than distal personality characteristics. Therefore, attitude theories have received a fair share of attention within the field of entrepreneurship.

Attitude theories have been predominantly used to explain entrepreneurship entry (Krueger, 1993; Davidsson, 1995; Kolvereid, 1996a; Kolvereid, 1996b) and business growth (Davidsson, 1989a, 1989b; Kolvereid, 1992; Kolvereid and Bullvag, 1996; Wiklund, 1998; Wiklund, Davidsson and Delmar, 2003). Here, we will concentrate on entrepreneurship entry.

Ajzen's theory of planned behaviour (1991) is the most applied model in entrepreneurship. Researchers such as Krueger and colleagues (Krueger and Carsrud, 1993; Krueger and Brazeal, 1994; Krueger, Reilly and Carsrud, 2000) have adapted this theory to explain engagement in entrepreneurship.

The theory of planned behaviour explains individual behaviour when actions are not under complete behavioural control and dependent on outside influence. Starting a business is an example of where actions are dependent on necessary resources and knowing the right people. The basic assumption is that people carefully assess the information they have about the behaviour and form beliefs about it, then try to act in accordance with these beliefs or attitudes. The theory postulates that the tendency to engage in a particular behaviour is determined by the individual's intention to do so. These behavioural intentions mediate the effects of attitudes on behaviour (Ajzen, 1995; Davidsson, 1995). This means that a person will start a business if they have:

- enough information to form an opinion
- the opinion regarding the behaviour of starting a business is favourable
- the person has a dominant intention to start a business.

Entrepreneurial behaviour is determined by the person's intention to act, which is influenced by personal attitudes. Entrepreneurial attitude is the first factor in the theory of planned behaviour and serves as a key construct to describe and analyse entrepreneurial behaviour (Thompson, 2009).

The second factor is a set of social norms that determine intentions and, consequently, actual behaviour. Social norms are defined as the perceived social pressure to perform or not to perform a specific behaviour (Bagozzi and Kimmel, 1995). To continue the venture-creation example, this means that a person will only try to start a new venture if its social environment encourages this kind of behaviour.

The third factor in predicting and explaining why people engage in a specific behaviour is perceived behavioural control. Perceived behavioural control is defined as the ease or difficulty a person experiences when performing a given behaviour. This concept reflects how anticipated problems and obstacles, as well as past experiences, influence individuals. Several studies found that perceived behavioural control was the single most important predictor of intentions and venture creation (Krueger, Reilly and Carsrud, 2000; Townsend, Busenitz and Arthurs, 2010).

Given a positive attitude towards entrepreneurship and favourable social norms, an individual is more likely to engage in entrepreneurial behaviour with higher levels of perceived behavioural control than without such an attitude. Furthermore, if perceived behavioural control is in accordance with actual behavioural control, this concept can help to predict the likelihood that intentions will realise into behaviour (Ajzen, 1991; Ajzen, 1995; Davidsson, 1995). Therefore, perceived behavioural control is key to explaining commitment to entrepreneurship (Keh, Foo and Lim, 2002).

Davidsson (1995) studied intentions to start new ventures in Sweden and found that men and women differed little in their attitudes, but women were low on perceived behavioural control. Consequently, because woman lack confidence in their own ability to start and operate a business, they are underrepresented among entrepreneurs.

Gupta and colleagues (2008) measured the entrepreneurial intention of 469 male and female business students and found that men and women had similar entrepreneurial intention scores when the researchers controlled for the activation of implicit and explicit gender stereotypes. In other words, there was no gender difference in entrepreneurial intention, granted that entrepreneurship was presented as gender neutral (see Chapter 12 for more detailed discussions of gender).

9.6.2 Achievement context models

The second group of cognitive models of entrepreneurial behaviour deal with motivation in achievement contexts. Achievement context models illustrate why and how individuals engage in situations with risks. They go further than attitude-based models by incorporating moods and emotions.

Two achievement context models dominate contemporary entrepreneurship research:

- perceived self-efficacy
- intrinsic motivation.

We will discuss how they have been applied to the field of entrepreneurship. The common denominator of these models is the concept of perceived control – i.e., we try to organise ourselves in ways that provide us with control over our lives. Furthermore, both models deal with behaviour and actual performance – i.e., achievement contexts models.

Perceived self-efficacy

We earlier discussed locus of control as a trait explaining why and how individuals engage in situations with the risk of failure. We also concluded that perceived behavioural control is an important determinant of entrepreneurial behaviour.

The theoretical roots of self-efficacy can be traced back to the concept of locus of control and, as such, it is closely related to behavioural control. Perceived self-efficacy is situation-dependent, whereas locus of control is situation-independent and can be seen as generalised self-efficacy. Perceived self-efficacy focuses more on the actual functioning of perceived capabilities (Krueger, Reilly and Carsrud, 2000). This difference is important as both perceived self-efficacy and locus of control are related to entrepreneurial task satisfaction and task performance (Judge and Bono, 2001). Perceived self-efficacy is 'concerned with people's beliefs about their capabilities to produce performances that influence events affecting their lives' (Bandura, 1995: 434). It is about our belief in our capabilities to mobilise the motivation, cognitive resources and courses of actions needed to control events in our lives (Bandura, 1977; Gist and Mitchell, 1992; Bandura, 2010). A belief in self-efficacy influences the decisions people make in a given situation, by affecting their levels of aspiration, mobilised effort, task persistence and use of self-hindering or self-aiding thought patterns (Phillips and Gully, 1997). Perceived self-efficacy is proximal in nature and, as such, situation- and context-dependent. For example, individuals may have a high level of perceived self-efficacy in rock climbing, while simultaneously having a low level of perceived self-efficacy in entrepreneurship matters, even though both situations involve considerable risktaking.

Due to its explanatory force, perceived self-efficacy has become a central concept in entrepreneurship (Boyd and Vozikis, 1994; McGee, Peterson, Mueller and Sequeira, 2009). Research has shown that a higher level of perceived self-efficacy is positively related to initiating and persisting in achievement-related behaviours, such as entrepreneurship settings (Wood and Bandura, 1989; Krueger, Reilly and Carsrud, 2000). Bandura and Locke (2003) found that perceived self-efficacy and personal goals are positively related to levels of motivation. People with a high level of self-efficacy approach difficult tasks as challenges to be mastered, rather than issues to be avoided. They set themselves challenging goals and maintain strong commitment to them (Gist and Mitchell, 1992). They are persistent in cases of adverse effects and they maintain an analytical distance that guides effective performance. They also tend to attribute failure to insufficient effort and poor knowledge.

Similar results were found in the entrepreneurship literature. Perceived self-efficacy was positively related to the intention of starting one's own business and exploring new opportunities (Krueger and Dickson, 1993, 1994; Chen, Greene and Crick, 1998; McGee, Peterson, Mueller and Sequeira, 2009). Moreover, the perceived self-efficacy of entrepreneurs has been proven to positively affect the strategy and performance of their ventures (Westerberg, 1998; Baum and Bird, 2010). In short, higher levels of perceived self-efficacy are associated with higher levels of entrepreneurial performance.

In these studies, performance was operationally defined as a function of profitability, customer satisfaction and venture survival.

There is also a dark side to self-efficacy. People with a low level of self-efficacy shy away from difficult tasks and perceive them as personal threats. They have a low level of aspiration, a low level of commitment and a low level of persistence. Failure is attributed to external obstacles and personal deficiencies. Therefore, they rapidly lose faith in their own capabilities.

Gist and Mitchell (1992) showed that task experience has a direct effect on perceived self-efficacy. A person's given level of self-efficacy is the result of previous successful and unsuccessful task experiences, which include both personal experience and experience from observing role models. Therefore, self-efficacy is malleable and has the tendency to be a pattern of a positive or negative cycle – success breeds success and failure breeds failure. In other words, if one has observed successful entrepreneurs or has made positive experiences personally, there is a high probability that one will again engage in entrepreneurial behaviour and be successful in it again. In the same manner, a person with low self-efficacy is unlikely to engage in this kind of behaviour, but, if he or she does nevertheless engage in entrepreneurial behaviour, there is a high probability of failure. However, the negative pattern of low self-efficacy can be broken through proper training (Bandura, 1986; Gist and Mitchell, 1992; Westerberg, 1998; Wilson, Kickul and Marlino, 2007).

To conclude, self-efficacy is related to perceived behavioural control, but the present concept focuses mainly on the actual functioning of perceived capabilities.

Intrinsic motivation

Intrinsic motivation is related to actions engaged in for their own sake and is closely related to concepts such as task interest and task enjoyment. Intrinsically motivated behaviour requires no reward except for the activity itself. For example, you enter into entrepreneurship because the task itself is attractive. In contrast, extrinsically motivated behaviour refers to behaviour that is motivated by an external controlling variable, such as rewards or sanctions that can readily be identified by the acting individual (Deci, 1992b; Amabile, Hill, Hennessey and Tighe, 1994). Extrinsically motivated people tend to perform less well in prescribed tasks than their intrinsically motivated peers.

Theories about intrinsic motivation or task interest have the capacity to integrate attitudes, goals and emotions. Enjoyment and personal interest are closely connected emotions. Interest is defined as what the individual likes or dislikes. This concept is an important factor in achievement settings, such as entrepreneurial activity.

Thus, certain events can be considered important, but not interesting and vice versa. Together, attitudes and interests form sets of preferences that guide goal-directed behaviour in the presence of options. Preferences are the result of rank ordering the available options. Put differently, preferences are assessments of the alternatives in a given choice situation.

In light of our earlier discussion, it is evident that interests, attitudes and preferences reflect the emotional value of individuals based on their cognitive representations of the world. In short, all three elements contribute to the individual's construction of reality. Interest functions primarily as a positive emotion motivating exploratory behaviour. This includes cognitive and motor searches, both of which are crucial to entrepreneurial behaviour. Interest is also a necessary condition for creativity. Task creativity demands a high level of devotion to a certain kind of activity, which itself depends on task interest (Izard, 1984; Csikszentmihalyi, 1990; DeTienne and Chandler, 2004). If the interest level is not sufficient, the lack of devotion to the task will hinder performance and creative contributions.

Finally, interest is also a significant determinant of selective attention and affects the contents of perception and cognition. As such, interest is a function of entrepreneurial challenge and perceived entrepreneurship ability. Interest determines which entrepreneurship tasks are perceived as moderate challenges and what is chosen during the entrepreneurship process. The relationship between goal-setting and task interest depends on which activities people perceive as interesting and in which they are engaged. Interest and engagement lead to the perception of challenging goals they want to accomplish (Epstein and Harackiewicz, 1992; Harackiewicz and Elliot, 1993; Elliot and Harackiewicz, 1994). Interest determines which tasks we engage in and how difficult and challenging we want them to be.

In the entrepreneurship context, interest plays a central role as it is closely connected to central entrepreneurial concepts, such as achievement, autonomy and creativity. For instance, task interest has been shown to predict entrepreneurial behaviour and how it is manifested (Delmar, 1996). In this study, entrepreneurs who were more interested in marketing issues were more growth-orientated and had more profitable businesses than those who weren't. One explanation for this behaviour is that interest determines the level and direction of attention. Thus, when the interests of entrepreneurs coincide with their achievement goals, such as business profitability and growth, it is likely that they will behave in ways that yield higher performance, compared to entrepreneurial peers who do not share the same interests.

Interest is also central to the entrepreneurial process, since an entrepreneur has to be interested in some aspect of entrepreneurship to undertake it. Again, the entrepreneur's interests are important because they are related to the goal that is chosen, the level of effort and sacrifices that are made and the task perception to identify moderate challenges. The direction and strength of interest is highly personal and varies strongly among individuals.

Researchers believe that the level and direction of interest are the result of internal and external factors (Lim, Morse, Mitchell and Seawright, 2010; Lee, Wong, Foo and Leung, 2011). Internal factors are embodied in the individual – e.g., inborn ability and sensitivity to stimuli. In contrast, external factors are the environmental factors that inhibit or enable the individual's personal development.

To sum up, the emotion of interest and its effect on entrepreneurial behaviour has been discussed. It was found that task interest affects the development of the entrepreneurial venture in terms of profitability and growth. Interest leads to higher levels of attention, better decisionmaking and increased performance.

9.6.3 Ability models

Performance is often said to be a function of skills and motivation. Some research has been focusing on skills and how they affect entrepreneurship. McCloy, Campbell and

Cudeck (1994) suggested three prerequisites for successful entrepreneurs, which are that they:

■ possess the relevant knowledge and cognitive ability

■ master the relevant skills

■ choose to work on the entrepreneurial task for some period of time with some level of effort.

The idea is to understand how successful entrepreneurs are different in terms of their skills in processing information, developing new opportunities and creating expertise in exploiting them (Sarasvathy, 2001; Baron and Ensley, 2006; Gustafsson, 2006; Baron, 2010). The hope is to use this knowledge to train potential entrepreneurs to develop an entrepreneurial mindset and thereby increase their chances of success (Read et al., 2011). A basic assumption is that the interaction between cognitive ability, skills, environmental possibilities and social support are likely to lead to a positive reinforcing spiral – i.e., entrepreneurs experience support to solve problems and can, therefore, develop specific skills. Basic intelligence coupled with an interest in becoming an entrepreneur leads the individual to develop the skills needed to become successful.

These task-specific skills have been termed successful intelligence (Sternberg, 1997; Sternberg, 2004). Successful intelligence is the ability to succeed in life according to one's life goals, which are established within one's environmental context (Baum and Bird, 2010). Here, entrepreneurial success can be defined in terms of personal goals, thus overcoming the problem of defining entrepreneurial performance.

Another type of ability or skill is social competence. Baron and Markman (2003) investigated the social competence of entrepreneurs (their ability to interact effectively with others based on discrete social skills). Based on a sample of 230 entrepreneurs taken from both cosmetics and high-tech industries, they found that the accuracy of their perceptions of others (e.g., their traits, intentions and behaviour) was positively associated with their financial success. Furthermore, they found that social adaptability (the ability to adapt or feel comfortable in a wide range of social situations) was important for entrepreneurs in the cosmetics industry, while expressiveness (the ability to express oneself clearly to generate enthusiasm in others) was important for entrepreneurs in the high-tech industries. This research indicates that an understanding of situational constraints is important, skills are developed over time and proximal measures are likely to generate important results for understanding the psychology of entrepreneurs.

9.6.4 Summarising cognitive models of entrepreneurial behaviour

Cognitive models – i.e. how we organise and come to understand the information surrounding us – provide better explanations and predictors of behaviour than earlier models. This section has reviewed three cognitive models that have greatly enhanced our understanding of entrepreneurship. Attitude-based models focus on how our attitudes to entrepreneurship shape our behaviour. Achievement context models are concerned with motivation in contexts where risk and performance are central. To understand why and how individuals engage in situations where they have to compete with others, perceived self-efficacy and intrinsic motivation were presented. Perceived self-efficacy and the related concept of behavioural control focus on the representation of one's own capabilities. Theories of intrinsic motivation focus on the representation of what one finds enjoyable and self-fulfilling. Bandura (1991, 1995) argues that both concepts show different aspects of the same phenomenon because intrinsic motivation is both an antecedent and a consequence of high self-efficacy.

Attitude-based and achievement context models have immense value because they enable actual tests of the proposed models, are proximal in nature and possess high explanatory power for entrepreneurial behaviour. Cognitive models possess a sophisticated theoretical frame of reference that incorporates the complexity of entrepreneurial behaviour and offers practical advice on how to train and educate future entrepreneurs (Hisrich, Langan-Fox and Grant, 2007). Cognitive models are more proximal by nature than distal traits or personality characteristics. This leads to a higher level of explanatory force when modelling entrepreneurial behaviour. Finally, research can offer better explanations for how entrepreneurs behave because we are focusing on their cognition – i.e., how we organise and come to understand the information around us. This shift towards cognitive models entails a number of practical consequences.

By focusing on how people think and react rather than on their personality, there has been a shift in focus from stable traits to more easily changeable cognitive processes. Thus, the practical value of this research is that there is an understanding of how entrepreneurs become who they are and this knowledge can be used to educate and train potential entrepreneurs. That is, in order to create an environment where more businesses are created and expanded, we need to have favourable attitudes and feelings towards the object. However, what leads to actual behaviour is the individual's feeling of control and whether or not they enjoy doing what they are doing. More precisely, individuals will engage in an entrepreneurial act if they believe that they know how to do it and this behaviour is intrinsically rewarding. This knowledge and feeling can, according to Bandura (1995), be obtained in four different ways:

- mastery experiences – personal experience
- vicarious experiences – experience by observing others
- social persuasion – reinforcing social support
- reduction of negative emotions towards the behaviour.

Mastery experience is the most effective way of accomplishing a high feeling of control. The reason is that personal experience offers the authentic evidence that one can master what it takes to succeed. Successes tend to build a strong belief in one's personal capabilities and failures tend to undermine it. This is true especially before one has established a strong sense of one's own capabilities.

The second way of creating and enhancing beliefs of capability and control is through vicarious experiences observing role models. Seeing people similar to oneself succeed by sustained effort raises an individual's beliefs about his or her own capabilities, whereas observing others fail, despite high levels of effort, lowers an individual's beliefs about his or her own capabilities. For the experience to be effective, too, it is important that the individual can identify him- or herself with the role model.

A third way, but less effective than the two previous ones, is through social persuasion – i.e., convincing people that they have what it takes to succeed.

The last way of modifying people's feeling of control towards a specific behaviour is to reduce the negative emotions, such as stress and anxiety. The reason is that people rely to a large extent on their somatic and emotional state (e.g., as having a gut feeling, nervousness, fatigue) in judging their capabilities. As a result, negative feelings are interpreted as having low capabilities.

Hence, it can be concluded that cognitive models such as the one presented here have several advantages compared to previous trait-based models. Instead of talking about a set of unchangeable traits, cognitive functions that can be altered should be discussed. Cognitive models have great power to explain entrepreneurial behaviour and offer practical advice on how to train and educate future entrepreneurs.

9.7 Chapter summary

The aim of this chapter was to review the research findings on entrepreneurial personality and behaviour. Studying entrepreneurship from a psychology perspective is essential because entrepreneurs are real objects of analysis and are seen as decision-makers who actively change their environment. This chapter was divided into four major parts. The first part covered the problems with explaining human behaviour as a function of individual differences, situational constraints or a mix of both. This was exemplified by our dart-throwing example that we then adapted back to entrepreneurial behaviour. Second, we covered the evolution of the field. The third part examined the trait research approach. Finally, the last part examined cognitive theory in entrepreneurship research, which is presently the predominant approach to studying the psychology of the entrepreneur. This theory is able to address individual differences in entrepreneurial behaviour and performance.

The development of the field from single trait theories to cognitive models is based on three shifts. At the beginning, traits were regarded as being stable over time, but this approach could offer only limited grounds for explaining the mechanisms involved. Due to its inability to explain the relationship between behavioural patterns and entrepreneurial performance, it was abandoned in favour of cognitive models that take into account the situation and the person's perception of the situation.

Cognitive models conceive human behaviour as directed by goal-setting, motivation and the perception of control. The advantage of cognitive models, compared to previous trait research, is the ability to address interpersonal differences in entrepreneurial behaviour and performance, which is the main objective of the research field. Cognitive theories that are able to explain and predict entrepreneurial behaviour thus possess explanatory force and practical value for entrepreneurial research.

However, there are limitations to cognitive models arising from the assumption that individuals construct their own realities. We find clear evidence that cognitive models offer a valuable path to theorybuilding that makes it possible to understand the interaction between the characteristics of the situation and characteristics of the entrepreneur. However, we are also likely to see the debate on whether entrepreneurship is innate or learned be revived as, increasingly, the results of research indicate that genetic components are playing an important role (Nicolaou and Shane, 2009a; Nicolaou and Shane, 2009b; Nicolaou, Shane, Cherkas and Spector, 2009), especially for female entrepreneurs (Zhang et al., 2009). Evidently much more work is needed to fully understand the complexity of entrepreneurial behaviour.

Questions

1 Discuss the traits approach to entrepreneurial personality and explain why it fails to properly predict the behaviour of entrepreneurs.

2 Discuss the similarities and differences of attitude-based and achievement context models as examples of cognitive motivation theories.

3 What are the theoretical and practical advantages of cognitive models in describing the psychology of the entrepreneur?

Weblinks

http://digitalknowledge.babson.edu/entrep/fer
This website contains a broad range of papers on the characteristics of the entrepreneur, which stem from the Annual Frontiers of Entrepreneurship Research Conference.

www.businessballs.com/davidmcclelland.htm
This article provides an introduction to David McClelland and his work on the need for achievement.

http://people.umass.edu/aizen
The homepage of Professor Icek Ajzen, who developed the theory of planned behaviour.

http://psychology.wikia.com/wiki/Entrepreneurship
This Wiki provides an overview of entrepreneurship from a psychological perspective. It focuses on the entrepreneurial personality and offers links to websites, books and other key resources.

www.des.emory.edu/mfp/self-efficacy.html
This Web page provides extensive resources on self-efficacy and Albert Bandura.

CHAPTER 10

Entrepreneurial failure

James E. Dever

10.1 Introduction

For many years the USA was the world leader in entrepreneurial activity, but according to a report released in September 2010 by the United States Small Business Administration Office of Advocacy (Acs and Szerb, 2010), both Denmark and Canada now outrank the USA. The USA continues to rank number one for entrepreneurial innovation, but has dropped to number six in entrepreneurial attitude rankings. Entrepreneurial attitude is the population's perceptions of entrepreneurs, opportunities and the risk of failure. It is this risk of failure, the precursors or antecedents to failure and the actual occurrence of failure that this chapter concerns.

10.2 Learning objectives

There are five learning objectives in this chapter:

1 to understand the meaning of a business failure, not only by definition but also by the actions that occur during the failure of a firm

2 to recognise the antecedents of a failure event

3 to enhance one's ability to recognise the cause of a failure event and take corrective actions to halt or lessen its severity

4 to differentiate between exogenous and indigenous failures, differentiate between large and small failures and understand the potential outcomes of each type of event

5 to understand the importance of exit strategies and determine which is best for the firm.

Key concepts
- entrepreneurial failure ■ exogenous or external ■ indigenous or internal
- bankruptcy or insolvency ■ exit strategies
- antecedents and perceptions of business failure

10.3 What is business failure?

In this chapter, failure includes closure of one's firm as a result of a bankruptcy or receivership, closure prior to bankruptcy to avoid further losses or an inability of the firm to operate in a manner that would enable the firm to produce sufficient capital in order to remain viable as a firm.

Since human trading activities began, success and failure have played an important part in these endeavours. Some enterprising individuals excelled at providing goods and possibly services to others, while some were not as successful and failure resulted.

Relative to the volume of research considering entrepreneurial success, very little work has been conducted that asks why entrepreneurial failures occur, what happens to the parties involved and how society is impacted. In spite of its magnitude as a research topic, entrepreneurial failure was not even considered until Mansfield (1962) encouraged academic studies of the birth, growth and death of firms. Despite this early encouragement, until very recently, remarkably little research has focused on the causes and consequences of business failure.

If you really want to know what causes a firm to fail, you have to begin by creating a list of reasons based on an independent investigation of any and all failed businesses you can locate. However, researchers have long pointed out that discovering reasons for failure is very difficult since many entrepreneurs, upon closing their firms, tend to disappear from view and are hard to locate. Even if they are found and prove willing to be interviewed, they may not be completely truthful when one enquires as to what happened to cause their company's failure.

The small number of studies considering entrepreneurial failure that have been conducted show failure occurs as a result of many differing causes and these include a lack of markets, competition, changes in customers' tastes, insufficient capital, ineffective planning and sometimes a lack of resolve on the part of the businessowner. There is no definitive reason for business or entrepreneurial failure, but it is imperative that, in order for one to find success in business, one must first understand failure and the many reasons it can occur.

The terms 'entrepreneurial failure' and 'business failure' have been used synonymously in research and been defined through the years in numerous fashions. Research has narrowed business failure down to 'failing to make a go of it' – a definition that includes bankruptcies, receiverships and the closure of a business, ceasing operation prior to bankruptcy due to losses (Mason, Carter and Tagg, 2008; Dever, 2009). Failure is also the termination of a business that has fallen short of its goals (McGrath, 1999; Politis and Gabrielsson, 2009) and fails to satisfy principal investors' expectations (Beaver, 1996). Notwithstanding bankruptcy or liquidation, failure includes the actual loss of capital and an inability of the company to flourish (Cochran, 1981). This will all eventually lead to a reduction in revenues due either to higher expenses or a decrease in income. In short, the current ownership cannot continue to operate the firm (Shepherd, 1999).

If you are planning to start a new business, failure should not and cannot be a major factor upon which you should dwell. However, one must be aware of the factors involved in failure in order to avoid it, as the consequences of failure can be unfortunate and ruinous for the entrepreneur. In spite of the negative connotations associated with failure, there is a positive side and that is an entrepreneur's ability to learn from his or her failure and, ultimately, find success. In order for one to find success in business, a complete understanding of failure, its antecedents, consequences and the ultimate outcomes must be understood.

Entrepreneurial research has long pointed to two major causes of entrepreneurial failure – a lack of capital and a lack of knowledge by the entrepreneur about the firm, its market and its industry. In addition to these widely held views, research has indicated that, among the personal traits, fear of failure is one of the major obstacles faced by start-up entrepreneurs and, in fact, is shown to be an actual hindrance to their starting a new company (Caliendo, Fossen and Kritikos, 2009). In a report released by the United States Small Business Administration Office of Advocacy (Acs and Szerb, 2010), the entrepreneurial fear of failure has risen since 2006 – attributed to the increase in the ageing population. As people grow older, they appear to become more risk-averse. When this fear of failure is compared to that in other countries of the world, the USA is lagging behind India and China, which both share an entrepreneurial system with little or no fear of failure – a fact presenting a real challenge to the USA.

Especially evident in today's economy is a lack of capital for start-ups or expansion of existing businesses. Due to stringent lending regulations and excessive demands for upfront capital, many entrepreneurs are turning to bootstrapping – an alternative method of raising capital (see Chapter 6 for a discussion of this concept). They are minimising costs by purchasing used equipment, delaying payments to suppliers and managers, borrowing equipment and attempting to obtain the lowest costs possible from suppliers (Winborg and Landström, 2001). The inability to raise or borrow sufficient capital is evident in the success of new start-ups, as well as the inability of the entrepreneur to successfully estimate start-up costs – a direct link to a lack of knowledge. In an interview with a successful entrepreneur, she indicated her rule of thumb for start-up costs was to attempt to determine every conceivable cost and, upon completion of the analysis, whatever the amount calculated, to add a minimum of 50 per cent more. This is neither scientific, nor probably even accurate, but is presented as a gentle reminder that entrepreneurial costs will probably exceed all expectations and it will require creativity and ingenuity from the entrepreneur in order to fund their start-up.

10.3.1 Large and small failures

Failures in business can be categorised. In addition to being internal or external, failures can be either large or small. This statement sounds innocuous, but, by understanding the various characteristics or types of failure, one can then begin to find success where previously only adversity existed. There is no exact measure for classifying whether an event is large or small since these are relative concepts, partly based on the viewpoint of the entrepreneur (Baumard and Starbuck, 2005), so the perceived magnitude of the dilemma is based on one's own perception of the problem. The importance of this discussion of large and small failures ties directly with the concept of failures being either internal or external.

To a multinational consortium, a difficulty may appear insignificant, while the same event may be catastrophic for an independent entrepreneur. The important factor one must understand is that the small failures which occur in a business may be antecedents to a much larger and devastating problem. It is the entrepreneur's duty to take aggressive and timely action to address all problems as they occur outside of or within his or her firm. Proactive measures can sometimes quickly remedy the small antecedents to a large failure and possibly closure of the firm; failure to act in a timely fashion can lead to a catastrophic failure.

Cannon and Edmonson (2005) identified large and small failures as being associated with business failure. Small failures, they concluded, may include a flaw in the design of equipment or an incident involving failure to give proper guidance to employees in need of assistance. These sometimes occur as a result of the firm failing to adhere to its core beliefs. These researchers refer to small failures as early warning signs that may provide management with a wake-up call, needed to prevent disaster in the future, hence, an antecedent to failure. Often these antecedents or small failures tend to be overlooked as minor mistakes or solitary anomalies that will go away in due time. It is the duty of the entrepreneur to recognise and act upon these minor mistakes.

Large failures within a firm can be traced to mostly exogenous or external origins, such as 'exceptional or historical conditions or society was undergoing large, dramatic change' (Baumard and Starbuck, 2005: 293). The larger the failure, the more dramatic and, therefore, the greater effect it will have on the external elements of the firm. There is a direct correlation between the cause and size of a failure – the larger the failure, the more external and more idiosyncratic.

When a firm has survived large failures in the past, there is usually no connection with current large events that are occurring in spite of the entrepreneur or management being involved in both of the situations. Future projects for firms are created slowly over time, just as large failures occur slowly over time. This 'slow growth' spreads the effect and ultimate cost of the failure over an extended period, thereby allowing it to draw less attention to the cause, cost and consequence of the event. Based on this, it can be assumed that the small failures affecting the entrepreneur and the company can be considered indigenous (i.e., internal to the firm and, presumably, within its control), while the large failures are exogenous (i.e., external to the firm and beyond its control; Baumard and Starbuck, 2005).

The results Baumard and Starbuck propound are interesting in that they found firms learned less from large failures than they did from small ones. The smaller problems tended to be more indigenous and, because they impacted their personal stakes in the firm, these were more closely monitored. Other researchers agree with this premise and state that distinguishing between large and small failures is important, but it is also important to 'learn to fail intelligently as deliberate strategy to promote innovation and improvement' (Cannon and Edmondson, 2005: 300). Regardless of the amount of learning that occurs during a failure event, whatever is learned will be beneficial to the future success of the entrepreneur.

10.3.2 Internal and external failures

The importance of this discussion of large and small failures is linked to the concept of them being either internal or external.

Based on the information shown in Box 10.1, the internal factors of failure include poor management – an event that occurs as a lack of entrepreneurial or managerial

Box 10.1 Internal and external factors contributing to failure

Internal failure factors	External failure factors
Poor management	Economy
Deficits in accounting practices	Change of buying patterns
Poor cashflow management	Decreased purchasing power of consumers
Inappropriate sources of finance	Shortage of raw materials
Dependency on customers or suppliers	Customers' strikes
Impending bad debt	Low-price competitors
Overtrading	Catastrophic unpredictable events
Poor marketing and research	Environmental protection and other
Fraud or collusion	regulatory requirements
Bankruptcy	Bankruptcy of main customer or supplier
	Governmental measures and international
	developments

Source: based on European Federation of Accountants, 2004: 7–17

attention or focus. This is confirmed by Beaver's (2003) study, which presented evidence that poor management is an internal problem and a major cause of failure in a firm. Another study found that two of the four major causes of failure among firms were internal problems or small failures, poor management function and working capital management (Gaskill, Van Auken and Manning, 1993). 'While everyone agrees that bad management is the prime cause of failure no one agrees what "bad management" means nor how it can be recognized except after the company has collapsed – then everyone agrees how badly managed it was' (Argenti, 1976: 3).

Being able to correctly handle the events caused by external factors may not be an easy undertaking. As Parsa, Self, Njite and King (2005: 316) reported, 'It is the individual's preparation or lack thereof that makes the difference in the severity of the impact'. One study found many external factors are beyond the control of even the most capable entrepreneur and will trigger problems in new firms (Osborne, 1993: 21). These external factors include strong competitor retaliation, ever-changing industries, loss of major customers, changes in technologies and market preferences, undercapitalisation and a reliance on unproductive or existing management.

Some failed entrepreneurs 'save face' by attributing their failures to others. One study found that entrepreneurs often attribute failure to external causes, such as market conditions and financial problems through a process known as attribution theory (see Chapter 9 for a longer discussion). This theory explains how people identify and make judgments about stimuli and entrepreneurs tie the failure of their enterprises to external factors, while attributing other firms' failures to internal causes. By doing this, entrepreneurs are able to save face. They can retain their perception of themselves as able businesspeople without admitting defeat – they would prefer to be victims of their circumstances rather than victims of their own actions (Zacharakis, Meyer and DeCastro, 1999).

Rogoff, Lee and Suh (2004) performed a matched pair analysis that analysed the attribution theory of entrepreneurial failure. They compared a group of entrepreneurs with a group of non-businessowners to confirm their theories. Their findings indicate that businesspeople do adhere to attribution theory and blame their failures on exogenous factors, while success is attributed to internal factors, such as their abilities to operate a business. They found attribution theory a useful means of conceptualising the attribution of success and failure. Their study indicated that 91.3 per cent of success was attributed to internal factors, while 81.4 per cent of failure factors were attributed to external factors. The findings further establish the premise set forth in this chapter that there are many external situations far beyond the control of an entrepreneur, such as social, legal, political, technological, economic, ethical and environmental events. Any of these externalities have the ability to create a business failure that may be beyond the extent of the entrepreneur's grasp or knowledge.

Rosa, Carter and Hamilton (1996) interviewed 600 UK small business owner-managers, 300 of each gender. They, too, found that most businesspeople tend to blame external factors for their possible shortcomings. The respondents were asked if their businesses were in trouble or faltering – almost 20 per cent said they were. The interesting characteristic of this survey is that both sexes blamed external factors, such as the recession and high interest rates that were prevalent in the United Kingdom at that time, rather than accepting blame for their own internal failures. Earning and maintaining respect from one's peers is important to everyone. This is why many people display an innate dislike of admitting, either privately or publicly, that they have failed as this may jeopardise their self-esteem (Cannon and Edmondson, 2005).

Contrary to what others have found concerning external problems, one study (Beaver, 2003) presents research that failure appears to be primarily caused by internal or endogenous factors, such as poor management within the firm. This study refers to Dun and Bradstreet research in 1991, in which the firm, without reservation, stated, 'the primary cause of business failure in the USA is due to management incompetence of the business owner' – an internal problem (Beaver, 2003: 120).

Another argument is that there is an 'executive limit', at which time the entrepreneur's ability to lead the firm becomes harmful. As Zacharakis, Meyer and DeCastro (1999: 3–9) state, 'This "executive limit" concept illustrates internal causes of failure, specifically, a management coordination and control problem . . . The examination of the aggregate frequency of the factors finds that internal factors were cited 58 per cent of the time.' Poor management strategy is the most frequently cited internal cause of venture failure; while the factor that is cited most frequently for complete entrepreneurial failure is poor external market conditions.

One can easily determine that there is no clear and definite position available regarding internal and external failure. Depending on the study, the people involved, the business type, market type and other factors, the results will differ. Some failure is internal and some is external, so this is a subject that will continue to be investigated as long as entrepreneurial research continues.

Fredland and Morris (1976: 7) argued that the causes of failure cannot be ascertained easily, and 'any attempt to do so is, at bottom, a futile exercise'. The weight of research evidence that has accumulated since then would uphold this statement.

The important issue one should take away from this section is that if the entrepreneur is unable or unaware of the events occurring in the firm and does not take positive action, an entrepreneurial failure will occur, harming the ability of the firm to continue to function properly, but may not necessarily lead to a catastrophic event such as closure. Whether or not external factors are beyond the control of the entrepreneur is a subject worthy of further research and if it is found that they are, in fact, beyond control, what can an entrepreneur do to lessen their effects?

10.4 Antecedents and perceptions of business failure

Earlier in this chapter we discussed the antecedents to failure as they pertain to an entrepreneur's observations of large and small failures. A more thorough discussion of the antecedents to failure is important as this phenomenon is so often overlooked or ignored by entrepreneurs, yet always seems to occur prior to a failure event.

Several questions must be answered in order to fully understand events that occur prior to a failure in a firm. Questioning the precursors to failure events will expose critical incidents or events, disclose what entrepreneurs were doing prior to the failure, how they perceived the problem and if certain types of antecedents were present prior to the actual failure event. One must ascertain what was occurring in the company prior to the event. Was management simply overlooking failure signals or did they incorrectly interpret them as flukes or simply ill fortune that would go away if they continued to adhere to the firm's core beliefs? In addition to ignoring problems, as we saw earlier, entrepreneurs will often attempt to blame others for their own shortcomings. In doing so, they are attempting to obtain a clear understanding of what had happened and yet remain outside the failure in their own company.

In order to fully understand the antecedents to a business failure and the perceptions an entrepreneur may hold, the following case is presented to illustrate these issues. The case was compiled from an interview undertaken for a doctoral dissertation that explored entrepreneurial failure (Dever, 2009: 237–9).

> Entrepreneur D stated he recognized few antecedents to failure at the time the failure was occurring; however, in hindsight he states, 'As I look back, I see that there were some signs (of failure) but most of that involved me'. The involvement he refers to is his own lack of focus. About this, he said: 'I was more interested in doing something else, and I was not paying as much attention to the company as I should. As far as big signs that stated, "this company is about to fail", there was none of that . . . I am not devoting enough time to my companies once they get started. I am always looking for another opportunity and as I look at this . . . maybe I need to devote myself more to my ventures'.
>
> Some of the antecedents to failure which Entrepreneur D does recognize include cashflow problems, an inability to attract outside investors, and a slowdown in business. None of the more obvious signs of failure have occurred in his businesses, according to Entrepreneur D. The lack of early warning signs, or perhaps his failure to recognize signs of failure, has prompted him to state the following: 'The death throes always occurred in my companies . . . prior to me having the opportunity to shut them down in order to create a new company'.
>
> Even though Entrepreneur D stated there were few, if any, antecedents in his businesses, he refutes this with his own statements, which indicate there were antecedents to failure occurring, but he chose to ignore them and, therefore, cannot discuss them as being prevalent in his firms. 'I think that businesspeople in general choose to ignore problems. I am not an exception to this. We all feel that if problems become too prevalent then we will do something about them, but small problems that perhaps will ultimately lead to failure are ignored a great deal of the time.'

A failure in one's firm will prompt an owner to offer a myriad of excuses as to why the firm failed, or why it was someone else's problem. In the case of Entrepreneur D, he readily admits, 'Even though my companies were discontinued, I don't consider them a closure, I consider them a failure'. This attitude sets this entrepreneur apart from most others and the following statement sums up his thoughts on the antecedents to failure, his perception of those antecedents, and what one must do to avoid failure: 'If we don't use the small failures as steering mechanisms to change the vision or the direction of the company, it will lead to catastrophic failure. If you take the small ones and use them to steer the vision, you could possibly avert catastrophic failure. If you ignore the little stuff you're going to get nailed. Little events tend to be swept under the carpet, ignored. If I have a problem with one of my employees, immediately that has to be handled. I cannot overlook anything like this as it will grow and become big. Put your problems behind you every day and then you don't have to worry about this. I also believe that if you don't handle a small problem as it arises, an unrelated problem will arise and increase the damage from that first problem that you ignored. If you own a business that provides a service and you start getting feedback that your (service is) not up to par, you'd better correct it immediately.'

Entrepreneur D has experienced more failures than all of the other entrepreneurs combined [who were interviewed for this doctoral dissertation], yet he appears less concerned than any of the others. He considers a failure as one of the basic components of business. His ability to ignore the antecedents has caused the failure of several firms, and in spite of those failures he states, 'I never looked at any of this as a personal failure. It is just one of those things that happen'.

As this entrepreneur illustrates, entrepreneurs possess an ability to recognise and acknowledge the antecedents to failure, yet they often choose to ignore the early warning signs that these present. They are ardent in their desire to divest themselves of firms that are not operating according to the standards they have created for themselves. These standards are based on their own perceptions of how a business should operate and also on the historical specifics of their other businesses. As is the case with all entrepreneurs, according to the literature, they can be subject to an ineffective management function, the difference between them being their willingness to discontinue operations without expending great energies and resources on trying to save their struggling firms (Gaskill, Van Auken and Manning, 1993).

10.5 Entrepreneurial risk

Failure in business can be tied directly to the amount of risk involved in the start-up or as the business grows. Failure serves as a training base for individuals wishing to go into industry by showing them it is a risky undertaking and may be much riskier than simply working for others (Storey, 1994). Business failure provides experience for the individuals involved in the failure. In spite of the risk of failure, 73 per cent of entrepreneurs have the impression that even more success, than they currently enjoy, is coming their way in the next five years (Brandstätter, 1997). The inverse of this finding would lead one to realise that, by the same token, 73 per cent of the entrepreneurs in the study felt they had no failures coming their way. Could this be how entrepreneurs see their future entrepreneurial plans?

As an investigation into entrepreneurial risk is carried out, it is important that one fully understands the results of a business failure and the part risk plays in failure and the long-term affect the failure will have on the entrepreneur. A discussion of one's business philosophies, perhaps, is the ideal way to examine the effect failure has on the entrepreneur. Some researchers have stated that entrepreneurs have one characteristic in common – their ability to use all of the talent at their disposal. Entrepreneurs utilise resources, energy and knowledge from everyone around them and the energies of many people both inside and outside their firms. This action is the creation of a network of relationships that enables the entrepreneur to utilise the best resources, while at the same time allowing those in the network to achieve their goals as well (McGrath and MacMillan, 2000). This is considered accepted wisdom and these actions further support risk-aversion on the part of entrepreneurs as they seek to minimise risk.

In business, there are often early warning signs of impending failure. Some of these phenomena are known as epistemic blindspots. This failure to recognise early problems and denial of risk are two of the impairments that cause disasters to occur in business (Choo, 2008). Often, these are ignored since the information does not agree with the entrepreneurs' existing beliefs or because they do not have the frame of reference needed to recognise the signs. Risk denial is defined as warning signs and actions that are not believed due to the priorities and values that are present and influence the interpretation of the signs, meaning no action is taken.

In addition to ignoring problems, it has been established that entrepreneurs engage in risky behaviour (Palich and Bagby, 1995). Past literature presents two diverse views of risk. The first viewed risk based on the variability of the returns an entrepreneur would expect from a new venture (Fisher and Hall, 1969), while the second avoided the variability aspect and indicated that entrepreneurs looked at risk from the standpoint of, 'If this fails, how much do I stand to lose?' (March and Shapira, 1987). Other literature states that entrepreneurs' propensities to take risk are contingent upon their perceived level of unpredictability in their choice of firms and, following a failure event, they tend to avoid jeopardising their future ventures due to the amount of risk they perceive (Forlani and Mullins, 2000).

Regardless of the perspective taken by entrepreneurs to risk, everyone will perceive an identical risk in differing ways (Nutt, 1993). Another study concluded that, 'entrepreneurs do not differ from non-entrepreneurs on risk taking propensity, and we find that entrepreneurs tend to assess risk more favorably' (Norton and Moore, 2006: 222).

Researchers (Shepherd, Douglas and Shanley, 2001; Hartog, Ferrer-i-Carbonell and Jonker, 2002) specified that, in spite of the identified views of risk, there has been little research into how entrepreneurs view, recognise or address the presence of risk. New venture creators do extensive work establishing an enterprise and it is reasonable to assume that they do not go into it without considering the risks that are inherent in business, especially in a new firm. The concept of risk reduction and the complexities that follow as one considers the complexity of the industry into which the entrepreneur is attempting to go is of great importance when attempting to determine the risk involved (Shepherd, Douglas and Shanley, 2001). One of the reduction methods would simply involve choosing an industry with less volatility. Perhaps an attempt at reducing risk could indicate that the entrepreneur is risk-averse or, perhaps, has past experience of or learning arising from failure, and has determined that, by reducing risk, chances of survival are increased.

Risk aversion is another important factor when considering the implications of failure. It has been shown that aversion to risk is much lower for individuals who are self-employed and more highly educated (Hartog, Ferrer-i-Carbonell and Jonker, 2002). This lower aversion to risk can explain a person's entrepreneurial activity.

Another group of entrepreneurs with a very low aversion to risk are inventors – the people who create new companies around their inventions. Studies have shown that when entrepreneurs start firms while trying to create a new invention, their chances of survival are lessened. However, if they have already established their inventions, their chances of survival are almost identical to the success rates of normal nascent firms. As Åstebro (1998: 45) concluded, 'Conditional on starting up, invention-based businesses are no more risky than other start-ups. Similarly, conditional on reaching the market, the gross profits from innovations developed by independent inventors are quite satisfactory. Very few are unprofitable, and for 70 per cent of the survey sample the gross profit margins are above 20 per cent'.

Based on the literature, it would seem that when entrepreneurs choose between various options for starting a new firm, those choices are based on the differences in their propensity to take risks, risk-aversion and the expected returns that the new company can offer them. All of this is based on their ability to understand and accept the inherent risks involved in the new venture. Numerous characteristics of an individual entrepreneur – e.g., age, family background, gender, previous work experience and education – are, oftentimes, indicated as factors that influence the risk propensity an entrepreneur can bear and, ultimately, performance can be affected by this, which can lead to entrepreneurial failure.

10.6 Liquidation or bankruptcy

As the definition of failure indicated, bankruptcy or liquidation is one of the paths to failure or dissolution of a firm. This usually occurs as a result of insolvency on the part of the individual or the firm. Insolvency is, quite simply, the inability to pay one's debts due to a lack of assets. This can be caused by cashflow shortfalls or excess liabilities. When liabilities are greater than tangible assets and an inability to pay current bills has occurred, the threat of bankruptcy may be imminent.

In the UK, the term bankruptcy relates only to individuals and partnerships. When firms are unable to continue to satisfy their liabilities, they enter into what is known as insolvency procedures, liquidation or administrative receiverships, with the exception of Scotland, where the correct terminology is sequestration. The media often incorrectly refer to these types of processes as bankruptcies (IVA, 2008). In the USA, business dissolution, according to the United States Small Business Administration (1996), consists of business failures, business bankruptcies, and business terminations. It defines bankruptcy as follows: 'A business bankruptcy is a legal recognition that a company is insolvent – that is, it cannot satisfy its creditors or discharge its liabilities. Therefore, the company must restructure (Chapter 11) or completely liquidate (Chapter 7)' (p. 7). Also, 'A business failure is defined as an enterprise that ceases operation with a loss to one or more creditors' (p. 8) and business termination is 'when a firm terminates operations, that is, ceases to employ people' (p. 9).

Table 10.1 Annual business and non-business bankruptcies filed, by year, in the USA (1980–2009)

Year	Total filed	Businesses filed	Non-businesses filed	Non-businesses filed as a percentage of total filed	Businesses filed as a percentage of total filed
1980	331,264	43,694	287,570	86.81	13.19
1985	412,510	71,277	341,233	82.72	17.28
1990	782,960	64,853	718,107	91.72	8.28
1995	926,601	51,959	874,642	94.39	5.61
2000	1,253,444	35,472	1,217,972	97.17	2.83
2005	2,078,415	39,201	2,039,214	98.11	1.89
2006	617,660	19,695	597,965	96.81	3.19
2007	850,912	28,322	822,590	96.67	3.33
2008	1,117,771	43,546	1,074,225	96.10	3.90
2009	1,473,675	60,837	1,412,838	95.87	4.13

Source: American Bankruptcy Institute

A controversy over the reporting of the frequency of small business bankruptcies has been ongoing. In the USA, according to raw statistical data, the numbers of business bankruptcies have been plummeting. This is due, in part, to what some refer to as an entrepreneur-friendly bankruptcy law. Table 10.1 indicates that, since 1980, business bankruptcies in the USA have declined from approximately 13.2 per cent of all bankruptcies to 4.1 per cent in 2009. This decrease occurred in a period during which total bankruptcies filed increased by almost 350 per cent, yet business bankruptcies increased by only 39.2 per cent.

According to Lawless and Warren (2005), this phenomenon is not factual. In the mid-1980s, the government in the USA streamlined the bankruptcy reporting process by simplifying the application software and, as a result, thousands of business bankruptcies

Table 10.2 Annual insolvency and bankruptcies filed in England and Wales

Year	Total filed	Businesses filed	Non-businesses filed	Non-businesses filed as a percentage of total filed	Businesses filed as a percentage of total filed
1980	10,928	6,890	4,038	36.95	63.05
1985	21,674	14,898	6,776	31.26	68.74
1990	29,038	15,051	13,987	48.17	51.83
1995	40,855	14,536	26,319	64.42	35.58
2000	43,845	14,317	29,528	67.35	32.65
2005	80,477	12,893	67,584	83.98	16.02
2006	120,425	13,137	107,288	89.09	10.91
2007	119,152	12,507	106,645	89.50	10.50
2008	122,079	15,535	106,544	87.27	12.73
2009	153,219	19,077	134,142	87.55	12.45

Source: The Insolvency Service, adapted from http://www.insolvency.gov.uk/otherinformation/statistics/historicdata/HDmenu.htm
© Crown copyright 2006

began to be classified as non-business bankruptcies. In 2005, official data indicated 39,201 business-related bankruptcies, but research indicates that there were, in fact, between 260,000 and 315,000 business-related bankruptcies. This flawed record keeping creates a predisposition for overconfidence and a lack of caution since many new entrepreneurs believe, as a result, that it is becoming safer to be in business for oneself, when, in fact, the opposite is true. Bankruptcies continue to rise annually, as indicated by Table 10.1 and 10.2, and it is only diligence, training and attention to detail can start to ensure that an entrepreneur's foray into the business world has a chance of success.

10.7 Fear of failure or comparative optimism

Just as the past successes and failures of entrepreneurs' businesses are tied, through an inextricable bond, to their entrepreneurs, their future entrepreneurial opportunities are linked in a similar manner. Entrepreneurs graciously accept this relationship and, as they create new business scenarios due to their past failures, they can see success only because of their newfound knowledge and greater confidence in their abilities.

This overconfidence is referred to as comparative optimism. It has been defined as 'the tendency of people to report that they are less likely than others to experience negative events, and more likely than others to experience positive events' (Ucbasaran, Westhead, Wright and Flores, 2010).

This finding agrees with that of another study, which concluded that entrepreneurs are more optimistic than non-entrepreneurs and 'they do not perceive themselves as being any more predisposed to taking risks' (Palich and Bagby, 1995: 426). This lack of perception sometimes results in them engaging in activities others may perceive as being overly risky. Also, this outlook of entrepreneurs can potentially lead to their perceiving certain situations as opportunities, while others would perceive the same situations as risky undertakings. However, as Dever (2009) concluded, entrepreneurs want to continue to build new firms and all seem to be confident in their ability to do just that.

According to Dever (2009), past failures are not seen as stumbling blocks to entrepreneurs but more as 'rites of passage' that will allow them to build in the future with no fear of failures yet to come. They do not believe that they will have another failure and, as a result, will move forward, perhaps with little or no regard to the risks. The learning process will protect them from future failure, so they surmise.

The traits that seem to emerge from interviews with active entrepreneurs indicate that they will rely on their perceptions of past experience for success and, as Stokes and Blackburn (2002: 18) state, 'Owners believe that they learn from the closure process so that they are better equipped to run businesses in future. Even those who have had unsuccessful ventures are motivated to start another enterprise and believe that they are more able to make it work next time because of lessons learned.'

10.8 Exit strategies

'Failure may lead to ultimate success in business by economizing on resources which leads to greater efficiencies' (Coelho and McClure, 2005: 13). Entrepreneurs often carry out an exit strategy to maximise those efficiencies and redirect their use, but such closures are sometimes mistakenly thought to be failures. The use of exit strategies sometimes occurs while the firm is earning a profit and prior to amassing large amounts of debt (Headd, 2003). A healthy economy requires pruning and the termination of uneconomic activities. Businessowners have been known, however, to time their departure from businesses when the economy is on an upswing and so take advantage of positive economic conditions. This would indicate that, in times of positively increasing economic activity, there will be an increase in business failures: 'There is certainly no point in trying to conserve obsolescent industries indefinitely; but there is point in trying to avoid their coming down with a crash and in attempting to turn a rout, which may become a centre of cumulative depressive effects, into orderly retreat' (Schumpeter, 1950: 90).

Based on this premise, as a business begins to decline or fail and an exit strategy is designed and implemented, one must question if this could then be considered a positive exit. Since profit is often the motive for one being in business and the entrepreneur chooses to close prior to losses mounting, could a sell-out be considered positive or is it still a negative event? Since a well thought out exit strategy is essential to a smooth discontinuance of business, it is important for entrepreneurs to design exit strategies that will allow them the flexibility to stop operations without losses.

Many feel that failure in a business is often automatically a negative event, but studies have shown that, often, by utilising an effective exit strategy, as suggested above, one can turn the perceived negative event into a positive one. Stokes and Blackburn (2002) analysed failure from a positive standpoint. Questioning entrepreneurs and associates of entrepreneurs, they were unable to ascertain whether or not closure is a negative event. Some 62 per cent of their respondents subsequently opened new businesses and 70 per cent were positively encouraged by the experience. The question is, therefore, by having an exit strategy in place and moving on to new achievements, can entrepreneurs avoid the negative effects of failure?

The following excerpts from a doctoral dissertation (Dever, 2009) examine the subject of an exit strategy, which was discussed with five entrepreneurs, all of whom had experienced a failure in their businesses. The strategies analysed in the dissertation for divesting oneself of an unwanted business were bankruptcy, closure, a sell-out and creative destruction (the closure of a business in order to move on to a more profitable venture).

[All five entrepreneurs] utilized closure as a strategy for discontinuance, with Entrepreneur B also using a sell-out for an additional business he did not close. According to the entrepreneurs, in spite of them all utilizing a closure, selling out was their preferred strategy. When questioned about this preference for selling out, each of the entrepreneurs offered varying reasons, but a common thread existed throughout their discussions: money. All of them equated selling out to making money. The exception to this profit perspective was Entrepreneur B, who approached this from the point of view, not how much could be made but how much could potentially be saved, if the business was a losing proposition. Of the four exit strategies investigated, sell-out was the sole strategy that ended with an absolute positive outcome. The entrepreneurs did state their closings were all positive, but their opinions should be considered an effort to 'save face'. This is not to say the strategy of closing was not positive, but it was positive in a way which allowed the entrepreneurs a freedom from a non-performing firm each so badly desired.

Another strategy which was common to all five entrepreneurs was a lack of the use of bankruptcy. As with the case of selling out, all of the entrepreneurs deemed bankruptcy as a viable tool to assist in exiting an unwanted business. Four of the five stated if they ever initiated a bankruptcy proceeding, they would still feel compelled to repay any debts that were removed in the procedure. The purpose of bankruptcy is to exorcise the unpayable debts of the filing party. Even though the four state every attempt would be made to repay debts, it is unlikely this would be the case. According to the United States Bankruptcy Courts, during a 12-month period ending September 30 2007, there were a total of 801,269 bankruptcy filings in the United States; of these, 25,925 were business filings, and there are no statistics indicating how much of the debt was repaid after the filing. Entrepreneur E is the only entrepreneur who indicated he would not repay any bankruptcy debt.

Three of the five entrepreneurs agreed on another exit strategy as being viable: creative destruction. Their comments ranged from it being the only way the economy can grow to creative destruction being second only to the sell-out as a strategy. The two dissenting entrepreneurs, Entrepreneur A and Entrepreneur D, were concerned the process would reverse all of the efforts of the entrepreneur. Entrepreneur A has seen creative destruction in the airline industry and does not feel it has proven successful. Entrepreneur D equates building a business with one's brand name and he is concerned, if the business is destroyed, the brand name would go with it. There is an ongoing discussion among researchers as to the benefits and liabilities of creative destruction. Knott and Posen (2005) argued the strategy is good for the economy while others, such as Meckstroth (2005), claim creative destruction is causing a serious decline in available jobs. Entrepreneur B is a rapt proponent of the strategy, having utilized it in the past, and believes communities must utilize creative destruction to maintain their viability.

Since all firms will eventually close for one reason or another – be it a failure, closure, sell-out or bankruptcy – everyone in business must have a stance on this issue and attempt to design a workable exit strategy in order to exit their firms with as little financial and personal damage as possible. Students of entrepreneurship are taught that one of the important parts of designing and creating a successful firm is to also design a workable exit strategy at the beginning of the start-up process.

10.9 Chapter summary

Entrepreneurial failure is a comprehensive and far-reaching subject and it is for this reason that this chapter has focused on the large – usually exogenous – and small – usually endogenous – failures within the firms and the effects of those failures upon entrepreneurs.

The overarching reasons for failure cannot be identified precisely due to the nature of business itself – no definite or clear factors can be determined. The only exception concerning failure is that it has the ability to affect all businesses and all entrepreneurs at one time or another. The failures may be due to small internal failures or external ones (Osborne, 1993; Cannon and Edmondson, 2005). Either way, failure will most likely affect every entrepreneur at some time in their career and could have devastating effects. The amount of damage the event will cause is based on individual entrepreneurs' abilities to recognise the antecedents of failure and their ability to take proactive and corrective actions in a timely, efficient and resourceful manner.

This chapter has addressed the antecedents of failure and it is worthy making a final review of these, as being able to recognise them may save entrepreneurs' firms, their self-esteem and ensure that they have the ability to continue to build companies. Key findings regarding entrepreneurs' perceptions of the antecedents to failure include:

- lack of interest or focus in the firm
- mismanagement by the entrepreneur
- insufficient time to devote to the firm
- thievery and inventory control shortcomings
- choosing to overlook the antecedents
- failure to dedicate sufficient resources to the firm
- lack of dedication and allegiance
- failure to act in a timely manner
- cashflow or funding problems
- inability to attract outside investors
- failure to recognise the signs of failure
- managerial ineptness.

Owners of small businesses are known for their outsized self-esteem and egos and, at times, failure to notice the small events that occur within their firms and to ask for help (see Chapter 9 for a discussion of over-optimism). Therefore, it is important for them to be aware of potential problems and take affirmative action when problems do arise. Entrepreneurs must have an understanding of the importance of their attentiveness to each of their ventures, especially new and vulnerable firms. This is not to say that entrepreneurs should spend all of their time at new firms searching for signs of failure, but they must, at the very least, be willing to devote ample quality time to ensuring the success of all of their ventures and future entrepreneurs must be aware of the importance of this to the success of any firm.

Questions

1 Discuss the ways in which entrepreneurs can exit their firms.

2 Discuss the difference between an internal and an external failure.

3 Explain the changes to the bankruptcy laws and what effects those changes have produced.

4 Write a synopsis of how an event occurring in a firm can lead to ultimate failure for the entrepreneur and the firm.

5 How do exit strategies play an important role in the success of an entrepreneurial venture?

Weblinks

www.onlinecollege.org/2010/02/16/50-famously-successful-people-who-failed-at-first
A fun page that reminds us how many successful people failed before they succeeded.

PART 3

Types of entrepreneurship

CHAPTER 11

Ethnicity and entrepreneurship

Monder Ram, Giles Barrett and Trevor Jones

11.1 Introduction

Ethnic minority-owned businesses are now an established and growing feature of many advanced industrial societies. In addition to fulfilling an important economic and social role for minority communities, ethnic minority-owned firms have become particularly conspicuous within the general small business population.

This chapter reviews a number of the often-contentious themes that have characterised this emerging field of enquiry. These include the myriad explanations of the formation of ethnic minority businesses, which range from 'culturalist' accounts to more structurally orientated responses, factors behind different levels of self-employment activity, the material basis of 'family' labour, the nature of the market environment, financial experiences and issues for business support agencies.

11.2 Learning objectives

There are four learning objectives for this chapter:

1 to account for different levels of self-employment among Britain's ethnic minorities
2 to understand the different explanations of the formation and development of ethnic minority firms
3 to describe the dynamics of financing ethnic minority businesses
4 to identify the challenges facing policymakers in supporting ethnic minority firms.

Key concepts
■ opportunity structure ■ culture ■ ethnicity ■ diversity ■ family

11.3 Ethnicity and enterprise

Throughout advanced industrial societies, the last two decades have witnessed a significant increase in self-employment and small business activity among ethnic minorities (Ram and Jones, 1998; Waldinger, Aldrich and Ward, 1990; Kloosterman and Rath, 2003). Many of these businesses are embedded (see Section 11.11.3 on the key concept of mixed embeddedness) in immigrant-origin communities that grew out of post-war demand for low-skill and low-paid labour, particularly in labour-intensive manufacturing industries. Since the 1970s, deindustrialisation and the growing importance of the service sector have reduced traditional job opportunities for immigrant labour, while simultaneously creating openings for self-employment (Phizacklea and Ram, 1996; Sassen, 1997).

In Britain, ethnic minority businesses have been the subject of growing interest. The media have not been slow to publicise the 'rags to riches' stories of conspicuously successful South Asian entrepreneurs, even though more careful accounts of this community in business convey a more complex picture. Researchers continue to offer competing explanations for the apparent entrepreneurial flair of some ethnic groups, noticeably South Asians, and the below-average propensity for self-employment among other communities, in particular African-Caribbeans. To varying degrees, business support agencies have attempted to respond, on the one hand, to high levels of unemployment in black communities and, on the other, to the increasingly significant phenomenon of ethnic enterprise in particular localities and economic sectors. These developments need to be set against a political context that, during the 1980s, was punctuated by civil disturbances in a number of British inner-city areas. A consensus among policymakers rapidly developed that exhorted the black population to engage in 'productive pursuits' (Scarman, 1981). Encouraging self-employment among ethnic minorities therefore emerged as a means of maintaining social harmony in urban areas.

This interest is testimony to the growing importance of the ethnic presence in the small firm population. In this chapter, key aspects of ethnic minority business activity in Britain are assessed. These include explanations of the different patterns of self-employment among ethnic minority groups, particularly African-Caribbeans and South Asians, the contentious question of entrepreneurial motivation and the apparent impact of 'cultural' resources on the business entry decision, the role of the often-lauded 'family' in the ethnic minority firm, the constraining nature of the market environment, the relationship between ethnic enterprises and high street banks and the role of business support agencies in ethnic minority business development. However, since ethnic minority entrepreneurship is not a peculiarly British phenomenon, we begin with a brief assessment of ethnic minority business activity from an international perspective.

11.4 Ethnic minority enterprises: an international perspective

Throughout virtually the entire economically advanced world, immigration has increased steadily from the mid-twentieth century onwards and immigrant-origin ethnic minorities have emerged as a burgeoning presence among the entrepreneurial self-employed. Indicative of a tension that permeates the ethnic business literature, some observers have argued that particular groups are culturally predisposed to engage in these types of activities (Werbner, 1984), whilst other contributors have stressed the importance of wider structures in shaping the entrepreneurial activity of ethnic minorities

(Jones, Barrett and McEvoy, 2000; Rath, 2000). For Kloosterman and Rath (2003: 10), ethnic enterprises arise out of 'the intersection of rising immigration and the post-industrial transition', immigration coinciding with a shift towards services and flexible production, which has created conditions for new small enterprise to flourish.

One important pattern that needs noting before this global review is the sharp contrast between high levels of ethnic minority enterprises in the Anglo-American realm and comparatively low levels throughout most of mainland Europe. According to Kloosterman and Rath (2003), this is largely due to structural factors with the laissez-faire deregulated commercial environments of the UK and USA offering a far more liberal opportunity structure than the much more restrictive mainland European countries. This reminds us of the way ethnic minority businesses are not solely products of their own community cultures but also vitally shaped by the surrounding political, market and legal environments. The recent development of mixed embeddedness theory analyses this interplay of forces in greater depth (see Section 11.11).

In France, high levels of business activity among individuals of Moroccan, Tunisian and Chinese origin have been noted. These enterprises tend to offer the same products as indigenously owned firms, but provide a different quality of service. Competitive advantage is achieved over their rivals through longer opening hours, easily available credit and the sale of products in very small quantities (Ma Mung and Guillon, 1986; Ma Mung and Lacroix, 2003).

The Tunisians are the smallest of the three groups, originating from North Africa, but they have the greatest affinity with self-employment. Research has shown a concentration of approximately 180 Tunisian catering establishments in only a few neighbourhoods of Paris. Within these outlets, strong traditions are fostered and the firms provide much-needed work for family members and co-ethnics (Boubakri, 1985).

Yet, despite their numerical profusion, ethnic minority firms in France are very much restricted to a 'narrow path' (Ma Mung and Lacroix, 2003), concentrated very much at the least profitable end of catering and retailing. It is important to note that this clustering in ill-rewarded labour-intensive sectors is a hallmark of ethnic minority businesses – an internationally recurrent pattern recorded for the UK (Barrett, Jones and McEvoy 2003), the Netherlands (Rath, 2000), Germany (Wilpert, 2003) and Austria (Haberfellner, 2003). In the latter two countries especially, this narrow focus is attributed to tight legal regulation of migration, citizenship and employment, emphasising that ethnic business patterns are subject to politics as well as economics and ethnic culture.

Mention of culture reminds us that, for historical reasons, the ethnic origins of entrepreneurs are variable from country to country. In Germany, it is Turkish entrepreneurs who occupy centre stage, with Turkish-owned businesses proliferating considerably since the 1980s. As elsewhere, this rise is explicable with reference to a combination of positive and negative factors. On the plus side, the Turkish community retains strong family traditions, with family members furnishing the valuable resource of labour power. Additionally, the presence of a large Turkish population creates a market demand for culturally specific products. At the same time, self-employment has also arisen as a means of material survival in the negative circumstances of rising unemployment. Over time, business activities have begun to break out of their reliance on the co-ethnic market and move towards providing such items as fast food and transport for the wider non-Turkish market (Wilpert, 2003). Turks in Belgium also appear to be following a similar trajectory, particularly in relation to restaurants (Kestleloot and Mistaanen, 1997).

The Netherlands, too, has witnessed growing ethnic minority business activity. Ex-colonial subjects constitute the largest ethnic minorities in the country and the Surinamese are the largest single group (Blaschke et al., 1990). Low levels of entrepreneurial activity have been officially noted for Turks, Moroccans, Chinese, Javanese and Creoles among other groups. However, more recently attention has turned to examining the informal economic activities of ethnic minorities in the Netherlands (Kloosterman, van der Leun and Rath, 1998; Rath, 1998).

'Informal activities' – defined as income-generating activities that do not meet the requirements of regulatory frameworks – are a feature of post-industrial urban economies throughout the world (Pugliese, 1993). They not only provide income for the businessowners but may also be instrumental in providing much-needed incomes for other ethnic minorities who may be, for example, between regular jobs or have no regular sources of income whatsoever.

The immigration of Surinamese to the Netherlands has been characterised by a stop–start process, with immigration peaking in 1974–1975 and then declining sharply following the independence of Surinam in 1975. The entrepreneurial behaviour of the Surinamese in Amsterdam reflects this pattern of migration, with the first wave of businesses established in the 1960s concerned with serving the dietary needs of the early migrants. As the numbers of co-ethnics rose in subsequent years, there was both a proliferation in the number of these tropical foodshops and a diversification into other activities. According to Blaschke et al. (1990), there were, in 1983, approximately 250 Surinamese ventures in Amsterdam, mostly occupying the cheapest sites in the older parts of the urban centre where Surinamese residents had settled (Byrne, 1998).

In North America, immigrant enterprises have, historically, been prominent for far longer than in Europe (Light, 1984) and often tend to be taken as a theoretical template for similar businesses elsewhere in the world. Business ownership has been repeatedly promoted as a self-help strategy through which oppressed American minorities can achieve economic advancement. Japanese-Americans, Chinese, Jews, Middle Easterners, French Canadians and Cubans, among others, have all been the focus of research studies into the business activities of these diverse ethnic minorities (Light, 1972; Razin, 1993; Light et al., 1993; Langlois and Razin, 1995; Portes and Bach, 1985).

Much of this interest in ethnic businesses has tended to focus on the question posed by Waldinger (1995: 62) as to 'why some visibly identifiable and stigmatized groups make it through business and others do not'. A more recent manifestation of this is the comparison between Koreans and African-Americans in business (as we shall see, this has echoes with the juxtaposition of South Asian and African-Caribbean entrepreneurship in Britain).

'Business-minded' Koreans have been presented as the archetypal role model for all disadvantaged minorities to aspire to in their logical quest for socio-economic advancement. Both Kim (1981) and Min (1991) discuss the propensity of Korean-owned businesses to become established in low-income black areas of central cities. Their decision to service the population in these areas is twofold. First, there is a desire to exploit the vacant niche that has not been filled by African-American entrepreneurs who (allegedly) lack the necessary cultural and class-based resources conducive to small business formation.

In New York, the emergence of these niches has been precipitated by an ageing population of Jewish and Italian businessowners whose fear of crime, age and the reluctance of heirs has prompted them to sell their businesses on.

Second, Korean entrepreneurs perceive that the black ghettos represent a relatively less hostile environment than predominately white areas. Whilst Korean entrepreneurs have brought much-needed services to central-city ghettos, their strong ethnic ties and cultural attachment has served to exclude others (Light and Rosenstein, 1995). These exclusionary practices have prompted violent responses from inner-city black communities angered by the failure of Korean-owned firms to employ African-American workers and contribute finances to African-American community organisations. The organised boycotts of Korean-owned outlets have also been a feature. Hence, the entrance of Korean businesses into African-American locales is often viewed as risky because of simmering inter-ethnic tensions (Jo, 1992; McEvoy and Cook, 1993; Ok Lee, 1995).

Bates (1994b) questions if the educational merits of Korean entrepreneurs are sufficiently rewarded in their business activities. Min (1991) notes that the vast majority of Korean immigrants have received a secondary school or college education in South Korea, hence their employment in retail and service activities represents an underutilisation of their human capital. Across the Atlantic, a similar argument has been proposed for South Asians in Britain (Aldrich, Cater, Jones and McEvoy, 1981, 1984; Srinivasan, 1995). Hence, self-employment has afforded entrepreneurs the opportunity to make their own decisions about the operations of their enterprises, but the wider structures of society regulates access to the different types of activities. Moreover, despite the ethnic and economic solidarity exhibited by Korean enterprises and their heavy investment in their ventures, actual returns on their human and physical capital are very small and inferior to the returns accruing to African-American-owned ventures (per dollar invested in capital; Asante and Mattson, 1992). This suggests that the appropriateness of the Korean entrepreneurship model as the benchmark for all marginalised minority groups to follow should be treated with caution.

As early as the 1880s, some intellectual African-American leaders in the USA, such as Booker T. Washington, propagated the rise and development of a black (African-American) bourgeoisie (Asante and Mattson, 1992). This emerging strand of the middle classes would lead to the full emancipation of African-American people as business opportunities and property ownership became widespread and an accepted facet of African-American culture. These developments would be underpinned by the bond of shared values, racial co-operation and self-help. However, Frazier (1957) points out that the capital mobilised within the African-American community was insignificant in relation to the American economy and African-American entrepreneurship provided very few jobs for co-ethnics. Hence, to promote African-American business activity as a panacea for the deep-seated and intractable problems of disadvantage and institutionalised racism is highly problematic.

Frazier (1957: 153) labels the belief that entrepreneurship represented an overarching solution to the endemic problems of racism as a 'Social myth . . . [and] . . . one of the main elements in the world of "make-believe" which the black bourgeoisie has created to compensate for its feeling of inferiority in a white world dominated by business enterprise'.

The comparatively low rates of African-American business ownership are generally attributed to the lack of sociocultural and class resources that can be mobilised in the pursuit of entrepreneurship. Both Light and Bonacich (1988) and Waldinger, McEvoy and Aldrich (1990b) affirm that the fragmented nature of African-American communities militates against the development of group social networks and mechanisms of in-group attachment, which help to nurture business opportunities. The absence of petty bourgeois values is also a serious setback to encouraging new firms (Cashmore, 1991). Low educational attainments among African-Americans, small amounts of financial capital and the absence of resource-generating mechanisms, such as rotating credit schemes, are among the class-related factors that severely hinder the processes of business formation (Bonacich and Modell, 1980; Curran and Burrows, 1986; Light and Rosenstein, 1995).

However, a fundamental hindrance to black progression is the persistence of racism. Unequal access to health, education, capital and labour market opportunities have stunted the growth of a black entrepreneurial class (Marable and Mullings, 1994; Waldinger and Perlmann, 1998). As Cashmore (1992) has observed, the promotion of an 'enterprise culture' during the 1980s under President Ronald Reagan actually involved considerable cuts in welfare and health expenditure and the proclaimed belief that poverty was a self-induced state of being. Hence socially, politically and economically marginalised groups, such as the homeless, un/underemployed and visible minorities, were held responsible for their own plight. So, neo-conservative thinking acted to create a pool of exploitable low-cost labour so that US industrial capital could begin to compete more readily with international companies (Kasarda, 1989; Sassen, 1991). Whilst, in the late 1990s, some economic progress is detected for ethnic minorities in the USA, this is extremely uneven. The recent founding of initiatives such as inner-city enterprise zones and Specialised Small Business Investment Companies (SSBICs) has failed to galvanise a new generation of black entrepreneurs in the USA (Bates, 1997).

11.5 Ethnic minority business activity: the British experience

As in the USA, one of the most debated features of the ethnic minority business population in Britain is the marked disparity between the circumstances of different groups, most clearly evident in the patterns of self-employment among ethnic minority communities. South Asians are particularly well represented in self-employment, with people of Pakistani or Bangladeshi origins three times as likely to be self-employed as West Indians or Guyanese. While there are inescapable transatlantic echoes here of the Korean/African-American gap, we shall see later that the picture has begun to change significantly. In the meantime, however, we shall concentrate on the 'Afro-Asian gap' – asking the question, 'Why so few black businessmen?' (Kazuka, 1980), which has attracted an almost obsessive interest since the 1980s (Ward, 1991; Soar, 1991).

11.5.1 African-Caribbean experiences

Many of the explanations accounting for African-Caribbean 'under-representation' in self-employment appear to make reference to the apparent lack of cultural resources that are often documented in other ethnic minority groups. Unlike Asians, who are invariably portrayed as richly endowed with family resources, communal networks and other forms of social capital (Metcalf, Modood and Virdee, 1996; Basu, 1998), African-Caribbeans are argued to be underendowed in various crucial respects. These include the different values base of the African-Caribbean family unit, which apparently does not predispose them to running a family business (Reeves and Ward, 1984), the legacy of slavery, which had a deleterious effect upon African-Caribbean culture (Rex, 1982; Fryer, 1984; Gilroy, 1987; Pajackowska and Young, 1992), and the absence of extended family and community networks (Blaschke et al., 1990).

However, explanations focusing exclusively on the absence or otherwise of 'cultural' resources often fail to appreciate the impact that the opportunity structure can have on the facilitation of business opportunities. Basu (1991), in particular, eschews culturalist interpretations and presents a cogent case for locating African-Caribbean under-representation in the social context of black people in Britain. To this end, a number of factors need to be considered.

First, many African-Caribbeans originally migrating to Britain were from a working-class background – essentially a 'replacement' workforce who came from working-class backgrounds to fill occupational and residential niches vacated by white people.

'Class' resources (Lights, 1984) are important in developing attitudes, beliefs, educational qualifications and social networks conducive to entrepreneurship. South Asian migrants in Britain appeared to have a broader socio-economic profile and, therefore, greater access to class resources. The greater entrepreneurial success of the more affluent blacks that migrated to the USA and Canada (Foner, 1979, 1987) would seem to bear out the importance of class background. Ethnic identity is cross-cut by class background in this as in many other instances.

Second, comparatively high levels of unemployment among the black community (Jones, 1993) serve to induce self-employment in low-skill, highly competitive and poorly rewarded industrial sectors. Often, such 'no choice' businesses operate in the informal economy (and, thus, are not accounted for in official statistics) or remain marginal concerns with little prospect of real progress (Basu, 1991).

Third, negative stereotyping of African-Caribbeans in British society impinges upon their capacity to mobilise resources that are potentially useful in business. Less preferential treatment by the banks (Jones, McEvoy and Barrett, 1994b) and racist customer behaviour (Jones, McEvoy and Barrett, 1992) are important business processes where such stereotyping has been noted.

Fourth, residential settlement patterns appear to influence business development among minority groups. For example, Reeves and Ward (1984) argue that the relative dispersal of African-Caribbean settlement (compared to the concentration of South Asians), their numerically smaller population and the apparent lack of culturally specific needs, combine to limit market potential for growth in small businesses. Finally, African-Caribbeans are further constrained by their comparatively low levels of home ownership, which diminishes their capacity to offer collateral for business start-up funding (Basu, 1991).

It appears, then, that this group is faced with a powerful combination of structural handicaps to entrepreneurialism, handicaps that in themselves have little directly to do with ethnic cultural attributes. This needs to be borne in mind in comparative assessments of ethnic minority entrepreneurship.

Also to be borne in mind are more recent trends that threaten to undermine many of the stereotypical assumptions about an Afro-Asian gap. Since the 1990s, there have been signs that the onward march of South Asian enterprise has gone into reverse, notably among Indians. Due, in part, to a supermarket-induced decline in small retailing, in part, to young Asians shunning self-employment for professional careers, there is now a palpable reduction in Asian self-employment (Jones and Ram, 2003). With African-Caribbean self-employment continuing to rise, however, any interethnic entrepreneurial gap can only diminish and even disappear. In any case, what matters in the final analysis is quality, not quantity. Though diminishing numerically, the signs are that Asian business is shifting away from low-profit, labour-intensive sectors into human capital-rich activities such as IT (Ram, Smallbone, Deakins and Jones, 2003).

A further relatively recent line of enquiry has focused on emerging differences within the South Asian entrepreneurial population itself. According to such sources as Metcalf et al. (1996), Indians and East African Asians are the real Asian entrepreneurial success stories in terms of business resources, good practice, positive motivations, earnings, profitability, growth and scale. Conversely, many Pakistani and Bangladeshi enterprises appear relatively weak in performance terms, economically marginal and arising out of a context of disadvantage. Once again, caution must be urged, however, since other researchers have found much less of an interethnic gap and identified many Pakistani firms as outstanding high-flyers (Ram et al., 2003).

11.6 The business entry decision

One of the most keenly debated issues within the ethnic business literature concerns the decision to become self-employed. Various explanations have been advanced outlining the processes that give rise to ethnic minority business ownership.

Jenkins (1984: 231–4), for instance, has identified three basic explanatory models of ethnic involvement in business. The 'economic opportunity' model regards ethnic minority business activity as essentially no different from routine capitalist activity, relying on the market for its fortunes. The 'culture' model asserts that some cultures predispose their members towards the successful pursuit of entrepreneurial goals. Finally, the 'reaction' model views self-employment by members of ethnic minority groups as a reaction against racism and blocked avenues of social mobility, a means of surviving at the margins of a white-dominated society.

Waldinger, McEvoy and Aldrich (1990b) have developed a more interactive approach for understanding ethnic business development. Essentially, it argues that ethnic enterprise is a product of the interplay of opportunity structures, group characteristics and strategies for adapting to the environment (for further evaluation of this, see Section 11.11).

A steady stream of studies since the 1980s have stressed the importance of external factors in their explanations of the proliferation of particularly South Asian-owned small enterprises (Mullins, 1979; Aldrich et al., 1981, 1982, 1984; Jones, 1981; Robinson and Flintoff, 1982; Nowikowski, 1984; Jones, Cater, De Silva and McEvoy, 1989). According to this perspective, self-employment is a survival strategy borne out of the persistent discrimination that ethnic minorities face within the wider labour market.

Compelling evidence for this view is presented by Jones, McEvoy and Barrett (1992) in their national study of 178 South Asian, 54 African-Caribbean and 171 white owners of small businesses. More than a quarter of the South Asian owners turned to self-employment because of blocked opportunities or unemployment. Furthermore, Jones et al. (1992: 186) believed this to be an underestimate:

> Since there were also many other Asian respondents who had experienced periods of unemployment or unsuitable employment even while giving positive entry motives like money or independence, we take this as a sure sign that Asians in Britain are no more culturally predisposed or voluntaristically oriented towards enterprise than any other group.

In contrast, there are strong proponents from a more 'culturalist' tradition who privilege what they regard as distinctively ethnic resources in their accounts of business formation (Werbner, 1980, 1984, 1990; Soni, Tricker and Ward, 1987; Srinavasan, 1992; Basu, 1995). For example, Werbner (1984) identifies a distinctive Pakistani ethos of self-sacrifice, self-denial and hard work that serves to fuel entrepreneurial activity. Basu (1995) also located a particular South Asian 'entrepreneurial spirit' in her survey of 78 South Asian retailers. Basu (1995: 16) maintained that, 'It is difficult to support the hypothesis that the small businessmen in our sample were driven or pushed into self-employment as the only alternative to escaping unemployment.'

The controversy shows little sign of abating. Nonetheless, it is clear that the simple concept of 'push' versus 'pull' (which has featured in some of the more quantitatively orientated studies of ethnic enterprise) is unlikely to grasp fully the complexity of entrepreneurial decisionmaking. As Granger, Stanworth and Stanworth (1995: 513) note in their study of freelances in the book publishing sector, 'research designs which simply focus on the moment of transition from one labour market state to another, without exploring background career histories, are unlikely to grasp the real dynamics of self-employment career changes.'

This point is given added resonance by Ram and Deakins' (1996) study of African-Caribbean entrepreneurs. From a reading of employers' initial responses (using pre-set statements), the findings indicated that African-Caribbean entrepreneurs had in common with the white owners of small businesses largely positive motivations for entrepreneurship (Curran, 1986). More qualitative accounts from respondents were also elicited, however, and they revealed that an unfavourable opportunity structure, in the guise of menial jobs or limited prospects at work, still had a bearing on the business entry decision.

From this review of the evidence, then, it would seem that pure culturalist explanations are not adequate in accounting for small business formation in ethnic minority communities. Indeed, more recent studies of entrepreneurial motivations suggest that ethnic culture is often overridden by *class* culture – a set of values common to all small business entrepreneurs (including white ones) in which independence and the desire to be one's own boss are paramount in influencing the decision to enter and continue in business (Ram et al., 2003). Where interethnic differences do apply, what is of more significance is the nature of the opportunity structure and what Light (1984) has called *class resources*. These are tangible material resources – e.g., property and accumulated finance – that can be used to spin off new firms or branches and less tangible resources – e.g., contacts and information networks and the self-confidence which goes with the possession of all these assets together with a track record. As noted above, such resources are not evenly spread across ethnic minority groups, though the signs are that a more educationally qualified and professionalised British-born generation of businessowners is steadily acquiring these resources (Ram et al., 2003).

11.7 Family and co-ethnic labour

A further prominent characteristic of ethnic minority businesses is the use made of family and co-ethnic labour. Such labour is often portrayed as a critical source of 'competitive advantage' for ethnic businesses since it is often cheap and the problem of supervision is made easier (Mitter, 1986). It is widely held that the rapid expansion of these groups into such labour-intensive lines as clothing manufacture, catering and, above all, convenience retailing is enabled by their superior capacity to tap into a ready supply of labour power, thus equipping them to work long antisocial hours at their customers' convenience (Ward, 1991).

South Asian-owned firms are often seen as the exemplars of the 'family business'. Very similar tendencies have also been attributed to Greek Cypriot and Chinese entrepreneurs. For the former, Curran and Blackburn (1994) observe that because these entrepreneurs are intensely concentrated in the restaurant trade, they work very long hours, boosted by ordering and collecting supplies. Chinese entrepreneurs are even more specialised in the restaurant and takeaway sector and, consequently, also exposed to extremely long hours of work in order to obtain a competitive cost advantage (Parker, 1994: 622). Among many factors, it is, above all, this competitive undercutting that has enabled the Chinese takeaway, in large part, to replace the traditional English 'chippy' in many areas (Liao, 1992). The personal toll on the families running these businesses, however, is often considerable. As Parker (1994: 622) notes, 'the whole of family life and the domestic economy [is] shaped by the takeaway'.

The facility of family labour does not appear to be as extensively utilised within African-Caribbean enterprises (Reeves and Ward, 1984). Explanations accounting for this include the more 'egalitarian' nature of the African-Caribbean family unit (Basu, 1991) and the lack of scope for enlisting unskilled family labour in the type of business sectors that the community tend to be involved in (Curran and Blackburn, 1993). Further corroboration is provided by Curran and Blackburn's (1993) study of Greek Cypriot, Bangladeshi and African-Caribbean businesses, in which it was found that family labour was used least by African-Caribbeans. Curran and Blackburn explain this by reference to not only the nature of family culture in this community but also its dispersed business activities. For instance, the types of unskilled or semiskilled family labour that characterise many ethnic minority firms may not be particularly appropriate in sectors like personal or professional services, where African-Caribbeans are involved.

However, two points that question the conventional wisdom on labour intensiveness and family labour, particularly in relation to South Asian businesses, need to be made. First, long working hours tend to be prevalent across the small firm population, irrespective of their ethnic origin (Curran and Burrows, 1988). When Jones et al. (1994a: 201) examined this question with South Asian, African-Caribbean and white owners of small businesses, they found that ethnic minority respondents operated more labour-intensive practices than is customary, but these 'were as much a function of sectoral distribution and of external pressures as of specific ethnic cultural and behavioural traits'. With regard to sectoral distribution, the simple fact is that Asians are very heavily concentrated in activities such as news agencies, which require very long hours of operation whatever the identity of their owner.

Second, the tendency to view the 'family' as an unqualified resource for the ethnic entrepreneur also needs to be more closely scrutinised. A growing body of evidence argues that 'culturalist' portrayals of the family at work are often one-dimensional; they fail to appreciate the extent to which primacy often accorded to the family can constrain business development (Ram, 1992, 1994a; Ram and Deakins, 1995; Barrett, Jones and McEvoy, 1996; Phizacklea and Ram, 1996). In other words, over-reliance on the family can actually get in the way of economic rationality. Ram's (1994b) ethnographic study of South Asian employers in the West Midlands' clothing sector documents many instances where family members were retained in the business despite a lack of competence, regular breaches of discipline were ignored and family workers secured equal remuneration despite making varying contributions to the business. Hence, the role of the family in ethnic minority enterprises is frequently 'double-edged' – a point that is rarely given sufficient attention in the more celebratory accounts of minority businesses (see Chapter 13 for a fuller discussion of the role of the family in business enterprises).

Further, more recent work emphasises the conflictual potential of gender and generational divisions (Jones and Ram, 2010; see also Mitter, 1986; Dhaliwal, 1998; Phizacklea, 1990). On gender, Barrett et al. (1996) speculate that many male-owned businesses conceal the extent of the centrality of women to these enterprises. It is also clear that women's contributions to the day-to-day activities of the businesses are often unacknowledged. Studies on the internal management processes in ethnic businesses (Ram, 1992, 1994; Phizacklea and Ram, 1996) and, indeed, small firms per se (Holliday, 1995; Fletcher, 1997) illuminate the often critical but not very visible contributions that women play in managing these businesses (see also Chapter 12).

Often the scale of an operation can be too large to be handled by family workers alone – as, for example, in many restaurants and clothing factories run by Asians in Britain. In order to maintain an essential degree of trust, such firms tend to restrict their hiring of non-family workers to members of their own ethnic community, using informal word-of-mouth methods of recruitment (Jones, McEvoy and Barrett, 1994a). Once again, it is often assumed that the bonds of common ethnic membership make for harmonious mutually beneficial working relationships, with paternalistic goodwill rendering unnecessary such practices as written contracts, formal pay bargaining and legal rights. However, evidence from employees themselves suggests that, in many instances, paternalistic benevolence provides a smokescreen for unacceptably low pay and long hours (Gilman, Edwards, Ram and Arrowswith, 2002), especially for low-skilled workers subject to discrimination in the mainstream labour market, whose job choices and bargaining leverage are minimal (Ram et al., 2001; Jones and Ram, 2010). It may be that labour processes of this kind are best viewed as not specifically 'Asian' but as more typical of the small firm generally (Jones and Ram, 2010).

More recently, too, researchers have highlighted a growing reliance on illegal immigrant workers by struggling firms desperate to cut costs in order to survive (Ram, Edwards and Jones, 2002; Jones, Ram and Edwards, 2006). As Jones et al. (2006) explain, this is a morally ambiguous situation where entrepreneurs are cutting legal corners in order to simply stay alive. Yet, even though this is more a commentary on the dire returns from some branches of catering and clothing than on the greed of employers, it nevertheless still victimises workers. Such workers represent the extremes of vulnerability, absolutely without any employment rights or bargaining power whatsoever (CARF, 1997; Staring, 2000).

11.8 Restricted spatial markets

Most ethnic minority businesses are located within Britain's inner cities, which is almost certainly an historic reflection of ethnic settlement patterns (Reeves and Ward, 1984; Basu, 1991). Labour Force Survey data indicates that 70 per cent of the economically active ethnic minorities live in metropolitan county areas, compared with 30 per cent of the white population (Daly, 1991: 68).

An inner-city location can have important implications for the viability and growth prospects of small businesses. It was often 'white flight' from decaying inner-city areas that provided the opportunity for ethnic minorities to take over businesses, particularly in the retail distributive sector (Jones et al., 1994a). Despite providing this initial opportunity, however, the problems inherent in an inner-city location often temper the potential for the development of such businesses. For example, local environmental conditions – e.g., physical dilapidation, inadequate parking and vandalism – are depressingly commonplace. They can often prove a major constraint on securing high-quality markets from outside the immediate locality (Basu, 1991). Moreover, they accentuate the problem of raising appropriate finance (Deakins, Hussain and Ram, 1994) and insurance cover (Patel, 1988).

Although co-ethnic consumer tastes may provide an initial opportunity for business activities, continued reliance acts as a major constraint on business development. This is due to the comparatively small size of ethnic minority communities. Furthermore, minority entrepreneurs tend to cater for mainly local residents within inner-city areas, but these customers have relatively low spending power (Basu, 1991). Moreover, such 'community markets' are likely to be in long-term decline since successive British governments have made immigration progressively more difficult and there is the likelihood of later generations of ethnic minorities being more integrated with the dominant white culture and economy (Curran and Blackburn, 1993). However, as Curran and Blackburn's (1993: 60) own findings show, breaking out may be less of an issue for minority firms located in areas where there is still a large ethnic minority population.

They found that businesses in London, where there is a very significant ethnic minority presence, were more dependent on co-ethnic markets for their sales than those in Sheffield and Leeds. Hence, demographic trends are likely to have a bearing on the urgency felt by ethnic minority businesses to break out.

In the light of such unpromising trading circumstances, encouraging these businesses to break out into majority markets has emerged as an issue of particular importance (Curran and Blackburn, 1993; Ram and Jones, 1998; Jones et al., 2000). What, though, actually constitutes a break-out?

Clearly, it involves rather more than simply servicing white markets. For instance, a corner shop in a white inner-city area may be in no better a position than a similar business situated in an ethnic enclave; in both cases, highly competitive market conditions and geographic location militate against any real prospects of substantial growth.

A study of African-Caribbean entrepreneurship in Britain (Ram and Deakins, 1996) cautions against simplistic notions of ethnic business development. Contrary to many previous studies, Ram and Deakins found that firms in their investigation had an average of 50 per cent sales to the majority population. Hence, at a basic level, many entrepreneurs may have heeded the advice of commentators advocating the servicing of 'white' markets as the way forward for ethnic enterprise, but it was not uncommon for these mixed market-orientated firms to remain low-yielding marginal concerns with little prospect for significant development in the future.

Curran and Blackburn (1993: 12) provide a rather more sophisticated view of breaking out. They argue for the assessment of plans for expansion with evidence of preparation for growth. Examples of the latter would include investigating sources of finance, planning for the refitting of premises to enhance the potential for growth and the revamping of existing products or services offered by the business to appeal to a wider market or achieve higher mark-ups. Precise measurement of these facets might be difficult, but, nonetheless, a genuine attempt at breaking out would need to address such issues. However, given the sectoral and spatial confines of many ethnic minority firms and their usually labour-intensive modus operandi, breaking out in these terms is likely to be highly problematic.

11.9 Funding ethnic minority enterprises

There can be little doubt that underfunding remains one of the most intractable problems facing the owners of ethnic minority small businesses. The difficult task of securing finance for a business start-up is the most documented problem facing both existing and potential ethnic minority businessowners, whether in Europe or North America (Jones et al., 1992, 1994b; Barrett, 1999; Woodward, 1997). Problems of undercapitalisation perpetually thwart the growth and threaten the survival of many ethnic minority businesses (Basu, 1991; Barrett, 1999). A major debate has been the extent to which the relationships between ethnic entrepreneurs and commercial banks serve to alleviate or exacerbate this problem.

The most comprehensive and up-to-date analysis of ethnic minority businesses was undertaken by Fraser (2009). The analysis used data from the 2004 UK Survey of SME

Finances (UKSMEF) and the UKSMEF Ethnic Minority Booster Survey 2005, both carried out for the Department of Trade and Industry's Small Business Service. These have a sufficiently large representative sample of SMEs from which to draw statistically significant conclusions. Fraser's analysis showed that credit outcomes were worse for entrepreneurs from several ethnic groups. For example:

■ black African firms were more than 4 times as likely as White firms to be denied a loan outright, black Caribbean firms 3.5 times as likely, Bangladeshi firms 2.5 times as likely and Pakistani firms 1.5 times as likely, while Indian firms had a slightly lower loan denial rate than white firms

■ interest rates for loans were higher for Bangladeshi, Pakistani, black Caribbean and black African businesses than for white and Indian enterprises (7.4–7.8 per cent compared to 6.8 per cent)

■ discouragement was highest amongst ethnic minority businesses (EMBs), with 44 per cent of black African, 39 per cent of black Caribbean, 31 per cent of Bangladeshi, 21 per cent of Pakistani and 9 per cent of Indian firms compared to 4 per cent of white firms reporting that fear of rejection had meant they had not applied for loans.

This data adds to the picture painted by earlier research, which, for example, suggested that about two-fifths of African-Caribbean and one-third of Asian applicants reported difficulties in securing loans compared with one-fifth of white applicants (Jones et al., 1994b). Another study showed that African-Caribbean EMBs had the lowest rate of access to bank finance at start-up, despite their owners being likely to have formal management qualifications (Smallbone, Ram, Deakins and Baldock, 2003).

Perceptions are important as well. According to the UKSMEF data, EMBs tend to report much greater problems with accessing finance than white firms – 11 per cent of Bangladeshi businesses, 16 per cent of African-Caribbean and 24 per cent of black African, compared with 1 per cent of white firms. In addition, 35 per cent of black-owned firms reported that their biggest problem at start-up was finding finance. As a result, two-thirds of black African firms used their personal savings as their main source of start-up funding compared with just over half of white firms and EMBs are more likely to use friends and family for finance than white firms, too.

Reasons for poorer creditworthiness suggested by the UKSMEF data include:

■ shorter financial relationships between banks and Pakistani, Bangladeshi, black African and Caribbean firms than with white and Indian firms

■ Indian and white firms tending to have longer business track records than Pakistani, Bangladeshi, black African and Carribean firms

■ Bangladeshi, African-Caribbean and African firms also have far less collateral to back up loan applications

■ very importantly, for the firms covered in the UKSMEF, there was a significantly greater likelihood of Bangladeshi, African-Caribbean and African firms having poorer financial records (missed loan repayments, exceeding overdraft limits and so on).

11.10 Ethnic minority businesses and enterprise support

Encouraging ethnic minority communities into self-employment has been a discernible feature of national and local policymaking since the early 1980s (see Chapter 4). There appear to be two particular reasons for this policy direction.

First, the civil disturbances in many inner-city areas that occurred in the early part of the decade focused attention on the often dire position of black racialised minorities (Cross and Waldinger, 1992). Following Lord Scarman's pronouncements in the wake of the disturbances in Brixton, promulgating self-employment among the black population was seen as an important means of tackling disadvantage and maintaining social harmony in urban areas.

Second, some minority communities – notably South Asian, Chinese and Cypriot communities – have come to dominate particular sectors and local economies. Often this position of prominence has been achieved without the assistance of business support agencies (Marlow, 1992).

A consistent finding of previous research on EMBs is their low propensity to use mainstream business support agencies, often relying instead on self-help and informal sources of assistance (see Ram and Jones, 1998; Ram and Smallbone, 2002; Deakins Ram and Smallbone, 2003 for reviews and Chapter 4 for a fuller discussion of support agency usage). Of course, it could be that the low take-up of business support from formal agencies reflects a low level of perceived need or a lack of interest by EMB owners in receiving external assistance. However, growing evidence (Marlow, 1992; Deakins et al., 2003) suggests that not using mainstream business support agencies cannot necessarily be put down to a lack of interest on the part of the businessowners. 'Supply side' issues – e.g., their inability to reach out to such firms, inadequate databases and the inappropriateness of the 'product-orientated' approaches used by many support agencies – are also pertinent factors.

The ostensibly low take-up of formal sources of business support draws attention to the capacity of these agencies to cater adequately for the needs of ethnic minority firms. The 'equality of access' approach that professes to 'treat all businesses the same' seems to founder on the reluctance of many EMB to utilise the services of mainstream agencies and is severely constrained on the practical grounds that such agencies often fail to capture the most basic data on the scale, dynamics and issues facing EMBs.

A key issue in the debate on appropriate policy support for EMBs is the extent to which their 'needs' are similar to, or different from, those of other SMEs. In practical terms, one of the distinctive characteristics of EMBs in Britain that has important potential implications for business support policy is their concentration in particular sectors – e.g., retailing, catering and personal services. This is important because the prospects for business development are heavily influenced by market and demand trends and the degree of competition in each of these sectors.

Size is another important characteristic of EMBs, which has implications for their access to finance and business support. Although the absence of comprehensive, large-scale business databases that include an ethnic variable makes it impossible to paint a totally accurate picture, it is widely accepted that most EMBs are not just small, but very small firms. This means that they share many of the characteristics, problems and support needs of micro-enterprises more generally. These include frequent problems in raising finance to start a business and/or expand (particularly in the early stages), as well as deficiencies in certain core management competencies – e.g., marketing and financial management skills. One of the consequences of their very small average size is that most EMBs fell outside the main target group of the mainstream business support agencies in England during the 1990s (i.e., Business Link), when the latter were mainly concerned with firms employing more than five (or ten) employees with growth potential (Ram and Smallbone, 2002).

Location is a further characteristic of EMBs, which may influence their support needs. Most ethnic minority businesses are located within Britain's inner cities, reflecting ethnic settlement patterns more generally. The negative consequences of such a location for trade has been documented since the first major study of Asian businesses in 1978 (Aldrich et al., 1984) and reinforced in more recent studies of other minority groups (Ram and Smallbone, 2002). As noted earlier, local environmental conditions such as physical dilapidation, inadequate parking and vandalism are commonplace in such settings. Furthermore, locational factors can add to the difficulties faced in raising finance, which is compounded by the tendency for minority entrepreneurs to cater for local residents who have relatively low spending power.

In interpreting such findings about ethnic minority businesses, it is important to recognise the reluctance of the owners of small firms per se to utilise external assistance. This resistance stems from doubts about value for money, scepticism regarding generalist advice (particularly where this is offered by advisers who lack detailed sectoral knowledge) and an emphasis on autonomy, which some owner-managers perceive is threatened when they use external advice. This may result in a greater use of informal rather than formal channels of support, particularly in cases where managers lack formal management training or qualifications, reflecting the importance of trust-based relationships in the effective delivery of advice and consultancy to small firms, regardless of the ethnicity of the owners (Ram and Smallbone, 2002).

Any contemporary discussion of publicly funded business support in Britain has to be set against the context of the current coalition government's enterprise policy. The Coalition government, elected in May 2010, has drastically reduced the amount of publicly funded business support for small firms and closed down Business Link branches and Regional Development Agencies, both of which provided considerable support for ethnic minority firms as part of their functions. New institutions – notably Local Enterprise Partnerships – are emerging, but, given their limited resources, their impact on small firms, let alone ethnic minority businesses, is unlikely to be significant.

11.11 Millennial shifts

Over approximately the past decade, three highly significant shifts have made themselves felt in the world of ethnic minority businesses. The first of these is historical in nature – a change in the world itself – while the other two are theoretical – changes in the way we explain the world.

11.11.1 Superdiversity

Over the past two decades or so, there have been drastic changes in migration flows to Britain, creating an unprecedented new migrant population. According to Vertovec (2007), the traditional migrant flows of replacement labour from a small handful of countries have been replaced by new migrants from dozens of geographical origins, driven by a host of different motives – what he calls 'superdiversity'.

Because these new populations tend to be highly educated and often have transnational contacts, some commentators see them as possessing good potential for mouldbreaking enterprises (Sepulveda, Syrett and Lyon, 2011). Others see them as destined to follow much the same disadvantaged enterprise path as the 'old' migrants (Jones and Ram, 2010).

11.11.2 The entrepreneurial transition

Falling levels of self-employment among young UK-born Indians, coupled with evidence that many are using their high-level qualifications to enter professional careers, calls for a rethink of the very meaning of enterprise for ethnic minorities. This has even led some writers to suggest that self-employment is no more than a transitional temporary solution for groups new to a society (Jones, Mascarenhas-Keyes and Ram, 2011). As suggested by groups like these in the past, such as Chinese Americans, abnormally high levels of self-employment are only necessary for groups yet to establish themselves in the host labour market and thereby realise their true potential.

11.11.3 Mixed embeddedness theory

Developed by Kloosterman, van der Leun and Rath (1999; see also Kloosterman, 2010), mixed embeddedness theory is a more realistic way of looking at structure versus culture in the creation of ethnic minority businesses. It argues that any firm is simultaneously grounded in both its own social capital – resources supplied by family, community and other social ties – and the wider surrounding economic and legal environment of markets and states. Thus, while explicitly acknowledging the entrepreneur's debt to social relationships, it equally insists that the firm must act within parameters laid down by this powerful context. One result of this is that there is no longer a temptation to see immigrant-origin firms as virtually unique and subject to their own rules rather than simply as special versions of a universal genre (Jones and Ram, 2007).

11.12 Chapter summary

The increasing importance of self-employment among ethnic minorities has been one of the marked features of labour market changes internationally over the past 20 years. As in many advanced industrial societies, ethnic minority-owned businesses are now an established and growing feature of contemporary Britain.

In addition to fulfilling an important economic and social role for the minority communities themselves, ethnic enterprises have also made a significant contribution to both the revival of the small business population and the revitalisation of depressed urban retail landscapes. There is little doubt that particular areas of economic activity – e.g., retailing, clothes manufacture and catering – have been transformed by the dynamic presence of minority communities. Groups such as the South Asian, Chinese and Greek Cypriot communities have been notably conspicuous in effecting such transformations in often adverse competitive environments.

Although African-Caribbean 'under-representation' in self-employment has precipitated much speculation, there is little doubt that they are an emerging presence on the small business scene. More recent evidence on African-Caribbean entrepreneurship (Curran and Blackburn, 1993; Ram and Deakins, 1996) points to the promising growth potential of this community in business.

In this chapter, we have attempted to scrutinise the growing literature on ethnic minority enterprises with a view to assessing some of the key debates that have dominated this subject. The processes that underpin small business formation have been shown to extend beyond pure culturalist arguments that, for instance, depict South Asians as natural entrepreneurs and African-Caribbean's as uninterested in entrepreneurial activities. The influence of the socio-economic context, or 'opportunity structure', continues to affect the life chances of Britain's ethnic minorities and its impact upon the decision to enter self-employment can rarely be discounted. The increasing sensitivity to the importance of context is manifested in the theoretical discussions on 'mixed embeddedness', 'super-diversity' and 'entrepreneurial transition'.

Investigation of family and co-ethnic labour inside the ethnic small business further exposes the fragility of popular stereotypes. It is undoubtedly the case that, in terms of hours worked, entrepreneurial rewards and commitment to the business, ethnic minorities (African-Caribbean as well as the more commonly noted South Asian communities) are remarkably industrious. It is equally evident, however, that such practices are characteristic of the harshly competitive economic sectors that such minority groups trade in rather than a culturally specific work ethic. Moreover, when the capacity of family labour to constrain business development and the often unequal nature of gender relations is highlighted, the image of the cosy, consensus-orientated ethnic minority firm becomes even more illusory. This is not to deny the importance of particular ethnic resources, which can often serve as an important source of competitiveness. Rather, it serves to reinforce the importance of the context in which such firms operate. Hence, a comprehensive synthesis of the multifaceted nature, ethnic minority business enterprise is incomplete without an elaborate understanding of the intricacies of economic change and how and why the proclivity to entrepreneurship in advanced market economies varies for different ethnic groups.

An important part of this context is the relationship with external agencies that are crucial to the development of small firms – notably the high street banks. Debate continues on whether the reported problems between ethnic minority firms and the banks are business- or 'race'-related. However, there is little doubt that underfunding remains one of the most serious problems facing ethnic minority small businesses. In attempting to assist with these and other problems, the 'mainstream' business support agencies appear to be constrained by major obstacles that seem endemic to the burgeoning 'enterprise' industry. These include a lack of clarity over objectives, interagency competition, scarce resources, inappropriate services and a lack of networking. The enterprise

216

policies of the Coalition government have, however, changed the landscape of business support in a way that is unlikely to benefit ethnic minority enterprises.

Questions

1 How adequate are 'culturalist' accounts in explaining ethnic minority involvement in self-employment?

2 What factors account for the different levels of self-employment among ethnic minorities?

3 How feasible is breaking out into majority markets for ethnic minority firms?

Web links

www.itzcaribbean.com/blackenterprise.php
An online resource celebrating caribbean culture in the UK, including business pages.

www.socialenterprise.org.uk/pages/black-asian-and-minority-ethnic-social-enterprises.html
The national body for social enterprise, with dedicated pages for black, Asian and minority ethnic (BAME) social enterprises in the UK.

CHAPTER 12

Gender and entrepreneurship

Sara Carter, Susan Marlow and Dinah Bennett

12.1 Introduction

Over the last 30 years, two parallel socio-economic trends have emerged. First, in almost every country in the world there has been growth in both the size and the relative importance of the small business sector. Second, female suffrage, achieved in many countries within the twentieth century, has been followed by a large-scale expansion in the economic participation of women in the labour market. Reflecting greater participation within paid employment, women have also increased their share of self-employment – although this remains at notably lower levels than that of their male counterparts.

Early research on gender and entrepreneurship – initially undertaken in the USA in the 1970s, but rapidly followed by further work from a diverse range of country contexts – at first initially generated descriptive and comparative analyses of male and female businessowners. Such studies portrayed the male entrepreneur as the 'norm', using gender as a variable to identify gender-specific barriers and constraints that women had to overcome in order to be credible entrepreneurs.

In light of feminist critiques of the detrimental influence of this normative, masculinised discourse of entrepreneurship upon analyses of women's business ownership, more recent research has focused upon the specificity of women's experiences of entrepreneurship. Such work has moved away from the descriptive 'gender as a variable' approach, instead exploring how gender subordination is produced and reproduced within normative accounts of entrepreneurship.

This chapter reviews the development of the research literature on women's entrepreneurship and highlights some of the main themes that have emerged. Finally, the chapter assesses the likely future development of research on women's entrepreneurship, identifying the need for greater theoretical engagement in order to unravel the causes and consequences of gender disadvantage within the context of entrepreneurship.

12.2 Learning objectives

There are three learning objectives for this chapter:

1 to understand the personal and business characteristics of women entrepreneurs and the main management constraints they may face

2 to review the historical development and status of research investigating female entrepreneurship

3 to understand the need for a greater theoretical engagement with the social sciences in order to unravel the causes and consequences of gender disadvantage.

Key concepts
■ women   ■ gender   ■ feminist analyses   ■ entrepreneurship

12.3 Gender and enterprise

Research investigating women's business ownership essentially dates from the mid-1970s. Prior to the pioneering studies of Schreier (1973) and Schwartz (1976), the contribution women made to the small firms sector, either as businessowners in their own right or, more commonly, as providers of labour to family-owned firms, was largely unrecognised. The growth in interest in the small business sector, coupled with a rise in the number of women moving into self-employment, prompted a number of studies investigating the issue of gender and enterprise. This research effort continues to this day, although the issues and themes being addressed by researchers have changed and developed over time. While many of the major studies have emanated from the USA and Western Europe, research investigating the characteristics and experiences of women businessowners has been drawn from a wide range of countries and socio-economic contexts (Al Dajani and Marlow, 2010).

A notable trend in more recent work on women's business ownership has been to move away from comparative work, where the male entrepreneur is presented as a proxy for normative standards, to greater recognition that women's entrepreneurial experiences are worthy of investigation in their own right. So, to take the example of a key theme for the entrepreneurship literature – finance – such work has moved away from comparing men's and women's access to finance. The focus has shifted, instead, to the influence of gender upon women's funding strategies, their use of debt and equity finance and relationships with bank officers. Within this chapter we consider the main research evidence relating to the female entrepreneurship and finance nexus as an illustration of how our approach to investigating the influence of gender upon business ownership has progressed.

Despite the development of an extant literature upon women businessowners during the late 1980s and early 1990s, it was argued that the study of female entrepreneurship was a neglected area (Baker, Adrich and Liou, 1997). More recent reviews of this area (Carter and Shaw, 2006; Neergaard, Frederiksen and Marlow, 2011) suggest that there is now a growing volume of theoretically informed material relating to this issue, but it still remains neglected, as the influence of this research remains limited in its reach and effects. Thus, whilst the volume and influence of research that considers gender is still somewhat limited, particularly that which considers the small business sector as a whole, there is evidence its quality and scope have developed greater sophistication and methodological maturity. In addition, key critiques from within the entrepreneurship subject domain (Ahl, 2006; Taylor and Marlow, 2010) and the broader social sciences (Bruni, Gherardi and Poggio, 2005) have outlined the need for future

219

research to contain stronger theoretical engagement, particularly in terms of employing feminist analyses to illustrate how female subordination is reproduced within the prevailing entrepreneurial discourse.

Within this chapter, we offer a broad overview of the development of this field of research. Drawing from this material, we then document trends in women's business ownership, noting the relatively static share of self-employment commanded by women. To offer a more nuanced account of how our understanding of the impact of gender upon entrepreneurial behaviour has evolved, we focus particularly on the issue of female entrepreneurship, finance and funding. The chapter concludes by considering if it is appropriate to single women out as a specific category worthy of consideration within this debate, the need for more theoretically informed analyses of the impact of gender upon entrepreneurship and potential future avenues for development.

12.4 The growth of female entrepreneurship

Over the past 30 years there have been increases in the number of women entering self-employment and business ownership, although the rate of increase has varied widely from country to country. Importantly, women have been identified as a largely untapped pool of entrepreneurial talent by national and international government agencies (OECD, 2003) – a view that is echoed by the Global Entrepreneurship Monitor (GEM), which highlights the importance of women's enterprises in the development of national economic growth. Despite this, studies have shown that, across the world, the number of women involved in entrepreneurial activities is notably lower than that of men, with almost twice as many men as women becoming entrepreneurs (Minniti, Arenius and Langowitz, 2005).

In the USA, women-owned firms are now estimated to number just over 8.1 million, generating nearly $1.3 trillion in revenues and employing 7.7 million workers. An analysis of US Census data on women-owned enterprises in the USA in 2011 by Womenable – the leading US-based think-tank on women's enterprise – found that the growth rate in the number of women-owned firms exceeds the national average and growth in revenue and employment kept pace with all firms, but only when they reach the 100-employees level or the $1 million revenue mark. Collectively, women-owned businesses in the USA have been estimated to spend $492 billion per year on salaries and employee benefits, $38 billion on IT, $25 billion on telecommunications, $23 billion on human resources services and $17 billion on shipping (National Women's Business Council, 2004).

A key issue in international comparative assessments of the numbers and trends relating to women's business ownership lies in the differences in the definitions of what constitutes women-owned businesses. In the USA, the term 'women-owned businesses' includes those solely owned by a woman or women, businesses that are majority (more than 51 per cent) owned by a woman or women and ones owned equally (50/50) by women and men. A more precise definition of women-owned businesses would include only those that are majority (more than 51 per cent) women-owned. However, international comparisons may be more accurately assessed through the use of self-employment data.

In 2002, the total number of people self-employed in the USA was 8,490,000 (6.4 per cent of total employment). Of this, male self-employment accounted for 5,124,000 (7.3 per cent of total male employment) and female self-employment accounted for 3,366,000 (5.4 per cent of total female employment). While male self-employment still accounts for a larger proportion of the self-employed total (60.3 per cent), the female share, which currently accounts for 39.6 per cent of the total, has expanded consistently over the past 30 years (US Bureau of Labor Statistics, 2005). In 1976, women constituted 26.8 per cent of total self-employment in the USA – a figure that has increased gradually year by year to its present level of nearly 40 per cent.

By comparison, within the UK, researchers have operated a more cautious definition of women-owned businesses, focusing their attention on businesses that are wholly owned by women. Survey data suggests that about 15 per cent of UK businesses are women-owned, 50 per cent are male-owned and 35 per cent are co-owned by males *and* females (Small Business Service, 2004).

Women currently account for 29 per cent of the self-employed total – a figure that has shown modest fluctuations but little change since 1984, when the female share of self-employment increased from 18 to 24 per cent of the total (ONS, 2005). Although remarkable increases in female self-employment have been seen within the USA over the past ten years, the UK situation is marked by more modest attainment. In 1999, there were 1.1 million self-employed females in the UK and more recent analysis of the Labour Force Survey (LFS) Annualised 2009–2010 data shows that this figure remains the same in 2011 (Arshed, 2011).

12.5 The characteristics and experiences of female entrepreneurs

As noted above, relatively little attention was afforded to the influence of gender upon entrepreneurship until the mid-1980s. Although many studies had been undertaken investigating owners of small businesses, the bulk of the work concentrated upon male-owned enterprises and there was an assumption that patterns of female behaviour conformed to those established using male samples.

The 1980s heralded the start of a new research interest in women's ownership of business, reflecting both the rise in the number of women starting in business in many Western economies and a growing academic interest in small businesses and the nature of entrepreneurship.

Influenced by the existing small business literature, early studies of female entrepreneurship concentrated mainly upon the motivations for starting a business (Schreier, 1973; Schwartz, 1976; Goffee and Scase, 1985; Hisrich and Brush, 1986) and, to a lesser extent, the gender-related barriers experienced during this phase of business ownership (Watkins and Watkins, 1984; Hisrich and Brush, 1986; Carter and Cannon, 1992).

In Europe, researchers focused their attention on trying to establish links between motivations for female self-employment and the overall position of women in the labour market (Goffee and Scase, 1985; van der Wees and Romijn, 1987; Cromie and Hayes, 1988; Carter and Cannon, 1992). As Berg's (1997: 259) critique highlighted, 'The aim of the majority of the studies [was] . . . mainly to make comparisons with male entrepreneurs and to make women entrepreneurs visible'. So, although women businessowners were afforded separate recognition, their activities and experiences were compared with those of their male counterparts, embedding masculinity as the normative standard (Ogbor, 2000; Marlow, 2002; Ahl, 2006). Thus, this stance was reflected in survey work encompassing both male and female entrepreneurs where the variable 'sex' was as another demographic variable, using the same questions that were posed to 'male-only' samples (Ahl, 2006). Notably, the limited gender-based differences that emerged from such studies were presented as 'challenges' for women to overcome rather than prompting critical reflections upon the prevailing epistemology informing the understanding of normative entrepreneurship.

It is acknowledged that early pioneering studies provided valuable descriptions of a group of entrepreneurs who had, hitherto, been overlooked by the mainstream small business research effort. Critics, however, drew attention to their descriptive nature, the small size and unrepresentative nature of the sample (Carter, 1993), the general lack of utility and rigour (Allen and Truman, 1988; Solomon and Fernald, 1988; Rosa and Hamilton, 1994) and the limited extent of their cumulative knowledge (Stevenson, 1983; Hamilton, Rosa and Carter, 1992).

By the late 1980s, it was becoming clear that the research debates surrounding the issue of gender and business ownership were continuing largely because of the difficulties for researchers of providing clear and unequivocal evidence, through either empirical investigation or more theoretical approaches. While several studies had suggested that it was considerably harder for women to both start and run their own enterprises, others had argued that start-up problems tended to be equally great for men and many women, 'far from being discriminated against, thought that being a woman gave them a positive advantage over men' (Birley, 1985: 36).

The tendency to use gender as a variable to describe, rather than explain, women's experiences of entrepreneurship was a consistent feature of early work (Neergaard et al., 2011). In a review of these trends, Ahl (2006) found that the female entrepreneur was uniformly represented as inferior to her male counterpart. In effect, women need 'fixing' to enable them to emulate and reproduce the behaviours of men (a difficult task in the face of social pressure for stereotypical gender conformity). In response to critical reviews such as those by Ogbor (2000) and Ahl (2006), the focus within the extant literature has shifted.

Moving into the twenty-first century, our understanding of the influence of gender upon women's entrepreneurship has developed in both depth and scope (Marlow, Henry and Carter, 2009). Moving on from small sample analyses of 'gender as a variable' added to the mix to search for differences between the entrepreneurial behaviours of men and women, the extant literature now focuses more clearly on gender as a socially constructed influence that critically shapes women's experiences of business ownership. In addition to using gender as a framework to position women within the entrepreneurial discourse, there is greater engagement with feminist analyses as a critical explanation for this positioning. So, for example, work by Calás and Smircich (2009) argues that entrepreneurship should be reconceptualised as 'entrepreneuring'.

As an ongoing activity, entrepreneuring is embedded within the social practices of society and, from this stance, we can use differing feminist perspectives to evaluate how gendered constructions situate women within the prevailing discourse. Thus, women's entrepreneuring subject position should be the focus of analysis rather than what men and women 'do' as entrepreneurs. As such, Calás and Smircich (2009) reframe entrepreneurship as a force for potential social change using feminist analytical lenses to illustrate this argument.

An emerging critique of the extant body of work on women's business ownership highlights the tendency towards a USA-Eurocentric approach, which assumes a normative context reflecting the institutional influences typical of Western developed economies (Al Dajani and Marlow, 2010). However, there is now an increasing, if still limited, literature exploring how context intersects with gender and entrepreneuring (Welter, 2011). For example, in an analysis of women businessowners in African and Asian countries, Marcucci (2001) described women as being more often pushed by severe economic conditions to create survival income than is the case in the West. Given the barriers to women in the formal sector and time constraints of domestic ties, many women start a business they can run from home using traditional skills. In such circumstances, entrepreneurship is seen as less a choice and more a 'desperate attempt by women with few alternatives' (Mayoux, 1995: 4). This contrasts with men, who are seen as pulled by the prospects of increased earnings, independence and the opportunity to directly benefit from their own work. Overall, however, the study found the gender differences to be marginal, with both sexes being 'pushed' into micro-enterprise creation. Women in Ethiopia, Tanzania and Zambia, however, more often proactively decided to be entrepreneurs rather than being driven by necessity arising from poverty. They also explicitly referred to their roles as mothers, wives and daughters and their need to generate income for the family as important motivations for business ownership.

In common with many descriptive studies emanating from more developed economies, studies of women entrepreneurs in Africa and Asia describe female-owned enterprises as being generally younger, smaller and requiring lower start-up resources than those owned by men (Marcucci, 2001; Richardson, Howarth and Finnegan, 2004). Women-owned enterprises were also less likely to be registered, more likely to be located in homes and operate in poorly remunerated, overcrowded sectors (Marcucci, 2001; Richardson et al., 2004). Richardson et al. (2004) also reported that these women started businesses with minimal social, human, financial, physical and natural resources. Having low levels of or no formal education, they were often illiterate and had limited or no experience of employment and limited networks. Women's enterprises also tended to operate in restricted locally based markets where access, mobility and networks were easier to negotiate, but with the consequence of excessive competition and underpricing (Zewde and Associates, 2002). They were also constrained by household and community roles, which restricted the time and acceptability of them travelling to conduct business.

Richardson et al. (2004) found men were four times more likely than women to be members of employers' organisations, Chambers of Commerce and small enterprise associations, prompting concern within the International Labour Organization (ILO) that women entrepreneurs were less able to express themselves through associations and decision-making forums. Access to information – in particular, market information – may also be problematic for women entrepreneurs. In Bangladesh, for example, women found it difficult to interact openly with men and sell their products in the markets (Marcucci, 2001).

223

Overall, these studies portray women-owned enterprises as being often undercapitalised and generating limited or no profits. However, as Downing and Daniels (1992: 2) noted in their study of women entrepreneurs in Southern Africa, 'when investments are made to increase profitability and decrease the labour intensity of the women's income-generating activities, the activities are frequently taken over by men'.

More recent work by Al Dajani and Marlow (2010) exploring the experiences of home-based self-employed Palestinian migrant women adds a further dimension to this debate. While acknowledging that these women experienced a matrix of disadvantage – being migrants, poor and subject to patriarchal regimes – self-employment offered vital financial independence and degrees of empowerment. Given the poverty of the Palestinian migrant community within Jordan, the income generated by women's self-employment was critical. However, financial benefits were accompanied by elevated status, opportunities to work with other women in their locality, plus, limited degrees of empowerment. This was enhanced by the women using highly skilled traditional craftwork as a base for their enterprises, so they were, generating income and conserving a heritage that celebrated their culture. This study is a useful illustration of the political, economic and social intersection of entrepreneuring behaviours that position self-employment as a potential empowering activity for women.

12.6 The management and financing of female-owned businesses

In an attempt to refocus the research effort away from broad descriptions of the personal and business characteristics of female entrepreneurs, increasing attention has been given to the attempt to understand the real nature – even the existence – of management differences in female-owned firms (Ahl, 2006; Carter and Shaw, 2006; Marlow et al., 2009). As the field has matured, studies have continued to explore the issue of management of female-owned businesses, but have developed to encompass more sophisticated methodologies and give critical appraisals of the effect of gender on both the experience of self-employment and the relative performances of male- and female-owned small businesses.

A recurrent theme throughout this body of research has been the focus on gender differences in the access to and usage of entrepreneurial finance. Following initial work by Buttner and Rosen (1989) and Riding and Swift (1990) in North America and Fay and Williams (1993) in New Zealand, researchers have highlighted differences in the financing patterns of male-owned and female-owned businesses (Brush, 1992; Coleman, 2000; Brush et al., 2001b). Women-owned businesses tend to start up with lower levels of overall capitalisation – on average, one-third of that of male-owned firms (Carter and Rosa, 1998), lower ratios of debt finance (Haines, Orser and Riding, 1999) and much less likelihood of using private equity or venture capital (Greene et al., 1999; Brush et al., 2001b).

As the most commonly used form of external finance, research has focused more on debt than equity finance (Greene, Brush, Hart and Saparito, 2001). Early studies investigating gender-based differences in debt financing focused on two related themes. First, researchers sought to unravel the complex relationship between the gender of entrepreneurs and bank finance with regard to the volume of finance lent, terms of credit negotiated and perceived attitudes of bank lending officers to female entrepreneurs (Fay and Williams, 1993; McKechnie, Ennew and Read, 1998; Haynes and Haynes, 1999; Coleman, 2000; Verheul and Thurik, 2000).

Second, researchers attempted to determine the root cause of gender-based differences in finance usage. Here, three main approaches have been taken to explain women's lesser likelihood of using external debt finance. The first explanation attributes differences to the presence of structural dissimilarities between male-owned and female-owned firms. The second approach points to (inadvertent) gender discrimination in the supply side. Finally, researchers have highlighted demand-side factors, pointing to apparently higher levels of debt aversion among women.

Structural dissimilarities of male-owned and female-owned businesses explain the most obvious differences between male and female finance patterns. In a large-scale survey analysing bank loan files, Haines et al. (1999) found initial differences between male and female entrepreneurs (lower sales levels and liabilities, lower levels of salary and drawings) to be a product of business size, age and sector. Fabowale, Orser and Riding (1995), similarly, argued that structural factors accounted for differences in rates of loan rejections between male and female entrepreneurs. Examining 282 matched pairs of male and female businessowners, McKechnie et al. (1998) found few substantial differences once structural factors had been taken into account.

Nevertheless, the view that structural dissimilarities explain gender differences has been countered by both empirical evidence and theoretical critiques. First, several studies have reported residual gender differences, even after structural factors had been controlled (Carter and Rosa, 1998; Verheul and Thurik, 2000; Fraser, 2005). Second, feminist critiques of entrepreneurship research have argued that the practice of statistically equalising structural dissimilarities between men and women in order to explain gender differences in bank borrowing suggest that 'it is business structure rather than gender that is the prime determinant of access to credit' (Mirchandani, 1999: 230).

In the absence of direct evidence of gender discrimination, researchers have suggested that differences in patterns of finance usage may be explained by supply-side practices that inadvertently disadvantage women businessowners. Using an experimental protocol, Fay and Williams (1993) presented bank loan officers with identical loan applications from male and female applicants. Gender-based differences were found when the applicant was described as having a high school education, but not when the applicant was university educated. They concluded that their study 'demonstrate[d] experimentally that some loan officers do employ differing evaluative criteria for female and male applicants, and that these differences in evaluative criteria may act to female disadvantage' (Fay and Williams, 1993: 304). Similarly, Orser and Foster (1994: 16) suggested that the standard 5Cs (character, capacity, capital, collateral and conditions) model of bank lending was applied in a 'subjective' manner to the detriment of female entrepreneurs. Coleman (2000), however, attributed women's lesser use of bank debt to the lower average size of women-owned businesses. So, rather than discriminating against women, Coleman (2000: 49) concluded that bankers 'discriminate on the basis of firm size, preferring to lend to larger and, one would assume, more established firms. This preference may put women at a disadvantage given that they are half the size of men-owned firms on average.'

A focus on supply-side discrimination has been countered by a focus on demand-side risk and debt aversion. Indeed, a lower preference for risk among women has been a recurrent conclusion of comparative analyses of male and female entrepreneurs (Sexton and Bowman-Upton, 1990; Watson and Robinson, 2003). The greater risk aversion of women is seen not only in their reluctance to assume the burden of business debt but also their reluctance to engage in fast-paced business growth (Cliff, 1998; Bird and Brush, 2002). Debt aversion among women entrepreneurs, often conceptualised as a quasi-psychological characteristic, is as likely to be rooted in socio-economic factors – women's comparatively lower earnings in employment (EOC, 2005) are reproduced among the self-employed (Marlow, 1997; Parker, 2004).

Overall, the weight of research evidence considering gender, entrepreneurship and bank lending suggests that, while the bank financing profiles of male and female entrepreneurs are distinctly different, much – but not all – of this is attributable to structural dissimilarities. The research evidence also suggests that while women entrepreneurs perceive that they are treated differently by bank lending officers, there is almost no evidence of systematic gender discrimination by banks. Indeed, there is a growing recognition that women entrepreneurs constitute an important new market for banks and so it is difficult to argue that it is within the banks' interest to deliberately, much less systematically, exclude this growing market. The debate has continued largely because of dissatisfaction with existing explanations, coupled with the methodological difficulties facing researchers in providing clear and unequivocal evidence.

While entrepreneurship researchers continue to debate the extent and causes of the gender, entrepreneurship and bank finance nexus, feminist analyses may provide new insights. In a review of the entrepreneurship research literature, Mirchandani (1999) points to the essentialism inherent in the construction of the 'female entrepreneur' category and stresses that gender should not be seen simply as a characteristic of individuals, but a process integral to business ownership, a critique developed by Ahl (2006) and Bird and Brush (2002). As Mirchandani (1999: 230) argued, the practice of statistically equalising structural dissimilarities between men and women in order to explain gender differences in bank borrowing suggest that 'it is business structure rather than gender that is the prime determinant of access to credit.'

One study of gender, entrepreneurship and bank finance (Carter, Shaw, Wilson and Lam, 2007; Wilson et al., 2007) attempted to bring further clarity to this debate. Replicating Fay and Williams' (1993) experimental protocol within a UK clearing bank, this study focused on both the sex of the loan applicant and the sex of the bank loan officer as key elements of the gender, entrepreneurship and bank lending nexus.

The results suggest that bank loan officers use a wide range of criteria to assess loan applications from entrepreneurs, but, for the most part, these do not vary by the sex of the applicant. Of 44 identified criteria used by bank loan officers, only 4 showed statistically significant differences by sex of the loan applicant.

It was found that female loan applicants were more likely to be assessed on whether they had undertaken sufficient research into the business, while male loan applicants were more likely to be assessed on whether they had supplied sufficient information about the business opportunity, the business' financial history and their general personal characteristics. Hence, gender plays a role in the credit decisionmaking process as loan officers evaluate male and female applicants not just on the merits of their individual case but also on the basis of their perceptions of men and women, which are imbued with gender socialisation processes.

These modest differences were complemented by differences in the criteria applied by male and female bank loan officers. Female bank loan officers were more likely to emphasise both the need to meet the applicant and the male applicant's marital status. In this context, marital status can be seen as a proxy for personal stability and financial responsibility – a characteristic that male loan applicants may be required to demonstrate more than women, for whom these characteristics are already conferred by gender stereotyping. In this regard, it is clear that male loan applicants are *also* affected by gender – an obvious point that is mostly overlooked within the research literature. Conversely, male bank loan officers were more likely to query the commitment of the loan applicant, especially when the loan applicant was female. This criterion and its specific application to female loan applicants raises concerns that the gendered stereotyping of female loan applicants persists.

12.7 The performance of female-owned firms

The performance of small businesses – that is, their survival, profitability, growth, wealth- and employment-generating capacities – is a fundamental and enduring focal point for policy development and academic debate.

Critically evaluating the contemporary data regarding small firm performance, Storey (2011) suggests that, despite the ambitions of governments for small firms to operate as an 'engine' of economic wealth and employment generation, very few will do so. Rather, the normative profile of the sector is one of marginal performance, limited growth on any scale and relatively high rates of closure and failure. So, although Storey's contemporary review of performance data suggests that very few small firms will exhibit sustained growth, women's enterprises are particularly singled out and labelled as 'underperforming', even though they largely reflect the normative profile of the sector as a whole. However, it is noted that there are specific gendered influences that compound general performance constraints within the sector.

So, for example, reflecting broader feminised working patterns, the data indicate that about half of self-employed women work part-time (less than 30 hours per week) and a third base their businesses within their homes. Men, however, reflect their stereotypical employment profile, with much lower rates of part-time and homeworking – 18 and 24 per cent, respectively (Bosma and Harding, 2006; Thompson, Jones-Evans and Kwong, 2009). Women adopt such operating profiles in an effort to combine economic activity, domestic labour and childcare (Belle and La Valle, 2003; Rouse and Kitching, 2006). This is despite evidence suggesting that self-employment provides a poor solution to such competing demands (Greer and Greene, 2003; Rouse and Kitching, 2006). Drawing from an econometric analysis of returns from self-employment, Hundley (2001: 825) notes unequivocally, 'the presence of small children and greater hours of housework have a negative effect on female earnings'. While such fragmented approaches to business operation may be a rational response to the positioning of self-employed women in a particular socio-economic context, they inevitably constrain both the performance and future prospects of the firm (Boden and Nucci, 2000; Marlow and McAdam, 2012). So, it is evident that the performance potential of women's businesses is constrained by specific socio-economic influences that position their firms in particular gendered spaces.

As we argue, such performance constraints should be assessed in the light of evidence that *most* small firms are marginal performers, but, clearly, the sustainability and potential of women's firms is further threatened by gendered influences. However, within the broader literature, there appears a determination to suggest that women themselves are responsible for poor performance profiles (Marlow and McAdam, 2012).

It is suggested that such performance deficiencies arise from gender-related risk aversion or a failure or inability to accrue appropriate levels of entrepreneurial capital to inform growth (Small Business Service, 2003; Department for Business, Enterprise and Regulatory Reform, 2008; Department for Business Innovation and Skills, 2011). The subtext of this argument suggests that women's firms exhibit *under*performance rather than *constrained* performance. This can be addressed and corrected by specific support and advice inputs, which, in turn, will equip women to emulate the (alleged) performance standards set by their male counterparts (Calás and Smircich, 2009; Ahl and Marlow, 2011). We suggest, however, that the underperformance label is a myth that has arisen, and persists, as an articulation of embedded socially situated gendered assumptions of female 'deficiencies'. As a result, there is scant evidence for critical reflexive interrogation of the associations between gender and firm performance because it is taken as a given that merely being female is the source of the problem (Watson, 2003; Watson and Newby, 2005, are exceptions). In essence, when uncritically subscribing to the female 'underperformance thesis', we contribute to and reproduce subordinating gendered assumptions regarding women's entrepreneuring.

Comparatively little rigorous and in-depth research has been undertaken on the issue of gender and business performance. Although many studies have made some mention of it, most shy away from a direct examination of quantitative performance measures, preferring instead to engage in discursive debate suggesting essential gender differences regarding qualitative assessments of success. These studies suggest that women perform less well on quantitative measures such as jobs created, sales turnover and profitability (as we would expect given their firm profiles). This, it is argued, is usually because women do not enter business for financial gain but to pursue intrinsic goals (for example, independence and the flexibility to run business and domestic lives) and so assess their success in relation to the extent that they attain these goals rather than in terms of the more usual economic or financial measures. However, following this argument to a logical conclusion suggests an unsustainable logic, given that independence is unlikely to accrue from economically unviable ventures and the evidence suggests self-employment is a very poor solution to flexible working.

The performance debate would appear to be embedded within gendered assumptions that, first, women-owned firms intrinsically underperform rather than that they are constrained by sector, market and gendered influences and, second, women willingly exchange performance attainments for greater flexibility and beneficial accommodation between domestic demands and income generation.

In summary, the limited evidence of weight-related performance profiles of female and male firms finds that – adjusting for resource inputs – the former typically perform on a par with and are sometimes stronger performers than the latter (Watson, 2003; Watson and Newby, 2005), so women-owned firms do *not* underperform. That women are more likely to adopt fragmented operating profiles and begin new firms in crowded elements of the service sector reflects socio-economic expectations and responsibilities and constrains performance. Suggesting that re-educating individual women entrepreneurs to be less risk-averse or accrue more entrepreneurial capital is unlikely to address this performance 'problem'. It is not an issue of the individual failing to fulfil her potential, but of embedded institutionalised gendered subordination that positions women as disadvantaged entrepreneurs.

12.8 Looking to the future: addressing neglect and advancing debate

This chapter has explored how gender influences women's experiences of entrepreneuring. In so doing, we have drawn upon a range of literatures and data, noting that the range and depth of this material has expanded considerably since the 1980s. Despite this growth, the issue of gender – articulated either as masculinity or femininity – as a critical influence upon entrepreneuring remains relatively neglected by the mass media and the academic community (Nicholson and Anderson, 2005; Ljunggren and Alsos, 2007; Radu and Redien-Collot, 2008; Larty and Hamilton, 2009).

Some years ago, Baker (with Aldrich and Liou 1997: 261) drew attention to this issue, noting how women were largely excluded as entrepreneurial subjects or actors because prevailing assumptions relied 'on notions of humanity and rationality that are masculinist'. As such, dualities such as the rational–irrational distinction may appear to have no apparent gender bias, but, in reality, are 'thoroughly imbued with gender connotations, one side being socially characterized as masculine, the other as feminine, and the former being socially valorized' (Massey, 1996: 113). Contemporary analyses suggest this neglect persists (Ahl, 2006; Calás and Smircich, 2009; Ahl and Marlow, 2011); it is embedded as an enduring feature of a discourse that portrays entrepreneurship as a particular form of masculinity. In effect, the experience of men is taken as a normative focus for analysis and theorybuilding; accordingly, the male norm persists within contemporary studies of entrepreneurship whilst the field itself masquerades as gender-neutral.

Further evidence of this neglect is reflected in the persistent tendency to silo research on women's business ownership, which suggests there is normative entrepreneurship (that done by men) and then there is *female* entrepreneurship. Thus, we see the 'othering' of women in this debate by marking them out as deficient or incomplete men (Taylor and Marlow, 2010). So, the increasing attention paid to female entrepreneurship has been positive in recognising that gender influences experiences of entrepreneuring, but counter-productive in further separating and identifying women as different/aside from/in contradiction to the norm. This epistemological assumption, bounding and limiting the field of entrepreneurship research, is rarely addressed in the broader literature (Calás and Smircich, 2009). A more critical and theoretically embedded analytical framing is now required to progress debate.

Thus, research has moved forward from early trends that recognised gender as a variable, so compared, described and measured differences, resting on the assumption of the male norm. This empiricist approach has been largely supplanted by more theoretically sophisticated work that recognises gender as a social construct subordinating the feminine and so generating gender-related challenges for women businessowners to address. Emergent analyses now acknowledge that for gender as a construct to act as an explanatory concept, it is necessary to draw upon feminist theorising to critically evaluate how the production and reproduction of female deficit within entrepreneurship arises from broader socio-economic institutional influences. Thus, entrepreneurship is but one site of female subordination – the interest lies in exploring the specifics of articulation, responses and denials in the broader research field and how feminist analyses can inform wider theory development surrounding the assumptions of who and what an entrepreneur is.

Studying the influence of gender upon entrepreneurship should not be seen as a woman's issue explored by women to find solutions whereby women can be more like men. Rather, it must move to act as critical analytical framing to challenge the normative epistemology inherent within the entrepreneurial discourse.

12.9 Chapter summary

The past two decades have seen a growth in the number of women entering self-employment and business ownership. During the same period, the growing interest in the role and importance of small businesses within the overall economy has led to an increase in the volume of research studies that focus on the small firms sector. Although the experiences of female entrepreneurs have been only a minority interest, research investigating the influence of gender on small business ownership has developed considerably over the past 15 years. While early research into female entrepreneurship focused on describing women's characteristics, motivations and experiences, the field has progressed beyond these exploratory and rudimentary studies. More recent research has not only developed a degree of methodological sophistication but also focused on increasingly specialised issues, such as the role of gender effects on the financing and performance of firms.

This chapter has provided an overview of the growing literature on female entrepreneurship, highlighting some of the key debates within the field. It has also highlighted more recent concerns that the female experiences of entrepreneurship and the effects of gender in small business management are seriously neglected areas of study. Studies that have started to investigate key issues, such as the management and performance of female-owned firms, have revealed the extent of female disadvantage in business financing and the related and relative underperformance of women-owned firms.

Although definitive results have yet to be attained, many recent studies unequivocally point to the same conclusion – that, as a relatively new group of entrepreneurs, operating significantly younger businesses, women-owned firms may not yet have attained the same level of achievement as those owned by men, but, as a group, they are catching up fast. Future research, however, must reveal the extent to which these women might catch up merely because they adopt and adapt to male norms or whether their increasing presence might challenge and change prevailing entrepreneurial norms.

Questions

1 Discuss the possible explanations for the growth in the numbers of women-owned enterprises varying so much in different countries.

2 Do women experience disadvantage in raising business financing? Explain the reasons that lead you to your conclusion.

3 What factors should be taken into account when considering the performance of female-owned businesses?

4 Given the widespread emancipation of women, do you believe that researchers should continue to investigate gendered experiences of entrepreneurship? Explain your reasoning.

Weblinks

www.womenable.com
The leading US think-tank that campaigns to improve the environment for women-owned businesses worldwide.

http://nawbo.org
National Association of Women Business Owners (USA).

http://ec.europa.eu/enterprise/policies/sme/promoting-entrepreneurship/women/portal
The European Commission's portal for women's enterprises.

http://ec.europa.eu/enterprise/policies/sme/promoting-entrepreneurship/women/ambassadors/index_en.htm
The European Commission's network of female entrepreneurship ambassadors.

CHAPTER 13

Family businesses

Carole Howorth and Eleanor Hamilton

13.1 Introduction

Entrepreneurship is often couched in terms of the heroic individual who seeks out opportunities that others cannot see. The reality is that many entrepreneurs found and develop their enterprises along with other family members. Indeed, any study of small enterprises that ignores the influence of family can only ever be a partial representation of reality, as family firms are so prevalent throughout the world. In fact, a high percentage of entrepreneurs found their businesses in the form of family firms and, for many more, families supply important resources, especially human capital (Aldrich and Cliff, 2003). Many smaller firms find it difficult to disentangle the firm from the family and there is an intertwining of family and business motivations, resources and dreams. Families are also crucial breeding grounds for enterprise and new businesses. Indeed, it has been suggested that families are 'the oxygen that feeds the fire of entrepreneurship' (Rogoff and Heck, 2003).

Following a fuller introduction of family businesses in section 13.3, this chapter is structured as follows. First, the scale and scope of family firms across the world is discussed. Second, some of the key theoretical approaches to understanding family firms are outlined. These include the three circles model, three-dimensional development model, Johannisson's model of the three ideologies, the F-PEC model and some insights from agency and stewardship theory that have helped to identify six conceptual 'types' of family firm. Third, important issues of gender relations in family firms and are introduced for discussion. Fourth, the dynamics of entrepreneurship and innovation across the generations is considered. Finally, we reflect on what could be argued as the defining theme in family business studies – succession.

13.2 Learning objectives

There are four learning objectives for this chapter:

1 to understand the significance of family businesses worldwide
2 to understand issues arising from the intertwining of families and businesses

3 to examine the major theoretical perspectives that guide our understanding of family enterprises

4 to understand innovation and entrepreneurship in family enterprises.

Key concepts

- family businesses ■ family enterprises ■ family firms ■ three circles model
- gender relations ■ innovation ■ succession

13.3 Family businesses

There is growing recognition of the prevalence of family businesses and their importance to economies throughout the world. It is estimated that, in most countries, family businesses represent two-thirds or more of all businesses (Howorth, Rose and Hamilton, 2006: 225). People are often surprised to learn that some of the largest corporations are family-owned businesses, firms such as IKEA, WalMart or Haribo. Other companies are more well-known for being family businesses because they stress their family roots and use them as a marketing tool; UK readers will be familiar with the Warburton family, who make a virtue of their 'familiness' in promoting their products. For many, though, family business is associated with small and medium-sized enterprises (SMEs) and, if you look around any town, you will discover a proliferation of family-owned SMEs. Box 13.1 suggests an exercise to investigate everyday interactions with the family-owned enterprises in your area.

Box 13.1 A week full of family enterprises

Consider your week and how you engage with family enterprises on a daily basis. A glance through my diary shows interaction with family businesses of all shapes and sizes.

Monday Filled up the car with fuel from my local garage, run by the Chippendale brothers, who also own and manage two other businesses in the town.

Tuesday Bought some cheeses from Butlers, owned and managed by Gillian Hall and her son Matthew.

Wednesday Ordered a new kitchen from Webbs. The firm was founded by Helen Monaghan's father. Helen and her husband Paul are moving to part-time working to allow their son Ben to take over.

Thursday Went to a Lancaster University workshop and met Alison Park, whose third-generation family business has just been sold to another company. Also met brothers Stuart and Jonathan Brakewell, owner-managers of an engineering company, Central Power Services.

Friday Meal out at a local restaurant – part of the Mitchells chain of pubs and restaurants, owned and managed by Jonathan and Andrew Barker, who, with their cousin, represent the fifth generation of family ownership.

Saturday Went shopping and bought vegetables from Bradshaw's farm shop, run by Bill and Jean and their son Alwyn, meat from the butchers, Singleton and Sons and groceries from Booths supermarket, fifth-generation family business.

Sunday Went for a drink at the local pub, run by husband and wife team, Ken and Hazel. Spent the evening chatting to Brenda, Jeannette and Abigail – a mother, daughter and granddaughter who run the local horse-riding school together.

In this chapter, we see how the intertwining of family and business provides a fascinating context for the study of enterprise. Family enterprises differ from other SMEs in that they are influenced by family – as well as business – objectives, values and relationships. For some family enterprises, the family dimension is openly acknowledged and made explicit and they might have formal family agreements or a family constitution. In many family enterprises, particularly the smaller ones, the family is not formally acknowledged or discussed until a critical juncture – e.g., succession – is looming or family issues become a problem.

In all family enterprises, the values, relationships and history of the family will influence how the firm operates and the organisational culture that predominates. Imagine going into business with your mother, father, brother, sister or other family members. Does it conjure up positive thoughts about how great that would be because you know each other so well, you have a high level of trust and you get on brilliantly or does it fill you with horror because you are bound to fall out or they would treat you as if you were still at school? Family enterprises bring all the baggage of family relationships into a business setting. The juxtaposition of the business as a performance-driven system, supposedly based on rational economic objectives, and the family, which is relationship-based and full of emotions, has all sorts of implications for the running of family businesses that do not apply to non-family businesses.

The extent of the family's influence varies from one business to another and over the life of an individual business. Later, this chapter explains how this impacts definitions of family businesses, as well as their operations and objectives. At one extreme, entrepreneurs may choose to exclude their families from every aspect of their businesses. In this case, the objectives of the business will likely be those of the entrepreneurs and their management teams. However, the majority of SMEs have a multiplicity of objectives that incorporate family, individual and business aspirations.

Box 13.2 Objectives of a family enterprise

Family objectives
- Avoid dilution of family ownership (and control).
- Protect or accumulate family wealth.
- Build family's reputation and status in the community.
- Pass the business on to the next generation.

Paternal objectives
- Provide employment for the family.
- Provide family members with careers.

Management objectives
- Increase profitability.
- Increase the value of the business.
- Grow and develop the business.
- Ensure independence.

Social objectives
- Employees' welfare.
- Social impact.

Box 13.2 provides examples of some of these, divided into family, paternal, managerial and social objectives. Any particular family enterprise may have a variety of these and other objectives guiding their activities. Objectives may also vary for each individual in a family business. For example, parents may see the employment of younger family members as important, whereas members of the junior generation may not.

Often, family businesses do not articulate these objectives and they remain implicit. One of the issues family enterprises face is that, because family members believe they know each other well, there are often (incorrect) assumptions about what another individual may want or expect. So, for example, it is not uncommon for a parent to assume that their eldest son will take over the family business without ever having discussed it with him or his siblings. It then comes as something of a shock when the son eventually plucks up the courage to tell his parents that this will not be the case or else if he does want to succeed, but a younger sibling argues that he or she should be the successor instead.

Communication is a bigger issue for family businesses than other organisations because they incorporate a broader range of interested parties, some of whom have formal roles and others who are less overtly prominent, but may, nevertheless, be very influential. Family businesses also bring together different generations and younger family members may have more of a voice in decisionmaking than they would normally have if they were employed in a similar role in another business. This interplay of different generations provides the defining aspect of family businesses across time. It brings an expectation of longevity that differentiates entrepreneurship in the family business context from other types of businesses.

One of the important theoretical models we shall examine in this chapter is the three circles model (see Figure 13.1 in Section 13.5.1), which is a fundamental diagnostic tool for family businesses and can be used, among other things, to analyse communication difficulties. The three circles model also helps to examine who is involved in the family business, either formally or informally. This is the starting point for considering whether there are important family members who may have an 'invisible' role in the business. The chapter discusses how this 'invisibility' has particularly applied to women in family businesses and why that might be the case. Our discussion highlights that it is therefore difficult to know the level of influence that family exerts on family businesses.

A widely used model for measuring different levels of family influence on the firm is the F-PEC model (see Box 13.3 in Section 13.5.4), which is also introduced and explained in this chapter. Family businesses provide a context where we can acknowledge and explore the influence of emotions, relationships and family dynamics that are so often swept aside in studies of business.

13.4 Family firms throughout the world

In most countries, family firms represent the majority of firms. The International Family Enterprise Research Academy (IFERA, 2003) conducted a poll of members to find out the distribution of family firms in their countries. Answers ranged from 60 per cent in Germany to 93 per cent in Italy. In the UK, it was estimated that 70 per cent of businesses were family firms. In many developing countries, family and enterprise are intertwined and difficult to separate or even imagine as independent and, therefore, studies report that over 95 per cent of firms are family enterprises. It is surprising, therefore, that the majority of management and entrepreneurship studies disregard the role of families. Students of business and entrepreneurship might pause to consider how many of the theories and models they have learned about include a family dimension.

A significant proportion of family businesses have been around for generations. The oldest recorded family business in the world – Hoshi Onsen – has been keeping inns in Japan for nearly 1500 years. It has survived through over 40 generations of family ownership. There are many other examples of family businesses that have prospered for hundreds of years. R. Durtnell & Sons, for example, is reputed to be Britain's oldest builder, established in 1591. The business has passed from father to son for 12 generations. Founder John Durtnell and his brother Brian built their first house in 1593 and this still stands and is occupied to this day. Similarly, the Whitaker family in Lancashire has been farming since the twelfth century, for 23 generations. Family businesses like these exist in all industries, all types of firms and they are young as well as old.

As we saw above, internationally, there are differences in the prevalence of family businesses. This could be related to a number of factors. Each country has a unique history that affects its style of government, the balance between public and private sectors, its laws, financial systems and industries, all of which may encourage or discourage the establishment of family businesses. As important, though, are the culture and attitudes towards families and being in business (Colli and Rose, 2008: 203). Countries with a stronger collectivist culture, where working together is the norm, appear to have more family businesses relative to countries with a more individualistic culture, where independence from the family is encouraged.

These factors not only affect the prevalence of family enterprises but also have implications for the types of family firms found, their longevity and governance structures. For example, countries with punitive inheritance tax regimes may be less likely to have multi-generational family businesses or they may have more complex ownership structures – e.g., shares are held in a trust rather than directly by family members. These influences are aspects of institutional theory, which considers how the broader environment influences organisations' structures and ways of working.

The number of family enterprises also depends on the definition employed. Westhead and Cowling (1998) showed that the percentage of family firms in their sample could range from 15 to 81 per cent if they varied the definition they used. Definitions of family businesses continue to be contested, particularly at the margins. Criteria that are included in such definitions, either singly or in a variety of permutations, include majority family ownership, family management, family succession or intention, family objectives and family influence.

In Europe, a group of family business experts undertook a study of family businesses in each of their home countries and agreed the definition that is detailed below. The European Expert Group definition of a family business (Mandl, 2008) includes the following criteria:

- the majority of decisionmaking rights are in the possession of the natural person(s) who established the firm or in the possession of the natural person(s) who has/have acquired the share capital of the firm or in the possession of their spouses, parents, child/children or their direct heirs

- the majority of decisionmaking rights are indirect or direct
- at least one representative of the family or kin is formally involved in the governance of the firm
- listed companies meet the definition of family enterprise if the person who established or acquired the firm (share capital) or their families or descendants possess 25 per cent of the decisionmaking rights mandated by their share capital.

It is important to have agreement and clarity on the definition because, otherwise, as Westhead and Cowling (1998) point out, studies are not comparing like with like and are in danger of reporting results that are definition-dependent (i.e. the results change if the definition is changed).

Whatever definition is employed, it should clearly differentiate between family and non-family enterprises. Good practice dictates that researchers, policymakers and other authors should clearly state what definition they are using so that when others make comparisons, they know what they are comparing them with and the body of knowledge is built up.

13.5 Theories of family firms

Studies of family businesses focus on the aspects that are distinct about them. These are factors that arise from the intertwining of family and business. In this section, some of the important studies that have attempted to capture and conceptualise that distinctiveness are introduced. The huge diversity in terms of age, sector, size, institutional and cultural context of family firms means that these models should be used to explore and understand variety rather than encourage any attempt to produce fixed categories.

13.5.1 The three circles model

The most commonly used theoretical model that captures the interwoven dynamics of family and business is the three circles model of family business (Tagiuri and Davis, 1982), mentioned earlier. This is shown in Figure 13.1, the model highlights the overlapping nature of the three main groups in family firms – the owners, family and managers.

A helpful way to use this model is to plot individuals by name in the segment that represents their position within the enterprise (the smallest family enterprises usually find it more helpful if the third circle is allocated to employees rather than managers). Some individuals will be family owner-managers, so are in the segment at the centre of the model, just as they are likely to be at the centre of the family enterprise itself. Others will have a dual role that means they straddle two of the circles – e.g., owner-managers, family managers who do not (yet) have any ownership and family owners who are not involved in the management of the firm. Other individuals will have only one role, so they will occupy the outer segments – i.e., family, owners or managers. It is especially important to include family members who may not have a *formal* role within the firm but who, nevertheless, have some influence. This includes a spouse or children who are involved in discussions about the business at mealtimes or parents who are used as a sounding board but do not have an ownership stake. There may also be other family members who have provided resources, loans or expertise to the

Figure 13.1 Three circles model of family businesses

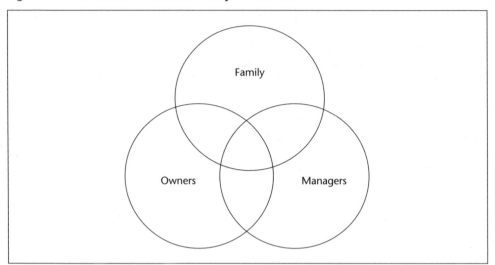

Source: Tagiuri and Davis (1982)

business. Later in this chapter we explain how some family members, particularly women, may be much more influential than their formal, externally perceived role suggests.

The three circles model is used to examine and explain relationships, motivations, communication, governance and decisionmaking, amongst other issues, within family enterprises. A much better understanding is provided by this model, which captures the overlapping roles of individuals, than can be gained from just differentiating between family and non-family members. An examination of the model as a whole can help to identify where there might be individuals on the periphery, which could have implications for inclusion, engagement and motivation. The family, its advisers or a researcher can then analyse how an issue might differ for people in each of the segments.

So, for example, if communication is being examined, we would first plot each person's location on the model and then examine how communication occurs in each of the circles. Typically, in a family business, communication about business issues often occurs within the family circle, in social settings, such as over the dinner table or at family events. Anyone who is in the management circle but not also in the family circle is therefore likely to be excluded from these discussions and could feel that they are not involved in the decisionmaking, which might eventually lead to disengagement and reduced motivation. Equally, if family business decisions are made exclusively in the management circle, there may be family owners who become disgruntled if they are not included in these meetings and so on.

This model is used often in family business consultancy as well as in research. In consulting, the three circles model is employed as a diagnostic tool. Family owner-managers are, by definition, in each of the three circles and they may be unaware of the implications of, for example, their style or method of communication and decisionmaking for individuals or groups of individuals in the peripheral segments. Just plotting each person's location on the model and discussing communication, decisionmaking or governance in relation to each of the circles can be a revelation to some family owner-managers.

The three circles model is also employed to examine the governance systems that are in place for each of the three groups. Elsewhere in this book there is a discussion of how, as small firms grow, they will formalise their management and ownership structures, with, for example, regular Board meetings and shareholder agreements. This is captured within the extensive literature on corporate governance. The three circles model highlights that, in family enterprises, there is a third group – the family – and its members also need to be clear about their rights and responsibilities. These can be clarified by drawing up a family constitution (also known as a family agreement) and larger family firms may also go so far as to have a family council, which operates in a similar manner to a Board of Directors, but with the remit of managing the family's interests rather than those of the business.

The three circles model is, thus, a very practical tool. However, it provides a static representation of the family business and one of its limitations is that it does not encompass changes and shifts over time. It has therefore been built on by family business researchers to provide insights into other aspects of family businesses, as described below.

13.5.2 The three-dimensional development model

Gersick et al. (1997) developed the three-dimensional development model (see Figure 13.2). As we can see, this is similar to the three circles model, in that it distinguishes between family, ownership and business dimensions. However, it goes a stage further by specifying some of the phases or stages that a family business might go through. The model is thus helpful in highlighting the dynamic nature of family businesses and the interplay between changes in the family, ownership and business dimensions. At any point in time, the family business could be experiencing changes in one, two or all of them. This model is particularly useful for highlighting that changes within the family are intertwined with what happens in the business.

However, the three-dimensional development model has many of the limitations associated with other 'stages models'. Such models suggest a linear progression in one direction from a specified start point. Obviously, this is a simplification of reality. It should not be assumed that all family businesses will start at the beginning stage and progress in one direction, from one stage to the next. For example, a family business may, when it is founded, use any of the three ownership forms. For example, although it is less common for a family enterprise to be founded as a cousin consortium than one of the other forms, it is not out of the question.

Ownership structures can progress in an evolutionary mode, as this model indicates, but they can also remain the same or change in a devolutionary direction – i.e., from more complex to simpler structures (Howorth and Ali, 2001). For example, a family business that is owned by a consortium of cousins may seek to simplify its ownership structure and move to a sibling partnership or jump back two stages to a single controlling owner. Similarly, the business may not progress to 'maturity' and it could be argued that there are more than three stages to business development. Thus, other stages models of small business development have a larger number of stages, with a variety of names (as explained elsewhere in this book).

Figure 13.2 Three-dimensional development model

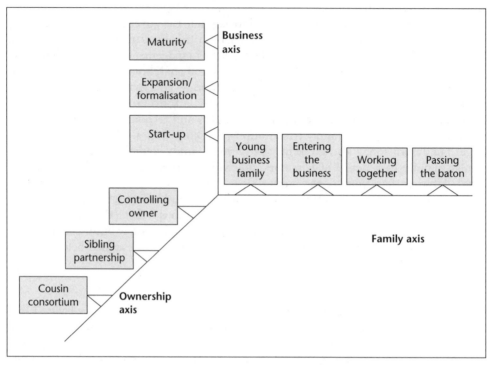

Source: *Generation to Generation: Life Cycles of the Family Business*, Harvard Business School Press (Gersick, K. E., Davis, J., Hampton, M. M. and Lansberg, I. 1997). Reprinted by permission of Harvard Business School Press. Copyright © 1997 by the Harvard Business School Publishing Corporation, all rights reserved.

13.5.3 Johanisson's model of the three ideologies

A further model that builds on the three circles pattern, as well as considering the multiplicity of objectives, is Johannisson and Huse's (2000) and Johannisson's (2002) model of ideological tensions that exist in family enterprises.

They identify three main ideologies that prevail in family enterprises, namely a paternal ideology, managerial ideology and an entrepreneurial ideology.

Successful family enterprises need to recognise the ideologies that underpin their activities and vision and gain a balance between them. Changes in the proportion of family to non-family members in the governance of family businesses shifts the balance of these competing ideologies. So, for example, a family business that brings in a non-family CEO could expect to see a shift towards a more managerialist ideology. Some more paternalistic family members may find this difficult to cope with and it could lead to tensions within the firm.

Where there are more family members in the governance structures of the firm, there is likely to be greater family influence on the business. This is one of the dimensions that is considered in attempts to measure family influence. Astrachan, Klein and Smyrnios (2002) argue that the essence of what makes family businesses different from other types of business is the influence that the family has. Many would agree, however, that family and non-family businesses do not represent a dichotomy and, instead, there are variations in the nature and level of family influence.

13.5.4 The F-PEC scale of family influence

Astrachan, Klein and Smyrnios (2002) developed the F-PEC scale of family influence, where F refers to family; P to power; E to experience and C to culture. Box 13.3 shows some of the elements that are included in the three dimensions of the F-PEC model.

Family power and family experience are based on the degree and length of family involvement in the formal structures and governance of the business. The points given in Box 13.3 for the family culture dimension provide an insight into the family values and attitudes towards the business that might influence its organisational culture. The points for this dimension are very typical of businesses that are characterised by a high level of family influence. Reading through the points listed will give you a bit more understanding of the attitudes and values that family members might have as a result of intertwining family and business over a long period of time. Positive attitudes include loyalty to and pride regarding the business. The points also involve identifying to what extent the family members are working in harmony.

F-PEC is useful for highlighting the dangers of assuming that family and non-family businesses represent two distinct groups. It is more realistic to recognise that degrees of 'familiness' exist in businesses. However, the culture dimension, in particular, is

Box 13.3 The F-PEC scale of family influence

Power
- Percentage of shares owned by members of the family.
- Percentage of family in the management team.
- Percentage of family on the Board.

Experience
- Generation that owns the company.
- Generation that manages the company.

Culture
- Family members agree with the business goals, plans and policies.
- Family members feel loyalty to the business.
- Family and business share similar values.
- Family members support the business in discussions with friends, employees and other family members.
- Family members really care about the fate of the business.
- Support family's decisions regarding the future of the business.
- Family members are proud to tell others that they are part of the business.
- Family members put in effort beyond that normally expected in order to help the business be successful.
- Being involved in the family business has a positive influence.
- There is a lot to be gained from participating in the family business in the long term.
- Family members share similar values.

Source: Astrachan, Klein and Smyrnios (2002)

biased towards capturing the positive influences of the family on the business, whereas there are a number of family businesses where, at certain points in time, the family has a strong but negative influence. The scale is also a static measure and does not incorporate the changes and dynamics that occur in family enterprises, many of which exist over a long period of time. Moreover, the scale works best in 'one family, one business' settings and it is more difficult to capture the variations that may arise when families have portfolios of businesses owned by different permutations of family members. As we see later, multiple business ownership is common among families in business.

It has also been argued that it is unrealistic to assume that 'family influence' or 'familiness' can be measured on a linear scale. Instead, researchers have attempted to identify different types of family firms. Sharma (2004) considered variations in performance alongside the financial and emotional capital of family businesses. From her experience and understanding of family businesses, she conceptualised four 'types' of family firms: warm hearts–deep pockets, pained hearts–deep pockets, warm hearts–empty pockets, and pained hearts–empty pockets. Sharma suggests that the first group of family businesses, which have positive emotional capital and financial capital, are likely to perform better than the others.

This conceptual framework is insightful as it captures, very simply, the essence of family influence on a business, but the typology was not theoretically grounded, nor empirically validated. Nevertheless, the study highlights the complexity of the family business sector and shows that we should be careful in making assumptions about what we perceive to the stereotypical family firm.

13.5.5 Insights from agency and stewardship theory

Clearly, family firms are not homogeneous entities – they encompass different motivations and ownership and management structures. Earlier in this chapter we stressed that family businesses bring with them a multitude of objectives and highlighted that there may be tensions between a family's relationship-based system and a business' performance focus.

If individuals are assumed to be self-serving within a performance-based system, agency theory suggests that there is more likely to be a focus on financial objectives, such as profit maximisation. Agency problems may occur if owners, who bear the risk, are separated from managers, who make the decisions, and each group has different objectives. Agency theorists assume that managers are opportunistic agents who might focus upon maximising their own welfare at the expense of shareholders. Where there is separation of ownership and control, owners may put agency control mechanisms in place to align the motivations and behaviour of managers with their own.

Agency theory may not apply to closely held and managed family firms, where the firm's objectives are intertwined with the family's objectives. Family firm managers may act as stewards and seek to protect the assets of the family firm rather than pursue interests that maximise their own personal gain. Where agency theory is 'silent' (Arthurs and Busenitz, 2003) – e.g., in some family firms (Zahra, 2003) – stewardship theory provides a useful counterpoint and suggests additional insights.

Stewardship theory assumes a relationship-based system with a focus on non-financial objectives, which is more representative of a family situation. It helps to explain contexts such as family business where the owners', managers' and employees' motives are aligned with those of the organisation (Davis, Schoorman and Donaldson, 1997). A strong psychological ownership of the firm and a high occurrence of altruism are assumed. 'Stewards' may want to manage the firm efficiently and be good stewards of corporate (and/or family) assets, often with a focus on the long term. Westhead and Howorth (2007) built on these theoretical foundations to illustrate different 'types' of family firms.

13.5.6 Westhead and Howorth's (2007) conceptualised 'types' of family firms

Westhead and Howorth (2007) identified six conceptualised 'types' of family firms in the literature, distinguishing between firms that have close family ownership, those diluted within the family and those diluted outside the family, as well as between firms that have family-dominated management and those that have non-family-dominated management (see Figure 13.3).

Figure 13.3 Conceptualised 'types' of family firms

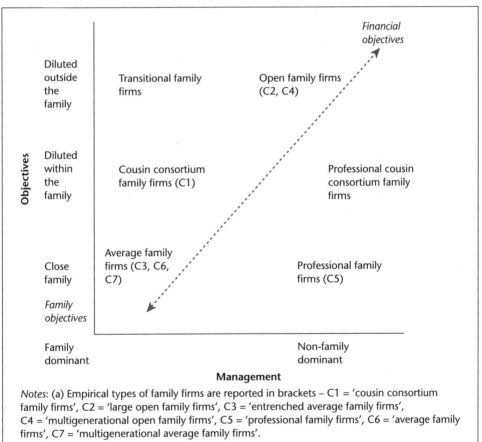

Notes: (a) Empirical types of family firms are reported in brackets – C1 = 'cousin consortium family firms', C2 = 'large open family firms', C3 = 'entrenched average family firms', C4 = 'multigenerational open family firms', C5 = 'professional family firms', C6 = 'average family firms', C7 = 'multigenerational average family firms'.

Source: Westhead and Howorth (2007, Table 1)

The relative importance of financial and non-financial (family) objectives is represented by the distance in a straight line between the ends of the arrow. Westhead and Howorth (2007) suggest that 'average family firms' emphasise family objectives and have closely held family ownership and family management. 'Professional family firms' report a mix of family and non-family objectives, but emphasise family objectives. They have closely held family ownership and management that is dominated by non-family members. 'Cousin consortium family firms' report a mix of family and non-family objectives. They have diluted ownership within the family and management that is dominated by family members. 'Professional cousin consortium family firms' have diluted ownership within the family and management that is dominated by non-family members. Furthermore, 'professional cousin consortium family firms' may place more emphasis on financial objectives and less emphasis on family objectives than 'cousin consortium family firms'. 'Transitional family firms' report both family and non-family objectives, but they place greater emphasis on financial objectives. They have diluted ownership outside the family but family members dominate the management. These firms are transitional because the management is expected to move towards less family dominance. Finally, 'open family firms' focus on financial objectives. They have diluted ownership outside the family and non-family management is dominant. Due to the separation of company ownership and control, the latter firms are most likely to report agency issues.

A total of 17 variables relating to company objectives (i.e., financial and family), ownership and management were used by Westhead and Howorth (2007) to derive an empirical taxonomy of family firm 'types' based on their conceptual representation. The seven 'types' of private family firms that were then identified empirically were as follows (see Figure 13.3):

- Cluster 1: cousin consortium family firms
- Cluster 2: large open family firms
- Cluster 3: entrenched average family firms
- Cluster 4: multigenerational open family firms
- Cluster 5: professional family firms
- Cluster 6: average family firms
- Cluster 7: multigenerational average family firms.

In line with agency theory, firms focusing more upon financial objectives generally reported organisational structures that suggest a self-serving culture – i.e., firms in Clusters 2 ('large open family firms'), 4 ('multigenerational open family firms') and 5 ('professional family firms'). Moreover, firms predominantly focusing upon non-financial objectives generally reported an organisation-serving culture as expected by stewardship theory – i.e., firms in Clusters 1 ('cousin consortium family firms'), 3 ('entrenched average family firms'), 6 ('average family firms') and 7 ('multigenerational average family firms). Two conceptualised 'types' – i.e., 'transitional family firms' and 'professional cousin consortium family firms' – were not validated in the empirical study. Westhead and Howorth's data were from small and medium-sized private family firms and it was expected that the two non-validated conceptualised types were likely to be the larger firms.

The performance of family firms varies across different types. Many studies have attempted to identify whether family firms perform better or worse than non-family firms. The discussion so far has highlighted that this approach is dangerous because family firms are not a homogeneous group and it probably explains why some studies show family firms have better performance, whereas others show the opposite. Westhead and Howorth (2007) show that family firms with the best performance have a mix of family and financial objectives and those with the worst performance have entrenched family objectives. The performance of the stereotypical family firm is no different from average. They also show that the best-performing family firms have non-family members on the management team or Board.

It should be clear by now that it is dangerous to assume family and non-family firms represent a distinct dichotomy. 'Types' studies also raise questions about the wider validity of a continuum or scale of 'familiness', such as the F-PEC (Astrachan et al., 2002; Klein, Astrachan and Smyrnios, 2005). Further analysis by Westhead and Howorth (2007) identified that their 'types' of family firms were empirically distinct from each other. This is an area of research that is currently being explored in different cultural, national and development contexts.

However, the typologies, taxonomies and F-PEC theories of family businesses tend to only capture the membership, influence and attitudes of a small number of family members. Sometimes, surveys only question one person in the business, which has huge limitations as an approach for family businesses as they are collective arenas by their very nature. Often, only those in formal, externally visible roles are included in studies of family businesses, yet, as stated earlier, one of the factors that makes family businesses particularly interesting is that there are many people influencing them who are not recognised formally, some of whom are key to the development of the business. This has been shown to apply in particular to women in family firms.

13.6 Gender relations in family businesses

Institutional, economic and social forces impacting the family and business forge gendered roles and identities, both masculine and feminine. The leadership, as well as the ownership, can be complex in family firms, reflected in patterns of everyday practice and shifting power in the family and the business over time. So, leadership in family firms may be more usefully understood as fundamentally collaborative and embedded in sets of relationships and family practices and the business.

In both the media (Nicholson and Anderson, 2005) and academia, the focus is, typically, on the individual, male entrepreneur. This reflects and reinforces the 'invisibility' of women. It consolidates the assumption that the entrepreneurial practice of founding and running a business is associated with masculinity – and the entrepreneur is a lone, heroic figure, individualised from his family, whereas the family and the business are often inextricably entwined.

It has been argued that gender in family businesses is under-researched (Sharma, 2004). It is all too easy to denigrate paternalistic regimes or primogeniture, for example, but there have been too few in-depth studies of the complexities of gender relationships in family businesses. The term 'invisible' or 'hidden' has been used to describe the role of women in family businesses. The 'invisibility' of roles is not a modern phenomenon, however – it has been recognised in historical studies of family businesses, where it is documented that women were vital sources of finance and access to networks, but their participation often went unrecorded (Colli, Fernández-Pérez and Rose, 2003).

The 'invisible' work of women is identified and studied broadly in organisational contexts, but there has been relatively little attention paid to family businesses by contemporary gender theorists. This is despite the fact that, as established earlier in this chapter, family firms represent such a significant organisational context and there have been calls for more attention to be given to gender theorising in the broader, overlapping field of entrepreneurship (Marlow, 2002; Ahl, 2006). From a sociological perspective, an analysis of the role of patriarchy in constructing 'entrepreneurial masculinities' offers a particular explanation of gender relations in the context of the family business (Mulholland, 1996). Patriarchy is a potent archetype that has explanatory power in relation to leadership in family businesses.

However, whilst it is possible to identify patriarchal practice in family businesses, patriarchy and entrepreneurial identities can be challenged. Hamilton (2006) presents intergenerational case studies where women were key players in founding or developing the family business. For example, in one family business where the founder described his wife as 'not business-minded', it emerged that she had suggested the setting up of two of the businesses and had raised finance allowing the expansion of the business through her earning as a headteacher. In another, where the husband said he thought of himself 'as a bit of an entrepreneur', it was his wife who went into business with him who looked after the financial matters and staffing policies.

It is interesting that the public accounts of family businesses are often contradicted by the private accounts of what really goes on. The traditional view of business – a view often reinforced by the existing entrepreneurship literature – tends to focus on an individual entrepreneur or leader. The media and researchers therefore seek out that person rather than adjust the frame of reference or unit of analysis to understand collaborative practices (Cramton, 1993). Within family businesses, this phenomenon is played out most obviously in studies and discussions of succession that focus primarily on the identification, preparation and implanting of the next (individual) leader.

13.7 Entrepreneurship and innovation in family businesses

The discussion of women's roles in family businesses has highlighted the importance of recognising collaborative practices. This is especially relevant in relation to entrepreneurship and innovation in family businesses.

As discussed earlier, many family businesses have been around for hundreds of years and across many generations. Often, these long-lasting family businesses were not innovative in the start-up phase, some very famous family businesses having started out with imitative products and business models. For example, the origin of Clark's shoes was as one of many tanners of sheepskin. Cadbury's, which, for many years, was an iconic family business, started out as a small shop alongside many other similar ones. William Grant's was just another whisky distillery.

246

What long-lasting family businesses tend to have in common, though, is an ongoing engagement in innovation and entrepreneurship and a series of incremental product and process innovations. Each new generation has the potential to bring renewed vigour, new ideas and innovations in collaboration with their older generations and peers. This mix of continuity and discontinuity is recognised in studies of innovation as providing the ideal conditions for incremental innovation. Studies of innovation in family businesses show a surge of new products and processes associated with transfers of ownership and management to the next generation. However, families can also stifle innovation, particularly where members of the older generation are very dominant and resist change.

Resource-based views of the firm suggest that the family represents a reservoir of resources, capabilities and knowledge that can be leveraged to create, identify and exploit a business opportunity. The family context can also provide a network with higher levels of trust than usually obtained in businesses. Family resources can reduce potential transaction costs and some of the risks associated with entrepreneurship because those involved have a good knowledge of each other that stems from a lifetime of social interaction and living together.

In the resource-based view, then, relationships are conceptualised as social capital. However, viewing social capital as an asset to be employed in the entrepreneurial process does not capture the affective bonds and complexities of family relationships. Stewardship theory (as discussed earlier), however, explains why family members work in the interests of an organisation rather than their own self-interests. In this context, the organisation is usually taken as the family business, but members' commitment may be to the interests of the family instead.

Stewardship theory, along with many of the theories of family business, is underpinned by trust. Family members with high levels of trust in their relationships are likely to be committed to each other and wish to serve the interests of the family. Family members may therefore aim to increase the wealth, welfare or provide opportunities, for the family rather than for a particular family business.

It has long been understood that families can be seedbeds of entrepreneurship, but most often this is assumed to be about the development of individuals and the propensity to become entrepreneurs if family members are also in business. There is growing recognition, however, that families often have portfolios of interconnected businesses ranging from formal family business groups (Carney and Gedajlovic, 2002) to family members helping each other out to set up individual businesses. Many families create teams of family members that found and develop several businesses over time, with various permutations of family members involved in the ownership and management of those businesses (Discua Cruz, Hamilton and Howorth, 2009; Iacobucci and Rosa, 2010).

Earlier studies of family businesses took the business as the unquestioned unit of analysis and tracked its successes and failures over the course of its existence. It has been assumed that if an individual family business does not grow, then succeeding generations are not entrepreneurial. Various versions of the phrase 'Clogs to clogs in three generations' are used to encapsulate the belief that one generation founds the business, the second generation manages it and uses up the resources and then, in the third generation, it will fail. In this view of family businesses only the first generation is seen as being entrepreneurial. However, this bears very little resemblance to the dynamic reality of families in business, where collective approaches, portfolio entrepreneurship and innovation are widespread.

Although the development of several ventures may be motivated by family circumstances, the enactment of opportunities is most often presented as being by individual family members, usually the senior generation. Instead, the pursuit of opportunities is assumed to be concentrated on the ruling members of existing family businesses and very few studies have considered the family in business as an entrepreneurial team (Discua Cruz, Howorth and Hamilton, 2010). Yet, throughout the world, there is evidence of family members coming together in a whole variety of permutations to develop portfolios of businesses.

Succession is closely linked with the reasons assumed to be linked to entrepreneurial activity in families. Earlier we discussed how new generations are often associated with a surge in innovations and entrepreneurial activity. Portfolio entrepreneurship has been associated with succession through the development of opportunities for offspring or wider family members, the division of the (existing) business to accommodate the succession of multiple siblings, as well as the search for alternative income opportunities when the core business faces unfavourable market conditions.

13.8 Succession

Succession is a defining issue for family enterprises. Some 40 per cent of family firms say that they intend to pass the firm on to the next generation, but only 4 per cent of them are in fact inherited (Harvey, 2004).

Whilst some businesses may fail before they can be passed on, many are put at risk due to a lack of succession planning. It has been suggested that thousands of owner-managed businesses in the UK expose their employees to the threat of unemployment because they have no succession plan (Harvey, 2004).

It is important, in considering succession, that we distinguish between management and ownership succession. Family business scholars suggest that families should first clarify their vision for ownership succession and then plan management succession to fit with this vision. It should be realised that succession is an ongoing process and not a one-off event. It is not uncommon for successful family businesses to plan an ownership succession over ten years in advance.

There are a number of reasons for the low levels of succession planning. Family owner-managers may be reluctant to let go, particularly if they are the founding generation. Many people do not enjoy change and this can create a resistance to succession planning. It requires an acknowledgement of mortality and ageing, which are uncomfortable subjects for many. In other cases, family owner-managers may be so wrapped up in the day-to-day running of their businesses that they never find the time to discuss succession or plan ahead. Nevertheless, a study by Morris et al. (1997) showed that the correlates of a successful succession were preparation, planning and relationships, which suggests family enterprises that prepare and plan for succession are more likely to be successful. Box 13.4 highlights some of the issues families in business need to consider when they are approaching the subject of succession.

A number of metaphors have been employed to illustrate and help understand the succession process. Wendy Handler (1991) likened it to a 'slow and subtle dance', in

Box 13.4 Recommendations for succession in family enterprises

- Start early:
  - plan knowledge transfer and reduce reliance on current owner-managers
  - identify and prepare heirs
  - plan for business objectives
  - plan regarding tax liabilities.
- Employ independent, non-family Board members or advisers to provide an external point of view.
- Share the family's vision:
  - discuss values and dreams
  - agree a family constitution to pre-empt or address conflict, jealousies, resentment
  - management succession should follow the vision for ownership succession
  - consider the needs of retiring as well as succeeding generations.
- Prepare a formal succession plan.
- Consider alternatives to direct intergenerational succession.
- Key to success is trust and communication.

that one person has to step back in order for the other person to step forwards. Her 'mutual adjustment model' allows for the transfer of experience, knowledge, authority, decisionmaking power and equity in a staged process of mutual adjustment as the successor steps forwards and the incumbent lets go, one stage at a time, with management succession preceding ownership succession. The model is most applicable to the scenario of a family member growing up to take over the leading position in the family enterprise (e.g., managing director).

Bruno Dyck and colleagues (2002) employed the metaphor of a relay race to understand the succession process. They suggest that, in a similar way to a relay race, succession requires planning of the sequence of events, timing and training in techniques and communication.

Succession studies have concentrated mainly on the longevity of firms, but, as discussed above, they should also consider the longevity of the family (in business) and the transfer of the firm from one generation of the same family to another as not the only solution, although it is the most obvious.

Succession can prove a trigger for entrepreneurial action. Whilst the founders of family firms are usually described as entrepreneurs, there is evidence of the transfer of entrepreneurial learning between family members (Hamilton, 2011) and the revitalisation of that entrepreneurial spirit through portfolio entrepreneurship and innovation (Discua Cruz et al., 2009, 2010).

The key success factor for long-lasting family businesses is a commitment to continuing in business together.

13.9 Chapter summary

This chapter has highlighted family businesses as a significant social and economic phenomenon. They contribute to wealth creation and economic performance worldwide. However, the intertwining of family and business presents complex issues for understanding family firms. Whilst acknowledging that family businesses are hugely diverse in terms of size, sector and their cultural and institutional situation, this chapter has presented some of the key conceptual models developed to guide our understanding of the family firm and the interwoven dynamics of families and businesses.

The family business context enriches our understanding of entrepreneurial behaviours and processes. Entrepreneurship is often couched in terms of the heroic individual, but the reality is that many firms are founded and developed with family members. Objectives, motivations, values and strategies are influenced by the family as well as the business. Theories of the family firm presented in this chapter help us to understand that interaction.

We also explored important themes that, it could be argued, are distinctive in the family firm. Historically, the role of women in family businesses has been described as 'invisible'. Gender relations in family firms are complex and, it has been argued, under-researched. Patriarchy has been introduced as an explanatory framework, but there is evidence that public accounts are often contradicted by what goes on behind the scenes.

This chapter has highlighted the importance of recognising collaborative practice in terms of founding and running businesses over time. The dynamic interactions between generations can be the spark for innovation and entrepreneurship. Indeed, the trigger for innovation can be the complex interplay between the old and the new generations.

This chapter challenged the 'clogs to clogs in three generations' view of family businesses, emphasising the reality of families in business, where collective approaches, portfolio entrepreneurship and innovation are widespread practices.

It was also noted that innovation and entrepreneurial activities are closely linked to issues of succession in family businesses. That is a fundamental issue, important at the level of the individual family firm but also in terms of economies worldwide. So, understanding succession as a process and not a one-off event is important. The question of how entrepreneurial practices, and spirit, are embedded in the intergenerational dynamics of families and their businesses is integral to understanding them.

Questions

1 Research and discuss whether or not the following can be defined as family businesses: Sainsbury's, A. F. Blakemore & Sons, Mitchells Hotels and Inns, Michelin.

2 Explain the family dynamics that may influence the creation or acquisition of additional businesses.

3 Why do some countries report higher percentages of family businesses than other countries?

4 How helpful is it to make a clear distinction between family and non-family firms?

5 Why has the role of women in family businesses been described historically as 'invisible'?

Weblinks

http://ffi.org
The Family Firm Institute – in Boston, USA, but it is an international organisation – provides training and guidance for advisers to family businesses. Its website contains a number of excellent resources.

http://ifera.org
The International Family Enterprise Research Academy (IFERA) is geared towards advancing family business research, theory and practice through enhanced collaboration and accelerated learning based on world best practice.

www.lums.lancs.ac.uk/departments/Entrep/family-business
The Lancaster University's Management School's Centre for Family Business aims to provide a vehicle for developing international research perspectives on family firms, large and small. It is the largest grouping of family business researchers in the UK.

CHAPTER 14

Habitual entrepreneurs

Mike Wright, Paul Westhead and Deniz Ucbasaran

14.1 Introduction

In this chapter, we analyse habitual entrepreneurs. The nature and extent of entrepreneurial experience – in particular, business ownership experience – is attracting research attention (Westhead, Ucbasaran and Wright, 2004).

We make a conceptual distinction between inexperienced novice entrepreneurs with no prior business ownership to leverage and habitual entrepreneurs with prior business ownership experience. Within the habitual entrepreneur category, we farther distinguish between serial and portfolio entrepreneurs (Westhead and Wright, 1998a, 1998b; Ucbasaran, Alsos, Westhead and Wright, 2008a). Also, an entrepreneur's business ownership experience may differ from that of others due to the number of private businesses the entrepreneur has established, inherited and/or purchased, the mode by means of which ownership took place and the degree of success or failure. It is reasonable to assume that an experienced entrepreneur may be able to identify profitable opportunities more clearly than novice entrepreneurs, who can only leverage the experience accumulated from their current venture to identify and exploit further entrepreneurial opportunities.

The resource needs, behaviour and contributions made by habitual entrepreneurs may differ significantly from those of novice entrepreneurs. Obstacles to subsequent business start-up and purchase, as well as barriers to growing the business thereafter may be circumvented more easily by habitual entrepreneurs, who have acquired resources and learning from prior experience. As a result of this expected learning, the potential for habitual entrepreneurs to create both greater personal financial returns and greater benefits for society through the development of businesses that create more employment and growth, as well as the generation of higher tax revenues, is of great interest (Westhead and Wright, 1998a; Westhead, Ucbasaran and Wright, 2003a; Rerup, 2005; Baron and Ensley, 2006).

In the sections that follow, we explore these dimensions of the habitual entrepreneurship phenomenon. First, we define habitual entrepreneurs, distinguishing between different types of habitual entrepreneurs – specifically, as mentioned, serial and portfolio entrepreneurs. We also elaborate a typology identifying that habitual entrepreneurs can involve different ownership modes. We then compare the information search and opportunity identification processes of habitual entrepreneurs with those of novice entrepreneurs. The resources of habitual entrepreneurs with regard to their human capital resources and cognitive behaviour, social capital and networks and access to financial resources are also examined. Performance aspects are then discussed in terms of the links between habitual entrepreneurship and superior firm and entrepreneur performance. Finally, we highlight several unresolved issues for further research.

14.2 Learning objectives

There are four learning objectives for this chapter:

1 to provide understanding of the distinctions between entrepreneurs who only (ever) own one business and those entrepreneurs who own more than one business
2 to provide theoretical and empirical insights into the entrepreneurial behaviour of habitual entrepreneurs and the subtypes of portfolio and serial entrepreneurs
3 to provide insights into whether or not and how habitual entrepreneurs learn from their previous success or failure
4 to obtain appreciation of the implications of habitual entrepreneurs for policymakers and practitioners.

Key concepts

- habitual entrepreneurs ■ novice, serial and portfolio entrepreneurs
- human capital ■ cognition ■ social and financial resources
- learning from experience ■ performance ■ business failure

14.3 Defining habitual entrepreneurship

Defining habitual entrepreneurs is conceptually difficult. Business ownership and a decisionmaking role within the venture are recognised as important dimensions of entrepreneurship. Further, given the prevalence of team-based entrepreneurship (Ucbasaran, Lockett, Wright and Westhead, 2003), this ownership may involve minority or majority equity stakes. Adopting a perspective recognising that ownership is a key element of entrepreneurship, the different types of entrepreneurs can be defined as follows (Westhead et al., 2003a; Ucbasaran et al., 2008a):

- *novice entrepreneurs* individuals with no prior minority or majority firm ownership experience, either as a firm founder or as purchaser of an independent firm, who currently own a minority or majority equity stake in an independent firm that is either new or purchased
- *habitual entrepreneurs* individuals who hold or have held a minority or majority ownership stake in two or more firms, at least one of which was established or purchased, and this group can be subdivided as follows:
  - *serial entrepreneurs* individuals who have sold/closed at least one firm that they had a minority or majority ownership stake in and currently have a minority or majority ownership stake in a single independent firm
  - *portfolio entrepreneurs* individuals who currently have minority or majority ownership stakes in two or more independent firms.

Table 14.1 Categorisation of habitual entrepreneurship

Nature of entrepreneurship		Serial entrepreneurs	Portfolio entrepreneurs
Involve new business(es)	De novo business	Serial founders (1)	Portfolio founders (6)
	Spin-off (including corporate and university spin-offs)	Serial spin-out entrepreneurs (2)	Portfolio spin-out entrepreneurs (7)
Involve existing business(es)	Purchase (including buyouts/buyins)'...	Serial acquirers (e.g., secondary management buyins or buyouts) (3)	Portfolio acquirers (e.g., leveraged build-ups) (8)
	Corporate entrepreneurship	Serial corporate entrepreneurs (4)	Portfolio corporate entrepreneurs (9)
Involve no new legal entity	Self-employment	Serial self-employed (5)	Portfolio self-employed (10)

Source: Adapted from Ucbasaran et al., 2008a, Table 7.1.

The emerging opportunity-based conceptualisation of entrepreneurship suggests that it involves the identification and exploitation of at least one business opportunity.

A business opportunity can relate to the formation of a new firm, the purchase of an existing private firm, identification of new opportunities in existing firms or for self-employment. This gives rise to a categorisation of the nature of habitual entrepreneurship in terms of the modes through which it can occur. A categorisation of habitual entrepreneurship is summarised in Table 14.1.

The serial habitual entrepreneurs engage in entrepreneurship sequentially, while the portfolio entrepreneurs engage in concurrent entrepreneurial activities. The serial and portfolio founders are involved in the founding of new independent firms, while the serial and portfolio spin-out entrepreneurs are involved in new firms that are spin-offs from other organisations. The serial and portfolio acquirers have become owners of established independent firms. These include individuals from outside the firm who undertake a straight purchase or a management buyin (MBI) and those from inside the firm who undertake a management buyout (MBO) of the firm. Some of these buyouts may involve founders selling their businesses and subsequently buying them back when the acquirers find themselves able to generate adequate performance because they do not possess the tacit knowledge of the founder. Some of them are secondary buyouts, where the same management acquire a larger stake in the firm through a financial restructuring, which may be associated with initial private equity investors selling their shares (Jelic and Wright, 2011). Serial and portfolio corporate entrepreneurs are engaged as corporate entrepreneurs within existing firms – they have not purchased them (Phan, Wright, Ucbasaran and Tan, 2009). Finally, the serial and portfolio self-employed entrepreneurs in cells are self-employed individuals who do not form a specific legal entity (Parker, 2010).

14.4 The habitual entrepreneur phenomenon

Habitual entrepreneurship is widespread. Differences in rates of habitual entrepreneurship between countries may, in part, be due to definitional and sample variations, including coverage of industry sectors and whether or not team ownership is encompassed. These differences may also be due to infrastructural and cultural variations, such as how active the capital market in each country is, government policies (e.g., towards failed businesses and entrepreneurs) and attitudes towards entrepreneurship and risk. Studies suggest that high proportions of habitual entrepreneurs among owners of private firms can be found in the UK (52 per cent), USA (51 to 64 per cent), Finland (50 per cent), Australia (49 per cent), Norway (47 per cent), Sweden (40 per cent) and Malaysia (39 per cent) (Ucbasaran et al., 2008a).

Studies have examined business groups under control of habitual entrepreneurs. Rosa (1998) mapped out business clusters in Scotland and noted a complex picture of portfolio entrepreneurship. Iacobucci (2002) observed that a quarter of Italian manufacturing firms were members of business groups created by habitual entrepreneurs (or their associated entrepreneurial team). Iacobucci and Rosa (2005) found that the formation of these business groups was a strategy to organise geographical extension, product diversification or market differentiation and their prevalence varied depending on sector.

Differences between novice and habitual entrepreneurs, as well as between novice, serial and portfolio entrepreneurs, with regard to demographic characteristics (i.e., gender, age and parental background), together with their general (i.e., education and managerial experience) and specific human capital profiles (i.e., entrepreneurial team experience, motivations, perceived skills and cognitive mindsets) have been identified. In general, evidence indicates that habitual entrepreneurs are fairly young when they start their first business and are male (Westhead and Wright, 1998b). Portfolio entrepreneurs are generally more likely than not to have parents who are businessowners (Westhead, Ucbasaran, Wright and Martin, 2003b). Habitual entrepreneurs have generally accumulated more different resource pools than novice entrepreneurs, which can impact their subsequent behaviour and performance. Regarding general human capital, habitual entrepreneurs tend to be more highly educated and have higher levels of managerial human capital than novice entrepreneurs (Westhead et al., 2003b; Ucbasaran, Westhead and Wright, 2006a).

14.4.1 Motivations for habitual entrepreneurship

The initial motivations for creating or purchasing a business may impact the opportunities identified and pursued by habitual entrepreneurs, as well as the strategies adopted by them to grow their ventures.

Habitual entrepreneurs report a variety of motivations, including a desire:

- for independence and autonomy
- for (personal) income and wealth creation (Wright, Robbie and Ennew, 1997a)
- to grow the activities of an existing business (Alsos and Carter, 2006).

The reasons leading to start-up vary, both with the type of entrepreneur and the type of locality where the surveyed business was located (Westhead and Wright, 1998a). Portfolio rural founders, for example, are markedly more likely than novice and serial rural founders to have started their businesses for wealth and/or welfare reasons. In contrast, novice and portfolio urban founders are more likely than serial urban founders to emphasise autonomy reasons (Westhead and Wright, 1998c). Habitual serial urban entrepreneurs are more likely than novice urban founders to start their latest business in order to develop an idea for a product. Portfolio and novice urban founders are more likely than serial founders to report they were taking advantage of an opportunity that appeared. A larger proportion of portfolio urban founders report that they were seeking tax benefits compared with novice and serial urban founders. Novice urban founders are more likely than portfolio urban founders to emphasise that they started a business to achieve something and get recognition for it. Serial urban entrepreneurs are more likely than novice urban founders to report that they started a business to continue a family tradition.

Evidence is mixed relating to the prevalence of materialistic and monetary motivations for starting or purchasing subsequent businesses. Several materialistic reasons coming to the fore when an entrepreneur establishes or purchases a subsequent business have been noted (Donckels, Dupout and Michel, 1987). However, other studies suggest that monetary gain may become less important in subsequent ventures, particularly if owners of second or later ones generally desire less novel ventures. In part, this is because they do not want to put at risk the wealth generated from an earlier successful venture (Wright et al., 1997a). Nevertheless, habitual entrepreneurs continue to report the desire to be independent and build a larger organisation.

Focusing specifically on the entrepreneurs' motivations for starting a group of businesses, Iacobucci (2002) found that the three main ones were growth, entrepreneurial dynamics, and a desire for capital accumulation. Portfolio entrepreneurs seem to be motivated to add new ventures to their business groups for the following reasons (Rosa, 1998):

- they want to diversify into a new market to spread risk or overcome potential adversity
- they see business creation as a challenge or a hobby
- they want to protect a new area or brand name
- they want to ringfence a geographical diversification or risk
- they seek to add value to existing ventures owned by the entrepreneur
- they want to assist a friend or relative
- they want to launder money, profits and/or family assets
- they want to avoid paying taxes
- because they want to cut costs and enhance internal efficiencies.

14.4.2 Information searches

Information is potentially valuable for entrepreneurs, particularly with regard to opportunity identification and exploitation (Shane, 2000).

Inexperienced entrepreneurs with less market knowledge may be more likely to engage in extensive searches (Woo, Folta and Cooper, 1992) than more experienced habitual entrepreneurs, who may be less likely to engage in proactive searches because they are able to adopt routines that previously worked well. However, information searches are part of the process of identifying or 'noticing' opportunities (Fiet, 2002). Novice entrepreneurs may utilise narrower search routines, relating to the amounts and sources of information. Being less attuned to market signals, though, these individuals have fewer benchmarks to assess whether or not the information they have gathered is suitable for identifying a novel business opportunity.

Habitual entrepreneurs who have multiple business experiences to draw upon may be more likely to rely on information-processing patterns based on heuristics (i.e., simplifying strategies or mental short cuts) to identify and exploit opportunities in complex and uncertain situations where complete information is not available. Notably, habitual entrepreneurs, who have learnt from their prior business experiences, may become experts in processing information relating to potential entrepreneurial opportunities. Experienced entrepreneurs may be better able than novice entrepreneurs to manipulate incoming information into recognisable patterns that generate novel insights (Baron and Ensley, 2006).

Studies have found that information searches vary from entrepreneur to entrepreneur. Although Cooper, Folta and Woo (1995) expected novice entrepreneurs to search for less information, due to their limited understanding of what was needed, they found the opposite – they generally sought more information than habitual entrepreneurs. Conversely, Westhead, Ucbasaran and Wright (2005a) found that, on average, habitual entrepreneurs used a wider range of information sources than did novice entrepreneurs. Ucbasaran et al. (2006a), however, failed to find a significant association between an entrepreneur's prior business ownership experience and the number of information sources utilised or the information search intensity.

14.4.3 Opportunity identification

Prior business ownership experience may allow habitual entrepreneurs to use information better, to be more alert to opportunities, than novice entrepreneurs. Habitual entrepreneurs can also leverage their experience-based knowledge to generate additional business ideas and spot opportunities. This is because they are more aware of and can better interpret market stimuli. Indeed, novice entrepreneurs, owning only one venture, are more likely than serial or portfolio entrepreneurs to have failed to identify any further opportunities for creating or purchasing a business within the last five years (Westhead et al., 2003b; Alsos, Kolvereid and Isaksen, 2006). Portfolio entrepreneurs are also more likely than serial entrepreneurs to have identified further opportunities.

Ucbasaran, Westhead and Wright (2008b) found that entrepreneurs with more business ownership experience identified significantly more opportunities and more innovative ones, too. However, beyond a certain point, the benefit of the number of previous businesses owned begins to decline. Up to a fairly high level (some 15 firms), prior business ownership experience may be a valuable resource for opportunity identification. Beyond this point, entrepreneurs may believe that they already have sufficient knowledge and so do not have to search for additional information, especially in new areas. Consequently, they may make biased or suboptimal decisions.

The outcomes of previous ventures owned by habitual entrepreneurs appears to influence their future opportunity identification and exploitation. Some learning from failure may occur as habitual entrepreneurs with higher proportions of prior business failure experience seem to identify significantly more business opportunities than those who haven't had these experiences (Ucbasaran et al., 2010). Again, however, this may be the case only up to a certain point as habitual entrepreneurs who reported that more than 26 per cent of their businesses had failed identified significantly fewer business opportunities than others who had been more successful. This evidence supports the view that business failure can be a traumatic event and hinder learning, as well as reducing an individual's self-confidence and motivation to own another business. Even when new businesses are created following such experiences, this evidence suggests that the new firm may not necessarily perform any better.

14.5 Resources and capabilities

Business ownership experience may provide habitual entrepreneurs with a variety of resources and capabilities that can be leveraged to identify and exploit subsequent ventures, such as enhanced human capital through direct entrepreneurial experience, additional managerial experience and an enhanced reputation, better access to and understanding of the requirements of finance institutions and access to broader social and business networks. We examine the human capital resources and cognition, access to financial resources and development of social capital and networks factors associated with habitual entrepreneurs in turn below.

14.5.1 Human capital resources and cognition

General human capital

Habitual entrepreneurs tend to have worked for more organisations prior to starting a business than novice entrepreneurs (Ucbasaran et al., 2006a).

Portfolio entrepreneurs proactively seek to fill gaps in their human capital resources by partnering with other team members. They are also more likely than other types of entrepreneurs to engage in team ownership to start or purchase surveyed businesses, with 34, 36 and 41 per cent of novice, serial and portfolio entrepreneurs, respectively, reporting doing so (Ucbasaran et al., 2006a). This may be because a partner could offer a wider range of skills and knowledge as well as financial resources than the entrepreneur. Also, the resources required to develop and coordinate a portfolio of businesses suggest that portfolio entrepreneurs are more likely to need contributions from more partners than serial or novice entrepreneurs. Further, habitual entrepreneurs, particularly portfolio entrepreneurs, whose comparative advantage is in *starting* businesses, may be able to delegate the running and development of their ventures to partners with more managerial skill once they are up and running.

Partners can also help mitigate liabilities associated with a new firm. If partners are selected to join a serial entrepreneur in a new venture and they have strong prior experience, they can give legitimacy to the serial entrepreneur, whose reputation may have been tarnished by prior business failure.

Managerial, technical and entrepreneurial capabilities

Managerial skills relate to the ability to manage and organise people and resources. Technical skills focus upon technical expertise. Repeated business ownership experience contributes to the development of these skills.

Entrepreneurial skills focus upon the perceived ability to create, identify and exploit opportunities. Entrepreneurs need to show skills relating to entrepreneurial, managerial and technical, functional areas. Perceived specific human capital skills have been shown to correlate highly with actual skills (Chandler and Jansen, 1992).

Portfolio entrepreneurs are more likely than novice entrepreneurs to report managerial capabilities relating to professionalised resource accumulation and management skills, as well as entrepreneurial capabilities relating to the alertness and developmental approach to opportunity identification (Alsos, Ljunggren and Pettersen, 2003; Westhead et al., 2003b). Conversely, serial entrepreneurs are more likely than novice entrepreneurs to perceive that they have entrepreneurial capabilities relating to customer focus and needs and be more likely than portfolio entrepreneurs to report that they believe they have technical capabilities in a technical or functional area. Even so, serial entrepreneurs, as might be expected, seem to have lower managerial skills than portfolio entrepreneurs. However, habitual entrepreneurs report lower levels of perceived technical skill than novice entrepreneurs (Ucbasaran, Westhead and Wright, 2006b).

How habitual entrepreneurs think, learn and process information may differ from how novice entrepreneurs do so. This is because experience can shape an entrepreneur's cognition (Ucbasaran et al., 2008a). Notably, experience may influence an individual's capacity to acquire and organise complex information and provide a framework for processing information. It thus allows experienced entrepreneurs with diverse knowledge and social capital to identify and exploit opportunities (Baron, 2004; Baron and Ensley, 2006). Dew et al., (2009) propose that 'expert' entrepreneurs are more likely than novices to display features of effectual reasoning in decisionmaking – i.e., identify more potential markets, focus more on building the venture as a whole, pay less attention to predictive information, worry more about making do with resources at hand to invest only what they can afford to lose and emphasise stitching together networks of partnerships. Experience-based knowledge may also create cognitive pathways that can lead to greater creativity.

Westhead, Ucbasaran, Wright and Binks (2005c) identified differences in the attitudes reported by novice, serial and portfolio entrepreneurs. Drawing upon prior business ownership experience, habitual entrepreneurs are more cautious and realistic than novices about the barriers they face. Habitual, particularly portfolio, entrepreneurs suggest that they are more creative than novice entrepreneurs. Portfolio entrepreneurs also report that they are more innovative than novice and serial entrepreneurs.

14.5.2 Access to financial resources

Prior business ownership experience may enable access to more capital to create or purchase subsequent ventures and from a wider range of external sources. If habitual entrepreneurs have successfully realised their investment in a previous venture, they can be in a strong personal financial position. Conversely, novice entrepreneurs with no entrepreneurial track record to leverage may find it difficult to access external funds, so they may have to rely upon finance from personal savings, family and friends.

Compared to novice entrepreneurs, portfolio and serial founders tend to invest significantly more money, particularly personal funds, in their firms at start-up (Westhead et al., 2003a; Alsos et al., 2006). There does appear to be a difference in the sources of funding obtained by portfolio and serial entrepreneurs, too.

Successful habitual entrepreneurs may be better placed to leverage their prior business ownership experience and obtain external financial resources from banks and venture capitalists for their subsequent ventures than habitual entrepreneurs who have previously failed. Portfolio entrepreneurs may be able to leverage the internal financial resources of their existing business(es), as well as make use of finance from existing customers and suppliers (Alsos and Kolvereid, 1998).

Serial entrepreneurs do not have such access, but they may have amassed significant personal financial wealth if they have successfully exited a previous business. However, evidence suggests that serial entrepreneurs are reluctant to become engaged in subsequent projects that involve putting a substantial portion of their newfound wealth at risk and potentially could undermine their reputation in the financial and business community (Wright et al., 1997a).

Financiers may take into account an individual's previous business ownership experience. They also need to be convinced that an entrepreneur is still motivated to succeed the next time around and has been able to identify a subsequent attractive opportunity (Wright et al., 1997b).

Prior founding experience – especially financially successful experience – increases the likelihood of venture capital funding (Gompers, Kovner, Lerner and Scharfsfein, 2007; Hsu, 2007). 'Failed' serial entrepreneurs, rather than 'successful' serial entrepreneurs, are more likely to obtain funding from the same venture capital firm that funded their first venture (Bengtsson, 2007). Successful serial entrepreneurs may be more aware of what is involved in raising venture capital and so may be in a stronger bargaining position to obtain better terms from venture capital firms than those with fewer start-ups to their name. A repeat venture capital relationship with the same investor seems more likely if an entrepreneur's subsequent start-up is similar to the previous one. The proximity of alternative venture capital investors may also be important (Bengtsson, 2007).

14.5.3 Development of social capital and networks

Entrepreneurs' social networks can provide access to information and new knowledge that facilitate the identification of novel opportunities (Davidsson and Honig, 2003). Habitual entrepreneurs may have already built up networks with regard to their prior venture ownership experience and may feel that they need to be subsequently less proactive in searching for information. Indeed, venture capitalists, advisers and others in the entrepreneur's network may bring new business proposals to habitual entrepreneurs who have developed a reputation for success.

The corridor principle suggests that entrepreneurs may not be able to identify the best new venture opportunities until they have become involved in an initial venture (Ronstadt, 1988). The notion of shadow options is a closely related concept (McGrath, 1999). That is, habitual entrepreneurs are seen to pursue ventures in order to gain access to further (more profitable) business opportunities that had not been previously recognised. Having become involved in one venture, further information becomes accessible regarding contacts, potentially attractive customers, new product opportunities and the resources needed to exploit further attractive business opportunities.

Two studies of habitual entrepreneurs illustrate this behaviour. First, farmers who identified opportunities based on the daily activities of the farm business have been found to be more likely to engage in the start-up of other new business activities (Alsos et al., 2003). Second, an entrepreneur's business networks and links with support agencies have been shown to be a significant predictor of habitual entrepreneurship (Wiklund and Shepherd, 2008).

Similarly, an academic entrepreneur's specific human capital associated with entrepreneurial experience can influence the ability to develop the social capital that is required to circumvent barriers to venture development. Mosey and Wright (2007) identified three types of academic entrepreneurs with differing levels of entrepreneurship experience – i.e., nascent, novice and habitual entrepreneurs. They proposed that habitual entrepreneurs have broader social networks and are more effective in developing network ties to gain equity finance and management knowledge than the other two types. Conversely, less experienced entrepreneurs are likely to encounter structural holes between their scientific research networks and industry networks, constraining their ability to recognise opportunities and gain credibility for their fledgling ventures.

14.6 Performance and strategy

It is reasonable to assume that entrepreneurs with prior business ownership experience will be subsequently associated with superior firm and entrepreneur performance outcomes. In reality, the picture is more complicated.

Some habitual entrepreneurs can accumulate liabilities as well as assets with regard to their prior business ownership experience (Starr and Bygrave, 1991). Notably, they may fail the first time around, but learn from their experience and become successful in their subsequent venture(s) as a result. However, the liabilities of prior business ownership experience may mean that some entrepreneurs fail to adapt to changed circumstances the next time around, so may pursue the same strategies and 'recipes' that worked before despite the changed market, technological and/or institutional conditions. If this is the case, habitual entrepreneurs may not necessarily outperform novice entrepreneurs (Ucbasaran et al., 2006a).

14.6.1 The firm

There is scant evidence relating to performance differences between novice, serial and portfolio entrepreneurs. A major challenge concerns assessing the full contribution of portfolio entrepreneurs because of the difficulties in obtaining a complete picture of the set of firms they own at consistent specific points in time (Carter, 1999; Rønning and Kolvereid, 2006).

Evidence on the link between entrepreneurs' prior business ownership experience and subsequent superior firm performance is mixed. Some studies have shown that more experienced entrepreneurs own firms that are more likely to survive and report superior performance across several outcomes than those with less experience (Dahlqvist, Davidsson and Wiklund, 2000; Delmar and Shane, 2004). Other studies have not identified any significant link between entrepreneurs' prior business ownership experiences and subsequent superior performance (Birley and Westhead, 1993; Kolvereid and Bullvåg, 1993; Westhead and Wright, 1998a, 1998c; Ucbasaran et al., 2006a). However, when compared to novice entrepreneurs, there is some evidence that firms owned by habitual entrepreneurs, especially portfolio entrepreneurs, report superior performance (Dahlqvist and Davidsson, 2000; Westhead et al., 2003a, 2003b; 2005a, 2005b), with there, for example, being markedly higher early new business employment growth (Alsos and Carter, 2006).

Habitual entrepreneurs appear to be significantly more likely to emphasise innovation and growth strategies than the other types of entrepreneurs (Westhead et al., 2003b). Perhaps this is because innovative opportunities with competitive advantages in domestic and international markets may have great wealth- and job-generation potential.

Robson, Akuetteh, Westhead and Wright (2012b) explored the propensity of novice, serial and portfolio entrepreneurs to introduce technological innovations, as well as new work practices and workforce organisation, new sources of supply or materials, the exploitation of new markets or means of reaching these markets and new administration and office systems. With reference to each of these seven types of innovation, a composite ordinal innovation outcome-dependent variable was computed.

A distinction was made between respondents who 'always not tried', 'tried and always failed', 'mixture of failed and introduced' and 'always introduced' the seven types of innovation. They identified that portfolio entrepreneurs were more likely than other entrepreneurs to report 'innovation tried and introduced'. Portfolio entrepreneurs were also less likely to report 'tried and always failed' or a 'mixture of failed and introduced' with reference to the composite index. Notably, portfolio entrepreneurs were more likely than other entrepreneurs to report innovation 'always introduced'.

Further, Robson, Akuetteh, Westhead and Wright (2012a) found that respondents reporting 'innovation not tried' reported lower exporting intensities, whilst those who had made investments in product, services and process innovations (i.e., distribution and work practices) reported higher exporting intensities. Notably, they showed that the nature rather than the extent of prior business ownership experience was linked to higher exporting intensities. Habitual (i.e., serial and portfolio) entrepreneurs reported higher exporting intensities than novice entrepreneurs. Further, they found that portfolio, rather than serial entrepreneurs, reported higher exporting intensities.

Perhaps reflecting the challenges of coordinating the multiple businesses they own concurrently, portfolio entrepreneurs tend to place greater emphasis on professionalised management practices than serial or novice entrepreneurs. Such management practices may contribute to portfolio entrepreneurs being able to generate synergies between the businesses they own, which results in improved performance (Rosa, 1998).

14.6.2 The entrepreneur

Performance indicators may relate to the entrepreneur rather than solely to the firm. Portfolio entrepreneurs tend to draw larger incomes than novice entrepreneurs (Westhead et al., 2005a; Rønning and Kolvereid, 2006). Evidence suggests that the overwhelming majority of habitual entrepreneurs are satisfied with their current businesses compared to their first business (Westhead et al., 2003b). An additional aspect of satisfaction relates to the willingness to start or purchase a business again in the future. Westhead et al. (2003a) found a larger proportion of portfolio, rather than novice and serial entrepreneurs, indicated that they intended to establish or purchase an additional business.

A certain amount of business failure can encourage entrepreneurs to learn from their mistakes and put into practice what they have learned. Ucbasaran, Westhead and Wright (2009) detected an inverse U-shaped relationship between the proportion of failed businesses relative to the number of businesses owned and the number of opportunities identified in a given period. They, however, failed to detect a significant link between the business failure experience and the subsequent ability to exploit innovative (i.e., potentially more wealth-creating) opportunities.

Business failure can be a traumatic event that hinders learning and reduces an individual's self-confidence and motivation to start another business. Although prior entrepreneurial experience has been linked with a greater intention to start a business again (Kolvereid and Isaksen, 2006), experience of business failure has been found to be associated with entrepreneurs being less likely to report comparative optimism. Ucbasaran et al. (2010), for example, detected that portfolio entrepreneurs are less likely to report comparative optimism following business failure, while serial entrepreneurs who have experienced business failure do not appear to adjust their comparative optimism. It may be that a business' failure in among a portfolio entrepreneur's set of activities may be a less traumatic event than for a serial entrepreneur who has only one current business and may seek to externalise blame for the failure.

14.7 Policy and practitioner implications

Policies have typically focused on increasing the stock of businesses in an economy through measures to stimulate new start-ups. Habitual entrepreneurs – and the presence of novice entrepreneurs who subsequently become habitual entrepreneurs – can distort new start-up rates. Ignoring habitual entrepreneurs, though, can lead to an underestimation of the contributions made by this numerically important subset of entrepreneurs to local and national economic development.

Practitioners promoting choice and opportunity, economic diversity, enterprise sustainability, wealth creation and innovative and knowledge-based firms need to understand the aspirations and resource needs of different types of entrepreneurs. Policies appropriate for encouraging people to become novice entrepreneurs may not be equally applicable to experienced habitual entrepreneurs, particularly those who want to grow their ventures, which can be associated with greater societal benefits. Evidence discussed above suggests that there is a case for customised support being made available to novice, serial and habitual entrepreneurs.

Recognising the heterogeneity of entrepreneurs may lead to the development of more fine-grained mechanisms that are targeted at enabling the different types of entrepreneurs to realise their wealth-generating potential (Westhead et al., 2003a). Such an approach may involve a shift in emphasis from support aimed at increasing numbers of new start-ups – only to see many of them fail shortly afterwards – towards including customised support that reflects entrepreneurs' track records from prior business ownership experience. Support could be allocated to growth-orientated entrepreneurs to ensure that the full economic and societal potential of all businesses they own are realised (Westhead et al., 2004). In particular, given that the benefits from prior business ownership seem to be stronger for portfolio entrepreneurs than serial entrepreneurs, there may be policy benefits to supporting portfolio entrepreneurs who are actively seeking to maximise wealth creation and job generation (Westhead et al., 2005c). Such a policy initiative may need to ensure that the private returns to entrepreneurs and their investors are reconciled with the social returns.

Evidence suggests that serial entrepreneurs are generally less successful than portfolio entrepreneurs. Schemes could be developed to enable serial entrepreneurs who have owned a previously unsuccessful venture to learn from their prior business ownership 'failure'. There may also be a case for providing habitual entrepreneurs with financial incentives through changes in the tax regime to encourage the investment of profits or funds realised from the sale of a business in subsequent ventures that have growth potential.

Policies might also be developed to enable novice entrepreneurs to learn from the best business practices of portfolio entrepreneurs, which could include assistance with developing networks and access to information. For example, Mosey and Wright (2007) have highlighted how nascent and novice academic entrepreneurs in universities may be able to learn from mentoring provided by more experienced habitual academic entrepreneurs, particularly if support from the university's technology transfer office is very limited.

Pursuit of such fine-grained policies would need to be carefully evaluated to guide the future resource allocation decisions of practitioners who need to repeatedly evaluate the total economic, societal and environmental contributions made by portfolio, serial and novice entrepreneurs to local and national economies.

14.8 Unresolved issues

Several unresolved issues remain in our understanding of habitual entrepreneurs. These concern the nature of opportunities, information searches, leveraging human capital, entrepreneurial teams, measures of habitual entrepreneurship, the role of the external environment, contexts for habitual entrepreneurship and data and method issues. Each of these is discussed, in turn, below.

Understanding the quality of the opportunities identified by different types of habitual entrepreneurs with regard to their first and subsequent venture(s) is limited.

A key challenge is assessing its quality ex ante, which is before the opportunity has been implemented on the market. Some studies have considered the innovativeness of an opportunity as a proxy for its quality (Shepherd and DeTienne, 2005; Ucbasaran et al., 2006b, 2008a; Robson et al., 2012b), but further research is needed to explore other dimensions of the quality of opportunities.

We noted earlier that there is limited evidence relating to the different motivations reported by habitual entrepreneurs with regard to their first and subsequent venture(s). Analysis of the connection between changes in the motivations of habitual entrepreneurs and the nature of opportunities subsequently identified and exploited is lacking. Such research does, however, face the challenge of dealing with potential retrospective biases. There is a need to monitor large cohorts of novice (and habitual) entrepreneurs over time before knowing how many of them will become habitual entrepreneurs. Further studies could examine if the motivations of habitual entrepreneurs remain constant once they have created or purchased more than one business and if this varies for portfolio and serial entrepreneurs, as well as the different modes of habitual entrepreneurship identified in Table 14.1. Research in this area may help shed light on whether habitual entrepreneurs are indeed undertaking further entrepreneurial activity out of 'habit' – i.e., they cannot help themselves – or it is a straightforward repeat of previous motivations and behaviour.

Additional research is warranted to explore whether and to what extent habitual entrepreneurs pursue the same or different information-searching activities to find new opportunities. For example, to what extent are the same networks used or new networks created? A major issue warranting further attention is that entrepreneurs may have needed to embed themselves in local networks to be able to identify and exploit their initial ventures, but this may create a paradox because such networks may be too restricting for the pursuit of additional opportunities (Meuleman, Lockett, Manigart and Wright, 2010), particularly innovative opportunities with more wealth-creation and job-generation potential. Further research is needed into how habitual entrepreneurs address this challenge.

The debate regarding policies in this area has focused upon encouraging entrepreneurs that have failed in business to re-enter the entrepreneurial pool by removing attitudinal, legal and resource barriers to establishing and/or purchasing ventures. This debate, thus far, has tended to be conducted at a quite general level. Evidence to support the contention that failed entrepreneurs should be supported the next time around is quite limited.

In this chapter, we have presented evidence that suggests entrepreneurs who have experienced business failure differ from each other with regard to the nature of their prior business ownership experience (Ucbasaran et al., 2010). There is, then, a requirement for a robust body of evidence that sheds light on if and, if so, what aspects of prior business failure are associated with different types of entrepreneurs. Studies using a variety of methods (Carter and Ram, 2003) are needed to explore the links between dimensions of entrepreneurs' prior business failure experience and their subsequent ability to identify more opportunities, novel opportunities and opportunities that are more (or less) likely to generate greater private and social returns.

Despite insightful studies relating to the genealogies of the portfolios owned by habitual entrepreneurs (Rosa, 1998), we know relatively little about organisational design issues facing habitual entrepreneurs. How do portfolio entrepreneurs, in particular, configure their portfolios of ventures? Similarly, we know little about the corporate governance mechanisms employed by portfolio entrepreneurs. A central issue that we also know little about concerns the processes by which these configurations and governance mechanisms emerge. This has important implications for the ways in which habitual entrepreneurship research is conducted. The notion of habitual entrepreneurship, by definition, introduces a time dimension, yet most studies in this area have been cross-sectional. Longitudinal studies offer the advantage of being able to examine the processes involved in the transformation of novice entrepreneurs into serial or portfolio entrepreneurs. A process approach would, in addition, enable understanding to be obtained of how habitual entrepreneurs learn from prior ventures, as well as why they change their decisions about whether or not to pursue similar opportunities the second time around.

Most of the research on habitual entrepreneurs has focused upon the kinds of serial entrepreneurs and their firms given in Table 14.1 and so relates to the ownership of new firms. There has been little research on habitual entrepreneurship that has distinguished these cases from the multiple purchases of firms through management buyins and buyouts. Similarly, there is an absence of research on habitual corporate entrepreneurship and multiple self-employment actions. There is, therefore, a need for further research that examines these different modes of habitual entrepreneurship and makes comparisons between them.

There are also important overlaps between habitual entrepreneurship and family firms that remain to be explored. While family firms are often thought of as single businesses, they may, in fact, involve a configuration of separate businesses run by different family members and different generations of family members. Research is lacking on understanding the nature of these configurations and the processes and reasons associated with their emergence. How these configurations are managed, in addition, poses interesting research questions concerning whether they operate, for example, as some form of holding company or a network of loosely connected (semi-) independent entities. The institutional environment may play an important role in the emergence and shape of this type of portfolio entrepreneurship. For example, are they more prevalent in contexts where extended families are an important cultural feature?

14.9 Chapter summary

We have distinguished between different types of habitual entrepreneurs – specifically, serial and portfolio entrepreneurs. Also, we have shown that habitual entrepreneurs can involve different ownership modes, including start-ups, acquisitions, corporate entrepreneurship and self-employment. We have compared the information search and opportunity identification processes reported by habitual and novice entrepreneurs. The resources of habitual entrepreneurs have been considered with reference to human capital resources and cognition, access to financial resources and the development of social capital and networks. Performance aspects have been discussed with regard to the links between entrepreneurs' prior business ownership experiences and their firms' performance, as well as entrepreneur performance indicators. Finally, we highlighted several unresolved issues worthy of additional research and practitioner attention.

Questions

1 Why have habitual entrepreneurs been presented as distinct from novice entrepreneurs? Discuss the extent to which you think this is a valuable theoretical and policy distinction.

2 Discuss the different challenges and benefits facing entrepreneurs who build portfolios of businesses concurrently in contrast to serial entrepreneurs who own one business at a time.

3 To what extent should policymakers offer customised support to novice and habitual entrepreneurs?

4 Consider the assets and liabilities associated with the experience of business failure. Should entrepreneurs who have experienced business failure try again?

Weblinks

www.seedinit.org
Founded by UNEP, UNDP and IUCN at the 2002 World Summit on sustainable development in Johannesburg, the SEED Initiative supports innovative small-scale and locally driven entrepreneurships around the globe that integrate social and environmental benefits into their business model.

www.highgrowthprogramme.co.uk
This is an example of business support and training offered in some regions for high-growth businesses.

CHAPTER 15

Technical entrepreneurship

Niall G. MacKenzie and Dylan Jones-Evans

15.1 Introduction

The development of Western economies in the post-war period has been characterised by the growth of knowledge-intensive industries, resulting in significant structural changes within these countries. At the heart of many of these changes have been technical entrepreneurs – individuals who operate within technologically advanced industries who, with a degree of technical expertise, have branched out by themselves and set up organisations focusing on their skills and experience gained in a variety of different environments. Such individuals can be found both in and creating a number of different industries.

With the rapid technological progress occurring in the last decade or so – particularly the growth of the Internet – technical entrepreneurship has become a primary consideration for governments at local, regional, national and even transnational levels that are seeking to encourage, stimulate and sustain increased levels of growth in the field. It has been said that the real source of power in newly developed knowledge economies is in combining entrepreneurship with technical expertise (Arora and Faraone, 2003). Arguably the most prominent examples of technical entrepreneurship can be found in Silicon Valley – the birthplace of modern computing, social networking and online searching – but there are examples to be found also, for example, in the two Cambridges – one in the UK and one in Massachusetts in the USA – both of which have world-class universities and an impressive array of start-ups.

As a result of the rapid growth and creation of new industries in recent years, the field of technical entrepreneurship has become of increasing interest to observers, scholars and policymakers, not least because of its ability to contribute to continued economic development and innovation.

This chapter examines the field of technical entrepreneurship, detailing the different approaches taken by researchers in the field and the development of our understanding of what constitutes technical entrepreneurship. It assesses the motivations, experiences, environment, background and expertise of the technical entrepreneur and how these filter into our understanding. The chapter identifies a number of different areas that may be of significance to interested observers of technical entrepreneurship, including policymakers, academics and other entrepreneurs, as well as, of course, technical entrepreneurs themselves. It compares the different types of technical entrepreneur and the different approaches taken to understanding them, as well as where they can be found, the kinds of environments in which they operate and the kinds of backgrounds they may have. It finishes with a discussion of policies that may be of use to policymakers seeking to stimulate increased levels of technical entrepreneurship and better understand these important actors in continued economic development and prosperity at all levels.

15.2 Learning objectives

There are six learning objectives for this chapter:

1 to understand the growth in technical entrepreneurship over the last 50 years
2 to identify what technical entrepreneurs are, how and why they act the way they do and in what markets
3 to understand how their backgrounds and experiences shape their approach
4 to discuss the role of technical entrepreneurs in economic development
5 to identify policies affecting technical entrepreneurship
6 to develop a typology for better understanding technical entrepreneurs.

Key concepts
■ innovation   ■ technology   ■ universities and economic development

15.3 Defining technical entrepreneurship

Technical entrepreneurs have been defined in a number of different ways over the years. One of the first studies (Schrage, 1965: 8) of small technology-based businesses envisaged technical entrepreneurship as the establishment of a new venture:

> Three physicists leave their positions with a large corporation or leading university to establish their own company. They pool their funds, secure a research contract from the government, obtain a loan from a friendly bank, and a so-called R&D company is born.

Subsequent studies (Roberts and Wainer, 1966, 1968; Cooper, 1970a, 1971b; Litvak and Maule, 1971, 1972; Braden, 1977) have also related 'technical entrepreneurship' directly to the founding of new ventures through 'spin-offs' from either university departments (Roberts, 1968; Lamont, 1972; Doutriaux, 1987; Samsom and Gurdon, 1990) or larger organisations (Cooper, 1971b; Draheim, 1972; Knight, 1988).

Further research has built on such definitions. For example, Jones-Evans (1995: 29) defined the technical entrepreneur as:

> the founder and current owner-manager of a technology-based business, i.e. primarily responsible for its planning and establishment, and currently having some management control within the organization.

An earlier study by Battelle Columbus Laboratories (1973) assessed technical entrepreneurs as product champions – those within organisations who champion a scientific or technical activity – whereas Smith (1967) defined them as those involved in setting up new ventures but not necessarily involved in their subsequent management.

What is clear from these definitions is that technical entrepreneurs are both entrepreneurs in the traditional sense but also involved closely with technology/technical expertise, be it championing it or possessing it. Jones-Evans' definition is similar to that which has been broadly used in the literature since its introduction in 1995 and so forms the basis for the analysis in this chapter.

15.4 Previous literature

The literature on technical entrepreneurship is still relatively young compared with its older, more established relation, general entrepreneurship. Still, the literature on technical entrepreneurs as agents of technical change and their role in economic development has a long and distinguished past, having attracted the attention of many of economics' most noted commentators – Schumpeter, Hayek, Turgot and Marx, to name but a few.

However, not all entrepreneurs who act as agents of technical change are necessarily technical entrepreneurs. Consequently, the study of technical entrepreneurship has been a relatively newer development, with a number of important insights being revealed in more recent years and an enhanced understanding of the place of the technical entrepreneur within the wider schema. The principal outcome of this period of analysis has been a recognition of the technical entrepreneur's role in industrial formation and growth (Cooper, 1970b; Rothwell and Zegveld, 1982; Cardullo, 1999; Oakey, 2003) and, consequently, in economic growth more generally.

Schumpeter (1947: 152) differentiated between inventors and entrepreneurs, arguing that 'an idea or a scientific principle is not, by itself, of any importance for economic practice' and that it is the entrepreneur who 'gets things done'. In the Schumpeterian sense, then, technical entrepreneurs are a combination of inventors and entrepreneurs – they have technical expertise and may have invented new processes or products, but it is the entrepreneurial side of their personality that moves them to bring this expertise to the marketplace in the form of their new organisation.

The orthodox view of technical entrepreneurs as having low management experience but possessing a high level of technological expertise was prevalent in work conducted in the 1960s by Schrage (1965), Roberts and Wainer (1966) and Wainer and Rubin (1969). However, research conducted by Cooper (1970b, 1973) improved understanding of technical entrepreneurship and demonstrated that another form of technical entrepreneur also exists – one who possesses previous experience within large industrial organisations. Further research revealed this to be technical corporate entrepreneurs – individuals or groups who create a new organisation or renewal of innovation within their existing organisation (Zahra and Covin, 1995; Sharma and Chrisman, 1999; Marvel, Griffin, Hebda and Vojak, 2007).

Research analysing the different types of technical entrepreneurs showed that significant differences exist in both the technical and management experience gained by each type (Jones-Evans, 1992, 1995, 1996). On one hand, studies of technical entrepreneurs based in academia often showed that they had little in the way of marketing, finance and other managerial skills, as well as little concept of business (Klofsten, Lindell, Olofsson and Wahlbin, 1988; Samsom and Gurdon, 1990; Costa, Fontes and Heltor, 2004). On the other hand, technical entrepreneurs coming from industrial organisations tended to have considerable managerial experience in interpersonal, decisionmaking and analytical skills, as well as marketing expertise (Braden, 1977; Knight, 1988). As a result, it can be posited that the type of organisation from which technical entrepreneurs emerge often directly affects their management and technical experience and, consequently, the management of the technology-based firm established by them.

There is also a line of thinking that suggests the level of management experience possessed by a technical entrepreneur may affect the way the new business develops and that, at a certain point in its life, the entrepreneur no longer has the management skills required to run it effectively. The lack of management experience may lead to problems if the company develops beyond the stage where strong leadership and delegation are needed (Greiner, 1972, 1998). A tangible, high-profile example of this is Steve Jobs' exit from Apple in 1985, when he was ousted from the company due to disagreements over product development amid claims of being an erratic and temperamental manager.

As Firnstahl (1986) has shown, technical entrepreneurs can face a number of problems as their businesses develop. For example, delegating tasks to other less competent employees in spite of being able to perform the role of specialist better than the employee, moving from their own role as specialist to a more generalist role and learning the new job of general manager and the requisite human resources and strategy roles it requires. These changes can often prove difficult for entrepreneurs with high levels of technical expertise but little managerial experience. Thus, if an entrepreneur with this kind of background and skillset continues to lead the venture beyond the start-up phase, then the organisational performance of the company can suffer (Flamholtz, 1986). This is one of many challenges facing technical entrepreneurs in their pursuits, the importance of delegation becoming clearer as the firm grows (Neergaard, 2005).

15.5 Methodologies for analysis

There are several methodologies for analysing technical entrepreneurship and these are based principally on quantitative or qualitative approaches, or a combination of the two. Much of the research in the field of entrepreneurship more generally has tended towards the use of quantitative methods (Churchill and Lewis, 1986) and this has also been the case in much of the analysis of the experiences of technical entrepreneurs.

A number of earlier American studies on technical entrepreneurship used quantitative tools, deploying questionnaires to sample hundreds of firms (Cooper, 1973; Roberts, 1991). One of the exponents of this approach was Ed Roberts (founder and chair of the MIT Entrepreneurship Center), who developed one of the most comprehensive databases on technology-based firms and their founders based on over 25 years of research in and around the Boston area, particularly around MIT. Principal amongst

Roberts' findings was that the failure rate of high-tech ventures after 5 years was only 15.5 per cent compared with the 90 per cent failure rate amongst new start-ups more generally.

Stuart and Abetti (1988) also used quantitative methodology to examine the characteristics of technical entrepreneurs and measured the amount (in years) of their experience and that of their new venture teams in an analysis of the impact of entrepreneurial and management experience on the early performance of technical ventures. Perhaps unsurprisingly, they concluded that it was not the amount but type of experience that was important in determining new venture success. This chimes with the approach of Bygrave (1988), who asserts that the heart of the entrepreneurship process is to be found in the descriptive backgrounds of entrepreneurs.

Several important exploratory studies in entrepreneurship and business development (Collins, Moore and Unwalla, 1964; Scase and Goffee, 1980) have adopted an inductive, qualitative methodological approach to the examination of small business owner-managers. Qualitative analysis can result in intensive and extensive studies of individuals or their situations and backgrounds, providing 'a wealth of information' for the development of hypotheses for later testing through quantitative studies (Smith, 1967).

Jones-Evans (1996) took a less prescriptive approach in terms of choosing one or the other, arguing that analysis of entrepreneurs' backgrounds should be 'largely exploratory' and not using an isolated quantitative or qualitative approach in order to provide a better understanding of the experiences of technical entrepreneurs and the processes in which they partake. The methodology chosen can have an effect on the outcome of any analysis, as Cooper's 1973 study showed.

Cooper compared the results from brief questionnaires for a large sample with those from more in-depth interviews with fewer respondents. The outcome of this was a clear demarcation between pull factors (e.g., desire for independence) and push factors (e.g., redundancy) in determining the motivations of the technical entrepreneurs, with the former appearing more regularly in responses to questionnaires and the latter in the more in-depth interviews.

In terms of what methodology should be used for researching technical entrepreneurship, there is no one 'correct' methodology as purely qualitative and quantitative approaches both have their own sets of benefits and drawbacks. For example, using qualitative analysis – e.g., in-depth interviews and/or participant observation – can result in a more multidimensional view of technical entrepreneurship, including of the actual start-up, role of the founder, subsequent development of the organisation and the influence of both internal and external actors. Combining quantitative survey research with these kinds of detailed follow-up interviews with a small number of survey participants can provide for a strong basis for research. There is the issue of 'research fatigue', however, as companies are being requested to contribute to increasing numbers of studies on technical entrepreneurship through the completion of both interviews and questionnaires. These, of course, take time, which is itself a precious commodity for businessowners, meaning companies often find it difficult to respond to all requests, particularly those companies targeted as a consequence of being located in directories of organisations in specific sectors or in popular locations, such as science parks.

15.6 The development of technical entrepreneurship

15.6.1 The growth of technical entrepreneurs

The increasing rate of technological change has, perhaps unsurprisingly, brought with it an increase in the number of technical entrepreneurs. With the decline in traditional manufacturing and other heavy industries in the Western developed world, a new emphasis on economic renewal through technology-focused industries has occurred. Conscious of the structural changes within their economies, developed nations have moved towards more technologically advanced forms of industry in order to develop knowledge economies.

The runaway success of areas such as Silicon Valley and Route 128 in Massachusetts over the last 50 years has brought much attention to the study of technical entrepreneurs and the benefits they can bring to bear on economic growth and renewal.

Europe has found itself playing catch-up, however, with growth in technology-focused start-ups only increasing over the last quarter century. With this has occurred a commensurate increase in European interest in the subject, with research being carried out in the UK, Sweden, Finland and other parts of Europe into the motivations and experience of technical entrepreneurs and the success of policy directed towards them. This research has filtered into public policies, with increasing levels of engagement between policymakers keen to establish appropriate support mechanisms for encouragement of technical entrepreneurship and researchers seeking to understand their subject matter.

Although the study of technical entrepreneurship is relatively new, technical entrepreneurs have been around for many years. The Industrial Revolution of the eighteenth and nineteenth centuries was a fertile breeding ground for technical entrepreneurs, for example, with the steam engine and telephone both making their appearance in history, their patents filed by James Watt and Alexander Graham Bell respectively.

With technological progress developing rapidly and increased awareness of what technical entrepreneurs are and what they bring to society and the economy, governments have placed creation of the knowledge-based economy at the heart of their policies in the developed world. Technical entrepreneurs lie at the centre of this focus due to their intrinsic role in the innovation process, with many acting as advisers to governments on policies at local, regional and national levels around the world, as well as pursuing their own entrepreneurial endeavours.

15.6.2 Characteristics of technical entrepreneurs

Technical entrepreneurs require a combination of skills and expertise in order for their businesses to survive and thrive. Some may learn by rote or doing (an idea first espoused by Arrow in 1962 on the effects of innovation and technical change), whereas others may adopt a systematic approach to developing the skills and knowledge base needed to result in moving into the entrepreneurial venture.

There are various requirements for any technology-focused business, including labour, capital and land (the last of which has diminished somewhat with the advent of the Internet, admittedly). The most important requirement though is the entrepreneur

– as Schumpeter said, the person who 'makes it happen'. There are myriad influences on technical entrepreneurs at any given moment. Cooper (1973) identified as key amongst these influences the organisation in which the technical entrepreneur previously worked and external factors in relation to the locality of the new firm as interacting to create a climate that is more or less favourable to entrepreneurial activity. Collins and Lazier (1993) identify the entrepreneur as being the leader and catalyst in this environment.

Technological development is a highly uncertain process, particularly within areas such as biotechnology, meaning that technical entrepreneurs often have to tolerate and endure significant levels of risk. Due to the environment in which they often operate, technical entrepreneurs almost have to be evangelical about the technology they are promoting and selling – they need to impart their understanding to others who may not have the same level of knowledge or competence and in such a way that it engenders trust in what they are doing, particularly with high-tech ventures. Technical entrepreneurs have to 'sell' their technology to other stakeholders and customers through their vision, spirit and enthusiasm for their work, especially when it comes to seeking finance for their ventures. The financiers are often invited to sink thousands, even millions, into these technological visions of the entrepreneurs, with no guarantee of return. Consequently, technical entrepreneurs have to be salesmen, visionaries, technical experts and risktakers all at once.

15.6.3 Where to find technical entrepreneurs

Technical entrepreneurship is not spatially bound, in the sense that it can and does occur all over and particularly so with the increasingly rapid development of information and communications technology (ICT). There are, however, certain conditions that can encourage technical entrepreneurs, including access to research-led universities, supportive enterprise policies, social and financial capital and a strong supporting infrastructure. Roberts (1991) and Best (2005, 2009) cite the example of Route 128 in the Boston area, where the supportive environment (helped by the presence of MIT and Harvard) contributed to its continued high incidence of spin-off entrepreneurs and the amount of success they enjoyed. Cooper (1996) writes that locations providing access to the right skills/knowledge base should facilitate the establishment of new businesses. So, areas with a strong presence of high-tech firms often establish a reputation for the quality of their local specialist support, particularly as there is not a plentiful supply of financial advisers with knowledge of technological sectors, for example. Thus, the development of a specialist support infrastructure, including accountants, venture capitalists, lawyers and other financial and business services, can be vital in the beginning stages of a technical entrepreneur's decision to create a new venture. This is often called the entrepreneurship 'eco-system'.

15.6.4 The environment for technical entrepreneurship

Although there is no one particular area where only technical entrepreneurs exist, there are physical locations where you are more likely to find technical entrepreneurs than others. One example is that of science/research parks. These are areas that often effectively bring together the important infrastructural requirements for stimulating and sustaining technical entrepreneurship, including government, universities, public-sector R&D performers, local authorities and finance, and the growth of new knowledge-focused companies, resulting in a positive contribution to the economy (Monck et al., 1988; Westhead and Storey, 1994; Barrow, 2001; Carayannis et al., 2006; McAdam and McAdam, 2008).

This approach is not without its problems, however. These kinds of parks are often 'sold' to technical entrepreneurs on the basis of offering access to other companies and university researchers working in the same field and the opportunity to collaborate (Oakey, 2008). Whilst this sounds good in theory, in practice it can prove quite different. Some authors have found that the reality of science parks is that the high-tech small firms located there rarely collaborate with similar firms operating in the vicinity (Oakey, 1984, 2008; Lindholm Dahlstrand and Klofsten, 2002). This is in direct contrast to Porter's well-documented cluster theory, which has dominated policy discussions around the world. Porter (1998b: 197) defines clusters as 'Geographic concentrations of inter-connected companies, specialised suppliers, service providers, firms in related industries, and associated institutions (for example, universities, standards agencies, and trade associations) in particular fields that compete but also co-operate'.

Whichever may be the case – and there are strong arguments for and examples of both – these kinds of developments have proved to be a popular approach by governments around the world. Notable success stories in respect of these parks can be found in the UK, with the Cambridge Science Park, Taiwan, with the Hsinchu Science Park, and over 140 parks in the USA. A report for the Association of University Research Parks by Battelle (AURP-Battelle, 2007) found that science/research parks were emerging as strong sources of entrepreneurship, talent and economic competitiveness for regions, states and nations.

Universities are now playing an increasingly important role in encouraging technical entrepreneurship through their provision of a physical incubator space and support. Further, they often provide these services at reasonably priced rates and include mentoring and other business support from experts. University linkages (either direct of through partial spin-off) have also been suggested as a positive factor in the probability of survival, smoother operation due to a lack of difficulty in attracting investment and developing the inherited and related knowledge base of technical (scientific) entrepreneurs' new companies (Anderson, Drakopoulou Dodd and Jack, 2010). Also, regional infrastructure tailored towards the encouragement of technical entrepreneurship and research-led universities can play a key role in encouraging the development and growth of new firms through knowledge diffusion (Castells and Hall, 1994; Keeble and Wilkinson, 2000; Lindholm Dahlstrand and Jacobsson, 2003), technology spillovers through agglomeration and clustering.

The impact of universities on technical entrepreneurship is best demonstrated by the effects of two universities in the USA on their economies. A report by Roberts and Eesley (2009) demonstrated that MIT alumni had created 25,800 active companies employing about 3.3 million people and generated annual world revenues of $2 trillion, producing the equivalent of the eleventh largest economy in the world. Yet, it could be argued that, whilst this result is impressive, the real hotbed of technology entrepreneurship is to be found on the other side of the USA, in California.

15.6.5 Silicon Valley

The USA lays claim to having the world's first science park – the Stanford Industrial Park (now Stanford Research Park), built in the grounds of Stanford University by the educational institution as a forerunner to the creation of Silicon Valley.

Stanford created its eponymous Industrial Park by leasing its land to companies identified as operating in industries in which the university was strong in terms of research, offering important synergies and helping create new spin-outs. It helped create Silicon Valley, which is arguably the most famous technological cluster in the world and the location of some of the most innovative and wealthy technical entrepreneurs, as well as a number of global brands. Many of the activities in Silicon Valley were originally centred around Stanford University and its Research Park, particularly on the development of high-tech industries such as the microprocessor.

The resulting technology cluster that developed is now home to a host of large and small companies and technical entrepreneurs who are engaged in a multitude of different pursuits and who often have strong links to the university. Consequently, there is now a supporting infrastructure of numerous business services that are designed specifically to meet the needs of nascent companies in the area and it has attracted global attention.

Although creating a 'new Silicon Valley' is an oft-cited aim of politicians and policymakers seeking to project images of modernity and being forward-thinking, there is no one, simplified way to develop the environment for technical entrepreneurship. Technology clusters are often developed as a result of the actions of a few individual firms, for example, rather than a deliberate outcome of policy.

Galbraith (1985) found that high technology firms often work according to a different set of factors from other types of manufacturing, with one shared feature being that they were in close proximity to complex local infrastructure, including governments, universities, government research labs and mature companies. Saxenian (2005) expanded on this, pointing out that, in spite of the higher costs of locating in areas with such complex infrastructure, the potentialities offered by doing so were considered to be of more value to technical entrepreneurs than locating in more peripheral areas, irrespective of the cheaper accommodation and services available if they did so.

15.6.6 Education and technical entrepreneurship

University science/research parks are not the only kind of relationship that occurs between technical entrepreneurs and education. Even without the formalised infrastructure of such parks, higher education often plays an important, multidimensional role in technical entrepreneurship, providing the expertise, environment, networks and facilities for technical entrepreneurs to develop and hone their business skills and create their new ventures (Keeble and Wilkinson, 2000). Educational institutions, including universities and research centres/institutes, provide both the entrepreneurs and knowledge from which new, technology-focused firms arise, as well as the technical assistance often required in the early stages of these new ventures (Lindholm Dahlstrand, 1999).

However, early studies on the development of new technology-based firms noted that these close links to academia meant that the majority of these small firms were founded by engineers and scientists with only a casual knowledge of the activities required to successfully run a business: 'While depth in technology is a source of strength for the university spin-off, the absence of business skills and lack of familiarity with business practices are perhaps the greatest weaknesses. Academic entrepreneurs, in particular, overlook the need for the functional business skills in their organisation' (Lamont, 1972: 121). In fact, many of the early studies identified that technical entrepreneurs rarely possessed management expertise that was comparable with their technical skills (Cooper, 1971b; Litvak and Maule, 1972), which was generally attributed to a lack of a formal business education, coupled with work experience that tended to be in the technical area.

Consequently, there have been specific policy interventions developed to address this issue and, during the last two decades, one of the principal contributions universities can make is, of course, through education provision in the form of entrepreneurship education and training (Siegel and Phan, 2005; Pittaway and Cope, 2007). Technical entrepreneurship education contributes to economic development in two main ways: encouraging and facilitating the creation of new ventures and growing existing businesses through adoption of new technical skills and technologies (Czuchry, Yasin and Gonzales, 2004). Not all technical entrepreneurship education has this effect, however.

A study by Kingdon (2002) found that the objective of technical entrepreneurship education for undergraduate engineers was often focused on creating awareness and enthusiasm for entrepreneurial activities rather than teaching the necessary business skills for creating and sustaining new ventures. The resultant outcome of this approach is awareness-raising rather than actual new venture creation.

There is, then, the question of whether or not entrepreneurship can be taught (Gibb, 1986) and, if so, what is the best way to do this? There is an increasing body of literature that suggests not only can technical entrepreneurship be taught but it can also, in turn, foster greater innovative cultural change through dissemination and symbiotic development of competition amongst entrepreneurs (Kingdon, 2002; D'Cruz and Vaidyanathan, 2003; D'Cruz, Shaikh and Shaw, 2006).

15.6.7 The motivations of technical entrepreneurs

Entrepreneurship is a risky venture with little or no guarantee of success, particularly within the dynamic and often volatile fields that technical entrepreneurs find themselves starting up a business in. It is thus pertinent to understand what motivations they have for jeopardising their often relatively stable career paths to set up on their own and take the financial and personal risks associated with their choice.

A number of studies in the 1960s detailed the different motivations of entrepreneurs and how they affect the growth of their companies (McClelland, 1961; Collins, Moore and Unwalla, 1964; Smith, 1967). Smith identified two types of owner-managers – the craftsman and opportunist entrepreneurs, suggesting that the motivations behind the start-up, by type of entrepreneur, would have a direct bearing on the growth of the ventures they established. Smith argued that, as a result of this, the craftsman entrepreneur would be motivated primarily not by profit, but the desire to show their skill's superiority over that of others. Thus, the type of organisation led by the craftsman entrepreneur is likely to be paternalistic, use very little in the way of external resources and have few or no plans to change the basic character of the organisation or attempt to bring about increases in the growth rate.

As a result of Smith's work, perceptions of entrepreneurial motivations and their effects on the growth and development of their companies changed. Follow-on work in the decades that followed, by Braden (1977) and Stanworth and Curran (1976), Davidsson (1988) and Jones-Evans (1995, 1996), all found similar results, establishing a clear understanding of the importance of motivation in determining the success and character of new firms.

In terms of technical entrepreneurship, the early US studies found that the motivations of such entrepreneurs were largely concerned with professional contentment and being their own boss rather than profit-seeking (Schrage, 1965). Again, these early findings panned out in subsequent studies in the following decades, which showed that, often, technical entrepreneurs' main aims in establishing and managing their new companies were independence and new technical challenges, with profit-seeking relegated to a secondary role (Litvak and Maule, 1971; Watkins, 1973; Davidsson, 1988; Roberts, 1989; Jones-Evans, 1995).

Cooper (1973) has shown that three important influences on the entrepreneur, especially within small technology-based firms, are familial influences, previous experience of entrepreneurship and educational ability.

- *Familial influence* Much of the early research examining entrepreneurial behaviour has indicated that owner-managers tend to have fathers who were themselves entrepreneurs (Collins et al., 1964; Komives, 1974), and that this was a major factor influencing their own decision to establish a new venture. More recent research has also found that self-employed fathers tend to encourage their children into entrepreneurship. A number of studies of technical entrepreneurs have found similar results. For example, Cooper (1986), in an examination of previous research into technical entrepreneurship, found that, across five different studies, 38 per cent of technical entrepreneurs were from families in which one of the parents was self-employed. Moreover, the major study by Roberts (1991) of technology-based entrepreneurs in the USA discovered that the majority of his sample had fathers who had been self-employed.

- *Entrepreneurial experience* Various researchers have also shown that previous organisational experience can be a major factor in influencing the success of start-ups (Cooper and Dunkelburg, 1986; Birley and Norburn, 1987; Steiner and Solem, 1988). For example, Plaschka (1990) demonstrated that previous experience in a similar line of business is more relevant to success than working experience in an unrelated business. It might be expected that technical entrepreneurs who had previous experience or knowledge of small business management might find this an influential factor in initiating their own entrepreneurial venture. A case study by Shane (2000) demonstrates, in detail, the importance of prior knowledge to the development of a new, innovative firm. The effect of experience on technical entrepreneurship is described in more detail in the next section.

- *Education* Earlier studies showed that entrepreneurs had comparatively fewer qualifications than the general working population (Collins et al., 1964; Deeks, 1972; Komives, 1974). In contrast, it has been postulated that *technical* entrepreneurs, because of the very nature of their businesses, are, on average, more highly educated than other types of entrepreneurs. Various studies have shown this to be the case (Brockhaus and Horwitz, 1986; Mayer, Heinzel and Muller, 1990; Roberts, 1991). For example, in Cooper's (1971a) sample of technical entrepreneurs, 28 per cent of them had PhDs, 28 per cent Master's degrees and 41 per cent BAs or BScs, whilst an examination of US entrepreneurs by Utterback, Reitberger and Martin (1982) found that 45 per cent had a BA or BSc degree, 35 per cent a Master's and 20 per cent a PhD or equivalent. Indeed, more recent research has suggested that entrepreneurs involved in developing new inventions and innovations are becoming more educated. Baumol, Schilling and Wolff (2009) suggest that inventors and entrepreneurs in the USA are better educated than the general population. Whilst the research points out that there are exceptions such as Steve Jobs, Larry Ellison and Bill Gates, technology entrepreneurs are becoming more educated. This is because technology is becoming more and more complex and for those entrepreneurs who wish to exploit new opportunities in emerging fields, more advanced education must be a prerequisite.

More recent literature has identified other push factors that are regularly reported by technical entrepreneurs as motivations for their career choices. The two main ones are purported to be the desire for autonomy and the wish to exploit a market opportunity (Oakey and Pearson, 1995; Cooper, Woo and Dunkelberg, 1998; Harrison, Cooper and Mason, 2004; Racine, 2010).

Push factors are often associated with previous disgruntlement on the part of technical entrepreneurs (Harrison, Cooper and Mason, 2004) – i.e., they had become disillusioned with their previous employment position or were forced into starting up their enterprises due to redundancy or a tight job market. Quite often, the idea of self-employment was not foremost in their minds and it took an exogenous event or shock to push them to take the plunge into entrepreneurship – e.g., redundancy or a period of unemployment meant it became apparent to them that self-employment was the answer to their position of difficulty.

There are a number of pull factors that act as motivations for technical entrepreneurs as well. These include the opportunity to control their future, take an active role in directing their companies through their strategic vision and controlling their time – a particularly important factor for some female entrepreneurs who have to balance family commitments with their entrepreneurial endeavours (Fielden et al., 2003; Aylward, 2007).

15.7 A typology of technical entrepreneurship by background and experience

It is clear that, although technical entrepreneurs all have in common the fact of having a notion to and then setting up their own businesses, they are not a uniform, homogenously defined, group.

Early studies into technical entrepreneurship initially identified the research-based academic environment – including non-profit organisations (namely, non-profit research institutes, government research centres and universities) – as the predominant background from which technical entrepreneurs emerged (Schrage, 1965; Roberts and Wainer, 1966; Wainer and Rubin, 1969). Subsequent studies, however, recognised a different type of technical entrepreneur – the individual who had 'spun out' from a large industrial organisation (Cooper, 1970a, 1970b). Such individuals were noted to have quite different characteristics from those originating in an academic environment. For example, a study by Knight (1988) of 133 spin-off ventures from large corporations showed that the entrepreneurs had gained considerable experience of interpersonal skills, decision and analytical skills and marketing management.

As well as differences in management experience between the two types, research by Roberts and Hauptmann (1986) has suggested that the organisational background may determine the degree of technological sophistication of the firms' products. In an examination of technological entrepreneurs in the biomedical field, a classification was devised according to the technological attributes of the founders' professional background and experience (Roberts and Hauptmann, 1986: 111–12):

> Entrepreneurs who held predominantly R&D or research positions were encoded as 'high' on technological sophistication of their professional background, and all the others were encoded as low . . . Entrepreneurs whose previous employment was predominantly in universities or hospitals were encoded as 'high' on relevance and technological sophistication of their industrial background, those with medical or pharmaceutical industrial experience were encoded as 'moderate', and the rest as 'low'.

In fact, depending on their background, technical entrepreneurs can act in very different ways and have different approaches to doing business. Subrahmanya (2005) in a comparison of North Eastern UK technical entrepreneurs and their Indian counterparts in Bangalore found that occupational background and experience were critical in the development of new product innovations and the growth of the firm. In addition, a more recent study by Salomo, Brinckmann and Talke (2008) suggested that technology management competence is a significant driver in the development of young technology-based firms – i.e., those firms run by a management team that is highly competent in technology management will progress more quickly through the early stages of development than those lacking such skills. The type of experience can also influence the type of innovation outcomes for technology-based businesses. For example, research by Marvel and Lumpkin (2007) suggests that individuals with greater depth of experience and higher levels of education are better suited to recognising and developing radical innovation.

In an earlier study, Jones-Evans (1996) separated technical entrepreneurs into four different types according to their occupational background, providing the basis for various subsequent analyses of the field. The different types are:

■ research entrepreneurs

■ producer entrepreneurs

■ user entrepreneurs

■ opportunistic entrepreneurs.

Technical entrepreneurs each have a unique background and take a variety of routes into self-employment. Occupational background is important, however, as it provides significant sectoral and market knowledge, as well as influencing the extent of commercial and business expertise that the technical entrepreneurs acquire during the course of their activities.

Below is a short analysis of each type of technical entrepreneur according to background, adapted from Jones-Evans' (1996) work.

- *Research entrepreneur* 'Research' technical entrepreneurs have a knowledge-focused background, usually in scientific or technical development, at an academic level, either in a higher educational establishment or within a non-commercial research laboratory (e.g., working for a government body). They often have little *traditional* management experience, but have strong *research* management and personnel skills. Many come from doctoral backgrounds so possess excellent technical competence and provide the technical vision for the business. Research entrepreneurs tend to collaborate with those with commercial management experience to make up for their lack of experience/familiarity with the more prosaic matters of business management – e.g., links with suppliers, customers and other external parties. This classification of technical entrepreneur is close to Samsom and Gurdon's (1990) definition of the academic entrepreneur.

- *Producer entrepreneur* 'Producer' technical entrepreneurs have an industrial organisational background and have been involved in the commercial production and development of technology products or processes, often within large organisations. The majority have a degree or higher qualification and the minority have served technical apprenticeships in technical subjects before moving into management later in their careers. Producer entrepreneurs usually possess extensive business-related contacts that they tap into when establishing their firms, making use of relationships with suppliers, customers and other service providers. They are more likely than other types of entrepreneur to retain their central role in the management of the company, partly as a result of their background of having the most developed all-round skills.

- *User entrepreneur* 'User' technical entrepreneurs also have an industrial organisational background, albeit in support services or technical sales environments – what can be described as peripheral technological experience. They may also have been end-users in the application of certain products or technology – e.g., technical support or other services – but without central involvement in their actual development. User entrepreneurs are often ill-equipped to set up organisations on their own, due to their lack of technical design and development expertise. Their sales experience does mark them out as being of potential high value to their new organisations, however, and they are often at ease with customers.

- *Opportunist entrepreneur* 'Opportunist' technical entrepreneurs are unlike the other types in that they have no industrial technical background at all, meaning their experience is in non-technical organisations. These entrepreneurs have simply identified a technology-based opportunity and acted on it. They tend to come from a predominantly middle-class background and identify strongly with management rather than a narrow technical discipline, picking up experience of physical and conceptual tools as they go along. Opportunist technical entrepreneurs often delegate far more tasks to employees and possess a different attitude towards the external environment than the other types, being proactive in marketing, with developed strategies for growth, and open to outside sources of finance.

Technical entrepreneurs play an important role in economic development, encouraging and using innovation and technology to create and grow businesses. The different kinds of technical entrepreneurs outlined above come from a wide variety of backgrounds and possess a range of different skillsets. This knowledge and typology allows us to formulate a better understanding of how background influences the way the technical entrepreneurs' organisations operate, in terms of their location and core focus. Furthermore, it allows us to pinpoint where certain kinds of entrepreneurs lack certain skills and knowledge and why they collaborate with others and how.

15.8 Examples of technical entrepreneurs

Below are four examples of technical entrepreneurs, spanning a period of almost 300 years. They – Josiah Wedgwood, William Shockley, Steve Jobs and James Dyson – are different types of technical entrepreneurs from very different industries with different motivations, backgrounds, environments, experience and results. They all share common traits, however, in terms of being experts in their technical fields and exhibiting clear entrepreneurial behaviour, albeit with different experiences in acting in this way and different outcomes.

15.8.1 Josiah Wedgwood

Josiah Wedgwood (1730–1795) has been described as 'the world's greatest innovator' (Dodgson, 2011).

Born into a family of Staffordshire potters, the youngest of 13 children, Wedgwood started in the industry at the age of just 11. Working in the family firm, he built up his expertise until, at the age of 29, he flew the coop of the family business to set up on his own, still based in Staffordshire.

By this time, Wedgwood had mastered the art of pottery and set about introducing new products, processes and services, which resulted in myriad inventions and commercial success on a hitherto unseen scale. He is credited with inventing the pyrometer (for measuring very high temperatures in kilns), money back guarantees, free delivery, illustrated catalogues, 'buy one get one free' offers, regular sales, travelling salespeople and self-service. He also created affordable yet desirable ceramics for the growing industrial classes who couldn't afford the expensive Chinese porcelain that had dominated the markets for the previous 200 years or so.

Rather than patenting (he only ever owned one patent), Wedgwood preferred to be first to market and was an early proponent of the open innovation model. He encouraged collaborative research, working with artists, customers, friends, rivals, architects and sculptors and was the first in the ceramic industry to mark his products with his name, denoting ownership of his designs.

Although Wedgwood made desirable pottery relatively affordable, he did so on the back of a demonstrable aptitude for marketing and branding, seeking patronage from politicians and royalty alike and using this in his advertising. He used the royal patronage to develop overseas clientele as well, resulting in 80 per cent of his total production being sold abroad by the mid-1780s.

Wedgwood's business expanded significantly during his stewardship of the company, resulting in him taking on a prominent role in public life, helping to create the first British Chamber of Manufacturers and playing an important role in the development of infrastructure in England during the period, including canals, turnpike roads and communications, often stemming from personal investment in the ports and towns in which his goods were transported through. From a modest start – inheriting £20 from his father – Wedgwood built up a very profitable and long-lasting dynastic firm that resulted in a personal fortune of £500,000 (equivalent to around £50 million today), in the process exhibiting numerous traits associated with technical entrepreneurship.

15.8.2 William Shockley

William Shockley (1910–1989) is perhaps less well known than Josiah Wedgwood, but has played a no less significant a role in the development of modern life as we know it.

Shockley was born in London to American parents before emigrating with them to Palo Alto, USA, as a child. Shockley gained his PhD from the Massachusetts Institute of Technology before joining Bell Labs in New Jersey. In 1945, he led the Solid States Physics Group in Bell Laboratories in Palo Alto, where early research was conducted into the development of transistors and, latterly, semiconductors. As a result of this research, Shockley, alongside John Bardeen and Walter Brattain, co-invented the transistor – a forerunner of the now ubiquitous semiconductor that is found in nearly all electronic devices, from aircraft to watches to cars to scales to calculators to mobile phones.

However, Shockley was a difficult and often domineering presence in the lab, leading to a great deal of contention and infighting amongst the researchers there. His abrasive style led to him being overlooked for promotion within Bell Labs and, eventually, he took a leave of absence in 1953 to become a visiting professor at Caltech before setting up his firm, the Shockley Transistor Company, and its lab, the Shockley Semiconductor Laboratory, back in California.

Shockley intended to realise the commercial benefits of semiconductors with his new venture and, having alienated his previous colleagues and his advances to recruit them refused, set about recruiting the brightest young graduates to work for him.

Shockley's company made a number of breakthroughs in the development of semiconductors, including using silicon (which would become the standard material for all semiconductors), but he became increasingly difficult to work with due to his paranoia, difficult personality and inability to delegate or share information and manage people. These failings, combined with his decision to stop the company's research into silicon-based transistors in 1957 (despite his original enthusiasm for the material), led to eight of his youngest and brightest researchers leaving his company to form their own company, a spin-off called Fairchild Semiconductor.

The eight who left Shockley's firm went on to found 65 other high-tech-based companies, including National Semiconductor and AMD processors (the second-largest supplier of microprocessors in the world) and created what would become the nucleus of Silicon Valley, as it is now known (Gromov, 2010). Indeed, three of those eight went on to found Intel, which is now the largest semiconductor chipmaker in the world, with revenues in the tens of billions of dollars.

Shockley continued to work on semiconductors but found his research outpaced by his former charges, who were realising the commercial potential of their research. This resulted in him eventually going back to academia, as a professor at Stanford University, before moving into research on the controversial topic of eugenics.

15.8.3 Steve Jobs

Steve Jobs (1955–2011) was the co-founder and CEO of Apple Inc, maker of the popular and critically lauded iPhone and Mac computer range.

Jobs was a college drop-out who developed a teenage interest in computing, attending after-school lectures at Hewlett-Packard before eventually taking a technician position at Atari, the computer games maker.

Whilst working at Atari, Jobs met Steve Wozniak at a computer hobbyist club in Palo Alto, where they found a common interest in developing computing technology. With funding from a former Intel executive, the two went on to form Apple Computer, Inc. in 1976 and, since then, it has become one of the most profitable and innovative companies on the planet, with very high brand awareness and award-winning designs and marketing.

Wozniak is no longer involved with the company, having left in 1981 after a plane crash, in which he lost part of his memory, short term, but Jobs is often cited as having been its leading visionary and driving force.

It wasn't all plain sailing for Jobs, however. He was forced out of the company in 1985, after a boardroom dispute, and went on to form another two companies – NeXT Computers and Pixar – almost immediately after. Jobs formed the latter after purchasing the graphics division of Lucasfilm (of *Star Wars* fame) for $10 million in 1986. He was welcomed back to Apple in 1996, with its purchase of his computing company, NeXT, for around $430 million. He later sold Pixar to Disney for $7.4 billion in shares in 2006, realising a massive return on his initial investment.

As successful an entrepreneur as Jobs was, he was not renowned for his financial savvy so much as his commitment to 'change the world' and 'put a dent in the universe'. Jobs has been described as the archetypal Silicon Valley entrepreneur – charismatic, egotistical, demanding, idiosyncratic, unyielding to opinion – but, more often than not, a visionary. He recognised the value of branding at an early stage in his Apple career, pitching the company as David to Microsoft's Goliath and aiming for 'cool' cachet amongst consumers. However, he also proved to be an adaptable CEO, since being reappointed by Apple to the position officially in 2000 (having been an interim prior). He kept the company focused more on the design of its physical products and software than in the past – its consumer electronics, including the iPod, iPhone and iPad – resulting in it dropping the 'Computer' from its name in 2007. These new products were all personally overseen by Jobs in their design and user experience, then launched by him to the world in dramatic presentations. Although he suffered from a rare pancreatic cancer towards the end of his life and having made enough money to retire decades before, Jobs continued to remain the focal point of Apple, driving it forward and ensuring its innovative edge remained a competitive asset.

15.8.4 James Dyson

James Dyson (1947–) is a British inventor and Managing Director of Dyson Ltd – best-known for commercialising the bagless vacuum cleaner.

Dyson originally started his career as an artist and designer before moving into engineering and creating his first prototype bagless domestic vacuum cleaner based on cyclone technology in 1979. Over the following five years, he continued to hone his invention with various prototypes that gained acclaim in design circles, but no commercial success. The release in 1983 of his G-Force vacuum was met with rejection in the UK – various larger, more established companies in the industry rejected it on the basis that it would disrupt the lucrative vacuum bag market, worth £250 million per annum at the time.

Having failed to bring his creation to the wider market, Dyson launched his new vacuum in Japan through a catalogue, retailing it at $2000. It gained much attention, design awards and, crucially, sales.

In 1986, he registered his bagless G-Force vacuum technology at the US patent office, having originally been rejected by the UK patent office for not providing a sufficiently different application from an existing patent. He then used the income from the sales of his G-Force vacuum to improve his other prototypes for an affordable bagless domestic vacuum cleaner, eventually producing the DC01 in 1993.

Dyson displayed a flair for marketing when releasing the DC01. Instead of concentrating on the superior suction power of his new product, he used the slogan 'Say goodbye to the bag', emphasising its bagless technology. Within 22 months, the vacuum became the market leader in the UK, realising the fears of the previously dominant industry leaders.

Dyson's bagless domestic vacuum has now become the industry standard, which has resulted in various patent disputes, including a notable success for Dyson when he successfully sued Hoover for a patent infringement, winning $5 million in damages in 1999. Ironically, Hoover was one of the companies that originally rejected Dyson's approach.

Dyson's company has gone from strength to strength, posting revenues of £770 million plus in 2010 and introducing other award-winning new products, including washing machines, hand dryers and fans. The company spends about 5.5 per cent of its total revenues on R&D. Dyson has a personal fortune estimated at anything between half a billion to a billion pounds, a reputation for being one of the most successful technical entrepreneurs in Britain and has been made the 'technology tsar' by the incumbent Coalition government in the UK.

15.9 Policy and technical entrepreneurship

New companies focused on technological innovation have been identified as playing a key role in economic growth, in both their direct contributions (jobs, wealth creation, export performance taxes, etc.) and indirect contributions, in terms of stimulating their competitors (Jones-Evans and Klofsten, 1997; Cardullo, 1999; Hart, 2003a; Oakey, 2003; Ulijn, 2007). Consequently, governments around the world are increasingly interested in developing policies geared towards encouraging the creation and growth of new technology-based firms (Oakey, 1985, 1991; Steil, Victor and Nelson, 2003; Khan, 2004; Li and Florida, 2006).

One important component of this encouragement is the development of efficient support programmes to facilitate firms in acquiring the knowledge and skills essential for a successful business (Jones-Evans and Kirby, 1995; Klofsten, 1995, 2000, 2008; Meyer, 2003; Mueller, 2006). These support mechanisms manifest themselves in a number of different ways, from the encouragement of university–industry relations to bespoke technology entrepreneurship action plans – all pursued with the explicit intention of harnessing new technological growth and development for economic growth.

However, Oakey and Cooper (1991) caution that governments seeking to exploit the opportunities afforded by new technologies considered to be important to economic growth should not simply assume that their encouragement will result in 'rapid and sustained growth' as there are no guarantees of this. Indeed, history is littered with examples of the 'next big thing' that governments have poured money into, encouraging new, emergent technologies, only to see their investments disappear down the drain.

Hart (2003a) and Acs and Stough (2008) have argued that there is no such thing as 'entrepreneurship policy' due to policy misalignments in recent years. Hay argues that what constitutes entrepreneurship policy has been swamped by other factors, although there are clear examples of when entrepreneurship policies have had a demonstrable effect. One such case of this is the rise in high-tech entrepreneurship in Washington DC in the late 1990s, where supportive social capital, venture capital, actively engaged research universities and enterprise support services were encouraged by regional government, resulting in significant growth in technical entrepreneurship in an area that was previously dominated by public-sector employment (Feldman, 2001).

Although the nature and effect of entrepreneurship policy is the subject of some debate in the literature, there is clear evidence to suggest that it has been pursued as an explicit policy objective by various governments around the world. The 2005 Vocational and Technical Entrepreneurship Development Act in the USA is one such explicit policy measure. Another, in the UK, is the creation of the Entrepreneurship Action Plan in Wales in the 1990s, as well as the development of 'enterprise zones' where financial (tax credits, grants and soft loans) and non-financial incentives (relaxation of planning regulations) were offered to encourage start-ups (Jones-Evans and Westhead, 1996).

The provision of supportive policies, environments and suitable physical infrastructure have also been found to be of benefit to the encouragement of technical entrepreneurship. Simply increasing the quantity of technical entrepreneurial start-ups should not be the main thrust of policy, however, as competitiveness and the technological and societal contributions of the new companies are determined by the quality of the firms (Jones-Evans and Westhead, 1996). As a result, it is more appropriate for policy to be both quantitatively and qualitatively focused. Oakey (2003) has written of the UK government accepting that, in order to improve both the quality and quantity of technical entrepreneurial 'spin-outs' from academia, improved business training for new and prospective faculty and student technical entrepreneurs is required – something that is often missing from science parks as well as academia more generally.

The delivery of policy in another important factor in determining the success of enterprise start-up and support programmes. A briefing by the National Endowment for Science, Technology and the Arts (NESTA, 2007) in the UK pointed out that engagement between technical entrepreneurs and policymakers is often fraught with difficulty. It noted how innovative new businesses are susceptible to frustrating engagements with policymakers due to the nature of their business position – new ideas, technology and processes often challenge the boundaries for policymakers, resulting in potentially difficult interactions between the two.

A longstanding concern in the literature regarding supply of and demand for enterprise support policies makes a similar point. Writers in the late 1980s and early 1990s (Gibb, 1992) noted that there was a gap between the demand from technical entrepreneurs for enterprise support services and the supply of these by the UK government. This was a result of not the amount of support provided, but the kind. There was a feeling amongst technical entrepreneurs that the services offered were not suited to businesses in general and particularly not to small firms.

Perhaps the most crucial lesson for policymakers in terms of encouraging and attracting technical entrepreneurs is the need to understand what influences technical entrepreneurs to set up new ventures in the first place and what persuades them to select particular locations in doing so. Without understanding these two factors, policy can often miss its intended targets.

15.10 Chapter summary

This chapter has demonstrated the importance of the technical entrepreneur as one of the key driving forces behind innovation within the economy. It began by focusing on the origins of academic research into technical entrepreneurship, examining the different motivational and personal influences on these entrepreneurs. In particular, it focused on previous experience as being a key characteristic that not only defines the different types of technical entrepreneurs but can also influence the businesses they develop and grow.

The four cases presented demonstrate that technical entrepreneurs have been at the forefront of major changes in a range of industries during the last 300 years. The fact that individuals with creativity, ingenuity, drive and talent can change the entire direction of industries and, in some cases, make significant contributions to the way we live our daily lives, is testament to the critical importance of entrepreneurship within the economy.

For policymakers, there are vital lessons that can be gained from observing the environments from which technical entrepreneurs emerge. In particular, these include the roles of innovation ecosystems in regions such as Cambridge in the UK and Cambridge, Massachusetts, and Silicon Valley, California. Indeed, with future growth in the world economy relying on knowledge-based sectors such as creative industries, information technology, clean technologies, biosciences and advanced manufacturing, it is critical that there is a greater understanding of technical entrepreneurs, the companies they lead and the environments which support their endeavours.

Questions

1 Identify the key characteristics of technical entrepreneurs and contrast them with those of entrepreneurs in general. Do they differ and, if so, how?

2 Select a technology-based business and develop a short case study profile of the firm and its founder (or principal founder in the case of a team-based start-up). How and in which areas of the firm is the influence of the founder's personal and employment background most apparent?

3 Which areas within your country have the greatest concentrations of technology-based firms? Why do you think that such firms are so common there and what resource or factor advantages exist?

4 How easy is it for technical entrepreneurs to set up firms in your local area? What forms of assistance are available to help them? What types of infrastructure, support and finance are provided by local and national government bodies and regional agencies to help potential founders and how supportive is the local business environment in terms of potential customers, suppliers and information providers?

Weblinks

www.deloitte.co.uk/fast50
An annual ranking of the UK's fastest-growing technology-based firms.

www.siliconvalley.com
A daily round-up of news from the companies that populate Silicon Valley.

www.nesta.org.uk
The UK innovation agency that supports policy and practice.

http://ec.europa.eu/enterprise/policies/innovation
The European Commission's homepage for industrial innovation policies.

CHAPTER 16

Social entrepreneurship

Dominic Chalmers and Simon Fraser

16.1 Introduction

The promise of social entrepreneurship as a mechanism for responding to growing poverty, inequality, exclusion and environmental degradation is vast.

Since 1997, when Leadbeater first published *The Rise of the Social Entrepreneur*, the approach has gained prominence as a viable method for tackling societal problems. One does not need to search far for evidence of this growing legitimacy. In academia, social entrepreneurship scholars have broken into mainstream management journals; in education, leading business schools are successfully delivering courses and modules on social and community enterprise; Muhammad Yunus, founder of the pioneering Grameen Bank, has been awarded the Nobel Prize for developing the concept of micro-finance; and, most importantly, across the EU and North America, policymakers are promising to put social innovation at the heart of rebalanced economic systems following the global recession.

This chapter provides an overview of current areas of discourse and debate, beginning with an examination of issues regarding definitions relating to social entrepreneurship. This is a much-contested area of the literature that continues to attract heated discussion amongst scholars. Next, a more detailed look at the dual tension that exists in social ventures between profit and mission, alongside the various legal forms and structures that are adopted by social firms. Then, to provide greater context for contemporary social entrepreneurship, the antecedents of the phenomena are explored. Finally, the chapter concludes with a critical examination of the domain and a reflection on the future trajectory of social entrepreneurship.

16.2 Learning objectives

There are four learning objectives for this chapter:

1 to understand the various concepts associated with social entrepreneurship
2 to understand the antecedents of social entrepreneurship
3 to understand the tensions between the social and entrepreneurial identities of social ventures

4 to critically examine the research field and examine controversial aspects of social entrepreneurship in practice.

Key concepts

■ social enterprise ■ social entrepreneurship ■ social innovation ■ civil society

16.3 The emergence of social entrepreneurship

Entrepreneurs have long been recognised as key catalytic figures in the economy (Schumpeter, 1934; Shane and Venkataraman, 2000). Increasingly, however, the notion of the entrepreneur as someone merely pursuing economic gain is being superseded by a broader notion of entrepreneurship that involves addressing issues of sustainability (Shepherd and Patzelt, 2011), the environment (Meek, Pacheco and York, 2010) and social needs (Leadbeater, 1997; Dees, 1998; Alvord, Brown and Letts, 2004). This is undoubtedly a profound development – one that has contributed to a shift in the way society views its political, social and economic systems. No longer do citizens passively expect governments or charities alone to tackle the most intractable social problems. There is, instead, recognition that these challenges are so vast and complex, new approaches and methods are required to conquer them. It is, therefore, at this nexus of government, civil society and the market that social entrepreneurs have emerged, creating sustainable new solutions to both global and niche social problems.

Although operating across the whole spectrum of human activities, social entrepreneurs find a natural home in the social economy. Situated in the space between the market and the State, neither privately held nor publicly controlled, the social economy includes non-profit associations, cooperatives, mutual organisations, associations and foundations (Haugh, 2007). An important development in this sector, largely emanating from the activities of social entrepreneurs, has been the emergence of social enterprises. These organisations – defined by UK government (DTI, 2002: 7) as businesses 'with primarily social objectives whose surpluses are principally reinvested for that purpose in the business or in the community, rather than being driven by the need to maximise profit for shareholders and owners' – are growing rapidly in number and have attained levels of legitimacy whereby they can compete for, and win, major government welfare contracts.

Characterised by their mission-driven behaviour, social enterprises fulfil needs that are simultaneously unmet by existing institutions and unattractive to the market (Seelos and Mair, 2005). They are manifest in a wide variety of organisational types and subtypes (Dees, 1996, 1998) and often employ diverse forms and structures (Low, 2006; Mason, Kirkbride and Bryde, 2007). Participating in an array of economic, educational, welfare, research, spiritual and social activities (Leadbeater, 1997), social enterprises cater for niche, often disenfranchised individuals suffering the consequences of market failure. By adopting revenue-generating business models and channelling the resourcefulness of commercial entrepreneurship, social entrepreneurs have been able to optimise social value-creation by drawing in talented innovators from beyond the traditional boundaries of the Third Sector. This cross-pollination of ideas has reinvigorated the social sphere and led to new mechanisms for tackling the most intractable problems.

The social entrepreneurship process is differentiated from traditional entrepreneurship primarily on the basis that a higher priority is afforded to creating social value as opposed to capturing economic wealth. These social ventures are seen as distinct from traditional non-profit and charitable organisations owing to their willing embrace of market-based approaches to achieving social impact. Indeed, many of the most active and influential funders of social entrepreneurship have successful commercial and technological entrepreneurship backgrounds, from which they draw extensively. These include, among others, familiar names such as Bill Gates (who established the Bill & Melinda Gates Foundation), Larry Page and Sergey Brin (who founded the philanthropic organisation Google.org) and Jeff Skoll (the Skoll Foundation).

16.4 Defining social entrepreneurship

Conceptual clarity for social entrepreneurship and its related terms appears to be as elusive as the phenomenon is omnipresent. Perhaps inevitably, given the broad multidisciplinary pool of researchers and practitioners who have contributed to shaping the field, different traditions, philosophies and priorities have, on occasion, butted heads. Meanwhile, anyone hoping to arrive at a neat definition of the highly loaded term 'social', is soon challenged to justify divisive examples of social entrepreneurship that are 'social' to some and not so to others.

Within this debate, there are voices who question the relevance of providing either a narrow or broad definition of social entrepreneurship (Jones, Keogh and O'Leary, 2007) – the vast majority of the extant literature agreeing, however, that precision is a desirable goal. As Bygrave and Hofer (1991: 15) note, 'good science begins with good definitions' and this is reflected in the academic work that has, thus far, attempted to bring clarity to the construct (Dees, 1998; Boschee and McClurg, 2003; Defourny and Nyssens, 2006; Peredo and McLean, 2006; Shaw and Carter, 2007). The case for a more robust definition of social entrepreneurship would appear to rest on two central arguments, which are: defining for practical reasons and defining for scholarly reasons.

For scholars, the future development of the paradigm is dependent on reaching a consensual approach towards terminology and conceptualisation (Nicholls, 2010). This would allow researchers to build knowledge effectively rather than work on divergent tangents. Bruyat and Julien (2001: 166) argue that:

> A research field can only be built and win legitimacy if it is differentiated from neighbouring fields. It can only impose its presence in the long term if it is able to establish its boundaries with other fields, even if those boundaries are, to some extent, fuzzy.

This need to differentiate and rationalise the field of social entrepreneurship as distinct from the entrepreneurship field is addressed in several papers (Peredo and McLean, 2006; Vega and Kidwell, 2007). Others, such as Weerawardena and Mort (2006) attempt to synthesise the various definitions that exist to create new multidimensional models to more accurately reflect the unique characteristics and contexts social entrepreneurs embody. Despite bringing a degree of improvement to conceptualisations, the field remains blurred and is often tricky to navigate.

In addition, and in parallel to these scholarly reasons for providing a more developed definition of social entrepreneurship, there is also a strong practical basis for doing so. Shaw and Carter (2007) highlight the quantitative problems that arise from discussing such a nebulous phenomenon. The fundamental difficulty of measuring the scale of social entrepreneurship is compounded by 'definitional differences of what constitutes a social enterprise', which, in turn, 'frustrate efforts to produce a comprehensive picture of the sector's size' (Shaw and Carter, 2007: 419). The implications of this are potentially significant: funding may be misallocated, service capacity may be overestimated and, ultimately, the credibility of the domain may be compromised. Taken to its extreme, this could see non-entrepreneurial organisations manipulating systems in order to access support allocated for 'genuine' social enterprises or social entrepreneurs, which, even if not done in a consciously deceptive way, risks confusing organisations that are doing good – though not generating an income – being considered entrepreneurial (Boschee and McClurg, 2003).

Despite the compelling case for tightly defining the phenomenon, there remains a risk that rushing towards consensual terminology threatens to preclude some of the most interesting emergent forms of social enterprise and social entrepreneurship that confound categorisation. Ultimately, however, as Martin and Osberg (2007: 36) conclude, 'failing to identify the boundaries would leave the term social entrepreneurship so wide open as to be essentially meaningless'.

16.5 Defining the social element

There is general acceptance that social entrepreneurs and their associated social enterprises are driven by social goals, although clarifying what constitutes 'social', can lead to some difficulty. This is perhaps unsurprising. As Seelos and Mair (2005) note, the term can take on a variety of personal and culturally bound meanings, yet, without addressing the social aspects properly, social enterprise is left subject to tautology (Cho, 2006).

At first glance, social entrepreneurship could be considered a more altruistic form of the predominantly 'self-concerned' commercial entrepreneur. This is disputed, however, by Mair and Martí (2006), who find that, despite a greater focus on ethical and moral responsibility, less altruistic drivers, such as personal fulfilment, come into play with some social entrepreneurs.

Several academics (Mair and Marti, 2006; Dahles, Verduyn and Wakkee, 2010) also claim that entrepreneurship, by its very nature, is a social activity and, therefore, it could be argued that attaching a prefix to the term is somewhat redundant. The term is sufficiently amorphous that most organisations could be considered 'social' in some regard through their everyday activities, which Leadbeater (2007) identifies as providing useful services for consumers, creating jobs, paying taxes, and through corporate socially responsible initiatives.

So, how are social entrepreneurs distinguishable from commercial entrepreneurs? Primarily, it would appear that a fundamental component is the centrality of the social mission to the social enterprise (Dees, 1998; Mort, Weerawardena and Carnegie, 2003). Dees (1998) highlights that, like traditional enterprises creating value for their customers, the focal mission for a social enterprise is creating social value for its clients or the community. Success, in turn, is measured by the creation of societal wealth rather than the economic wealth of traditional enterprises.

16.6 Defining the entrepreneurial element

The entrepreneurial element of social enterprise is a similarly problematic construct to define. Despite it being a far more developed paradigm, there is still debate surrounding the very nature of entrepreneurship (Anderson and Marzena, 2008; Sarasvathy and Venkataraman, 2011; Wiklund, Davidsson, Audretsch and Karlsson, 2011), which, in turn, contributes to a tenuous understanding of social entrepreneurship.

Early studies of the phenomenon, for instance, are generally limited to identifying the drivers and personality types of the entrepreneurs behind the organisations. According to Mair and Martí (2006), this stream of research describes social entrepreneurs as characterised by particular traits (Drayton, 2002), possessing special leadership skills (Thompson, Lees and Alvy, 2000), having a passionate approach to their vision (Bornstein, 1998) and a strong ethical core (Drayton, 2002).

The social entrepreneur, therefore, much like the commercial entrepreneur in early research, is cast as an heroic figure who enacts socio-economic change 'against the odds'. While this particular narrative may have proven useful for drawing attention and resources to social entrepreneurship in practice, it fails to account for the collective and collaborative community-based nature of many social ventures (Peredo and Chrisman, 2006; Haugh, 2007).

Moving beyond this 'heroic individual' approach, there is a desire in some sections of the academic community to widen the often simplistic understanding of social entrepreneurship that is grounded in a 'business methods' context. Peredo and McLean (2006), for instance, outline the theoretical roots of entrepreneurship in their attempt to craft a more nuanced understanding of the entrepreneurial component of the phenomenon. Dees (1998), meanwhile, adopts a 'pick-and-mix' approach to his definition, taking unique elements from seminal contributions by Say (1767–1832), Schumpeter (1883–1950) and Drucker (1909–2005) and synthesising them into a new definition of social entrepreneurship:

Social entrepreneurs play the role of change agents in the social sector, by:

- adopting a mission to create and sustain social value (not just private value)
- recognizing and relentlessly pursuing new opportunities to serve that mission
- engaging in a process of continuous innovation, adaptation, and learning
- acting boldly without being limited by resources currently in hand and
- exhibiting heightened accountability to the constituencies served and for the outcomes created.

What emerges from these contributions is a wider understanding of the entrepreneurial component that privileges the role of innovation and acknowledges the undertaking of risk by the social entrepreneur.

The entrepreneurial component has been refined further still, by Zahra, Gedajlovic, Neubaum and Shulman (2009) and Di Domenico, Haugh and Tracey (2010), who both use the concept of bricolage to explain the entrepreneurial process (see Chapter 6 for further elaboration of this concept). Here, social entrepreneurs are understood as those who 'make do' and 'improvise' with whatever resources are available to them – a description that will resonate with those who have direct experience of working in the social sector.

Zahra et al. (2009) goes further, distinguishing two other forms of social entrepreneur operating on different scales from those of social bricoleurs. First, there is the social constructionist, influenced by a Kirtznerian view of entrepreneurship, in which entrepreneurs focus on addressing opportunities and market failures. Next, there are social engineers, influenced by Schumpeter, who recognise issues within existing social structures and attempt to introduce innovations that will lead to revolutionary change.

16.7 Hybridity in social enterprise

From a scholarly perspective, besides these definitional discussions, an enduring and important area of enquiry remains that of understanding the hybrid nature of socially entrepreneurial ventures.

The hybridity in question refers to the manner in which organisations straddle both commercial and social realms by adopting elements of each to achieve optimum social outcomes. This diversity has been conceptualised by some as a continuum (Dees and Elias, 1998; Austin, Stevenson and Wei-Skillern, 2006; Peredo and McLean, 2006), ranging from purely charitable organisations to for-profit social and commercial ventures. Between each extreme, there exists a multitude of organisational forms and structures that blend varying levels of economic and socially driven activity (Atler, 2007; Kistruck and Beamish, 2010).

In more recent times, a shifting socio-economic and political environment has driven many traditionally grant-seeking or charitable non-profits to source new and sustainable income streams. Owing to squeezed fiscal priorities and some notable ideological shifts, traditional funders such as governments and philanthropic organisations are less willing, or able, to dispense money simply to 'uphold' the status quo. There is now an implicit demand that social organisations 'professionalise' and adopt more market-based approaches in both their internal organisation and service provision.

For many social organisations, this change has precipitated a move towards ensuring alternative means of funding and long-term viability. Dart (2004) argues that the increased market orientation of society has legitimated the use of business methods in the social sector. Examples such as the Energy Savings Trust (which is becoming a social enterprise owing to public funding cuts) point to ways in which the mindset of an organisation can change by making it more alert to opportunities and more operationally efficient.

The structural changes have also had a countervailing impact on the social economy, with many commercial ventures having been drawn into this previously 'sacrosanct' sector. Large private-sector service organisations, outsourcing firms and management consultancies, such as Deloitte (in partnership with Ingeus) have identified profitable contracting opportunities in the public and social sectors, while grocery retailers such as Tesco, Asda and Sainsbury's have reacted to changing customer demand and shifted towards more ethical business approaches, such as Fairtrade, in doing so, further obfuscating the traditional boundaries between economic sectors.

Most importantly, there has been an injection of new life and vitality into the social arena as individuals, inspired by the promise of social entrepreneurship as a mechanism for change, have formed ventures that are hybrid at conception. These organisations have been able to move more nimbly than either of the more established for-profits or non-profit organisations, as they are unencumbered by the baggage associated with changing the existing organisational orientation towards either more social or more economic goals (Smith et al., 2010).

16.8 Competing logics and multiple identities

While it is evident that many organisations have benefited from adopting a dual social and economic purpose, others have encountered significant challenges and resistance. This has led some to question the appropriateness of concurrently pursuing purportedly dichotomous profit and social goals (Peattie and Morely, 2008) – particularly in cases where commercial activities threaten to undermine the legitimacy of the social mission (Pache and Santos, 2011).

This tension is best characterised by Cooney (2006: 137), who speaks of hybrid organisations as being 'caught between two fields' – a notion that has resurfaced with some regularity in the literature (Cho, 2006; Grimes, 2010; Miller and Wesley, 2010; Bacq and Janssen, 2011). At the core of this strain, sit two markedly different institutional logics: commercial and social.

Factors such as governance structure, accountability, competing goals and ownership (Di Domenico, Tracey and Haugh, 2009) go some way to explaining why those operating at the nexus of these two worlds can be found to exhibit multiple organisational identities (Smith et al., 2010). Taking governance as an illustrative example, it becomes clear that the established structures in place for running a commercial venture may fail to sufficiently account for organisations that choose to shift to a hybrid organisational form (Low, 2006). While corporations operate under a stewardship model of governance, traditional voluntary groups and non-profits tend towards more democratic and representative stakeholder models (Mason, Kirkbride and Bryde, 2007).

It is likely that, as social enterprises professionalise, they will move towards the more business-focused stewardship model (Mason et al., 2007), but it is argued that this may threaten to alienate and disenfranchise key groups of stakeholders from participating in decisionmaking.

Tied to this issue of governance – and compounding issues of management – is a failure to arrive at a set of generally accepted performance measures in social enterprise (Paton, 2003). While it is relatively easy to measure the economic impact of a particular activity, the social element has been described as 'intangible, hard to quantify, difficult to attribute to a single organization, best evaluated in the future and open to dispute' (Dees and Anderson, 2003: 7). Looking towards the future, Nicholls (2009) proposes a move to blended value accounting, which takes account of both the social and financial aspects of an organisation – though, to date, there remains no consensus on reporting methods.

16.9 Antecedents of social entrepreneurship

When reflecting on the more recent interest in social entrepreneurship, one would be forgiven for assuming that it is somehow a new phenomenon. This is far from accurate. Contemporary social entrepreneurship draws on a rich and storied heritage, dating back as far as Victorian-era Britain and the great entrepreneurial philanthropists, such as Andrew Carnegie (Harvey et al., 2011). Pioneers such as Robert Owen (Banks, 1972), who turned a mill in New Lanark, Scotland, into a utopian workers' community, provide an early archetype for those seeking to combine dual economic and mission-based activities. It was also during this period that worker co-operatives, charitable bodies and non-profit organisations emerged as institutional forms for tackling the social squalour and poverty associated with the Industrial Revolution. Such was the impact of this early social innovation, that many organisations established by the Victorians, such as the Joseph Rowntree Foundation and the Co-operative Group, continue to thrive to this day.

Antecedents of social entrepreneurship can also be found in unexpected places. In the profit-centred world of modern European football, for example, it is possible to find examples of historically hybrid social organisations. FC Barcelona, fêted as one of the sport's greatest teams, expertly embodies combined commercial and social activities. Defined by its motto, '*Més que un club*' (more than a club), the team, which is owned entirely by its supporters (or members as they are known), has been responsible for maintaining Catalan culture and defending democratic rights and freedoms in the region for over 100 years. Similarly, in the UK, Celtic FC, formed in 1888 by a Marist Brother, originally sought to raise funds for inhabitants of the impoverished east end of Glasgow while also facilitating greater integration of Irish immigrants into the area. Over time, the club has drifted towards a more commercial orientation, though it remains guided by the founding principles established by Brother Walfrid and maintains a social charter and social mission statement to carry out this legacy.

Current developments in social entrepreneurship also remain heavily indebted to the strong European tradition of workers' cooperatives, particularly those in Spain, Italy and France. Defourny and Nyssens (2006) discuss the way that these organisations have evolved to cater for the needs of regional communities while remaining economically credible. The Mondragon Corporation (www.mondragon-corporation.com) in Spain, for instance, looks at first glance like any other global conglomerate. With interests ranging from the manufacturing of domestic appliances through to banking and an employee roll of 83,859 people (Mondragon, 2011), it is only on closer inspection that it is revealed the company is a workers' cooperative, guided by principles of cooperation, participation, social responsibility and innovation.

16.10 Drivers of contemporary social entrepreneurship: a UK perspective

Following the global economic crash, there has been a renewed focus on civil society and the Third Sector as creative spaces for tackling issues of social welfare and well-being. Political rhetoric from across both the EU and the USA espouses a new language of localism and community-based action (Taylor et al., 2011), while, concurrently, many vestiges of the traditional post-war welfare system are being dismantled or radically restructured (Smith, 2010). However, this shift has not been as abrupt as the surface level would indicate. Rather, it is the culmination of a longer change in the needs and wants of citizens played out against a continuously evolving backdrop of political and economic change.

To understand this progression – and appreciate why social entrepreneurship has emerged as an approach to solving social problems – it is necessary to look as far back as the aftermath of the Second World War. During this period, William Beveridge produced a document that outlined radical social reform, leading directly to the introduction on the National Health Service (NHS), family allowances and provisions for the elderly. This was an era of almost full employment where families largely retained a traditional nuclear structure, making central planning and undifferentiated services feasible.

Following the unravelling of the economy in the early 1970s, neo-Marxists and Conservatives alike criticised these Keynesian economics on the basis that 'the welfare state impinged on the profitability of the capitalist sector by acting as a disincentive both to work and investment' (Quadagno, 1987: 110). The welfare state, as initially conceptualised, was designed to provide only in situations where 'family failed' and sexual divisions of welfare were clearly delineated (Clark and Newman, 1997). Large-scale immigration, female emancipation and the breakdown of traditional family structures challenged this system and undermined the State's ability to provide homogenous services.

The advent of Thatcherism in 1979 was a milestone in the development of social enterprise, as it signalled a dramatic shift away from the omnipotent State and towards a more minimalist form of government that fervently adopted the free-market doctrine. Termed neoliberalism, the approach went on to become the economic orthodoxy in vast areas of the world and is guided by five core principles. These involved (Birch and Mykhenko, 2010: 5):

> privatisation of State-run assets (firms, council housing et cetera); liberalization of trade in goods and capital investment; monetarist focus on inflation control and supply-side dynamics; deregulation of labour and product markets to reduce 'impediments' to business; and, the marketization of society through public–private partnerships and other forms of commodification.

The intention was to liberate individual entrepreneurial freedoms by establishing a pro-business institutional framework (Harvey, 2005), while at the same time, Clarke and Newman (1997) argue, 'Its distinctive combination of anti-welfarism and anti-statism means that it has sought to dismantle welfare states and the social, political, economic and organisational settlements that sustained them'. These institutions, according to neoliberals, created a culture of dependency and expectancy and failed to adequately stimulate entrepreneurship in the cities and regions (Amin, 2005). Indeed, it was believed that profligate public spending and lack of inflationary control were at the root of Britain's stagnating economy and government was subsequently reorientated towards business and supporting growth in prosperous regions (Amin, 2005). While it has been recognised, even by ex-Labour prime minister Tony Blair (2003), that many of these changes were necessary – in particular, opening State-owned industries to competition – it is also widely considered to have wrought considerable damage to health, education and the public realm.

As the deficiencies of neoliberalism became increasingly apparent to the electorate, the Left – under the intellectual guidance of Anthony Giddens – attempted to introduce a new type of politics, blending aspects of neoliberal economic policy with strong social democratic overtones. Termed the Third Way, it was an attempt by Labour in 1997 to overcome the 'ideological paralysis' of its past – one that had left voters unwilling to trust the party with public spending or the economy. Labour adopted an increasingly neoliberal attitude towards the markets and won over 'the City' with light touch laissez-faire regulation. Blair continued with privatisation of public goods and a raft of public–private partnerships (PPPs) – in doing so, presiding over a term of strong economic growth (Smith, 2010).

The New Labour reign also coincided with the publication of perhaps the most influential document on social entrepreneurship – *The Rise of the Social Entrepreneur* (Leadbeater, 1997), produced by influential think-tank Demos. The central idea in this piece – that Schumpeterian entrepreneurship could be applied to the social sphere to enact structural changes to service provision – chimed with the rhetoric of the incumbent government. This new approach, however, involved changing the fundamental economics of the Third Sector by introducing a neoliberal market logic that brought competition, innovation and efficiency to the provision of social care. The complexity of these changes is described by Leys (2001: 4):

> For a non-market field to be successfully transformed into a market, four requirements need to be met. First, the goods or services in question must be reconfigured so that they can be priced and sold. Second, people may be induced to want to buy them. Third, the workforce involved in their provision must be transformed from one working for collective aims with a service ethic into one working to produce profits for owners of capital and subject to market discipline. Finally, capital moving into a previously non-market field needs to have the risk underwritten by the State.

This radical approach not only demanded a significant change in the mindset of those providing the services but also the general public, who were sceptical of previous privatisation projects such as the shambolic break-up of the rail network. The social entrepreneurship agenda, however, had strong support within 10 Downing Street through advisers including Geoff Mulgan, one-time director of policy for New Labour, currently Chief Executive of NESTA and leading propagator of social innovation and social entrepreneurship ideals. On reflection, it appears this was an extremely fertile period for both the theoretical development of the paradigm and the actual practice of creating the institutional conditions that would facilitate social entrepreneurship across the UK in forthcoming years.

Despite moving to a Conservative–Liberal coalition government in 2010, many of the reforms started by Labour were continued under the auspices of the Conservative's Big Society policy (Cameron, 2010b):

> Big Society – that's not just two words. It is a guiding philosophy – a society where the leading force for progress is social responsibility, not State control. It includes a whole set of unifying approaches – breaking State monopolies, allowing charities, social enterprises and companies to provide public services, devolving power down to neighbourhoods, making government more accountable. And it's the thread that runs consistently through our whole policy programme – our plans to reform public services, mend our broken society, and rebuild trust in politics. They are all part of our Big Society agenda.

The Big Society has proved a useful narrative for promoting the proliferation of social enterprise, sometimes into areas that may be unpalatable for some sections of the public still sceptical of private-sector interference in social welfare. It harks back to traditional Conservative values of 'public duty and the responsibility of the well-off to the disadvantaged' (Smith, 2010: 830) and creates the institutional environment and legislative power to deconstruct barriers commonly faced by social enterprises.

Clearly, there has never been greater political will behind the notion of a more widely engaged and enterprising social sector and this is reflected in the way political and economic structures are shifting to accommodate more socially enterprising activities.

16.11 Social entrepreneurship: an international perspective

Despite this increasingly fertile political and economic environment for social entrepreneurship in developed areas such as the UK, Europe and North America, it is by no means a Western phenomenon. It is, instead, in developing regions such as Africa and Asia that perhaps some of the most powerful and scalable social innovations are emerging. No example of these latter innovations remains more potent than Bangladesh's Grameen Bank, founded in 1976 by a professor of economics, Muhammad Yunus.

The simple principle behind Grameen – that providing small loans to poor Bangladeshis would unlock the entrepreneurial potential of the region – has proved to be a model rapidly adopted in areas of extreme poverty. Termed microfinance, over 7.5 million individuals (Yunus, Moingeon and Lehmann-Ortega, 2010) have now accessed funds directly from the Grameen Bank, allowing the organisation to expand and diversify into other socially innovative activities. The list of spin-offs is as long as it is impressive. Examples range from partnership arrangements with food producer Danone, which seeks to address the dietary needs of Bangladeshi children, to collaboration with Veolia, providing water treatment facilities for rural areas.

A further interesting dynamic of microfinance is the manner in which innovative solutions to problems experienced in developing countries have been adopted in more prosperous developed countries. ACCION USA, for instance, has provided over 18,000 loans to micro-entrepreneurs in America who would otherwise have been unable to obtain capital investment for their business. This is a neat illustration of scalability (long a preoccupation of funders, philanthropists and scholars alike) in action.

Amidst the publicity and plaudits awarded to the Grameen Bank, it is often easy to forget the multitude of other innovators who have brought entrepreneurial approaches to addressing social problems. Organisations such as Sekem, founded in Egypt, have matured from providing agricultural solutions to creating educational centres, schools, a university and a medical centre (Seelos and Mair, 2005). Similarly, Vila das Canoas, in Brazil, have launched a community-based tourism venture that enables travellers to lodge with local residents. This has had the dual effect of opening a revenue stream for villagers while allowing them to share their knowledge and culture with foreign visitors. It is this willingness to exploit new opportunities in a creative manner that is the hallmark of socially entrepreneurial behaviour.

16.12 Social entrepreneurship: a critical approach

For all the excitement and enthusiasm social entrepreneurship has generated – in both research and practice – it remains, for now, at the margins of the entrepreneurship paradigm. As an academic field, it is only slowly developing the theoretical foundations that will help elucidate and explain the phenomenon more effectively.

Short, Moss and Lumpkin (2009: 167) provide a reality check of sorts in their authoritative 'state of the field' literature analysis. Of 152 journal articles published on social entrepreneurship, 'only 3% set forth operational hypotheses that may be rigorously tested' and there remains an abundance of papers presenting descriptive case studies. Weaknesses were also found with sample sizes and a perceived lack of generalisability from findings across the research output.

While the patterns that emerged from Short et al.'s (2009) analysis may be symptomatic of a paradigm going through the early stages of maturation, the lack of definitional clarity and impact measurement may withhold precious resources from being diverted to the field. Reflecting on this paradigmatic development, Nicholls (2010) concludes that the domain is currently at a pre-paradigmatic stage. Following Kuhn (1962), this means that actors are actively engaged in shaping the discourses, methods and narratives that will fully establish the paradigm.

At present, some researchers have focused on using available data as opposed to building new data sets and, as a result, empirical work draws repeatedly on the same small set, while theoretical work lacks empirical support (Nicholls 2010). Nicholls (2010) identifies two discourses clustered around social entrepreneurship – one relating to the 'hero' social entrepreneur and one that locates social entrepreneurship in community settings and networks of action. These competing logics are awkward as, on one hand, social entrepreneurship can be viewed as invoking advocacy and social change while, on the other, it can be about the marketisation of services and sustainable funding models.

It is precisely this 'marketisation' of the social sector that draws the most ire from those actively involved in the field, with some (Davies, 2007; Public Administration Select Committee, 2008) noting the view that social enterprise and the Third Sector are being used as a Trojan Horse to put an 'acceptable face' on outsourcing and greater private-sector involvement in welfare provision (Walker, 2006). This accusation taps into deeper fears that social enterprise and the commodification of social welfare threatens to undermine civil society as, traditionally, it has been a sphere of public life that has been separate from the market and the State (Salamon and Anheier, 1997; Jenei and Kuti, 2008).

Eikenberry and Kluver (2004) argue that the self-interested outlook of an entrepreneurial mindset is incompatible with principles of democracy. Notions of fairness and justice, they claim, are restricted in market-based systems and it would appear to be antithetical to the ethos of the Third Sector. Whether the argument by Alexander, Nank and Stivers (1999) that the increasingly business-like practices of non-profits poses a threat to civil society is of any substance ultimately, however, remains to be seen.

16.13 Chapter summary

Social entrepreneurship has rapidly infiltrated mainstream consciousness in both the developed and developing worlds. It can be viewed as a grass roots movement, where active citizens use their skills, expertise and resourcefulness to tackle the most pressing societal and environmental problems. These entrepreneurs, through vehicles such as social enterprises, blend commercial and social objectives to varying degrees in order to achieve operational sustainability and social impact.

The emergence of social entrepreneurship can be attributed, in part, to profound changes in the political and economic structure of society – in particular, to a general trend for smaller, more minimalist approaches to State welfare provision and governance. This reduction in public provision has created a gap, which is increasingly being filled by socially enterprising individuals. Much like the earlier examples of Robert Owen and the Victorian philanthropists, the onus for tackling social problems has once more shifted back to the citizen.

Social entrepreneurship is not, however, without its obstacles or critics. Research has consistently shown that social ventures often struggle to effectively balance the competing commercial and social activities necessary for achieving social impact. Judged in some quarters to be too revenue-focused and, in others, too socially driven, a lack of definitional clarity hinders robust empirical assessment of the phenomenon. Others still see the increased marketisation of the social sphere as a threat to civil society and propose that it is evidence of a creeping commodification of public life.

Whatever the personal views held by individuals, there unquestionably remains much still to learn about what social entrepreneurship means and what its implications may be. Analysing the field as a whole, Gras, Masakowski and Lumpkin (2011) identify three dominant future research directions: financing/funding, innovations and general contexts. As the years pass, we will undoubtedly come to a greater understanding and acceptance across all of these areas.

Questions

1 Why is the debate regarding definitions surrounding social entrepreneurship and social enterprise important?

2 Why do social ventures pursuing both economic *and* social purposes often experience identity tension?

3 What are the political and economic factors that have led to the emergence of social entrepreneurship as a promising method of addressing social ills?

4 What are the challenges facing the social entrepreneurship research community?

5 What do critics believe are the drawbacks and limitations to social entrepreneurship?

Weblinks

http://nyustern.campusgroups.com/sea/home and www.sbs.ox.ac.uk/centres/skoll
The NYU Stern Social Enterprise Association and Skoll Centre for Social Entrepreneurship, University of Oxford, are two of the world's leading academic centres researching and teaching about social enterprise.

http://ashoka.org
Founded in 1981, Ashoka is one of the key foundations leading social transformation, using citizens rather than government to stimulate change.

www.youngfoundation.org
The Young Foundation brings together insights, innovation and entrepreneurship to meet social needs. It works across the UK and internationally, undertaking research, influencing policy, creating new organisations and supporting others to do the same, often with imaginative uses of new technology.

http://socialinnovationexchange.org
Social Innovation eXchange (SIX) is a global community committed to promoting social innovation and growing the capacity of the field. Its aim is to improve the methods used by our societies to find better solutions to challenges such as ageing, climate change, inequality and healthcare.

CHAPTER 17

Community entrepreneurship

Ingebjørg Vestrum, Gry Agnete Alsos and Elisabet Ljunggren

17.1 Introduction

Community entrepreneurship is not a new phenomenon. Community ventures have long made valuable contributions to society by promoting economic and social renewal in communities all over the world. Job-creating organisations and business networks have facilitated new commercial activities and job opportunities (Johannisson, 1990; Johnstone and Lionais, 2004). Cultural festivals and events as well as rehabilitation centres are found to increase the quality of life (Haugh, 2007; Thompson, Lees and Alvy, 2000) and to bridge and link social capital within communities (Teasdale, 2010).

Although community entrepreneurship is a phenomenon that has been around for a long time, research interest in it is quite new. In contrast to commercial entrepreneurship, where societal wealth is seen as a consequence of private and economic goals, community entrepreneurship views societal wealth creation as the main goal, where economic values are used as a means to develop collective values. Through individual and collective action, community entrepreneurs pursue opportunities to generate an entrepreneurial environment, redeploy local resources, create social change, create employment and income for community members or in other ways create new opportunities for the community.

This chapter provides a brief review of the research on community entrepreneurship. First, the community entrepreneurship concept is discussed. Next, the types of community ventures, actors in the process, and the entrepreneurship process and resource acquisition of community ventures are discussed. In this section, examples from community ventures in rural communities are given. Finally, the chapter is summarised and its implications set out.

17.2 Learning objectives

There are four learning objectives for this chapter:

1 to understand what community entrepreneurship is
2 to understand which actors may participate and how they participate
3 to understand how community entrepreneurship processes can be started
4 to understand how resource acquisition processes in community ventures may take place.

Key concepts
- community entrepreneurship ■ community ventures ■ embeddedness
- collective processes

17.3 The role of community entrepreneurship

As mentioned above, the idea that entrepreneurs may play an important role in social change in communities is not new. Stories of community entrepreneurs as important actors in community change processes have long roots in the literature.

Social anthropologists have used the term 'entrepreneur' in a broader sense than within economics and management research. The social anthropologist Fredrik Barth's (1963) description was someone who acted as an agent of social change by being active in the transformation of a community. He saw entrepreneurs as individuals who maximise not only profits but also prestige, information and social assets.

In their discussion of entrepreneurship, social anthropologists have been more interested in community-based and group solutions than individual economic solutions. They have seen the community context within the entrepreneurship process as significant (Lindh de Montoya, 2000). On one hand, an entrepreneur needs to be able to interpret the culture embedded in the community context to be able to develop a business. On the other, community change processes may be driven by entrepreneurs acting as initiators for community-based venturing. Economic sustainability of local communities depends, to a large extent, on business activities that develop and adapt to changing markets and other external conditions. Entrepreneurial activities are needed to enable the community to take advantage of development options that rise.

Within management and economic research, the community entrepreneurship concept was introduced as a response to restructuring and the closure of industries in Western economies, leading to unemployment and societal crisis during the 1970s and 1980s (Johannisson and Nilsson, 1989; Lotz, 1989; de Bruin and Dupuis, 2003). Communities were left with only some businesses, high unemployment and social problems. One example of this is the closure of coalmines in the UK. Earlier attempts to solve societal problems within communities by 'top-down' efforts driven by the government had failed to develop the new social structures that were needed to stimulate economic development (Lotz, 1989). The social life and the commercial activities of a community were seen as closely connected and local mobilisation and grass roots actions were needed to be able to create new jobs and stimulate economic development. As the OECD (1986: 4) expressed it:

> Community entrepreneurship is essential and means both a large number of individuals acting in an entrepreneurial manner, not only in the private but also in the voluntary and public sector, as well as an entrepreneurial opportunity-seeking attitude in community processes, local organisation and within the broader local community. Community entrepreneurship is the motor that activates and utilises the indigenous potential of a locality and can bring about locally generated development.

Another stimulus for community entrepreneurship was the decline in public support for non-profit organisations in the 1980s, leading to new forms of leadership within non-profits. To be able to access resources and create social change in communities, interorganisational leadership and new forms of collaboration between different actors emerged in the community (Selsky and Smith, 1994).

Literature on community entrepreneurship has particularly focused on communities in difficult economic situations and demonstrated how individuals or groups with a commitment to community interests through different modes of action contribute to economic regeneration (e.g., Johannisson and Nilsson, 1989; Haugh and Pardy, 1999; Johnstone and Lionais, 2004; Peredo and Chrisman, 2006). In such situations, new types of collaboration were developed and local economic initiatives were formed as joint ventures involving public, private and voluntary sectors (Waters, 1985). Consequently, new structures and socio-economic networks necessary for economic development and social change in the community were developed.

Community entrepreneurship within Western economics emphasised the leadership by an entrepreneur or a group of entrepreneurs as a critical entrepreneurial act. Charismatic, communicative and local legitimacy were seen as important characteristics of the entrepreneurs who were socially and morally motivated (Johannisson, 1990; Selsky and Smith, 1994; Haugh and Pardy, 1999). Furthermore, community entrepreneurship became connected to rural communities, since these communities were more vulnerable when industries closed down and more likely to act collectively. Community entrepreneurship has also become a popular research area within poor indigenous communities – e.g., Latin America and New Zealand (Dupuis and de Bruin, 2003; Peredo, 2003). Peredo and Chrisman (2006) studied indigenous communities in postcolonial states. Community entrepreneurship within these communities was pushed forward because of civil wars, repression and unemployment. Local economic and social development became important and the community is seen as both the entrepreneur and the result of the entrepreneurship process. The emerging activities created during the entrepreneurship process are owned, managed and governed by the people and have become synonymous with the local community.

17.4 What is community entrepreneurship?

As with many concepts that have emerged from multiple disciplines and empirical settings, there exist a variety of different definitions of community entrepreneurship. However, common to all of them is a focus on the local community as important – as a context, actor and result of the entrepreneurship process. In other words, community entrepreneurship is embedded in a specific geographical reality and bridges community and business practices. Through individual or collective action, community entrepreneurs pursue opportunities to generate an entrepreneurial environment (Johannisson and Nilsson, 1989), redeploy local resources (Haugh and Pardy, 1999), create and organise social change (Selsky and Smith, 1994; Haugh, 2007), create employment and income for community members (Peredo and Chrisman, 2006) or create new development opportunities within the community (Johnstone and Lionais, 2004).

To define community entrepreneurship here, it makes sense to start with the entrepreneurship literature. The opportunity-based conceptualisation of entrepreneurship focuses upon entrepreneurial opportunities and how these are identified, evaluated and used (Shane and Venkataraman, 2000; Eckhardt and Shane, 2003).

While this perspective on entrepreneurship is widely applied as a means of generating new business activity, Steyaert and Katz (2004) claim that the concept of entrepreneurship can be applied more diversely. They see it as the process of reorganising the established and crafting the new across a broad range of settings and spaces, with a variety of aims. Entrepreneurship can thus be a means for social change and transformation.

Acquisition and organisation of resources are core elements in the entrepreneurial process (Stevenson and Jarillo, 1990; Shane, 2003). In fact, they are so central that some scholars include them as part of the definition of entrepreneurship (Landström and Johannisson, 2001; Ucbasaran, Westhead and Wright, 2001). As individual entrepreneurs do not possess all the resources required to launch a venture, they have to acquire them from people and institutions in their surroundings. From the opportunity-based view of entrepreneurship, community entrepreneurship can be seen as the organisation of resources to pursue opportunities to fulfil community objectives. This can include a range of opportunities within different sectors.

Next, the concept of community is central to the definition of community entrepreneurship. Tapsell and Woods (2010) argue that innovative activities occur in an historical and cultural context of communities.

A community can be defined as (Peredo and Chrisman, 2006: 315):

> an aggregation of people that is not defined initially by the sharing of goals or the productive activities of the enterprise but, rather, by shared geographical location, generally accompanied by collective culture and/or ethnicity and potentially by other shared relational characteristic(s).

A community can be described as an integrated system of jointly interrelated and interdependent parts (Arensberg and Kimball, 2001) where the relationships are based upon family, kinship and trust (Tönnies, 1887/1963). The members of the community have something in common with each other that distinguishes them in a significant way from the members of other groups (Bell and Newby, 1971).

Although 'community' can also refer to a specific interest or religion, we define the characteristics of a place as important. A community might be a municipality, village, region or town. However, in large cities, the interrelationships can become fragmented and 'the community' might then be an urban quarter with distinct identity. This chapter, however, gives examples of community entrepreneurship from small, rural municipalities or villages, where the inhabitants are close connected to each other and form distinct communities, often quite geographically delimited.

Over the last decade, there has been growing interest in another concept related to entrepreneurship with social aims, namely social entrepreneurship (see Chapter 16). Community entrepreneurship can be viewed as a branch of social entrepreneurship (Tracey, Phillips and Haugh, 2005) – as social entrepreneurship happening at the community level, where the entrepreneurs are driven by a social vision and committed to improving the environment of their communities (Cooney, 2008). Community entrepreneurship, however, is closely connected to the community that it enfolds. Also, it encompasses activities that are broader than those undertaken by the charitable and non-profit organisations so often associated with social entrepreneurship.

A community venture is a new activity, network or organisation likely to contribute to the quality of life (Thompson, Lees and Alvy, 2000; Haugh, 2007), new commercial activities and job opportunities (Johannisson and Nilsson, 1989; Johannisson, 1990;

Johnstone and Lionais, 2004) or cultural growth within a community. Community entrepreneurship activities may take place within existing organisations or be organised as new enterprises, originating from the voluntary, business or governmental sectors (Austin, Stevenson and Wei-Skillern, 2006; Shaw and Carter, 2007; Borch, Huse and Senneseth, 2008). Lindgren and Packendorff (2006: 230) explain community entrepreneurship as 'an eternal balancing act between deviation and belonging – constantly striving to make history without being able to leave anyone or anything behind.'

We conceptualise community entrepreneurship as the process of pursuing opportunities by recombining resources within the community to develop economic and social wealth for the inhabitants (Perrini, 2006; Perrini, Vurro and Constanzo, 2010; Tapsell and Woods, 2010). Community entrepreneurs acquire, organise and leverage resources to set up ventures for the common good of a local community. These processes result in a community venture or ordinary businesses supported by the community. Table 17.1 summarises the most important characteristics of community entrepreneurship and compares it with social and commercial entrepreneurship.

In contrast to community entrepreneurship, commercial entrepreneurship focuses on the development of individual wealth. The development of social and economic

Table 17.1 Comparing social, community and commercial entrepreneurship

	Commercial entrepreneurship	Social entrepreneurship	Community entrepreneurship
Main goals	Creating profit and personal wealth for shareholders and owners	Creating social wealth for a client group	Creating social and economic wealth for the inhabitants within a particular community
Distribution of profit	Profit is distributed to shareholders and owners	Profit is reinvested in the venture or to benefit client groups	Profit is reinvested in the venture or to benefit the local community
Community venture	Autonomous, for-profit business organisation	Autonomous, profit or non-profit organisation	Embedded in a community, voluntary organisation, community business, business/social networks
Actors	Business actors	Actors in the social economy, outside the public and economic sectors	Actors in business, the municipality and social economy
Entrepreneurship process	Commercial entrepreneurs in the creation of business ventures	Social entrepreneurs in the creation of social ventures	Creation of community ventures in a collective process or commercial businesses supported by communities with resources needed being embedded in the community

wealth within the community, however, is seen as a *consequence* of the entrepreneurship process rather than its *goal* (Venkataraman, 2002). In other words, the aim of commercial entrepreneurship is to provide personal gain and profits for the entrepreneur and shareholders, but community ventures aim at developing collective values for a range of stakeholders within the local community. Economic values are viewed as means of developing the community rather than goals in themselves.

This distinction between community and commercial entrepreneurship might not be dichotomous, but could be conceptualised as a continuum ranging from individual and economic focus to collective and social focus. For example, it often occurs that local governments engage in community entrepreneurship to directly and indirectly develop business activities.

A further distinction is that commercial ventures are limited to for-profit organisations, whilst community ventures can employ a range of organisational forms to achieve their objectives. A commercial venture emerges within the business sector, whilst community ventures can emerge within or across non-profit, business and government sectors. The structure of a community venture is likely to be formed in a way that ensures the pursuit of community benefit over personal gain (Johnstone and Lionais, 2004). In contrast to commercial entrepreneurs, community entrepreneurs are able to engage volunteers, access capital from non-traditional sources and attract customers because of the community benefits associated with the community venture (Johnstone and Lionais, 2004).

As mentioned, community entrepreneurship is often understood as a specific type of social entrepreneurship and possesses many similarities to it – e.g., the focus on social wealth creation. However, as Table 17.1 indicates, community entrepreneurship emphasises the development of a specific community, whilst social entrepreneurship focuses upon clients that might not be connected to a specific community. Community entrepreneurs identify and pursue the needs of a locally defined set of individuals (Seelos, Mair, Battilana and Dacin, 2010) and members of the community become instrumental in the decisionmaking processes and the ownership of the community venture (Tracey Phillips and Haugh, 2005; Haugh, 2007). A social venture might be formed as an independent organisation, whilst community ventures are embedded within a community and characterised as having a democratic structure, multistakeholder structure and collective decisionmaking process (Tracey et al., 2005; Teasdale, 2010).

Central elements of community entrepreneurship are the *actors* involved – i.e., the community entrepreneurs – and the entrepreneurial *processes* by means of which these actors identify opportunities for community development, gather resources to pursue the opportunities and carry on organising efforts to fulfil community goals (see Chapter 6 for an account of the entrepreneurial process). The results of these processes are community *ventures*. Next, we will discuss each of these important elements in more detail, starting with community ventures.

17.5 Community ventures

The community venture is a result of an entrepreneurial process and can be in the form of a new organisation, networks, initiative or project (Johannisson, 1990; Peredo and

Chrisman, 2006; Haugh, 2007). Common for community ventures is that they are embedded in the local community and likely to involve a range of stakeholders with different aims – e.g., social, economic, environmental and cultural goals. Their result may be social innovation or increasing local economic sustainability. Some ventures are non-profit, where eventual profit is reinvested in the venture or invested to facilitate other community goals (Haugh, 2007). Other ventures might take a for-profit form, but with strong local linkages and a community goal.

A challenge can be to balance private and collective interests as well as economic and non-economic goals (Peredo and Chrisman, 2006). Typically, though, the ventures are organised to ensure the collective interest and not the individual interest – e.g., cooperatives or community-owned ventures (Johnstone and Lionais, 2004; Tracey et al., 2005). Also, since the venture is rooted in the community, it might be difficult to separate the activities and actors within the community venture from activities in the local community.

Three types of community ventures can be identified:

- community enterprises
- community networks
- public community ventures.

Some examples of these types of community ventures are given below.

17.5.1 Community enterprises

Community businesses or enterprises are one possible product of community entrepreneurship (Haugh and Pardy, 1999; Johnstone and Lionais, 2004). Hayton (1995) describes the development of community businesses as a process of identifying service gaps in a local economy.

Community enterprises are distinguished from other third sector and voluntary organisations by their generation of income through trading rather than philanthropy and/or government subsidy to finance their social goals (Novy, 1990; Tracey et al., 2005; Haugh, 2007). This hybrid form motivates community enterprises to think and act like businesses by focusing on the market and customers (Johnstone and Lionais, 2004), but, to ensure that the collective interests are in focus and not the individual interests, the governance structures are democratic, allowing community members to participate in the management of the organisation. Johnstone and Lionais (2004) studied a special form of corporation that distributed the profits to worker-owners and the community rather than a few shareholders.

Community enterprises are likely to work in partnership with the corporations and public-sector organisations (Tracey et al., 2005). They are often orientated towards marginalised groups, such as the unemployed, young people, ethnic minorities or disabled people.

Community businesses can be organised as cooperatives, self-managed firms or non-profit organisations (Novy, 1990). They are unique to their contexts (Peredo and Chrisman, 2006).

Haugh and Pardy (1999) studied a boat festival that was a community business within rural communities in Scotland. The festival used existing resources, but also identified innovative opportunities and recombined pre-existing elements of activities within the area in innovative ways. The goal of the festival was to benefit the community and it generated revenues from the visitors who came. In addition, social benefits were also developed, such as gaining a new deal within the community.

Peredo and Chrisman (2006) argue that the emerging enterprise can build upon local culture and, conversely, the enterprise is likely to strengthen or create new social and cultural systems. The Skiippagurra Festival serves as an example of such a community enterprise as it builds upon existing traditions and, at the same time, stretches existing structures within the community.

The Skiippagurra Festival emerged within a small, rural community in a northern part of Norway with about 3000 inhabitants. The community has a mixed population of the Sami people (the indigenous people of north Scandinavia) and Norwegians. The community had attracted negative media attention nationwide because of social problems.

The Skiippagurra Festival was set up as a rock-festival for the youth of the area on one weekend in July every year and started as a project to change the negative focus on the community. The Festival celebrated the local Baltic and Sami traditions and was organised as outdoor concerts on a river beach. International and national rock artists and groups performed at the Festival. A class for children in the chanting song of the Sami people (the *joik*) was arranged. In addition, activities such as a sandcastle-building competition, a volleyball competition and horseriding were offered.

The Festival attracted significant media coverage, regionally and nationally, and successfully changed the media focus on the community. The Festival became an important part of the community and, today, the youth in the region associate the area with a 'cool festival'. In the process, one of the outcomes of this community enterprise has been that the Sami culture became more visible and has been strengthened.

17.5.2 Community networks

Unlike the process of community business creation, where the entrepreneurs are at the centre of the process, the entrepreneur developing community networks is not engaged in the new businesses directly. Instead, Johannisson and Nilsson (1989) explained, the community entrepreneurs share and develop their extensive networks with commercial entrepreneurs to assist them in starting new businesses. These networks include significant actors at local, regional and national levels (Johannisson 1990). Networked businesses are found to provide more support for their communities than non-networked businesses (Besser, Miller, and Perkins, 2006).

The development of networks in a small fishing island, Lovund, in Norway, is a good example. As a response to the low profitability of existing fisheries and depopulation of the island, two inhabitants started a salmon-farming project to develop new job opportunities and attract inhabitants to the island. The entrepreneurs linked different sectors and actors to develop new structures and improve the infrastructure of the island. The network became embedded in the community and consisted of local businesses, politicians, voluntary organisations and villagers, as well as external linkages to regional and national politicians and business actors.

As a result of the business networks, new businesses connected to the salmon-farming project were launched. A collective form of business establishment became the practice and, when one of the villagers had a business idea, all the firms started the business together until the initiator could continue alone. Simultaneously, the business networks realised that they needed to develop leisure activities to attract new inhabitants and hold onto the present ones, so new social and cultural activities – e.g., a fitness studio, museum and squash hall – were established.

17.5.3 Public community ventures

As mentioned above, community ventures can be established with the aid of, and also run by, a public body – i.e., local government.

There are several examples of different forms of initiatives by public bodies. In their study of community entrepreneurship as a facilitator of local economic development, Rønning, Ljunggren and Wiklund (2010) found quite a few ways in which this had been carried out. They studied a rural community striving to bring about economic development. Local government decided to support efforts to advance certain industries where it was perceived the community possessed the necessary resources – primarily physical resources – and that had potential, economically.

Tourism was one of the industries selected and, as there are many caves within the community's geographic boundaries (a natural resource), caving was thought to be an experience that could complement other outdoor experiences already available in the community – e.g., hiking, salmon fishing and hunting. The local government invested in the necessary equipment to enable guided cave tours (hard hats, ropes, headlamps, etc.) and, together with the local caving club, which had certified guides, guided cave tours were offered to tourists.

This joint effort between public community entrepreneurship and actors from the voluntary sector generated a new source of economic activity in the community. The equipment and the business idea were later given to a private entrepreneur who possessed the qualifications to lead groups in cave visits and who had access to caves at her property.

17.6 Community entrepreneurship actors

Community entrepreneurs have been identified as being individual charismatic leaders (Johannisson, 1990), groups of entrepreneurs (Haugh and Pardy, 1999) or communities acting corporately as entrepreneurs in pursuit of the common good (Peredo and Chrisman, 2006). Often they come forward with the initial idea for community entrepreneurship, although the exact role played differs from community to community. Sometimes, it can be difficult to identify any one entrepreneur, since the entrepreneurship process is embedded in the local community. The initiative for the process might come from local government, the voluntary sector, business sector or, often, a combination of different sectors is necessary for the development of the venture (Austin, Stevenson and Wei-Skillern, 2006). Volunteers are a key labour resource in the establishment of community ventures.

Local government is often viewed as a significant actor in community entrepreneurship, especially in contexts where there is a well-developed welfare system and a strong public sector, such as within the Nordic countries. Dupuis, de Bruin and Cremer

(2003) argue that 'municipal community entrepreneurship' was forced by localisation, decentralisation and delegation of responsibility from central government to regional and local government level during 1980s. The basic assumption is that local and regional development should be promoted by local approaches to local situations and, indeed, local government has been increasingly involved in enterprise initiatives and searching out new means to promote their communities as desirable locations for economic and social activities. When local government takes an entrepreneur role, it is likely to do best when it develops partnerships, especially public–private partnerships. Studies show that it may take on the role of an entrepreneur or be an important key actor in the initiation of both community and business entrepreneurship.

An example from Norway (Rønning et al., 2010) shows how the local government of one municipality derised a strategy to promote business development and actively involved people from its administration in this process. It had found that there was the potential to develop small hydroelectric power plants that have little impact on the landscape, unlike large hydroelectric power plants with large dams and piped rivers. Within the boundaries of the municipality there were many small waterfalls owned by local farmers that had the potential to be exploited to produce electricity and, thereby, generate income for the farmers, who needed additional ways to increase the revenue from their farms and, thereby, benefit the local economy, too. Local government acted as a community entrepreneur, informing the farmers of the money-making potential of their water resources and providing them with administrative and technological knowledge on how to exploit these resources. It held monthly meetings for the waterfall owners and technical consultants and representatives from the directorates came to tell the farmers how to apply for approvals and give them suggestions for good technical solutions to any problems that arose. In addition, they were given the chance to meet and discuss things among themselves. This was a good community entrepreneurial strategy that resulted in several new small hydroelectric power plants being installed, which boosted the total economy.

Community entrepreneurship is, as other types of social entrepreneurship, also often associated with the 'Third Sector' (Shaw and Carter, 2007; Zografos, 2007) and voluntary organisations. The growing literature on social entrepreneurship addresses the magnitude of the Third Sector and the role of voluntary organisations in the achievement of societal goals (see Chapter 16). Community entrepreneurs originating from the voluntary sector often may have such goals as their main focus. They earn legitimacy from the community based on the visibility of these societal goals. They may, therefore, be more able to draw on voluntary resources than community entrepreneurs stemming from the public or business sectors.

The Concerten Ensemble in Tynset, Norway, is an example of such an initiative by a voluntary organisation. The community, with about 5400 inhabitants, faced depopulation. The local school band took the initiative to develop new cultural activities in the community. The result, Concerten Ensemble, is an organisation that created a festival of nine musical concerts during two weekends in May every year. The local school band – the Concerten Ensemble – brought together cultural organisations within the community – e.g., school bands, choirs, theatre and dance groups and the music school – and the young people got a chance to develop their artistic talents together with adults and professional artists at the festival. The festival developed positive associations for the local community among the younger generation. In addition, it gave the voluntary organisations income to develop other new cultural activities during the rest of the year.

Community ventures can also emerge from within the business sector. Community entrepreneurs may regard commercial spin-offs as an important part of their ventures and develop the local community by using some for-profit entrepreneurs' tools (Johnstone and Lionais, 2004) or individual commercial entrepreneurship may be a by-product of community ventures (Johannisson, 1990; Peredo and Chrisman, 2006). Equally, some business entrepreneurs aiming to create new business ventures also seek revitalisation of the local community (Lotz, 1989; Johnstone and Lionais, 2004). Such an outcome can be the main purpose of the entrepreneurial activity, but it can also be parallel to other goals. Johnstone and Lionais (2004: 229) explain that community entrepreneurs can use 'the sense of community to access social capital and lever it into economic capital'. Similarly, Johannisson and Nilsson (1989) found that community ventures aiming to develop a business and revitalise the community need to build both social *and* commercial networks.

In this regard, we return to the example of the salmon fisheries and community networks in Lovund, Norway, discussed earlier. The two community entrepreneurs involved were from the business sector and had worked as fishermen before they started the salmon-farming (aquaculture) project.

Lovund had experienced hard times since the mid-1960s due to the low profitability of the existing fisheries and depopulation of the area. The entrepreneurs started farming salmon to develop new employment and business opportunities. They explained that the opportunities for generating income would have been better in another location because of the unsatisfactory level of communication on the island. However, their aim was to develop job opportunities for the inhabitants of the island and attract new inhabitants, which was more important to them than generating profit. The profit they later gained from salmon farming, however, was used to develop and stimulate the local infrastructure and social and cultural activities of the island. This effort made the community more attractive and so more people moved to the island. Furthermore, they stimulated new business spin-offs by supporting the inhabitants' new business initiatives by linking them to their own network.

17.7 The process of community entrepreneurship

The emergence of a new venture is a significant part of the entrepreneurship process (Gartner, 1985). During its initial phases of development, a new venture needs access to financial, physical, human, intangible and other resources (Brush, Greene and Hart, 2009; Zott and Huy, 2007). The entrepreneurship process starts with the discovery of an opportunity and ends when a sustained resource base for the new venture has been established. This process can be characterised as a recombination of local resources and activities with the aim of developing social and/or economic value within the community (Moss, Short, Payne and Lumpkin, 2010; Perrini, Vurro and Costanzo, 2010). The community entrepreneurs may take the role as change agents who aim to build new structures and develop new activities (Shaw and Carter, 2007).

To be able to identify the needs and problems within their local community, the entrepreneurs are found to be closely linked to it. The scope and progress of the entrepreneurship process will differ according to the needs and access to resources within the specific context, but a common characteristic is that the emerging community venture becomes embedded in the local structures (Jack and Anderson, 2002) to motivate the community members to take collective action (Peredo and Chrisman, 2006).

Social capital is seen as a community's major resource (Coleman, 1988) and this is developed during the day-to-day relationships between the community members. Social capital is generated by networks of relationships, reciprocity, trust and social norms and will facilitate individual or collective action. The social capital and social structures of the community are used as a means of organising new activities (Johannisson and Nilsson, 1989; Peredo and Chrisman, 2006). Hence, it may be difficult to separate the economic and social dimensions of the community in the entrepreneurship process (Johannisson and Nilsson, 1989).

Acquisition, organising and leveraging of the resources needed are crucial parts of the process of new venture creation (Stevenson and Jarillo, 1990; Landström and Johannisson, 2001; Shane, 2003). To set up a new venture, then, an entrepreneur needs to acquire and organise a variety of resources, including human, social, physical, cultural and financial resources. A central role for community entrepreneurs is to build social, aesthetic and environmental capital, as well as acquire the financial capital required to achieve the primary objectives of the community venture (Cooney, 2008), attracting these resources for a community purpose rather than financial return. They will rely on networks of contacts to provide them with financial and human resources and need a strong reputation that engenders trust and legitimacy among potential contributors (Austin, Stevenson and Wei-Skillern, 2006).

Teece, Pisano and Shuen (1997) make a distinction between resources and production factors. While the latter can be easily purchased in the marketplace, resources become organisation-specific assets that carry values greater than their market values since others will have difficulties in purchasing, copying or substituting them. Thus, to acquire and assimilate resources into a new community venture becomes a complex, iterative process. Some resources – e.g., network contacts – may be needed only to access the resources that are later organised into the new venture.

While previous studies have found many similarities between community/social entrepreneurship and commercial entrepreneurship (Austin et al., 2006; Shaw and Carter, 2007), there are reasons to assume that the resource acquisition process of community entrepreneurs differs from that of commercial entrepreneurs in essential ways. Community ventures will probably not attract investors seeking return, as any financial surplus is often reinvested in the venture. Further, community ventures may often not be able to pay market prices for key resources or market salaries for employees (Austin et al., 2006).

The centrality of the social purpose, however, may attract investors with a non-profit motivation and give access to other types of resources, such as philanthropic capital, public support, gifts and contributions from volunteers. Haugh (2007) suggests that, unlike for-profit ventures, community ventures may rely on volunteers as human resources and purchase other resources at below the market rate or receive donations. Stakeholder mobilisation may be used as a strategy to gather human, physical, financial and technological resources, particularly in the pre-venture phase (Haugh, 2007). Legitimacy may be crucial for the community entrepreneur to be able to gather resources and it is critical to develop a large network of strong supporters (Austin et al., 2006).

The lack of a track record and the non-profit status of community ventures may make community ventures dependent upon external sources of volunteer support, staff, funding and founders (Thompson, 2002; Sharir and Lerner, 2006). Campi, Defourny and Grègoire (2006) found that most community ventures across Europe were multi-stakeholder enterprises and the participation of stakeholders led to their influences within the ventures' Boards. Di Domenico, Haugh and Tracey (2010) found that engaging and convincing stakeholders were important means of accessing resources and ensuring that community ventures were embedded in their communities. Also, the involvement of the stakeholders themselves in the community is important, to identify the needs, access needed resources and operate the venture (Haugh, 2007). These are important but time-consuming processes. Consequently, the entrepreneurial process may take longer in community ventures compared to commercial ventures.

It has been suggested that community entrepreneurs prosper by attracting resources from a broad range of sectors and combine resources, people and sectors that traditionally have been dispersed (Leadbeater, 1997). Austin et al. (2006) argue that, to obtain critical resources, community entrepreneurs need to move between the voluntary, business and public sectors. This might be especially important in rural communities, where the available resources are likely to be scarce.

17.8 Chapter summary

This chapter has discussed community entrepreneurship – defined as the process of organising resources to pursue opportunities to fulfil community goals. Community entrepreneurs can originate from the public sector, private businesses or voluntary organisations. Their ability to bridge these sectors and utilise resources from the private sector, public organisations as well as the Third Sector and voluntary work, is likely to be crucial if they are to successfully pursue the opportunity and achieve the desired outcomes for the community.

Drawing boundaries around the new organisation has been considered a crucial aspect of the commercial entrepreneurial process (Katz and Gartner, 1988), but doing so in a community venture environment might be difficult since it is embedded in the community it has evolved out of (Peredo, 2005).

Three types of community ventures were presented: community enterprises, community networks and public community ventures. The community entrepreneurship process was described and, as was seen, this process may be initiated from the bottom up or the top down. Regardless of their origins, community ventures often rely on strong relations to the public, business and voluntary sectors.

Resource acquisition is an important part of the process of entrepreneurial community ventures. As their focus is on community rather than commercial goals, community ventures may be less successful in obtaining financial resources and start-up capital from banks and investors as they generally want a return on their capital. Community entrepreneurs may also lack the resources to fully interact with the market. If, however, they are able to communicate their community goals well, they may achieve legitimacy and engagement with other types of resources – e.g., philanthropists, sponsors, local municipality government administrators and voluntary workers. This may give community ventures the advantage of having access to resources that commercial entrepreneurs are unable to benefit from.

Questions

1 Find examples of community ventures in your own local community. Try to identify their actors, what their goals are and how they acquire resources.

2 Why do you think some entrepreneurs engage in community entrepreneurship rather than using their skills and effort to create a commercial venture?

3 Where do you think community entrepreneurship is more relevant – in poor or rich communities? In urban or rural communities?

4 How can community entrepreneurship benefit from the business, voluntary and public sectors?

Weblinks

www.cedcentre.org

The Community Empowerment and Development Centre in Nakasongola, Uganda, was founded in 2009 by Simon Levin Mugabi to contribute to and make a difference in the lives of the disadvantaged women, youth and children in the rural communities of Uganda. Its goals are to empower the disadvantaged women and youth to become self-reliant, implement interventions to support the orphans and vulnerable children in an effort to keep children in school and host volunteer vacations for interested people from overseas to share their skills in Nakasongola communities.

www.mycei.org

The Community Entrepreneurship Institute, Inc. (CEI) is a non-profit organisation in the USA that is dedicated to advancing social and economic well-being in urban communities through entrepreneurship. The CEI was developed with the philosophy that sustainable urban districts can best be created when entrepreneurs have a strong commitment to the customers and communities where they operate their businesses.

PART 4

Entrepreneurial management

CHAPTER 18

Entrepreneurial marketing

Eleanor Shaw

18.1 Introduction

The concept of entrepreneurial marketing has emerged in response to the recognition that small firms are not simply scaled-down versions of their larger counterparts (Wynarczyk et al., 1993; Storey, 1994).

Research has established that, within the context of micro- and small-sized firms, marketing is approached, managed and implemented in significantly different ways from the management of marketing within a large-firm context (Hills, 1987; Carson, Cromie, McGowan and Hill, 1995; Morrish, Miles and Deacon, 2010; Jones and Rowley, 2011). Specifically, it has been found that the characteristics of micro- and small-sized firms – including the conditions they experience regarding their customers and competitors, the restricted nature of their resource base, their typically flatter organisational structures, absence of management systems and preference for developing networks of reciprocal relationships – combine to identify that an alternative, entrepreneurial approach to marketing is effective in building and maintaining sustainable competitive advantage (Carson et al., 1995; Collinson and Shaw, 2001). Most recently it has been argued that entrepreneurial marketing might, in fact, offer an antidote to growing concerns regarding the appropriateness of marketing theory's relevance to the practical management and implementation of the types of marketing activities employed by organisations competing in the challenging environment of the twenty-first century (Brownlie and Saren, 1997; Varadarajan, 2003; Morrish et al., 2010).

This chapter considers the theory and practice of marketing within the context of small firms. It aims to encourage awareness of the significant contribution that marketing can make to the competitiveness of small firms and discusses in detail the nature, role, management and implementation of marketing within the context of micro- and small-sized firms. It also reviews the theory of entrepreneurial marketing and related concepts, including networking, interaction and word of mouth, while emphasising the link between the theory and practice of marketing within small firms. Recognising the nascent nature of the academic study of this subject, the chapter concludes with suggestions for future studies of entrepreneurial marketing.

18.2 Learning objectives

This chapter has four learning objectives:

1 to identify the implications that firm size and related characteristics have for the marketing approach adopted by micro- and small-sized firms

2 to appreciate the critical role of marketing within micro- and small-sized firms and the contribution that it can make to a firm's success

3 to develop an understanding of the distinctions and similarities between entrepreneurial and traditional approaches to marketing

4 to acquire an awareness of the tools of entrepreneurial marketing and the ways in which these can be used by small firms to exploit opportunities and contribute to sustainable competitive advantage.

Key concepts

- entrepreneurial marketing ■ the entrepreneurial marketing process
- the tools of entrepreneurial marketing ■ networks ■ word of mouth

18.3 The characteristics of small firms: implications for marketing

There is ample and longstanding research evidence that indicates the importance of marketing for small firms (Hills, 1984; Hisrich, 1989; Hills and LaForge, 1992). For example, Hills (1984) found that experienced venture capitalists rate marketing as more important than any other business function in the success of new ventures. His research also established that venture capitalists believe that the failure rates of young ventures could be reduced by as much as 60 per cent if they engaged in better market analysis in the early stages. Based on such figures, Hills (1984) concludes that new ventures face significant marketing challenges that are unique to their small size. Hisrich's (1989) review of the challenges that entrepreneurs identify as critical to their businesses revealed marketing and finance to be of particular relevance and research has consistently demonstrated the critical impact of a marketing orientation on firms' survival and the success rates of new businesses (Morris and Lewis, 1995).

It is interesting that, in the face of such compelling research findings, our knowledge and theory of marketing has, in the main, been informed by research on the marketing practices and processes of *large* firms (Cravens, Hills and Woodruff, 1987; Kotler, 2003). Such research suggests that marketing can be defined as both an orientation and as a business function (Webster, 1992).

As an *orientation*, marketing is regarded as an organisational approach that is organised around the consumer, with a keen focus on identifying customer needs, wants and demands and matching these to the features and benefits of the products contained within an organisation's portfolio. Organisations embracing a marketing orientation often regard themselves as customer-focused or customercentric and typically rely upon extensive market research to be able to identify and then target those market segments that offer greatest potential for profitability and growth.

As a *business function*, marketing is concerned with management of the marketing mix – the variety of marketing tools that can be used to make products attractive to consumers by satisfying their needs, wants and demands. Included within this mix are the:

- *product*, particularly the unique selling propositions that distinguish it from other offerings in the marketplace
- *price* charged for the product
- *promotions* or marketing communications that organisations direct towards their customers in an effort to make them aware of their products
- *place* where products can be purchased or experienced – e.g., can the product be purchased from a high street retailer or is it only available online?

Particularly for services – e.g., a meal in a restaurant or a haircut, the marketing mix also includes decisions about the:

- *processes* involved in providing the service
- *physical environment* in which the service is made available
- *people* who provide the service.

Conceived of in these ways, this suggests that marketing, as both an organisational orientation and a business function, is supported by an extensive resource base including significant people resources, such as a marketing manager or marketing director responsible for the management of a team of staff located within a dedicated marketing department.

This depiction of marketing contrasts sharply with the characteristics of micro- and small-sized firms and the implications of these for the marketing approaches and activities that they use. It also suggests the need to acquire a clear understanding of approaches to and the use of marketing in small firms (Hills and LaForge, 1992; O'Dwyer, Gilmore and Carson, 2009). The characteristics of small firms and the implications of these for marketing are summarised in Table 18.1 and expanded upon below.

Table 18.1 Implications of firm size for marketing approach adopted

Characteristics of small firm	Implications for marketing
Restricted resource base	No dedicated marketing department
	No dedicated marketing staff
	The owner is also the sales and marketing 'director' and all staff are involved in marketing
Combined ownership and management	Concentration on current and future market opportunities and latent demand
	The owner is the brand
Flat organisational structures and informal processes	Little planning of marketing
	Able to quickly respond to changing market conditions
Local embeddedness	Benefits of interactions and transactions arranged through network mechanisms rather than market dynamics of organisational hierarchies
	Buffer to support vulnerable market position

18.3.1 Restricted resource base

Research within the field of entrepreneurship has long established the liabilities of smallness that can be experienced by small firms. Building upon such work, more recent research has recognised that, as a consequence of their smaller size, micro- and small-sized firms possess a restricted resource base (Carson et al., 1995; Shaw 2006). Relative to their larger counterparts, micro-sized firms employing no more than 10 people and small firms employing no more than 49 rarely possess the financial or people resources needed to establish a separate marketing department, employ dedicated marketing staff or invest in the structured, routine processes involved in developing, implementing and evaluating annual marketing plans.

Writing on this, Hills and LaForge (1992: 45) argue that, while the 'normative academic literature places considerable emphasis on the development of detailed marketing and business plans, as well as on the conduct of market research . . . many new ventures do not have detailed marketing plans'. Moreover, they suggest that owner-managers often regard traditional approaches to marketing in negative terms, particularly marketing research, which, they argue, is, at best, regarded by entrepreneurs in 'lukewarm' terms.

This should not, however, be interpreted as suggesting that smaller firms do not engage in marketing. Quite the contrary. Instead, research suggests that the more restricted resource base of small firms implies the necessity to adopt an entrepreneurial approach to the creative and effective use of their resources, including for marketing purposes (Guersen, 1997; O'Dwyer et al., 2009). For example, research has revealed that, within smaller-sized firms, the owner often assumes the role of sales and marketing director and *all* members of staff are involved in marketing (Carson et al., 1995; Stokes, 1995). It has also been established that, despite their restricted resource base and lack of sophisticated planning, small firms use marketing to generate sales (Carson, 1990; Guersen, 1997; Stokes, 2000).

This approach contrasts starkly with our understanding of marketing as it is practiced within the context of larger firms, in which only dedicated marketing staff are involved in marketing a firm's products and services. The more restricted resource base of small firms dictates, however, that *all* members of staff become ambassadors for the firm and the building of relationships with customers is the responsibility of the owner and the staff they employ. In this way, marketing within the small firm context can often be more effective than that in a large firm environment as, when a customer interacts with the firm, all members of the firm are aware of the necessity of being consumer-centred and considering the needs, wants and demands of consumers.

18.3.2 Combined ownership and management

A unique characteristic of small firms is that their ownership is rarely separated from their management. Research that has distinguished between managers and business-owners regards the former as being involved in managing resources and the latter as searching for and subsequently marshalling resources to exploit market opportunities (Gibb, 1984).

This distinction has important consequences for marketing within the context of micro- and small-sized firms. One of these is that, within smaller firms, the owners' concentration on searching for opportunities can help their firms maintain a competitive advantage in the long run (Day and Wensley, 1988). Miles and Darroch (2006) suggest that, by concentrating on both current and emerging market opportunities, small firms can accrue important benefits over their larger counterparts. They argue that, in small firms, the owners' keen focus on current and future market opportunities ensures that small firms can prepare for and meet latent demand. In contrast, they argue, traditional approaches to marketing that encourage a focus on satisfying the well-defined demands of well-defined target markets can, in the long run, restrict the success of larger firms. They (Miles and Darroch, 2006: 488) suggest that much of 'traditional marketing management has, however, focused exclusively on reactively meeting explicit customer needs, while ignoring latent demand'. Emphasising this, they cite Hayes (1988: 12), who has noted that, by encouraging a focus on current customer needs, wants and demands, the 'marketing concept . . . has contributed to the death of true product innovation'. Taking this further, Harvey, Lusch and Cavakapa (1996: 4) argue that 'under the marketing concept, the customer is king, and the practice of marketing is held hostage by the king'.

A second implication of combined ownership and management is that, for small firms, the owner is often the brand. Research indicates that customers often transact with and develop a relationship with a small firm because they regard the entrepreneur as a legitimate, credible businessperson (Zott and Huy, 2007). In other words they 'buy into' the entrepreneur and trust that he or she will provide them with a product or service that will satisfy their needs, wants and demands.

This can be illustrated by thinking about how you might select business services such as those offered by an accountant or a lawyer. Typically one might ask for the recommendations of colleagues, friends and neighbours. Also important will be the first point of contact when meeting with potential accountants or lawyers. It is very likely that how they present themselves during this initial encounter will determine whether or not you intend to develop the relationship by commissioning them to work for you.

In this way, the characteristics of owners' impression-management skills can dictate the extent to which they are able to convince the marketplace that they and their businesses are credible brands with which customers will want to transact and build relationships.

18.3.3 Flat organisational structures and informal processes

Small firms are also characterised as possessing flat organisational structures and adopting ad hoc, informal management approaches, both of which can have significant implications for the organisation and management of marketing within them (Carson and Cromie, 1989; Carson et al., 1995; Stokes, 1995; Collinson and Shaw, 2001).

The flatter structures adopted by smaller firms mean that owners are much closer to the marketplace and, given the absence of organisational hierarchies, they are able to maintain regular, typically daily, contact with their customers. In this way, the owners of small businesses can immerse themselves in the market, gleaning constant information about emerging customer trends and competitor activities. In so doing, they are able to exploit their 'closeness' to the market and use this to gather up-to-date, accurate and reliable customer and competitor information without incurring the costs of market research, which can often generate information that is both inaccurate and, by the time it reaches a firm, out of date (Carson et al., 1995; Shaw, 2006).

Strong empirical evidence for this is provided by Hills and Narayana's (1989) study of 100 small and young entrepreneurial firms, which identified a passionate responsiveness to customers to be within the top two of 26 factors underpinning the success of their firms. More recently, Zontanos and Anderson (2004) have commented that the marketing advantages enjoyed by small firms are related to the very close relationships they share with customers.

The informal management approach preferred by owners of small businesses also has implications for marketing. Combined with research indicating they tend to be more generalist in their management approach and often lack specific marketing skills, this further emphasises that, within the context of small firms, marketing is managed, organised and implemented in ways that are significantly different from marketing within large firms.

With little formal knowledge of how to organise and manage marketing, research has found that the owners of small businesses rely upon their knowledge of their customers and the marketplace, together with their intuition, sound judgement and excellent communication skills, to be able to identify market opportunities and then exploit these by marshalling the required resources (Carson et al., 1995). This is in stark contrast to the more rigorous planning process, informed by detailed market research, that large organisations use to guide the selection of target markets and management of a marketing mix with which to (hopefully) competitively position products within the marketplace. Instead, research indicates that small firms tend to adopt a much more informal marketing approach.

The flatter organisational structures of small firms, combined with their more informal management processes, often create an additional benefit: the ability to quickly respond to changing market conditions. Research indicates that, despite increasingly dynamic and competitive environments, small firms' ability to survive can be credited, at least in part, to their flexibility and market responsiveness (Covin and Miles, 1999). This ability to quickly adapt to changing market demands is particularly relevant in today's turbulent markets. This has been commented upon by researchers located within both marketing and entrepreneurship disciplines. For example, marketing scholars Addis and Podesta (2005) have used the words 'change', 'complexity', 'chaos' and 'contradiction' to describe what they regard as the characteristics of postmodern markets. Building on this, scholars within the field of entrepreneurship have suggested that the more flexible marketing approaches favoured by small firms are effective in guiding responses to market changes, complexities, contradictions and chaos (Morris, Schindehutte and LaForge, 2002).

18.3.4 Local embeddedness

Research within the field of industrial marketing has long recognised the importance of networks for organising and negotiating transactions and relationships between industrial organisations (Håkansson, 1987; Axelsson and Easton, 1992; Håkansson, 2009). Similarly, there is a recognition that smaller-sized firms are typically embedded within local markets and communities (Storey, 1994; Jack and Anderson, 2002). Such embeddedness has been found to be especially important for small firms. In contrast with larger organizations, which can select to organise their transactions either through market mechanisms that involve buying products and goods at their market price or through organisational hierarchies encouraging both collaboration and competition between different departments or business units, small firms often select to arrange their exchanges through networks of relationships.

As a consequence of their restricted resource base, small firms are often unable to purchase goods and services at their market price. To overcome this, they may develop informal, reciprocal relationships with other firms and engage in mutually beneficial transactions that do not incur market costs. An example of this might be a small communications agency that has strong competencies in design and copywriting, but does not have a permanent photographer. It may develop a relationship with a local photographer, who will provide photographic services in exchange for the agency designing leaflets, brochures or a website to help communicate his or her services. In this scenario, no money is exchanged and, instead, both small firms benefit by engaging in reciprocal exchange behaviour. Such exchanges have been found to be beneficial in extending the resource base of small firms without increasing their cost base (Shaw, 2006).

Given their scale and flatter organisational structures, small firms do not have the option of arranging their transactions through organisational hierarchies. Instead, they may decide to develop strategic alliances with other small firms and enter into agreements to share their distinct yet complementary products, knowledge and resources for the purposes of individually enhancing their competitiveness. Such behaviour can be described as 'collaborating to compete'. Take, for example, two small life science firms located in the same business park or incubation centre involved in distinct yet complementary research. As the owners of the firms get to know one another, they may start to discuss their expertise, knowledge and/or technology. Over time, as they become more familiar with one another and their respective businesses, they may decide to form a strategic alliance that encourages the exchange of knowledge, information, expertise and so on. Again, no money is involved in such exchanges, but, by sharing their resources, both firms benefit and enhance their potential for market success.

These examples illustrate that small firms can be embedded within different types of networks, including informal bartering exchanges, strategic alliances, industrial districts and business associations (Saxenian, 1990; Gulati and Gargulio, 1999; Shaw, 2006; Anderson, Drakopoulou Dodd and Jack, 2010). Importantly, the extensive body of research on this topic indicates that being embedded within such relationships can generate multiple benefits for small firms, including such marketing benefits as access to market opportunities and information (Birley, 1985; Aldrich and Zimmer, 1986; Nahapiet and Ghoshal, 1998; Hite and Hesterly, 2001; Casson and Giusta, 2007; Ozcan and Eisenhardt, 2009), enhanced innovation (Saxenian, 1990; Batterink, Emiel, Lerkx and Omta, 2010), organisational learning (Rae, 2005; Lee and Jones, 2008) and, ultimately, competitive advantage (Joyce, Woods and Black, 1995; Ostgaard and Birley, 1996; Uzzi, 1996).

Particularly as a consequence of their restricted resource base, small firms have been found to benefit from networks in so many ways that networks have been referred to as *the* most important resource for small firms (Johannisson, 1986; Ostgaard and Birley, 1994). It has also been argued that if small firms are to survive today's turbulent environments, they *must* engage in networks (Huggins, 2000b). The key reason for this is that the networks within which small firms are embedded provide access to a wide variety of resources at minimum additional cost. As Slotte-Kock and Coviello (2009: 33) have argued, 'networks have been shown to improve entrepreneurial effectiveness by providing access to resources and competitive advantage without capital investment'.

Another important marketing benefit of the typically local networks within which small firms are embedded is the 'buffer' that such networks can provide. As small firms often occupy insignificant spaces within the market and so possess little market share (Storey, 1994), they can be vulnerable to the effects of tough competitive dynamics. Particularly in times of recession, it can be difficult for small firms to compete with price cuts and other promotional measures that, drawing on their considerably greater resources, their larger competitors are able to implement.

Yet, often, small firms are still able to survive and an important reason for this is the established reciprocal relationships that they share with other firms, customers and stakeholders embedded within the same locality (Jack and Anderson, 2002; Shaw, 2006). Such relationships can ensure firms continue to engage in reciprocal behaviours that help maintain their competitiveness. In particular, established relationships with local networks of customers can provide small firms with an important defence against challenging competitive dynamics. These relationships have been found to not only provide access to regular business but also provide referrals and the supply of informed, relevant market and competitive information (Carson et al., 1995; Shaw, 2006).

Considered collectively, research evidence regarding the networks in which small firms are embedded suggests that small firms do not need to engage in traditional approaches to environmental scanning and market research as such information can be provided by their networks at a cost below that which they would have to pay were they to acquire such information and research through market mechanisms. Writing on this, Hills and Hultman (2008: 222) argue that, within small firms, marketing tactics are often based upon two-way communications with customers and marketing decisions are typically based on daily contact with customers and other relevant stakeholders in their environments.

18.3.5 Summary of the characteristics of small firms and their implications for marketing

Despite the very clear implications the characteristics of micro- and small-sized firms have for marketing, it is recognised that, until more recently, both the mainstream marketing and entrepreneurship literatures had paid scant attention to marketing within the context of small firms (Davis, Hills and LaForge, 1985; Jones and Rowley, 2011). That is despite a significant body of research evidence identifying the critical relevance of marketing for small and ventures (Hills and LaForge, 1992; Morris and Lewis, 1995; Morris et al., 2002; Morrish et al., 2010; Jones and Rowley, 2011).

Recognising both this research gap and the contributions that small firms can make to economic and social wealth, interest in the marketing practices and activities of small firms has attracted significant research attention. In particular, scholars researching the interface between entrepreneurship and marketing have recognised the similarities and dynamics between these two disciplines and their work has encouraged the development of an alternative management paradigm known as 'entrepreneurial marketing' (Hills, 1987; Hills and LaForge, 1992; Carson et al., 1995; Miles and Darroch, 2006). It is to this concept and its practice that this chapter now turns.

18.4 Entrepreneurial marketing: theory and practice

Entrepreneurial marketing (EM) has been variously defined. For example, Kotler (2003) regards it as a 'stage' or type of marketing that organisations tend to adopt either at their initiation or during the latter stages of their evolution. Conceived of in this way, Kotler views EM as belonging within what Hills, Hultman and Miles (2008) refer to as traditional or administrative marketing.

In contrast, a growing number of scholars regard EM as being very different from the traditional approaches to marketing espoused by marketing textbooks, which typically describe the marketing principles and practices of large firms. Such scholars argue that the concept of EM has emerged in recognition of two important realisations. The first, as stated above, is the recognition that small firms are *not* simply scaled-down large firms (Storey, 1994) and, as a consequence, marketing within small firms differs fundamentally from marketing within large-sized firms (Hills, 1987; Hills and LaForge, 1992; Stokes, 2000; Collinson and Shaw, 2001; Jones and Rowley, 2011). The second realisation is that, while entrepreneurship and marketing have developed as distinct disciplines, they share much in common, as entrepreneurship and innovation are not only relevant for success within the marketplace but also marketing is essential to the creation, development and sustainability of entrepreneurial ventures (Davis et al., 1985; Stokes, 2000; Collinson and Shaw, 2001). As Hills and LaForge (1992: 33) argue, 'the underlying philosophy and orientation of the [marketing] discipline are attuned to market and customer needs, which have direct applicability to entrepreneurship'. They also identify marketing and entrepreneurship as being similar in multiple ways, including the boundary-spanning nature of their activities, extensive interplay with the environment and their capacity to absorb risk and uncertainty.

Contemporary discussions within the marketing literature suggest that the purpose of marketing is to create value-rich, mutually beneficial exchange relationships (Keefe, 2004). Acknowledging this, Miles and Darroch (2006) argue that, by leveraging innovation to create goods and services of superior value (Covin and Miles, 1999), entrepreneurship can provide a critical way of achieving such relationships.

Considered in these terms, this suggests that EM is *distinct from* traditional approaches to marketing rather than being what Kotler describes as a '*stage*' within organisations' marketing evolution. Recognising this and the nexus between marketing and entrepreneurship, a body of research positioned at the marketing/entrepreneurship interface has developed and the concept of entrepreneurial marketing has become accepted as a recognised approach to marketing, distinct from traditional approaches historically favoured by large firms. Significantly, EM is regarded as an important concept that *integrates* the disciplines of entrepreneurship and marketing rather than considering either how entrepreneurship can *assist* marketing or how marketing can *assist* entrepreneurship. Instead, in its simplest form, EM is a concept that recognises both entrepreneurship and marketing are interested in identifying and exploiting opportunities located within the marketplace.

In this section, we look more closely at definitions, principles and practices of EM and consider its distinctions from traditional marketing approaches.

18.4.1 Defining entrepreneurial marketing (EM)

As a subject area, EM involves the study of the interface between entrepreneurship and marketing (Hills, 1987; Carson et al., 1995; Collinson and Shaw, 2001). As research at this interface has developed, definitions of EM have evolved to become more sophisticated.

Initial definitions concentrated on identifying areas of distinction and overlap between marketing and entrepreneurship (Omura, Calantone and Schmidt, 1993). Noted differences included assumptions made about the environment. For example, while traditional marketing presumes that market conditions are continuous and firms are able to satisfy clearly defined customer needs, wants and demands, entrepreneurship is often regarded as operating within uncertain environments in which market conditions are discontinuous and the needs of the market are often unclear.

Similarities identified between entrepreneurship and marketing include a focus on opportunities. Omura et al. (1993) have argued that, when market conditions are continuous, entrepreneurship can aid the process of identifying new, future and latent demand in existing markets and, when market conditions are less predictable, entrepreneurship can help identify opportunities existing in developing and new markets.

Building upon Omura et al.'s (1993) discussions of the entrepreneurship/marketing interface, Carson et al. (1995) and Collinson and Shaw (2001) identify three areas of commonality between entrepreneurship and marketing – that both are change-focused, opportunistic in nature and innovative in their approach to management. Specifically, they suggest, in difficult to determine, changing market environments, the search for innovative solutions that create value for customers are central to both entrepreneurship and marketing and, as such, form the basis of EM. Figure 18.1 captures early discussions

Figure 18.1 The entrepreneurship/marketing interface

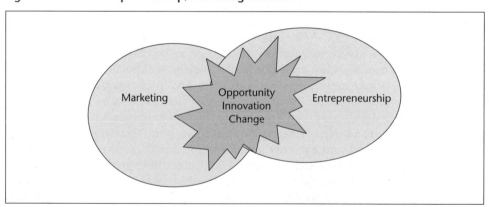

Source: Adapted from Carson et al. (1995)

of the EM interface, highlighting entrepreneurship and marketing's shared focus on opportunity, innovation and change.

As knowledge and understanding of EM have evolved, so too have definitions of it. Researchers have moved beyond discussing the entrepreneurship marketing interface to conceiving of EM as a concept or unique management paradigm.

In their discussion of EM, Morris et al. (2002) emphasise the role of innovation in identifying and creating unique propositions that are valued by consumers. Specifically, they (2002: 5) define EM as the 'proactive identification and exploitation of opportunities for acquiring and retaining profitable customers through innovative approaches to risk management, resource leveraging and value creation'. Building on this, Miles and Darroch (2006: 488) argue 'that a firm with an entrepreneurial approach to marketing will proactively leverage innovation and manage risks' in an attempt to create and deliver value for customers while benefiting the organisation. Hills and Hultman (2008: 19) provide an even more comprehensive definition when they describe EM as 'a spirit, an orientation as well as a process of passionately pursuing opportunities and launching and growing ventures that create perceived customer value through relationships by employing innovativeness, creativity, selling, market immersion, networking and flexibility'.

Having explored how definitions of the EM concept have evolved since Hills (1987) initiated discussions of the entrepreneurship/marketing interface, it can be concluded that innovation, opportunity and change remain central tenants of this unique management paradigm. Acknowledging this, Morrish et al. (2010: 306) comment that, 'critical aspects of marketing and entrepreneurship are synthesised into a comprehensive conceptualisation where marketing becomes a proactive opportunity-focused process that firms can use to act entrepreneurially'.

Despite recognising the dynamic between marketing, entrepreneurship and innovation, it is acknowledged that research has concentrated on exploring the interface between *entrepreneurship* and innovation and less is understood about the interface between *marketing* and innovation, particularly within the context of small firms (Hills and LaForge, 1992; Kleindl, Mowen and Chakraborty, 1996; O'Dwyer et al., 2009). This is regardless of the suggestion that innovation is the 'most significant factor that can be used by SMEs to compensate for any disadvantages experienced because of their size' (O'Dwyer et al., 2009: 55).

18.4.2 Entrepreneurial marketing competencies

Differences between the entrepreneurial and more usual kinds of marketing suggest a number of implications for the competencies required when EM is embraced. Boyatzis (1992: 21) defines competencies as 'an underlying characteristic of a person, which results in effective and/or superior performance'.

Research has identified a number of competencies as being associated with EM and stressed the similarity of these to those characteristics typically associated with entrepreneurs, including innovative, risky, creative and adaptable behaviours (Collinson and Shaw, 2001). Writing on this, Carson, Gilmore and Grant (1997: 463) explain that EM involves searching for 'creative, novel or unusual solutions to problems [and] demonstrates a willingness to commit resources to less than fool-proof opportunities'. Interestingly, when discussing the relationship between EM and innovation, O'Dwyer et al. (2009: 53) suggest that, while 'SME marketing activities can be highly innovative, they are not necessarily based on originality, and are more likely to be an adaptation of an existing concept or situation'. This adaptation of existing innovations is, they suggest, a central element of SME marketing.

Described in these terms, the competencies for EM contrast with those required when approaching marketing from a traditional or administrative perspective (Hills et al., 2008). Collinson and Shaw (2001) identify careful planning, rigour in research and decisionmaking and familiarity with statistics and figures as important competencies associated with traditional marketing. In contrast, they (2001: 763) argue that 'the management of entrepreneurial marketing is characterised by intuition, informality and speed of decision making, all of which require different competencies'.

Grant et al. (2001) have identified the continual development of entrepreneurs' experiential knowledge as central to EM and O'Dwyer et al. (2009: 47) note that the 'formation and depth of experiential knowledge is the key competence of the entre-preneur'. This builds on recognition of the critical role that human capital plays in the entrepreneurial process. An emergent, significant body of research has identified entrepreneurs' experiences and acquisition of knowledge relevant to the market and associated product, technology, competitive and customer dynamics in which their firm competes as critical to the establishment and sustainability of small firms (Shaw, Lam and Carter, 2008).

O'Dwyer et al. (2009: 47) argue that the marketing characteristics of small firms are derived from both the experiential knowledge of the owner-manager and the unique characteristics inherent in small firms including their restricted resource base, informal management style and combined ownership and control. They suggest that this com-bination of experiential knowledge and firm characteristics encourage 'an inherently innate method'. They further suggest that the knowledge and experience of owners provide key sources of successful innovation for small firms.

18.5 The process and tools of entrepreneurial marketing

This chapter has so far identified that, as a consequence of unique characteristics, marketing within small firms is approached from and implemented in ways that are significantly different from those found in large firms. Specifically, it has been argued that, for small firms, the concept of (EM) may be more relevant to acquiring a sustain-able market advantage given small firms' restricted resource bases, flatter organisa-tional structures, informal management processes and local embeddedness. Having explored the evolution of the EM concept, associated definitions and implications for the types of competencies required when EM is embraced, the chapter now turns to issues related to the practical adoption, management and implementation of EM and considers its process, tools and underlying dimensions.

18.5.1 The process of EM

Discussions of marketing typically highlight both the marketing management process and the tools of marketing.

Figure 18.2 The traditional marketing management process

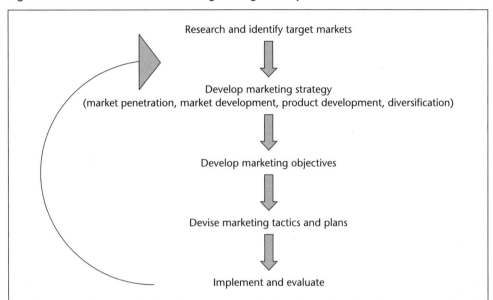

As depicted in Figure 18.2, the process tends to start by carrying out detailed research of markets and buyer behaviour to help identify target markets and familiarise organisations with the needs, wants and demands of consumers. Once a target market has been identified and customer requirements have been established, the next stage involves selecting an effective marketing strategy. Typically, firms are depicted as selecting from one of four possible marketing strategies: market penetration, market development, product development or diversification into new product markets. Once a strategy has been identified, the process continues by selecting marketing objectives, targets and developing a detailed marketing plan, which guides the implementation of these tactics and indicates measures and timeframes for evaluation.

This process suggests the need for a dedicated marketing team and significant resources to facilitate detailed, formal marketing research and associated planning decisions. However, as has been discussed, the characteristics of small firms – in particular, their restricted resource base, informal managerial processes and flatter organisational structures – indicate that this traditional marketing management process is neither possible nor favoured by small firms.

An important reason identified for this is that, when firms adopt EM, they are typically located within fluctuating, changing environments, which limit opportunities for engaging in the timely and detailed planning of marketing (Carson et al., 1995). Collinson and Shaw (2001: 763) argue that, in such environments, 'if time is taken to engage in a rigorous planning process, by the end of that process it is likely that market conditions will have changed sufficiently to render any decision resulting from this process as no longer relevant'. They suggest that, instead, EM is typically implemented with the minimum amount of planning.

Figure 18.3 The EM process (Stokes, 2000)

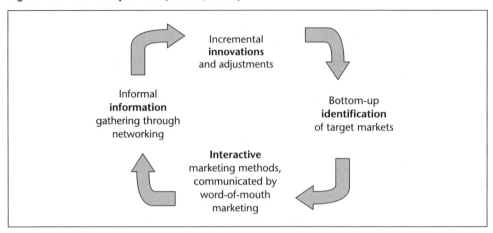

Supporting this is research that suggests, rather than engaging in detailed market research to identify target markets and profile groups of consumers, small firms often 'arrive at' their target market by a process of elimination rather than the more traditional approaches involving market segmentation, targeting and positioning (O'Dwyer et al., 2009).

Stokes' (2000) research on the marketing practices used by small firms (involving in-depth interviews and focus groups with 40 entrepreneurs) has been significant in developing our understanding of the EM process.

Stokes was especially interested in understanding the ways in which marketing as an organisational philosophy, marketing as a strategy, the marketing mix and marketing intelligence are manifest in small firms. During interviews, he deliberately avoided the use of marketing terminology so as not to influence the respondents' comments.

The findings of his study established that, for each of the aspects of marketing in which he was interested, distinct variations were found 'between what successful entrepreneurs actually do and what marketing theory would have them do' (Stokes, 2000: 50). Figure 18.3 captures the process of EM as revealed by Stokes (2000) and this is discussed in more detail below.

- *Marketing as an orientation* Stokes found that, while literature on marketing as an organisational philosophy indicates market needs will be assessed before engaging in product development, the reality for entrepreneurs is often the other way round. He established that entrepreneurs often conceive of an idea before then collecting information and feedback from potential customers. As such, he suggests that, for many small firms, an innovation rather than customer orientation is adopted. However, he does caution that such innovation is rarely radical and, instead, is more commonly focused on incremental change and imitative innovation, involving, for example, the introduction of an existing product or good to a new market.

- *Marketing as strategy* As depicted in Figure 18.2, the dominant marketing perspective suggests that, as a strategy, it adopts a 'top-down' approach, which makes use of extensive market research and customer profiling. Stokes' research did not find this. Instead, entrepreneurs in his study described a more 'bottom-up' approach, which, initially, involves serving the needs of a few customers and, over time, as experience and resources permit, serving the needs of a larger customer base.

■ *The marketing mix* Stokes found little evidence that the entrepreneurs involved in his study made use of the 4 or 7 Ps. He did, however, find that a concentration on sales encouraged by the use of promotions, together with entrepreneurs' preferences for personal contact and direct interactions with customers, were instrumental in the choice of the types of marketing techniques they employed. Stokes (2000: 51) found that, for many of the entrepreneurs he spoke with, 'the nature of their personal contact with customers represented the unique selling point' of their business and they identified personal relationships as a key way of developing their customer base. Indeed, some of the entrepreneurs involved in his research 'regretted that the growth of their businesses reduced their opportunities for direct customer contact' (2000: 52).

■ *Marketing intelligence* Contrasting with traditional approaches to managing marketing, Stokes found very little evidence of the use of formal market research. While participating entrepreneurs spoke of the need to monitor the market and had strategies in place to gather marketing intelligence, they regarded formal market research as unnecessary, expensive and unhelpful. Instead, they reported that informal methods, including networking with relevant individuals, were valuable in informing them of important market and competitive changes.

18.5.2 The tools of EM

The process of EM as described by Stokes (2000) suggests that the tools of EM differ significantly from the marketing mix favoured by the traditional marketing approaches often used by large firms. As discussed, traditional marketing theory suggests that marketing managers, supported by a dedicated team of marketing staff, will make use of a mix of either the 4 (product, price, promotion, place) or, for services, 7 Ps (which, also include people, processes and physical environment) to implement well-crafted marketing strategies. Specifically, marketing textbooks suggest that manipulation of the marketing mix can be used to help competitively position products within the marketplace.

In contrast, EM research suggests that, for entrepreneurs, personal contact with customers and encouragement of word-of-mouth recommendations are essential marketing tools (Carson et al., 1995; Stokes, 2000; Shaw, 2006). Stokes refers to these as a set of *interactive* marketing tools, highlighting the reliance of EM on the abilities of entrepreneurs and their staff to engage in relationships with customers and other stakeholders relevant to the success of their firms. Indeed, research has shown that, by developing and maintaining mutually beneficial relationships with customers, small firms can grow their business base. Specifically, positive word-of-mouth communications have been found to encourage customer referrals (File, Judd and Prince, 1992; Stokes, 2000; Stokes and Lomax, 2002; Shaw, 2006).

The benefit of word-of-mouth marketing is that firms not only grow their business but also do so without incurring additional costs – e.g., those associated with advertising and direct mail. Moreover, when firms grow their customer base as a result of referrals encouraged by word-of-mouth communications, this supports a 'slow build-up of new business' (Stokes, 2000: 53), which many small firms prefer as they find it easier to manage than a sudden spike in demand resulting from advertising.

There are, however, disadvantages associated with an over-reliance on word-of-mouth communications. Not only can it restrict growth to those networks within which this occurs but also it can be difficult to control. Addressing the first of these limitations, many entrepreneurs will engage in active networking to diversify and enlarge the networks within which they and their firms are embedded (Shaw, 2006). In particular, entrepreneurs seem to be effective in identifying both areas within their network that need to be strengthened and those brokers who can provide introductions and connections to individuals and organisations located outside their networks.

Extensive research on entrepreneurial networks has established that networks and networking activities – e.g., attending business and social events – have significant, positive marketing benefits for small firms (Shaw, 1998; Hill and McGowan, 1997; Jack and Anderson, 2002; Shaw, 2006; Shaw et al., 2008). For example, entrepreneurial networks have been found to be a key source of access to marketing intelligence, customer referrals, various resources and other opportunities (Carson, Cromie, McGowan and Hill, 1995; Gilmore, Carson and Grant, 2001; Shaw, 2006). Importantly, the information and advice provided to entrepreneurs from their networks is trustworthy, reliable and can be used to inform a variety of marketing decisions, ranging from the location of market opportunities and customer demand to how to price, distribute and even package goods and services (Hill and McGowan, 1997; Collinson and Shaw, 2001).

To overcome the challenges associated with controlling word-of-mouth communications, research indicates that entrepreneurs will often adopt creative approaches to encouraging *positive* ones. For example, Stokes and Lomax (2002) used case study research within the hotel industry to demonstrate how the use of corporate gifts and honesty bars were used to encourage positive word-of-mouth communications, which resulted in increased customer loyalty and referrals. This suggests that methods for controlling word-of-mouth communications may be specific to particular industries as, while corporate gifts may work well within the hotel industry, it may be that other approaches are more effective in other industry sectors. As discussed below, it is also likely that the widespread adoption of social networking sites, including Twitter, LinkedIn and YouTube, are likely to have significant implications both for entrepreneurial networking and approaches used to encourage positive word of mouth.

18.5.3 Seven core dimensions of EM

In their seminal paper, Morris et al. (2002) argue that the adoption of an EM orientation requires more than a distinct marketing process and set of tools and unique competencies. Going further, they (2002: 5) suggest that an EM orientation also requires changes 'in the underlying attitudes held by those responsible for marketing activities'. Specifically, they identify seven interrelated dimensions of entrepreneurial marketing, each of which are now briefly considered.

- *Proactive orientation* Building on the recognition that EM does not regard the environment as static and predictable, and acknowledging that entrepreneurs view the environment as containing opportunities, Morris et al. (2002: 6) argue that entrepreneurs will make use of marketing activities 'as a means of creating change and adapting to change'.

- *Opportunity-driven* Morris et al (2002: 6) suggest that the 'recognition and pursuit of opportunity is fundamental to entrepreneurship, and is a core dimension of EM'. They argue that when EM is embraced, an external focus and continuous external scanning become critical marketing activities, essential to identify current, future and latent demands. This, they argue, distinguishes EM from traditional approaches to marketing, which encourage a concentration on the demands of current customers and restrict considerations about changing and future demands that may emerge in the market.

- *Customer intensity* Morris et al. (2002: 7) suggest that 'EM incorporates the need for creative approaches to customer acquisition, retention and development' and a 'philosophy of customer intensity produces a dynamic knowledge base of changing customer circumstances and requirements'. Such a philosophy, they argue, is essential in ensuring entrepreneurial ventures are prepared for evolving and latent customer demands – something that can be restricted by the lengthy and detailed marketing planning processes favoured by traditional marketing theory.

- *Innovation-focused* Recognising the intimate relationship between entrepreneurship and innovation, Morris et al. (2002) reason that, when EM is embraced, marketing becomes integral to sustainable innovation. They explain that, when firms adopt an EM orientation, they adopt a philosophy that encourages a steady stream of new ideas to be translated into valuable product, service and technological improvements, which can result in benefits for both customers and the firm.

- *Risk management* It is recognised that effective entrepreneurs engage in calculated risks. Reflecting this, Morris et al. (2002) indicate that, when an EM orientation is adopted, it encourages an approach to allocating and managing resources and this allows firms to respond quickly and flexibly to changing market conditions. It also reduces the risks associated with tying resources too closely to specific product markets and technologies and, instead, encourages flexibility by combining resources in different and unique ways.

- *Resource leveraging* Related to risk management is the resource leveraging encouraged by an EM orientation. This suggests that entrepreneurial marketers 'are not constrained by the resources they currently have at their disposal' (Morris et al., 2002: 7). Instead, often drawing upon reciprocal relationships with others in their networks, firms are able to leverage resources and relationships to expand their restricted resource base, incurring minimal costs as they do so.

- *Value creation* Morris et al. (2002) argue that, unlike traditional marketing, the focal point of EM is not on the transaction or relationship shared with customers. Rather, they believe a prerequisite of market exchanges is the availability of a good or service that can deliver benefits valued by the customer, so the focus of EM is on innovative value creation. This, they explain, can be acquired by identifying unmet customer demands and combining resources in unique ways to provide distinct value for customers.

335

18.6 Future research

While research interest in EM is growing and a now sizeable body of literature on the subject exists, relative to other research areas, including entrepreneurship and marketing, studies of EM are at an early stage, with significant potential for further theoretical and empirical developments.

A number of potential avenues for fruitful research can be identified. Included amongst these is the potential for EM to provide a viable marketing alternative for large firms. While there is some recognition within the literature of the applicability of EM in large firms (Morrish et al., 2010; Jones and Rowley, 2011), empirical studies have tended to concentrate on its relevance in small firms. However, more recent developments within the mainstream marketing literature are growing in their support for the suggestion that future research on the benefits that an EM orientation can provide to large firms is timely.

An emerging theme within the marketing literature is a growing frustration with the applicability and relevance of existing marketing theory to the marketing practices and approaches used by contemporary organisations (Brownlie and Saren, 1997; Brown, 2002; Addis and Podesta, 2005; Cova and Pace, 2006; Cova, Pace and Park, 2007). Adding weight to these arguments are the turbulent environments within which firms of all sizes and at all stages of development find themselves at the time of writing. Entrepreneurship has long been recognised as flourishing within such dynamic and changing environments (Morris and Lewis, 1995) and it is increasingly evidenced that those firms with flexible approaches to marketing, encouraging adaptability and quick-moving responses to often hostile market environments, are best positioned to enjoy sustainable market success. This also suggests that future research might usefully consider the value of EM for large firms.

It is likely that, when faced with significant and far-reaching market changes, including increasingly threatening competitor tactics, market fragmentation, consumer resistance and disruptive technological and demographic developments, that the adoption of an EM orientation, with its focus on creating customer and organisational value by engaging in innovative, proactive opportunity-focused processes (Morrish et al., 2010), will be of benefit to contemporary organisations regardless of their size.

A second key area of future research is to consider the implications of digital and online environments for the implementation of EM. Given the interactive nature of the tools preferred by EM, it is likely that future EM studies will contribute to our knowledge and practice by considering the implications that significant growth in online communities such as Twitter, LinkedIn and YouTube have for the use of networks and word of mouth as critical EM tools.

18.7 Chapter summary

This chapter has considered the implications that the characteristics of micro- and small-sized firms have for the approaches to marketing they adopt. Specifically, the chapter has argued that, as small firms are not simply scaled-down versions of their larger counterparts, the nature of marketing within the context of small firms differs considerably from the one experienced by larger firms, supported by access to plentiful resources.

Entrepreneurial marketing (EM) has been identified as a valid, alternative approach to marketing that is very well suited to the unique characteristics of small firms and, indeed, may offer an antidote to increasingly outdated marketing practices suggested by traditional marketing theory – even for large firms.

The implications that EM has for firm competencies, together with the process and tools of EM, have been described in detail and contrasted with their counterparts within the mainstream marketing literature.

The chapter concluded by identifying those dimensions that Morris et al. (2002) regard as central to the concept of entrepreneurial marketing and indicating potential areas for future research.

Questions

1 In what ways do the characteristics of small firms impact upon the marketing approaches and activities that they adopt?

2 How can Entrepreneurial Marketing be defined and what are the central tenets of this unique management paradigm?

3 Compare and contrast traditional with entrepreneurial approaches to marketing highlighting both commonalities and distinctions.

4 In what ways might small firms use word of mouth and networks as critical marketing resources? What market benefits can be acquired from networking and encouraging word of mouth?

Weblinks

www.entrepreneurship.org
This is as a free online international resource, designed to help build entrepreneurial economies.

www.academyofmarketing.org/entrepreneurial-small-business-marketing-sig
The Academy of Marketing's special interest group, entrepreneurial and small business marketing.

www.marketingpower.com
The American Marketing Association (AMA) is the professional association for individuals and organisations leading the practice, teaching and development of marketing worldwide.

CHAPTER 19

Entrepreneurial networks and the small business

Steve Conway and Oswald Jones

19.1 Introduction

The study of entrepreneurship has often concentrated on either the personality traits of entrepreneurs or neoclassical views of rational economic activity. Critics have long argued that both approaches are inadequate in explaining entrepreneurial behaviour that is embedded in networks of social relations (Aldrich and Zimmer, 1986). Indeed, research has highlighted the importance of social networks and networking as entrepreneurial tools for contributing to the establishment, development and growth, of small firms. Social networks, for example, have been found to assist small firms in their acquisition of information and advice (Birley, 1985; Carson, Cromie, McGowan and Hill, 1995; Shaw, 1998, 2006; Mohannak, 2007), sourcing finance (Aldrich, 1989; Jenssen and Koenig, 2002; Jones and Jayawarna, 2010), supplementing internal resources (Aldrich and Zimmer, 1986; Jarillo, 1989; Hite and Hesterly, 2001; Zhang, 2010), in their ability to compete (Brown and Butler, 1995; Chell and Baines, 2000; Lechner and Dowling, 2003) and development of innovative products (Birley, Cromie and Myers, 1991; Rothwell, 1991; Conway, 1997; Jones, Cardoso and Beckinsale, 1997; Freel, 2003; Varis and Littunen, 2010). Gibson (1991: 117–18) contends that 'the more extensive, complex and diverse the web of relationships, the more the entrepreneur is likely to have access to opportunities, the greater the chance of solving problems expeditiously, and ultimately, the greater the chance of success for a new venture'. Thus, paradoxically, whilst entrepreneurs may be characterised by their autonomy and independence, they are also 'very dependent on ties of trust and co-operation' (Johannisson and Peterson, 1984: 1).

Johannisson (2000) argues that the concept of networking helps us focus on entrepreneurship as a collective, rather than an individualistic phenomenon. Similarly, Jones, Conway and Steward (2001: 13) see networks as a way of understanding the 'embeddedness' of entrepreneurial activity, where 'Embeddedness refers to the fact that economic action and outcomes, like all social actions and outcomes, are affected by actors' dyadic (pairwise) relations and by the structure of the overall network of relations'

(Granovetter, 1992b: 33). Jones and Conway (2004: 91) view the network perspective as providing a 'conceptualization of the entrepreneurial process as a complex and pluralistic pattern of interactions, exchanges, and relationships between actors'.

To demonstrate this perspective on entrepreneurship, we draw upon the well-known UK case of James Dyson.

At one level, Dyson illustrates the traditional viewpoint of entrepreneurs as 'heroic' individuals who achieve success as a result of their motivation, persistence and hard-work. However, a close reading of Dyson's autobiography, *Against the Odds* (1997), reveals that, at crucial stages in all of his business ventures, he made extensive use of his wide and diverse social network. The autobiography, for example, highlights the important contribution of Dyson's personal network to his access to finance, legal advice, social and emotional support, marketing and public relations services, as well as talented young design engineers.

Drawing upon this example, as well as other empirical work, we argue that the personal or social network should be viewed as an important, sometimes critical, resource of the entrepreneur. Indeed, for Leonard-Barton (1984: 113), 'entrepreneurs who, for geographic, cultural or social reasons, lack access to *free* information through personal networks, operate with less *capital* than do their well-connected peers'. However, as Birley, Cromie and Myers (1991: 58) warn, 'networks do not emerge without considerable endeavour'. Indeed, networkbuilding is a dynamic process, where relationships can be both destroyed as well as developed (Bowey and Easton, 2007; Casson and Giusta, 2007).

Interestingly, despite the extensive empirical evidence to the contrary (which we explore in the second half of this chapter), the myth of the entrepreneur as 'heroic individual' persists in the popular imagination. In attempting to explain this phenomenon, Dodd and Anderson (2007: 352) contend that:

> The popular vision of the entrepreneur has been shown to be profoundly individualistic: people may have difficulty in understanding the concept of entrepreneurship, but they readily identify with the entrepreneur. A commonsense understanding of entrepreneurship infers an individual.

19.2 Learning objectives

This chapter has three learning objectives:

1 to understand the alternative foci of network research in the area of entrepreneurship

2 to appreciate the social network perspective through examining the Dyson story and focusing on the role and contribution of Dyson's personal network to his entrepreneurial activities

3 to be aware of the key findings from academic research on entrepreneurial networks.

Key concepts

■ entrepreneurship ■ social networks ■ relationships in small firms

19.3 Alternative foci of network research in entrepreneurship

The study of 'the entrepreneur' and 'entrepreneurship' from a network perspective originates in the mid-1980s, with the work of academics such as Howard Aldrich, Sue Birley, Dorothy Leonard-Barton and Bengt Johannisson. Over the last decade or so, there has been an increasing body of research concerning the role, nature and dynamics of the entrepreneur's network.

However, within the entrepreneurship and small firm literature, the term 'network' has been used to describe a variety of phenomena. In particular, the notion of entrepreneurial or small firms' networks have been employed with reference to industrial districts (Piore and Sabel, 1984; Saxenian, 1985, 1990; Pyke, 1992), support structures (Chaston, 1995) and the personal contacts of entrepreneurs and small business' owner-managers (Birley, 1985; Aldrich and Zimmer, 1986). For example, studies have explored the networks of small firms within industrial districts such as Emilia-Romagna in Northern Italy (Piore and Sabel, 1984; Pyke, 1992) and Silicon Valley in California (Saxenian, 1985, 1990). This research has sought to develop an understanding of the networking patterns and collaborative arrangements present within such networks to inform policymakers of their impact upon the competitiveness of small firms.

Similar interests have motivated research concerning the networks of support organisations, such as Business Links in England and Local Economic Companies in Scotland, which exist to support the creation and growth of small firms. Encouraged by government enthusiasm for collaborative relationships between small firms, this branch of research has sought to inform policy of the nature and extent to which umbrella organisations such as local chambers of commerce and business clubs serve as a catalyst for small firms' networking activities and, thus, indirectly assist in the establishment and subsequent development and growth of small firms (Chaston, 1995).

Research centred on the personal or social networks of the entrepreneur and the small firm's owner-manager has long been motivated by an interest in understanding the impact that these networks have upon the ability of such individuals to create, develop and grow their small firms (Birley, 1985; Aldrich and Zimmer, 1986; Aldrich, Rosen and Woodward, 1986, 1987; Carsrud, Gaglio and Olm, 1987; Birley et al., 1991; Dubini and Aldrich, 1991; Mohannak, 2007; Lee and Jones, 2008; Jones and Jayawarna, 2010). A number of these studies have focused on the impact of nationality (Aldrich and Sakano, 1995; Dodd and Patra, 2002; Greve and Salaff, 2003; Stephan and Uhlaner, 2010), gender (Aldrich, 1989; Katz and Williams, 1997; Greve and Salaff, 2003; Hampton, Cooper and McGowan, 2009; Roomi, 2009) and ethnicity (Zimmer and Aldrich, 1987; Peterson and Roquebert, 1993; Smallbone, Berlotti and Ekanem, 2005; Deakins et al., 2007) on the nature and role of the entrepreneur's social network. Such research is interested in exploring the full breadth of relationships of entrepreneurs, rather than just the narrower set of 'business' relationships in which small firms are involved. Thus, in contrast to studies concerning industrial districts and support networks, this area of research does not separate or 'abstract' the business relationships of entrepreneurs and small firms' owner-managers from the ongoing, social relationships within which small firms' activities occur.

In more recent years, the social networks of entrepreneurs have been increasingly viewed through the lens of 'social capital' (Abell, Crouchley and Mills, 2001; Greve and Salaff, 2003; Tötterman and Sten, 2005; Anderson, Park and Jack, 2007; Bowey and Easton, 2007; Casson and Giusta, 2007; Deakins et al., 2007; Lee and Jones, 2008; Lee, 2009; Fang, Tsai and Lin, 2010; Ramos-Rodriguez et al., 2010). Social capital is viewed as a resource that can be nurtured and mobilised. It has three inter-related dimensions or components:

- the *structural* dimension, which concerns the nature of the network ties and network structure or configuration
- the *cognitive* dimension – i.e., the shared codes and language employed within a network
- the *relational* dimension, referring to the presence of trust, norms and obligations within a network (Nahapiet and Ghoshal, 1998).

The application of this perspective has provided interesting new insights into the 'inner workings' of entrepreneurial networks. For example, Lee and Jones (2008) found that the emergence of 'positive coded behaviours' in online communications (i.e., the development of cognitive capital), enabled trust to be built between a group of entrepreneurs and their contacts (i.e., the development of relational capital). This helped entrepreneurs develop their networks and gain access to more extensive resources (i.e., the development of structural capital).

This emphasis on the networking process alongside network structure is an important advance and helps address one of the critiques of the earlier literature – its overemphasis on structure (O'Donnell et al., 2000).

19.4 An overview of the social network perspective

The 'network' metaphor is a powerful way of viewing social groupings – it changes the imagery from a focus on pairs of relationships to one of 'constellations, wheels, and systems of relationships' (Auster, 1990: 65).

It is perhaps not surprising, then, that the social network perspective has been employed extensively since the 1960s to reveal the patterns of relationships and inter-action within a wide range of communities and organisations. Whilst the network perspective can and has been used, for example, to study the network of relationships between individuals, groups and organisations (i.e., various units of analysis), the social network perspective focuses on the relationships between individuals.

It is useful to distinguish between 'networks' and 'networking'. The network is a social structure comprised of a set of relationships between a set of individuals that is viewed as being 'greater than the sum of its parts', whilst networking can be seen as the activity by means of which these network relationships are built, nurtured and mobilised and the 'flows' through these relationships – e.g., information, money, power and friendship. However, there is also an interplay between a network and the networking that occurs within that social structure. On the one hand the network may constrain or liberate the patterns of interaction and exchanges between network members, while, on the other, networking behaviour may serve to either ossify the existing network membership and relationships or create a dynamic in the membership and relationships within the network.

Thus, when researching social networks and social networking activity, there are four key components that need to be investigated (Conway, Jones and Steward, 2001: 355):

- *actors* the individuals within the network
- *links* the relationships between the individuals within the network
- *flows* the exchanges between the individuals within the network
- *mechanisms* the modes of interaction employed by the network members.

We will now introduce the various dimensions of each of these network components (for further details, see Conway and Steward, 2009: 81 – 8) and networks themselves.

19.4.1 Dimensions of actors

There is a wide range of dimensions for categorising individuals – from the generic (e.g., age, gender, family membership, nationality, ethnicity and educational level), to the more specific (e.g., functional background – finance, marketing, engineering, etc.) or sectoral background. All of these dimensions can tell us something interesting about the membership and potential of the networks of entrepreneurs and owners of small businesses.

19.4.2 Dimensions of links and relationships

The nature of a link or relationship between network members may also vary along a number of dimensions. Perhaps the most relevant here are the following.

- *Formality* distinguishes between informal or social relationships and formal links (e.g., in a written contract).
- *Intensity* indicated by the frequency of interactions and the amount of flow or transactions between two actors over a given time period (Tichy, Tushman and Fombrun, 1979).
- *Trust* this is central to the maintenance and development of relationships and the sharing of information, knowledge and other resources between actors. Trust may be viewed as 'a state of mind' regarding the expectation that 'the other' will act reliably and fairly, exhibiting goodwill when unforeseen circumstances arise. Within social networks, trust is higher where the ties between individuals are strong rather than weak and is reinforced in dense networks where an individual has more to lose if he or she acquires a reputation of low trustworthiness (Castilla et al., 2000; Roomi, 2009).
- *Multiplexity* signifies the degree to which two actors are linked by multiple role relations (e.g., friend, brother and business partner). The greater the number of role relations linking two actors, the stronger and more durable is that link (Boissevain, 1974; Tichy et al., 1979).
- *Origin* the identification of the events leading to the origin of a link. It is intended that this dimension incorporates, factors such as the context in which the relationship originated and the initiator of the relationship.

- *Motive* the functional significance of networking does not qualify as a convincing explanation of its occurrence. In addressing this issue, Kreiner and Schultz (1993: 201) argue that 'one must determine the motives and perspectives of the actors who reproduce such [networking] patterns'.

19.4.3 Types of 'flow' within a network

One can distinguish between various types of flow within a network:

- *affect* the exchange of friendship between actors
- *power* the exchange of power and influence between actors
- *information* the exchange of ideas, information and know-how between actors
- *goods* the exchange of goods, money, technology or services between actors.

Individuals may 'exchange' any one of these types of transaction content for another (e.g., goods for money, information for friendship), although, in many cases, this may be implicit rather than explicit. It is also worth pointing out here that the perceived *value* of the flow or flows between two actors within a network may vary greatly for the sender/giver and the recipient and, indeed, for others in the network.

19.4.4 Mechanisms of interaction and network maintenance

There are a number of ways in which individuals can interact with one another, including telephone conversations, e-mails, documents and face-to-face meetings. Kelley and Brooks (1991) dichotomise these mechanisms of interaction into 'active' – referring to those modes involving personal interaction, whether face-to-face or over the phone – and 'passive' – essentially referring to documents and other textual material, where there is no direct interaction between the 'sender' and 'receiver' of the information.

As noted in the introduction, 'networks do not emerge without considerable endeavour' (Birley et al., 1991: 58) and, thus, we are interested in not only the mechanisms for the exchange of information and goods through the network but also the mechanisms and forums by which entrepreneurs build and nurture their networks.

19.4.5 Dimensions of networks

The overall network or set of relationships may also be seen to vary along a number of dimensions. The most relevant for our concerns include the following.

- *Size* this dimension simply refers to the number of actors participating in the network (Tichy et al., 1979; Auster 1990). However, the size of the network under investigation is frequently influenced by some arbitrary boundary set by the researcher (see discussion below).
- *Diversity* this network characteristic most frequently refers to the number of different types of actor (Auster, 1990), which, as discussed above, may be measured along a number of dimensions, such as age, gender, education, etc.

- *Density* this refers to the number of actual links in the network as a ratio of the total number of possible links. This dimension is also sometimes termed 'connectedness' (Tichy et al., 1979; Rogers and Kincaid, 1981). However, Boissevain (1974: 37) argues, 'It must be stressed . . . that network density is simply an index of the potential not of the actual flow of information' (i.e., it is a measure of network structure, not networking activity).

- *Openness* in the entrepreneurship literature, the distinction is often made between strong ties (e.g., with family, friends and close work colleagues) and weak ties (e.g., with business acquaintances). Strong ties are found in cliques and associated with dense networks (i.e., relationships with individuals who are also linked to each other), whereas weak ties connect to individuals outside of a clique and, thus, create 'openness' in the network (i.e., they are boundary-spanning relationships or links between different networks (Burt, 1992).

- *Stability* Tichy et al. (1979: 508) define this dimension as 'the degree to which a network pattern changes over time'. Auster (1990) expands on this, referring to both the frequency and magnitude of change of the actors and links in a given network.

19.4.6 Setting boundaries for network research

One of the key problems in undertaking a network study is determining its boundary, since this establishes the sample of actors and links under investigation. Mitchell (1969: 12) distinguishes between the 'total' network of a society – i.e., 'the general ever-ramifying, ever-reticulating set of linkages that stretches within and beyond the confines of any community or organisation' – and the 'partial' network the researcher abstracts from that total network.

This process of 'abstraction' (Scott, 1991) is problematic, since social networks have little regard for boundaries, whether defined by the network members themselves (e.g., teams, groups and organisations) or the network researcher. Thus, when undertaking or reviewing a network study, it is essential to be aware of the potential limitations of the sample of the study.

Network researchers may focus on either a group of individuals (e.g., a team of scientists within an organisation and the relationships of each of them, termed a 'sociocentred' network or the network of an individual termed an 'egocentred' network, since it centres on the relationships of a central or key individual, such as an entrepreneur, but not on the relationships between those he or she is linked to. See Figure 19.1 for an example of a 'network map' of an ego-centred network.

A network map is simply a graphic representation of a network (Conway and Steward, 1998: 223). A particularly useful feature is that it allows for the network to be tracked over time, so, different stages in the life of an entrepreneurial firm can be compared. An excellent example of this is provided by Blundel (2002), who studied the network evolution of two small regional cheesemaking firms in the UK.

Figure 19.1 James Dyson's social network

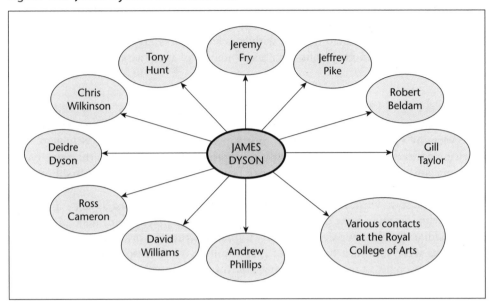

19.5 Retelling the Dyson story from a social network perspective

We believe that the Dyson case is important to the study of entrepreneurship for a number of reasons. First, James Dyson is an accomplished designer, innovator and entrepreneur and all of his entrepreneurial ventures – the Sea Truck, Ballbarrow and Dual cyclone vacuum cleaner – illustrate that creative thinkers can identify exceptional opportunities in very mature sectors.

Second, Dyson is, in some regards, a modern reincarnation of the traditional inventor-entrepreneur, as exemplified by Richard Arkwright, Robert Stephenson, James Watt and Isambard Kingdom Brunel. This role is such a feature of the UK's economic history (Mathias, 1969).

Third, the case highlights the importance of self-belief, persistence and sheer hard work in the creation of new businesses.

Fourth, and perhaps most importantly, the case illustrates the role played by informal or social networks in providing support, information and knowledge for even the most individualistic of entrepreneurs.

19.5.1 Case background and chronology of key events

After leaving school, where he studied humanities at A level, James Dyson first went on to art school in London, then later was accepted on to a Masters degree course in design at the Royal College of Art (RCA). He became particularly inspired by Buckminster Fuller – the American engineer dismissed by many as a 'dreamer' – and the great Victorian engineer Isambard Kingdom Brunel, who was responsible for many of the railways, steamships and bridges that symbolise the UK's industrial power.

Dyson's father had died when he was young and this, he believes, accounts for his own self-sufficiency and identification with 'external figures'. Dyson's subsequent business career can be roughly split into three major phases, which we shall address chronologically.

Phase 1: Rotork and the development of the Sea Truck

Whilst still a student at the RCA, James Dyson began to work for an entrepreneur named Jeremy Fry, who manufactured motorised valve actuators for pipelines.

Fry encouraged him to adopt a hands-on approach to design rather than one based on theory and this is an approach that has been the hallmark of Dyson's subsequent entrepreneurial ventures.

Dyson was soon working on one of his innovative ideas – the Sea Truck – and, over the following months, went on to build a prototype. He patented his idea and Fry set up a subsidiary of his company – Rotork – to manufacture the product. More than 250 Sea Trucks were sold at a turnover of many millions, but Dyson soon began to feel that he had been away from the drawing board for too long.

Phase 2: Kirk-Dyson and the development of the Ballbarrow

Whilst working for Rotork, Dyson and his family had moved from London to a 300-year-old farmhouse in the Cotswolds. Undertaking most of the rebuilding work himself, he became familiar with the failings of the traditional wheelbarrow: unstable when fully laden, tyres prone to puncture, liable to sink into soft ground and with a steel body that damaged doorframes and human limbs. He considered these problems for around a year before hitting upon the idea of reinventing the wheelbarrow by replacing the wheel with a ball.

It was at this point that Dyson decided to set up his own manufacturing company, which was to become Kirk-Dyson. Dyson's company launched the Ballbarrow and it soon became a commercial success. However, the idea was soon stolen by a US company and Kirk-Dyson lost the subsequent legal case. This failure led to tension between the Board members of the company, with the result that Dyson was voted out of the company by his business associates.

Phase 3: Dyson and the development of the Dual Cyclone vacuum cleaner

Undeterred, Dyson then decided to investigate why the performance of the household vacuum cleaner declined so rapidly after fitting a new dustbag. He found that only a thin layer of dust inside the bag would clog the pores and reduce performance to 'an enfeebled suck'. Experience with industrial cyclone technology provided Dyson with the idea for a cyclone vacuum cleaner.

Using an old vacuum cleaner, cardboard and industrial tape, Dyson spent one evening constructing a fully working model of the world's first bagless cleaner – the prototype for the Dual Cyclone.

After two years of trying to convince British and European companies of the Dual Cyclone's potential, Dyson decided to try the USA. Yet, despite the optimism and 'can-do' spirit of the USA, which he found refreshing after the negativity he had experienced in the UK, no company was willing to manufacture the Dual Cyclone.

In November 1984, after five years of trying to gain interest in the Dual Cyclone among European and US manufacturers, Dyson received an informal approach from a Japanese company, Apex, which agreed to produce the Dual Cyclone for the Japanese market under the G-Force brand name. He then, once again, turned to the US market and eventually set up a deal with Iona, a Canadian company, which agreed to produce the Dual Cyclone for the US market under the Drytech brand name. However, as the product was about to be launched on to the US market, Dyson discovered that Amway, a US company that had originally rejected the Dual Cyclone concept several years before, had unlawfully launched its own version.

Reluctantly, Dyson, once again, found himself involved in a long-running and extremely expensive legal battle with a US company.

In 1991, after almost five years of litigation, Amway agreed to a deal over its patent infringement and the haemorrhage of legal fees stopped.

Finally, in July 1993, 15 years after his original idea, the first DC01 Dual Cyclone vacuum cleaner rolled off Dyson's own assembly line and the innovation was successfully launched in the UK.

Dyson's social network and the development of the Sea Truck and the Ballbarrow business ventures (Phases 1 and 2)

Dyson's most significant and influential contact was Jeremy Fry, who inspired and supported his early ventures. While studying at the RCA, Dyson had met Joan Littlewood, the theatre and film impresario, who invited him to design a new theatre that she was planning to build. Dyson, operating under the influence of Buckminster Fuller, created a 'mushroom-shaped auditorium built of aluminium rods'. He sought financial support from British Aluminium and, during his first meeting, a manager suggested he contact Jeremy Fry, which was the start of a career-long relationship (Dyson, 1997: 47):

> I had shown Fry my model of the proposed theatre, and I think he rather liked it, if not enough to cover me with gold. What he *did* offer me, however, was to prove far more useful in the long run: work [at Rotork], and the first of many collaborations.

Having developed the Sea Truck at Rotork, Dyson describes his mistakes in attempting to market it by conveying a message that was too complicated for potential buyers. At the same time, he makes reference to the support of his wife in overcoming this problem (Dyson, 1997: 62):

> For each function Deidre designed a brochure, and they began to sell. And it all seemed so obvious: you simply cannot mix your messages when selling something new.

Dyson eventually left Rotork to set up his own company to manufacture and market the Ballbarrow, which he had been working on over the previous year. He once again acknowledges the considerable emotional support Deidre offered him when he first left Rotork to work for himself (Dyson, 1997: 78):

> I still marvel at Deidre's encouragement of me at that time. It could have meant losing everything. But she was always philosophical, and insisted that if everything failed she could paint pictures for money and I could make furniture.

Although he had made money from the Sea Truck he needed financial support to establish a company to manufacture the Ballbarrow. Perhaps not surprisingly, as with many entrepreneurs, he turned to his family (Dyson, 1997: 79–80):

> I went to see a lawyer friend of my brother-in-law . . . Andrew Phillips not only helped with the formation of the company, but fell in love with the Ballbarrow and persuaded said brother-in-law (Stuart Kirkwood) to invest in it. Stuart was the son of one Lord Kirkwood, former chairman of the mining company RTZ. He and his brother . . . as a result, inherited some family money. Which is always nice.

These contacts were fundamental to the setting up of Kirk-Dyson as they provided legal advice on forming the company and funding to develop the Ballbarrow and invest in production equipment. Even with this support, though, things did not progress smoothly and the new entrepreneurs had considerable difficulty in finding a market for their revolutionary barrow, but help was at hand (Dyson, 1997: 82):

> I had a friend called Gill Taylor whom I had met at Badminton and just so happened to have been Miss Great Britain in 1964. She was blond, attractive, curvaceous and a typical 'travel around the world and help people' beauty queen. She was also at a loose end and quite prepared to tour the garden centres of the West Country touting Ballbarrows.

Gradually, the partners managed to make the Ballbarrow a success and began considering ways in which they could expand the business. They wanted to increase output by acquiring a 'proper' factory and invest in some injection-moulding equipment. George Jackson, a local property developer, was approached and subsequently sold a third share in the company. Dyson does not explain how this particular contact was made, nor why he was judged to be an appropriate member of the Board (other than having the required £100,000). In addition, his social network was important in providing industrial expertise (Dyson, 1997: 87):

> I brought in an old friend of my father's, Robert Beldam, to have a bit of moral support on the Board. He was chairman of the CBI small companies section, and though his presence created a little, never expressed, resentment on the Board, having him there made me feel somewhat better.

Eventually, tension between Board members meant that James Dyson was voted off the Board and out of the Kirk-Dyson company.

Dyson's social network and the development of the Dual Cyclone business venture (Phase 3)

Following his departure from Kirk-Dyson, Dyson decided to concentrate his efforts on developing the Dual Cyclone vacuum cleaner. However, he needed finance to proceed and, thus, sought a partner to invest in the setting up of the 'Air Power Vacuum Cleaner Company' (Dyson, 1997: 120):

> Fry . . . was always likely to be my best hope. And so it proved. With £25,000 from Jeremy, and £25,000 from me, £18,000 of which I raised by selling the vegetable garden at Sycamore House and the rest borrowed with my home as security . . . I was in the vacuum cleaner business.

Dyson eventually built around 5000 prototypes over a three-year period and, by 1982, he had a Dual Cyclone that was 100 per cent efficient, but debts of more than £80,000.

He had also spent a considerable amount of time trying to persuade various European companies, including Hoover, Hotpoint, Electrolux, AEG and Zanussi, to manufacture his vacuum cleaner, but to no avail.

The Fry connection once again proved invaluable, as Rotork's chief executive, Tom Essie, was persuaded by Fry to provide further funding (Dyson, 1997: 138):

> Together we drew up a business plan for the production of an upright Dual-Cyclone vacuum cleaner, and the Rotork Board of directors, swayed presumably by Jeremy's dual involvement, approved it. We thrashed out an agreement that paid me £20,000 and gave me a 5 per cent royalty, and I went off to develop the vacuum cleaner.

Ultimately, Tom Essie was replaced by what Dyson describes as a 'money man' and Rotork did not proceed with manufacturing the Dual Cyclone. The company did, however, provide Dyson with financial support at a crucial time in the development of the Dual Cyclone.

A new opportunity was soon at hand. It was not only his extensive social network that proved of value to Dyson – serendipity also seemed to play a part in the story. A key element in the ultimate success of the Dual Cyclone was the deal he established with a Canadian company that took over responsibility for the North American market. The company was run by an Englishman (Dyson, 1997: 175):

> Jeffery Pike, with whom I had become friendly quite by chance after we sat next to each other on an aeroplane in May 1986, and both turned out to be reading the same novel by Fay Weldon. Having flunked English A level all those years before, my fortune looked as if it was about to be made by a novel.

In 1991, Dyson decided that he would set up production in the UK himself, but, once again, he was hampered by the lack of capital. As usual in times of crisis, he was able to make use of his extensive network as a way of resolving the problem (Dyson, 1997: 186):

> When I started with the Ballbarrow I had approached a man called David Williams, whose plastics company, WCB, built all our tooling and then recouped the money in instalments as we began to sell . . . He was now running a company called Linpak which, quite handily for me, was Britain's biggest plastic producer.

As plans for the manufacture of the Dual Cyclone in the UK progressed, Dyson was keen that it embody the very latest technological developments. By this time, he had a healthy stream of royalties from Japan and the USA, so could afford to hire designers from his alma mater (Dyson, 1997: 192):

> The team consisted of four design engineers straight out of the RCA – Simeon Jupp, Peter Gammack, Gareth Jones and Mark Bickenstaffe – all in their twenties, a marvellous bunch, whose presence made me feel as if I was freshly sprogged from the Royal College myself . . .

Even when Dyson's business venture was well-established, he still retained links with the RCA, which illustrates the importance of utilising long-standing social networks (Dyson, 1997: 239):

> Round about the time I was planning the DC02, I was at the RCA degree show – for I had since become an internal examiner on their product design course – and I went around offering one or two of the graduates jobs, as is my habitual wont.

The RCA connection continued to be of value to Dyson after the company became highly successful. By 1995, demand meant that he had to move out of the Chippenham factory because it had a limited capacity of 30,000 units per week (Dyson, 1997: 246):

> A fantastic new factory was designed for us by my old tutor Tony Hunt, and a whizzkid architect called Chris Wilkinson, but we expanded so fast that we had outgrown it before it was even built . . . Wilkinson and Hunt were back though in the Autumn of 1996, drawing up plans to treble the 90,000-square-foot factory space by extending over more of our 20-acre site.

By 1996, Dyson was considering ways in which he could extend into the increasingly global market for consumer products. After considering the attractions of Germany and France as the first step in his expansion, he eventually settled on Australia (Dyson, 1997: 252–3):

> I got a call from a man called Ross Cameron. Cameron was an Australian who had seen a presentation of mine at Johnson-Wax in Racine, Wisconsin. 'Why not start up in Australia?' I asked. A couple of days later Ross rang back to say 'OK'. He was that sort of man, not one to mess about.

Yet again, Dyson's social network proved to have a major impact on the direction and fortunes of his business venture.

19.5.2 Case summary

Through a 'retelling' of Dyson's autobiography *Against the Odds* (1997) from a social network perspective, we have sought to demonstrate that the creation of Dyson's various business ventures has been heavily dependent upon both family and friends (strong ties), as well as acquaintances and serendipitous meetings (weak ties). Dyson's large and diverse social network incorporates relationships that originated in various stages and facets of his life and career, many of which have been long-term and multiplex in nature.

We see from this case, for example, that Dyson's family and friends provided him with financial and knowledge-based resources that helped ensure he was able to turn his various novel ideas into successful business ventures. Of course, not all potential entrepreneurs will be fortunate enough to be able to call upon an ex-Miss Great Britain to sell their products or a senior member of the CBI to provide business expertise, but perhaps what distinguishes entrepreneurs is their ability to maintain and make use of their strong ties, as well as their effectiveness in initiating, nurturing and mobilising weaker ties. As this case illustrates, contacts made on aeroplanes and in business meetings and seminars can eventually become extremely important elements in business success.

The point of these examples is not to suggest that Dyson overemphasised the importance of his own contribution to the success of his various business ventures; rather, what we are trying to illustrate is that it is all to easy to attribute the success of entrepreneurial ventures to the sole efforts of the man or woman responsible for founding a new business. In Dyson's case, persistence, hard work and self-belief obviously made a massive contribution to his ultimate success. At the same time, it is important to recognise that, at crucial points in the Dyson story, his extensive and diverse social network provided him with considerable financial, legal, business and emotional support. Without these networks, it is unlikely that Dyson would have overcome what were, no doubt, formidable odds.

19.6 What has research told us about entrepreneurial networks?

Following seminal studies in the mid- to late 1980s, there has been an increasing interest in the social networks of entrepreneurs on the part of both academics and policymakers. Indeed, there now exists an extensive body of work concerning the social networks or capital of entrepreneurs. This academic research has sought to reveal the nature of the actors, relationships, flows and role of the entrepreneur's network, as well as its overall features – e.g., network size, diversity, membership, openness (incidence of weak ties) and stability.

Whilst a number of studies have been cross-sector (Birley, 1985; Conway, 1997; Greve and Salaff, 2003), research has also focused on a wide variety of business sectors – e.g., computing and IT (Saxenian, 1985, 1990; Collinson, 2000; Lechner and Dowling, 2003), wine (Brown and Butler, 1995), specialist cheesemaking (Blundel, 2002), business services (Chell and Baines, 2000) and oil (MacKinnon, Capman and Cumbers, 2004). This research has highlighted the importance of entrepreneurial networks across a broad range of business sectors.

Over the last decade or so, research has also indicated the importance of social networks to entrepreneurial activities in a wide range of countries, including the USA (Saxenian, 1985), UK (Shaw, 1998, 2006), Australia (Mohannak, 2007), Japan (Aldrich and Sakano, 1995), Singapore (Zhang, 2010), Greece (Dodd and Patra, (2002), Norway, Sweden and Italy (Greve and Salaff, 2003), Germany (Brüderl and Preisendörfer, 1998), Russia (Rehn and Taalas, 2004), Belgium (Donckels and Lambrecht, 1997), Slovakia (Copp and Ivy, 2001), Sri Lanka (Premaratne, 2001) and Taiwan (Lin and Zhang, 2005). However, these studies also reveal some degree of variation in the social networking patterns of entrepreneurs from different countries, which will be discussed in the following sections. Similarly, differences between the social networking patterns of female and male entrepreneurs (Aldrich, 1989; Aldrich, Reese and Dubini, 1989; Katz and Williams, 1997; Greve and Salaff, 2003; Neergaard, Shaw and Carter, 2005; Hampton, Cooper and McGowan, 2009; García and Carter, 2009; Klyver and Grant, 2010) and ethnic minority entrepreneurs (Zimmer and Aldrich, 1987; Gold, 1992; Dhaliwal, 1998; Peterson and Roquebert, 1993; Ram, 1994a; Smallbone, Berlotti and Ekanem et al., 2005; Deakins et al., 2007) will also be highlighted in the following discussion.

19.6.1 The size, diversity and stability of entrepreneurial networks

Several studies have sought to reveal the size and membership of the networks of entrepreneurs and small firms. Some of these have focused on specific activities, such as innovation (Rothwell, 1991; Conway, 1997; Freel, 2000), though most are more general in nature and look at the overall composition of the entrepreneurial network (Birley et al., 1991; Donckels and Lambrecht, 1997). What is common amongst the findings of such studies, is the importance of the diversity of actors within the network of the entrepreneur or small firm (Beesley and Rothwell, 1987; Dodgson, 1989; Conway, 1997; Shaw, 1998, 2006). This network diversity allows small firms to draw upon a range of external resources – e.g., technical knowledge, market information and finance – to supplement the internal resources of the organisation.

In the more general studies of entrepreneurial and small firm networks, the importance of family and friends has been highlighted, particularly during the early phase of entrepreneurial activity. However, as the enterprise evolves, the network grows and the entrepreneur increasingly develops and utilises more formal business relationships (Jarillo, 1989; Birley et al., 1991; Larson and Starr, 1993; Donckels and Lambrecht, 1997; Hite and Hesterly, 2001; Greve and Salaff, 2003; Hampton et al., 2009). This pattern is articulated clearly by Birley et al. (1991: 59), who note that:

> entrepreneurs, at an early stage of enterprise development, rely heavily on an informal network of friends, family members and social contacts from the local neighbourhood to gather relevant data. At a later stage, entrepreneurs rely increasingly on professional bankers, accountants, lawyers, suppliers, government agencies, etc. to gain access to requisite business information.

The diversity of the entrepreneurial network is highlighted by Conway (1997) in a study of the relationships mobilised in the development of a sample of successful technological innovations. The networks revealed were often found to be large, predominately informal, localised and diverse, stretching 'upstream' along the supply chain to suppliers, 'downstream' to various users and distributors and incorporating other individuals, such as university academics. Of particular importance to the innovation process were links with users and suppliers. The research also revealed that the 'egocentred' networks of entrepreneurs frequently plugged into a series of important and extensive 'secondary' networks (i.e., the networks of those to whom they were linked). These weak ties allow them to tap into knowledge, information and resources from a wider set of relationships than those with whom they are directly connected. Five broad categories of 'secondary' network were identified:

- *scientific and technical* these are organised around scientific or technological domains and include academic and corporate researchers
- *professional* these are comprised of individuals within a given profession – e.g., medicine or education – bound by 'professional ethics of cooperation'
- *users* these evolve with the end-users of a firm's products
- *friendship* this refers to the personal networks of individuals, based predominantly on friendship
- *recreation* this is a particular type of friendship network, the cohesion of which arises from the mutual sense of attachment to some recreational activity (e.g., sailing, mountaineering or rugby) where the feelings of challenge, achievement and comradeship through participation create and maintain personal bonds.

Research has also highlighted a number of factors that promote the geographical 'reach' of the network of an entrepreneur. For example, a study by Donckels and

Lambrecht (1997) revealed that highly educated entrepreneurs were significantly more likely to have personal networks that spanned national boundaries into the international arena and the bias towards local contacts in the network was lower for small businesses of more than ten employees and growth-orientated small firms.

In their critique of the literature, O'Donnell et al. (2001: 755) contended that many studies provide 'an overly static analysis' of the entrepreneur's network, leading to a 'snapshot' of the network structure at a single point in time. As a result, they argued for more longitudinal research, in order to deliver greater insight into the dynamic nature of entrepreneurial networks. In more recent years, there has been an increasing emphasis on addressing this issue. For example, Jack, Moult, Anderson and Dodd (2010) studied the network of a group of new entrepreneurs in North East Scotland over a six-year period and, as a result, were able to map the dynamic nature of the network and associated change processes overtime.

19.6.2 The nature of relationships in entrepreneurial networks

Research has also focused on the nature of the links between actors within entrepreneurial networks. A key distinction is made between informal or personal relationships and formal ones – e.g., joint ventures, licensing agreements and supply chain links with either suppliers or users.

The importance of informal or personal relationships, and the role of trust, has long been cited (Leonard-Barton, 1984; Birley, 1985; Dubini and Aldrich, 1991; Conway, 1997; Hampton et al., 2009). Informality would appear to play an important role in allowing entrepreneurs to resolve the apparent paradox raised earlier in this chapter: that while, on the one hand, the entrepreneur personifies individualism and independence, on the other, he or she is very dependent on ties of trust and cooperation.

Studies have also highlighted the different roles played by strong and weak ties within the entrepreneur's network. Strong ties – e.g., those with family and friends – are useful for providing knowledge, information, skills, finance and emotional support (Jack, 2005), whilst weak ties – e.g., those with business acquaintances, including customers and suppliers – can provide access to unique opportunities and resources by acting as 'brokers' with other actors and networks (Burt, 1992; Kirkels and Duysters, 2010).

In their study of the use of 'bootstrapping' techniques for obtaining resources (i.e., imaginative techniques for acquiring resources, such as speeding up invoicing, seeking advance payments, using a personal credit card, sharing or borrowing equipment and/or premises, etc.), Jones and Jayawarna (2010) found that strong ties were important for sharing resources, whilst weak ties were key for 'bootstrapping' financial resources.

Furthermore, the reliance of entrepreneurs on strong and weak ties varies during the different phases of the entrepreneurial process, with strong ties being more important during the start-up phase and weak ties becoming more important as the small firm grows and matures (Brüderl and Preisendörfer, 1998; Elfring and Hulsink, 2003, 2008; Smith and Lohrke, 2008).

Drawing upon past research, Hung (2006) posits a three-stage model of network development. In the first, 'preventure' stage, entrepreneurs rely on their social or interpersonal networks to provide resources. In the second, 'venture formation' stage, they seek to develop more formal interorganisational networks to supplement their interpersonal networks. Finally, in the third, 'venture development' stage, the interorganisational networks become increasingly important for the survival and growth of their ventures.

However, whilst there is evidence to support such a model (Hampton et al., 2009), there is also evidence to suggest that this development is more nuanced. For example, Johannisson and Peterson (1984: 3) argue that the individual links in entrepreneurs' social networks 'are multi-stranded involving unique syntheses of instrumental, affective [friendship] and moral [bonds]', in contrast to the bureaucratic desire 'to separate the strands and in particular to focus in on instrumental [bonds] only', whilst, for Freeman (1991: 503), 'behind every formal network, giving it the breath of life, are usually various informal networks . . . Personal relationships of trust and confidence . . . are important both at the formal and informal level.'

Indeed, in reviewing existing research concerning the evolution of the network relationships of entrepreneurs, Hite (2005: 116) notes that 'work-related ties may evolve . . . as social exchanges are layered over the business relationship' and Conway (1997), in his study of successful small firm innovations, found evidence that, whilst, in some cases, friendships emerged from formal relationships, in others, friendships spilled over into more formal joint projects.

19.6.3 The types of flow and interaction in entrepreneurial networks

We saw in the Dyson story that an extensive and diverse social network provided James Dyson with considerable financial, legal, business and emotional support. A number of studies have shown that such a diversity of flow through entrepreneurs' networks is important to successful entrepreneurial activity.

Birley (1985), for example, found that the social networks of entrepreneurs – incorporating family, friends and contacts – were more important than formal relationships in sourcing raw materials, equipment, premises, employees and finance. Equally, in her work on the networking behaviour of small service firms in the UK, Shaw (1998; 2006) highlights the variety of flow through their networks – e.g., information, advice, friendship and economic exchanges. She also found that each of these flows had an important impact on the innovation processes of these small service firms. Similarly, in his study of successful technological innovation by small entrepreneurial firms, Conway (1997) revealed the importance of a variety of flows, including technical knowledge and solutions, market information and prototype feedback, for example, from contacts in universities, suppliers, customers and even competitors. Studies have also shown that social networks play an important role in providing emotional support, especially in the early stages of the business venture (Ibarra, 1997; Hampton et al., 2009).

However, in a study of a 128 high-tech entrepreneurs in Singapore, Zhang (2010) reveals a number of problems associated with employing social networks to acquire such resources. He highlights 'information' problems (e.g., the limited information that is generally available through personal networks, the time taken in communicating and the lack of novelty that can characterise these often dense networks), 'influence' problems related to customers, due to the difficulty in 'leveraging the reputation or authority of referrers' (p. 353), and, constraints resulting from the 'social consensus discouraging business based on personal relationships' (p. 354) and, finally, what he terms 'solidarity' problems, associated with the possibility of harming relationships as a result of business failure, leading to a more conservative use of strong ties.

In their critique of the literature, Hoang and Antoncic (2003: 1977) argue that there remains 'considerable conceptual vagueness regarding the resources that are both rare and valuable to success, and how we measure the networks that provide those resources. Mapping networks of general information flows may be too far removed from resource flows more closely linked to an outcome such as business performance'. Recent research, such as that by Jones and Jayawarna (2010) mentioned above, has started to address this. Their investigation (2010: 127), for example, focuses on 'how social networks can help new ventures to acquire bootstrapped resources and how these resources influence business performance'. Their study reveals that the mobilisation of entrepreneurs' social networks to 'bootstrap' resources was found to enhance the performance of their businesses.

We noted earlier in this chapter that considerable effort is required to create, nurture and maintain network relationships. Indeed, research indicates the importance of 'active' modes of interaction – in particular, face-to-face interaction – in the development, nurturing and utilisation of entrepreneurial networks (Conway, 1997; Donckels and Lambrecht, 1997; Dodd and Patra, 2002). Research by Donckels and Lambrecht (1997), for example, found that the educational level of the entrepreneur and the growth-orientation of the firm can positively impact the use of certain forums of interaction (e.g., trade fairs and business seminars), whilst Conway (1997) noted that relationships with users, in particular, tended to be informal, with the principal mechanisms for interaction being customer site visits, chance meetings at exhibitions and contact over the phone.

19.6.4 The role of the entrepreneurial networks

The personal or social networks of entrepreneurs can be seen to play a number of important roles:

- they generate social support for the actions of the entrepreneur
- they help extend the strategic competence of the entrepreneur in response to opportunities and threats
- they supplement the often very limited resources of the entrepreneur, allowing the resolution of acute operating problems (Johannisson and Peterson, 1984).

For Donckels and Lambrecht (1997: 13), 'the fragility which accompanies small size can be offset by the supportive environment provided by resilient networks'. Thus, the function or role of the social network can range from the more general (e.g., supporting firm development or competence building), to the more specific (e.g., supporting the development of particular instances of innovation).

Entrepreneurial networks, new venture formation and survival

Johannisson (2000) argues that all start-up firms need an 'organising context' as a means of helping to structure exchanges within the broader environment. This context helps the entrepreneur cope with ambiguity, provides a shelter against uncertainty and aids with reactions to unexpected changes in the marketplace.

In this regard, entrepreneurial networks can be particularly important during the start-up phase of a new venture (Birley, 1985; Aldrich and Zimmer, 1986; Larson and Starr, 1993; Johannisson, 2000). With reference to university 'spin-outs', a particular type of new venture, Nicolaou and Birley (2003) argue that the nature of the networks of the key academics involved in the spin-out can have profound impacts on the future relationship between the new venture and the university and, hence, may be associated with different growth trajectories.

There is substantial evidence to indicate that entrepreneurial networks are also important to the growth of a firm, since they open up new opportunities and resources (Aldrich and Zimmer, 1986; Jarillo, 1989; Brown and Butler, 1995; Shaw, 1998; Chell and Baines, 2000; Hite and Hesterly, 2001; Lechner and Dowling, 2003; Hite, 2005). However, in her research on small service firms, Shaw (1998, 2006) reveals that social networks may play both positive *and* negative roles in the development of the firm, depending on network membership and the nature of what flows through the network. Specifically, it was found that the more heterogeneous or diverse the social network in which the small firm was embedded and the greater the variety of information and advice flowing through the network, the more positive the impact the social network was found to have on the firm's development.

In an interesting longitudinal study of two regional specialist cheesemakers in the UK, Blundel (2002) demonstrates how stable entrepreneurial networks may evolve to enable a firm to adapt to major changes in its environment – what he terms 'episodes'. We also see, as noted earlier, that the survival and growth of a new venture following formation is likely to require a shift from a reliance on social or interpersonal networks to an increasing dependence on more formal interorganisational networks (Hampton et al., 2009).

Entrepreneurial networks and the building of technological competence

Research has also highlighted the role that networks play in the building of technological competence within small firms. In their study of the influence of networks on new biotechnology firms in the UK and France, Estades and Ramani (1998) develop a typology of three technological competence trajectories:

- *competence 'widening'* a diversification of the technological competence of a firm
- *competence 'deepening'* an improvement of existing technological competencies of a firm
- *competence 'narrowing'* an abandoning of a set of existing projects, processes or products without the development of new technological competencies.

Estades and Ramani (1998) found that the decisive networks associated with the deepening or widening of technological competence in these small firms were scientific (i.e., those linking them to scientific communities) and interfirm networks (i.e., those linking them to large firms).

Entrepreneurial networks and the innovation process

The importance of networks to the innovation process has already been noted. This holds true for both small and large firms, although small firms are more reliant on such boundary-spanning networks to overcome internal resource constraints (Conway, 1994). However, the importance of the small firm network, and of particular actors within it, will vary depending on the task at hand (Conway, 1997; Freel, 2000, 2003; Mohannak, 2007). In his study of technological innovation in a cross-sector sample of small firms, introduced earlier, Conway (1994, 1997) distinguished between the nature and importance of the contribution of the network towards different stages or activities in the innovation process – i.e.:

- project stimuli
- concept definition
- idea-generation, regarding features and functionality of innovation
- technical problemsolving
- field-testing, prior to commercialisation.

Users were found to be a major source of inputs in the idea-generation phase and this was particularly evident during 're-innovation' – i.e., the modification of earlier models. In addition, users were also seen to represent a major source for the pre-commercialisation field-testing of the innovations. Field-tests were seen not only as an important test-bed for the technical performance of the innovations but also the suitability of the embodied features and functionality. The study also highlighted the key role played by suppliers in providing inputs into the technical solutions embodied in the commercialised innovations, sometimes developing critical components in response to specific requests from the small firm innovators. The cases in the study provide clear illustrations of both the 'complementary' and 'substitutive' nature of external sources of knowledge and technology in relation to indigenous innovative activity in small entrepreneurial firms.

However, other studies have shown marked sectoral differences in the degree of importance of networks to the innovation process. For example, in his study of small Sydney-based biotechnology firms and small Melbourne-based ICT firms, Mohannak (2007) found that, whilst the former regularly carried out R&D through collaboration and networking with universities, customers, suppliers and consultants, the latter relied primarily on in-house capability and expertise. Similarly, in his study of a large sample of small manufacturing firms in the UK (nearly 600 firms), Freel (2003: 766) found 'considerable sectoral variation, but also variation by innovation type'. With regard to innovation type, Freel (2003: 767) reveals, for example, that 'Novel innovators . . . are marked by the greater geographical reach of their innovation networks, whilst incremental product innovators appear to be more locally embedded' – a finding that, he argues, 'raises concerns over the appropriateness of cluster-driven network formation policies', such as the promotion of science parks.

19.6.5 Variations in entrepreneurial networks due to gender, ethnicity and nationality

Studies comparing the networks of entrepreneurs of different nationalities have suggested variations exist in their size and membership, as well as in patterns of networking activity.

In their study of US, Norwegian, Swedish and Italian entrepreneurs, for example, Greve and Salaff (2003) found that US entrepreneurs had the largest networks, followed by the Swedes and Italians, with the Norwegians having the smallest networks. They also found that US entrepreneurs had a significantly smaller proportion of family within their network compared to the other three nationalities in their study (6 per cent as compared to 22–25 per cent).

This complements earlier research by Leonard-Barton (1984), who found that US entrepreneurs were more likely to draw upon informal personal relationships, as opposed to more formal channels, than their Swedish counterparts.

Studies of Northern Irish entrepreneurs (Birley et al., 1991) and Greek entrepreneurs (Dodd and Patra, 2002) indicate that their social networks are relatively small, being similar in size to those of Italian entrepreneurs, although Dodd and Patra (2002) also found that Greek entrepreneurs had extremely extensive 'secondary' networks – i.e., they combined small yet strong circles of contacts with weak ties to the networks of others. Greek entrepreneurs also have a large percentage of family members in their networks, accounting for approximately a third (Dodd and Patra, 2002).

In comparing the networking activity of US, Norwegian, Swedish and Italian entrepreneurs, Greve and Salaff (2003) found that Italian entrepreneurs spent significantly more time both developing and maintaining their relationships, whilst Norwegian entrepreneurs were found to spend significantly less time maintaining their relationships.

Research by Dodd and Patra (2002) found that Greek entrepreneurs also spent substantial time developing and maintaining relationships – some 44 hours per week, which is much more than that spent by Italian entrepreneurs. They also found that roughly 40 per cent of this networking activity by Greek entrepreneurs occurred in a social setting, with roughly 40 per cent in a business office and 20 per cent over the phone. In sharp contrast, Japanese entrepreneurs reported very low levels of networking activity compared to other nationalities (Aldrich and Sakano, 1995).

The evidence regarding gender differences in network size, formality, membership, density and role is more mixed (Neergaard et al., 2005) and may vary for different countries. For example, Aldrich et al. (1989) found marked gender differences in networking activity and network density among US entrepreneurs (lower for females), whereas Cromie and Birley (1992) found far fewer differences in their study of entrepreneurs in Northern Ireland. In a more recent study of male and female entrepreneurs, García and Carter (2009) found little difference in resource mobilisation through their respective networks, although male entrepreneurs were able to gain greater contact referrals.

Greve and Salaff (2003) did, however, find some evidence that female entrepreneurs had slightly larger networks than their male counterparts and these often included a higher proportion of kin. This latter finding ties in with the contention of Renzulli et al. (2000), that female entrepreneurs often find it difficult to expand their networks into male-dominated business circles. Similarly, in their longitudinal, cross-national study (embracing 35 countries), Klyver and Grant (2010) found that those who personally knew an entrepreneur were more likely to be involved in entrepreneurial activity, but female entrepreneurs were less likely to be so acquainted. Hampton et al. (2009) have also revealed that female entrepreneurs found family commitments reduced the amount of time they had available for networking and confidence was sometimes a barrier to pursuing more mixed-gender, formal networks at the early stages of the new venture process. As a result, Hampton et al. (2009: 204) found that female entrepreneurs initially relied on all-female informal networks for '[addressing] feelings of isolation and boosting confidence', although, in the longer term, such networks were seen as 'holding less worth in assisting them to develop and grow their business'. Interestingly, Ibarra (1997) found that, in contrast to male entrepreneurs, who employed only one network, female entrepreneurs often employed two networks – one for friendship and emotional support, composed largely of females, and a second for advice and information, consisting largely of males. Such evidence suggests that female entrepreneurs would benefit from policies that encourage mentoring and/or promote female entrepreneurial role models (García and Carter, 2009; Klyver and Grant, 2010).

There is a well-established lineage of research concerning ethnic minority businesses. Within this literature, the importance of social networks to the success of small businesses has been firmly established.

However, in an extensive review of this literature, Menzies, Brenner and Filion (2003) were able to distil a more nuanced picture of the nature and role of such entrepreneurial networks. For example, they found that, whilst research has indicated many ethnic minority groups are characterised by entrepreneurs with high-density networks (e.g., Tunisians in France, Indians and Pakistanis in the USA and UK, Bangladeshis in the UK, Vietnamese, Chinese and Italian in Canada, Hong Kong, the UK and USA, Jewish and Korean in the USA and Canada, plus Iranian, Cuban, Haitian and Taiwanese in the USA), examples also exist of low-density networks (e.g., Vietnamese, Latino and African-Americans in the USA and Haitians in Canada) and the social networks of refugees are smaller than those of established immigrant groups (for a full summary of these studies, see Table 7.2 in Menzies et al., 2003: 135–40). Despite these differences, such networks were found to play a number of important roles, such as providing informal advice, support and mentoring.

This review also revealed, however, that reliance on such social capital was inversely related to the level of education and resources (including finance) at the disposal of the ethnic minority entrepreneur.

These key findings continue to be supported in more recent studies (Smallbone et al., 2005; Deakins et al., 2007), although Deakins et al. (2007: 320) note from their in-depth qualitative study that, 'Potentially the importance of social capital is both a help and a hindrance to EMB [ethnic minority business] owners. For example, there is no doubt that the ability to call upon sources of advice and the accumulated learning . . . is invaluable to new start EMB owners and even well-established owners . . . yet strong ties may be restrictive as well as being beneficial'.

19.7 Chapter summary

The study of entrepreneurship from a social network perspective is an important contribution to our understanding of entrepreneurial behaviour, supplementing more long-standing psychological approaches, which emphasise the sources of individual motivation (McLelland, 1961; Manimala, 1999), and economic theories, concentrating on the economic rationality of those starting their own businesses (Casson, 1982, 1990). Indeed, the contention of Aldrich and Zimmer (1986: 9) that 'comprehensive explanations of entrepreneurship must include the social context of [such] behaviour, especially the social relationships through which people obtain information, resources and social support', is now broadly accepted in the entrepreneurship literature.

For some, perhaps, the concept of networking takes us a step further; it helps us move away from the traditional view of entrepreneurs as resourceful individualists to an image of entrepreneurship as a collective phenomenon (Johannisson, 2000). We are, however, not suggesting that the motivation of individual entrepreneurs can be discounted in explaining the creation of new business ventures. Rather, we agree with Wickham (2006: 98) that the characteristics of successful entrepreneurs include hard work, self-starting, goal-setting, resilience, confidence, assertiveness and comfort with power.

It is certainly the case that James Dyson demonstrated all of these characteristics over a considerable amount of time. At the same time, we have illustrated how Dyson's entrepreneurial activities were heavily embedded in an extensive network of family, friends and casual acquaintances. Although, clearly, this network would not have developed in the way that it did without Dyson's ability (agency) to maintain and utilise existing strong ties while, at the same time, initiating, nurturing and mobilising a range of weaker ties.

Since the seminal work on entrepreneurial networks in the mid- to late 1980s by the likes of Howard Aldrich, Sue Birley, Dorothy Leonard-Barton and Bengt Johannisson, there has been an increasing interest and burgeoning body of empirical work in the area. This work has provided insights into the size, diversity, stability, membership and morphology of entrepreneurial networks and how these evolve over time. It has highlighted the range of important roles and functions for which it is nurtured and mobilised and informed us of the variety of the flows through the network, the mechanisms and forums for interaction and the often informal and multiplex nature of many of the network relationships. This empirical work has also highlighted differences in the nature and role of the network and networking activity between entrepreneurs of different nationalities, between male and female entrepreneurs and ethnic minority entrepreneurs. Importantly, more recent research has provided a more nuanced view of the role and nature of entrepreneurial networks and networking patterns, as well as revealing sectoral variations in the importance of such networks.

Questions

1 Why might entrepreneurship be considered a 'collective' phenomenon?

2 If entrepreneurship is to be considered a 'collective' phenomenon, what would you think are the key roles, skills and resources of entrepreneurs?

3 In what ways might an entrepreneur's social network be mobilised during the entrepreneurial process?

4 What characteristics of an entrepreneur's social network are likely to promote successful entrepreneurial activity.

Weblinks

www.unc.edu/~healdric
Homepage of Howard Aldrich, containing a range of articles and publications.

http://socialnetworks.org
Contains a range of references on social networking.

www.dyson.co.uk
The corporate website for James Dyson's company, with information on the entrepreneur himself, his products and his company.

CHAPTER 20

Finance and the small business

Robin Jarvis and Emmanouil Schizas

20.1 Introduction

The information available on how small firms are financed is limited because little is in the public domain. However, through a careful search of the literature a picture emerges that indicates small firms use different types of finance from large firms. Large firms benefit from established markets where they can raise funds. There are no similar markets for the vast majority of small firms. Therefore, the proportion of equity invested in small firms by third parties is much less than that of large companies. In general, small firms tend to rely on other types of financial products, such as bank loans, as well as credit from their suppliers, retained earnings and, often, the savings of owner-managers themselves.

The question of whether or not a finance gap exists for small firms has been examined and debated over many years and much has been written on the subject (OECD, 2006). Through government initiatives and the introduction of new products by financial institutions, much has been done to bridge any gap. However, many argue that a gap still exists, particularly for firms starting up or wishing to grow.

The influential variables in the capital structure decisions of large firms, such as the market values of debt and equity, are not available to small firms, as neither their debt nor their equity are tradeable in liquid markets. The markets in which small firms operate, their lifecycles, plus the preferences and desires of the owner(s) are influential.

The research also shows that there is an important link between small firms' annual reports and accounts and the supply of finance. A number of studies have identified that this information is used by the providers in their decisions to grant credit and monitor the firms' progress.

20.2 Learning objectives

This chapter has five learning objectives:

1 to understand the arguments as to whether or not a finance gap exists for small firms
2 to appreciate the types of finance used by small firms

3 to understand the reasons why small firms and large firms are financed differently

4 to recognise that capital structure theory is not influential when small firms make capital structure decisions

5 to appreciate the importance of small firms' annual reports and accounts to the providers of finance.

Key concepts
- finance gap ■ capital structure decision
- the separation of ownership and management
- the importance of annual reports to finance providers

20.3 Finance and the small firm

It is important, when examining the financing of small firms, to recognise that there are distinct differences between the financing of large, quoted companies and small firms. The majority of the literature relating to finance, however, focuses on large, quoted firms and, to a great extent, implies that it is relevant to small firms. This reflects the commonly held notion that small firms are only smaller versions of large firms.

From a financial–economic perspective, the main difference lies in the lack of capital markets where small firms can raise funds compared with their larger counterparts, which have access to established markets such as the London Stock Exchange. The differences, from a socio-economic perspective, are primarily associated with the relationship between the finance provider and the enterprise. In the case of small firms, the owners normally represent the enterprise in the capacity of both owner and manager. In large firms, which are invariably quoted companies, the relationship is between the providers of finance (the shareholders, who are the owners of the company) and the directors (the managers), who are invariably separate from the owners (shareholders). The significance of these differences will be a theme running throughout this chapter.

Although much has been written about the different types of finance employed by small businesses, only limited information is available on the extent to which each type is actually used. This is because, as previously mentioned, not all the information relating to the financing of small businesses is in the public domain. By contrast, information relating to the different types of finance used by large companies is publicly available from a variety of sources, including these companies' own annual reports and accounts.

The research and the surveys examining the financing of small firms should be interpreted with caution for two reasons. The first is that there is no universal definition of a 'small' business; the second is connected to the aggregation of the data. This is particularly important when examining how small businesses are financed because it is likely that the extent and source of funds will depend upon the size of a business. For example, small firms with a turnover of £50,000 are likely to have very different capital structures from small firms with a turnover of £1 million. Another important factor that tends to affect the type of finance employed by a small enterprise is the industrial sector in which it operates. For example, a firm that has tangible assets (e.g., land and buildings) that can be offered as security is likely to find it easier to obtain funds than is a firm in a sector the assets of which, in the main, are intangible in nature – e.g., an advertising firm's main assets will tend to be creative, reflecting the skills of the personnel it employs. These problems will result in reducing the validity of a comparative analysis between research and surveys.

This chapter begins by examining what is referred to as the 'finance gap'. This is followed by a review of the main sources of finance employed by small enterprises and an examination of the relative risk from the perspective of the providers of the finance and the owner-managers of the firms receiving the funds.

Next, the capital structure of small enterprises is examined and this focuses on the critical issue of the choice of financing the firm with equity only or with both equity and debt. This section looks at some theoretical models, followed by some evidence of practice.

Finally, the role of financial information is considered, with specific reference to financial reporting, and comparisons are made with the users and uses of large company financial reports.

20.4 The finance gap

The finance gap refers to a situation where a firm has profitable opportunities but there are no, or insufficient, funds (either from internal or external sources) to exploit those opportunities. In finance theory, this situation is known as hard capital rationing, as opposed to soft capital rationing, which, to a great extent, is a self-imposed restriction.

Hard capital rationing occurs when there is a mismatch between the supply and demand for finance from equity and debt sources. The term 'equity gap' is also commonly used and specifically refers to the gap between funds that can be profitably employed by the firm and the funds they are able to raise from equity markets or investors. Similarly, the inability to raise debt finance is commonly referred to as the debt gap. Clearly, if a gap in the funding of small businesses exists, it may seriously curtail the growth of such enterprises, which could adversely affect the economy. Not surprisingly, the subject has attracted much attention from government, policymakers and academia.

Historically, the existence of a finance gap was formally recognised 80 years ago. In 1931, the government-sponsored Macmillan Committee reported that the financing needs of small business were not well served by the then existing financial services institutions. The Committee, consisting of such eminent academics as John Maynard Keynes and politicians such as Ernest Bevin, illustrates the importance given to the subject of financing small firms by government in the 1930s. Since then, this criticism of financial institutions has been echoed by other important inquiries (Bolton Committee, 1971; Wilson Committee, 1979).

In response to this, successive governments have introduced a number of initiatives with varying success. For example, the Enterprise Finance Guarantee (formerly Small Firms Loan Guarantee) is a guarantee scheme for firms that can only offer limited security as collateral for bank loans (this scheme is examined in more detail in Section 20.5.3). In more recent years, financial services institutions have broadened their scope and, for commercial reasons, introduced new products that have made access to funds easier for smaller firms. It has been argued that if a finance gap still exists, it has been substantially narrowed because of these initiatives and other responses by the market since the 1930s (Deakins, 1996). However, others dispute this claim, on both empirical and theoretical grounds (Harrison and Mason, 1995). The following examines the nature of a gap and some of the evidence as to whether it exists or not and if it is a constraint on the financing of small enterprises.

In terms of equity capital, most small firms depend on the capital the owner or owners (and often their friends and family) put into the business at the start-up stage, together with a proportion of the profit retained to develop the business. There are very limited opportunities for small firms to raise funds in the equity markets. The main one is the Alternative Investment Market (AIM), but only a very small proportion of small business in the UK are eligible for listing. In addition, there is some evidence to suggest that a large proportion of owner-managers of small firms are reluctant to seek equity finance from external sources (Binks, Ennew and Reed, 1990b; Cowling, Samuels and Sugden, 1991). This reluctance is primarily due to owner-managers' desire to maintain their independence and control of their businesses (Keasey and Watson, 1993), although disproportionate listing costs and a lack of liquidity can put off even owner-managers who have no such preoccupations. AIM is discussed in Section 20.5.6.

In terms of debt finance (e.g., bank loans), financial institutions should assess the application for funds from small firms by applying the principle of a risk–return trade-off. Figure 20.1 illustrates the relationship between risk and return. Simply, the economic rationale of the principle dictates that the higher the risk, the higher the return that can be expected. With reference to Figure 20.1, point 'a' on the graph is the base rate and the gradient from points 'a' to 'b' represents the increase in interest

Figure 20.1 The relationship between risk and return

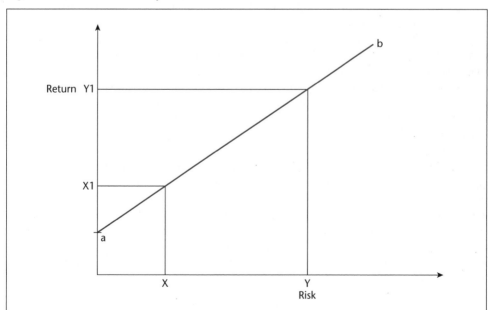

rates as the risk increases. The point X on the horizontal risk axis represents the risk associated with Firm X, while X1 indicates the interest rate (the return) relating to that level of risk. In contrast, point Y on the horizontal axis indicates the risk associated with the much riskier Firm Y and point Y1 on the vertical axis the interest rate related to this higher level of risk.

Risk is conventionally measured in terms of the variability in returns of a firm and, the greater the variability of the returns, the greater the risk and vice versa. The variability in a firm's returns and, thus, risk is a function of the type of business, structure of the industry and other similar business characteristics.

Whilst this explanation of the relationship between risk and return is blessed with sound economic logic and widely used when assessing large firms, it suffers from one major problem when applied to small firms – it is impossible to measure risk in a small firm with any reasonable accuracy. At first sight, this is not necessarily apparent because the word 'risk' in this context is very much a part of institutional financiers' rhetoric, whether referring to large or small firms. For example, the phrase 'well, it all depends upon the risk' is commonly heard from clearing bankers when considering business loans. The inability of financial institutions to measure risk and make some assessment of the debt interest that should be charged has resulted in the use of secured lending and crude credit-scoring systems to control exposure to risk.

Security is normally based on the assets of the borrower or a personal guarantee and the amount of security available is clearly a constraint on borrowing by small business owners. Banks also typically use credit scoring – a system of analysing information when making lending decisions. Points are allocated based on the characteristics of the applicant and the sum of the points is the credit score, which indicates the degree of risk associated with lending to that person or firm (Berry, Faulkner, Hughes and Jarvis, 1993a: 202).

Security and credit scoring both limit the extent to which small firms can borrow and, therefore, contribute to the finance gap.

On the whole, the small business sector is not as dependent on bank loans as is commonly thought. Most SMEs have no loans on their balance sheets and only a minority will seek finance in any given year. In fact, since 1997, bank deposits by small enterprises (note that banks use their own definitions for small and medium-sized business, which do not always match the official government definitions, but, in the UK, the British Bankers' Association/Bank of England convention is for businesses with less than £1 million of account turnover to be considered 'small' and businesses with less than £25 million of account turnover to be considered 'medium-sized', though, in practice, each bank applies its own thresholds for operational purposes, with the majority still setting the small business threshold at below £5 million (Capgemini et al., 2010)) have, with the exception of four quarters in 2008 and 2009, exceeded total lending (British Bankers' Association, 2011). Because of this, only a small number of SMEs will, at any given moment, report any difficulties accessing debt finance. Clearly, the demand for finance in general is disproportionately influenced by a small minority of firms, which makes aggregated figures for small business lending particularly misleading.

This conclusion can also be extended to other sources of finance: no more than 21 per cent of SMEs cited access to finance as one of their top three concerns at any point during the 2008–2009 recession and its aftermath (Open University, 2010). Between 2004 and 2007, the 12 per cent of SMEs that were consistently profitable, cash-positive and had plans to grow, generated 58 per cent (this figure is derived from a modelling exercise carried out by the Association of Chartered and Certified Accountants (ACCA) as part of its response to the Rowlands review of growth capital, the terms of reference of which were modelled against data from the BIS 2007 survey of SME finances, discussed in Cosh et al. (2008)) of the sector's total demand for finance (ACCA, 2010). This suggests that, in general, a so-called 'finance gap' does not exist for small firms. However, there is evidence that a number of groups and sectors, categorised within most definitions as small firms, face distinct challenges when accessing finance. Some of the firms subject to these challenges are discussed below.

It would appear a subset of small businesses that wish to grow have more acute financing problems because of their need for development finance (Buckland and Davis, 1995). The Wilson Committee, some 28 years ago, for example, recognised that the finance gap was a particular problem for such firms. Research shows that only those in a very small subset of the SME population have the potential to grow substantially – NESTA (2009) identifying a 'vital 6 per cent', Experian (2010)'s slightly different methodology identifying a tenth of the business population that constitute high-impact firms.

This subset of small, high-impact firms has long attracted attention (Buckland and Davis, 1995) because of their significant actual or perceived contribution to the economy, as well as the difficulties involved in financing them. Between 2004 and 2007, the 50,000 UK SMEs that were consistently profitable and cash-positive – and had plans for very strong growth – were unable to raise over 19 per cent of the finance they originally sought, against 5.4 per cent for the total SME population (ACCA, 2010).

A particular problem for policymakers wishing to support growth firms is the low levels of supply and take-up of equity capital (HM Treasury and Department for Business, Innovation and Skills, 2010). The problem is that businesses can only increase loan capital in proportion to assets held and the equity interest prevailing. Therefore, these firms are effectively constrained in accessing debt finance and the only way the firm can increase capital is through injections of equity.

In recognition of the difficulties faced by small enterprises, capital market institutions such as the AIM have emerged, while financial institutions have developed products collectively referred to as venture capital or even debt/equity hybrids called mezzanine finance. Venture capital normally takes the form of equity in high-risk small firms. These firms are characterised by high growth and are often in the high-tech industries, even though high-growth firms are not necessarily concentrated in this sector (Experian, 2010). Mezzanine products are aimed at established but growing firms with a similar risk profile, but are used by more risk-averse providers of finance because they are senior to common shares (i.e., creditors are paid before common shareholders in the event of default). Mezzanine finance is, however, still junior to the firm's other obligations, such as loans.

The shortage of start-up and early stage equity capital in general, not necessarily only in the case of growth firms, has also been cited as a particular problem for small enterprises (Robson Rhodes, 1984; ACOST, 1990). This often relates to an insufficient amount of start-up capital (the amount owner-managers initially invest in the enterprise) and, subsequently, this affects the ability to raise loan capital as well, as this is typically reserved for cash-positive businesses with an existing sales pipeline.

Women setting up in business have been identified as a particular group facing challenges in raising finance to get started. A study by Carter, Anderson and Shaw in 2001 indicated that women only use one-third of the funding compared to men when starting up in business. The reasons for this are not fully understood, but there is some evidence that women are active in less capital-intensive sectors (Minitti et al., 2005), and are less willing to take on debt or cede control to finance providers than men.

Female entrepreneurship is a key issue on the UK government's small business agenda. It has been claimed by successive UK governments (Brown, 2005) that, if women set up businesses at the same rate as men in the UK, there would be another 150,000 businesses created every year and, if women set up businesses at the same rate as they do in the USA, there would be another extra 750,000 businesses. Undercapitalisation at the start of the business' lifecycle may lead to long-term under-capitalisation problems and put women at a disadvantage in terms of being able to grow their businesses.

Another group that the evidence suggests is facing challenges in raising finance for start-ups are university graduates. The Global Entrepreneurship Monitor (GEM), 2001 (Reynolds et al., 2001) indicated that graduates are one of the most entrepreneurial groups of people and research shows that nearly half of undergraduates would consider setting up their own businesses after university. However, higher education can also discourage entrepreneurial graduates from starting up in business by increasing the earnings they can expect as employees. Moreover, average levels of student debt are burdensome and a constraint to raising finance. This is increasing year on year and had reached almost £25,000 per student by 2011 (Push, 2011). New graduates with significant levels of student debt may be more inclined to enter paid employment than start their own businesses. Lending institutions may not be able to provide funds to new graduates to start up in business, given their levels of debt. This could have a significant detrimental effect on the economy.

Much attention has been given to informal risk capital provided by investors – known as business angels – as a means of providing small amounts of equity to close the gap. A number of initiatives have been developed to make this form of finance more accessible. However, the main problem is one of matching potential investors with the firms that need the funds. Business angels are considered in more detail in the next section.

Research into the finance gap has also highlighted an 'information gap'. It is claimed that the reason small enterprises have problems raising finance is because owner-managers are insufficiently informed about funding opportunities, with regard to both equity and loan capital, plus the quality and cost of information, which can drive and sustain bank lending decisions (Bovaird, Hems and Tricker, 1995; Binks and Ennew, 1995). In more recent years, the information flows and advice available have improved substantially, with initiatives from the British Bankers Association and the growing amount of literature on the range of sources of finance available to small firms. That said, creditworthiness and investment-readiness among small businesses is still a matter of interest to finance providers and government policy alike.

It would appear that the evidence from research on whether or not there is a finance gap is inconclusive. However, the attention of successive governments to the problems faced by small businesses with regard to raising finance has resulted in a number of initiatives that have improved matters for some owner-managers. At the same time, financial institutions have developed a number of products that have increased the range of options for financing small enterprises.

20.5 Sources of finance

In this section, empirical evidence is drawn upon in order to provide an overview of the nature and usage of varying types of finance employed by small businesses. In so doing, we assume that usage is a reasonable surrogate for importance, although it is clear that businesses unable to source particular types of finance will resort to substitutes (ACCA and CBI, 2010). As already mentioned, the results of the surveys reviewed must be interpreted with care, due to the problems associated with the lack of a standard definition for what constitutes a 'small' business or an SME and other limitations of survey methods. The main sources of finance are reviewed.

20.5.1 Suppliers

Although rarely acknowledged as such, suppliers are the most important providers of short-term finance to SMEs. More than 80 per cent of all business-to-business sales are made on credit (Wilson and Summers, 2002; Paul and Wilson, 2006; Paul and Boden, 2008), allowing SMEs to tap suppliers for twice as much short-term credit as they obtain from banks (Wilson, 2008). Small- and medium-sized companies in the UK typically owe their suppliers an amount equal to 19 per cent of their total assets (Wilson, 2008). As of the second half of 2010, 24 per cent of UK SMEs were planning to tap their suppliers for additional credit in the coming year (ACCA and CBI, 2010; Forbes Insights, 2010).

On average, small- and medium-sized enterprises in the UK settle invoices 58–61 days after receipt (Wilson, 2008), which is typically the agreed limit plus half again (Intrum Justitia, 2010). Firms are more likely to extend credit to their SME suppliers if they themselves are cash-positive or have good access to finance and, therefore, act, in a way, as financial intermediaries (Garcia-Teruel and Martinez-Solano, 2010). In theory, suppliers can extend credit to their customers where a bank would not, because their commercial relationship gives them a greater amount of information on and control over the recipient than a bank would have. This means that a trade credit facility is less risky than an equivalent overdraft facility would have been. However, as suppliers are typically undercapitalised by the standards of a lending institution, the supply of trade credit is very sensitive to economic and liquidity conditions. Hughes, Cosh, Bullock and Milner (2009) found that fewer than 50 per cent of SMEs were able to obtain trade credit during the 2008 credit crunch, while ACCA and CBI (2010) reported a 91 per cent success rate in the 12 months to August/September 2010.

Late payment or payment outside of agreed credit terms is used by businesses to extract additional credit out of suppliers, as the trade credit equivalent of an unauthorised overdraft. Late payment is seen as a major problem by policymakers in Britain and abroad as it can directly endanger the survival of even the most productive and profitable firms. UK SMEs were collectively owed £24 billion in overdue payments in late 2009 and the amount they owed to their own suppliers is likely to have been in the same order of magnitude. However, despite being controversial and damaging to business relationships, late payment is so widespread that 17 per cent of businesses would readily admit to using it as a financing strategy in 2010 and 9 per cent intended to use it in 2011. Of those attempting late payment, 89 per cent were successful (ACCA and CBI, 2010).

20.5.2 Banks

The importance of bank lending as a primary source of small business finance is widely acknowledged (Berry, Faulkner, Hughes and Jarvis, 1993a; Keasey and Watson, 1993; Binks and Ennew, 1995; Cruickshank, 2000). British banks lent £66 billion to SMEs in 2010 (HM Treasury, 2011), of which 10 per cent went to small businesses, as defined by the banks (British Bankers' Association, 2011). Bullock, Cosh and Hughes (2007) estimate that bank lending accounted for over 55 per cent of all external finance used by SMEs in 2004 – down from an estimated 61 per cent of external finance in 1997–1999, but up significantly from 48 per cent in 1995–1997. SMEs' reliance on bank loans is not surprising as they are rarely able to access the capital markets for funding. Generally, reliance on lending will tend to fall after a recession or downturn and then rebound as the economy recovers. In later years, it appears that microenterprises contributed significantly to the recovery in SMEs' use of bank finance after 2001, suggesting their demand for and access to bank loans might be more strongly cyclical than that of other SMEs.

The pattern of bank lending to small firms has changed dramatically in recent years, even before the financial crisis of 2008 hit the UK. As of late 2010, 85 per cent of outstanding loans by the UK clearing banks were on a fixed-term basis, while just over 15 per cent were in the form of overdrafts (British Bankers' Association, 2011). This very low figure is the outcome of a steady fall in the share of overdrafts, from 58 per cent in late 1991 (ACCA SME Committee, 2008). An overdraft is a short-term loan that banks grant customers, giving them the right to overdraw their bank account by an agreed amount, and is normally repayable on demand.

The fallout from the recession of the early 1990s, when banks took substantial losses on small business overdrafts, set in motion a trend away from overdraft lending. Since then, however, successive sets of quantitative rules on capital requirements have made it increasingly costly for banks to make funds available on demand in this way, as a certain amount of capital needs to be set aside against these facilities even if the customer isn't using them. This trend has combined with the effects of the Brumark case (see Section 20.5.9, Factoring), which effectively turned much of what were hitherto secured overdrafts into unsecured ones. The 2008–2009 recession and its aftermath shifted this balance further by forcing banks to economise sharply on their capital.

The term of any loan should, ideally, be matched to the life of the investment for which the loan is required. For example, if finance is required to purchase a printing machine, the term of the loan, ideally, should match the commercial life of the machine. This ensures that monies generated from the use of the machine are available to repay the loan. The lives of the assets used by businesses to generate funds should be for periods commensurate with long- or medium-term loans that have fixed terms. If finance is required to fund working capital, however, a short-term loan – perhaps in the form of an overdraft – is likely to be more appropriate.

Although matching the term of the loan to the life of the investment makes commercial sense, this does not always take place in practice because time is associated with uncertainty and, therefore, risk. The longer the time period, the greater the uncertainty and the risk associated with predicting outcomes. This notion of uncertainty due to the passing of time is extremely relevant to the lending decision. The length of the loan – in terms of the period for repayment – will be strongly influenced by the other perceived risks associated with the applicant for the loan and the purpose of the loan. Therefore, in the case of riskier (but still acceptable) applications, the banker is likely to lend only for a short period, ignoring the matching principles relating to the life of the investment and the repayment period for the loan. Smaller businesses are generally perceived as being riskier than their larger counterparts and this generally leads banks to offer shorter-term loans to younger and smaller firms or businesses with which they have not worked very much in the past (Hernandez-Canovas and Koeter-Kant, 2008).

As UK banks and SMEs recovered from the recession of the early 1990s, criticism of past excesses in short-term lending and competitive pressures forced banks to extend longer-term loans to SMEs, while taking on more risk in the process (Bevan and Danbolt, 2000). Indeed, the provision of finance and other services offered by the clearing banks to small firms has been subject to much criticism since the early 1970s and has typically grown in response to credit crunches. As far back as 1979, the Wilson Committee concluded that bank managers tend to be overly cautious in their lending decisions, finding evidence of banks demanding a high level of security as collateral for loans, which constrained the financing of small firms in the economy. More recent research (Binks, Ennew and Reed, 1988, 1990b, 1993) provides evidence that banks have continued to demand high levels of security. Since the 2008–2009 recession hit, more evidence has emerged of lenders' increasing emphasis on collateral and guarantees, with lenders ranking these as the most important considerations in post-recession lending to SMEs and secured term loans emerging as the most commonly used type of credit in 2010 (International Federation of Accountants and *The Banker*, 2009; Forbes Insights, 2010).

Lenders and policymakers have sought to reduce the sector's reliance on security by introducing behavioural scoring and two loan guarantee schemes, which are examined in the following section. Behavioural scoring is a type of credit scoring that monitors customers' credit risk in the light of the activity in their bank accounts. This type of scoring is concerned with helping banks to decide specific terms for individual accounts, based on their risk assessment. For example, customers going into overdraft on their accounts without previous agreement with the bank is likely to go against those customers in terms of their future relationship with the bank. Most of the information banks use in their lending decisions is actually acquired internally in this manner (Capgemini et al., 2010). Despite these efforts, it seems that collateral never ceased to be a major consideration in successfully accessing finance (Graham, 2004b) and, with the growing uncertainty surrounding small business lending after the 2008 financial crisis, it has risen dramatically in importance (International Federation of Accountants and *The Banker*, 2009).

There has been a concern for many years regarding the lack of competition for bank lending to small firms in the UK, prompting a number of formal inquiries – most recently by the House of Commons Treasury Select Committee in 2011. In the large corporate lending market, the effects of deregulation created an open and competitive environment for UK clearers through competition from overseas financial institutions based in London (Berry, Citron and Jarvis, 1987). With the advent of the European internal market, as well as the number of overseas banks in the UK, there was an expectation that at least the European banks based in the UK would compete in the UK small business lending market, which would enhance competition.

However, only a very small proportion of these European banks managed to enter the small business market (Berry, Grant and Jarvis, 2003). The Competition Commission (CC) (2002) estimated that the big four UK clearers controlled 90 per cent of the SME market and, on the basis of this and other similar evidence, the CC introduced price controls in 2002 to reduce the dominance of the big four banks.

By 2007, these measures had been judged sufficiently successful, even though the share of the big four had only fallen to 85 per cent. Some commentators have suggested that such concentration levels are detrimental to competition, although empirical data also exists to suggest that bank consolidation is actually associated with better access to finance, as long as it doesn't interfere with relationship banking (Canton et al., 2010).

20.5.3 Loan guarantee schemes (EFG/SFLG)

The Small Firms Loan Guarantee scheme (SFLG) was originally introduced in 1981, based on a recommendation of the Wilson Committee of 1979 to address the high levels of security required of small enterprises as collateral for a loan. Famously, it helped companies such as Waterstones and the Body Shop get off the ground.

Loan guarantees are aimed at small firms that have a viable business proposal, but have tried and failed to obtain a conventional loan from a bank, either because of the lack of security or business track record or both. The provision by government to guarantee against the potential default by borrowers enables banks to reduce their exposure to risk and addresses market failure. Under the SFLG, the government would guarantee 75 per cent of the loan, with the remaining 25 per cent being taken on by the banks. The maximum amount of the loan was £250,000 for a maximum term of 10 years.

When the UK went into recession in late 2008, the government announced its intention to replace the SFLG with the Enterprise Finance Guarantee (EFG), which was eventually launched in January 2009. Unlike the SFLG, which mostly targeted start-ups and very small firms, the EFG was aimed at more established and larger firms and, therefore, allowed for a much higher upper loan threshold of £1 million. With subsequent revisions, it is intended to have enabled £2 billion-worth of loans by the end of 2011; subject to demand it will be kept in operation until 2015.

Guarantee schemes are intended to be in addition to normal commercial finance and are not available if a conventional loan can be obtained. Strictly speaking, it is impossible to *apply* for a guaranteed loan. Under the scheme, the applicant applies initially to a bank and, once the loan officer has decided that the applicant has a viable business proposal and is eligible for a loan under the scheme, the bank applies to the Department for Business, Innovation and Skills (BIS) for a guarantee.

The intention is for the scheme to be self-financing and a premium is charged on top of the normal interest rate to recover bad debts. The EFG premium currently stands at 2 per cent, which is higher than that of the old SFLG, while the main cost to the programme is defaults. The SFLG faced a very high level of defaults, though this fell gradually from 45 per cent in 1984–1998 to 26.1 per cent by 2006 (Cowling, 2010). The EFG, however, targeted much more established firms and, hence, the government has aimed at a 13 per cent default rate (Allinson et al., 2010).

As of mid-2010, awareness of the EFG among SMEs was reasonably high, at 43 per cent (ACCA and CBI, 2010), but less than a third of those aware of EFG were interested in it and the success rate of applications was low. Only about 1 per cent of SMEs were actually using the scheme (Forbes Insights, 2010). On reflection, it was widely felt that, although the scheme was well conceived and well designed, the government had failed to communicate its precise purpose and features or to manage expectations ahead of the launch (House of Commons Business and Enterprise Committee, 2009).

20.5.4 Leasing and hire purchase

Leasing and hire purchase (HP) are often considered together in surveys and, excluding equity, studies show that, after bank loans and overdrafts, leasing and HP represent the second most important source of finance to small firms. In this section, further evidence is considered with regard to the use of leasing and HP by small firms, the nature of leasing and HP and the main reasons for it being an attractive source of finance for small firms.

Leasing can be described as a form of renting. The ownership of the asset rests with the lessor, who allows the lessee the use of the asset for an agreed period. There are two types of lease: an operating lease and a finance lease.

Under an operating lease, the asset is leased for a period that is substantially shorter than its useful economic life. The responsibility, in this case, for servicing and maintenance normally rests with the lessor. Typically, equipment such as photocopiers, computers and cars are acquired by firms under operating leases. Such leases are very attractive to small businesses, not only because they are convenient but also, by leasing instead of buying, small firms can insure against the risk of future uncertainty as to the assets' values (e.g., changes in technology) as the risk is transferred to the lessor.

A finance lease is a lease that transfers substantially all the risks and rewards of ownership to the lessee. It is a contractual commitment to make a series of payments for the use of an asset over the majority of the assets' life, which, normally, cannot be cancelled. The lessee therefore acquires most of the economic value of the ownership, although the lessor retains the title. Finance leases are long-term and very similar, apart from the question of ownership, to purchasing an asset with a bank loan.

HP is a method of buying goods in which the purchaser takes possession of them as soon as an initial instalment of the price (known as the deposit) has been paid. Ownership of the goods passes to the purchaser when all the agreed number of subsequent instalments, which include an interest charge, have been made. The purchaser has the use of the goods over the period that he or she is making the payments and, as with leasing, benefits from being able to use the asset without incurring a large capital outlay. It is because of this similarity that HP and leasing are often grouped together when considering the sources of finance of firms, as in the studies discussed next.

Although now dated, research by Berry, Jarvis, Lipman and Macallan in 1990 gives good insight into the usage of leasing by small firms in the absence of any more recent study. In a survey of 90 small businesses, 70 per cent had some assets financed by leasing or HP, with 12 per cent of the total value of assets leased and 65 per cent acquired via HP. Of 238 different assets acquired by the sample businesses in a year, 45 per cent were financed by leasing or HP.

The sample comprised firms in printing, computer services and professional services and some significant variation was found in the relative importance of leasing compared with HP. In the printing industry, only 9 per cent of the total value of the assets was leased, whilst 77 per cent were acquired using HP. The main reason for this difference was because the assets acquired (in this case, printing machines) tended at the time to appreciate in value and there was a very active second-hand market for them. Therefore, printers preferred to use HP as a source of finance since the ownership of the asset eventually transferred to them. If firms in the printing industry are excluded from the analysis because of this particular preference for HP, the percentage of the value of the assets leased by the remaining sample would be just above 20 per cent.

The study demonstrated that the use made of leasing and HP was related to certain characteristics of both the business and the asset. The larger the size of the firm, the more likely it was to use both leasing *and* HP. The firms' past experiences of various sources of finance, in negative or positive terms, was also found to affect the firm's future preference for a particular source of finance. Of the sample firms, 21 per cent expressed negative attitudes towards leasing whilst only 4 per cent of the sample responded negatively to HP. Also, the type of asset was found to influence the type of finance used – e.g., assets such as photocopiers and cars have traditionally been marketed via leasing. Finally, the study found that the number of firms using leasing appears to increase with the upward growth rate of the firm, although the number using HP does not.

Previous research, which was mainly focused on large firms, indicates that the influence of tax is the most significant factor influencing the decision to lease. This relates to tax benefits via capital allowances, which are obtainable when using finance leases as opposed to operating leases (Drury and Braund, 1990). Interestingly, a study by Jarvis, Lipman, Macallan and Berry (1994) gathered the views of owner-managers of small firms on the perceived advantages of leasing and their findings showed that tax was *not* important in the leasing decision. They suggested that few owner-managers could undertake the complex tax computations necessary to establish the cost of leasing compared to other forms of finance. The main advantages to owner-managers in leasing were that it avoids a large capital outlay, it is cheaper, it helps cashflow and it is easier to arrange.

20.5.5 Equity

The term equity is used here to mean the finance contributed by the owner(s) of the enterprise. This definition ignores whether the enterprise is a company, partnership or sole trader. Although funds from business angels and venture capital could be included within this definition, these forms of finance are considered in detail separately.

Individuals starting a business normally need to invest a certain amount of their own money in the business, whether they are a sole trader, partnership or a company. After start-up, owners can choose whether to withdraw profits from the business or reinvest these funds. Funds retained in the business are another form of equity finance, which, together with start-up funds, are often referred to as internal equity. Finally, during the life of the business, owners may make further investments from their own personal funds to finance the business.

The amount of equity invested by the owners in the business depends on a number of factors, the most influential of which are the owners' wealth and the profitability of the business' activities. From a survey of small firms, Keasey and Watson (1992) estimated that internal equity contributed approximately 30 per cent of the capital structure. This suggests that the amount of equity contributed to the business after start-up from owners, and funds derived from the retention of profits, is relatively low compared to other sources of finance. Indeed, another survey (Cosh and Hughes, 1996) estimated that only 6 per cent comes from this source. The 2008–2009 financial crisis, however, may have done much more to shift business owners' attitudes by introducing a high degree of debt-aversion. Forbes Insights (2010) found that about 57 per cent of SMEs reinvested earnings into the business in 2010 and almost all of these (93 per cent) would continue to do so in the future. An ad hoc survey by Hiscox (2010) estimated that owner-managers provided their firms with £16 billion in capital out of their own savings in 2009, while both Hiscox (2010) and the ACCA and CBI (2010) estimate that additional owners' equity was used by about 20 per cent of SMEs in that year. Forbes Insights (2010) estimates this figure at 26 per cent. ACCA (2010) also suggests that small business' deposits have been used extensively to finance working capital in the recession.

Access to sources of equity other than that contributed by the original owners (external equity), is limited to formal venture capital and informal venture capital (business angels) and raising finance from the Alternative Investment Market (AIM). All of these sources will be discussed separately. However, it should be borne in mind that, as already mentioned, the overriding evidence is many owner-managers resist any form of external involvement and, therefore, do not seek external equity sources.

The extent of a small firm's overall funding generally depends on the owner-manager's wealth and the equity in the business. Other forms of finance, such as bank lending, normally depend on the security provided by the business. Such collateral usually takes the form of a charge on the firm's assets or the personal assets of the owner-manager or a combination of the two. The limitations of equity sources for small firms therefore constrain the assets acquired by the business and the wealth of the owner-manager further limits his or her ability to raise finance elsewhere. Binks (1990b) argues that this reliance on collateral effectively creates a 'debt gap'.

20.5.6 The Alternative Investment Market (AIM)

When AIM was established in 1995, Michael Heseltine (then President of the Board of Trade in the UK) said:

smaller and growing firms are critical to Britain's long term economic prosperity and that a market which will enable them to raise capital for investment and have their shares more widely traded can only help to strengthen this sector of the economy.

The support of the government was an important factor in the initial success of the market, but perhaps more so was the timing of its launch – in the middle of a bull market, when investors had been lured by easy profits made from sensational share price gains. For example, the shares of ViewInn were placed at 100p in December 1995 and in June 1996 were traded at 650p.

In the first 12 months of its existence, 162 companies obtained a listing on AIM and, by 1998, the number had grown to more than 260. This high volume of companies joining AIM in its short lifetime provided evidence, for most, of the need for an alternative market for small companies. However, during 1998, a series of companies crashed shortly after listing and then the end of the dotcom bubble came in 1999–2000.

These two developments put a dent in, but did not stop, AIM's growth trajectory. Prospective companies considering joining – in particular, computer and high-tech companies – are looking for a higher profile and a wider source of funds and not generally considering any alternatives (Burton, Helliar and Power, 2003). The number of AIM-listed companies peaked at 1694 in 2007 and has been falling since. It should be noted that most of the new funds raised on AIM so far were in the three peak-of-the-cycle years from 2005 to 2007 (London Stock Exchange, 2011).

Conditions for listing on AIM are that companies must have a nominated adviser, broker and reporting accountant in order to give investors some degree of reassurance about the quality of the company. Once listed, the company must appoint, and retain at all times, a nominated adviser and nominated broker. The nominated adviser is selected by the corporation from a register of firms approved by the Stock Exchange. The adviser and broker are required to ensure that the company has complied with the listing rules for AIM. The reporting accountant is required to ensure that the company complies with the rules regarding the publication of price-sensitive information and the quality of the interim and annual reports. A prospectus must be produced, but not necessarily a trading record.

Listings currently carry a fixed cost element of approximately £370,000, plus an additional 6.7 per cent of funds raised (AIM Advisers, 2011), and costs have been rising year on year as a share of proceeds since 2005 (Bates, 2010). Hence, it is generally claimed that AIM is suitable for companies wishing to raise between £1 and £50 million, particularly the larger small companies. That said, the AIM has been known to list firms with as little as £20,000 in tangible assets, only a single employee and no sales (Colombelli, 2009).

At this stage in its life, it would appear that AIM makes very little contribution to the overall funding of small enterprises in the UK. This is typical of lightly regulated specialist exchanges, which generally suffer from a lack of liquidity. This makes them unattractive to both institutional investors, who are relatively risk-averse, and entrepreneurs, who are afraid that they will not be able to obtain a fair valuation due to excess volatility in the stock price.

Overall, Demarigny (2010) calculates that Europe's exchanges direct more than 93 per cent of their liquidity to the top 7 per cent of listed companies by capitalisation.

20.5.7 Venture capital

Venture capital is finance provided to companies by specialist financial institutions. Venture capitalists tend to be very selective, concentrating on fairly risky investments, typically in the form of backing for entrepreneurs, financing a start-up or developing business or assisting a management buy-out (MBO) or management buy-in (MBI). Usually the venture capital is represented by a mixture of equity, loans and mezzanine finance. Mezzanine finance is usually provided by specialist institutions and is neither pure equity nor pure debt. It can take many different forms and can be secured or unsecured. It normally earns a higher rate of return than pure debt, but less than equity, yet carries higher risk than debt although less than equity. It is often used in the financing of MBOs. It is used for medium- to long-term investments where the venture capitalist is looking eventually for an exit route.

Venture capital has not, to this day, recovered from the exuberance of 1999–2000, when the dotcom bubble delivered quick exits (two to three years) and quadruple-digit returns for the top quartile of deals. Since then, the median return has not exceeded 34 per cent and the number of companies invested in has remained at less than half of what it was in 2000. Venture capitalists remain invested for around five years. However, investment was also hit hard by the 2008–2009 recession as a lack of funding and opportunities reduced the supply of venture capital by some 40 per cent. (Pierrakis, 2010). Forbes Insights (2010) found that approximately 3 per cent of SMEs used venture capital to finance their business in 2010.

Although much is written about venture capital as a major source of funds for small enterprises, the evidence is that the majority of firms receiving funds from this source are relatively large enterprises and venture capitalists are increasingly either abandoning early stage investment or relying on business angels (in 40 per cent of instances) to identify good investments (Pierrakis, 2010). The average investment of venture capitalists is £1 to £2 million and the smallest investment £100,000 and they typically remain invested for just under 6 years (Pierrakis, 2010). A large, and increasing, proportion of capital has been invested in MBOs. Although Murray (1995: 125) contends that venture capital 'represents a small but important part of the finance for new firm formation and industrial restructuring in both the UK and continental Europe', earlier in the same paper he graphically shows start-ups and other early stage finance as representing 6 per cent of UK venture capital investments, as opposed to MBO/MBI investments of over 50 per cent in 1991. The European Venture Capital Association (2010) stated that 70 per cent of all venture capital flows in 2010 went into MBO/MBI investments, with only 5 per cent in early stage companies.

Other more recent research has suggested (HM Treasury/SBS, 2003) that the reason for venture capital playing very little part in the financing of small enterprises is largely the high fixed transaction costs associated with the provision of small amounts of capital, a shortage of available exit routes and, historically, lower returns from early stage finance. In addition, there is also evidence that owner-managers of small businesses do not want equity for fear of diluting ownership and control (Bank of England, 2002).

In more recent years, a number of schemes have been introduced by the public sector to inject venture capital funds into the small business economy in an attempt to bridge the equity gap. These include the Enterprise Capital Funds (ECFs), Early Growth Funds (EGFs), Regional Venture Capital Funds (RVCFs) backed by Scottish Enterprise and Welsh Hybrid Funds, as well as the University Challenge Funds (UCFs), all of which are aimed roughly at the presumed 'equity gap' for firms looking to raise £0.5 to £2 million. Although only one in five SMEs is aware that there is a local publicly funded venture capital fund (Cosh et al., 2008), Pierrakis (2010) finds that public funds are involved in about 40 per cent of all venture capital deals and 56 per cent of all early stage deals – a trend that has mostly come about as conventional venture capitalists withdrew from early stage deals.

While it is difficult to reach a general conclusion relating to the performance of these funds, it is clear that they achieve exits less frequently but are more successful at attracting partners than conventional venture capitalists. As per the intentions of policymakers, they emphasise investment in technology, especially in low-tech regions (Munari and Toschi, 2010) and there is evidence that recipients of public venture capital would rarely have been able to obtain the same funds in other ways (North, Baldock and Ekanem, 2010). This suggests that the funds are a qualified success.

20.5.8 Business angels

Business angels are a source of informal venture capital that is distinct from 'love money' from friends and family. Mason and Harrison (2010: 1) define a business angel as:

> an individual, acting alone or in a formal or informal syndicate, who invests their own money directly in unquoted businesses in which there is no family connection in the hope of financial gain and who, after making the investment, takes an active involvement in the business, for example, as mentor, adviser or member of the Board.

Angel investment is 'informal' in the sense that it is individuals rather than financial institutions who invest venture capital in a more controlled environment. Although informal venture capital is well developed in the USA and could also be a significant source of finance in the UK, it has only been in the last ten years that it has attracted much attention from academics and policymakers (Mason and Harrison, 1992).

It has been argued (Harrison and Mason, 1995) that the use of informal venture capital provides an appropriate resolution for the new small business equity gap because it lowers the information and monitoring costs that are incurred in borrowing from external sources and there is less likelihood of owner–equity value dilution. Loans and other forms of finance from external sources normally involve the preparation of detailed credit reviews and the collection of information for formal reviews and monitoring of the progress of the enterprise. However, informal venture capitalists normally have prior knowledge of the industry, which is a crucial factor in their investment decision, and benefit from private disclosures that are both informal and more informative. Hence, angels are generally able to materially improve their chances of a profitable investment by carrying out a mere 20 hours or so of due diligence (Wiltbank, 2009). Business angels, additionally, seek a greater degree of direct control over the recipient business than other sources of capital and, in fact, often emphasise physical proximity precisely for this reason. Also, as they invest their own funds, they are generally able to take on extremely risky propositions for substantial returns: the average angel investment delivers an internal rate of return (IRR) of 22 per cent, but the majority of individual investments fail to ever turn a profit (Wiltbank, 2009).

Harrison and Mason (1995) claim that informal venture capitalists are more patient than other venture capitalists and willing to invest smaller amounts of capital in line with the needs of the owner-managers of small firms. As Wiltbank (2009) explains, business angels tend not to look for quick exit routes and typically invest approximately £42,000 each per deal for 3.6 years, often including a number of unforeseen investment rounds.

Business angels sometimes join together to become investment syndicates and, in such cases, the sums invested can be relatively large.

Collectively, business angels are thought to have invested £800 million to £1 billion per year in early stage companies in the UK in the heady days of 1999–2000, but investment has fallen since and suffered particularly in the adverse credit and economic environment of 2008–2009 – with only approximately £400 million thought to have been invested during the 2010/2011 tax year (Mason and Harrison, 2010).

The major problem associated with informal venture capital is that of matching investors with smaller firms seeking finance. For some time, the main way in which firms and business angels could find one another was through friends, family and business connections. In recognition of the importance of this source of income, formal networks started to form as early as the 1980s to aid this matching and provide some degree of due diligence for investors or even investment-readiness training for entrepreneurs. The British Business Angels Association (BBAA), while not representative of all the angel networks in the UK, nonetheless boasts 22 member networks around the UK. Networks appear to add value through their services, but, even so, only a small proportion of proposals are attractive to business angels – over 97 per cent of proposals are rejected (Mason and Harrison, 2010).

There is more detailed discussion of informal and formal venture capital and its role in the development of entrepreneurship and small firms in Chapter 19.

20.5.9 Factoring

Factoring is the purchase by a factor of the trade debts of a business, usually for immediate cash. The sales accounting functions are then provided by the factor who will manage the sales ledger and collection accounts, under terms agreed by the seller. The factor may agree to take the credit risk within certain limits or this risk may be retained by the seller. This source of finance is, to a certain extent, dependent upon the nature of the business (i.e., where the business has a reasonably high debtors balance). In the right circumstances, factoring can provide a significant source of finance on a continuing basis to firms.

The ACCA and CBI (2010) argue that credit management in small firms leaves much to be desired, overlooking valuable credit-scoring information and using severely dated information. Good credit management itself is, of course, a source of finance. Research shows that small firms in particular suffer from late payment and tend to have weak credit management. Factors employ specialist credit controllers and tend to use the state-of-the-art computer software, which enables them to manage efficiently the credit given to the customers of small firms. The effectiveness of factors in credit management is demonstrated by figures published by the Factors and Discounters Association (FDA) in 1995: the average waiting period for payment was 75 days; the factoring industry's own average was 58 days.

Factoring saw an increase in popularity in the past. For example, turnover in the factoring industry rose from £4.4 million in 1984 to £47.2 million in 1997. Use of factoring and invoice discounting was further boosted at the expense of overdraft lending in 2001 by the landmark 'Brumark' case heard by the House of Lords (and subsequently upheld by the courts in 2005), which established that banks could not claim a fixed charge over book debts if they allowed the borrower to use the proceeds from those debts as they pleased, effectively converting much of the existing overdraft lending from secured to unsecured.

Despite these trends, it would appear that only between 6 and 8 per cent of small- and medium-sized firms in the UK currently use factoring (Forbes Insights, 2010; ACCA and CBI, 2010), a figure unchanged since the late 1990s (Grant Thornton, 1998), and only about half of these facilities appear to be new ones (Cosh et al., 2008; IFF, 2010). In a survey of the perceptions of accountants, Berry and Simpson (1993) identified three main reasons why small- and medium-sized enterprises do not use factoring: the high cost, reduced customer relations and the issue of confidentiality. There is, however, very little independent evidence on the perceptions of owner-managers of small enterprises since much of the literature in this area tends to be anecdotal and speculative.

Invoice discounting is normally classified as a form of factoring, but it simply relates to the raising of finance from customers and excludes all the credit management functions that are normally associated with factoring. With invoice discounting, therefore, invoices are pledged to the finance house in return for an immediate payment of up to 90 per cent of the face value. It will then be the responsibility of the finance house to collect the debt.

Invoice discounting has grown significantly over the years and, as of late 2010, it provided just under £1.1 billion of finance for firms with an annual turnover of less than £1 million (Asset-based Finance Association 2011), a figure that has declined steadily since peaking in mid-2006. The typical facility appears to provide about £20,000 per month, although, once heavy users are considered, the average rises to £79,000 (Cosh et al., 2008).

20.5.10 Other sources of finance

As Section 20.5.1 on trade credit demonstrated, some of the most commonly used methods of financing businesses are not seen by researchers and policymakers as part of the mainstream of small business finance. One particularly important example is credit card debt: business credit cards were the most commonly used type of credit among UK SMEs in 2010 (Forbes Insights, 2010; IFF, 2010). Perhaps more importantly, 16 per cent of SMEs made use of the owners' or directors' personal credit cards – taking an expensive and risky route in order to bypass the bank's application process (Forbes Insights, 2010). For the most part, however, credit card debt is repaid immediately so is not really used to finance the business (ACCA, 2010), but a substantial and growing number of SMEs are resorting to this option. It is worth noting that demand for credit card debt has been unaffected by the financial crisis of 2008–2009 and the subsequent recession. If anything, it has increased, and is the element of demand that lenders are best at anticipating (Bank of England, 2011). In a similar vein, there is reason to believe that home equity was frequently used to finance businesses in the last decade – a hypothesis for which there is solid evidence in the USA (Schweitzer and Shane, 2010).

More importantly, there is a fairly large proportion of SMEs that make a point of not using external finance and resort instead to a range of internal financing techniques collectively known as 'bootstrapping'. These include not only retained earnings but also the use of personal savings and finance as described above, the use of trade credit and late payment, as well as shared use of assets and resources. The population of bootstrappers is not precisely known, but data from Forbes Insights (2010) suggests that about 10 per cent of UK SMEs did not seek any kind of finance in 2010, despite expecting to grow, and another 4 per cent sought more than 3 out of 6 types of finance identifiable as means of bootstrapping (personal savings, personal credit card, friends and family, trade credit, retained earnings and government guarantees).

20.6 The capital structure decision

Finance theory assumes that the firm is a vehicle for shareholders to maximise their wealth and ignores other stakeholders. Much of the finance literature also assumes there is a separation of ownership and the control of the entity by directors and managers. Therefore, it is not surprising that the main question, when deciding how the firm should be financed, is whether or not there is an optimal capital structure that will maximise the value of the firm and, hence, shareholders' wealth. To put it another way, does the way in which the firm is financed affect its value?

Traditionally, the starting point for examining the capital structure decision is the seminal paper by Modigliani and Miller (1958). They demonstrated that, assuming a perfect capital market with no information costs, the value of the firm is independent of its capital structure. Thus, there is no optimal capital structure, therefore the financing decision is irrelevant and the value of the firm is solely dependent upon firms' abilities to generate profits (cashflows) from operations. Their assumptions, importantly, include a world with no taxes.

Since this paper, a number of researchers have examined the effect on the capital structure decision by relaxing one or more of the market imperfections that Modigliani and Miller in their 1958 paper assumed did not exist (Ross, 1970; Myers, 1984). Perhaps the most influential research that did allow for one of these market imperfections was by Modigliani and Miller themselves in 1963, considering the effect of corporate and personal taxes on the capital structure decision.

Modigliani and Miller in this latter paper demonstrate that, when other things are held constant, firms with high tax rates should use more debt than firms with low rates, because the value of debt financing is tax deductibility vis-à-vis equity and the value of this benefit increases with the tax rate. Therefore, financing the firm using debt rather than equity implies that firms should obtain as much debt finance as possible. Clearly this does not happen in practice, primarily because of the countering effects of other market imperfections, such as insolvency. However, this is not to say that this tax effect is not influential to some extent on the overall capital structure decision.

Despite these developments in finance theory, it does not yet fully explain the different capital structures that firms adopt in practice, nor do we know how firms choose the debt, equity or hybrid securities they issue (Myers, 1984). Nevertheless, from a careful inspection of real-world market imperfections, we get a good idea of the factors that will affect the capital structure decision (Higson, 1993). Large firms have been the main focus of research on the capital structure decision (Michaelas, Chittenden and Poutziouris, 1996) and, thus, the literature relating to small firms' capital structure is less well developed and restricted to a few papers (Keasey and Watson, 1993).

Small firms, of course, are subject to very different financial economic and socio-economic structures from those of large firms. For example, as previously mentioned, there tends not to be a separation between ownership and control of firms and large firms are listed and quoted on markets. These are two significant characteristics of large firms that are not likely to influence the capital structure decision of small firms. Therefore, capital structure decision theory related to large firms has very limited applicability to small firms.

Norton (1990, 1991a and 1991b) is one of a few researchers who have examined the capital structure decision from the perspective of the small firm. In examining a number of market imperfections that, it is claimed, are influential in the capital structure decision of large firms, Norton argues that bankruptcy costs, agency costs and information asymmetries seem to have very little affect on small firms' capital structure decisions. He also highlights the importance of certain factors relating to the market the firm operates in and the preferences and desires of the owner(s). Small firms, Norton concludes, are less likely to have target debt ratios and there is a preference for using internal finance rather than external finance.

Michaelas, Chittenden and Poutziouris (1996) conducted a study of the financial and non-financial factors that determine the capital structure of small, privately owned firms. Their findings show that the lifecycle of a small firm is influential in determining its capital structure. When firms start up and as they grow, they use debt finance. However, as they mature, the reliance on debt declines. A positive relationship was found between gearing and the collateral value of the assets and this emphasises the importance of security in the banks' lending decisions.

The research also found that tax and bankruptcy costs were not influential in the decision making-process and no relationship was found between gearing levels and profitability, growth, risk and the level of debtors. Firms in different industrial sectors seem to differ in their capital structure preferences and it was found that economic conditions also had a bearing on their decisions in this area.

Research to date, from a small firms' perspective, does highlight that financial theory related to large firms – particularly that related to the theory of the capital structure decision – is not necessarily appropriate to smaller enterprises.

20.7 Financial reporting considerations

An important link between the sources of finance for a business, particularly for small firms, are the financial reports produced periodically by firms. These primarily give an account of the performance for a stated period – normally a year (an income statement) – and the financial position of the business on a stated date (the balance sheet).

The main use of published financial statements of small businesses that are companies is for assessing lending and credit risk (Stanga and Tiller, 1983; Berry, Faulkner, Hughes and Jarvis, 1993b; Berry, Grant and Jarvis, 2004; Roberts and Sian, 2006; Collis, 2008) . However, lenders, major suppliers and customers have the power to demand special-purpose financial statements that meet their own requirements rather than general-purpose statements, as reflected in published financial statements (Berry et al., 2004; Marriott, Collis and Marriott, 2006). Therefore, they are not solely reliant on the published accounts.

Table 20.1 identifies who normally receives a copy of the company's accounts (apart from shareholders and Companies House) and supports the conclusion that banks are important users of financial statements. It also shows that lenders and the tax authorities are the main non-statutory recipients.

Sole traders and partnerships are not required by statute to disclose such information, but may do so in order to satisfy the needs of creditors. In contrast, companies are required by statute to file annual accounts (whether or not they are seeking external finance) with the Registrar of Companies and give copies to their shareholders in companies where there is a separation of ownership and management.

In more recent years, it has been recognised that the needs of users of large, listed financial reports are growing complex and the information requirement with the financial reports have reflected this complexity. As a result, many jurisdictions have introduced accounting standards that set the framework for which transactions are reported in the financial reports specifically for small companies. In particular, in 2009, the International Accounting Standards Board (IASB) introduced IFRS for SMEs.

The findings of research into bankers' use of financial reports recognise that the use of financial information is dependent upon a number of contingent variables (Berry and Waring, 1995). An influential factor in the use of financial information is whether

Table 20.1 Users of financial statements

Recipients	Percentages of companies
The bank and other lenders	67
Tax authorities	50
Directors or other employees who are *not* shareholders	31
Major suppliers and trade creditors	12
Major customers	10
Credit-rating agencies	9
Industry regulators (e.g., FSA, CAA, ABTA)	5

N = 1294 (NB: more than one response was possible)

Source: Collis, 2008: 34

or not the applicant is currently a customer with the bank and the business in question is new or existing (Berry, Faulkner, Hughes and Jarvis, 1993b). For example, if the application is from an owner-manager of a new business, no financial reports would be available. There is also evidence that this user group can obtain additional information in support of figures in financial statements (e.g., management accounting information and valuation reports commissioned by the business). Banks are able to successfully demand this information because they are in a relatively powerful position within the relationship.

From a survey of directors' views on who the major users of SME financial reports are, suppliers (Collis, 2008), customers, competitors and credit-rating agencies were also identified as important users of small firms' financial reports.

A literature review by Jarvis (1996) identified that a study by Mitchell, Reid and Terry (1995) identified venture capitalists as users of financial reports in their investment decisions. The financial statement was seen as an important source of information in the process of making decisions. Research (Collis and Jarvis, 2000) provides evidence of owner-managers' use of financial reports.

It is clear that managers recognise the importance of financial statements to creditors of their businesses. In that context, it is likely that they, the owner-managers, will monitor the reports to ensure that everything looks all right regarding creditors, otherwise this may cause concern (Jarvis, 1996).

20.8 Chapter summary

This chapter has examined the types and sources of finance used by small firms and three important related issues: the finance gap, capital structure decision and financial reporting. Small firms use different types of finance than large firms. Large firms have established markets where they can publicly raise funds. There are no similar markets for the majority of small firms. The proportion of equity invested in small firms has lessened and there is more reliance on bank lending.

Over the years, the question as to whether a finance gap exists or not has been debated. Although any finance gap is never likely to completely disappear, through the introduction of government initiatives and new products by financial institutions, it has become much less of a constraint for the majority of firms.

Finance theory relating to the capital structure decision was found to be not wholly applicable to small firms. A significant influential variable is the lifecycle of small firms. When firms start up and as they grow, they tend to rely on debt, but when the firm matures, this reliance on debt declines. The amount of security available, however, restricts the extent to which the firm can obtain debt financing. The type of finance available to small firms has changed over time because of the changing economic environment, capital markets and government intervention. This was reflected on in the Section 20.5.

It was also argued that the capital structure decision for small firms was very different from that for large firms. Primarily, this was due to large listed companies trading on the capital markets, which subsequently results in the very different sources of finance used by small firms compared to large, listed companies.

Financial reports are an important source of information for financial institutions when making credit decisions and monitoring the client's progress. It was recognised, however, that the users of these reports and their needs differed if they were small firms.

Therefore, it is clear that, from a number of perspectives, the financing of small businesses differs significantly from the ways in which large firms are financed.

Questions

1 Are small enterprises constrained in their operations by a lack of finance?

2 Why do large companies use different types of finance from those used by small firms?

3 From a financial perspective, compare businesses where there is a separation between the owners and managers and the owner is also the manager.

4 What are the influential variables in the capital structure decision of businesses? Do they differ according to the size of the business (i.e., whether it is small or large)?

5 Small businesses invariably have higher gearing levels than large businesses. Discuss.

6 Why are the financial reports of small businesses used by banks when making lending decisions?

Weblinks

www.acca.co.uk/general/activities/library/small_business
The ACCA (Association of Chartered and Certified Accountants) site for small business policy and resources.

www.bankofengland.co.uk/publications/financeforsmallfirms
A range of reports, published by the Bank of England between 1991 and April 2004, that monitored the availability of finance to small- and medium-sized enterprises (SMEs) in the UK

www.bbaa.org.uk
The British Business Angels Association's website has lots of information about this source of funding.

www.evca.eu
The European Venture Capital Association undertakes a range of studies into areas such as venture capital, corporate entrepreneurship and management buyouts across the continent.

CHAPTER 21

Strategy and the small firm

Colm O'Gorman

21.1 Introduction

This chapter introduces the concepts of strategy and competitive advantage and their relationship to the management of small firms.

Small businesses face distinct strategic challenges. Many small firms are character-ised by low levels of profitability and limited managerial resources (Storey, 1994). The majority in developed economies operate in mature conventional industries (OECD, 1997a). Many of these industries are characterised by low barriers to entry, high rates of entry and high failure rates. In many of these industries, owner-managers pursue a 'me too' strategy. The cycle of 'me too' new start-ups results in low profitability and high failure rates for small businesses.

Small firms are also found in other contexts – e.g., new emerging sectors are often characterised by new small firms. These contexts present a different set of strategic challenges for the owner of a small firm, such as market and technological uncertainty. However, even in these contexts the small firm typically faces financial and manage-ment resource constraints.

Small size need not be a competitive disadvantage. Small size can increase the flexibility of the business in responding to customer requests and market changes (Stevenson and Gumpert, 1985), increase flexibility in terms of production systems (Fiegenbaum and Karnini, 1991) or price and lead to faster responses to changes in the market. Small firms may also be less risk-averse and more inclined to initiate competitive actions (Chen and Hambrick, 1995).

Given the differences between small and large businesses, it is important to consider strategy specifically in the context of the small firm. In reading this chapter you should ask yourself some of the following questions.

- What does strategy mean in the context of a small firm?
- Do the characteristics of the small firm impact how strategy is made?
- What strategies are associated with success?
- Is it realistic for the small business to define its strategy and strategic position?
- Should a small business have a formal strategy?

- Should a small firm 'plan' its strategy?
- What strategies should a small firm pursue?
- Can a small business reposition itself strategically?

In the first part of the chapter, we outline the strategymaking process in small businesses, highlighting the fact that this is a highly informal and ad hoc process in most small businesses. The advantages of a formal strategymaking process are discussed.

The second part of the chapter reviews research on the success strategies of small businesses. This review suggests that successful small businesses pursue 'focused' strategies and emphasise competitive advantages such as flexibility, fast response times and closeness to the customer. Innovation can also provide the small business with an important competitive advantage.

The chapter concludes by highlighting structural and the strategic weakness that impact the choice of strategy and the strategymaking processes of small businesses. These weaknesses make it difficult for the manager of the small business to develop a clear competitive advantage. One of the most significant structural characteristics of small businesses that influences the strategymaking process is the centrality of the owner-manager. Strategic weaknesses include the lack of financial and managerial resources, reliance on a small customer base and poor technological competence.

21.2 Learning objectives

This chapter has four learning objectives:

1 to appreciate the strategymaking process in small businesses
2 to recognise the importance of focused and differentiated strategies for small businesses
3 to understand the strategies that are associated with success in small businesses
4 to consider the strategic weaknesses of small businesses.

Key concepts
- strategy ■ competitive advantage ■ focus strategy
- the strategymaking process

21.3 What is strategy?

Strategy is about two questions: 'What business(es) should we be in?' and 'How do we compete in a given business?' (Hofer, 1975). Drucker (1977) referred to these two challenges in terms of effectiveness and efficiency. Efficiency means doing things right – ensuring that day-to-day operations are managed well; effectiveness is ensuring that the business is doing the right things – that the focus of the business is correct in the context of customers, competitors and industry trends. Efficiency ensures short-term survival by producing a profit from existing activities, while effectiveness ensures long-term survival by focusing the business on activities that will continue to produce profits in the future.

The essence of a good strategy is that it is feasible – i.e., it is consistent with the resources and skills of the business – it provides a clear competitive advantage and there is a 'fit' between the business and its external competitive environment (Rumelt, 1991).

The outcome of a strategy should be a clear competitive advantage. A competitive advantage is an advantage that is valued by customers and distinguishes the business from its competitors. The source of a competitive advantage can be conceptualised in terms of the strategic positioning of the business or its resources and skills. The positioning approach emphasises the need for the business to achieve 'fit' with the external environment. To develop a strategy, the business must have a clear understanding of its market and its competitors. The ongoing success of the business is dependent on the ability of the business to maintain the 'fit' between the business and the changing environmental context.

The resource-based perspective argues that the source of a competitive advantage is the resources and capabilities of the business (Barney, 1991). By developing or acquiring resources, the business can develop sustainable competitive advantages. Resources confer competitive advantage if they are hard to imitate, heterogeneous (i.e., different from the resources that other businesses have) and there is uncertainty as to their value. However, the value of resources can only be understood in the context of the market in which the business is operating and a particular moment in time.

Of particular advantage to firms is having what are referred to as superior core competences and capabilities (Prahalad and Hamel, 1990). Core competences and capabilities are areas of activities within the firm that deliver added value to customers or allow the firm to operate more efficiently. In the context of small firms, it is necessary to consider both superior competences and areas where the firm might have inferior competences and capabilities relative to competitors (Almor and Hashai, 2004).

The concept of strategy has different meanings in different contexts. Mintzberg (and Quinn, 1991) proposed that strategy can be defined in five different ways:

- as a plan
- as a ploy
- as a pattern
- as a position
- as a perspective.

Strategy as a plan refers to the intended actions that management has developed. When these plans refer to a specific decision, they can be described as ploys.

Mintzberg argues that not all strategies are planned, but, in many situations, they can be inferred from a pattern in a stream of decisions that management has made over time.

Strategy can also refer to the position that the business has adopted in the external environment. This position can be defined in terms of the market that the business serves and the position that competitors have adopted.

Finally, strategy can be conceptualised in terms of how a business perceives itself and its external environment – that is, in terms of the shared values and beliefs guiding the decisions made by the business.

21.4 Strategymaking in small businesses

How do owner-managers make strategic choices?

There is a strong relationship between the strategy pursued by a small firm and the experiences of the owner-manager. For example, where the firm competes – i.e., the initial opportunity pursued by the owner-manager – may be the result of the owner-manager's prior work experience (Shane, 2000). The strategy chosen by the owner-manager, then, most likely reflects his or her personal priorities and goals (Kisfalvi, 2002). These personal priorities are likely to be determined by the owner-manager's own life experiences, education, functional work experiences and prior work experiences (Schrader and Siegel, 2007). The influence of the entrepreneur on the choices a firm makes may last for long periods of time. The entrepreneur may place a lasting 'stamp' on the company that influences the choice of strategy, organisational culture and managerial behaviours within the firm (Mullins, 1996).

Bhide (1994) argues that new businesses typically lack a planned strategy. Strategy in the businesses he studied emerged over time, with entrepreneurs responding flexibly to customers' requirements. The businesses he studied typically faced significant capital constraints at start-up leading him to argue that, in the context of new firms, the key strategic challenge is the acquisition of resources. So, rather than focusing on market position and competitive advantage, Bhide suggests that the entrepreneur engages in creative ways of attracting resources and generating sales. He argues that this process is unplanned and is typically characterised by 'guesswork'.

In some new and small firms, strategymaking is characterised by improvisation (Baker, Miner and Eesley, 2003). Improvisation describes a process whereby strategy is developed as it is implemented – i.e., where design and execution of a strategy occur simultaneously. Small firms may also be characterised by bricolage, which is defined as 'making do with current resources, and creating new forms and order from tools and materials at hand' (Levi-Strauss, 1966). Baker et al. (2003) observed improvisation in many aspects of the venture-creation process, including the very founding of the new venture. Improvisation also occurs in established ventures, where day-to-day improvisation can lead to the emergence of new strategic positions (Baker et al., 2003).

During the initial creation of the new firm, Sarasvathy (2001, 2008) provides a distinction between two processes that describe how new firms come about, labelling them as effectuation and causation processes. A causation logic in the venture-creation process suggests that an entrepreneur 'takes a particular effect as given and focus on selecting between means to create that effect' (Sarasvathy, 2001: 245). This is the typical 'planning' approach, whereby the owner-manager identifies a goal and then seeks the resources needed to achieve this goal. In contrast, effectuation is defined as a process where an entrepreneur takes 'a set of means as given and focuses on selecting between possible effects that can be created with that set of means' (Sarasvathy 2001: 245).

Strategy is also influenced by who controls the firm. In the context of family-controlled businesses, it is argued that family pressures influence strategic choices. Family controlled businesses may seek to balance the needs of the family with the 'strategic' needs of the business.

One approach to developing a strategy is to engage in a formal planning process. However, there is evidence to suggest that formal and comprehensive planning systems are rare in small businesses. In many cases, the owner-manager may not formally articulate a business strategy or engage in any formal planning. The planning processes observed in most small businesses have been described as 'informal, unstructured, and sporadic' (Cohn and Lindberg, 1972) and as 'a passive search for alternatives' (Bracker, 1982). The structure of the small business and the centrality of the entrepreneur mean that all 'strategic planning' is typically concentrated on the owner-manager. The owner-manager may see no advantage in formalising the planning process that they use to develop the strategy of the business and often will, in fact, see disadvantages, such as the potential loss of control, secrecy and flexibility.

The reality of strategymaking and planning in the new venture context is that it is opportunistic and informal rather than formal. Founders analyse ideas parsimoniously and integrate analysis and implementation (Bhide, 1994). However, the lack of formal planning does not imply the absence of strategic thinking. Planning can be thought as any reflective activity that precedes the making of decisions (Foster, 1993). Strategy change in new and small businesses may reflect a process of experimentation (Nicholls-Nixon, Cooper and Woo, 2000). As such, the owner-manager seeks to determine the nature of the competitive environment and how best to compete in this environment by engaging in a process of trial-and-error learning.

21.4.1 The arguments in favour of adopting a formal planning system

While formal planning systems may be uncommon in small firms, there are some reasons for advocating that owner-managers engage in more systematic planning.

Planning is generally perceived as a crucial element in the survival of new and small businesses (Hisrich and Peters, 1992; Kinsella et al., 1993). Ensley (2006) argues that the capacity to engage in strategic debate is critical to a firm's performance as it allows management to understand the relative costs and benefits of strategic choices that focus on maintaining a consistent, long-term strategy, as compared to making short-run changes to strategy.

The models of planning suggested for small businesses have been adopted from the strategic management literature. However, small businesses differ from large businesses with regard to their planning needs and processes (Curtis, 1983). They generally do not have the resources to plan and purchase external advice and support, are very susceptible to small environmental changes and owner-managers may not have the necessary experience for managing all aspects of a small business and cannot devote a lot of time to consciously working through plans because of day-to-day pressures of work. A consequence of this is that owner-managers tend to take a shorter and more functional approach to planning.

The essential components of a successful planning process in a small business are that the owner-manager is central to the planning process, the owner-manager and, where relevant, managers have sufficient time to devote to the planning process and it is clear effective planning will only be possible if sufficient internal information is available. This means that an adequate financial recordkeeping and a financial control system should be in place in the business. Financial information must also be timely and accurate.

Business plans are essential if entrepreneurs are to acquire external financial support. By planning you increase your chances of success by choosing the right battlefield to suit your skills (Hay, Verdin and Williamson, 1993). Timmons (1994) argues that plans give a new business a results orientation that it would otherwise not have and force it to work smarter so goals can be attained in the most effective and efficient manner possible. Also, the process results in the consideration of alternatives that may not otherwise have been thought of, which allows planners to choose the optimum way of approaching a problem and, at the same time, it also makes them think ahead.

There are two main roles and uses of plans – as communication devices and aids to controlling the business' factors of production (Baker, Miner and Eesley, 1993; Mintzberg, 1994). The preparation of a business plan by an owner-manager is often seen as an exclusively external communications device. For some owner-managers, a plan is written merely to improve legitimacy and satisfy demands from external agencies in order to acquire funding (Frank, Plaschka and Roessl, 1989). A clear description of how the entrepreneur will exploit the business opportunity does indeed allow investors to decide whether or not the project is a worthwhile investment and what risk is attached to it.

The second role of a plan is as a control device. Plans provide benchmarks against which subsequent performance can be evaluated. This is particularly important in small businesses as the owner-manager's time tends to be consumed by day-to-day management issues. The benefits of formal planning for small businesses are the following.

- *Statement of goals and objectives* A formal planning system will require key managers and promoters to state the goals and objectives of the business. Essential to planning is the choice of a future direction, for, 'if you do not know where you are going, any road will take you there' (The Koran). By clearly specifying objectives, promoters and staff should be more focused in their daily work activities.

- *Efficient use of time* By engaging in a planning process, the owner-manager and, where appropriate, directors, managers and so on should improve how they use their management time. Planning should result in the identification and monitoring of a small number of key success factors.

- *Consideration of alternatives* A formal planning system allows the small business to explicitly consider alternatives for the development of the business. Smith (1999) argues that, for very small new firms (micro-businesses), a higher awareness by the owner of the threats the firm faces and the firm's own strengths leads to better initial performance. This may include addressing issues such as succession planning in family businesses.

- *Better internal management and staff development* By focusing on the future development of a business, a planning system should highlight its need for internal systems and processes and future staff and managerial requirements. The owner-manager should be able to develop these processes and systems in advance of them actually being needed. In many cases, the development of these internal systems and structures will facilitate the strategic development of the business.

- *Better financial management* Planning systems are closely tied to financial systems. In order to plan, a small business will need a basic financial system that provides timely information on current performance. This should improve the financial control of the business and result in improvements in decisionmaking.

21.4.2 Planning and financial performance

Within the literature on small businesses, research on planning has concentrated on establishing a link between planning and performance. Many researchers make the inference that the ultimate survival of a small business is dependent on the presence of formal planning activity (Bracker and Pearson, 1986). There is evidence that small business failure is linked to a lack of planning activity (Bracker and Pearson, 1986). However, this research on the significance and impact of planning in small businesses has proved to be inconclusive (Schwenk and Shrader, 1993; Cragg and King, 1988; Stone and Brush, 1996).

Schwenk and Shrader (1993) reviewed studies on the relationship between planning and financial performance and found conflicting results. In a comparative study between planners and non-planners, Cragg and King (1988) found no correlation between planning activities and financial performance. They also found a negative correlation between planning and the size of the sales and marketing team. Within this sample, however, younger firms performed better than older ones. Bracker and Pearson (1986) compared small, mature firms in terms of age, size and planning history. They concluded that level of sophistication of planning had a positive impact on financial performance, younger firms performed better than older firms and firms with a longer planning history performed better than those which had done less planning.

In many cases, the act of planning cannot necessarily be correlated with the success of a business venture (Robinson and Pearce, 1984). It is possible that the contribution of planning to new and small businesses cannot be measured quantitatively. Rather than compare planning and financial performance, a more useful measure of planning might be the amount of vicarious experience that the owner-manager acquires by undertaking the planning process. Planning helps focus owner-managers on their resources, market and product(s). In this way, it could be argued that the main contribution of planning to a business is an increased level of environmental awareness. Similarly, the absence of planning cannot be used as the sole explanation for business failure. In fact, it has been argued that a higher proportion of unsuccessful firms than successful ones coordinate written plans and performance, set goals and monitor goal achievement (Frank, Plaschka and Roessl, 1989).

21.4.3 Reasons for the absence of formal strategic planning

Research suggests that most new and small businesses do not plan (Curtis, 1983; Robinson and Pearce, 1984; Stratos Group, 1990; Bhide, 1994). In many cases, the structure of the small business is such that the owner-manager is intimately linked to all day-to-day activities. This allows the entrepreneur to control the direction of the business on a day-to-day basis. Where there is a planning process, it is often seen as a separate activity from this kind of management of the business rather than a tool for improving it.

There are several factors that inhibit the practice of planning in new and small businesses.

- *Clear sense of strategic direction/position* Most owner-managers have a clear sense of the strategic position and direction of their business, so do not feel that it is necessary to plan. Management activity is typically focused on striving to implement more effectively the strategy chosen at start-up.

- *Centrality of the owner-manager* The close proximity of the entrepreneur to environmental issues often makes objective judgement difficult.

- *Environmental context* Many small businesses operate in highly turbulent environments. Formal planning may be counterproductive, therefore, as it reduces the strategic flexibility of the business (Fredrickson and Mitchell, 1984; Chaffee, 1985).

- *Rigidity of formal systems* They often rely on their lack of rigidity and speed of response as a competitive strength and a formal planning system with tight financial controls may restrict its responsiveness. Once a plan is developed, there are so many links between issues and areas, one change can upset the whole plan. In addition, some goals are planned in 'lock step immutable order', which means that the entire plan can be ruined by one unexpected difficulty (Timmons, 1994).

- *Lack of time* The owner-manager is, typically, involved in the day-to-day management of the business and may not have enough time to invest in formal planning. Many owner-managers have to complete administrative and recordkeeping activities outside of work hours.

- *Lack of experience* Owner-managers typically have little formal management training and limited exposure to budgeting, controlling or planning systems.

- *Lack of openness* Owner-managers, typically, are sensitive about their business plans and the business' performance. They are slow to share this information and key decisions with staff or external advisers.

- *Fear of failure* The explicit statement of goals and objectives – an essential element in a planning process – may result in failure to achieve these goals and a sense of overall failure for the entrepreneur. By avoiding stating the goals and objectives of the business, the entrepreneur can avoid commitment to any one direction or goal.

21.5 Success strategies in small firms

The owner-manager must choose where to compete and then, given a particular environmental or industry context, how to compete (McDougall and Robinson, 1990). These choices have a significant and lasting effect on the organisation and its performance (Mintzberg and Waters, 1982; Quinn and Cameron, 1983). The choice of competitive strategy within a market determines the financial performance of the organisation. If the 'wrong' market is chosen, performance may be low, but most owner-managers of small businesses adopt a 'me too' or 'copycat' strategy, replicating what has been done before.

The performance of small firms can also be explained in terms of other factors, such as industry structure and the entrepreneurial orientation of their owner-managers. Industry structure impacts the success of new ventures and has a critical impact on the choice of strategy (Sandberg and Hofer, 1987). Periods of high-demand conditions – e.g., industry growth and industry maturity – offer better opportunities for small businesses than do periods of low demand, such as the emergent stage of the product lifecycle (Carroll and Delacroix, 1982; Romanelli, 1989). However, while market choice is a critical managerial decision, it is not a choice that is, or can be, subject to frequent change. The choice of environment is constrained by owner-managers' past experiences and previous choices, so is not an active decision variable (Eisenhardt and Schoonhoven, 1990).

Some research has argued that firms characterised by an 'entrepreneurial strategic orientation' have improved levels of performance (Covin and Slevin, 1991). An entrepreneurial strategic orientation means that the firm is more willing to innovate, more prepared to take risks and more proactive than its competitors. As such, entrepreneurial orientation captures aspects of the firm's decisionmaking styles, methods and processes (Wiklund and Shepherd, 2005).

More commonly, researchers focus on the strategic attributes of *successful* small businesses. Success is typically measured in terms of existing competitive position and the change in this position over time. Some research suggests that the ability to maintain a stable strategic focus over time is an advantage of smaller and family-controlled firms (Le Breton-Miller and Miller, 2006). However, this is balanced by the risk of strategic inertia, with the firm failing to respond to changing market needs. Measuring success in a small business context is inherently difficult, as success should be related to the owner-manager's objectives rather than measured in terms of competitive, financial or market success. Studies on the strategies pursued by small businesses typically focus on some measure of success in terms of these latter criteria rather than in terms of the owner-manager's personal definition of success.

21.5.1 Choosing 'where' to compete: a broad or narrow focus?

The small firm might choose to appeal to a narrow market niche, hoping to capture a relatively high market share within it, or compete by appealing to a broader range of customers. That is, the firm can choose to be a specialist or a generalist. The appeal of focusing on a narrow segment is that the small firm's resources can be targeted or concentrated and the firm can build a strong reputation and customer loyalty with this targeted customer base. The prescriptive advice from the strategy literature is typically that small businesses should focus on market niches – i.e., they should be specialists.

Porter (1985) argues that a focus strategy is most appropriate for smaller businesses. According to Porter, the business pursuing a focus strategy competes by selecting a segment or group of segments in its industry and tailoring its strategy to serving these segments to the exclusion of others. By optimising its strategy in the target segments, the business with a focus strategy achieves a competitive advantage, even though it does not possess a competitive advantage for the *whole* market.

Some research suggests small firms that focus achieve superior performance. For example, research studies of micro-breweries and local wineries suggest small firms that compete more narrowly are more successful than those which try to satisfy a broader market. Other research suggests that high-growth small businesses pursue market niche strategies. The essence of a market niche strategy in the context of many small businesses appears to be the avoidance of direct competition with both larger and smaller competitors. The evidence from the studies of fast-growth businesses in Ireland and the UK suggests that, despite attempts in the research to control for sector influences on growth by choosing 'matched pairs', high-growth companies rarely competed directly with low-growth companies (Kinsella and Mulvenna, 1993; Storey, 1994).

Research on low market share competitors has suggested a number of strategies that the smaller-share business can successfully employ. The most common conclusion of these studies is that the smaller business should avoid head-to-head competition by seeking out protected market niches (Buzzell and Wiersema, 1981; Cooper, Willard and Woo, 1986). Combined with this strategy of segmentation, the smaller-share competitor should seek to differentiate its product offering and deliver a high-quality product.

Studies of successful medium-sized companies have suggested that a market niche strategy is an important characteristic of these companies. Cavanagh and Clifford (1986: 10) concluded that 'most winning companies are leaders in market niches, often in markets they have created through innovation'. Research evidence from the UK suggests that market position is an important characteristic of fast-growth businesses (Solemn and Stiener, 1989; Macrae, 1991). This research suggests that, while the choice of overall sector may influence profitability and growth, the choice of specific market position is more important to the performance of an individual enterprise.

The empirical identification of a market niche strategy in small businesses is fraught with operational and definition difficulties. It is difficult for researchers to precisely define the product market a business is competing in. For example, how does a small food manufacturer producing speciality-frozen desserts for supermarkets define its product-market arena? Such a business could define its business very narrowly as 'a producer of premium frozen desserts for supermarkets' or broadly as 'a dessert producer'. The classification of its competitive strategy will be a function of the choice of business definition and, more importantly, this may broaden as the business seeks to grow and expand.

Neither Kalleberg and Leicht (1991) nor Westhead and Birley (1993) were able to provide conclusive evidence of market niche strategies among fast-growth small businesses in the UK. Biggadike (1976) compared the relative attractiveness of a niche strategy and an aggressive market share-seeking entry strategy and suggested that the latter is more appropriate for new ventures seeking to establish themselves. He suggested that the poor performance of many new ventures is the direct consequence of limiting market focus at the time of entry.

The dangers of pursuing a focus strategy are that the business may incorrectly identify a market niche. Unless the business gets a competitive advantage by focusing on the niche, then it should pursue a more broadly based strategy. An additional problem with pursuing a focused strategy is that the chosen market niche may be too small for the business to survive or may require that the small business becomes involved in export markets at a stage when they lack the resources to support these markets.

Rather than focusing on a market niche, the entrepreneur might try to gain a large share of the market. Some new businesses must pursue a broad entry strategy because of the large capital investment required at start-up. These businesses are only viable if they achieve high utilisation of their large capital investment.

The advantage of a broad market strategy is that if the business is successful, it will be on a large scale. Additionally, a broad strategy might be more attractive to distributors, retailers or consumers. It suggests that there will be continuity in the business and it might include a more comprehensive service for the customer.

Most new businesses do not have the resources to pursue such a strategy and, therefore, start on a small scale. Despite inconclusive empirical evidence, the prevailing wisdom in the strategy literature is that small businesses should indeed optimise the use of their limited resources by competing in a limited market niche. In the literature on small businesses, too, the prescriptive advice is that the best way to avoid direct competition with larger competitors is to pursue a niche strategy (Vesper, 1990).

21.5.2 Choosing 'how' to compete: cost or differentiation

Having chosen *what* market to compete in, the small firm must choose *how* it is going to compete within it. Porter (1985) identified two types of competitive advantage, which he termed cost leadership and differentiation. Based on these two advantages and the competitive scope of the business, which he classified as either industrywide or focused, he developed three generic competitive strategies – namely cost leadership, differentiation and focus. According to Porter, businesses must choose one of these generic strategies. Failure to do so results in below-average profitability.

Research suggests that a differentiation strategy is the most appropriate strategy for small businesses. The limited resources of small businesses suggest that the owner-manager should focus resources and pursue a differentiation strategy. A large number of firms pursuing a variety of differentiation strategies may be successful in the same environment (Porter, 1980; Eisenhardt and Schoonhoven, 1990; McDougall and Robinson, 1990).

Product quality was the most important competitive advantage identified by SMEs across a number of European countries (Bamberger, 1989). In addition, factors such as reliability of delivery, reputation of firm and the competence of the workforce were ranked as important competitive advantages. Interestingly, pricing factors were only rated 16 out of the 26 factors important to the development of competitive advantage. New ventures pursuing undifferentiated strategies performed less well than new ventures pursuing differentiated strategies (Sandberg and Hofer, 1987).

There are many ways in which a business may offer a better product or service. These include superior product or service performance, faster delivery service, better location, wider product range, personal advice and after-sales service, longer credit terms, more flexible service, personalised attention, etc. It is important that the entrepreneur tries to maximise the number and extent of advantages the product or service has. This strategy is often not successful because the 'better' service or product that the business is offering is not of value to customers. Another reason why this strategy is unsuccessful is because the small business fails to communicate its better service or product to its customers. This may be because of the financial investment and time required for promotion, advertising and sales support – activities and areas of expenditure that most small businesses consider a luxury.

Porter (1985) proposes that a business differentiates itself from competitors by being unique at something of value to buyers. To be sustainable, a business' differentiation must perform unique activities that impact customers' purchasing criteria. To this end, Porter (1985: 152) identifies several methods that a business can employ to enhance its differentiation:

- enhance its sources of uniqueness
- make the cost of differentiation an advantage

- change the rules of competition to create uniqueness
- reconfigure the value chain to be unique in entirely new ways.

Intuitively, most owner-managers believe that a low-cost strategy will be successful – customers *should* be willing to pay *less* for the same product or service. However, this strategy is not that easy to pursue and many owner-managers fail to do so successfully, so their business performs poorly.

To pursue a low-priced strategy, the new business should have a lower cost base than its competitors. Many small businesses pursue this strategy of lower costs by ensuring that they have lower overheads, operating outside the tax system or using low-cost labour and not costing their own time at the market rate. The danger with this approach is that the entrepreneur may not have identified all the overheads that the business will incur and, as the business develops, these overheads will increase.

The advantage of a low-price strategy is that the new business should be able to attract customers. Lower prices should encourage customers to try the new business and may encourage new customers into the business. However, this does not always work for small businesses. Often, the net effect of lower prices is lower profits for the entrepreneur rather than increased sales. There are several reasons for this strategy not working for the small business. The first is that, for many products, the price charged is assumed by customers to be a reflection of its quality. So, customers may interpret low prices as a sign of lower-quality service rather than the supplier is more efficient than its competitors. To overcome this, it might be necessary for the entrepreneur to inform customers *why* the products are cheaper – e.g., 'they are cheaper because we buy direct from the factory'.

The second reason for this strategy not working is that the owner-manager fails to invest in promotion and advertising. The owner-manager may incorrectly assume that a low-cost strategy means *not* investing in marketing and selling costs. The net effect of this is that the customer is unaware of the lower-cost alternative and the new business remains small. Indeed, many small businesses fail to generate revenues to invest in advertising and promotion because of their low prices and low turnover.

21.5.3 Operational strategy: efficiency or flexibility

Strategy in small firms can also be considered in terms of efficiency and flexibility (Ebben and Johnson, 2005). A firm may choose to compete on efficiency by producing its products in a standard format or in terms of flexibility by producing products to customers' requirements. As noted above, the flexibility to respond to customers' requirements can be an advantage smaller firms have relative to larger ones. A firm that seeks to compete with operational flexibility will, typically, have general-purpose equipment and utilise unit or small batch production with skilled labour.

In contrast to competing on flexibility, the small firm seeking to compete on efficiency focuses on producing a standardised product. These firms will, typically, have specialised equipment, and utilise long production runs with lower-skilled direct labour.

This categorisation of strategy is different from Porter's categorisation discussed above. While efficiency and flexibility might appear to be the same as low cost and differentiation, the focus in the former is on the operational strategy of the firm. So, for example, a firm producing a standardised product can still seek to differentiate this in the market through marketing activities, payment options, etc.

Do small firms that pursue flexible strategies outperform those using efficiency strategies? Ebben and Johnson (2005) do not find performance advantages for either of these two 'pure' operational strategies. However, they find that when small firms combine these strategies, performance is lower. That is, a strategy based on either efficiency *or* flexibility is associated with higher performance. Why, then, might a firm mix these strategies? Often, smaller firms have to pursue flexible strategies to attract customers (Bhide, 2000). As they grow, they might be drawn to seek increased efficiencies by standardising production. However, small firms attempting to pursue an efficiency strategy based on standardised products may decide to respond to customers' demands for greater product variety in an attempt to increase sales volumes.

21.5.4 Innovation as a source of advantage

Within the literature on innovation, researchers have sought to establish a relationship between business size and the level of innovation. An alternative perspective is to compare the level of innovation with business profitability, growth and survival. To the extent that this has been done – mostly indirectly by studies examining the characteristics of better-performing companies in a particular size/industry sector – it appears that there is a relationship between better performance and a higher levels of innovation. Scherer (1980: 422) concluded:

> what we find . . . is a kind of threshold effect. A little bit of bigness – up to sales levels of $250 million to $400 million at 1978 price levels – is good for invention and innovation. But beyond the threshold further bigness adds little or nothing, and it carries with it the danger of diminishing the effectiveness of inventive and innovative performance.

Innovation may manifest itself in terms of the introduction of new products. Research suggests that the ability to introduce new products is positively related to performance in small businesses (Woo et al., 1989; Cambridge Small Business Research Centre, 1992; Kinsella et al., 1993; Wynarczyki et al., 1993; Murray and O'Gorman, 1994). Other evidence suggests those businesses that are technically more sophisticated or technologically more innovative are likely to grow faster than those which are not (Boeker, 1989; Phillips and Kirchhoff, 1989). However, it may be that these technically more sophisticated sectors are experiencing faster growth than other sectors.

Buzzell and Wiersema (1981) used the PIMS database to test what strategies were characteristic of businesses that were increasing their market share position. They found that the strategic factors generally involved in market share gains included increases in new product activity, relative product quality and sales promotion, relative to the growth rate of the served market.

Small businesses face a number of disadvantages in trying to be innovative. Most small businesses lack the financial, technical and human resources needed. The lack of time owner-managers have for long-term thinking prevents the development of both technical and market-led innovations. The absence of a marketing function and marketing expertise restricts the development of customer-driven innovations.

Even those small businesses that are technologically competent (e.g., small engineering or software firms) face problems in the management of technology. The competitive strength of these small businesses, their specialist technical knowledge, exposes them to the possibility of technical developments outside their area of expertise. This problem is particularly apparent in sectors where developments have been driven by the fusion of two or more existing technologies. The small business typically does not have the expertise or the financial resources to cope with external developments.

The solution to this problem often is to cooperate with other businesses or universities or technical institutes. However, small businesses are reluctant to cooperate with other businesses. While universities may provide technical assistance, they seldom provide access to investment and, therefore, can only partially solve the problems facing the small business.

Should small firms seeking to pursue a strategy based on innovation formalise their innovation strategy and structures? While it is argued above that flexibility and informality may be an advantage for some small firms competing in small niche markets, Bessant and Tidd (2007) have argued that there are advantages to small firms doing exactly that. Terziovski (2010) argues that small manufacturing firms in Australia would benefit from replicating the approach of larger firms and formalising their approach to innovation. This, they argue, is particularly important if the firm is competing in a mature market with a competitive strategy that is focused on cost.

21.5.5 Exporting and internationalisation strategies

Exporting or internationalisation can provide small businesses with access to larger and more attractive markets (see Chapter 23). However, most small businesses do not engage in any exporting or international activities. In particular, those in the services sector have very low levels of direct international activity.

Small firms face significant barriers in trying to internationalise their activities. Of particular significance are a lack of knowledge and resources (Johanson and Vahlne, 1990). However, it is important to note that many small businesses are involved indirectly in international markets through their sub-supply activities with larger indigenous and multinational companies. The globalisation of some new high-tech sectors facilitates small companies internationalising at an earlier stage of development than is typical among small businesses (see Chapter 23).

21.6 The strategic problems of small businesses

Developing a sustainable competitive strategy entails not only developing superior competences and capabilities in some aspects of the business but also minimising the impact of areas of the small firm where there are inferior competences and capabilities (Almor and Hashai, 2004). The strategic weaknesses that characterise most small businesses are the consequence of any deficiencies in the managerial skills of the owner-managers and the firms' resources.

21.6.1 Lack of financial resources

Most small businesses are under- and inappropriately capitalised, in terms of both a high debt–equity ratio and an over-reliance on short-term debt (Davidson and Dutia,

1991). Inadequate and inappropriate capitalisation are significant contributory factors to the high levels of failure among new businesses. Poor capitalisation may be the result of the difficulties that new businesses face in raising capital (Hall, 1989) and the low levels of profitability in small businesses (Davidson and Dutia, 1991). When capital is available, entrepreneurs may choose debt capital in preference to equity capital, due to its perceived lower cost (Brigham and Smith, 1967).

However, the capital structure decision is not purely a financial one. Strategic factors also determine debt–equity ratios (Chaganti, DeCarolis and Deeds, 1995). The desire to maintain control of the business may increase the use of personal equity investment. The level of personal equity investment by the entrepreneur may reflect his or her 'insider' knowledge of the business and evaluation of the likelihood of success, with low levels of investment resulting in non-value-maximising behaviours, such as higher CEO salaries. Entrepreneurs may substitute cheaper 'sweat equity' for financial capital.

21.6.2 Marketing problems and customer concentration

Small businesses engage in little marketing activity. Most have few resources to devote to it and many owner-managers have no experience and prefer to devote their time to activities that are more familiar – e.g., production – with the result that little time is spent on either marketing or selling activities.

Some of the marketing problems of small businesses relate to their lack of product differentiation. This makes it difficult for the owner-manager to position the product or service as a distinctive offering.

A distinguishing characteristic of small businesses is their high dependency on a small number of customers. Research evidence suggests that as many as one-third of all small businesses are dependent on one customer for 25 per cent or greater of their sales (Cambridge Small Business Research Centre, 1992). This is a high-risk strategy for small businesses as the loss of just one customer may result in business failure.

Finally, owner-managers tend to have very little knowledge of export markets.

21.6.3 Management and human resources

By their nature, most small businesses are owner-managed. That person is required to manage all functions of the business, including operations, finance, staff and marketing. However, the narrow expertise of owner-managers and a lack of management skills can mean that small businesses are deficient in a number of these functional areas.

Most small businesses do not have the resources to hire outside managers to strengthen functional areas of the business. Where resources *are* available, the pervasive involvement of the entrepreneur in the business may make it difficult for outside managers to function properly in the business.

Small firms have difficulty in attracting good staff. For many potential employees, a small business will not offer the scope for training and development. Additionally, potential employees perceive it as a risky career move, as the business may subsequently fail. Also, due to a lack of resources and low levels of profitability, small businesses often pay lower salaries than competing larger businesses.

21.6.4 Over-reliance on the entrepreneur

Most small businesses are characterised by what Mintzberg (1979) refers to as a 'simple' structure. This reflects the personality traits of their owner-managers (Miller and Droge, 1986). Typically, they are actively involved in the day-to-day management of their businesses and often involved in the direct production of products or provision of services. The customer base of these businesses is typically limited and known directly to the entrepreneurs. They rely on informal channels to communicate internally and externally. Due to a lack of time, many entrepreneurs keep incomplete and outdated financial records and/or spend 'out of work' hours updating financial accounts.

The benefits of this 'simple' structure is that entrepreneurs are in close contact with the key issues of the business and 'on the spot' to deal with problems, quality standards are maintained through their direct supervision and staff are involved in the business and engage in frequent informal communication with the owner-managers. These advantages allow the business to respond to the needs of customers in a quick, innovative and flexible manner. It is these latter qualities that many larger bureaucratic organisations are now trying to emulate by delayering, downsizing and teamwork (Kanter, 1984).

Others argue that small firms exhibit diversity in how they are organised – i.e., in how jobs are divided, grouped and coordinated (Barth, 2003). However, in many cases, it appears that the management style of the owner-manager is the antithesis of good management practices. The skills, competencies and behaviours necessary for successful new venture creation later become barriers to the growth and development of a business (Churchill and Lewis, 1983; Kazanjian, 1988). Traits such as a strong need for control and a high sense of distrust can result in owner-managers engaging in behaviours that prevent the organisation from growing (Churchill and Lewis, 1983; Kets De Vries, 1985; Baumback and Mancuso, 1987). Such behaviours might include the centralisation of control and 'scapegoating' when activities are not successful (Kets De Vries, 1985). The pervasive involvement of the entrepreneur in the business means that it is difficult for him or her to attend to important, though non-urgent, issues. The high need for achievement that drives the entrepreneur may result in the centralisation of decisionmaking (Miller and Droge, 1986).

21.6.5 Lack of systems and controls

Small businesses are characterised by informality and poor information systems. Specifically, they have poor formal control systems (Huff and Reger, 1987). During the start-up period, informality dominates in many aspects of the new business, including its control systems (Quinn and Cameron, 1983; Walsh and Dewar, 1987). The lack of information results in poor decisionmaking.

21.6.6 Technological skills

The majority of small businesses can be classified as technological contingent, having no influence on the technological trends and innovations that impact the business. Most small businesses lack the capacity to investigate and assess new technical developments that might impact their competitive position. In many cases, they operate in sectors that have a stable technological trajectory, allowing them to pursue a reactive strategy – i.e., respond to external changes as they happen. However, with technological developments, the technical demands on many small businesses has increased significantly and technological competence has become a prerequisite to survival in many sectors.

21.7 Chapter summary

This chapter has outlined research exploring how strategies generally and success strategies are arrived at, as well as the strategic weaknesses, in small firms.

Most small businesses face significant strategic and structural weaknesses. In particular, they lack the managerial skills necessary to develop and implement a strategy. The strategymaking process is typically ad hoc and informal and, frequently, the entrepreneur's personality prevents the sharing of information about the business' strategic position.

There is some evidence to suggest that some strategies – e.g., a focused market position and differentiated competitive advantage – are positively associated with success in small businesses. In addition, the importance and significance of innovation as a means of developing competitive advantage was discussed.

Strategic weaknesses also prevent the implementation of strategies. Small businesses are typically characterised by insufficient financial and managerial resources. The lack of financial resources prevents investment in activities such as product development and marketing. The owner-managers' lack of financial skills mean that the information necessary to make managerial decisions is not available.

The implications of the research presented in this chapter for owner-managers are that the development of a clear competitive advantage is essential for both short- and long-term survival. Owner-managers must understand that choices in relation to 'where' and 'how' they compete impact the viability and performance of the business. In addition, they need to understand that the structural characteristics of their businesses and their own managerial styles may restrict the development of both an effective strategymaking process and effective strategies.

The implications of these points for policymakers are that most small businesses are characterised by significant strategic and structural weaknesses. For individual small businesses to develop and prosper, these deficiencies must be reduced. Clearly, the role of policymakers is to facilitate owner-managers in their development of strategies and competitive advantage. It is important that policymakers appreciate the problem is not with the strategy formulation process but, rather, the development of a clear competitive advantage. Pressurising owner-managers to produce formal plans does not assist them in addressing the strategic and structural deficiencies of their small businesses. Policymakers need to systematically address the strategic and structural deficiencies of small businesses by providing owner-managers with opportunities to develop the skills and acquire the resources that are needed for the development and implementation of effective strategies.

Questions

1 What strategic and structural weaknesses impact the development and implementation of effective strategies in small businesses?

2 What strategies are associated with success in small businesses?

3 How appropriate is it for policymakers to require owner-managers of small businesses to prepare formal business plans prior to receiving any financial assistance?

4 Given the strategic and structural weaknesses of small businesses, do the concepts of 'strategy' and 'competitive advantage' have any relevance to small businesses?

Weblinks

www.entrepreneur.com
The website of *Entrepreneur* magazine contains a range of information for small businesses, including some about strategic planning.

www.inc.com
The website of *Inc.* magazine also contains information about growing new businesses and some dos and don'ts for entrepreneurs.

CHAPTER 22

Growth and development in the small firm

David Smallbone and Peter Wyer

22.1 Introduction

There has probably been more written about small business growth in recent years than any other aspect of the development or management of small firms, with the possible exception of finance. One of the reasons for this is the contribution of growing firms to economic development and employment generation, which has attracted the attention of both academics and policymakers in many countries. In this regard, there is a growing body of research evidence that demonstrates a positive relationship between entrepreneurship and economic growth (Wennekers and Thurik, 1999; Carree, van Stel, Thurik and Wennekers, 2002; Acs, 2006; Acs, Parsons and Tracy, 2008; Levie and Autio, 2008). At the same time, there is limited understanding of precisely how this occurs and what the nature of the causal relationships is. Nevertheless, the issue is very topical in the early years of the twenty-first century, evidenced by the widespread interest and support from policymakers for the Global Entrepreneurship Monitor (GEM) (Bosma, Jones, Autio and Levie, 2008).

Results from GEM emphasise that the relationship between entrepreneurship and economic growth varies with the level of economic development. Levels of so-called necessity entrepreneurship (that is, in the GEM framework, individuals become entrepreneurs either because they start a new business to exploit a perceived business opportunity or they are pushed into it because all other options for work are either absent or unsatisfactory) are high at low levels of economic development, but decline as the economy develops and production sectors create more jobs. At higher levels of economic development, so-called opportunity-driven entrepreneurship increases, which means that there is a qualitative change in the nature of entrepreneurship as an economy grows (Bosma et al., 2008).

For private-sector business service providers such as banks, growing businesses are potentially attractive customers because business growth is likely to be associated with a demand for finance and other services. For some individual businessowners, the high casualty rates among new firms in particular focuses attention on the elusive 'success factors', the identification of which have been the subject of a large number of studies undertaken over many years (Smallbone, Leigh and North, 1995; Warren and Hutchison, 2000; Delmar, Davidsson and Gartner, 2003; Barringer, Jones and Neubaum, 2005; Davidsson, Delmar and Wiklund, 2006). Whilst growth may be judged by some as an indicator of business success, it can also present managers with challenges, which often focus on the need to relate expansion to the resources available or those that can be realistically mobilised.

In this context, we consider some of the main issues relating to growth that confront small businessowners, as well as those individuals and organisations concerned with assisting or doing business with them. After a brief discussion of what is meant by 'growth' in small firms, the question of how it can be explained is considered, drawing on a number of major research studies. The second half of the chapter focuses on some of the management issues associated with growth in small firms, including the main barriers to growth and how these can be managed.

22.2 Learning objectives

This chapter has four learning objectives:

1 to understand what is meant by growth in small firms
2 to consider some of the theories and concepts used to help explain growth in small firms
3 to assess the main barriers to and constraints on growth in small firms
4 to identify some of the main issues facing managers in growing small firms and discuss ways in which these may be successfully dealt with.

Key concepts

■ business growth ■ business development ■ management constraints
■ external environment

22.3 Growth and development in the small firm

Much of the literature on small business growth defines growth in terms of employment (Storey, 1994; Schutgens and Wever, 2000; Hoogstra and van Dyk, 2004). Part of the reason for this is the interest of public policymakers in facilitating growth in employment opportunities. In this context, various studies have demonstrated the disproportionate contribution of a minority of fast-growth firms to employment generation (see Chapter 3). For example, among new firms, it has been suggested that 'out of every 100 created, the fastest-growing four firms will create half the jobs in the group over a decade' (Storey, Keasey, Watson and Wynarczyk, 1987). Another study concerned with the development of a group of 306 mature manufacturing SMEs over an 11-year period showed that 23 per cent of the firms (i.e., those achieving high levels of growth) contributed 71 per cent of all new jobs created in the panel (Smallbone, Leigh and North, 1995).

The dynamism of high-growth enterprises and their disproportionate contribution to employment generation and economic development more widely has contributed to a resurgence of interest in these firms in both the scientific (Delmar, Davidsson and Gartner, 2003; Barringer, Jones and Newbaum, 2005; Acs et al., 2008) and policymaking communities. This has led to studies being commissioned by policymakers seeking to identify the characteristics and support needs of high-growth firms (Ministry of Trade and Industry, Finland, 2007; Department for Business, Enterprise and Regulatory Reform, 2007a; OECD, 2007; SBRC, Kingston University, 2008).

Although a variety of approaches and criteria have been used to define high-growth enterprises – which raises questions about whether like is being compared with like (Shepherd and Wiklund, 2009) – policy-orientated studies increasingly use the OECD definition (OECD Eurostat, 2007: 61), which is that firms:

> with average annualised growth greater than 20 per cent per annum, over a three-year period should be considered as high-growth enterprises. Growth can be measured by the number of employees or by turnover.

At the same time, there is evidence that where growth occurs in small firms, it is, typically, discontinuous (Smallbone, Leigh and North, 1995; Smallbone and Massey, 2010; Storey, 2010). This means the concept of a high-growth enterprise may be challenged if it is taken to mean that high-growth firms are a distinctive subset of the business population. It may be more realistic to think in terms of high-growth *phases* that some firms may pass through, which has implications for policymakers.

Although employment generation may be an appropriate growth criterion for public policy, for most SME owners-managers, it is a *consequence* of growth rather than a prime objective of business development. Where owners seek to expand their businesses, this is more likely to be in terms of profitability, sales turnover or net assets than employment per se, since few set them up primarily to create employment for others. At the same time, a number of studies have demonstrated the close correlation that typically exists between employment growth and sales growth in small firms over a long period of time (Smallbone, Leigh and North, 1995; Delmar, Davidsson and Gartner, 2003), although increased employment is less clearly related to a growth in profitability.

Although the policy context is one of the reasons many academic studies define small business growth in terms of increased employment, another is related to data availability and reliability. Financial data (e.g., sales turnover or profits) are notoriously less reliable in small firms than large ones and also less commonly available, particularly in countries (e.g., the UK) where the smallest firms are exempt from annual financial reporting requirements. This means that, typically, researchers have to rely on self-reported financial data, which presents both confidentiality and reliability issues, particularly with respect to sales and profitability.

One of the issues that needs to be recognised in any discussion of small business growth is that not all owners see it as an important business objective. One of the reasons is that there are a variety of factors that contribute to individuals starting and running businesses, which means that lifestyle and non-business objectives may result in a lack of growth orientation (Shane, Locke and Collins, 2003). As others have emphasised, the rational actor model of traditional economic theory simply does not hold for small businesses (Dobbs and Hamilton, 2007).

In assessing the role of the growth motivation of businessowners in relation to actual business growth, it is important to take into account the effects of previous motives, as well as previous business performance. In this regard, Delmar and Wiklund (2008) found a strong empirical relationship between growth motivation and growth performance, particularly when the latter was measured in terms of employment growth. This suggests that the importance of business growth in relation to other goals that individual entrepreneurs may aspire to can change over time.

The growth orientation of an individual small firm can also vary at different stages of business development, as well as in response to changes in external factors. For example, in a newly established business, some growth is likely to be a necessity for survival, although a period of rapid growth may need to be followed by a period of consolidation, if expansion is not to outstrip the ability of the firm's resource base to support it.

For all these reasons, the extent to which the owner of a small firm is seeking to grow (i.e., growth orientation) can vary over time as well as from firm to firm.

22.4 Explaining growth in small firms

Although a great deal has been written about the growth of small enterprises, there is no single theory that can adequately explain growth patterns in small businesses, nor, as Gibb and Davies (1990) have suggested, is there much likelihood of such a theory being developed in the future.

The main reason for the absence of such a growth model is the variety of different factors that can affect the growth of small firms, as well as the way in which these factors interact with one another. At the same time, there is broad agreement about what the main influences on small business growth are, summarised in the framework developed by David Storey (1994). As a result, a slightly modified version of the Storey framework is used in this chapter to consider the factors influencing small firm growth. This will incorporate aspects of the four main theoretical approaches to small business growth identified by (Gibb and Davies, 1990) – namely entrepreneurial personality, organisation development, functional management skills and sectoral studies – as well as selected empirical evidence, where appropriate. The aim is to highlight those aspects that appear to be characteristic of growing and high-growth enterprises.

Our framework includes the three influences on growth identified by Storey (1994) – namely characteristics of the entrepreneur, the firm and management strategies – but also the influence of the external environment, which Storey does not separately consider. The external environment is separately identified here in order to emphasise its influence, since one of the size-related differences between large and small firms is connected with their differing abilities to control or shape external environmental influences. Hence, it is our intention to make explicit that a prime influence on the growth performance of small firms is the way in which their managers address the enabling and constraining forces emanating from their operating context (Figure 22.1). Each of the four components identified in Figure 22.1 will be discussed in turn.

22.4.1 Characteristics of the entrepreneur

Since one of the distinguishing characteristics of small firms, when compared with large firms, is the close correspondence between ownership and management, the

Figure 22.1 Growth in small firms

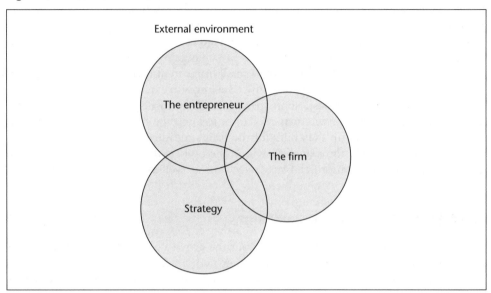

Source: This Figure is based on Fig. 5.1 in Storey (1994), p.124.

characteristics of individuals who start and run small firms can have a major impact on their growth orientation and performance, as well as on their organisational culture (see Chapter 9 for a more detailed discussion).

In this context, one of the approaches to understanding small business growth identified by Gibb and Davies (1990) is the so-called 'personality-dominated approach', in which the entrepreneur is seen as the key to the development of the business. For example, the personal goals of an entrepreneur are likely to influence why a business was started in the first place, as well as the strength of the firm's growth orientation once it is established. A priori, one might expect a business that was set up to exploit a clearly defined market opportunity for a product or service (and/or because the entrepreneur is strongly motivated to make money) to show a higher propensity to grow than a start-up where the main drivers are 'push' factors (e.g., unemployment, or the threat of it, dissatisfaction with present employment or personal lifestyle reasons).

This distinction refers to what is described in the GEM research programme as 'opportunity-driven' and 'necessity-driven' entrepreneurship (Bosma et al., 2008). At the same time, such concepts are open to question since they only capture the motives of businessowners at one point in time (i.e., at start-up) and motives can change over time, for a variety of reasons.

In their seminal work on small business growth, Stanworth and Curran (1976) distinguished three different identities of owners of small businesses, thus emphasising the variety of goals that are apparent in relation to why individuals start and run businesses (see also Chapter 9). The identities were defined as:

- *artisan*, where the owner's role centres on the intrinsic satisfaction associated with the personal autonomy that running one's own business can entail

- *classical entrepreneurial*, where the owner's role emphasises earnings and the generation of profits
- *managerial*, where it is suggested that the owner's priorities are focused on looking for the recognition of others.

Empirical evidence suggests that, while growth orientation (in the sense of growth being actively sought as a business objective) does not necessarily lead to actual growth performance, one of the characteristics that distinguishes high-growth firms from other firms is the commitment of the owner(s) to expanding the business. For example, in Smallbone, Leigh and North's (1995) study of 306 established manufacturing SMEs (up to 100 employees) referred to at the beginning of this chapter, it was found that the propensity to achieve high growth between 1979 and 1990 was significantly associated with the strength of their commitment to growth, with 70 per cent of high-growth firms referring to strong commitment to growth during this period compared with 32 per cent of other firms with weaker growth performance (Smallbone et al., 1995).

Some insight into the distinctive characteristics of entrepreneurs involved in high-growth small businesses can be obtained from research undertaken in relation to a government initiative in England to provide targeted support for start-ups with the potential for high levels of growth. The research involved surveying young businesses that had actually achieved high growth during the first years of trading – defined as reaching annual sales of £150,000 by the end of the first year and/or £1 million by the end of the third year (Smallbone, Baldock and Burgess, 2002). By surveying a sample of businesses with these characteristics, drawn from Dun and Bradstreet, it was found that 75 per cent of these businesses were started by people with previous management experience, which was typically gained in a medium or large enterprise. In fact, 29 per cent had been developed out of a previous business, which, typically, reflected a situation where the entrepreneur had worked in a larger firm in a related activity, but had reached a stage where he or she felt that they could start their own firm (sometimes with others) in a similar or related business activity, either in competition with their previous employer or as a supplier or by exploiting a new market niche. The profile of entrepreneurs in high-growth businesses that emerges from this research appears distinctive, in comparison with the small business population as a whole.

Researchers who have focused on the role of the entrepreneur's personality on the firm's growth performance (Smith-Hunter, Kapp and Yonkers, 2003; Chell, 2008), have highlighted its influence on attitudes to risk (which can affect the willingness of a businessowner to use external finance), the emphasis placed on personal autonomy (which can affect the willingness of the entrepreneur to collaborate with other firms or even use consultants) and managerial competencies, particularly in relation to strategic management skills.

With regard to the role of the entrepreneur's personality, a European-wide study of fast-growing enterprises found the most successful firms to be characterised by 'strong leadership' and pursuing highly outward-looking, customer-focused strategies (European Foundation for Entrepreneurial Research, 1996).

However, researchers have been unable to reliably identify a personality trait that distinguishes entrepreneurs from other people, perhaps because of the tendency for personality traits to interact with situational modifiers of behaviour. Whilst such factors

409

can undoubtedly affect the performance of the firm in a number of respects, some types of research in this paradigm are more controversial. These include attempts to use typologies based on profiling the personality traits of entrepreneurs to predict business success, which tend to ignore the capacity of people to learn and change over time or, indeed, their motivation. For example, owners' motivation for expanding a business may decline once they have achieved what they consider to be a satisfactory level of income from their enterprises and/or their personal/family circumstances change as they grow older. Alternatively, some businessowners may become more growth-orientated over time, as their aspirations rise with growing self-confidence. In this respect, Chell and Haworth (1992) have pointed to an association between the age and experience of the leader of the firm and the stage of development of the business has reached.

Some of the manufacturing SMEs that achieved high growth in the longitudinal study referred to previously (Smallbone, Leigh and North, 1995), were started by what Stanworth and Curran characterised as 'artisans', but they changed to a more entrepreneurial stance over time. This is an important point because it demonstrates how individuals can change their orientation to growth in response to changes in external circumstances, as well as their own learning experiences and/or their personal circumstances. An example includes a business started by a founder from a craft printing background but who, ten years later, was beginning to think like an entrepreneur seeking to manage the assets of the business to increase his returns, rather than simply to run a production plant. This had involved firms setting up a property management arm to the business, which the owner ran himself, recruiting a production manager to run the core printing activity, which the owner had become increasingly bored with.

Storey's emphasis on the role of the characteristics of entrepreneurs on business performance places less emphasis on personality per se and more on those personal characteristics that influence access to resources. These include educational background and qualifications, which can affect the management resource base of the business, as well as the entrepreneurs' motivations for running it, because of the higher earnings expectations of the more educated businessowners. Whilst recognising that educational qualifications are no guarantee of business success, Storey (1994) suggests that their role is likely to vary between sectors, tending to be higher in technology and knowledge-based activities and lower in the more traditional and craft-based sectors (see Chapter 15). Other personal characteristics of entrepreneurs considered by Storey include:

- previous management and/or entrepreneurial experience (if any) prior to establishing the current enterprise
- family history
- functional skills and previous training
- previous knowledge and/or experience of the sector in which the business has been established.

However, whilst most of these factors have been shown to contribute to small business growth in one or more major empirical study, none appears to make a *consistent* contribution. Indeed, the search for the identikit picture of 'successful entrepreneur' has not proved fruitful and, whilst undoubtedly relevant, the characteristics and previous experience of the founder appear to have only a modest effect on the success of the business in terms of its growth performance. Moreover, for many of us, who have spent some years researching the behaviour of small businesses, it is the unpredictability and variety of conditions associated with their success that help to make this topic so fascinating.

One characteristic that has been attracting increasing attention in the entrepreneurship literature has been portfolio ownership (Carter and Ram, 2003), which refers to the fact that some entrepreneurs may be involved in the simultaneous ownership of a number of enterprises. Some studies have suggested that portfolio entrepreneurs are more likely to be associated with growth-orientated firms than those running a single business, since multiple ownership is itself a sign of entrepreneurial flair. It has also been pointed out that, whilst early studies of portfolio entrepreneurship tended to emphasise its role in reducing business risk, it has been increasingly recognised as an important growth strategy, particularly in sectors where economies of scale can be achieved at a low level (Carter, 1998a, 1998b). Perhaps the key point is that a focus on the entrepreneur rather than the firm as the unit of investigation may produce a more comprehensive picture of small business growth than we have now (Scott and Rosa, 1996).

22.4.2 Characteristics of the firm

Although organisational characteristics may reflect those of their entrepreneurs, they are different in the sense that they are based on decisions made by the owners either at the time the businesses were started or at some time afterwards.

Storey's review of the relationship between organisational profile characteristics and the propensity of small firms to grow includes age and size, as well as other variables. With respect to age, Storey (1994) reports that most UK and US research shows that younger firms grow more rapidly than older firms (Lotti, Santarelli and Vivarelli, 2003). Whilst this may be statistically accurate as far as surviving businesses are concerned, it partly reflects the need for newly established firms to increase the scale of their operations if they are to accumulate sufficient resources to be able to withstand unforeseen external shocks (see Chapter 6).

At the same time, other research has demonstrated that even some very mature firms can grow strongly, sometimes following a long period of stagnation (Smallbone and North, 1996). Indeed, growth in small firms (where it occurs) is rarely a continuous and sustained process, so a firm's age will never be a completely reliable predictor of its growth prospects.

One of the approaches used to explain small business growth identified by Gibb and Davies (1990) is the so-called 'organisational' approach, which emphasises the development sequences of a firm as it passes through a series of stages at different points in its lifecycle. The original idea was that, since every product or service faces a lifecycle, then so do businesses.

There are a number of variants of the 'lifecycle' or 'stages of growth' models. Churchill and Lewis (1983) propounded a five-stage developmental model, which considers each development stage of a firm in terms of enterprise and management factors, the nature, form and significance of which change over time as the firm develops.

Application of such a model (see an example in Figure 22.2) might, for instance, highlight the pivotal management roles and activities of the owner-manager at the start

Figure 22.2 An indicative 'stages' of growth/lifecycle model

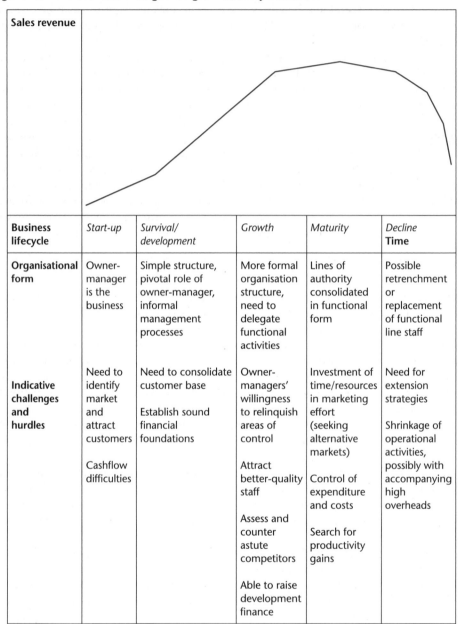

Sales revenue					
Business lifecycle	*Start-up*	*Survival/ development*	*Growth*	*Maturity*	*Decline* **Time**
Organisational form	Owner-manager is the business	Simple structure, pivotal role of owner-manager, informal management processes	More formal organisation structure, need to delegate functional activities	Lines of authority consolidated in functional form	Possible retrenchment or replacement of functional line staff
Indicative challenges and hurdles	Need to identify market and attract customers Cashflow difficulties	Need to consolidate customer base Establish sound financial foundations	Owner-managers' willingness to relinquish areas of control Attract better-quality staff Assess and counter astute competitors Able to raise development finance	Investment of time/resources in marketing effort (seeking alternative markets) Control of expenditure and costs Search for productivity gains	Need for extension strategies Shrinkage of operational activities, possibly with accompanying high overheads

and during the survival phases of the business, when simple organisation structure and informal management processes predominate. Significantly, the model focuses attention on the ways in which these enterprise and management factors will need to be adapted through the various development stages of the firm. Corresponding development hurdles that the small firm may face at identified development phases and the likely changing nature of impacting problems are also mapped on to some models.

Typical of such models is their highlighting of the inadequacy of informal management approaches as a small business strives to grow, with a subsequent need for the owner-manager to relinquish all-embracing control of management tasks and begin to formalise the organisational structure. As the business progresses towards a sustainable growth path, recruitment of quality staff may become a priority and further formalisation of the organisational structure necessary, including the increasing delegation of management responsibilities. Tighter control over day-to-day operations and finances may be required, as may the ability to identify and act upon development opportunities, together with a more formalised approach to planning and monitoring activities and assessment of competitors' actions.

Although critical thresholds separating distinctive phases of the development of a small firm often exist, the formalised 'stages' models, such as those of Churchill and Lewis (1983) or Steinmetz (1969), have little application as tools to explain the growth of small firms for a number of reasons. In practice, boundaries between phases may be fuzzy rather than distinct and some small businesses commonly develop more rapidly in relation to certain functions or dimensions than others. As a result, it is often difficult to position firms empirically and, thus, apply the model in practice.

More fundamentally, such an approach implies that a firm's development path is determined, whereas, in practice, the number of stages that can be identified is variable. Moreover, the order of stages is not fixed, which means that some firms may ultimately grow further, move back then forwards and so on rather than continuously forwards in a set sequence of stages. Overall, the value of such models lies more in helping to diagnose organisational problems and bottlenecks that need to be addressed by owner-managers if their firms are to grow further than as explanations of what actually occurs. In addition, such models are only concerned with internal constraints and thresholds, divorcing the firms' development path from any interrelationship with their external environments.

Lichenstein and Levie (2009) have undertaken a comprehensive review of 'stages' models in which they examined 104 published examples. Having emphasised the lack of consensus in relation to the basic constructs of the approach, the authors present what they describe as a new dynamic state approach, which views the firm as operating in an open system, incorporating the external environment and emphasising the typical disequilibrium that exists between the firm and its operating conditions.

Despite the lack of consensus emphasised by Lichenstein and Levie, empirical studies have shown that one of the most critical thresholds with respect to growth as far as organisational development is concerned, relates to the willingness of the owner to delegate decisions (Storey, 1994). This can be illustrated with reference to an analysis of the distinctive characteristics and strategies of a group of high-growth SMEs over an 11-year period, referred to earlier in the chapter (Smallbone, Leigh and North, 1995).

One of the most significant differences between high-growth firms and their low-growth or non-growth counterparts was their propensity to have made changes that were designed to create more time for the leaders to manage the firm strategically. Other writers have suggested that 'creating time to manage is one of the key internal factors influencing the process of change in small firms' (Gibb and Dyson, 1982). The results from the longitudinal research showed it to be a key discriminating feature between firms that were able to achieve high growth over the 11 years and those that were simply able to survive. Whether this is a cause or effect of growth is less important in practical terms than recognising that the issue needs to be prioritised by entrepreneurs if sustained growth over a long period of time is to be achieved.

22.4.3 Management strategy

In considering the role of strategy as a factor influencing the growth of small firms, we refer to management actions taken by the owners once the business has started to trade that affect the development path of their firms. These actions may be planned and explicit, but, more typically, are implicit and emergent in smaller companies (see Chapter 21).

David Storey's (1994) review of key empirical studies, looking at areas where management strategy may influence the growth of small firms, found that they include product development and innovation, market strategy, business planning, production technology, the financial base and external equity, management training and recruitment, workforce training and the use of external advice and assistance. As a result, strategies for mobilising resources are included and, by implication, management competence, since this underpins management actions and is central to the way in which finance, labour and other resources are mobilised.

Several key strategy factors that are evident in growing firms were identified by Storey. First, a willingness to share equity with external individuals or organisations was frequently identified in small firms that actually achieved high rates of growth. A second factor relates to the ability of rapidly growing firms to identify market segments or niches where they can build customer bases founded on their distinct advantages and selling points (see Chapter 6). Moreover, exploitation of this type of non-price-competitive advantage will often relate to the utilisation of relevant technologies and a willingness to introduce new products. Finally, an owner-manager's willingness to delegate and devolve decisionmaking was found to be a crucial facilitator of growth in a number of studies, which would also require an ability to attract, retain and enthuse managerial personnel who are capable of accepting this delegated authority.

Whilst not explicitly recognised by either Gibb and Davies (1990) or Storey (1994), a resource base perspective on small business growth is long established in the literature, stemming from the work of Edith Penrose (1959). As Dobbs and Hamilton (2007) explain, the essence of a resource base perspective, when applied to small enterprises, is that growth depends on the managerial resources available to plan and manage any future growth *in addition* to maintaining current operations. Linked to this is the ability of managers of small firm, to identify opportunities for growth.

One of the main approaches to understanding the growth process identified within the literature is characterised by Gibb and Davies (1990) as the 'business management' approach, which focuses on the importance of business skills and the role of functional management, planning, control and formal strategic orientations.

This body of literature offers valuable guiding insights into how a growing business might achieve sustainable development by making internal adjustments that are commensurate with identified opportunities in its external environment. In this regard, informative works on business strategy, such as that of Johnson and Scholes (2008), emphasise the growing need for managers to sensitise themselves to what is an increasingly turbulent operating environment, offering management approaches and techniques to aid them in this respect.

Certainly, the work of Johnson and Scholes offers support for Storey's propositions with respect to key strategy factors. However, much work within the 'business and management' field continues to be based on assumptions that organisations utilise rational decisionmaking approaches to identify, and act upon, development opportunities within their external change environment. This rationality manifests itself in recommendations and prescriptions with regard to the essential roles of long-term planning and financial control to underpin organisational growth. However, such prescription seems to overlook the inability of management tools of this nature to accommodate the nature, form and variety of change situations that impact contemporary businesses. This particularly applies in the case of smaller firms, which have limited ability to shape or control external environmental influences (see Chapter 19).

Whilst management activities such as 'strategic planning' and 'control' may have a part to play in sustaining the growth of some small businesses, the use of formal planning is much less common in small firms than in large firms. This is partly because of the higher propensity of large firms to employ managers that are professionally trained, although it also reflects a greater ability to reduce some of the uncertainties in the external environment that is typical in the case of small firms.

It appears, therefore, that, whilst management approaches contained in the wider business literature have some potential for aiding our understanding of organisational growth, there is a need to be selective in applying this knowledge to the small business context, where owners and managers typically face an uncertain external environment with a limited resource base.

22.4.4 External environmental influences

Arguably, it is the impact of external influences and the unpredictable manner in which they emerge, and change over time, that has the greatest influence on the nature and pace of small business growth. Small businesses can face major problems in identifying and dealing with environmental change because of a lack of understanding, management expertise and a shortage of time. Yet, given that most small firms concentrate on a narrower range of activities and markets and rely on fewer suppliers and customers, it can be argued that identifying, understanding and acting upon key changes in external factors impacting their business is even more important than it is for large companies. In relation to finance, for example, external volatility tends to have more impact on small businesses than on large businesses, with changes in, for example, interest rates or government regulations potentially affecting a significant percentage of small firms' costs (see Chapter 4).

Certainly, two of the approaches to explaining growth in small firms, identified by Gibb and Davies (1990), can incorporate the impact of the external environment upon organisations. These are, first, the so-called 'business management' approaches discussed above and, second, the so-called 'sectoral and broader market-led approaches'.

For Gibb and Davies (1990), sectoral studies concentrate on the identification of external constraints and opportunities facing small firms. For example, within the context of small high-tech businesses, the need to keep abreast of technological change and 'the importance of building marketing into quality, design and development from the early stages' are key sectoral conditions affecting potential business success (see Chapter 15). In other sectors, the position and role of large firms in the external operating environment can exert considerable influence over the ability of small firms to grow, because of the dominance of supply chain-based relationships. In some cases, this can result in highly dependent relationships between small firms and their large firm customers. For example, the strategies of large firms with regard to subcontracting, 'make or buy' decisions and strategic partnerships can be key influences on the growth potential of individual small firms. Partnership implies a more interdependent than dependent relationship in which small firms may normally access know-how and resources from large firms, in relation to R&D, technology and/or management skills. While Gibb and Davies emphasise that the existing literature does not provide clear guidelines in the form of predictive theory, the existing knowledge base provides some insight that may be used as a guiding frame of reference with regards to the processes involved in the growth of small firms.

In relation to external environmental influences, sectoral variations in the growth rates of small firms are to be expected because of differences in market trends and competitive conditions for different activities, which may themselves vary over time (see Chapter 22). However, since market conditions can vary for individual product markets, the amount of sectoral variation in growth performance, which is identified in practice, tends to vary according to the level of sectoral disaggregation. This is because the narrower the sectoral definition that is used, the less variety there is within sectoral categories, which means there is less of a tendency for buoyant conditions in one product market to be offset by weak trends in another and vice versa.

A firm's location is another characteristic that can affect its growth prospects, since it reflects spatial variations in local environmental conditions. On the demand side, variations in the size, scope and buoyancy in local markets might be expected to affect a firm's opportunities to grow. On the supply side, variations in the cost and availability of some factors of production (e.g., labour and premises) and resources (e.g., access to information and business services) may also be an influence.

At the same time, the ability of SMEs to adapt local external conditions should not be underestimated (Smallbone, North and Kalantaridis, 1999). Whilst the employment growth of small firms may vary considerably for different types of location (Hoogstra and van Dijk, 2004) because of differences in labour market conditions, the growth performance of small firms, measured in terms of sales growth, tends to show much less variation. This is because of differences in the types of strategy used by SME owner-managers to develop their businesses in different locations, which is an indication of how well successful SMEs adapt to local conditions (North and Smallbone, 1996).

22.5 Barriers and growth constraints – the external operating context

In this section, we consider the main external barriers that may constrain small business development and have to be circumvented or managed if growth is to be achieved and sustained.

22.5.1 A rapidly changing environment

If business organisations are to survive and prosper, their managers must learn to cope with unprecedented levels of change. The origins of such change are multisourced, deriving from factors such as increasing globalisation associated with the emergence of new sources of production, developments in information and communications technology and the emergence of the better-educated and more discerning consumers in mature market economies. In combination, such factors have contributed to a more competitive and rapidly changing environment facing business managers.

For small businesses, the low level of their ability to control external environmental forces is a key distinguishing characteristic. Moreover, when one conceptualises 'change' at a more specific level, the complexity of the management task in small firms becomes readily apparent. Change situations may be conceptualised in terms of closed, contained and open-ended change (Stacey, 1990).

Faced with a closed change situation, a firm can predict events and actions with regard to timing and consequences – e.g., if a major customer increases an order. In such circumstances, the form and timing of its consequences are knowable and allow for prediction in terms of the required resources and cashflows.

Contained change relates to events occurring that involve repetition of past events – e.g., where a seasonal pattern of sales allows for a degree of predictability. In the case of both closed and contained change situations, managers of small businesses can undertake rational short-interval planning activities in order to underpin organisational control.

However, as Stacey and others have emphasised, much of the change that faces contemporary business organisations is unknowable and unpredictable, in terms of both its timing and consequences. Such change may be considered open-ended, in that it is often unclear to managers what is changing or why it is changing, thus making it virtually impossible to predict the consequences for the operating environment of individual businesses. For example, the unanticipated emergence of cost reductions and quality-improving technology from overseas competitors can have an indeterminate impact on a small business. Under such operating conditions, sustainable business development can only be effected by management processes that are able to facilitate the identification and understanding of open-ended change situations as a basis for determining appropriate internal adjustment activities within the small firm.

22.5.2 Industry structure, competition and market limitations

Porter (1980) emphasises that the key aspect of a firm's operating environment is the industry or industries in which it competes. For Porter, the competitive rules of the game and strategies potentially available to a firm are substantially influenced by industry structure. He sees the intensity of competition in an industry transcending the behaviour of current competitors, with its roots in the industry's underlying economic structure. For him, it is the collective strength of five basic competitive forces that determine the profit potential in an industry. These forces, which drive industry competition, are:

- the threat of new entrants
- bargaining power of suppliers

- bargaining power of buyers
- the threat of substitute products or services
- the intensity of rivalry among existing firms.

In order to effect sustainable development within a given industry, a small firm would need to build up an understanding of the underlying structural features that underpin the basic competitive forces described above. This is because knowledge of the underlying sources of these competitive forces allows a firm to determine its critical strengths and areas of weakness.

For the smaller business, one keystone to growth may be a recognition that (Borch, Huse and Senneseth, 1999; Moen, 2002):

> markets tend to become more heterogeneous over time, evolving into progressively finer segments as buyer tastes and technological opportunities change . . . [Such] . . . heterogeneity of the market permits market segmentation and the use of product differentiation to create 'specialist' or 'niche' strategies by firms.

At the same time, significant potential barriers often exist that may prevent the small firm from effecting such development. These barriers include the need to identify and respond to such market segments or niches, requiring both the determination of the form of the 'distinctiveness' that will provide the differentiation of product to match the customer needs and the ability to produce and sustain that distinctiveness. In this context, it has been suggested firms that achieve growth can identify the key criteria upon which to compete in certain segments (including design, price, quality, delivery) and are then able to develop and sustain a competitive advantage around these criteria (Martin, Martinand and Minnillo, 2009). The barriers also include the difficulty of coping with direct competitors that may ultimately be attracted by the returns associated with the emerging segment or niche as well as the broader forces of competition, as discussed above.

At the same time, even where a small business has appropriately identified underlying industry and market structure characteristics in a manner that continues to facilitate ongoing sustainable development, the unfolding of unknowable open-ended change situations can confound that development without warning. For example, the effect of 9/11 2001 on the willingness of many US citizens to travel abroad had sudden and significant effects on firms engaged in tourism in London and other major tourist centres.

22.6 Barriers and growth constraints – the internal operating context

This section reviews some of the major internal constraints that affect growth in the small firm. These relate to the influence of the owner-manager and the relative small scale of the enterprise.

22.6.1 Owner-manager and size-related constraints

For many small and medium-size enterprises, 'size-related factors affect their ability to identify and respond to developmental opportunities in their external environment' (Wyer and Smallbone, 1999). This emphasises how owner-manager and size-related characteristics help to shape the enabling and constraining forces that affect the ability of smaller firms to identify, cope with and positively respond to external environmental changes. Size-related characteristics thus contribute substantially to shaping strategic activity and underlying management actions. Relevant owner-manager and size-related characteristics include the following.

Organisational culture

In an owner-managed business, the 'organisational culture' typically reflects the personality traits and aspirations of the owner-manager who, in turn, shapes the enabling and constraining forces affecting the firm. The pervading sets of norms and values, ways of doing things and the freedoms afforded to different individuals are often reflected in informal and idiosyncratic structures, systems and processes, which themselves often reflect the personality traits of the owner-manager. In this context, a key potential constraint on future development can be the extent to which the small business culture/structure remains embedded in the owner-manager. We address this issue later in this chapter.

Finance

A well-documented constraint on small business growth is that of an inadequate financial resource base (see Chapter 20), which can be particularly so for growing firms, where an ongoing need for development funds creates a strong demand for finance.

Financial constraints can result from a lack of the required levels of collateral (perhaps because the firm's assets are already being used to secure existing debt) combined with the absence of a proven track record in the case of new and young firms. This can affect their ability to raise external finance. Firms' financial management skills can also affect their ability to generate investment funds internally (Hamilton et al., 2002).

Whilst David Storey (1994) has identified a willingness to share equity as a factor influencing the growth potential of small firms, the operation of the formal venture capital markets makes it difficult for them to raise sums of less than approximately £250,000 from this source. The potential importance of equity financing to high-growth small firms is emphasised, however, by the fact that, for risky projects and those requiring long-term funding, equity capital is often the only possible source. Whilst informal risk capitalists (or business angels) are a possible source of such finance, as well as publicly funded venture capital funds that, in some cases, may be specifically targeting seed and early stage financing, entrepreneurs must have the knowledge and ability to identify a feasible development project and produce a supporting business plan to realise finance from these sources. As it is, an ignorance of formal and informal sources of risk capital and/or the non-financial value-adding benefits that business angels can bring to the business such as business contacts, commercial experience and complementary expertise, may itself be a constraint on the growth of many otherwise potentially successful small businesses.

Attracting and retaining quality people

Many small businesses face a marginal labour market, as they cannot offer the same levels of pay or the career path opportunities large companies can. This can affect their ability to attract the most able, committed and/or experienced workers, which can, in turn, impact the consistency of product or service quality. The latter is essential for building a good image and a satisfied customer base, but it can be difficult to realise if there are staffing problems.

The solution must be to encourage more owners to adopt a more staff-focused approach to human resource management (Carlson, Upton and Seaman, 2006), recognising that, potentially, the workforce can be one of the firm's most important assets.

Marketing problems

Developing effective marketing and distribution systems can represent a particular challenge for small businesses, especially those attempting to grow through market development activities in overseas markets (see Chapter 23).

Small firms often face difficulties in obtaining information about foreign markets, which is partly due to their tendency to rely on informal marketing methods (Smallbone et al., 1999), which they may get away with in some domestic markets, but probably not abroad. Carson and Gilmore (2000) highlight that marketing processes in small businesses are different from those in larger companies and our understanding of them will derive from greater consideration of factors such as the character and personality of the owner-manager and the inherent flexibilities and informalities of small business management.

The distinctive characteristics of small businesses, described in this section, may threaten their potential flexibility and responsiveness. If such problems are not circumvented or effectively managed, they are likely to prove a major constraint on the ability of the small business to grow.

22.6.2 Inadequacy of existing assets to underpin growth

Many of the above size-related constraints can exert pressure on management to attempt to squeeze more out of existing assets in order to facilitate the growth path to which they are committing themselves. For example, rapidly growing small businesses are particularly vulnerable to the need for increased working capital to support growth in business activity and turnover. This can lead to a phenomenon known as overtrading (Thomas, 2011), which can result from a failure to plan the underlying financial requirements of a development project or an attempt to expand too rapidly. For instance, taking on additional customer orders on the assumption that existing resources can cope (when, in practice, they are insufficient) can lead to cashflow problems. This, in turn, may contribute to relations with the firm's workforce and suppliers being soured as the firm finds itself unable to pay staff or suppliers.

Growth can also lead to pressure on the firm's human resource base, which is exacerbated if management is either unwilling or unable to recruit externally. Such firms must focus on existing human resources within the firm, placing an emphasis on getting the best out of those workers. For example, in order to motivate and enthuse management and supervisory level staff and fully utilise their expertise and capabilities, it may be necessary to give them more responsibility, involving them more substantially in management decisionmaking processes. However, the management style of many owner-managers can be autocratic and/or underpinned by the ineffective delegation of decisionmaking (Johnstone, 2000).

A further issue concerns the confidence and capability levels of staff (including the owner-manager) to undertake new tasks, which they will inevitably be asked to complete as the firm proceeds along its growth path.

This, in turn, raises the issue of the need to upgrade management skills, although a number of constraints have been found to restrict the uptake of management training within small firms. These include owner-managers' reluctance to utilise outside advice, time constraints, unwillingness to pay the market price and the inadequacy (Small Business Service, 2002a) or inappropriateness of much of the training provided to the actual needs of a heterogeneous small business sector. One of the biggest challenges for those providing training is the proposition that the most effective learning mode for small firms may be gaining experience rather than undertaking formal external training (Gibb, 1997).

The pace of growth can also exert pressure on physical resources. For example, a reluctance to invest in additional or new machinery may be the result of a lack of confidence, ability to assess new available technologies or reflect concern with regard to the integration of new systems and processes into existing activities. In this regard, Ekanem and Smallbone (2007) have demonstrated the key role of experiential learning in relation to investment decisionmaking in small manufacturing firms rather than using appraisal methods based on formalised learning.

A further developmental difficulty revolves around premises, since the pace of growth may result in a small business outgrowing its existing facilities. Both availability and cost of alternative premises can result in a firm attempting to utilise existing premises to the limit, which may have severe repercussions, in terms of efficiency of operation and the firm's ability to meet customer demands with regard to quality and delivery. Moreover, a fear that increased overheads associated with expansion may not be adequately covered can also result in a reluctance to take up new premises (Wyer and Smallbone, 1999).

22.6.3 Difficulties associated with teambuilding and team management

In order to establish a newly developing firm as an effective organisation capable of sustaining itself in the marketplace, owner-managers have to ensure that all tasks are appropriately allocated on an individual and/or small group basis. At an early stage in a firm's development, those 'subunits' of individuals, organised to work together, may appear to be working as a 'team', but, in practice, may be no more than a 'group', lacking a collective rationale, but it needs to be clearly understood that individual performance contributes directly to the overall good (Ensley and Pearce, 2001; Ucbasaran, Lockett, Wright and Westhead, 2003).

Whilst recognising that the transition from 'group' to 'team' working is a precondition for effecting sustainable small business development, the problems associated with teambuilding and team management can prove a major constraint on organisational development in practice.

22.7 Managing growth

Since one of the major challenges facing the contemporary small business is that of coping with unknowable, unpredictable open-ended change, a key issue relates to how small firms attempt to strategically control their operations. This section first considers the potential and limitations of formal, rational long-term planning modes of management to underpin small firm development. Empirical insight is then utilised to suggest the potential utility of an organisational learning perspective to effecting small business growth.

22.7.1 The uses and limitations of rational long-term planning modes of management

Considerable support continues to be afforded to the view that a rational, systematic step approach to managing the dynamic, volatile and fast-changing operating environment in which the modern-day small business finds itself is the most effective way to underpin sustainable long-term development. Some academics and practitioners propound that, whilst business problems are less amenable to the highly structured analytical methods utilised in the sciences, the high-level complexity of many business problems may, instead, be effectively approached through some kind of structured procedure to help identify and deal with key issues.

Within a strategic planning context, it is assumed that a small business can approach the strategic control of its fast-changing operating environment through undertaking a series of rational, systematic steps (see Box 22.1).

The propounded strength of this model lies in its processual form. Strategic planning encourages a careful and systematic reading of shifts in technology, competitor position and customer tastes, leading to the formulation of actions in response. Moreover, it has been suggested that strategic planning can help the small business to concentrate its competitive nature by encouraging an external focus on key environmental factors to determine where the firm fits, as well as internally focusing on the firm's strengths and weaknesses. The overall analytical and evaluatory process should then lead to the setting of a formal direction for the business, helping to determine where the business is going (Fry, Stoner and Weinzimmer, 1999).

However, the real utility of rational planning models in microfirms and small organisations is debatable (Liberman-Yaconi, Hooper and Hutchings, 2010). First, the utility of rational analytical planning should be considered within the context of the assumptions upon which the approach is based, which include the quality of the information and an ability to extrapolate future events from past experiences. Its value is also affected by the fact that resource constraints limit the ability of most small firms to formally scan their external environment. Much of the change that contemporary

Box 22.1 Indicative steps in strategic control

- External analysis – reveals opportunities and threats in the operating environment.
- Internal analysis – identifies the organisation's strengths and weaknesses.
- SWOT analysis.
- Formulate long-term development objectives.
- Choose strategies – to achieve objectives.
- Develop action plans.
- Implement strategies – through action plans.
- Control and review – monitor progress and feedback.

small businesses must be able to cope with is open-ended, which is unknowable and unpredictable, rather than closed or contained change. In addition, coping must be undertaken in the context of limited internal resources that are available compared with large firms. As a consequence, it is questionable whether formal, rational, long-term planning methods of management are compatible with the challenges facing small business managers, and the idiosyncrasies and informalities of small firm management processes, or they are, in fact, adequate for dealing with open-ended change situations (Stacey, 1990).

A further question mark against the promotion of a rational planning model in small firms is that, although some studies suggest a positive correlation between formal planning activity and growth (Schwenk and Shrader, 1993) and some association is suggested between strategic planning intensity and success in achieving primary business objectives (Peel and Bridge, 1998), there is still little evidence of a causal relationship between planning and long-term business performance. Moreover, as Shane (2003) points out a similar correlation has been found in studies that have examined founders who have a tendency to plan, rather than the creation of business plans per se (Miner, Smith and Bracker, 1989, 1994), thereby emphasising the role of planning as a process. A more recent study of 153 small Finnish firms emphasises that 'strategic plans as such are not sufficient to improve business performance unless they are carefully integrated into the actual processes and behaviour of the firm' (Kohtamaki, Kautonen and Kraus, 2010).

22.7.2 An organisational learning perspective

Drawing upon personal construct theory (Kelly, 1955) and contemporary learning theory (Hawkins, 1994), Wyer and Boocock (1998) have offered insights into the ways in which the owner-managers of small businesses learn, providing foundations for considering how small firms cope with open-ended change.

The thrust of their work is founded on Kelly's proposition that all individuals utilise a personal construct system (derived from inherent personal characteristics and accumulated experience) and this is used as a frame of reference when interpreting the world. In brief, we all have personal constructs that act as frames of reference to help us view the world that confronts us and deal with new situations as they arise.

If change situations impact the owner-managers of small firms, they will use their existing personal constructs to cope with the change. On many occasions, minor adjustments to the constructs may allow them to deal with it, simply because a *similar situation* has been dealt with in the past. This can be characterised as *simple* learning (Stacey, 1996), which takes place when the owner-managers have confirmed the validity of their current constructs by using them to make sense of a new situation. However, sometimes change situations arise for which existing constructs are inadequate. This requires the constructs to be extended through a process that involves questioning the underlying assumptions on which the existing constructs are based. It is a more *complex* learning process, which is why simple learning is more common (Stacey, 1996).

Such a conceptualisation of how individuals cope with change has far-reaching implications for growth-orientated small businesses. If the owners are confronted by unknowable, unfolding change forces, success in coping with such challenges in a manner that can lead to sustainable business development will depend, to a considerable extent, on their ability and willingness to 'extend' their personal construct systems – i.e., to change their mindset or frames of reference and engage in complex learning. This may include an ability and willingness to anchor the understanding and learning of other key members in and around the organisation to enhance collective organisational understanding. This means that the role of dialogue, both between internal organisational members and with key external informants on the boundaries of the small firm's operating environment, is a crucial learning activity (Wyer, Donohoe and Matthews, 2010).

In-depth case studies that have drawn on an organisational learning perspective to investigate strategic *development* processes in small firms have revealed a number of insights into strategic *management* processes (Wyer, Mason and Theodorakopoulos, 2000). They confirm that, while few small firms have written short- or long-term plans, many owner-managers demonstrate strategic awareness (Gibb and Scott, 1985), in the sense of having a mental image of the preferred development path for their businesses.

Studies have also demonstrated the role of informal networking with key external actors and informants in contributing to an emergent strategy, which, typically, is developed in a trial and error way (see Chapter 19).

Significantly, some of the most successful firms in the study were able to loop back the results of what they had learned to make adjustments to their strategic or operational activities. In other words, successful SMEs were led by owner-managers who appeared to have learned how to learn. This proposition has been reiterated by Unger et al. (2009: 38), whose findings 'suggest the acquisition of expertise and business growth largely remains the responsibility of the owners themselves to deliberately engage in a variety of quality learning activities . . . business owners need to learn how to learn'.

22.7.3 Managing finance to facilitate expansion

In order to facilitate sustainable growth, it is necessary for small firms' management to progressively enhance its financial management capabilities (see Chapter 20). As a business grows, it becomes increasingly necessary to formalise the approach to financial management, but also recognise the interdependencies between finance and other areas of functional activity within the firm. For example, the projection of financial requirements to underpin a period of expansion must derive, to a considerable extent, from the forecasting of future sales and determination of income and costs associated with that sales expansion. This requires a marketing capability to provide an understanding of the target customer base and change forces that may affect it in order to provide such estimates. In other words, effective financial management depends, to some extent, on other functional management capabilities.

With regard to the financing of growth, two crucial areas are the management of fixed and working capital. Expansion will require close attention to be paid to fixed capital needs in terms of the firm's ability to acquire requisite premises, plant and/or equipment. In this context, the firm's management has to acquaint itself with the various methods of raising long-, medium- and short-term finance and develop understanding of what an appropriate mix of these categories of finance would be to effectively underpin development, which may include innovative 'finance packages' (CEEDR, 2007) that can be used to leverage further funds from elsewhere.

A crucial ability in this regard relates to the need to consider the appropriate balance of external and internal funds. For example, the balance of debt (long- and medium-term external funding) to equity (the owner's own internal funding) is a key issue. The ratio of this funding (known as the gearing ratio) can be critical in terms of facilitating or constraining small firm growth. With a high gearing ratio (where the firm is relying on external interest-bearing borrowings), in times of slow sales and high interest rates, a firm may find its potential for future growth severely constrained because of the financial drain imposed upon it by having to meet high interest costs on borrowings.

The small business will also have to make sufficient provision for working capital in order to facilitate growth. Working capital relates to the ongoing provision of stocks of appropriate levels of raw materials and component parts, financing of debtors and access to cash to meet day-to-day expenditures and running costs. It thus incorporates the firm's current assets and current liabilities.

The complexity of the management tasks underpinning the determination of the forms and levels of working capital to facilitate growth include the need to forecast sales, from which estimates of the costs likely to be incurred and anticipated income can be made; plans for future growth, including the timescales of each step and an estimation of all inherent costs; consideration of possible developmental problems, which may result in delay (hold-ups and inefficiencies); and examination of the current and likely costs of borrowing and consideration of repayment periods (Bennett, 1989).

Inevitably, over time, growth will require additional fixed and working capital and the ability to ensure that adequate and appropriate funding underpins that growth clearly points to the need for an ongoing enhancement of financial capabilities. For example, stock levels must be managed to ensure a free-flowing production activity and an ability to serve customers in a timely manner, whilst not at a level that results in stocks of raw materials or component parts idling on the shelves and, thus, tying up cash. With regard to creditors, there is a need to negotiate credit periods that contribute effectively to a positive cashflow, whilst, at the same time, recognising creditors should not be exploited, resulting in a souring of the relationship and leading to a deterioration in the quality or timing of supplies or precluding the uptake of discounts for early settlement.

22.7.4 Developing the marketing function

Analysis of small businesses in the early stages of their development is unlikely to reveal a marketing approach or activity that even vaguely reflects formal marketing management, as represented in the mainstream marketing literature (Jocumsen, 2004; see Chapter 20). Instead, it is an understanding and application of the concept of marketing that is important – namely, 'a matching between a company's capabilities and the wants of customers in order to achieve the goals of the firm' (McDonald, 2002). There is considerable evidence of small firms going out of business because of a failure to fully understand the needs of their targeted customers and firms founded on the mistaken premise that they have the 'company capability' to serve the needs of an identified group of customers (Smallbone, 1990).

In the early stages of the development of small businesses, the nature and form of marketing are often embedded in the owner-managers themselves. In many instances, it is the owner-managers' close interface and relationship with their customers that allows for the matching processes of small firms' capabilities to the wants of customers to be effectively achieved.

Whilst an informal 'market orientation' may be a keystone for sustainable growth and development of small firms, the effective facilitation of sustainable growth may require an increasing formalisation of their marketing activities. For McDonald (2002), it is not essential for firms to have formalised marketing departments for the analysis, planning and control of the matching processes. However, with growth in firms' product ranges and customer types, the management of marketing may need to be brought within one central control function.

Growth brings with it the need to coordinate all functional activities within the firm that participate in the matching process. The crucial issue is not whether a department or an individual or group of individuals is responsible for a firm's marketing, but the extent to which marketing is embedded within the organisation. This means that key individuals within the firm have to have a clear understanding that the profit the company strives to earn is a return founded on a depth of understanding of the needs of the firm's target customer groups, as well as the ability to organise the firm's resources in their totality so as to satisfy those needs.

Within the context of a growing small business, a key management art is being able to extend the marketing concept in the business as it develops. Market orientation needs to be deeply rooted in the organisation's culture (Martin, Martin and Minnillo, 2009). Achievement of effective market orientation will require the implementation of processes across a small firm's value-creating activities, with comprehensive links between those processes (Golann, 2006).

22.7.5 Broadening the customer base whilst coping with existing customers

A major challenge facing growth-orientated small businesses is sustaining the level of service provision to an existing clientele, which may be making increasing demands, both quantitatively and qualitatively, while at the same time seeking to broaden their customer base. However, as we have already seen, the process of identifying opportunities, which can facilitate a widening of the customer base, is itself a difficult one. It is likely to exert considerable strain upon small firms' abilities to continue to serve the increasing demands of their existing customer base. The broadening of firms' product –market definitions will require the expansion of physical, financial and human resources at a time when their existing customer base may be demanding ongoing management attention and additional resource allocations.

Within a highly competitive environment, small firms will find themselves having to continuously seek efficiency improvements, both within their businesses and in their interfacing with service providers, such as suppliers and distributors, in order to maintain a competitive edge in their existing markets. This, together with the need to improve their existing products, will be a prerequisite for protecting existing customer bases and market shares so as to cement current foundations – to both maintain current levels of activity *and* facilitate any future expansion. A key challenge during growth, therefore, is recapturing the entrepreneurial spirit that underpinned the firm's early stage development and nurture the coexistence of an entrepreneurial and market orientation to facilitate serving existing customer bases *and* the creation of new markets in parallel (Miles and Darroch, 2008).

22.7.6 Deciding when to introduce new managers and modify organisational structure

A key developmental issue is to what extent small businesses striving for growth can continue to rely on organisational frameworks in which the owner-managers are the pivotal centre of all activities, based on informal structures for the direction and fulfilment of the firms' operational activities. The answer is likely to be contingent upon the individual business and its personnel, the nature of the firm's development path and the environment and markets in which it is operating.

Handy (1993) explains how 'each organisation, each part of an organisation has a culture, and a structure and systems appropriate to that culture'. Thus, in a large company, we may find several subcultures and different forms of structure throughout the organisation. However, in small businesses it is common to find culture in a form that Handy terms a *power* culture, its structure being depicted by a *web*. In other words, 'the culture depends on a central power source, with rays of power and influence spreading from that central figure. They are connected by functional or specialist strings but the power rings are the centre of activity'. These organisations, with their few rules and procedures, tend to work on precedent, with staff often anticipating the wishes and decisions of the owner-managers, who are the central power source. The owner-managers often exercise control by selecting key individuals for particular activities or 'occasional summonses to the centre'.

As small businesses grow, this approach is likely to prove inadequate to facilitate a rapid pace of development. Indeed, as reported earlier in the chapter, firms that are successful in achieving high growth over an extended period are characterised by an ability to modify the structure to accommodate an evolving role for the leaders. A typical evolving response by owner-managers might be to gradually formalise the structure, in terms of the allocation of responsibilities and the development of linking mechanisms between the newly emerging roles.

The result is a formal *hierarchy*-type structure and an underpinning *role*-type culture (see the pioneering work in this area by Taylor, 1947, and Fayol, 1949). However, for small businesses to evolve into formal hierarchical structures in pure form would be to overlook the inherent weaknesses of such structures. Thus, the timings and forms of adjustment to organisational structures in a small firm context are complex issues. There is also a danger that adjustment towards a formal hierarchy – with its rigidity and inward-focusing tendency – may reduce the ability of these firms to relate and adapt to their fast-changing environments. In such a context, it is crucial that a cultural environment is created and maintained that supports idea-generation and creativity to facilitate innovation (Cakar and Erturk, 2010), supported by the development of a structure and systems appropriate to that culture.

22.8 Chapter summary

Growth-orientated small businesses make a major contribution to economic development and employment generation within local communities and are a crucial engine for the development of national and regional economies. For this reason, they attract a great deal of attention – not least from policymakers and support providers hoping to encourage and influence their ongoing growth. However, the existing knowledge base, about how successful growth businesses effectively sustain development, is limited, although there have been growing numbers of empirical studies.

Commencing from the premise that there is no single theory to adequately explain the growth of small firms, this chapter, first, sought to draw upon major research studies to highlight aspects that appear to be characteristic of growing enterprises.

Crucial in many small firms is the central and pivotal role of the owner-manager, though research studies have had limited success in their attempts to identify key personality traits and characteristics that can be said to typify owner-managers of growth-orientated firms. Nevertheless, the combination of ownership and management – quite often in a single individual – is a recurrent feature distinguishing small firms from large companies. As a result, the characteristics and capabilities of individuals operating small firms impact substantially the form of organisational culture that obtains in particular small firms and their orientation towards, and success in achieving, sustained growth.

Many studies have focused on the characteristics and development issues of small firms themselves. One such approach is the lifecycle or stages model approach, which, whilst a useful vehicle for aiding the diagnosis of organisational problems and difficulties that owner-managers may have to circumvent if growth is to be achieved, is of less value when seeking to explain growth. Similarly, the body of 'business management' literature provides guiding insights to enhance understanding of the ways in which organisations may sustain growth through the adoption of development choices regarding potential adjustments to their markets, products and/or process activities, but many of these so-called insights appear overly rational and systematic when trying to apply them to the reality of small business management. In addition, they may be inappropriate as a way of coping with the unpredictable contemporary change environment with which modern-day managers of small businesses must struggle. Indeed, an emphasis throughout this chapter has been on the point that a prime determinant of growth is the way in which growth-orientated small businesses must successfully address the enabling and constraining nature of their external operating context.

It appears, therefore, that the literature provides foundation insight and guiding frames of reference for enhancing our understanding of key issues underpinning the growth of small firms, without providing an integrated growth theory. Moreover, a lot of those areas of literature that are 'business management' based seem to be substantially large company-orientated, failing to fully address the idiosyncrasies and problems impacting smaller firms. As a result, this chapter has made a selective utilisation of relevant literature that has facilitated a consideration of major barriers that may constrain small business development and must be circumvented or managed if effective growth is to be sustained.

Commencing with the external operating context, emphasis is placed on the predominance of totally unpredictable open-ended change and how this must be identified and understood if small firms are to grow effectively. With regard to the competitive environment, small businesses need to be sensitive to underlying industry and market structure characteristics if they are to understand the broad sources of competition.

In terms of the internal management operations of small firms, it is suggested that these businesses can be viewed as a 'potential unique problem-type', facing problems and barriers to growth that are owner-manager- and/or size-related. Particular attention has been afforded to internal barriers impacting growth, in the form of the potential inadequacy of existing assets, as well as the ability of management to teambuild and manage in order to effectively facilitate the nature and pace of development.

Having focused on key barriers that can potentially impede growth, the final section of the chapter considered, first, the limited utility of rational long-term planning in a small business context and, second, an alternative organisational learning perspective to effecting sustainable strategic development in small businesses.

In total, the chapter has provided an overall context for considering key management issues facing growing small firms.

Questions

1 To what extent do lifecycle and stages models of business development help in enhancing understanding of the growth process in small firms?

2 In what ways may rational long-term planning modes of management be inadequate for aiding small businesses to effect sustained growth?

3 What are likely to be the key constraints impacting small businesses in their attempts to effect growth through the broadening of their customer base?

Weblinks

www.inc.com/inc500
Inc magazine's list of the fastest-growing firms in the USA.

www.europes500.com
A list of the 500 fastest job creators in Europe.

www.fasttrack.co.uk
A list of the fastest-growing companies in the UK.

www.fastgrowth50.com
A regional barometer of fast-growing firms.

CHAPTER 23

Internationalisation and entrepreneurial businesses

Kevin Ibeh

23.1 Introduction

This chapter is concerned with the internationalisation of entrepreneurial small- and medium-sized enterprises (SMEs). It starts with some reflections on the widely acknowledged status of entrepreneurial SMEs as international actors and the economic and technological imperatives that have shaped policymaking and research on entrepreneurial internationalisation over the past few decades.

It next considers theoretical perspectives relevant to understanding the internationalisation of businesses, including the stage models, network theories and resource-based approaches. Further discussions centre on the factors that trigger internationalisation among entrepreneurial SMEs, the range and variety of internationalisation barriers faced by these businesses, the key characteristics associated with successful internationalisation among entrepreneurial SMEs and the policy support measures available across OECD countries to facilitate the internationalisation of entrepreneurial SMEs.

23.2 Learning objectives

This chapter has five learning objectives:

1 to explain internationalisation and discuss the various ways in which it can be achieved

2 to discuss the changing face of international entrepreneurship, including its underlying dynamics

3 to present the major theoretical explanations for the internationalisation of firms and identify the critical decisionmaker, firm and environmental influences on the phenomenon

4 to examine the major internationalisation barriers and challenges faced by entrepreneurial SMEs

5 to review policy and institutional measures commonly employed to promote internationalisation among entrepreneurial SMEs.

Key concepts
- entrepreneurship ■ internationalisation ■ 'stages' ■ networks ■ barriers
- policies

23.3 Internationalisation and entrepreneurial SMEs

Internationally focused entrepreneurship has witnessed a phenomenal level of growth since the latter part of the twentieth century. Driven largely by the remarkable, even revolutionary, changes in their external environments, entrepreneurial businesses and other companies, large and small have increasingly embraced the international growth path as a way of leveraging technological, organisational and interorganisational resources and reducing business costs and risks (Ibeh, 2006).

SMEs are not insignificant actors in this changing landscape. Indeed, their prevalence among the relatively recent category of firms referred to as born globals, global start-ups, international new ventures or micromultinationals (McDougall and Oviatt, 2000a; Borchert and Ibeh, 2008; Ibeh, Borchert and Wheeler, 2009) has given rise to a substantive research field, international entrepreneurship (Jones and Coviello, 2005; Zahra, 2005).

International entrepreneurship (IE) has been defined as a combination of innovative, risk-seeking behaviour that crosses national borders and is intended to create value for an organisation (McDougall and Oviatt, 2000b). Its essential contribution has been to illuminate a phenomenon – 'international new ventures' (INV) – that has been largely ignored by the entrepreneurship and international business theories. The former generally views new firm formation as a locally embedded process, while the latter does not really posit a role for smaller and inexperienced firms in the international markets (McNaughton, 2003).

What the IE research field has done, therefore, is make INVs, born globals and internationalising SMEs the main focus of concerted scholarly attention. This, as McDougall and Oviatt (2000a) noted, implies a search for more INVs and international entrepreneurs and, more importantly, understanding the key facilitating factors associated with this category of firms.

This seems very different from the period, not too long ago, when internationalisation was regarded as the domain of large corporations. Based on their presumed lack of internationalisation potential, small firms were largely ignored by most governments, policymakers and researchers seeking to promote a national economic position through greater firm-level internationalisation. This explains why the dominant theories and models of internationalisation – product lifecycle, market imperfection, internalisation/ transaction cost and the eclectic paradigm – have an essentially multinational enterprise (MNE) focus, explaining the conditions under which multinational enterprises (MNEs) extend and establish their activities – particularly production – overseas.

The serious difficulties experienced by Western MNEs during the 1970s and early 1980s, as well as the knock-on effects on their national economies, however, served to expose the weakness of this exclusive reliance on larger firms. Assailed by such developments as the oil crisis of 1973/1974, depressed global demand, intense international competition from Japan and newly industrialising countries and revolutionary new technologies, Western MNEs lost their grip on world trade and were forced into plant closures, downsizing and process re-engineering. Their governments soon reacted with massive programmes of deregulation and privatisation.

From the ashes of resulting redundancies, however, emerged many new small firms – their formation fuelled by rising trends in outsourcing, greater demand for services and micro-electronics (Bell, 1994; Ibeh, 2006). Subsequent evidence of the small firm sector's economic contribution was reported in a number of studies, notably the Bolton Committee's (1971) in the UK, Birch's (1979, 1981) in the USA and Storey and Johnson's (1987) in the European Community.

Concerns were expressed, however, about the disproportionate under-representation of smaller firms in the international market. The Bolton Commission, for example, reported that a significant proportion of SMEs with exporting potential had restricted themselves to domestic operations in the erroneous 'belief that size is an insuperable disadvantage' in internationalisation (Bolton Committee, 1971). Faced, therefore, with burgeoning trade deficits and an inert large-firm sector, policymakers began to focus on developing the little-tapped export potential of smaller firms (Bell, 1994). This favourable policy climate transformed SME internationalisation into an important area of enquiry – a situation that has continued to date (Ibeh, 2006).

23.4 Internationalisation and entrepreneurial SMEs: concepts, context and extent

The term 'internationalisation' commonly refers to the process of increasing involvement in international operations (Welch and Luostarinen, 1988; Bell, Crick and Young, 2004). It describes the continuum that stretches from the firm's first import activity or extra-regional expansion or domestic internationalisation to full globalisation (Wiedersheim-Paul, Olsen and Welch, 1978; Luostarinen, 1994).

Full company globalisation is characterised by the establishment of manufacturing plants and marketing affiliates across major international regions, extensive outsourcing of inputs and marketing of outputs across borders and worldwide integration and coordination of resources and operations in pursuit of global competitiveness. Sometimes used interchangeably with globalisation (its most evolved form), internationalisation is attained through a variety of international market entry and development modes (Young, 1990; Welch, Benito and Petersen, 2007). These include direct and indirect exporting, licensing, franchising, management contract, turn-key contract, contract manufacturing/international subcontracting, industrial cooperation agreements, project operations, contractual joint venture, equity joint venture, strategic alliances, mergers and acquisitions and wholly owned subsidiaries.

A number of authors have tried to classify internationalisation modes. This chapter employs Luostarinen's (1980) approach, whose distinctions between home and overseas production, plus direct and non-direct investments, offer useful insights into understanding SME versus large-firm internationalisation. In general terms, the progression from home-based internationalisation modes to overseas production modes and from non-direct investment modes to direct ones, is marked by increased resource commitments/ transfer and risks. Given their obvious resource (financial and managerial) and attitudinal (towards risk/control) differences, small and large firms have tended to adopt divergent internationalisation modes. Indeed, SMEs are more likely to supply their international markets from domestic production bases (through indirect and direct exporting and sales/service subsidiaries). This explains why the bulk of the literature on SME internationalisation originates from exporting research.

According to a classic OECD (1997a) report, SMEs' share of exports in each of the surveyed OECD and Asian economies range between 15 and 50 per cent, with 20 and 80 per cent being active exporters (see Table 23.1). In general, SME internationalisation

Table 23.1 Estimates of the extent of SME internationalisation

	Percentages of exports from SMEs	Percentages of SMEs exporting	Notes
Australia	n.a.	5 to 10	0–100 employees
Belgium		20	0–500 employees
Canada		14	5–200 employees
Denmark	46		< 500 employees
Finland	23		
France	26		
Greece	n.a.	n.a.	SME exports as percentage of industry turnover = 15–20 per cent
Ireland		25	
Italy	52.7		< 500 employees
		68	51–100 employees
		80	101–300 employees
		83	301–500 employees
Japan	13.5		< 300 direct
	30–35		< 300 indirect
Netherlands	26		< 100 indirect + direct
		17	0–9 employees
		43	10–99 employees
		67	100+ employees
Portugal	–	–	No figures available
Spain		18	< 20 employees
		50	51–100 employees
		70	101–200 employees
Sweden	36		< 200 employees
Switzerland	40		
United Kingdom		16–20	
United States	11	12*	
China	40–60		
Republic of Korea	40		
Indonesia	10.6		
Chinese Taipei	56		
Thailand	10		
Malaysia	15		
Singapore	16		
Vietnam	20		

Source: Ibeh, 2006 and OECD, 1997a

is greater in small, open economies and less in larger, more self-contained economies. This, however, is not always the case. France and Italy still have 30 and 70 per cent of exports, respectively, contributed by SMEs, while internationalisation in small, open economies such as Australia, Malaysia and Greece is less than might be expected (Ibeh, 2006).

That entrepreneurial SMEs are not restricting their internationalisation forays to exporting, however, is evident in the rising trend towards small firms' adoption of more direct forms of international marketing, including low-level foreign direct investments (FDI), strategic alliances, licensing, joint ventures and similar cooperation-based modes (Dimitratos, Johnson, Slow and Young, 2003; Ibeh, Borchert and Wheeler, 2009). OECD (1997a) statistics indicate the extent of SME internationalisation thus (Ibeh, 2006):

> about 10% of SMEs are engaged in FDI and about 10% or more foreign investment appear to be attributable to SMEs. Around 10 to 15% of SMEs have licences, franchises or other arrangements with firms outside their home country . . . It is estimated that about 1% or less of SMEs (30,000 to 40,000) can be said to be global, in the sense of being active in multiple countries and/or across several continents, or having the ability to operate wherever they see fit . . . another 5 to 10% of SMEs in manufacturing . . . can be said to be extensively inter-nationalized . . . [with] a further 10 to 20% . . . active in up to three foreign countries.

These internationally active SMEs are growing faster than their domestic counterparts. Those in niche markets and new (including high-tech) industries constitute the fastest-growing segment (20 per cent), while those in traditional industries (around 50 per cent) internationalise incrementally via exporting. It would, indeed, appear that most SMEs now see internationalisation as not only fashionable but also imperative. This is based on the realisation that pressures from inward internationalisation are likely to be most unkind to firms that stand still and are not internationally active.

As the OECD (1997a) reports, probably less than 40 per cent of SMEs are insulated from any effects of globalisation and the proportion of such firms (mainly small service providers) is expected to contract further to 20 per cent. This does not imply that service firms are not active internationally – many play an increasingly important international role (Erramilli and Rao, 1990; Sharma, 1993; Hellman, 1996; Deprey, 2011) – but measurement difficulties prevent us from having an overall picture of the extent of service SMEs' internationalisation. It should be noted, nevertheless, that the easily measured physical, manufactured exports are often accompanied by significant international SME service activity, including customer service, design, distribution, marketing, etc. (Ibeh, 2006).

23.5 Explaining SME internationalisation

Firm internationalisation has been studied from both the perspective of export development (involving mostly SMEs) and the emergence of the MNEs (Bell and Young, 1998). Focusing on SME internationalisation, three theoretical approaches can be identified:

- incremental internationalisation (or stage of development) models
- network theory
- resource-based perspectives, including international entrepreneurship and dynamic capability/knowledge-based perspectives.

23.5.1 Incremental internationalisation – or stage of development – models

The literature accommodates a number of 'stage' models that have been advanced to explain the process of a firm's development along the internationalisation route. Common to all these models is the view of the firm's international market development as a sequential, 'staged' process. All have their roots in the behavioural theory of the firm (Cyert and March, 1963) and Penrose's (1959) theory of the growth of the firm.

According to the 'stage' theorists, firms adopt an incremental, evolutionary approach to foreign markets, gradually deepening their commitment and investment as they gain in international market knowledge and experience (Johanson and Vahlne, 1977, 1990). Firms are also believed to target neighbouring, 'psychically close' countries initially and, subsequently, enter foreign markets with successively larger psychic distance. 'Psychic distance' refers to the extent of proximity in geography, language, culture, political systems and business factors – e.g., industry structure and competitive environment (Ibeh and Kasem, 2011).

Pioneering this approach was Johanson and Vahlne's (1977) model of knowledge development and increasing foreign market commitment, which built on Johanson and Wiedersham-Paul's (1975) study of the internationalisation behaviour of four Swedish firms from their early beginnings. They found that the internationalisation process was the consequence of a series of incremental decisions, rather than large, spectacular foreign investments. Four different stages were identified in relation to a firm's international involvement:

1 no regular exports

2 exports via independent representation (agents)

3 sales subsidiaries

4 production/manufacturing.

As Johanson and Vahlne (1990: 13) stated:

> the firm's engagement in a specific foreign market develops according to an establishment chain, i.e. at the start no export activities are performed in the market, then export takes place via independent representatives, later through a sales subsidiary, and, eventually manufacturing may follow.

A further dimension was added to the internationalisation process model by Wiedersheim-Paul, Olson and Welch's (1978) work. They extended the establishment chain backwards to include a pre-export-stage. Starting to export was found to be influenced by the interplay between 'attention-evoking factors' and the individual decisionmaker, the environment and history of the firm, including experience in extra-regional expansion (domestic internationalisation). Thus, the establishment chain model attempts to explain the *whole* process of a firm's internationalisation, from the pre-export to post-export stages, including FDI.

Cognisance should be taken of the differences in perspectives adopted by these 'stage theorists'. Anderson (1993), for example, distinguished between the Uppsala internationalisation (U) models and innovation-related (I) models. While the former clearly refers to the models that emerged from a Swedish school of that description, the composition of the latter is not so clear. It seems appropriate, however, to include as innovation-related models those works that present export development as an innovation–adoption cycle (Lee and Brasch, 1978; Reid, 1981) and those which see it as a 'learning curve', influenced by external, attention-evoking stimuli (e.g., unsolicited orders or enquiries) and internal factors (e.g., managerial ambitions and excess capacity; Bilkey and Tesar, 1977; Cavusgil, 1980; Czinkota and Johnston, 1982; Crick, 1995).

The actual number of 'stages' undergone by internationalising firms also differs according to the model, but this, as observed by Anderson (1993: 212), 'reflect[s] semantic differences rather than real differences concerning the nature of the internationalization process'. Anderson's (1993: 227) major criticisms, however, are 'the lack of proper design to explain the development process', the absence of clear-cut boundaries between stages and the lack of 'tests of validity and reliability'.

The incremental internationalisation models have also been faulted on grounds of having limited applicability. Indeed, many studies involving firms from small domestic markets, service firms, high-tech, knowledge-intensive and entrepreneurial firms, subcontractors and international new ventures have reported evidence that counters the incremental approach (Bell, 1995; Etemad, 2004). As Bell (1995) explains, that is because stage theories use linear models to explain dynamic, interactive, non-linear behaviour.

Clark, Pugh and Mallory (1997: 616) observed that the establishment model was one of several paths to FDI, noting that 'firms often bypass the intermediate stages to FDI'. The remarks by Bell and Young (1998) – that the incremental internationalisation models merely identify the internationalisation patterns of certain firms, but not of others and they fail to adequately explain the processes involved – seem to reflect the consensus position on the topic.

Madsen and Servais (1997) sought to clarify the situation by categorising internationalising firms into three kinds. First, the traditional exporters with internationalisation patterns largely reflecting the traditional stages model. Second, firms that leapfrog some stages – e.g., late starters that have only domestic sales for many years, but then suddenly invest in a distant foreign market. Third, the born global firms. Suffice it to say that 'the stages theory has merit in its use as a framework for classification purposes rather than for an understanding of the internationalization process' (Turnbull, 1987: 21).

Findings supportive of the 'psychic distance' concept have been reported in a variety of studies, including Styles and Ambler's (1994: 40) research, which concluded that 'firms should focus on those countries which are closest in "psychic distance" for early export endeavours'. There have, however, been refutations of the psychic distance concept, most notably by Czinkota and Ursic (1987) and, to a lesser degree, by the 'network school' (Johanson and Mattsson, 1988). The latter ascribe limited relevance to the concept in the face of vastly improving global communications and transportation infrastructures, as well as increasing market convergence. Evidence of 'client followership' has also been reported (Bell, 1994), which is inconsistent with the 'intuitive logic' (Sullivan and Bauerschmidt, 1990) of the psychic distance concept. O'Grady and Lane's (1996) Canadian study further identified a 'psychic distance paradox' – that operations in psychically close countries are not necessarily easy to manage because assumptions of similarity can prevent executives from learning about critical differences.

Despite valid criticisms, the stage of development perspective remains a significant contribution to the understanding of SME internationalisation – a fact reinforced by the more recent refinement of the approach by Johanson and Vahlne (2009). Prior to its emergence, internationalisation was essentially theorised and discussed in terms of the MNE. It is also the case that its focus on initial internationalisation attracted considerable research attention and illumination to SME internationalisation, extending even to the pre-export stage.

The postulations on psychic distance may now appear dated, given the more recent advancements in ICT, including social media, but few would disagree that they resonate with the market selection pattern intuitively associated with exporters (Madsen and Servais, 1997). Criticisms of the model, based on its failure to reflect the internationalisation behaviour of rapidly internationalising entrepreneurial firms, including knowledge-intensive and service firms, are acknowledged. Nevertheless, most studies involving firms in mature industries have largely supported the model's basic propositions.

23.5.2 Network theory

Another significant strand of internationalisation research was the development, from international industrial marketing, of the network or interaction and relationship concepts. The basic tenet is that internationalisation proceeds through an interplay between increasing commitment to and evolving knowledge about foreign markets, gained mainly from interactions in the foreign markets. These interactions – dynamic, evolving, less structured – yield increased mutual knowledge and trust between international market actors and, subsequently, greater internationalisation commitment. In summary, a firm begins the export process by forming relationships that will deliver experiential knowledge about a market and then commits resources in accordance with the degree of experiential knowledge it progressively gains from these relationships (Styles and Ambler, 1994; Vissak, Ibeh and Paliwoda, 2007; Johanson and Vahlne, 2009).

In network theory, markets are seen as a system of relationships between a number of players, including customers, suppliers, competitors, family, friends and private and public support agencies. Strategic action, therefore, is rarely limited to a single firm and the nature of relationships established with others in the market influences and often dictates future strategic options. For example, firms can expand from domestic to international markets through existing relationships that offer contacts and help to develop new partners and positions in new markets. At the same time, network relationships may restrict the nature of a firm's growth initiatives (Ibeh, 2006; Ibeh and Kasem, 2011).

Internationalisation driven by customer/client followership or what Hellman (1996) referred to as 'customer-driven internationalisation' has been seen in service, high-tech and knowledge-intensive sectors (Bell, Crick and Young, 2004; Ibeh, Young and Lin, 2004). As observed by Johanson and Mattsson (1988), a firm's success in entering new international markets is more dependent on its relationships with current markets, both domestic and international, than it is on the chosen market and its cultural characteristics. This subtle shift from the core Uppsala internationalisation model (the psychic distance concept) was further endorsed by Johanson and Vahlne's (1992) remarks that many firms enter new foreign markets almost blindly, propelled not by strategic decisions or market research, but social exchange processes, interactions and networks.

A growing body of evidence exists on the role of network relationships in SME internationalisation. Coviello and Munro (1995, 1997), for example, found that successful New Zealand-based software firms are actively involved in international networks and outsource many market development activities to network partners. As Coviello and Munro (1997: 366) observed, 'the network perspective goes beyond the models of incremental internationalization by suggesting that firms' strategy emerges as a pattern of behavior influenced by a variety of network relationships'. Coviello and Munro's evidence, while supportive of network theory, recognised the occurrence of internationalisation stages, albeit in a much-condensed and accelerated form. This attempt to reconcile the network perspective with the work of the stage theorists and the 'international new venture' scholars also formed the substance of Madsen and Servais (1997) theory-building effort.

There is no doubt that the network perspective has brought immense value to the understanding of the internationalisation process, particularly among SMEs. It presents a view of SME internationalisation that should be seen more as a complement than an alternative to the incremental internationalisation model – a point reinforced by Johanson and Vahlne's recent refinement of the Uppsala internationalisation model and its focus on business networks (Johanson and Vahlne, 2009).

23.5.3 Resource-based perspectives (knowledge-based and international entrepreneurship perspectives)

A major recent development in the SME internationalisation research has been the increasing adoption of the resource-based theory as an integrative platform for explaining firm-level internationalisation (Bell and Young, 1998; Peng, 2001; Ibeh, 2001, 2005). As Bell and Young (1998) explained, the resource-based perspective presents a holistic view of the firm, such that key internationalisation decisions are made within a coordinated framework of resources and capabilities (whether internal or externally leveraged), as well as environmental (including competitive) realities. They elaborated that firms will have a different mix of resources/competencies/capabilities and resource/competence/capability gaps, and their strategic responses to these allow for the possibility of different paths to growth and internationalisation. It could be argued that the resource-based theory of internationalisation is actually a more grounded restatement of the business strategy and contingency frameworks. It would appear to have met the need to root contingency frameworks within an underlying theory. As its proponents observe, there is a close relationship with contingency approaches that are designed to show the influence of a range of internal and external variables. This perspective is equally implicit in the business strategy frameworks and more recent work on international entrepreneurship.

The business strategy perspective proposes a strategically planned, rational approach to internationalisation, such that decisions on foreign market entry and servicing strategies (entry mode) are made in the context of the firm's overall strategic development and guided by rigorous analysis of relevant internal and external environmental factors (Young, 1987; Young, Hamill, Wheeler and Davis, 1989).

This is consistent with Chandler's (1962) view that structure follows strategy. It also reflects Turnbull's (1987) conclusion that a company's stage of internationalisation is largely determined by the operating environment, industry structure and its own marketing strategy. The business strategy perspective is implicit in much of the mainstream export literature, notably Aaby and Slater's (1989) model (widely referred to as the 'strategic export model'), Namiki's (1994) taxonomic analysis of export marketing strategy, Cavusgil and Zou's (1994) path analysis of export marketing strategy and performance, as well as Reid's (1983a) contingency framework.

International entrepreneurship researchers have generally sought to explain the behaviour of such recently identified firm categories as 'born globals', 'global start-ups', 'international new ventures', 'born-internationals', 'rapidly internationalising firms', 'committed internationalists' and 'micromultinationals' by highlighting the quality of their knowledge assets (including the knowledge and experiential resources embedded in their top management), internationally focused entrepreneurial orientation, privileged access to network resources, social capital and other market-based assets, among others (Oviatt and McDougall, 1994a, 1994b; Bell, 1995; Knight and Cavusgil, 1996; Madsen and Servais, 1997; Jones, 1999; Dimitratos, Johnson, Slow and Young, 2003; Etemad, 2004; Ibeh, Young and Lin, 2004; Ibeh, Johnson, Dimitratos and Slow, 2004). According to this literature stream, firms, including SMEs, would seem to have become more entrepreneurial and sophisticated with regard to their appreciation of international growth opportunities and feasible entry mode options. This has resulted in a faster pace of internationalisation (rapid internationalising firms) and more ambitious entry mode selection behaviour (micromultinationals).

A common denominator of these frameworks is the recognition that internationalisation is affected by multiple influences and a range of the firms' internationalisation decisions are made in an holistic way. There appears to be an increasing realisation of this extended base of internationalisation parameters.

Having identified partial and situational relevance for each of the existing internationalisation models, Bell and Young (1998) invited more attention to be given to their 'potential complementarities'. Researchers seem to have accepted this challenge. For example, Coviello and Munro's (1997) study of New Zealand software SMEs reported evidence of incremental internationalisation, network-driven internationalisation, as well as accelerated internationalisation (international new ventures), which is similar to the range of propositions offered by Madsen and Servais (1997) in their conceptualisations of 'born globals'.

It will be interesting to see what other explanatory frameworks will emerge in the growing area of the internationalisation of small firms. Of more immediate relevance, however, is the role of internal (firm or decisionmaker) and external (environmental) factors that stage theorists, network scholars, resource-based theorists, business strategy and international entrepreneurship scholars have identified as significant to SMEs' initial internationalisation decisions.

23.6 Stimulating international entrepreneurship

To initiate and subsequently develop international activity, a firm must first be influenced by stimulating or 'attention-evoking' factors. The nature of these stimuli may offer invaluable insights into why some SMEs successfully internationalise while others do not. Building on previous typologies of internationalisation stimuli, Albaum, Strandskov, Duerr and Dowd (1994) identified the following four categories:

- *internal-proactive* factors associated with the SME's own initiative to exploit its unique internal competencies – e.g., potential for export-led growth
- *internal-reactive* responding to pressures from the internal environment – e.g., accumulation of unsold goods
- *external-proactive* active exploitation by management of market possibilities – e.g., identification of better opportunities abroad
- *external-reactive* reaction to factors from the external environment – e.g., receipt of unsolicited foreign orders.

Nevertheless, research on initial internationalisation suggests that stimuli are not sufficient on their own. They need to be supported by facilitating factors associated with the decisionmaker, organisation and environment. These broad factors are also thought to facilitate successful international entrepreneurship activity (Ibeh and Analogbei, 2010).

23.6.1 Decisionmaker characteristics

Decisionmaker characteristics are generally considered to have, in Brooks' and Rosson's (1982) words, 'a decided impact on export decision'. All the major review articles on empirical exporting research have, similarly, concluded on the decisive importance of decisionmakers' characteristics (Wheeler, Ibeh and Dimitratos, 2008; OECD, 2009). As Reid (1981: 109) noted, too, 'empirical evidence points conclusively to the decisionmakers' attitude, experience, motivation and expectations as primary determinants in firms engaging in foreign marketing activity'.

This is particularly so in small firms, where power – particularly decision-making power – is generally concentrated in the hands of one or very few persons. According to Miesenbock (1988: 42), 'the key variable in small business internationalization is the decision maker of the firm. He or she is the one to decide starting, ending and increasing international activities'. Empirical findings on the specific decisionmaker characteristics that increase the likelihood of SME internationalisation have, however, been inconsistent. This is particularly true of findings on decisionmakers' age and level of educational attainment. Garnier's (1982) remarks that it was not possible to ascertain whether or not there were statistically significant differences between managers of internationalised and non-internationalised firms with respect to age and level of education would appear to reflect the available evidence.

With regard to international orientation – variously defined as foreign education or work experience, travel, foreign birth, world-mindedness (Boatler, 1994) – the balance of empirical evidence is that decisionmakers of internationalised SMEs are likely to have spent part of their lives abroad and be generally not very affected by foreign business-related uncertainties. Miesenbock (1988: 42) concluded, from an extensive review of the literature, that 'the external contacts of the decision maker seem to be the most important objective characteristic'.

Closely related to international orientation is another characteristic that may be referred to as international ethnic ties or contact networks. There is growing evidence that decisionmakers whose contact networks are internationally spread are more likely to exploit international market opportunities than those who lack such ties (OECD, 2009). Indeed, Jackson (1981) found the Zionist links of British Jews to be significant in explaining the flow of Israeli exports into Britain. Further supportive evidence has been reported by Crick and Chaudhry (1995) and Zafarullah, Ali and Young (1998) in their respective studies of British-Asian and Pakistani SMEs (see Chapter 11).

Decisionmakers' psychological traits provide a further set of variables that have been widely studied. A large number of empirical findings have associated decision-makers of internationalised SMEs with such characteristics as:

- favourable perception of exporting risks, costs, profits and growth
- positive attitudes toward exporting
- aggressiveness and dynamism
- flexibility
- self-confidence.

As observed by Ford and Leonidou (1991: 3), 'firms with a decision maker perceiving risk in the export market as being lower versus risk in the domestic market, profits in the export market as being higher versus profits in the domestic market, and costs in the export market as being lower versus costs in the domestic market are more likely to become exporters'. Nevertheless, as Miesenbock (1988: 43) stated 'the explanatory power of psychologically-oriented research in internationalization . . . [is] controversial'.

23.6.2 Firm characteristics and competencies

Very few issues in SME internationalisation research have as much empirical support as the positive link between management support, commitment, perceptions and attitude and internationalisation behaviour (Wheeler, Ibeh and Dimitratos, 2008). As Aaby and Slater (1989: 16) remarked, 'management commitment and management perceptions and attitudes towards export problems and incentives are good predictors of export [behaviour]'. Studies have also found a much higher propensity to internation-alise (export) among firms with market (or organisational) planning or exploration. As Aaby and Slater (1989: 19) concluded, 'the implementation of a process for system-atically exploring, analysing, and planning for export seems to be a very powerful discriminator between . . . exporters and non-exporters'.

Findings on the impact of firm size (whether measured by employee numbers, sales, ownership of capital equipment, financial capability or a combination of criteria) on internationalisation behaviour have been mixed, if not outright controversial. The balance of evidence, however, suggests the importance of size, particularly in initiating international activity. As a general rule, larger firms are more likely to internationalise than small firms. Beyond some point, however, exporting would appear not to be correlated with size – a view corroborated by Withey's (1980) critical mass of 20 employees for crossing the internationalisation threshold. Reid (1982: 101) explained it thus: 'absolute size using traditional indicators (assets, employees, functional specialisation, and sales) predominantly affect . . . [small firms'] export entry'. This standard does not, however, apply to SMEs in high-tech, knowledge-intensive and service sectors (Bell, 1994). Indeed, the use of e-commerce and online marketing via the World Wide Web and internet is increasingly removing whatever deterrence size brings to the internationalisation of SMEs, even in traditional industries.

The SME's industry or product type has also been found to influence international market entry. As Tybejee (1994) remarked, industry membership or the structural characteristics of the industry determine the conditions in which a firm competes and, consequently, its internationalisation. Garnier (1982: 113), for example, in a study of Canadian printing and electrical industries, reported that 'the most immediate cause of export[ing] . . . is the nature of the product or service offered by the exporting firm'. While SMEs in industries characterised by low skill level, low intrinsic value, bulkiness and high transportation costs are less likely to internationalise, those in sectors marked by short lifecycles are motivated to accelerate their entry into the international markets (Tybejee, 1994; McGuinness and Little, 1981). Another firm characteristic that appears to influence an SME's internationalisation is its history, including previous experience of extra-regional expansion, importing experience or 'inward internationalisation'. Such experiences and attendant (network) relationships have been found to be significant precursors of internationalisation.

Empirical studies on SME internationalisation have also underscored the importance of firm competencies. Indeed, it has been suggested that 'firm competencies are probably more important than firm characteristics' (Aaby and Slater, 1989: 21). The specific dimensions of firm competencies that, on balance, have been empirically supported include:

- technology intensity
- R&D
- systematic market research
- product development
- unique product attributes and quality
- distribution, delivery and service quality
- advertising and sales promotion.

23.6.3 Characteristics of the firm's environment

Relative to larger firms, SMEs tend to lack the necessary resources and political clout to control their operating environment. Empirical findings can broadly be categorised as either those related to the firm's domestic environment or those concerned with foreign (target) market attractiveness.

As observed by Miesenbock (1988: 44), 'the home country of the firm also determines the performed export behavior'. The legal system 'may facilitate (e.g. tax advantages in exporting) or complicate (e.g. foreign exchange regulations) international business. The same holds for infrastructure (e.g. distribution facilities or impediments)' (Miesenbock, 1988: 44). Wiedersheim-Paul, Olson and Welch's (1978) model of pre-export behaviour and Garnier's (1982) theoretical model of the export process in a small firm, both reflect this impact of the domestic environment. The former suggests that firms' location within an 'enterprise environment' facilitates an efficient exchange of information, as well as creates 'possibilities for "contagion transmission" of ideas from other firms, in different stages of expansion' (Wiedersheim-Paul, Olson and Welch, 1978: 47). Garnier (1982) also sees general characteristics of the environment, as well as the industry in which small firms operate, as affecting their decision to export or refrain from so doing. Bilkey (1978) and Pavord and Bogart (1975) identified 'adverse home market conditions' as a push factor in export initiation, one example being 'home market saturation'.

With respect to foreign (target) market environments, studies have reported foreign government-imposed barriers and poor infrastructure – road and telephone systems – to be significant impediments to export market choice. Ford and Leonidou (1991: 3) concluded that 'firms producing products which have to be modified in order to conform with the rules and regulations of foreign governments . . . are less likely to become exporters'. Further discussions on these and related issues are undertaken in the next section.

23.7 Barriers to SME internationalisation

SMEs typically face several obstacles and challenges as they attempt to initiate, develop or sustain international entrepreneurship activities (Ibeh, 2006; OECD, 2009). Leonidou (1995: 29) defined these barriers as 'all those attitudinal, structural, operational, and other constraints that hinder the firm's ability to initiate, develop, or sustain international operations'.

Different classification schemes have been used in the literature with respect to these challenges. In an extensive review of export barrier research, Leonidou (1995) combined his earlier framework with Cavusgil's (1984), giving a 'two-dimensional export barrier schema' (Kaleka and Katsikeas, 1995). This identified four categories of problems:

- internal-domestic
- internal-foreign
- external-domestic
- external-foreign.

23.7.1 Internal-domestic

The problems in this category encompass obstacles emanating from within the firm and relating to its home country environment. They include:

- a lack of personnel with the requisite information and knowledge of export marketing, including expertise in handling such problems as foreign government regulations
- negative perceptions of risks involved in selling abroad
- management emphasis on developing domestic market activities, particularly a large-sized domestic market.

These kinds of internationalisation barriers, including limited firm resources and international contacts and lack of requisite managerial knowledge, were highlighted in an OECD (2009) report.

23.7.2 Internal-foreign

This category of problems includes those that arise mainly from SMEs' limited marketing ability and are experienced in the foreign (target) market environment.

For some SMEs, international market entry is inhibited if product modifications are required to meet foreign safety or health standards or customers' specifications. As Moini (1997: 86) remarked, 'adapting a product to foreign standards may require a large initial investment which many non-exporters lack'. Similar difficulties have also been reported with regard to providing repair and technical services, pricing and communicating with overseas customers.

Other typical obstacles here include both high transportation costs and transportation, service and delivery-related difficulties.

23.7.3 External-domestic

The problems that are grouped in this category emanate from SMEs' domestic environments, but are typically beyond their control. Among the most-cited obstacles are the vast amount of time and complex documentation involved in international marketing. Also, often, the absence of adequate government support – relating to incentives and infrastructure – to overcome internationalisation barriers and the lack of reasonable access to (or prohibitive cost of) capital needed to finance internationalisation.

23.7.4 External-foreign

This category of problems relates to those that originate outside SMEs and are, typically, experienced in international markets.

Several studies have reported on the inhibiting impact of foreign government-imposed restrictions, including exchange rate, import and tariff regulations.

Equally problematic for SMEs is the development of reliable overseas contacts/distributors/representatives, due to difficulties with overcoming language and cultural differences, for example.

Other often-cited internationalisation barriers in this category are the intensity of competition in international markets or SMEs' lack of price competitiveness and the difficulties of obtaining payments.

23.7.5 How SMEs deal with barriers to internationalisation

The nature of firms' responses to these obstacles depends broadly on the background decisionmaker and firm characteristics, specifically the organisations' size, international business experience, international market research orientation and export involvement. For example, inexperienced exporters, relative to regular exporters, perceive strict import quotas and confusing import regulations as much more important in hindering their entry into the Japanese market (Namiki, 1988). Similarly, marginal exporters, compared to their more active counterparts, have significantly different perceptions – the former finding shipping and trade documentation complex and feeling uncertain about shipping costs. Similar conclusions were reached by Tesar and Tarleton (1982), with respect to passive and aggressive exporters among their

Wisconsin and Virginia sample, and Bell (1997), with regard to occasional, frequent and aggressive exporters.

It also appears that firms at different stages of internationalisation face problems of differing types and severity (Bilkey and Tesar, 1977; Bilkey, 1978; Bell, 1997). A three-nation study by Bell (1997: 602), for example, reported that, while finance-related problems 'often intensify with increased international exposure, . . . marketing-related factors tend to decline as firms become more active in export markets'. The OECD (2009) also found resource limitations, especially of a financial kind, to be particularly prevalent among smaller, newly internationalising firms.

23.8 Policy and institutional support for SME internationalisation

This section highlights the existing policy frameworks and support programmes that underpin SME internationalisation in most OECD countries. Currently used measures can be classified as direct or indirect, in terms of whether they are specifically designed for export development or with a general aim of enhancing SMEs' overall competitiveness – internationalisation benefits being only implied (OECD, 2009).

As observed by Seringhaus and Rosson (1991: 3), direct assistance encapsulates 'an array of programmes that range from awareness-creating, interest-stimulating, research support, export preparation, export market entry, to export market development and expansion-focused activities'. These have broadly been categorised by Crick and Czinkota (1995) as export service programmes (e.g., seminars for potential exporters, export consultancy and export financing) and market development programmes (e.g., dissemination of sales leads to local firms, participation in trade shows and preparation of market analyses).

Indirect assistance extends to those aspects described as economic infrastructure (Owualah, 1987), whether hardware (financial, fiscal and plant and machinery leasing) or software (training, advice, information). They are generally aimed at effecting structural and process change within companies (Seringhaus and Rosson, 1991) and are often integrated into the industrial policies implemented by various governments at central and/or regional levels (Bell, 1994). Such programmes also, increasingly, seek to facilitate the adoption of innovative new technologies and best practices (including networking) by firms.

Programmes of direct and indirect support include:

- providing access to foreign market information
- providing some form of financial assistance (e.g., export credit or foreign investment guarantees, venture capital, grants and subsidies)
- improving SMEs' capabilities through management advisory services and help with R&D and technology
- providing SMEs with a better business environment, by facilitating networking and subcontracting arrangements and offering simplified, one-stop assistance units, industrial parks and arbitration assistance.

Importantly, the extent of the involvement of the government and private sector in terms of the actual support they provide varies from country to country. While government involvement appears to be dominant in countries such as the UK, Ireland and Canada, others, such as Finland, Denmark and Germany, tend to emphasise private-sector leadership in providing support. Yet, a few others – notably, France, The Netherlands and Austria – seem to provide highly rated support at both public- and private-sector levels.

Given that no firm conclusions have been reached regarding the relative merits of public versus quasi-public sector support mechanisms (Bell, 1997), it is safe to suggest 'delivery systems that make use of existing and potential private-sector activities are more likely to be cost-effective' (OECD, 1997a: 14).

Despite the sophistication and comprehensiveness of policy measures available in advanced (as well as developing) economies, empirical findings on SMEs' level of awareness of usage and satisfaction with these programmes have been generally negative. This highlights the challenging nature of the task of seeking to improve SME internationalisation policy – a task that the summary below attempts to address.

23.9 Chapter summary

It would appear from the unremitting pressures of globalisation that the trend towards SMEs undertaking international entrepreneurship can only intensify. The prognosis of a continuing shrinkage in the percentage of SMEs insulated from (inward) globalisation effects implies, also, that SMEs ignoring internationalisation realities risk losing their competitiveness. This situation makes it even more imperative that as many SMEs as possible are given whatever support is necessary to encourage their internationalisation.

A consensus appears to have emerged among academic researchers and policymakers that SMEs negotiate varying paths to internationalisation. Having been extensively and successfully challenged, the 'stage' approach would seem to have lost its traditional hegemony to a more inclusive, integrative view of SMEs' internationalisation. This perspective, articulated by Bell and Young (1998) among others, presents extant frameworks – incremental models, a network-driven, resource-based computer app, including knowledge-based/dynamic capability and international entrepreneurship perspectives – as complementary rather than competing explanations. While some SMEs internationalise in an incremental manner, others may accelerate through the process – driven, possibly, by their differential resource factors, unique knowledge or capabilities or existing network relationships. Thus, it behoves policymakers to seek greater understanding of SMEs as the objects of their policy measures. Such an under-standing should inform the segmentation of these SMEs for policymaking purposes and, subsequently, lead to needs-based targeting of appropriate assistance and support (Ibeh, 2006).

The idea of segmenting assistance targets is not new in the literature – it is integral to the much-criticised stage models. What should, perhaps, be new is a rethinking of the segmentation framework, such that the 'stage-by-stage' approach is seen not as 'the way', but as *one* of the ways to internationalise on a spectrum that includes network-driven and accelerated internationalisation, as well as strategy/resource-based internationalisation. Hopefully, this perspective would translate as a broadening of the focus of programmes supporting SME internationalisation beyond their traditional exporting emphasis (Bell, 1994).

Whatever the approach taken, policymakers should recognise the existence of different internationalisation pathways. For incrementally inclined firms, the usual methods of targeting assistance, based on stages of internationalisation, may be appropriate. SMEs at the lower stages may need intensive information support and one-to-one counselling to nudge them along their learning curve, while those at more advanced stages may require more experiential-type knowledge and, perhaps, assistance aimed at easing the financial obstacles facing them as they target foreign customers (Crick and Czinkota, 1995).

Proper acknowledgement of the reality of accelerated internationalisation should imply, for example, programmes of support for networkbuilding and activation among SMEs. Existing efforts in this direction – at industry, national and regional levels – should be strengthened. It seems appropriate, also, to widen the assistance programmes on offer to reflect a more diversified mix of internationalisation possibilities than is currently the case, such that SMEs wishing to establish joint venture operations overseas or engage in strategic alliances or even acquire a production plant abroad would find the requisite support and encouragement (Ibeh, Johnson, Dimitratos and Slow, 2004).

Given, also, the widely appreciated opportunities offered by e-commerce and online marketing, SMEs should be supported by having access to appropriate training and consultancy to optimise the benefits of Internet-based internationalisation.

To effectively target SMEs and their decisionmakers with the appropriate kind of competence-enhancing support, it may be useful to employ a classification scheme built on their current characteristics and competencies – i.e., internationalised entrepreneurial firms, internationalised less entrepreneurial firms, non-internationalised entrepreneurial firms and less internationalised non-entrepreneurial firms (see Figure 23.1).

Figure 23.1 Sample recommendations for categories of SMEs

	Entrepreneurial	Less entrepreneurial
Internationalised	[IV] * Encourage best practice – R&D, IT, innovation * Facilitate participation in network structures * Mitigate operational problems, assist foreign customers, ease market access	[III] * Seek positive reinforcement * Deploy liasion officer/problemsolver * Encourage networking; export clubs * Establish mentoring scheme
Non-internationalised	[I] * Assist to redress competency gap * Provide consultancy support and training * Ease access to available support * Introduce mentoring scheme * Encourage best practice – R&D, IT, innovation, networking	[II] * Introduce change agents * Provide training/information support * Help with foreign market contacts * Encourage networking * Establish and utilise international market brokers

For the non-internationalised, less entrepreneurial SMEs, the focus should be on improving the entrepreneurial and international orientation of their key decisionmaker(s) through seminars and workshops, export information provision, sponsorship to trade fairs and 'experiential knowledge assistance programmes' (Knight, Bell and McNaughton, 2003). This should also involve introducing an external agent (Wiedersheim-Paul, Olson and Welch, 1978) on a part-time or consultancy basis. Ideally, non-internationalised SMEs lacking an entrepreneurial orientation should be assisted in the search for, and employment of, managers with the requisite profiles – i.e., experienced, internationally orientated and connected decisionmakers.

Other measures that may be useful here include encouraging networking and linking them with foreign customers. The latter could be particularly crucial, given the strength of empirical evidence on the impact of unsolicited orders from abroad in stimulating initial internationalisation.

Clearly, non-internationalised entrepreneurial SMEs have not yet internationalised, but they do appear to have the right entrepreneurial disposition to do so. This group of firms, by definition, are likely to have top management or key decisionmakers with the requisite characteristics. Their resource gap, therefore, may arise from firm competencies such as product quality and technology, market intelligence or their intermediaries' networks. These would have to be addressed in order to enable them to internationalise as they apparently wish to do. Potentially useful support measures may comprise providing access to market survey reports, assisting with consultancy or foreign market contacts and networks, including mentoring relationships.

Internationalised, but less entrepreneurial SMEs are those which have found themselves in the international market, but appear to lack a strong motivation to be there. Such firms may have started exporting accidentally, through the receipt of unsolicited foreign orders or allied external-reactive stimuli (Albaum et al., 1994). The policy focus here should be on ensuring that such SMEs receive positive reinforcement from their international market experience. Suggested measures include providing requisite assistance – information, training and counselling, easing operational problems, seconding 'change agents' or helping them to employ more decisionmakers with the requisite qualities and encouraging private-sector organisations to draw them into their networks, hence availing them of useful opportunities for sharing experiences and learning.

Finally, the policy focus with respect to internationalised entrepreneurial SMEs should be on shoring up their key competencies and renewing their international and entrepreneurial vision. Such firms should be equipped to continually respond to the inevitable competitive challenges of an increasingly globalised market through appropriate adjustments and innovations in products, processes, organisations, markets and technology (Hyvarinen, 1990; OECD, 1997a). Increased attention needs to be paid to relationships with key market actors (regular market visits and so on), particularly given the strength of empirical support for the potential benefits of so doing (Bell, 1994; Styles and Ambler, 1994, 1997).

Internationalised entrepreneurial SMEs, relatively speaking, need less assistance from the government and its relevant agencies than other SMEs. Where government assistance would, nonetheless, be most appreciated is in the minimisation of operational or access problems for foreign markets (Katsikeas, 1994; Morgan and Katsikeas,

1995). This is the standard service provided by government to its businesses, the most notable example, arguably, being the US government's deployment of its might in favour of its international companies.

Policymakers can also make a real difference by facilitating sectoral and/or industry-level export cooperative arrangements between SMEs to assist them in meeting the increasingly stiff competition from other regions (Arnould and Gennaro, 1985). The potential benefits of such initiatives may be quite immense, extending to cost-sharing in terms of R&D and technology sourcing, more innovative and quality products, a better reputation for the country's products in export markets, better leverage in relationships with distributors, agents, government officials (domestic and foreign) and, indeed, a whole lot of other network-related spin-offs (Ibeh, 2006).

Questions

1 Many SMEs are often constrained from internationalising by managerial and external factors. What are the implications of this statement for government policy making and support provision?

2 A fuller understanding of SME internationalisation can be gained by focusing on the potential complementarities of existing theoretical perspectives, as opposed to the current practice of viewing them as competing alternatives (Bell and Young, 1998). Discuss.

3 Internationalised SMEs have progressed from being a rarity, to a significant exporting presence and are now serious contributors to direct foreign investments, especially the cooperation-based modes. Fully explain this statement.

4 Share your thoughts on the probable future implications of continuing advances in information and communication technologies on the internationalisation of entrepreneurial SMEs.

Weblinks

www.ukti.gov.uk
Official website of the UK government organisation promoting international trade – UK Trade & Investment – jointly operated by the Foreign Office and the Department of Trade and Industry.

www.oecd.org
The Organisation for Economic Co-operation and Development, which has published a number of reports on the impact of globalisation on the small firm sector.

www.export.org.uk
The Institute for Export, which has as its mission to enhance the export performance of the UK by setting and raising professional standards in international trade management and export practice.

References and further reading

Aaby, N. and Slater, S. F. (1989) 'Management influences on export performance: A review of the empirical literature 1978–1988', *International Marketing Review*, 6 (4): 7–23.

Abell, P., Crouchley, R. and Mills, C. (2001) 'Social capital and entrepreneurship in Great Britain', *Enterprise and Innovation Management Studies*, 2 (2): 119–44.

ACCA (2009) 'Response to the Rowlands review of growth finance'. London: ACCA. Unpublished.

ACCA (2010) 'ACCA quarterly SME credit update, Q1 2010'. London: ACCA.

ACCA and CBI (2010) 'Small business finance and the recovery'. London: ACCA.

ACCA SME Committee (2008) 'Financing SMEs in the recession'. London: ACCA.

Ackerman, P. L. and Heggestad, E. D. (1997) 'Intelligence, personality, and interests: Evidence for overlapping traits', *Psychological Bulletin*, 121 (2): 219–45.

Ackerman, P. L. and Humphreys, L. G. (1990) 'Individual differences theory in industrial and organizational psychology', in M. D. Dunnette and L. M. Hough (eds), *Handbook of Industrial and Organizational Psychology*. Palo Alto, CA: Consulting Psychologists Press. pp. 223–82.

Ackerman, P. L., Kanfer, R. and Goff, M. (1995) 'Cognitive and noncognitive determinants and consequences of complex skill acquisition', *Journal of Experimental Psychology: Applied*, 1 (4): 270–304.

ACOST (1990) 'The enterprise challenge: Overcoming barriers to growth in small firms', Advisory Council on Science and Technology, Cabinet Office. London: HMSO.

Acs, Z. J. (2002) *Innovation and the Growth of Cities*. Cheltenham: Edward Elgar.

Acs, Z. J. (2006) 'How is entrepreneurship good for economic growth?', *Innovations*, 1 (1): 97–107.

Acs, Z. J. and Audretsch, D. B. (1990) *Innovation and Small Firms*. Cambridge, MA: MIT Press.

Acs, Z. J. and Audretsch, D. B. (2001) 'The emergence of the entrepreneurial society', prize lecture, The International Award for Entrepreneurship and Small Business Research, Stockholm, May 2001.

Acs, Z. J. and Megyesi, M. I. (2009) 'Creativity and industrial cities: A case study of Baltimore', *Entrepreneurship and Regional Development*, 21 (4): 421–39.

Acs, Z. J. and Plummer, L. A. (2005) 'Penetrating the knowledge filter in regional economies', *The Annals of Regional Science*, 39 (3): 439–56.

Acs, Z. J. and Stough, R. (eds) (2008) *Public Policy in an Entrepreneurial Economy*. Cheltenham: Edward Elgar.

Acs, Z. J. and Szerb, L. (2007) 'Entrepreneurship, economic growth and public policy', *Small Business Economics*, 28 (2/3): 109–22.

Acs, Z. J. and Szerb, L. (2010) 'Global entrepreneurship and the United States', US Small Business Administration, US Office of Advocacy, Washington, DC.

Acs, Z. J., Audretsch, D. B. and Feldman, M. P. (1994) 'R&D spillovers and recipient firm size', *Review of Economics and Statistics*, 76: 336–40.

Acs, Z. J., Braunerhjelm, P., Audretsch, D. B. and Carlsson, B. (2009) 'The knowledge spillover theory of entrepreneurship', *Small Business Economics*, 32 (1): 15–30.

Acs, Z. J., Parsons, W. and Tracy, S. (2008) 'High impact firms: Gazelles revisited', Paper 328, US Office of Advocacy, Washington, DC.

Addis, M. and Podestà, S. (2005) 'Long life to marketing research: A postmodern view', *European Journal of Marketing*, 39 (3/4): 386–413.

Adler, P. and Kwon, S. W. (2002) 'Social capital: Prospects for a new concept', *Academy of Management Review*, 27 (1): 17–40.

Ahl, H. (2006) 'Why research on women entrepreneurs needs new directions', *Entrepreneurship, Theory and Practice*, 30 (3): 595–621.

Ahl, H. and Marlow, S. (2011) 'Exploring the intersectionality of feminism, gender and entrepreneurship to escape the dead end', EGOS Symposium, Gothenburg, Sweden.

AIM Advisers (2011) 'IPO Activity – 2010', AIM Advisers, Santa Monica, CA.

Ajzen, I. (1991) 'The theory of planned behavior', *Organizational Behavior and Human Decision Processes*, 50 (2): 179–211.

Ajzen, I. (1995) 'Attitudes and behavior', in A. S. R. Manstead and M. Hewstone (eds), *The Blackwell Encyclopedia of Social Psychology*. Oxford: Blackwell. pp. 52–7.

Albaum, G., Strandskov, J., Duerr, E. and Dowd, L. (1994) *International Marketing and Export Management* (2nd ed.). Wokingham: Addison-Wesley.

Al Dajani, H. and Marlow, S. (2010) 'The impact of women's home based enterprise on marriage dynamics: Evidence from Jordon', *International Small Business Journal*, 28 (5): 360–78.

Aldrich, H. E. (1979) *Organizations and Environments*. Englewood Cliffs, NJ: Prentice Hall.

Aldrich, H. E. (1989) 'Networking among women entrepreneurs', in O. Hagen, C. Rivchum and D. Sexton (eds), *Women Owned Business*. New York: Praeger. pp. 103–32.

Aldrich, H. E. (2009) 'Lost in space, out of time: Why and how we should study organizations comparatively', in B. G. King, T. Felin and D. A. Whetten (eds), *Studying Differences between Organizations: Comparative approaches to organizational research: Research in the sociology of organizations* (vol. 26). Bingley: Emerald. pp. 21–44.

Aldrich, H. E. (2010) 'Beam me up, Scott(ie)!: Institutional theorists' struggles with the emergent nature of entrepreneurship', *Research in the Sociology of Work*, (21): 329–64.

Aldrich, H. E. and Auster, E. R. (1986) 'Even dwarfs started small: Liabilities of age and size and their strategic implications', *Research in Organizational Behavior*, 8: 165–98.

Aldrich, H. E. and Cliff, J. E. (2003) 'The pervasive effects of family on entrepreneurship: Toward a family embeddedness perspective', *Journal of Business Venturing*, 18 (5): 573–8.

Aldrich, H. E. and Fiol, C. M. (1994) 'Fools rush in? The institutional context of industry creation', *Academy of Management Review*, 19 (4): 645–70.

Aldrich, H. E. and Martinez, M. E. (2001) 'Many are called but few are chosen: An evolutionary perspective for the study of entrepreneurship', *Entrepreneurship Theory and Practice*, 25 (4, Summer): 41–56.

Aldrich, H. E. and Sakano, T. (1995) 'Unbroken ties: How the personal networks of Japanese business owners compare to those in other nations', in M. Fruin (ed.), *Pacific Rim Investigations*. New York: Oxford University Press. pp. 17–45.

Aldrich, H. E. and Whetten, D. (1981) 'Organisation-sets, action-sets, and networks: Making the most of simplicity', in P. Nystrom and W. Starbuck (eds), *Handbook of Organizational Design* (vol. 1). New York: Oxford University Press. pp. 385–408.

Aldrich, H. E. and Wiedenmayer, G. (1993) 'From traits to rates: An ecological perspective on organizational foundings', in J. A. Katz and R. H. Brockhaus (eds), *Advances in Entrepreneurship, Firm Emergence, and Growth*: Greenwich, CT: JAI Press. pp. 145–195.

Aldrich, H. E. and Zimmer, C. (1986) 'Entrepreneurship through social networks', in D. Sexton and R. Smilor (eds), *The Art and Science of Entrepreneurship*. Cambridge, MA: Ballinger. pp. 3–24.

Aldrich, H. E., Cater, J., Jones, T. and McEvoy, D. (1981) 'Business development and self-segregation: Asian enterprise in three British cities', in C. Peach, V. Robinson and S. Smith (eds), *Ethnic Segregation in Cities*. London: Croom Helm. pp. 170–90.

Aldrich, H. E., Cater, J., Jones, T. and McEvoy, D. (1982) 'From periphery to peripheral: The South Asian petite bourgeoisie in England', in R. Simpson and I. Simpson (eds), *Research in the Sociology of Work* (vol. 2). pp. 1–32. Greenwich, CT: JAI Press.

Aldrich, H. E., Jones, T. and McEvoy, D. (1984) 'Ethnic advantage and minority business development', in R. Ward and R. Jenkins (eds), *Ethnic Communities in Business*, Cambridge: Cambridge University Press. pp. 189–210.

Aldrich, H. E., Rosen, B. and Woodward, W. (1986) 'Social behaviour and entrepreneurial networks', Summary in *Frontiers of Entrepreneurship Research 1986*. Wellesley, MA: Babson College.

Aldrich, H. E., Rosen, B. and Woodward, W. (1987) 'The impact of social networks on business foundings and profit: A longitudinal study', in *Frontiers of Entrepreneurship Research 1987*. Wellesley, MA: Babson College.

Aldrich, H. E., Reese, P. and Dubini, P. (1989) 'Women on the verge of a breakthrough: Networking among entrepreneurs in the United States and Italy', *Entrepreneurship & Regional Development*, 1: 339–56.

Aldrich, H. E., Renzulli, L. and Laughton, N. (1997) 'Passing on privilege: Resources provided by self-employed parents to their self-employed children', Paper presented at the American Sociological Association.

Alexander, J., Nank, R. and Stivers, C. (1999) 'Implications of welfare reform: Do nonprofit survival strategies threaten civil society?', *Nonprofit and Voluntary Sector Quarterly*, 28: 452–75.

Allen, S. and Truman, C. (1988) 'Women's work and success in women's businesses'. Paper presented to 11th UK National Small Firms Policy and Research Conference, Cardiff Business School, November.

Allen, W. D. (2000) 'Social networks and self-employment', *The Journal of Socio-Economics*, 29 (5): 487–501.

Allinson, C. W., Chell, E. and Hayes, J. (2000) 'Intuition and entrepreneurial behaviour', *European Journal of Work and Organizational Psychology*, 9 (1): 31–43.

Allinson, G., Stone, I., Braidford, P. and Houston, M. (2010) 'Early stage assessment of the impact of the Enterprise Finance Guarantee (EFG) on recipient firms'. London: BIS.

Almor, T. and Hashai, N. (2004) 'Competitive advantage and strategic configuration of knowledge-intensive small- and medium-sized multinationals: A modified resource-based view', *Journal of International Management*, 10: 479–500.

Alsos, G. A. and Carter, S. (2006) 'Multiple business ownership in the Norwegian farm sector: Resource transfer and performance consequences', *Journal of Rural Studies*, 22 (3): 313–22.

Alsos, G. A. and Kolvereid, L. (1998) 'The business gestation process of novice, serial and parallel business founders', *Entrepreneurship Theory and Practice*, 22 (4): 101–14.

Alsos, G. A., Kolvereid, L. and Isaksen, E. J. (2006) 'New business early performance: Differences between firms started by novice, serial and portfolio entrepreneurs', in P. R. Christensen and F. Poulfeldt (eds), *Managing Complexity and Change in SMEs: Frontiers in European research*. Cheltenham: Edward Elgar. pp. 35–49.

Alsos, G. A., Ljunggren, E. and Pettersen, L. T. (2003) 'Farm-based entrepreneurs: What triggers the start-up of new business activities?', *Journal of Small Business and Enterprise Development*, 10 (4): 435–43.

Alvarez, S. A. and Barney, J. B. (2004) 'Organizing rent generation and appropriation: Toward a theory of the entrepreneurial firm', *Journal of Business Venturing*, 19 (5): 621–35.

Alvarez, S. A. and Barney, J. B. (2007) 'Discovery and creation: Alternative theories of entrepreneurial action', *Strategic Entrepreneurship Journal*, 1: 11–26.

Alvarez, S. A. and Barney, J. B. (2010) 'Entrepreneurship and epistemology: The philosophical underpinnings of the study of entrepreneurial opportunities', *The Academy of Management Annals*, 4 (1): 557–83.

Alvarez, S. A. and Busenitz, L. W. (2001) 'The entrepreneurship of resource-based theory', *Journal of Management*, 27: 755–75.

Alvord, S. H., Brown, L. D. and Letts, C. W. (2004) 'Social entrepreneurship and societal transformation', *The Journal of Applied Behavioral Science*, 40: 260–82.

Amabile, T. M. (1988) 'A model of creativity and innovations in organizations', in B. M. Staw and L. L. Cummings (eds), *Research in Organizational Behavior*. Greenwich, CT: JAI Press.

Amabile, T. M., Hill, K. G., Hennessey, B. A. and Tighe, E. M. (1994) 'The work preference inventory: Assessing intrinsic and extrinsic motivational orientations', *Journal of Personality and Social Psychology*, 66 (5): 950–67.

Ambler, T., Chittenden, F. and Miccini, A. (2010) 'Is regulation really good for us?'. London: British Chambers of Commerce.

Amin, A. (1999) 'An institutionalist perspective on regional economic development', *International Journal of Urban and Regional Research*, 23 (2): 365–78.

Amin, A. (2005) 'Local community on trial', *Economy and Society*, 34: 612–33.

Amin, A. and Thrift, N. (1992) 'Neo-Marshallian nodes in global networks', *International Journal of Urban and Regional Research*, 16: 571–87.

Amit, R. and Zott, C. (2001) 'Value drivers in e-business', *Strategic Management Journal*, 22: 493–520.

Anderson, A., Park, J. and Jack, S. (2007) 'Entrepreneurial social capital: Conceptualizing social capital in new high-tech firms', *International Small Business Journal*, 25 (3): 245–72.

Anderson, A. R. and Marzena, S. (2008) 'Research practices in entrepreneurship: Problems of definition, description and meaning', *International Journal of Entrepreneurship and Innovation*, 9: 221–30.

Anderson, A. R., Drakopoulou Dodd, S. and Jack, S. (2010) 'Network practices and entrepreneurial growth', *Scandinavian Journal of Management*, 26: 121–33.

Anderson, D. E. (2005) 'The spatial nature of entrepreneurship', *The Quarterly Journal of Austrian Economics*, 8 (2): 21–34.

Anderson, O. (1993) 'On the internationalization process of firms: A critical analysis', *Journal of International Business Studies*, Second Quarter: 209–31.

Anderson, O. and Striegel, W. H. (1981) 'Business surveys and economic research: A review of significant developments', in H. Laumer and M. Ziegler (ed.), *International Research on Business Cycle Surveys*. München: Springer-Verlag. pp. 25–54.

Anderson, P. and Tushman, M. (1990) 'Technological discontinuities and dominant designs: A cyclical model of technological change', *Administrative Science Quarterly*, 35: 604–33.

Anderson, P. H., Blenker, P. and Christensen, P. R. (1995) 'Generic routes to subcontractors' internationalization', paper presented at the RENT IX Conference on Entrepreneurship and SMEs, November, Milano, Italy.

Andersson, M. and Ejermo, O. (2005) 'How does accessibility to knowledge sources affect the innovativeness of corporations?: Evidence from Sweden', *Annals of Regional Science*, 39: 741–65.

Andersson, M. and Karlsson, C. (2007) 'Knowledge in regional economic growth: The role of knowledge accessibility', *Industry and Innovation*, 14 (2): 129–49.

Ardichvili, A., Cardozo, R. and Ray, S. (2003) 'A theory of entrepreneurial opportunity identification and development', *Journal of Business Venturing*, 18 (1): 105–23.

Arensberg, C. M. and Kimball, S. T. (2001) *Family and Community in Ireland*. Ennis, County Clare, Ireland: CLASP Press.

Argenti, J. (1976) *Corporate Collapse: The causes and symptoms*. New York: McGraw-Hill.

Arnould, O. and Gennaro, E. (1985) 'Enhancing the market for new products and services by export co-operation between innovative SMEs', in 'Developing markets for new products and services through joint exporting by innovative SMEs', Commission of the European Community, Report EUR 9927. pp. 27–32.

Arora, V. K. and Faraone, L. (2003) '21st century engineer-entrepreneur', *IEEE Antennas and Propagation Magazine*. 4: 106–14.

Arrow, K. (1983) 'Innovation in small and large firms', in J. Ronen (ed.), *Entrepreneurship* Lexington, MA: Lexington Books. pp. 15–28.

Arrow, K. J. (1962) 'The economic implications of learning by doing', *Review of Economic Studies*, 29 (3): 155–73.

Arshed, N. (2011) 'The formulation of enterprise policy in the UK: An institutional theoretical perspective'. Unpublished PhD thesis, University of Strathclyde, Glasgow.

Arthurs, J. D. and Busenitz, L. W. (2003) 'The boundaries and limitations of agency theory and stewardship theory in the venture capitalist/entrepreneur relationship', *Entrepreneurship Theory and Practice*, 28 (2): 145–62.

Asante, M. K. and Mattson, M. T. (1992) *The Historical and Cultural Atlas of African Americans*. New York: Macmillan.

Asheim, B. and Isaksen, A. (2003) 'SMEs and the regional dimension of innovation', in B. Asheim, A. Isaksen, C. Nauwelaers, F. Tödtling (eds), *Regional Innovation Policy for Small–medium Enterprises*, Cheltenham: Edward Elgar. pp. 21–48.

Asset Based Finance Assocation (2011) 'Statistics' (produced by FLA). Richmond: ABFA. Available online at: www.abfa.org.uk/public/statistics.asp

Åstebro, T. (1998) 'Basic statistics on the success rate and profits for independent inventors', *Entrepreneurship: Theory and Practice*, 23 (2): 41–8.

Astrachan, J. H., Klein, S. B. and Smyrnios, K. X. (2002) 'The F-PEC scale of family influence: A proposal for solving the family business definition problem', *Family Business Review*, XV (1): 45–58.

Athayde, R. (2009) 'Measuring enterprise potential in young people', *Entrepreneurship Theory and Practice*, 33 (2): 481–500.

Atherton, A. (2006) 'Should government be stimulating start-ups?: An assessment of the scope for public intervention in new venture formation', *Environment and Planning C: Government and Policy*, 24 (1): 21–36.

Atler, K. (2007) *Social Enterprise Typology*. Portland, OR: Virtue Ventures LLC.

Audit Commission (1999) 'A life's work: Local authorities, economic development and economic regeneration'. London: Audit Commission.

Audretsch, D. B. (2003) 'Entrepreneurship policy and the strategic management of places', in D. M. Hart, *The Emergence of Entrepreneurship Policy: Governance, start-ups and growth in the U.S. knowledge economy*. Cambridge: Cambridge University Press. pp. 20–38.

Audretsch, D. B. (2007) 'Entrepreneurship capital and economic growth', *Oxford Review of Economic Policy*, 23 (1): 63–78.

Audretsch, D. B. and Feldman, M. P. (1996) 'R&D spillovers and the geography of innovation and production', *American Economic Review*, 86 (3): 630–40.

Audretsch, D. B. and Fritsch, M. (2002) 'Growth regimes over time and space', *Regional Studies*, 36 (2): 113–24.

Audretsch, D. B. and Keilbach, M. (2004) 'Entrepreneurship and regional growth: An evolutionary interpretation', *Journal of Evolutionary Economics*, 14 (5): 605–16.

Audretsch, D. B. and Keilbach, M. (2005) 'Entrepreneurship capital and regional growth', *The Annals of Regional Science*, 39 (3): 457–69.

Audretsch, D. B. and Thurik, A. R. (2001) 'Linking entrepreneurship to growth', STI working paper. Paris: OECD.

Audretsch, D. B., Grilo, I. and Thurik, A. R. (2007) 'Explaining entrepreneurship and the role of policy: A framework', in D. B. Audretsch et al. (eds), *The Handbook of Research on Entrepreneurship Policy*. Cheltenham and Northampton, MA: Edward Elgar. pp. 1–17.

Audretsch, D. B., Keilbach, M. and Lehmann, E. (2006) *Entrepreneurship and Economic Growth*. Oxford: Oxford University Press.

Audretsch, D. B., Lehmann, E. E. and Warning, S. (2005) 'University spillovers and new firm location', *Research Policy*, 34 (7): 1113–22.

Audretsch, D., Thurik, R., Verheul, I. and Wennekers, S. (2002) *Entrepreneurship: Determinants and policy in a European–US comparison*. Boston, Dordrecht, London: Kluwer.

AURP-Battelle (2007) 'Characteristics and trends in North American research parks: 21st century directions'. Tucson, AZ, and Columbus, OH: AURP and Battelle.

Auster, E. (1990) 'The interorganizational environment: Network theory, tools, and applications', in F. Williams and D. Gibson (eds), *Technology Transfer: A communication perspective*. London: Sage. pp. 63–89.

Austin, J., Stevenson, H. and Wei-Skillern, J. (2006) 'Social and commercial entrepreneurship: Same, different, or both?', *Entrepreneurship Theory and Practice*, 30 (1): 1–22.

Axelrod, R. (1985) *The Evolution of Cooperation*. New York: Basic Books.

Axelsson, B. and Easton, G. (eds) (1992) *Industrial Network: A new view of reality*. London: Routledge.

Aylward, Elaine (2007) *Traditional and Non-traditional Female Entrepreneurs: An exploration into what influences their selection of industry sector*. Waterford, Ireland: Waterford Institute of Technology.

Bacq, S. and Janssen, F. (2011) 'The multiple faces of social entrepreneurship: A review of definitional issues based on geographical and thematic criteria', *Entrepreneurship and Regional Development*, 23: 373–403.

Bagozzi, R. P. and Kimmel, S. K. (1995) 'A comparison of leading theories for the prediction of goal-directed behaviours', *British Journal of Social Psychology*, 34: 437–61.

Bagozzi, R. P. and Warshaw, P. R. (1992) 'An examination of the etiology of the attitude–behavior relation for goal-directed behaviors', *Multivariate Behavioral Research*, 27 (4): 601–34.

Baines, S. and Wheelock, J. (1998) 'Working for each other: Gender, the household and micro-business survival and growth', *International Small Business Journal*, 17 (1): 16–35.

Baker, T., Aldrich, H. E. and Liou, N. (1997) 'Invisible entrepreneurs: the neglect of women business owners by mass media and scholarly journals in the USA', *Entrepreneurship and Regional Development*, 9 (3): 221–38.

Baker, T. and Nelson, R. E. (2005) 'Creating something from nothing: Resource construction through entrepreneurial bricolage', *Administrative Science Quarterly*, 50 (3): 329–66.

Baker, T., Gedajlovic, E. and Lubatkin, M. (2005) 'A framework for comparing entrepreneurship processes across nations', *Journal of International Business Studies*, 36 (5): 492–504.

Baker, T., Miner, A. S. and Eesley, D. T. (2003) 'Improvising firms: Bricolage, account giving and improvisational competencies in the founding process', *Research Policy*, 32 (2): 255–76.

Baker, W. H., Adams, L. and Davis, B. (1993) 'Business planning in successful small firms', *Long Range Planning*, 26 (6): 82–8.

Bandura, A. (1977) 'Self-efficacy: Toward a unifying theory of behavioral change', *Psychological Review*, 84 (2): 191–215.

Bandura, A. (1982) 'The psychology of chance encounters and life paths', *American Psychologist*, 37 (7): 747–55.

Bandura, A. (1986) *Social Foundations of Thought and Action*. Englewood Cliffs, NJ: Prentice Hall.

Bandura, A. (1991) 'Social cognitive theory of self-regulation', *Organizational Behavior and Human Decision Processes*, 50 (2): 248–87.

Bandura, A. (1995) 'Perceived self-efficacy', in A. S. R. Manstead and M. Hewstone (eds), *The Blackwell Encyclopedia of Social Psychology*. Oxford: Wiley-Blackwell. pp. 434–6.

Bandura, A. (2010) 'Self-efficacy', in I. B. Weiner and W. E. Craighead (eds), *The Corsini Encyclopedia of Psychology* (vol. 3). New York: Wiley. pp. 1534–6.

Bandura, A. and Locke, E. A. (2003) 'Negative self-efficacy and goal effects revisited', *Journal of Applied Psychology*, 88 (1): 87–99.

Bank of England (1996) 'Finance for small firms: A third report'. London: Bank of England.

Bank of England (2002) 'Finance for small firms: Ninth report'. London: Bank of England.

Bank of England (2011) 'Credit conditions survey: Survey results: 2010 Q4'. London: Bank of England. Available online at: www.bankofengland.co.uk/

publications/other/creditconditionssurvey110106.pdf

Banks, J. (1972) *The Sociology of Social Movements*. London: Macmillan.

Bannock, G. (1990) *Taxation in the European Community: The small business perspective*. London: Paul Chapman.

Bannock, G. and Peacock, A. (1989) *Government and Small Business*. London: Paul Chapman.

Barker, R. G. and Gump, P. V. (1964) *Big School, Small School*. Stanford, CA: Stanford University Press.

Barkham, R., Gudgin, G., Hart, M. and Hanvey, E. (1996) *The Determinants of Small Firm Growth: An inter-regional study in the UK 1986–90*. London and Bristol, PA: Jessica Kingsley.

Barney, J. B. (1991) 'Firm resources and sustained competitive advantage', *Journal of Management*, 17 (1): 99–120.

Barney, J. B. (1997) *Gaining and Sustaining Competitive Advantage*. Menlo Park, CA: Addison-Wesley.

Baron, R. A. (1998) 'Cognitive mechanisms in entrepreneurship: Why and when entrepreneurs think differently than other people', *Journal of Business Venturing*, 13 (4): 275–94.

Baron, R. A. (1999) 'Counterfactual thinking and venture formation: The potential effects of thinking about "what might have been"', *Journal of Business Venturing*, 15: 79–91.

Baron, R. A. (2004) 'The cognitive perspective: A valuable tool for answering entrepreneurship's basic "why" questions', *Journal of Business Venturing*, 19 (2): 221–39.

Baron, R. A. (2007) 'Behavioral and cognitive factors in entrepreneurship: Entrepreneurs as the active element in new venture creation', *Strategic Entrepreneurship Journal*, 1 (2): 167–82.

Baron, R. A. (2008) 'The role of affect in the entrepreneurial process', *Academy of Management Review*, 33 (2): 328–40.

Baron, R. A. (2009) 'Effectual versus predictive logics in entrepreneurial decision making: Differences between experts and novices: Does experience in starting new ventures change the way entrepreneurs think? Perhaps, but for now "caution" is essential', *Journal of Business Venturing*, 24 (4): 310–15.

Baron, R. A. (2010) 'Effectual versus predictive logics in entrepreneurial decision making: Differences between experts and novices: Does experience in starting new ventures change the way entrepreneurs think?: Perhaps, but for now "caution" is essential', *Journal of Business Venturing*, 24: 310–15.

Baron, R. A. and Ensley, M. D. (2006) 'Opportunity recognition as the detection of meaningful patterns: Evidence from comparisons of novice and experienced entrepreneurs', *Management Science*, 52 (9): 1331–44.

Baron, R. A. and Markman, G. D. (2003) 'Beyond social capital: The role of entrepreneurs' social competence in their financial success', *Journal of Business Venturing*, 18 (1): 41–60.

Baron, R. A. and Markman, G. D. (2005) 'Toward a process view of entrepreneurship: The changing impact of individual-level variables across phases of new firm development', in R. T. Golembiewski and K. D. MacKenzie (eds), *Current Topics in Management*. New Brunswick, NJ: Transaction. pp. 45–64.

Baron, R. A., Frese, M. and Baum, J. R. (2007) 'Research gains: Benefits of closer links between I/O psychology and entrepreneurship', in J. R. Baum, M. Frese and R. A. Baron (eds), *The Psychology of Entrepreneurship*. Mahwah, NJ: Lawrence Erlbaum. pp. 347–73.

Barreto, H. (1989) *The Entrepreneur in Microeconomic Theory: Disappearance and explanation*. New York: Routledge.

Barrett, G. A. (1999) 'Overcoming obstacles: Access to bank finance for African-Caribbean enterprise', *Journal of Ethnic and Migration Studies*, 25 (2): 303–22.

Barrett, G. A., Jones, T. P. and McEvoy, D. (1996) 'Ethnic minority business: Theoretical discourse in Britain and North America', *Urban Studies*, 33 (4/5): 783–809.

Barrett, G. A., Jones, T. and McEvoy, D. (2003) 'United Kingdom: Severely constrained entrepreneurialism', in R. Kloosterman and J. Rath (eds), *Immigrant Entrepreneurship: Venturing abroad in the age of globalisation*. Oxford: Berg.

Barringer, B. R., Jones, F. F. and Neubaum, D. O. (2005) 'A quantitative content analysis of the characteristics of rapid growth firms and their founders', *Journal of Business Venturing*, 20 (5): 663–87.

Barrow, C. (2001) *Incubators: A realist's guide to the world's new business accelerators*. New York: John Wiley.

Barth, F. (1963) *The Role of the Entrepreneur in Social Change in Northern Norway*. Bergen: Norwegian Universities Press.

Barth, H. (2003) 'Fit between competitive strategy, administrative mechanisms and performance: A comparative study of small firms in mature and new industries', *Journal of Small Business Management*, 41 (2): 133–47.

Basu, A. (1995) 'Asian small businesses in Britain: An exploration of entrepreneurial activity'. Paper presented at the Second International Journal of Entrepreneurial Behaviour and Research Conference, Malvern, 18–20 July.

Basu, A. (1998) 'An exploration of entrepreneurial activity among Asian small businesses in Britain', *Small Business Economics*, 10: 313–26.

Basu, D. (1991) 'Afro-Caribbean businesses in Great Britain: Factors affecting business success and marginality'. Unpublished PhD thesis, Manchester Business School.

Bates, T. (1994a) reported in *The Franchise Update Report*, 94–1.

Bates, T. (1994b) 'An analysis of Korean-immigrant-owned small-business start-ups with comparisons to African-American and non-minority-owned firms', *Urban Affairs Quarterly*, 30 (23): 227–48.

Bates, T. (1997) 'Financing small business creation: The case of Chinese and Korean immigrant entrepreneurs', *Journal of Business Venturing*, 12 (2): 109–24.

Bates, T., Jackson III, W. E. and Johnson, J. H. (2007) 'Introduction to special issue on minority entrepreneurship', *Annals of the American Academy of Political Science and Social Science*, 10–17.

Bates, V. (2010) 'Cost of listing on AIM soars', *City A.M.*, 25 February.

Bathelt, H. and Glückler, J. (2003) 'Toward a relational economic geography', *Journal of Economic Geography*, 3 (2): 117–44.

Bathelt, H., Malmberg, A. and Maskell, P. (2004) 'Clusters and knowledge: Local buzz, global pipelines and the process of knowledge creation', *Progress in Human Geography*, 28 (1): 31–56.

Battelle Columbus Laboratories (1973) 'Interactions of science and technology in the innovative process: Some case studies', National Technical Information Service, US Department of Commerce, Springfield, VA. p. 218.

Batterink, M. H., Emiel, F. M., Lerkx, L. and Omta, S. W. F. (2010) 'Orchestrating innovation networks: The case of innovation brokers in the agri-food sector', *Entrepreneurship and Regional Development*, 22 (1): 47–76.

Battilana, J., Leca, B. and Boxenbaum, E. (2009) 'How actors change institutions: Towards a theory of institutional entrepreneurship', *Academy of Management Annals*, 3: 65–107.

Baum, J. R. and Bird, B. J. (2010) 'The successful intelligence of high-growth entrepreneurs: Links to new venture growth', *Organization Science*, 21 (2): 397.

Baum, J. R. and Locke, E. A. (2004) 'The relationship of entrepreneurial traits, skill, and motivation to subsequent venture growth', *Journal of Applied Psychology*, 89 (4): 587–98.

Baum, J. R., Locke, E. A. and Kirkpatrick, S. A. (1998) 'A longitudinal study of the relation of vision and vision communication to venture growth in entrepreneurial firms', *Journal of Applied Psychology*, 83 (1): 43–54.

Baum, J. R., Locke, E. A. and Smith, K. G. (2001) 'A multidimensional model of venture growth', *Academy of Management Journal*, 44 (2): 292–303.

Baumard, P. and Starbuck, W. H. (2005) 'Learning from failures: Why it may not happen', *Long Range Planning*, 38 (3): 281–98.

Baumback, C. and Mancuso, P. (1987) *Entrepreneurship and Venture Management*. Englewood Cliffs, NJ: Prentice Hall.

Baumol, W. J. (1990) 'Entrepreneurship: Productive, unproductive and destructive', *Journal of Political Economy*, 98 (5): 893–921.

Baumol, W. J., Schilling, M. A. and Wolff, E. N. (2009) 'The superstar inventors and entrepreneurs: How were they educated?', *Journal of Economics and Management Strategy*, 18 (3): 711–28.

Beaver, G. (2003) 'Small business: Success and failure', *Strategic Change*, 12 (3): 115–22.

Beaver, G. and Jennings, P. L. (1996) 'The abuse of entrepreneurial power: An explanation of management failure?' *Strategic Change*, 5 (3): 151–64.

Becker, G. S. (1996) *Accounting for Tastes*. Cambridge, MA: Harvard University Press.

Becker, G. S. and Murphy, K. M. (2000) *Social Economics: Market behavior in a social environment*. Cambridge, MA: Belknap Press.

Beesley, M. and Rothwell, R. (1987) 'Small firm linkages in the UK', in R. Rothwell and J. Bessant (eds), *Innovation, Adaptation and Growth*. Elsevier: Amsterdam.

Begg, I. (1999) 'Cities and competitiveness', *Urban Studies*, 36 (5/6): 795–810.

Begley, T. M. and Boyd, D. P. (1987) 'Psychological characteristics associated with performance in entrepreneurial firms and smaller businesses', *Journal of Business Venturing*, 2 (1): 79–93.

Bell, C. and Newby, H. (1971) *Community Studies: An introduction to the sociology and the local community*. London: Unwin.

Bell, J. (1995) 'The internationalization of small computer software firms: A further challenge to "stage" theories', *European Journal of Marketing*, 29 (8): 60–75.

Bell, J. (1997) 'A comparative study of the export problems of small software exporters in Finland, Ireland and Norway', *International Business Review*, 6 (6): 585–604.

Bell, J. and Young, S. (1998) 'Towards an integrative framework of the internationalization of the firm', in G. Hooley, R. Loveridge and D. Wilson (eds), *Internationalization: Process, context and markets*. London, Macmillan.

Bell, J., Crick, D. and Young, S. (2004) 'Small firm internationalization and business strategy: An exploratory study of knowledge-intensive and traditional manufacturing firms in the UK', *International Small Business Journal*, 22 (1): 23–54.

Bell, J., McNaughton, R., Young, S. and Crick, D. (2003) 'Towards an integrative framework of small firm internationalization', *Journal of International Entrepreneurship*, 1 (4): 339–62.

Bell, J. D. (1994) 'The role of government in small-firm internationalization: A comparative study of export promotion in Finland, Ireland and Norway, with specific reference to the computer software industry', unpublished PhD thesis, Department of Marketing, University of Strathclyde, Glasgow.

Belle, A. and La Valle, I. (2003) 'Combining self-employment and family life'. Bristol and York: Policy Press and Joseph Rowntree Foundation.

Bellu, R. R. (1988) 'Entrepreneurs and managers: Are they different?', in *Frontiers of Entrepreneurship Research 1988*. Wellesley, MA: Babson College.

Bellu, R. R. (1993) 'Task role motivation and attributional style as predictors of entrepreneurial performance: Female sample findings', *Entrepreneurship and Regional Development*, 5 (4): 331–44.

Bellu, R. R. and Sherman, H. (1995) 'Predicting firm success from task motivation and attributional style: A longitudinal study', *Entrepreneurship and Regional Development*, 7 (4): 349–64.

Bengtsson, O. (2007) 'Repeated relationships between venture capitalists and entrepreneurs', University of Chicago working paper.

Bennett, J. and Estrin, S. (2007) 'Informality as a stepping stone: Entrepreneurial entry in a developing economy'. Rochester, NY: SSRN eLibrary.

Bennett, M. (1989) *Managing Growth: NatWest Small Business Shelf*. London: Pitman. pp. 85–114.

Bennett, R. J. (1997) 'The relations between government and business associations in Britain: An evaluation of recent developments', *Policy Studies*, 18 (1): 5–33.

Bennett, R. J. (1999) 'Business associations: their potential contribution to government policy and the growth of small and medium-sized enterprises', *Environment and Planning C: Government and Policy*, 17: 593–608.

Bennett, R. J. (2008) 'Government SME policy since the 1990s: What have we learnt?', *Environment and Planning C: Government and Policy*, 26: 375–97.

Bennett, R. J. and McCoshan, A. (1993) *Enterprise and Human Resource Development: Local capacity building*. London: Paul Chapman.

Bennett, R. J. and Payne, D. (2000) *Local and Regional Economic Development: Renegotiating power under Labour*. Aldershot: Ashgate.

Bennett, R. J. and Robson, P. J. A. (1999a) 'The use of external business advice by SMEs in Britain', *Entrepreneurship and Regional Development*, 11: 155–80.

Bennett, R. J. and Robson, P. J. A. (1999b) 'Business Link: Use, satisfaction and comparison with Business Connect', *Policy Studies*, 20 (2): 107–32.

Bennett, R. J. and Robson, P. J. A. (2000) 'The Small Business Service: Business support, use, fees and satisfaction', *Policy Studies*, 21 (3): 173–90.

Bennett, R. J. and Robson, P. J. A. (2003) 'Business Link: Use, satisfaction and the influence of local governance regime', *Policy Studies*, 24 (4): 163–86.

Bennett, R. J. and Robson, P. J. A. (2004) 'Support services to SMEs: Does the "franchisee" make a difference to the Business Link offer?', *Environment and Planning C: Government and Policy*, 22: 859–80.

Bennett, R. J., Wicks, P. J. and McCoshan, A. (1994) *Local Empowerment and Business Services: Britain's experiment with TECs*. London: UCL Press.

Berg, N. G. (1997) 'Gender, place and entrepreneurship', *Entrepreneurship & Regional Development*, 9 (3): 259–68.

Berry, A. and Simpson, J. (1993) 'Financing small and medium-sized businesses and the role of factoring: the view of accountants and user companies'. Brighton Business School Research Papers, Brighton University.

Berry, A., Citron, D. and Jarvis, R. (1987) 'The information needs of bankers dealing with large and small companies'. ACCA Research Report No. 7. London: ACCA.

Berry, A., Faulkner, S., Hughes, M. and Jarvis, R. (1993a) *Bank Lending: Beyond the theory*. London: Chapman & Hall.

Berry, A., Faulkner, S., Hughes, M. and Jarvis, R. (1993b) 'Financial information: The banker and the small business', *British Accounting Review*, 25 (2): 131–50.

Berry, A., Grant, P. and Jarvis, R. (2003) 'Can European banks plug the finance gap for UK SMEs?'. ACCA Research Report No. 81, London: ACCA.

Berry, A., Jarvis, R., Lipman, H. and Macallan, H. (1990) 'Leasing and the smaller firm'. ACCA Occasional Paper No. 3. London: ACCA.

Berry, M. (1997) 'Government objectives and the "model" trade association', in R. J. Bennett (ed.), *Trade Associations in Britain and Germany: Responding to internationalisation and the EU*. London and Bonn: Anglo-German Foundation.

Berry, R. H. and Waring, A. (1995) 'A user perspective on "making corporate reports valuable"', *British Accounting Review*, 27: 139–52.

Bessant, J. and Tidd, J. (2007) *Innovation and Entrepreneurship*. Chichester: Wiley.

Berry, R. H., Crum, R. E. and Waring, A. (1993) 'Corporate performance appraisal in bank lending decisions'. London: CIMA.

Besser, T. L., Miller, N. and Perkins, R. K. (2006) 'For the greater good: Business networks and business social responsibility to communities', *Entrepreneurship and Regional Development: An International Journal*, 18 (4): 321–39.

Best, M. (2005) 'Regional specialization and cluster drivers: Medical devices in Massachusetts', *Business and Economic History On-line* (Vol. 3). Available online at: www.thebhc.org/publications/BEHonline/2005/best.pdf

Best, M. (2009) 'Massachusetts high tech: A "manufactory of species"', in G. Becattini, M. Bellandi and L. De Propris (eds), *A Handbook of Industrial Districts*. Cheltenham: Edward Elgar. pp. 648–55.

Better Regulation Task Force (2000) 'Helping small firms cope with regulations'. London: Cabinet Office.

Better Regulation Task Force (2004) 'The challenge of culture change'. London: Cabinet Office.

Bevan, A. A. and Danbolt, J. (2000) 'Capital structure and its determinants in the UK: A decompositional analysis', *Applied Financial Economics*, 12 (3): 159–70.

Bhave, M. P. (1994) 'A process model of entrepreneurial venture creation', *Journal of Business Venturing*, 9: 223–42.

Bhide, A. V. (1994) 'How entrepreneurs craft strategies that work', *Harvard Business Review*, 72 (2): 150–62.

Bhide, A. V. (2000) *The Origin and Evolution of New Businesses*. Oxford: Oxford University Press.

Biggadike, R. (1976) 'Corporate diversification: Entry, strategy and performance'. Division of Research, Graduate School of Business Administration, Harvard University, Boston, MA.

Bilkey, W. J. (1978) 'An attempted integration of the literature on the export behavior of firms', *Journal of International Business Studies*, 9 (1, spring/summer): 33–46.

Bilkey, W. J. and Tesar, G. (1977) 'The export behavior of smaller-sized Wisconsin manufacturing firms', *Journal of International Business Studies*, 8 (1, spring/summer): 93–8.

Binks, M. and Vale, P. (1990) *Entrepreneurship and Economic Change*. Maidenhead: McGraw-Hill.

Binks, M. R. and Ennew, C. T. (1995) 'Bank finance for growing small businesses' in E. W. Davis (ed.), *Finance for Growing Enterprises*. London: Routledge. pp. 40–54.

Binks, M. R., Ennew, C. T. and Reed, G. V. (1988) 'The survey by the forum of private business on banks and small firms', in G. Bannock and E. V. Morgan (eds), *Banks and Small Businesses: A two nation perspective*. London: Forum of Private Business/National Federation of Small Business.

Binks, M. R., Ennew, C. T. and Reed, G. V. (1990a) *Small Business and their Banks, 1990*. Knutsford. Forum of Private Business.

Binks, M. R., Ennew, C. T. and Reed, G. V. (1990b) 'Finance gaps and small firms'. Paper presented to the Royal Economics Society Annual Conference, Nottingham.

Binks, M. R., Ennew, C. T. and Reed, G. V. (1993) *Small Business and their Banks, 1992*. Knutsford: Forum of Private Business.

Birch, D. (1979) *The Job Generation Process*. Cambridge, MA: MIT Programme on Neighbourhood and Regional Change.

Birch, D. (1981) 'Who creates jobs?', *The Public Interest*, 65: 3–14.

Birch, K. and Mykhenko, V. (2010) 'Introduction', in K. Birch (ed.), *The Rise and Fall of Neoliberalism: The collapse of an economic order?* London: Zed Books.

Bird, B. J. (1988) 'Implementing entrepreneurial ideas: The case of intention', *Academy of Management Review*, 13 (3): 442–53.

Bird, B. J. (1992) 'The operation of intentions in time: The emergence of the new venture',

Entrepreneurship Theory and Practice, 17 (1): 11–20.

Bird, B. and Brush, C. (2002) 'A gendered perspective on organizational creation', *Entrepreneurship Theory and Practice*, 26 (3): 41–65.

Bird, B. J. and West, G. P. (1997) 'Time and entrepreneurship', *Entrepreneurship Theory and Practice*, 22 (2): 5–10.

Birley, S. (1985) 'The role of networks in the entrepreneurial process', *Journal of Business Venturing*, 1: 107–18.

Birley, S. and Norburn, D. (1987) 'Owners and managers: The Venture 100 vs. The Fortune 500', *Journal of Business Venturing*, 2: 351–63.

Birley, S. and Stockley, S. (2000) 'Entrepreneurial teams and venture growth', in D. Sexton and H. Landström (eds), *The Blackwell Handbook of Entrepreneurship*. Oxford: Wiley-Blackwell.

Birley, S. and Westhead, P. (1993) 'A comparison of new businesses established by "novice" and "habitual" founders in Great Britain', *International Small Business Journal*, 12 (1): 38–60.

Birley, S., Cromie, S. and Myers, A. (1991) 'Entrepreneurial networks: Their emergence in Ireland and overseas', *International Small Business Journal*, 9 (4): 56–74.

Bjenning, B. and Bjärsvik, A. (1999) 'En marknadsundersökning av en innovationsprodukt: En studie av de potentiella konsumenterna till Husqvarna AB's automatiska gräsklippare, Auto Mower' [Market research for an innovative product: A study of the potential buyer's of Husqvarna's robotic lawnmower, Auto Mower], Bachelor's thesis, Jönköping International Business School, Jönköping.

Blair, T. (2003) 'The third way: New politics for the new century', in A. Chadwick and R. Heffernan (eds), *The New Labour Reader*. Cambridge: Polity Press.

Blaschke, J. and Ersoz, A. (1986) 'The Turkish economy in West Berlin', *International Small Business Journal*, 4 (3): 38–47.

Blaschke, J., Boissevain, J., Grotenberg, H., Joseph, I., Morokvasic, M. and Ward, R. (1990) 'European trends in ethnic business' in R. Waldinger, H. Aldrich and R. Ward (eds), *Ethnic Entrepreneurs: Immigrant business in industrial societies*. London: Sage. pp. 79–105.

Blundel, R. (2002) 'Network evolution and the growth of artisanal firms: A tale of two regional cheese makers', *Entrepreneurship and Regional Development*, 14 (1): 1–30.

Boatler, R. (1994) 'Manager worldmindedness and trade propensity', *Journal of Global Marketing*, 8 (1): 111–27.

Bock, B. B. (2004) 'Fitting in and multi-tasking: Dutch farm women's strategies in rural entrepreneurship', *Sociologia Ruralis*, 44 (3): 245–60.

Boden, R. J. and Nucci, A. (2000) 'On the survival prospects of men's and women's new business ventures', *Journal of Business Venturing*, 15 (4): 347–62.

Boeker, W. (1989) 'Strategic change: The effects of founding and history', *Academy of Management Journal*, 32: 489–515.

Boissevain, J. (1974) *Friends of Friends: Networks, manipulators and coalitions*. Oxford: Blackwell.

Bolton Committee (1971) 'Report of the Committee of Enquiry on Small Firms', Cmnd 4811. London: HMSO.

Bonacich, E. and Modell, J. (1980) *The Economic Basis of Ethnic Solidarity*. Berkeley, CA: University of California Press.

Bontis, N., Crossan, M. M. and Hulland, J. (2002) 'Managing an organizational learning system by aligning stocks and flows', *Journal of Management Studies*, 39 (4): 437–69.

Borch, O. J., Huse, M. and Senneseth, K. (1999) 'Resource configuration, competitive strategies, and corporate entrepreneurship: An empirical analysis', *Entrepreneurship: Theory & Practice*, 24 (1): 51–72.

Borchert, O. and Ibeh, K. I. N. (2008) 'The quintessential born-global: Case evidence from a rapidly internationalising Canadian small firm', in Ndubisi N. (ed.), *Internationalisation of Business*. Kuala Lumpur: Arah Pendidikan Books.

Bornstein, D. (1998) 'Changing the world on a shoestring', *Atlantic Monthly*, 281: 34–9.

Boschee, J. and McClurg (2003) *Towards a Better Understanding of Social Entrepreneurship: Some important distinctions*. Minnetouka, MN: Social Enterprise SE Alliance.

Bosma, N., Acs, Z., Autio, E., Coduras, A. and Levie, J. (2008) 'Global Entrepreneurship Monitor: Executive summary 2008'. Babson College, Universidad del Desarrollo, Santiago, Chile, London Business School.

Bosma, N. and Harding, R. (2006) 'Global Entrepreneurship Monitor: GEM 2006 summary results'. Global Entrepreneurship Monitor Consortium at: www.gemconsortium.org

Bosma, N. and Levie, J. (2009) 'Global Entrepreneurship Monitor: 2009 Global Report'. Global Entrepreneurship Monitor Consortium at: www.gemconsortium.org

Bosma, N., Jones, K., Autio, K. and Levie, J. (2008) 'Global Entrepreneurship Monitor: 2007 executive report'. Global Entrepreneurship Monitor Consortium at: www.gemconsortium.org

Boubakri, H. (1985) 'Mode de gestion et reinvestissement chez les comercants Tunisiens a Paris', *Revue Européene des Migrations Internationales*, 1 (1): 49–66.

Bovaird, T., Hems, L. and Tricker, M. (1995) 'Market failures in the provision of finance and business services for small and medium-size enterprises', in R. Buckland and E. W. Davis (eds), *Finance for the Growing Enterprise*. London: Routledge.

Bowen, H. P. and De Clercq, D. (2008) 'Institutional context and the allocation of entrepreneurial effort', *Journal of International Business Studies*, 39: 747–67.

Bowey, J. L. and Easton, G. (2007) 'Entrepreneurial social capital unplugged: An activity-based analysis', *International Small Business Journal*, 25: 273–306.

Boyatzis, R. E. (1992) *The Competent Manager*. New York: Wiley.

Boyd, N. G. and Vozikis, G. S. (1994) 'The influence of self-efficacy on the development of entrepreneurial intentions and actions', *Entrepreneurship Theory and Practice*, 18 (4): 63–77.

Bracker, J. (1982) 'Planning and financial performance among small entrepreneurial firms: An industry study'. *Unpublished PhD thesis*, Georgia State University, Atlanta, GA.

Bracker, J. and Pearson, J. (1986) 'Planning and financial performance of small mature firms', *Strategic Management Journal*, 7: 503–22.

Braden, P. L. (1977) 'Technological entrepreneurship: The allocation of time and money in technology-based firms', Michigan Business Reports No. 62, University of Michigan, MI.

Brandstätter, H. (1997) 'Becoming an entrepreneur: A question of personality structure?', *Journal of Economic Psychology*, 18 (2–3): 157–77.

Braunerhjelm, P., Acs, Z. J., Audretsch, D. B. and Carlsson, B. (2009) 'The missing link: Knowledge diffusion and entrepreneurship in endogenous growth', *Small Business Economics*, 34 (2): 105–25.

Brazeal, D. and Herbert, T. (1999) 'The genesis of entrepreneurship', *Entrepreneurship Theory and Practice*, 23 (3): 29–44.

Breschi, S. and Malerba, F. (2001) 'The geography of innovation and economic clustering: Some introductory notes', *Industrial and Corporate Change*, 10 (4): 817–34.

Bresnahan, T., Gambardella, A. and Saxenian, A. (2001) '"Old economy" inputs for "new economy" outcomes: Cluster formation in the new Silicon Valleys', *Industrial and Corporate Change* 10 (4): 835–60.

Bridge, S., O'Neill, K. and Cromie, S. (2003) *Understanding Enterprise, Entrepreneurship and Small Business*. Basingstoke: Palgrave Macmillan.

Brigham, E. and Smith, K. (1967) 'Cost of capital to the small firm', *The Engineering Economist*, 13 (3): 1–26.

Brinckmann, J., Grichnik, D. and Kapsa, D. (2010) 'Should entrepreneurs plan or just storm the castle?: A meta-analysis on contextual factors impacting the business planning–performance relationship in small firms', *Journal of Business Venturing*, 25 (1): 24–40.

British Bankers' Association (2011) 'Small business support: November 2010'. London: BBA. 8 February.

Brockhaus, R. H. and Horwitz, P. S. (1986) 'The psychology of the entrepreneur', in D. L. Sexton and R. W. Smilor, *The Art and Science of Entrepreneurship*. Cambridge, MA: Ballinger. pp. 25–48.

Brockhaus Sr, R. H. (1980) 'Risk taking propensity of entrepreneurs', *Academy of Management Journal*, 23 (3): 509–20.

Brockhaus Sr, R. H. (1982) 'The psychology of the entrepreneur', in C. A. Kent, D. L. Sexton and K. H. Vesper (eds), *Encyclopedia of Entrepreneurship* (vol. 1). Englewood Cliffs, NJ: Prentice Hall. pp. 39–57.

Brooks, M. R. and Rosson, P. J. (1982) 'A study of behavior of small and medium-sized manufacturing firms in three Canadian provinces', in M. R. Czinkota and G. Tesar (eds), *Export Management: An international context*. New York: Praeger. pp. 39–54.

Brown, B. and Butler, J. (1995) 'Competitors as allies: A study of the entrepreneurial networks in the US wine industry', *Journal of Small Business Management*, 33 (3): 57–6.

Brown, G. (2005) Speech to the Advancing Enterprise Conference, London, December.

Brown, L. and McDonald, M. H. B. (1994) *Competitive Marketing Strategy for Europe*. London: Macmillan. p. 4.

Brown, S. (2002) 'Vote, vote, vote for Philip Kotler', *European Journal of Marketing*, 36 (3): 313–24.

Brownlie, D. and Saren, M. (1997) 'Beyond the one-dimensional marketing manager: The discourse of theory, practice and relevance',

International Journal of Research in Marketing, 14 (2): 147–61.

Brüderl, J. and Preisendörfer, P. (1998) 'Network support and the success of newly founded businesses', *Small Business Economics*, 10 (3): 213–25.

Bruni, A., Gherardi, S. and Poggio, B. (2005) *Gender and Entrepreneurship: An ethnographic approach*. Abingdon: Routledge.

Brush, C. G. (1992) 'Research on women business owners: Past trends, a new perspective, future directions', *Entrepreneurship Theory and Practice*, 16 (4): 5–30.

Brush, C. G., Carter, N., Greene, P., Gatewood, E. and Hart, M. (2001b) 'An investigation of women-led firms and venture capital investment'. Report prepared for the US Small Business Administration Office of Advocacy and the National Women's Business Council.

Brush, C. G., Carter, N. M., Greene, P. G., Mart, M. M. and Gatewood, P. (2002) 'The role of social capital and gender in linking financial suppliers and entrepreneurial firms: A framework for future research', *Venture Capital: An International Journal of Entrepreneurial Finance*, 4: 305–23.

Brush, C. G., Greene, P. G. and Hart, M. M. (2001a) 'From initial idea to unique advantage: The entrepreneurial challenge of constructing a resource base', *Academy of Management Executive*, 15 (1): 64–78.

Bruyat, C. and Julien, P.-A. (2001) 'Defining the field of research in entrepreneurship', *Journal of Business Venturing*, 16: 165–80.

Buchanan, J. M. and Di Pierro, A. (1980) 'Cognition, choice, and entrepreneurship', *Southern Economic Journal*, 46: 693–701.

Buckland, R. and Davis, E. W. (1995) *Financing for Growing Enterprises*, London: Routledge.

Bullock, A., Cosh, A. and Hughes, A. (2007) 'Finance for SMEs' in A. Cosh and A. Hughes (eds), *British Enterprise: Thriving or surviving?: SME growth, innovation and public policy 2001–2004*. Cambridge: Centre for Business Research.

Burns, P. (1989) 'Strategies for success and routes to failure', in P. Burns and J. Dewhurst (eds), *Small Business and Entrepreneurship*. London: Macmillan. pp. 32–67.

Burt, R. (1992) *Structural Holes: The social structure of competition*. Cambridge, MA: Harvard University Press.

Burton, B., Helliar, C. and Power, D. (2002) 'A behavioural finance perspective on IPOs and SEOs'. ACCA Research Report No. 82. London: ACCA.

Busenitz, L. W. (2007) 'Progress in understanding entrepreneurial behavior', *Strategic Entrepreneurship Journal*, 1 (1–2): 183–85.

Busenitz, L. W. and Barney, J. B. (1997) 'Differences between entrepreneurs and managers in large organizations: Biases and heuristics in strategic decision-making', *Journal of Business Venturing*, 12: 9–30.

Busenitz, L. W. and Lau, C.-M. (1996) 'A cross-cultural cognitive model of new venture creation', *Entrepreneurship Theory and Practice*, 20 (4): 25–39.

Buttner, E. H. and Rosen, B. (1988) 'Bank loan officers' perceptions of the characteristics of men, women, and successful entrepreneurs', *Journal of Business Venturing*, 3: 249–58.

Buttner, E. H. and Rosen, B. (1989) 'Funding new business ventures: Are decision makers biased against women entrepreneurs?', *Journal of Business Venturing*, 4 (4): 249–61.

Buzzell, R. D. and Wiersema, F. D. (1981) 'Successful share-building strategies', *Harvard Business Review*, 53 (1): 135–44.

Bygrave, W. (1988) 'The structure of investment networks of venture capital firms', *Journal of Business Venturing*, 3 (2): 137–57.

Bygrave, W. D. (1989) 'The entrepreneurship paradigm (I): A philosophical look at its research methodologies', *Entrepreneurship Theory and Practice*, 14 (1): 7–26.

Bygrave, W. D. and Hofer, C. W. (1991) 'Theorizing about entrepreneurship', *Entrepreneurship Theory and Practice*, 16 (2): 13–22.

Byrne, D. (1998) 'Class and ethnicity in complex cities: The cases of Leicester and Bradford', *Environment and Planning A: Government and Policy*, 30: 703–20.

Cabinet Office (1996a) 'The government response to the Deregulation Task Force Report 1996'. London: Cabinet Office.

Cabinet Office (1996b) 'Sector challenge: Bidding guidance'. London: Cabinet Office.

Cakar, N. D. and Erturk, A. (2010) 'Comparing innovation capability of small and medium-sized enterprises: Examining the effects of organisational culture and empowerment', *Journal of Small Business Management*, 48 (3): 325–9.

Calás, M. B. and Smircich, L. (2009) 'Extending the boundaries: Reframing entrepreneurship as social change through feminist perspectives', *The Academy of Management Review*, 34 (3): 552–69.

Caliendo, M., Fossen, F. M. and Kritikos, A. S. (2009) 'Risk attitudes of nascent entrepreneurs:

New evidence from an experimentally validated survey', *Small Business Economics*, 32 (2): 153–67.

Camagni, R. (1991) 'Local "milieu", uncertainty and innovation networks: Towards a new dynamic theory of economic space', in R. Camagni (ed.), *Innovation Networks: Spatial perspectives*. London: Belhaven Press. pp. 121–44.

Camagni, R. (2002) 'On the concept of territorial competitiveness: Sound or misleading?', *Urban Studies*, 39 (13): 2395–411.

Cambridge Small Business Research Centre (1992) 'The state of British enterprise'. Department of Applied Economics, University of Cambridge, Cambridge.

Cameron, D. (2010a) 'PM and Deputy PM's speeches at Big Society launch'. Number 10 website, 18 May, at: www.number10.gov.uk/news/pm-and-deputy-pms-speeches-at-big-society-launch

Cameron, D. (2010b) 'Our "Big Society" Plan'. Conservatives' website, 31 March, at: www.conservatives.com/News/Speeches/2010/03/David-Cameron_Our_Big_Society_plan.aspx

Campbell, D. J. (1988) 'Task complexity: A review and analysis', *Academy of Management Review*, 13 (1): 40–52.

Campi, S., Defourny, J. and Grègoire, O. (2006) 'Work intergration social enterprises: Are they multiple-goal and multi-stakeholder organizations?', in M. Nyssens (ed.), *Social Enterprise: At the crossroads of market, public policies and civil society* (vol. 7). Abingdon and New York: Routledge. pp. 29–49.

Cannon, M. D. and Edmondson, A. C. (2005) 'Failing to learn and learning to fail (intelligently): How great organizations put failure to work to innovate and improve', *Long Range Planning*, 38 (3): 299–319.

Cannon, T. and Willis, M. (1981) 'The smaller firm in overseas trade', *European Small Business Journal*, 1 (3): 45–55.

Cantillon, R. (Higgs, H., trans.) (1732/1931) *Essai Sur la Nature du Commerce en Général*. London: Macmillan.

Canton, E., Grilo, I., Monteagudo, J. and van der Zwan, P. (2010) 'Investigating the perceptions of credit constraints in the European Union'. Research Paper ERS-2010-001-ORG, January, Erasmus Research Institute of Management, Rotterdam.

Capello, R. (1999) 'Spatial transfer of knowledge in high technology milieux: Learning versus collective learning processes', *Regional Studies*, 33 (4): 353–65.

Capgemini, UniCredit and European Financial Management and Marketing Association (2010) 'World retail banking report: Special edition 2010: Small business banking and the crisis: Managing development and risk'. Capgemini.

Cappelli, P. and Sherer, P. D. (1991) 'The missing role of context in OB: the need for a meso-level approach', *Research in Organizational Behavior*, 13: 55–110.

Caprara, G. V. and Cervone, D. (2000) *Personality: Determinants, dynamics, and potentials*. Cambridge: Cambridge University Press.

Caputo, R. K. and Dolinsky, A. (1998) 'Women's choice to pursue self-employment: The role of financial and human capital household members', *Journal of Small Business Management*, 36 (3): 8–17.

Carayannis, E. G., Popescu, D., Sipp, C. and Stewart, M. (2006) 'Technological learning for entrepreneurial development (TL4ED) in the knowledge economy (KE): Case studies and lessons learned', *Technovation*, 26 (4, April): 419–43.

Cardullo, M. (1999) *Technological Entrepreneurism Enterprise formation, financing and growth*. Baldock, Hertfordshire Research Studies Press.

CARF (1997) 'Commentary', *Race & Class*, 39 (1): 85–95.

Carland, J. W., Hoy, F. and Carland, J. A. (1988) '"Who is an entrepreneur?" is a question worth asking', *American Journal of Small Business*, 13 (spring): 33–9.

Carland, J. W., Hoy, F., Boulton, W. R. and Carland, J. A. C. (1984) 'Differentiating entrepreneurs from small business owners: A conceptualization', *Academy of Management Review*, 9 (2): 354–9.

Carlson, D. S., Upton, N. and Seaman, S. (2006) 'The impact of human resource practices and compensation design on performance: An analysis of family-owned SMEs', *Journal of Small Business Management*, 44 (4): 531–43.

Carney, M. and Gedajlovic, E. (2002) 'The co-evolution of institutional environments and organizational strategies: The rise of family business groups in the ASEAN region', *Organization Studies*, 23 (1): 1–29.

Carree, M. and Thurik, A. R. (2006) 'Understanding the role of entrepreneurship for economic growth', in M. A. Carree and A. R. Thurik (eds), *The Handbook of Entrepreneurship and Economic Growth* (International Library of Entrepreneurship Series). Cheltenham: Edward Elgar. pp. ix–xix.

Carree, M., van Stel, A., Thurik, R. and Wennekers, S. (2002) 'Economic development and business ownership: An analysis using data of 23 OECD countries in the period 1976–1996', *Small Business Economics*, 19: 271–90.

Carroll, G. and Delacroix, J. (1982) 'Organisational mortality in the newspaper industries of Argentina and Ireland: An ecological approach', *Administrative Science Quarterly*, 27: 169–98.

Carroll, G. R. (ed.) (1988) *Ecological Models of Organizations*. Cambridge, MA: Ballinger.

Carson, D. (1990) 'Some exploratory models for assessing small firms' marketing performance (a qualitative approach)', *European Journal of Marketing*, 234 (11): 8–51.

Carson, D. (1991) 'Research into small business marketing', *European Journal of Marketing*, 9: 75–91.

Carson, D. and Cromie, S. (1989) 'Marketing planning in small enterprises: A model and some empirical evidence', *Journal of Marketing Management*, 5 (1): 33–49.

Carson, D. and Gilmore, A. (2000) 'Marketing at the interface: Not what but how', *Journal of Marketing Theory and Practice*, 8 (2): 1–7.

Carson, D., Cromie, S., McGowan, P. and Hill, J. (1995) *Marketing and Entrepreneurship in SMEs: An innovative approach*. Upper Saddle River, NJ: Prentice Hall.

Carson, D., Gilmore, A. and Grant, K. (1997) 'Qualitative marketing factors which contribute to growth in the developing small firm: A discussion and proposed methodology', in G. E. Hills, J. J. Giglierano and C. M. Huffman (eds), *Research at the Marketing/Entrepreneurship Interface*. Conference Proceedings. Chicago, IL: University of Illinois at Chicago. pp. 461–72.

Carsrud, A. L. and Johnson, R. W. (1989) 'Entrepreneurship: A social psychological perspective', *Entrepreneurship and Regional Development*, 1 (1): 21–31.

Carsrud, A., Gaglio, C. and Olm, K. (1987) 'Entrepreneurs, mentors, networks and successful new venture development: An exploratory study', *American Journal of Small Business*, Fall: 13–18.

Carswell, P. and Rolland, D. (2004) 'The role of religion in entrepreneurship participation and perception', *International Journal of Entrepreneurship and Small Business*, 1 (3–4): 280–6.

Carter, N. M. and Allen, K. R. (1997) 'Size determinants of women-owned businesses: Choice or barriers to resources?', *Entrepreneurship and Regional Development*, 9 (3): 211–20.

Carter, N. M., Gartner, W. B. and Reynolds, P. D. (1996) 'Exploring start-up event sequences', *Journal of Business Venturing*, 11: 151–66.

Carter, N. M., Gartner, W. B., Shaver, K. G. and Gatewood, E. J. (2003) 'The career reasons of nascent entrepreneurs', *Journal of Business Venturing*, 18: 13–39.

Carter, S. (1993) 'Female business ownership: Current research and possibilities for the future' in S. Allen and C. Truman (eds), *Women in Business: Perspectives on women entrepreneurs*. London: Routledge. pp. 148–60.

Carter, S. (1998a) 'Portfolio entrepreneurship in the farm sector: Indigenous growth in rural areas?', *Entrepreneurship & Regional Development*, 10 (1): 17–32.

Carter, S. (1998b) 'The economic potential of portfolio entrepreneurship: Enterprise and employment contributions of multiple business ownership', *Journal of Small Business and Enterprise Development*, 5 (4): 297–306.

Carter, S. (1999) 'Multiple business ownership in the farm sector: Assessing the enterprise and employment contributions of farmers in Cambridgeshire', *Journal of Rural Studies*, 15 (4): 417–29.

Carter, S. (2011) 'The rewards of entrepreneurship: Exploring the incomes, wealth, and economic well-being of entrepreneurial households', *Entrepreneurship Theory and Practice*, 35 (1): 39–55.

Carter, S. and Cannon, T. (1988) 'Female entrepreneurs: A study of female business owners; their motivations, experiences and strategies for success'. Department of Employment Research Paper No. 65. pp. 1–57.

Carter, S. and Cannon, T. (1992) *Women as Entrepreneurs*. London: Academic Press.

Carter, S. and Jones-Evans, D. (2006) *Enterprise and Small Business: Principles, practice and policy* (2nd edn). Harlow: Prentice Hall.

Carter, S. and Ram, M. (2003) 'Reassessing portfolio entrepreneurship', *Small Business Economics*, 21 (4): 371–80.

Carter, S. and Rosa, P. (1998) 'The financing of male- and female-owned businesses', *Entrepreneurship and Regional Development*, 10 (3): 225–41.

Carter, S. and Shaw, E. (2006) 'Women's business ownership: Recent research and policy developments'. DTI Small Business Service Research Report, November.

Carter, S., Anderson, S. and Shaw, E. (2001) 'Women's business ownership: A review of the academic, popular and internal literature'. Report to the DTI Small Business Service.

Carter, S., Shaw, E., Wilson, F. and Lam, W. (2007) 'Gender, entrepreneurship and bank lending: The criteria and processes used by bank loan officers in assessing applications', *Entrepreneurship Theory and Practice*, 31 (3): 427–44.

Cashmore, E. (1991) 'Flying business class: Britain's new ethnic elite', *New Community*, 17: 347–58.

Cashmore, E. (1992) 'The new black bourgeoisie', *Human Relations*, 45 (12): 1241–58.

Casson, M. (1982) *The Entrepreneurs: An economic theory*. Oxford: Martin Robertson.

Casson, M. (1990) *Entrepreneurship*. Cheltenham: Edward Elgar.

Casson, M. and Giusta, M. D. (2007) 'Entrepreneurship and social capital: Analysing the impact of social networks on entrepreneurial activity from a rational action perspective', *International Small Business Journal*, 25 (3): 220–44.

Castells, M. and Hall, P. (1994) *Technopoles of the World*. London: Routledge.

Castilla, E., Hwang, H., Granovetter, E. and Granovetter, M. (2000) 'Social networks in Silicon Valley', in C. Lee, W. Miller, M. Hancock and H. Rowen (eds), *The Silicon Valley Edge*. Palo Alto, CA: Stanford University Press. pp. 218–47.

Cavanagh, R. E. and Clifford, D. K. (1986) *The Winning Performance*. London: Sidgwick & Jackson.

Cavusgil, S. T. (1980) 'On the internationalization process of firms', *European Research*, 8 (November): 273–81.

Cavusgil, S. T. (1984) 'Differences among exporting firms based on their degree of internationalization', *Journal of Business Research*, 12 (2): 195–208.

Cavusgil, S. T. and Zou, S. (1994) 'Marketing strategy–performance relationship: An investigation of the empirical link in export market ventures', *Journal of Marketing*, 58 (January).

CEEDR (2007) 'The impact of perceived access to finance difficulties on the demand for external finance: Literature review for the small business service'. CEEDR, Middlesex University, April.

Chaffee, E. (1985) 'Three models of strategy', *Academy of Management Review*, 10: 89–98.

Chaganti, R., DeCarolis, D. and Deeds, D. (1995) 'Predictors of capital structure in small ventures', *Entrepreneurship Theory and Practice*, 20 (7): 7–18.

Chandler, A. (1962) *Strategy and Structure*. Cambridge, MA: MIT Press.

Chandler, A. (1977) *The Visible Hand: The managerial revolution in American business*. Cambridge, MA: Belknap Press.

Chandler, G. N. and Jansen, E. (1992) 'The founder's self-assessed competence and venture performance', *Journal of Business Venturing*, 7 (3): 223–36.

Chandler, G. N. and Lyon, D. W. (2001) 'Issues of research design and construct measurement in entrepreneurship research: The past decade', *Entrepreneurship Theory and Practice*, 25 (4): 101–13.

Chandler, G. N., Dahlqvist, J. and Davidsson, P. (2002) 'Opportunity recognition processes: A taxonomy and outcome implications', in *Frontiers of Entrepreneurship 2002*. Wellesley, MA: Babson College.

Chandler, G. N., Dahlqvist, J. and Davidsson, P. (2003) 'Opportunity recognition processes: A taxonomic classification and outcome implications'. Academy of Management meeting, Seattle.

Chandler, G. N., DeTienne, D. and Lyon, D. W. (2003) 'Outcome implications of opportunity creation/discovery processes'. Paper presented at the Babson College, Babson Kauffman Entrepreneurship Research Conference, 2002–2006.

Chaston, I. (1995) 'Small firm growth through the creation of value-added networks'. Proceedings of the 18th ISBA National Small Firms Policy and Research Conference, Paisley, Scotland. pp. 45–57.

Chell, E. (1985) 'The entrepreneurial personality: A few ghosts laid to rest?', *International Small Business Journal*, 3 (3): 43–54.

Chell, E. (2008) *The Entrepreneurial Personality: A social construction*. Abingdon: The Psychology Press/Routledge.

Chell, E. and Baines, S. (2000) 'Networking, entrepeneurship and microbusiness behaviour', *Entrepreneurship and Regional Development*, 12: 195–215.

Chell, E. and Haworth, J. (1992) 'A typology of business owners and their orientation towards growth', in K. Calay, E. Chell, F. Chittenden and C. Mason (eds), *Small Enterprise Development: Policy and practice in action*. London: Paul Chapman.

Chell, E., Haworth, J. and Brearley, S. (1991) *The Entrepreneurial Personality: Concepts, cases and categories*. London: Routledge.

Chen, C. C., Greene, P. G. and Crick, A. (1998) 'Does entrepreneurial self-efficacy distinguish entrepreneurs from managers?', *Journal of Business Venturing*, 13 (4): 295–316.

Chen, M. and Hambrick, D. (1995) 'Speed, stealth and selective attack: How small firms differ from large firms in competitive behaviour', *Academy of Management Journal*, 38 (2): 118–27.

Cho, A. H. (2006) 'Politics, values and social entrepreneurship: A critical appraisal', in J. Mair, J. Robinson and K. Hockerts (eds), *Social Entrepreneurship*. Houndmills, Basingstoke: Palgrave Macmillan.

Choo, C. W. (2008) 'Organizational disasters: Why they happen and how they may be prevented', *Management Decision*, 46 (1): 32–45.

Chrisman, J. J., Chua, J. H. and Litz, R. (2003) 'A unified systems perspective of family firm performance: An extension and integration', *Journal of Business Venturing*, 18 (4): 467–72.

Christensen, C. and Bower, J. (1996) 'Customer power, strategic investment, and the failure of leading firms', *Strategic Management Journal*, 17: 197–218.

Churchill, N. C. and Lewis, V. (1983) 'The five stages of small business growth', *Harvard Business Review*, 61 (3): 30–9.

Churchill, N. C. and Lewis, V. L. (1986) 'Entrepreneurship research: Directors and methods', in D. L. Sexton and R. M. Smilor (eds), *The Art and Science of Entrepreneurship*, Cambridge, MA: Ballinger. pp. 333–65.

Cialdini, R. B. (1988) *Influence: Science and practice*. London: HarperCollins.

Ciavarella, M. A., Buchholtz, A. K., Riordan, C. M., Gatewood, R. D. and Stokes, G. S. (2004) 'The big five and venture survival: Is there a linkage?', *Journal of Business Venturing*, 19 (4): 465–83.

Clark, T. (1995) *Managing Consultants: Consultancy as the management of impressions*. Buckingham: Open University Press.

Clark, T., Pugh, D. S. and Mallory, G. (1997) 'The process of internationalization in the operating firm', *International Business Review*, 6 (6): 605–23.

Clarke, J. and Newman, J. (1997) *The Managerial State: Power, politics and ideology in the remaking of social welfare*, London: Sage.

Cliff, J. (1998) 'Does one size fit all?: Exploring the relationship between attitudes towards growth, gender and business size', *Journal of Business Venturing*, 13 (6): 523–42.

Cochran, A. B. (1981) 'Small business mortality rates: A review of the literature', *Journal of Small Business Management*, 19 (4): 50–9.

Coelho, P. R. P. and McClure, J. E. (2005) 'Learning from failure', *Mid-American Journal of Business*, 20 (1): 13–20.

Cohn, T. and Lindberg, R. (1972) *How Management is Different in Small Companies*. New York: Harper & Row.

Cohn, T. and Lindberg, R. A. (1974) *Survival and Growth: Management strategies for the small firm*. New York: Amacom.

Coleman, J. S. (1988) 'Social capital in the creation of human-capital', *American Journal of Sociology*, 94: S95–S120.

Coleman, J. S. (1990) *Foundations of Social Theory*. Cambridge, MA: Harvard University Press.

Coleman, J. S. (2000) 'Social capital in the creation of human capital', in P. Dasgupta and I. Serageldin (eds), *Social Capital: A multifaceted perspective*. Washington, DC: World Bank.

Coleman, S. (2000) 'Access to capital and terms of credit: A comparison of men- and women-owned small businesses', *Journal of Small Business Management*, 38 (3): 37–52.

Colli, A. and Rose, M. B. (2008) 'Family business', in G. Jones and J. Zeitlin (eds), *The Oxford Handbook of Business History*. Oxford: Oxford University Press. pp. 194–218.

Colli, A., Fernández Pérez, P. and Rose, M. B. (2003) 'National determinants of family firm development?: Family firms in Britain, Spain and Italy in the nineteenth and twentieth centuries', *Enterprise and Society*, 4 (1): 28–64.

Collins, C. J., Hanges, P. J. and Locke, E. A. (2004) 'The relationship of achievement motivation to entrepreneurial behavior: A meta-analysis', *Human Performance*, 17 (1): 95–117.

Collins, J. C. and Lazier, W. C. (1992) *Beyond Entrepreneurship: Turning your business into an enduring great company*. Paramus, NJ: Prentice Hall.

Collins, O. F., Moore, D. G. and Unwalla, D. B. (1964) 'The enterprising man'. Bureau of Business and Economic Research, Michigan State University, East Lansing, MI.

Collinson, E. and Shaw, E. (2001) 'Entrepreneurial marketing: A historical perspective on development and practice', *Management Decision*, 39 (9): 761–6.

Collinson, S. (2000) 'Knowledge networks for innovation in small Scottish software firms', *Entrepreneurship and Regional Development*, 12: 217–44.

Collis, J. (2008) 'Directors' views on accounting and auditing requirements for SMEs'. London: BERR. Available online at: www.bis.gov.uk/policies/business-law/research/audit-accounting-and-reporting-research

Collis, J. and Jarvis, R. (2000) 'How owner-managers use accounts'. Centre for Business Performance, ICAEW.

Colombelli, A. (2009) 'Entrepreneurial dimensions of the growth of small business'. Paper in series provided by Dipartmento di Economia, University of Turin, Italy, No. 200902.

Companys, Y. E. and McMullen, J. S. (2007) 'Strategic entrepreneurs at work: The nature, discovery, and exploitation of entrepreneurial opportunities', *Small Business Economics*, 28: 301–22.

Competition Commission (2002) 'The supply of banking services by clearing banks to small and medium-sized enterprises'. London: Competition Commission.

Conway, S. (1994) 'Informal boundary-spanning links and networks in successful technological innovation', unpublished PhD thesis, Aston Business School, Birmingham.

Conway, S. (1997) 'Informal networks of relationships in successful small firm innovation', in D. Jones-Evans and M. Klofsten (eds), *Technology, Innovation and Enterprise: The European experience*. London: Macmillan. pp. 236–73.

Conway, S. and Steward, F. (1998) 'Mapping innovation networks', *International Journal of Innovation Management*, 2 (2): 165–96.

Conway, S. and Steward, F. (2009) *Managing and Shaping Innovation*. Oxford: Oxford University Press.

Conway, S., Jones, O. and Steward, F. (2001) 'Realising the potential of the social network perspective in innovation studies', in O. Jones, S. Conway and F. Steward (eds), *Social Interaction and Organisational Change: Aston perspectives on innovation networks*. London: Imperial College Press. pp. 349–66.

Cooke, P. (1997) 'Regions in a global market: The experiences of Wales and Baden Württemberg', *Review of International Political Economy*, 4 (2): 349–81.

Cooke, P. (2004) 'Regional innovation systems: An evolutionary approach', in P. Cooke, M. Heidenreich and H. Braczyk (eds), *Regional Innovation Systems: The role of governance in a globalized world*. Abingdon: Routledge.

Cooke, P. and Huggins, R. (2003) 'High-technology clustering in Cambridge', in F. Sforzi (ed.), *The Institutions of Local Development*. Aldershot: Ashgate. pp. 51–74.

Cooney, K. (2006) 'The institutional and technical structuring of nonprofit ventures: Case study of a U.S. hybrid organization caught between two fields', *Voluntas: International Journal of Voluntary and Nonprofit Organizations*, 17: 137–55.

Cooney, T. M. (2008) 'Why is community entrepreneurship worth debating?', *Journal of Enterprising Communities: People and Places in the Global Economy*, 2 (2): 97–9.

Cooper, A. C. (1970a) 'The Palo Alto experience', *Industrial Research*, May: 58–60.

Cooper, A. C. (1970b) 'Incubator organisations, spin-offs and technical entrepreneurship'. Proceedings of the Indiana Academy of the Social Sciences, 3rd Series. p. 4.

Cooper, A. C. (1971a) 'Spin-offs and technical entrepreneurship'. IEEE Transactions on Engineering Management, EM18, No. 1. pp. 2–6.

Cooper, A. C. (1971b) *The Founding of Technologically-based Firms*. Milwaukee, WI: Center for Venture Management.

Cooper, A. C. (1973) 'Technical entrepreneurship: What do we know?', *R & D Management*, 3 (2): 59–65.

Cooper, A. C. (1986) 'Entrepreneurship and high technology', in D. L. Sexton and R. W. Smilor (eds), *The Art and Science of Entrepreneurship*. Cambridge, MA: Ballinger. pp. 153–68.

Cooper, A. C. and Bruno, A. V. (1977) 'Success among high technology firms', *Business Horizons*, 20 (2): 16–22.

Cooper, A. C. and Dunkelburg, W. C. (1986) 'Entrepreneurship and paths to business ownership', *Strategic Management Journal*, 7: 53–68.

Cooper, A. C., Dunkelberg, W. C. and Woo, C. Y. (1986) 'Optimists and pessimists: 2994 entrepreneurs and their perceived chances for success', in *Frontiers of Entrepreneurship Research 1986*. Wellesley, MA: Babson College.

Cooper, A. C., Folta, T. B. and Woo, C. (1995) 'Entrepreneurial information search', *Journal of Business Venturing*, 10: 107–20.

Cooper, A. C., Willard, G. E. and Woo, C. Y. (1986) 'Strategies of high-performing new and small firms: A re-examination of the niche concept', *Journal of Business Venturing*, 1 (3): 247–60.

Cooper, A. C., Woo, C. Y. and Dunkelberg, W. C. (1988) 'Entrepreneurs' perceived chances for success', *Journal of Business Venturing*, 3 (1): 97–108.

Cooper, S. Y. (1996) 'Small high technology firms: A theoretical and empirical study of location issues'. Unpublished PhD thesis, Department of Business Organisation, Heriot-Watt University, Edinburgh.

Cope, J. (2003) 'Entrepreneurial learning and critical reflection: Discontinuous events as triggers for "higher-level" learning', *Management Learning*, 34 (4): 429–50.

Cope, J. (2005) 'Toward a dynamic learning perspective of entrepreneurship', *Entrepreneurship Theory and Practice*, 29 (4): 373–97.

Copp, C. and Ivy, R. (2001) 'Networking trends of small tourism businesses in post-socialist Slovakia', *Journal of Small Business Management*, 39 (4): 345–53.

Corbett, A. C. (2007) 'Learning asymmetries and the discovery of entrepreneurial opportunities', *Journal Business Venturing*, 22 (1): 97–118.

Cornett, A. P. (2009) 'Aims and strategies in regional innovation and growth policy: A Danish perspective', *Entrepreneurship & Regional Development*, 21: 399–420.

Cosh, A. and Hughes, A. (eds) (1996) 'The changing state of British enterprise'. Cambridge: ESRC Centre for Business Research, University of Cambridge.

Cosh, A. and Hughes, A. (eds) (2000) 'British enterprise in transition: Growth, innovation and public policy in the small and medium-sized enterprise sector, 1994–1999'. Cambridge: ESRC Centre for Business Research.

Cosh, A. and Hughes, A. (eds) (2003) 'Enterprise challenged: Policy and performance in the British SME sector 1999–2002'. Cambridge: ESRC Centre for Business Research.

Cosh, A., Hughes, A., Bullock, A. and Milner, I. (2008) 'Financing UK small and medium-sized enterprises: The 2007 survey'. Cambridge: ESRC Centre for Business Research, University of Cambridge.

Costa, C., Fontes, M. and Heltor, M. (2004) 'A methodological approach to the marketing process in the biotechnology-based companies', *Industrial Marketing Management*, 33 (5, July): 403–18.

Cova, B. and Pace, S. (2006) 'Brand community of convenience products: New forms of customer empowerment – the case of "my Nutella The Community"', *European Journal of Marketing*, 40 (9/10): 313–29.

Cova, B., Pace, D. J. and Park, D. J. (2007) 'Global brand communities across borders: The Warhammer case', *International Marketing Review*, 24 (3): 99–127.

Coviello, N. and Munro, H. (1995) 'Growing the entrepreneurial firm: Networking for international marketing development', *European Journal of Marketing*, 29 (7): 49–61.

Coviello, N. and Munro, H. (1997) 'Network relationships and the internationalization process

of small software firms', *International Business Review*, 6 (4): 361–86.

Covin, J. G. and Miles, M. (1999) 'Corporate entrepreneurship and the pursuit of competitive advantage', *Entrepreneurship Theory and Practice*, 23 (3): 47–63.

Covin, J. G. and Slevin, D. P. (1991) 'A conceptual model of entrepreneurship as firm behavior', *Entrepreneurship: Theory and Practice*, 16 (1): 7–24.

Cowling, M. (2010) 'Economic evaluation of the Small Firms Loan Guarantee (SFLG) scheme'. London: BIS.

Cowling, M., Samuels, J. and Sugden, R. (1991) 'Small firms and clearing banks', Report prepared for the Association of British Chambers of Commerce.

Cragg, P. and King, M. (1988) 'Organisational characteristics and small firms' performance revisited', *Entrepreneurship Theory & Practice*, winter: 49–64.

Cramton, C. D. (1993) 'Is rugged individualism the whole story?: Public and private accounts of a firm's founding', *Family Business Review*, VI (3): 233–61.

Cravens, D. W., Hills, G. E. and Woodruff, R. B. (1987) *Marketing Management* (3rd edn). Homewood IL: Richard D. Irwin.

Cressy, R. (2000) 'Tax assistance, compliance and the performance of the smaller business'. London: Federation of Small Businesses.

Crick, D. (1995) 'An investigation into the targeting of UK export assistance', *European Journal of Marketing*, 29 (8): 76–94.

Crick, D. and Chaudhry, S. (1995) 'Export practices of Asian SMEs: Some preliminary findings', *Marketing Intelligence and Planning*, 13 (11): 13–21.

Crick, D. and Czinkota, M. R. (1995) 'Export assistance: Another look at whether we are supporting the best programmes', *International Marketing Review*, 12 (3): 61–72.

Cromie, S. and Birley, S. (1992) 'Networking by female business owners in Northern Ireland', *Journal of Business Venturing*, 7 (3): 237–51.

Cromie, S. and Hayes, J. (1988) 'Towards a typology of female entrepreneurs', *Sociological Review*, 36 (1): 87–113.

Cross, M. and Waldinger, R. (1992) 'Migrants, minorities and the ethnic division of labour', in S. Feinstein, I. Gordon and M. Harloe (eds), *Divided Cities: New York and London in the contemporary world*. Cambridge, MA: Blackwell.

Crossan, M. M., Lane, H. W. and White, R. E. (1999) 'An organizational learning framework:

From intuition to institution', *Academy of Management Review*, 24 (3): 522–37.

Cruickshank, D. (2000) 'Competition in UK banking: A report to the Chancellor of the Exchequer', March. London: HM Treasury.

Csikszentmihalyi, M. (1990) 'Flow: The psychology of optimal experience'. New York: HarperCollins.

Cumming, D. (2007) 'Government policy towards entrepreneurial finance: Innovation investment funds', *Journal of Business Venturing*, 22 (2): 193.

Curran, J. (1986) *Bolton 15 Years On: A review and analysis of small business research in Britain 1971–86*. London: Small Business Research Trust.

Curran, J. and Blackburn, R. (1993) *Ethnic Enterprise and The High Street Bank*. Kingston Business School, Kingston University.

Curran, J. and Blackburn, R. (1994) *Small Firms and Local Economic Networks: The death of the local economy?* London: Paul Chapman.

Curran, J. and Burrows, R. (1986) 'The sociology of petit capitalism: A trend report', *Sociology*, 20 (2): 265–79.

Curran, J. and Burrows, R. (1988) 'Enterprise in Britain: A national profile of small business owners and the self-employed'. London: Small Business Research Trust.

Curtis, D. A. (1983) *Strategic Planning for Smaller Businesses*. Toronto: Lexington Books.

Cyert, R. M. and March, J. G. (1963) *A Behavioral Theory of the Firm*. Englewood Cliffs, NJ: Prentice Hall.

Czinkota, M. R. and Johnston, W. J. (1982) 'Exporting: Does sales volume make a difference?: A reply', *Journal of International Business Studies*, summer: 157–61.

Czinkota, M. R. and Ursic, M. L. (1987) 'A refutation of the psychic distance effect on export development', *Developments in Marketing Science*, X: 157–60.

Czuchry, A., Yasin, M. and Gonzales, M. (2004) 'Innovative entrepreneurial education: Design and implementation'. Paper presented at the Eighteenth Annual National Conference of the United States' Association for Small Business and Entrepreneurship Conference, also published in the Conference Proceedings of the Eighteenth Annual National Conference of the United States Association for Small Business and Entrepreneurship, Dallas, Texas, January.

D'Cruz, C. and Vaidyanathan, P. (2003) 'A holistic approach to teaching engineering entrepre-

neurship and technology commercialization'. Proceedings of the ASEE National Conference, Nashville, TN, June.

D'Cruz, C., Shaikh, M. and Shaw, W. (2006) 'Taking engineering entrepreneurship education to the next level with systems engineering entrepreneurship at Florida Tech'. Paper presented at the NCIIA Conference.

Daft, R. and Huber, G. (1987) 'How organizations learn: A communication framework', in B. Staw and L. Cummings (eds), *Research in the Sociology of Organizations* (vol. 5). Greenwich, CT: JAI Press. pp. 1–36.

Dahles, H., Verduyn, J. K. and Wakkee, A. M. (2010) 'Introduction', 'Soci(et)al entrepreneurship special issue', *Journal of Enterprising Communities: People and Places in the Global Economy*, 4 (1): 1–10.

Dahlqvist, J. and Davidsson, P. (2000) 'Business start-up reasons and firm performance', in P. D. Reynolds, E. Autio, C. G. Brush, W. D. Bygrave, S. Manigart, H. J. Sapienza and K. G. Shaver (eds), *Frontiers of Entrepreneurship Research 2000*. Wellesley, MA: Babson College. pp. 46–54.

Dahlqvist, J., Chandler, G. N. and Davidsson, P. (2004) 'Patterns of search and the newness of venture ideas'. Paper presented at the Babson College/Kauffman Foundation Entrepreneurship Research Conference, Glasgow.

Dahlqvist, J., Davidsson, P. and Wiklund, J. (2000) 'Initial conditions as predictors of new venture performance: A replication and extension of the Cooper et al. study', *Enterprise and Innovation Management Studies*, 1: 1–18.

Daly, M. (1991) 'The 1980s: A decade of growth in enterprise', *Employment Gazette*, March: 109–34.

Dart, R. (2004) 'The legitimacy of social enterprise', *Nonprofit Management and Leadership*, 14: 411–24.

Davidson, W. and Dutia, D. (1991) 'Debt, liquidity, and profitability problems in small firms', *Entrepreneurship Theory & Practice*, fall: 53–64.

Davidsson, P. (1988) 'Type of man and type of company revisited: A confirmatory cluster analysis approach'. Frontiers of Entrepreneurship Research, Babson Centre for Entrepreneurial Studies, Wellesley, MA. pp. 88–105.

Davidsson, P. (1989a) 'Continued entrepreneurship and small firm growth', unpublished PhD thesis, Stockholm School of Economics.

Davidsson, P. (1989b) 'Entrepreneurship – and after?: A study of growth willingness in small firms', *Journal of Business Venturing*, 4 (3): 211–26.

Davidsson, P. (1994) 'Husqvarna forest and garden (a marketing case)'. Mimeo. Jönköping International Business School, Sweden.

Davidsson, P. (1995) 'Determinants of entrepreneurial intentions'. Paper presented at the Rent IX Conference, Piacenza, Italy, November.

Davidsson, P. (2000) 'Three cases in opportunity assessment: The sports bra, the solar mower, and a decent cup of coffee'. Mimeo. Brisbane: Queensland University of Technology.

Davidsson, P. (2003) 'The domain of entrepreneurship research: Some suggestions', in J. Katz and D. Shepherd (eds), *Advances in Entrepreneurship, Firm Emergence and Growth: Cognitive approaches to entrepreneurship research* (vol. 6). Oxford: Elsevier/JAI Press. pp. 315–72.

Davidsson, P. (2004) *Researching Entrepreneurship*. New York: Springer.

Davidsson, P. and Delmar, F. (1997) 'High growth firms: Characteristics, job contribution and method observations'. Paper presented at the RENT XI Conference, Mannheim, Germany, 27–28 November.

Davidsson, P. and Honig, B. (2003) 'The role of social and human capital among nascent entrepreneurs', *Journal of Business Venturing*, 18 (3): 301–31.

Davidsson, P. and Klofsten, M. (2003) 'The business platform: Developing an instrument to gauge and assist the development of young firms', *Journal of Small Business Management*, 41 (1): 1–26.

Davidsson, P. and Wiklund, J. (2001) 'Levels of analysis in entrepreneurship research: Current research practice and suggestions for the future', *Entrepreneurship Theory and Practice*, 25 (4): 81.

Davidsson, P., Delmar, F. and Wiklund, J. (eds) (2006) *Entrepreneurship and the Growth of Firms*. Cheltenham: Edward Elgar.

Davidsson, P., Low, M. B. and Wright, M. (2001) 'Editor's introduction: Low and MacMillan ten years on: Achievements and future directions for entrepreneurship research', *Entrepreneurship Theory and Practice*, 25 (4): 5–15.

Davies, S. (2007) 'Research for Unison: Third sector provision of local government and health services'. London: Unison.

Davis, C. D., Hills, G. E. and LaForge, R. W. (1985) 'The marketing/small enterprise paradox: Research agenda', *International Small Business Journal*, Spring: 31–42.

Davis, J. H., Schoorman, F. D. and Donaldson, L. (1997) 'Toward a stewardship theory of management', *Academy of Management Review*, 22 (1): 20–47.

Day, G. and Wensley, R. (1988) 'Assessing advantage: Framework for diagnosing competitive superiority', *Journal of Marketing*, 52 (2): 1–20.

de Bruin, A. and Dupuis, A. (2003) 'Introduction: Concepts and themes', in A. de Bruin and A. Dupuis (eds), *Entrepreneurship: New perspectives in a global age*. Aldershot: Ashgate. pp. 1–24.

de Bruin, A. and Mataira, P. (2003) 'Indigenous entrepreneurship', in A. de Bruin and A. Dupuis (eds), *Entrepreneurship: New perspectives in a global age*. Aldershot: Ashgate. pp. 169–84.

De Carolis, D. M. and Saparito, P. (2006) 'Social capital, cognition, and entrepreneurial opportunities: A theoretical framework', *Entrepreneurship Theory and Practice*, 30: 41–56.

de Koning, A. (2003) 'Opportunity development: A socio-cognitive perspective', in J. Katz and D. Shepherd (eds), *Advances in Entrepreneurship, Firm Emergence and Growth: Cognitive approaches to entrepreneurship research* (vol. 6). Oxford: Elsevier/JAI Press. pp. 265–314.

Deakins, D. (1996) *Entrepreneurs and Small Firms*. Maidenhead: McGraw-Hill.

Deakins, D., Hussain, G. and Ram, M. (1994) *Ethnic Entrepreneurs and Commercial Banks: Untapped potential*. Birmingham: University of Central England Business School.

Deakins, D., Ishaq, M., Smallbone, D., Whittam, G. and Wyper, J. (2007) 'Ethnic minority businesses in Scotland and the role of social capital', *International Small Business Journal*, 25 (3): 307–26.

Deakins, D., Ram., M. and Smallbone, D. (2003) 'Addressing the business support needs of ethnic minority firms in the United Kingdom', *Environment and Planning C: Government and Policy*, 21: 843–59.

Deci, E. L. (1992a) 'Commentary: On the nature and functions of motivation theories', *Psychological Science*, 3 (3): 167–71.

Deci, E. L. (1992b) 'The relation of interest to the motivation of behavior: A self-determination theory perspective', in K. A. Renninger, S. Hidi and A. Krapp (eds), *The Role of Interest in Learning and Development*. Hillsdale, NJ: Erlbaum. pp. 43–70.

Deeks, J. (1972) 'The small firm: Asset or liability?', *Management Decision*, 10 (1): 52–70.

Dees, G. (1996) 'Social enterprise spectrum: Philanthropy to commerce'. Boston, MA: Harvard Business School.

Dees, G. and Elias, J. (1998) 'The challenges of combining social and commercial enterprise', *Business Ethics Quarterly*, 8 (1): 165–78.

Dees, J. G. (1998) 'The meaning of "social entrepreneurship"'. Paper with comments and suggestions contributed from the Social Entrepreneurship Funders Working Group. Kansas City, MO: the Kauffman Foundation.

Dees, J. and Anderson, B. (2003) 'Sector-bending: Blurring lines between nonprofit and forprofit', *Society*, 40: 16–27.

Defourny, J. (2011) 'Concepts and realities of social enterprise: A European perspective', in A. Fayolle and H. Matley (eds), *Handbook of Research on Social Entrepreneurship*. Cheltenham: Edward Elgar.

Defourny, J. and Nyssens, M. (2006) 'Defining social enterprise', in M. Nyssens (ed.) *Social Enterprise: At the crossroads of market, public policies and civil society*. Abingdon and New York: Routledge.

Delmar, F. (1996) 'Entrepreneurial behavior and business performance', unpublished PhD thesis, Economic Research Institute, Stockholm School of Economics.

Delmar, F. (1997) 'Measuring growth: Methodological considerations and empirical results', in R. Donckels and A. Miettinen (eds), *Entrepreneurship and SME Research: On its way to the next millenium* (vol. 1). Aldershot: Ashgate. pp. 199–216.

Delmar, F. and Shane, S. (2003a) 'Does business planning facilitate the development of new ventures?', *Strategic Management Journal*, 24: 1165–85.

Delmar, F. and Shane, S. (2003b) 'Does the order of organizing activities matter for new venture performance?', in *Frontiers of Entrepreneurship 2003*. Wellesley, MA: Babson College.

Delmar, F. and Shane, S. (2004) 'Legitimating first, organizing activities and the survival of new ventures', *Journal of Business Venturing*, 19 (3): 385–410.

Delmar, F. and Shane, S. (2006) 'Does experience matter?: The effect of founding team experience on the survival and sales of newly founded ventures', *Strategic Organization*, 4 (3): 215–47.

Delmar, F. and Wiklund, J. (2008) 'The effect of small business managers' growth motivation on firm growth: A longitudinal study', *Entrepreneurship Theory and Practice*, 32 (30): 337–57.

Delmar, F., Davidsson, P. and Gartner, W. (2003) 'Arriving at the high-growth firm', *Journal of Business Venturing*, 18 (2): 189–216.

Demarigny, F. (2010) 'An EU listing Small Business Act: Establishing a proportionate regulatory and financial framework for small and medium-sized issuers listed in Europe (SMILEs)'. Report to the French Minister of Economy, Industry and Employment, Brussels.

Demmert, H. and Klein, D. B. (2003) 'Experiment on entrepreneurial discovery: An attempt to demonstrate the conjecture of Hayek and Kirzner', *Journal of Economic Behavior and Organization*, 50 (3): 295–310.

Department for Business, Enterprise and Regulatory Reform (2007a) 'Enterprise and Growth: Discussion paper', September. London: HMSO. Available online at: http://webarchive.nationalarchives.gov.uk/+/http://www.berr.gov.uk/files/file42806.pdf

Department for Business, Enterprise and Regulatory Reform (2007b) 'VAT registrations in deprived areas'. London: HMSO.

Department for Business, Enterprise and Regulatory Reform (2007c) 'A government action plan for small business'. London: Department for Business, Enterprise and Regulatory Reform.

Department for Business, Innovation and Skills (2010) 'Local growth: Realising every place's potential', Cm 7961, 28 October. London: Department for Business, Innovation and Skills.

Department for Business, Innovation and Skills (2011) 'Bigger better business: Helping small firms start, grow and prosper'. London: HMSO.

Department for Education and Skills (2003a) '21st century skills: Remaking our potential (individuals, employers, nation)', Cm5810. London: Department for Education and Skills.

Department for Education and Skills (2003b) 'Skills for life: National needs and impact survey of literacy, numeracy and IT skills', RR490, October. London: Department for Education and Skills.

Department of Employment (1989) 'Small firms in Britain'. London: Department of Employment.

Deprey, B. (2011) 'The internationalization of management consultancy SMEs', unpublished PhD thesis, Anglia Ruskin University, Cambridge.

Deregulation Task Force (1996) 'Report 1995/96'. London: Cabinet Office.

DeTienne, D. R. and Chandler, G. N. (2004) 'Opportunity identification and its role in the entrepreneurial classroom: A pedagogical approach and empirical test', *Academy of Management Learning & Education*, 3 (3): 242–57.

DeTienne, D. R., Shepherd, D. A. and De Castro, J. O. (2008) 'The fallacy of "only the strong survive": The effects of extrinsic motivation on the persistence decisions for under-performing firms', *Journal of Business Venturing*, 23 (5): 528–46.

Dever, J. E. (2009) 'An analysis of the antecedents and consequences of entrepreneurial failure on the portfolio entrepreneur', unpublished PhD thesis, University of Strathclyde, Glasgow, Scotland.

Dew, N., Read, S., Sarasvathy, S. D. and Wiltbank, R. (2009) 'Effectual versus predictive logics in entrepreneurial decision-making: Differences between experts and novices', *Journal of Business Venturing*, 24 (4): 287–309.

Dhaliwal, S. (1998) 'Silent contributors: Asian female entrepreneurs and women in business', *Women's Studies International Forum*, 21 (5): 463–74.

Di Domenico, M., Haugh, H. and Tracey, P. (2010) 'Social bricolage: Theorizing social value creation in social enterprises', *Entrepreneurship Theory and Practice*, 34: 681–703.

Di Domenico, M., Tracey, P. and Haugh, H. (2009) 'The dialectic of social exchange: Theorizing corporate social enterprise collaboration', *Organization Studies*, 30: 887–907.

Dickson, P. R. and Giglierano, J. J. (1986) 'Missing the boat and sinking the boat: A conceptual model of entrepreneurial risk', *The Journal of Marketing*, 50 (3): 58–70.

Dimitratos, P., Johnson, J. E., Slow, J. and Young, S. (2003) 'Micromultinationals: New types of firms for the global competitive landscape', *European Management Journal*, 21 (2): 164–74.

Dimov, D. (2007a) 'Beyond the single-person, single-insight attribution in understanding entrepreneurial opportunities', *Entrepreneurship Theory and Practice*, 31 (5): 713–31.

Dimov, D. (2007b) 'From opportunity insight to opportunity intention: The importance of person–situation learning match', *Entrepreneurship Theory and Practice*, 31 (4): 561–83.

Dimov, D. (2010a) *The Glasses of Experience: Opportunity enactment, experiential learning, and human capital.* Saarbrucken: Lambert Academic Publishing.

Dimov, D. (2010b) 'Nascent entrepreneurs and venture emergence: Opportunity confidence, human capital, and early planning', *Journal of Management Studies*, 47 (6): 1123–53.

Dimov, D. (2011) 'Grappling with the unbearable elusiveness of entrepreneurial opportunities', *Entrepreneurship Theory and Practice*, 35 (1): 57–81.

Discua Cruz, A., Hamilton, E. and Howorth, C. (2009) 'Opportunity evaluation in business families: The case of Honduran business groups'. Paper presented at the IFERA Global Perspectives on Family Business Developments Conference, Cyprus, 24–27 June.

Discua Cruz, A., Howorth, C. and Hamilton, E. (2010) 'Family entrepreneurial teams: A vehicle for portfolio entrepreneurship'. Paper presented at the Theories of Family Enterprise Conference, University of Alberta, Edmonton.

Dobbs, M. and Hamilton, R. (2007) 'Small business growth: Evidence and new directions', *International Journal of Entrepreneurial Behaviour and Research*, 13 (5): 296–322.

Dodd, S. and Anderson, A. (2007) 'Mumpsimus and the mything of the individualistic entrepreneur', *International Small Business Journal*, 25 (4): 341–60.

Dodd, S. and Patra, E. (2002) 'National differences in entrepreneurial networking', *Entrepreneurship and Regional Development*, 14: 117–34.

Dodgson, M. (1989) 'Celltech: The first ten years of a biotechnology company'. Special report, Science Policy Research Unit, University of Sussex.

Dodgson, M. (2011) 'Exploring new combinations in innovation and entrepreneurship: Social networks, Schumpeter, and the case of Josiah Wedgwood (1730–1795)', *Industrial and Corporate Change*, 20 (4): 1119–51.

Doll, J. and Ajzen, I. (1992) 'Accessibility and stability of predictors in the theory of planned behavior', *Journal of Personality and Social Psychology*, 63 (5): 754–65.

Donckels, R. and Lambrecht, J. (1997) 'The network position of small businesses: An explanatory model', *Journal of Small Business Management*, April: 13–25.

Donckels, R., Dupont, B. and Michel, P. (1987) 'Multiple business starters: Who? Why? What?', *Journal of Small Business and Entrepreneurship*, 5 (1): 48–63.

Doutriaux, J. (1987) 'Growth pattern of academic entrepreneurial firms', *Journal of Business Venturing*, 2: 285–97.

Downing, J. and Daniels, L. (1992) 'The growth and dynamics of women entrepreneurs in

Southern Africa'. Gemini Technical Report 47, US Agency for International Development, Washington, DC.

Draheim, K. P. (1972) 'Factors influencing the rate of formation of technical companies', in A. C. Cooper and J. L. Komives (eds), *Technical entrepreneurship: A symposium*. Milwaukee, WI: Center for Venture Management. pp. 3–27.

Drakopoulou Dodd, S. and Gotsis, G. (2007) 'The interrelationships between entrepreneurship and religion', *The International Journal of Entrepreneurship and Innovation*, 8: 93–104.

Drayton, W. (2002) 'The citizen sector: Becoming as entrepreneurial and competitive as business', *California Management Review*, 44: 120–32.

Drucker, P. F. (1977) *Management: Tasks, responsibilities, practices*. London: Pan.

Drucker, P. F. (1985a) 'The discipline of innovation', *Harvard Business Review*, May–June (reprint 98604).

Drucker, P. F. (1985b) *Innovation and Entrepreneurship*. Oxford: Butterworth-Heinemann.

Drury, C. and Braund, S. (1990) 'The leasing decision: A comparison of theory and practice', *Accounting and Business Research*, 20: 179–91.

DTI (1992) 'A prospectus for one-stop shops for business'. London: DTI.

DTI (1996) 'The model trade association'. London: DTI.

DTI (2002) 'Social enterprise: Strategy for success'. London: DTI.

DTI (2003) 'DTI: The strategy'. London: DTI.

DTI (2007) 'Simplifying business support: A consultation'. London: DTI.

Dubini, P. and Aldrich, H. (1991) 'Personal and extended networks are central to the entrepreneurial process', *Journal of Business Venturing*, 6: 305–13.

Dupuis, A. and de Bruin, A. (2003) 'Community entrepreneurship', in A. Dupuis and A. de Bruin (eds), *Entrepreneurship: New perspectives in a global age*. Aldershot: Ashgate. pp. 109–27.

Dupuis, A., de Bruin, A. and Cremer, R. D. (2003) 'Municipal–community entrepreneurship', in A. de Bruin and A. Dupuis (eds), *Entrepreneurship: New perspectives in a global age*. Aldershot: Ashgate. pp. 128–47.

Durand, R. and Coeurderoy, R. (2001) 'Age, order of entry, strategic orientation, and organizational performance', *Journal of Business Venturing*, 16: 471–94.

Dutta, D. K. and Crossan, M. (2005) 'The nature of entrepreneurial opportunities: Understanding the process using the 4I organizational learning framework', *Entrepreneurship Theory and Practice*, 29 (4): 425–49.

Dyck, B., Mauws, M., Starke, F. A. and Mischke, G. A. (2002) 'Passing the baton: The importance of sequence, timing, technique and communication in executive succession', *Journal of Business Venturing*, 17 (2): 143–62.

Dyson, J. (1997) *Against the Odds: An autobiography*. London: Orion.

Eagly, A. H. and Chaiken, S. (1993) *The Psychology of Attitudes*. Fort Worth, TX: Harcourt Brace Jovanovich.

Ebben, J. and Johnson, A. (2005) 'Efficiency, flexibility, or both?: Evidence linking strategy to performance in small firms', *Strategic Management Journal*, 26: 1249–59.

Eckhardt, J. T. and Shane, S. A. (2003) 'Opportunities and entrepreneurship', *Journal of Management*, 29 (3): 333–49.

European Foundation for Entrepreneurial Research (1996) 'Europe's 500 dynamic entrepreneurs and job creators'. Brussels: EFER.

Egge, K. A. (1987) 'Expectations vs. reality among founders of recent start-ups', in N. C. Churchill, J. A. Hornaday, B. A. Kirchhoff, O. J. Krassner and K. H. Vesper (eds), *Frontiers of Entrepreneurship Research*. Wellesley, MA: Center for Entrepreneurial Studies, Babson College. pp. 322–36.

Eikenberry, A. M. and Kluver, J. D. (2004) 'The marketization of the nonprofit sector: Civil society at risk?', *Public Administration Review*, 64: 132–40.

Eisenhardt, K. and Schoonhoven, C. (1990) 'Organisational growth: Linking founding team, strategy, environment, and growth among US semiconductor ventures, 1978–1988', *Administrative Science Quarterly*, 35: 504–29.

Ekanem, I. and Smallbone, D. (2004) 'Investment decision-making in small manufacturing firms: A learning approach'. Paper presented at the 27th ISBA Annual Small Firms Research and Policy Conference, University of Teesside.

Ekanem, I. and Smallbone, D. (2007) 'Learning in small manufacturing firms: The case of investment decision making behaviour', *International Small Business Journal*, 25 (2): 107–29.

Elam, A. and Terjesen, S. (2010) 'Gendered institutions and cross-national patterns of business creation for men and women', *European Journal of Development Research*, 22: 331–48.

Elfring, T. and Hulsink, W. (2003) 'Networks in entrepreneurship: The case of high-technology firms', *Small Business Economics*, 21 (4): 409–22.

Elfring, T. and Hulsink, W. (2008) 'Networking by entrepreneurs: Patterns of tie formation in emerging organizations', *Organization Studies*, 28 (12): 1849–72.

Elliot, A. J. and Harackiewicz, J. M. (1994) 'Goal setting, achievement orientation, and intrinsic motivation: A mediational analysis', *Journal of Applied Psychology*, 66 (5): 968–80.

Emirbayer, M. (1997) 'Manifesto for a relational sociology', *American Journal of Sociology*, 103 (2): 281–317.

Engwall, L. and Wellenstal, M. (1988) 'Tit for tat in small steps: The internationalization of Swedish banks', *Scandinavian Journal of Management*, 4 (3/4): 147–55.

Ensley, M. D. (2006) 'Family businesses can outcompete: As long as they are willing to question the chosen path', *Entrepreneurship Theory and Practice*, 30 (6): 747–54.

Ensley, M. D. and Pearce, C. (2001) 'Shared cognition in top management teams: Implications for new venture performance', *Journal of Organisational Behaviour*, 22 (2): 145–60.

Epstein, J. A. and Harackiewicz, J. M. (1992) 'Winning is not enough: The effects of competition and achievement orientation on intrinsic interest', *Personality and Social Psychology Bulletin*, 18 (2): 128–38.

Equal Opportunities Commission (2005) 'Facts about women and men in Great Britain'. Manchester: Equal Opportunities Commission.

Erramilli, M. K. and Rao, P. (1990) 'Choice of foreign market entry modes by service firms: The role of market knowledge', *Management International Review*, 30 (2): 135–51.

Estades, J. and Ramani, S. (1998) 'Networks and technological competence: An analysis of some NBFs in the biotechnology sectors in France and Britain', *Technology Analysis and Strategic Management*, 10 (4): 483–95.

Etemad, H. (2004) 'Internationalization of small and medium-sized enterprises: A grounded theoretical framework and an overview', *Canadian Journal of Administrative Sciences*, 21 (1): 1–21.

Etzkowitz, H. (2003) 'Innovation in innovation: The triple helix of university–industry–government relations', *Social Science Information*, 42: 293–337.

Etzkowitz, H. and Leydesdorff, L. (2000) 'The dynamics of innovation: From national systems and "Mode 2" to a triple helix of university–industry–government relations', *Research Policy*, 29: 109–23.

European Commission (2000) 'Presidency conclusions: Lisbon Council of Ministers Bulletin EU 3-2000'. Brussels: European Commission.

European Commission (2003) 'Green Paper: Entrepreneurship in Europe', COM (2003) 27. Brussels: European Commission.

European Commission (2004) 'Action plan: The European agenda for entrepreneurship', COM (2004) 70. Brussels: European Commission.

European Commission (2008) 'Small Business Act'. Brussels: European Commission.

European Federation of Accountants (2004) 'Avoiding business failure: A guide for SMEs'. Brussels: European Federation of Accountants.

European SMEs Observatory (1994) 'First report'. Zoetermeer, The Netherlands: EIM.

European SMEs Observatory (1995) 'Second report'. Zoetermeer, The Netherlands: EIM.

European SMEs Observatory (1996) 'Third report'. Zoetermeer, The Netherlands: EIM.

European Venture Capital Association (2011) 'EVCA yearbook 2011'. Brussels: EVCA. Available online at: www.evca.eu/uploadedfiles/Home/Knowledge_Center/EVCA_Research/Statistics/Yearbook/Evca_Yearbook_2011.pdf

Experian (2010) 'Tomorrow's champions: Finding the small business engines for economic growth'. Nottingham: Experian.

Fabowale, L., Orser, B. and Riding, A. (1995) 'Gender, structural factors, and credit terms between Canadian small businesses and financial institutions', *Entrepreneurship: Theory and Practice*, summer: 41–65.

Fagenson, E. A. (1993) 'Personal value systems of men and women entrepreneurs versus managers', *Journal of Business Venturing*, 8 (5): 409–30.

Fang, S., Tsai, F. and Lin, J. (2010) 'Leveraging tenant-incubator social capital for organizational learning and performance in incubation programme', *International Small Business Journal*, 28 (1): 90–113.

Fay, M. and Williams, L. (1993) 'Sex of applicant and the availability of business "start-up" finance', *Australian Journal of Management*, 16 (1): 65–72.

Fayol, H. (1949) *General and Industrial Management*. London: Pitman.

Feldman, M. P. (2001) 'The entrepreneurial event revisited: Firm formation in a regional context', *Industrial and Corporate Change*, 10 (4): 861–91.

Feldman, M. P., Francis, J. and Bercovitz, J. (2005) 'Creating a cluster while building a firm: Entrepreneurs and the formation of industrial clusters', *Regional Studies*, 39: 129–41.

Fiegenbaum, A. and Karnini, A. (1991) 'Output flexibility: A competitive advantage for small firms', *Strategic Management Journal*, 12: 101–14.

Fielden, S. L., Davidson, M. J., Dawe, A. J., Makin, P. J. (2003) 'Factors inhibiting the economic growth of female owned small businesses in North West England', *Journal of Small Business and Enterprise Development*, 10 (2): 152–66.

Fiet, J. O. (2002) *The Systematic Search for Entrepreneurial Discoveries*. Westport, CT: Quorum.

File, K. M., Judd, B. B. and Prince, R. A. (1992) 'Interactive marketing: The influence of participation on positive word-of-mouth and referrals', *Journal of Services Marketing*, 6 (4): 5–14.

Finegold, D. and Soskice, D. (1988) 'The failure of training in Britain: Analysis of prescription', *Oxford Review of Economic Policy*, 4 (3): 21–53.

Finke, R. A. (1995) 'Creative insight and pre-inventive forms', in R. J. Sternberg and J. E. Davidson (eds), *The Nature of Insight*. Cambridge, MA: MIT Press. pp. 255–80.

Firnstahl, T. W. (1986) 'Letting go', *Harvard Business Review*, 64 (5): 14–18.

Fisher, M. (1996) Member of Deregulation Task Force, quoted in, 'Campaign to cut red tape "is a sham"', *Financial Times*, 6 December.

Fisher, N. and Hall, G. R. (1969) 'Risk and corporate rates of return', *Quarterly Journal of Economics*, 83: 79–92.

Flamholtz, E. G. (1986) *How to Make the Transition from an Entrepreneurship to a Professionally Managed Firm*. San Francisco, CA: Jossey-Bass.

Fletcher, D. E. (1997) 'Organisational networking, strategic change and the family firm', unpublished Phd thesis, Nottingham Business School.

Fletcher, D. E. (2006) 'Entrepreneurial processes and the social construction of opportunity', *Entrepreneurship Theory and Practice*, 18 (4): 421–40.

Florida, R. (2002) *The Rise of the Creative Class, and How It's Transforming Work, Leisure, Community and Everyday Life*. New York: Basic Books.

Fombrun, Charles (1982) 'Strategies for network research in organisations', *Academy of Management Review*, 7 (2): 280–91.

Foner, N. (1979) 'West Indians in New York and London: A comparative analysis', *International Migration Review*, 13: 284–95.

Foner, N. (1987) 'The Jamaicans: Race and ethnicity among migrants in New York City', in N. Foner (ed.), *New Immigrants in New York*. New York: Columbia University Press. pp. 195–217.

Fong, C. T. (2006) 'The effects of emotional ambivalence on creativity', *Academy of Management Journal*, 49 (5): 1016–30.

Food & Drink Weekly (2002) 'Ocean Spray Cranberries Inc. close to sale of Nantucket Nectars', *Food and Drink Weekly*, 1 April. Available online at: http://findarticles.com/p/articles/mi_m0EUY/is_13_8/ai_84376816

Forbes Insights (2010) 'Small and medium-sized enterprises: Rebuilding a foundation for post-recovery growth'. Forbes Insights: New York.

Ford, D. and Leonidou, L. (1991) 'Research developments in international marketing', in S. J. Paliwoda (ed.), *New Perspectives on International Marketing*. London: Routledge.

Forlani, D. and Mullins, J. W. (2000) 'Perceived risks and choices in entrepreneurs' new venture decisions', *Journal of Business Venturing*, 15 (4): 305–22.

Foster, M. J. (1993) 'Scenario planning for the small business', *Long Range Planning*, 26 (1): 123–9.

Frank, H., Plaschka, G. and Roessl, D. (1989) 'Planning behaviour of successful and non-successful founders of new ventures', *Entrepreneurship & Regional Development*, 1: 191–206.

Fraser, S. (2005) 'Finance for small and medium-sized enterprises: A report on the 2004 UK survey of SME finances', Warwick Business School, University of Warwick, Coventry.

Fraser, S. (2009) 'Is there ethnic discrimination in the UK market for small business credit?', *International Small Business Journal*, 27: 583–607.

Frazier, E. F. (1957) *Black Bourgeoisie*. Glencoe, IL: Free Press.

Frederking, L. C. (2004) 'A cross-national study of culture, organization and entrepreneurship in three neighbourhoods', *Entrepreneurship and Regional Development*, 16 (3): 197–215.

Fredland, J. E. and Morris, C. E. (1976) 'A cross section analysis of small business failure', *American Journal of Small Business*, 1 (1): 7–18.

Fredrickson, J. and Mitchell, T. (1984) 'Strategic decisions processes: Comprehensiveness and performance in an industry with an unstable environment', *Academy of Management Journal*, 27 (2): 399–423.

Freel, M. (2000) 'External linkages and product innovation in small manufacturing firms', *Entrepreneurship and Regional Development*, 12: 245–66.

Freel, M. (2003) 'Sectoral patterns of small firm innovation, networking and proximity', *Research Policy*, 32: 751–70.

Freeman, C. (1991) 'Networks of innovators: A synthesis of research issues', *Research Policy*, 20 (5): 499–514.

Frensch, P. A. and Sternberg, R. J. (1989) 'Expertise and intelligent thinking: When is it worse to know better?', in R. J. Sternberg (ed.), *Advances in the Psychology of Human Intelligence*. Hillsdale, NJ: Erlbaum. pp. 157–88.

Frese, M. (2007) 'The psychological actions and entrepreneurial success: An action theory approach', in J. R. Baum, M. Frese and R. Baron (eds), *The Psychology of Entrepreneurship*. Mahwah, NJ: Erlbaum. pp. 151–88.

Fritsch, M. and Schmude, J. (2006) *Entrepreneurship in the Region: International studies in entrepreneurship*. New York: Springer Science.

Fry, F. L. and Stoner, C. R. (1995) *Strategic Planning for the New and Small Business*. Chicago, IL: Upstart. pp. 3–19.

Fry, F. L., Stoner, C. R. and Weinzimmer, L. G. (1999) *Strategic Planning for New and Emerging Businesses: A consulting approach*. Chicago, IL: Dearborn Financial Publishing. pp. 3–19.

Fryer, P. (1984) *The History of Black People in Britain*. London: Pluto.

Fukuyama, F. (1996) *Trust: The social virtues and the creation of prosperity*. New York: Free Press.

Furnham, A. and Steele, H. (1993) 'Measuring locus of control: A critique of general, children's, health- and work-related locus of control questionnaires', *British Journal of Psychology*, 84 (4): 443–79.

Furr, N. R. (2009) 'Cognitive flexibility: The adaptive reality of concrete organizational change', unpublished PhD thesis Stanford University, Palo Alto, CA.

Gaddefors, J. and Cronsell, N. (2009) 'Returnees and local stakeholders co-producing the entrepreneurial region', *European Planning Studies*, 17 (8): 1191–203.

Gaglio, C. M. (1997) 'Opportunity identification: Review, critique, and suggested research', in J. A. Katz (ed.), *Advances in Entrepreneurship, Firm Emergence, and Growth*. Greenwich, CT: JAI Press.

Gaglio, C. M. (2004) 'The role of mental simulations and counterfactual thinking in the opportunity identification process', *Entrepreneurship Theory and Practice*, 28 (6): 533–52.

Gaglio, C. M. and Katz, J. A. (2001) 'The psychological basis of opportunity identification: Entrepreneurial alertness', *Journal of Small Business Economics*, 16: 95–111.

Galbraith, C. S. (1985) 'High-technology location and development: The case of Orange County', *California Management Review*, 28: 38–58.

Galbraith, J. K. (1956) *American Capitalism: The concept of countervailing power*. Boston, MA: Houghton Mifflin.

Garcia-Teruel, P. and Martinez-Solano, P. (2010) 'Determinants of trade credit: An investigation of European SMEs', *International Small Business Journal*, 28(3): 215–33.

García, M. and Carter, S. (2009) 'Resource mobilization through business owners' networks: Is gender an issue?', *International Journal of Gender and Entrepreneurship*, 1 (3): 226–52.

Gargiulo, M. and Benassi, M. (2000) 'Trapped in your own net?: Network cohesion, structural holes and adaptation of social capital', *Organization Science*, 11: 183–96.

Garnier, G. (1982) 'Comparative export behavior of small Canadian firms in the printing and electrical industries', in M. R. Czinkota and G. Tesar (eds), *Export Management: An international context*. New York: Praeger Publishers. pp. 113–31.

Garofoli, G. (2002) 'Local development in Europe: Theoretical models and international comparisons', *European Urban and Regional Studies*, 9: 225–39.

Gartner, W. B. (1985) 'A conceptual framework for describing the phenomenon of new venture creation', *The Academy of Management Review*, 10 (4): 696–706.

Gartner, W. B. (1989a) ' "Who is an entrepreneur?" is the wrong question', *Entrepreneurship Theory and Practice*, 13 (4): 47–68.

Gartner, W. B. (1989b) 'Some suggestions for research on entrepreneurial traits and characteristics', *Entrepreneurship Theory and Practice*, 13 (1): 27–37.

Gartner, W. B. (2001) 'Is there an elephant in entrepreneurship?: Blind assumptions in theory development', *Entrepreneurship Theory and Practice*, 25 (4): 27–39.

Gartner, W. B. and Carter, N. M. (2003), 'Entrepreneurial behaviour and firm organizing processes', in Z. J. Acs and D. B. Audretsch (eds), *Handbook of Entrepreneurship Research: An interdisciplinary survey and introduction*. Dordrecht, Netherlands: Kluwer. pp. 195–221.

Gartner, W. B., Davidsson, P. and Zahra, S. A. (2006) 'Are you talking to me?: The nature of community in entrepreneurship scholarship', *Entrepreneurship Theory and Practice*, 30 (3): 321–31.

Garud, R. and Karnoe, P. (2003) 'Bricolage versus breakthrough: distributed and embedded agency in technology entrepreneurship', *Research Policy*, 32 (2): 277–300.

Gaskill, L. R., Van Auken, H. E. and Manning, R. A. (1993) 'A factor analytic study of the perceived causes of small business failure', *Journal of Small Business Management*, 31 (4): 18–31.

Gatewood, E. J., Shaver, K. G. and Gartner, W. B. (1995) 'A longitudinal study of cognitive factors influencing start-up behaviors and success at venture creation', *Journal of Business Venturing*, 10 (5): 371–91.

Gatewood, E. J., Shaver, K. G., Powers, J. B. and Gartner, W. B. (2002) 'Entrepreneurial expectancy, task effort, and performance', *Entrepreneurship Theory and Practice*, 27 (2): 187–206.

George, G. and Zahra, S. A. (2002) 'Culture and its consequences for entrepreneurship', *Entrepreneurship: Theory & Practice*, 26 (4): 5.

Gersick, K. E., Davis, J., Hampton, M. M. and Lansberg, I. (1997) *Generation to Generation: Life cycles of the family business*. Boston, MA: Harvard Business School Press.

Gibb, A. (1983) 'The small business challenge to management education', *Journal of European Industrial Training*, 7 (5): 6–8.

Gibb, A. (1984) 'The small business challenge to management', *Journal of European Industrial Training*, 7: 3–41.

Gibb, A. (1986) 'Graduate career aspirations, education and entrepreneurship', in T. Faulkner, G. Beaver, A. A. Gibb and J. Lewis (eds), *Readings in Small Business*. Aldershot: Gower.

Gibb, A. (1992) 'Introduction' and 'The small firms growth programme, Part III' in 'Networking for Entrepreneurship Development'. Geneva: ILO.

Gibb, A. (1997) 'Small firms' training and competitiveness: Building upon the small firm as a learning organisation', *International Small Business Journal*, 15 (3): 13–29.

Gibb, A. (2002) 'In pursuit of a new "enterprise" and "entrepreneurship" paradigm for learning: Creative destruction, new values, new ways of doing things and new combinations of knowledge', *International Journal of Management Reviews*, 4 (3): 233–69.

Gibb, A. and Davies, L. (1990) 'In pursuit of frameworks for the development of growth models of the small business', *International Small Business Journal*, 9 (1): 15–31.

Gibb, A. and Davies, L. G. (1991) 'Methodological problems in the development and testing of a growth model of business enterprise development' in L. G. Davies and A. A. Gibb, *Recent Research in Entrepreneurship*. Aldershot: Avebury. pp. 286–323.

Gibb, A. and Dyson, J. (1982) 'Stimulating the growth of the owner-managed firms'. Paper presented at the UK National Small Firms' Policy and Research Conference, Glasgow, September.

Gibb, A. and Dyson, J. (1984) 'Stimulating the growth of owner-managed firms', in J. Lewis, J. Stanworth and A. Gibb (eds), *Success and Failure in Small Business*. Aldershot: Gower. pp. 249–58.

Gibb, A. and Scott, M. (1985) 'Strategic awareness, personal commitment and the process of planning in small business', *Journal of Management Studies*, 22 (6): 597–632.

Gibson, D. (ed.) (1991) *Technology Companies and Global Markets: Programs, policies and strategies to accelerate innovation and entrepreneurship*. Lanham, MD: Rowman & Littlefield.

Gilbert, B. A., Audretsch, D. B. and McDougall, P. (2004) 'The emergence of entrepreneurship policy', *Small Business Economics*, 22 (3/4): 313–23.

Gillman, M., Edwards, P., Ram, M. and Arrowsmith, J. (2002) 'Pay determination in small firms in the UK: The case of the response to the national minimum wage', *Industrial Relations Journal*, 33 (1): 52–68.

Gilmore, A., Carson, D. and Grant, K. (2001) 'SME marketing in practice', *Marketing Intelligence and Planning*, 1: 6–11.

Gilroy, P. (1987) *There Ain't No Black in the Union Jack: The cultural politics of race and nation*. Houndmills, Basingstoke: Macmillan.

Gist, M. E. and Mitchell, T. R. (1992) 'Self-efficacy: A theoretical analysis of its determinants and malleability', *Academy of Management Review*, 17 (2): 183–211.

Gladwell, M. (2010) 'The sure thing', *The New Yorker*, 18 January.

Glaeser, E. L. (2002) 'Learning in cities', *Journal of Urban Economics*, 46 (2): 254–77.

Glaeser, E. L. (2005) 'Review of Richard Florida's *The Flight of the Creative Class*', *Regional Science and Urban Economics*, 35 (5): 593–6.

Glaeser, E. L. (2007) 'Entrepreneurship and the city', Harvard Institute of Economic Research, Discussion Paper No. 2140.

Glaeser, E. L. and Sacerdote, B. (2000) 'The social consequences of housing', *Journal of Housing Economics*, 9 (1/2): 1–23.

Glaeser, E. L., Kallal, H. D., Scheinkman, J. A. and Shleifer, A. (1992) 'Growth in cities', *Journal of Political Economy*, 100 (6): 1126–52.

Godfrey, P. (1990) 'Management: Theories and practice', in M. Armstrong (ed.), *The New Manager's Handbook*. London: Kogan Page. pp. 37–49.

Godwin, L., Stevens, C. and Brenner, N. (2006) 'Forced to play by the rules?: Theorizing how mixed sex founding teams benefit women entrepreneurs in male dominated contexts', *Entrepreneurship, Theory and Practice*, 30 (5): 623–42.

Goffee, R. and Scase, R. (1985) *Women in Charge: The experience of female entrepreneurs*. London: Allen & Unwin.

Golann, B. (2006) 'Achieving growth and responsiveness: Process management and market orientation in small firms', *Journal of Small Business Management*, 44 (3): 369–85.

Gold, S. (1992) 'The employment potential of refugee entrepreneurship: Soviet Jews and Vietnamese in California', *Policy Studies Review*, 11 (2): 176–85.

Goldberg, L. R. (1993) 'The structure of phenotypic personality traits', *American Psychologist*, 48 (1): 26–34.

Gompers, P., Kovner, A., Lerner, J. and Scharfstein, D. (2007) 'Skill vs. luck in entrepreneurship and venture capital: Evidence from serial entrepreneurs'. NBER Working Paper. Available online at: http://papers.nber.org/papers/W12592.

Graham, T. (2004a) 'Task force studies new ideas to reduce regulatory and administrative burden', press release 6 December, Better Regulation Task Force. London: Cabinet Office.

Graham, T. (2004b) 'Graham review of the Small Firms Loan Guarantee'. London: HM Treasury.

Granger, B., Stanworth, J. and Stanworth, C. (1995) 'Self-employment career dynamics: The case of "unemployment push"', *Work, Employment and Society*, 9 (3): 499–516.

Granovetter, M. (1973) 'The strength of weak ties', *American Journal of Sociology*, 78 (6): 1360–80.

Granovetter, M. (1983) 'The strength of weak ties: A network theory revisited', *Sociological Theory*, 1 (1): 201–33.

Granovetter, M. (1985) 'Economic action and social structure: The problem of embeddedness', *The American Journal of Sociology*, 91 (3): 481–510.

Granovetter, M. (1992a) 'Economic institutions as social constructions: A framework for analysis', *Acta Sociologica*, 35 (1): 3–11.

Granovetter, M. (1992b) 'Problems of explanation in economic sociology', in N. Nohria and R. Eccles (eds), *Networks and Organizations: Structure, form and action*. Boston, MA: Harvard Business School Press.

Grant, K., Gilmore, A., Carson, D., Laney, R. and Pickett, B. (2001) 'Experiential research methodology: An integrated academic–practitioner "team" approach', *Qualitative Market Research: An International Journal*, 4 (2): 66–75.

Grant, P. and Perren, L. (2002) 'Small business and entrepreneurial research: Meta-theories, paradigms and prejudices', *International Small Business Journal*, 20 (2): 185–211.

Gras, D., Mosakowski, E. and Lumpkin, G. (2011) 'Gaining insights from future research directions in social entrepreneurship: A content-analytic approach', in G. Lumpkin and J. Katz, (eds), *Advances in Entrepreneurship, Firm Emergence and Growth* (vol. 13). pp. 25–50.

Greene, F. J., Mole, K. F. and Storey, D. J. (2004) 'Does more mean worse?: Three decades of enterprise policy in the Tees Valley', *Urban Studies*, 41 (7): 1207–28.

Greene, F. J., Mole, K. F. and Storey, D. J. (2007) *Three Decades of Enterprise Culture?: Entrepreneurship, economic regeneration and public policy*. Houndmills, Basingstoke: Palgrave MacMillan.

Greene, P., Brush, C., Hart, M. and Saparito, P. (1999) 'An exploration of the venture capital industry: Is gender an issue?' in P. D. Reynolds, W. Bygrave, S. Manigart, C. Mason, G. D. Meyer, H. Sapienza and K. G. Shaver (eds), *Frontiers of Entrepreneurship Research*. Wellesley, MA: Babson College.

Greene, P., Brush, C., Hart, M. and Saparito, P. (2001) 'Patterns of venture capital funding: Is gender a factor?', *Venture Capital: An International Journal of Entrepreneurial Finance*, 3 (1): 63–83.

Greer, M. and Green, P. (2003) 'Feminist theory and the study of entprepreneurship', in J. Butler (ed.), *New Perspectives on Women Entrepreneurs*. Greenwich, CT: IAP.

Gregoire, D. A., Barr, P. S. and Shepherd, D. A. (2010) 'Cognitive processes of opportunity recognition: The role of structural alignment', *Organization Science*, 21 (2): 413–31.

Greiner, L. E. (1972) 'Evolution and revolution as organizations grow', *Harvard Business Review*, 50 (4): 37–46.

Greiner, L. E. (1998) 'Evolution and revolution as organizations grow', *Harvard Business Review*, 76 (3): 55–68.

Greve, A. and Salaff, J. (2003) 'Social networks and entrepreneurship', *Entrepreneurship Theory and Practice*, 28 (4): 1–22.

Grimes, M. (2010) 'Strategic sensemaking within funding relationships: The effects of performance measurement on organizational identity in the social sector', *Entrepreneurship Theory and Practice*, 34: 763–83.

Gromov, G. (2010) 'A legal bridge spanning 100 years: From the gold mines of El Dorado to the "Golden" startups of Silicon Valley', NetValley. Available online at: www.netvalley.com/silicon_valley/Legal_Bridge_From_El_Dorado_to_Silicon_Valley.html

Guersen, G. (1997) 'Marketing theory: Its importance and relevance to entrepreneurs and small business', in Hills, G. E., Giglierane, J. J. and Hultman, C., *Research at the Marketing/Entrepreneurship Interface*. Chicago, IL: University of Illinois at Chicago. pp. 145–64.

Gulati, R. and Gargulio, M. (1999) 'Where do interorganizational networks come from?', *American Journal of Sociology*, 103 (5): 177–231.

Gupta, V. K., Turban, D. B. and Bhawe, N. M. (2008) 'The effect of gender stereotype activation on entrepreneurial intentions', *Journal of Applied Psychology*, 93 (5): 1053–61.

Gurdon, M. A. and Samsom, K. (1991) 'Entrepreneurial scientists: Organizational performance in scientist-started high technology firms' in *Frontiers of Entrepreneurial Research, 1991*. Wellesley, MA: Babson College.

Gustafsson, V. (2006) *Entrepreneurial Decision-making: Individuals, tasks and cognitions.* Cheltenham: Edward Elgar.

Haberfellner, R. (2003) 'Austria: Still a highly regulated economy', in R. Kloosterman and J. Rath (eds), *Immigrant Entrepreneurship: Venturing abroad in the age of globalisation*. Oxford: Berg.

Haines, G. H., Madill, J. J. and Riding, A. L. (2003) 'Informal investment in Canada: Financing small business growth', *Journal of Small Business and Entrepreneurship*, 16 (3/4): 13–40.

Haines, G. H., Orser, B. J. and Riding, A. L. (1999) 'Myths and realities: An empirical study of banks and the gender of small business clients', *Canadian Journal of Administrative Sciences*, 16 (4): 291–307.

Håkansson, H. (ed.) (1987) *Industrial Technological Development: A network approach*. London: Croom Helm.

Håkansson, H. (2009) 'Comment on actors, resources, activities and commitments', *Industrial Marketing Management*, 38: 562.

Hall, G. (1989) 'Lack of finance as a constraint on the expansion of innovative small firms', in J. Barber, J. Metcalfe and M. Porteous (eds), *Barriers to Growth in Small Firms*. London: Routledge.

Hamilton, D., Rosa, P. and Carter, S. (1992) 'The impact of gender on the management of small business: Some fundamental problems' in R. Wetford (ed.) *Small Business and Small Business Development: A practical approach*. Bradford: European Research Press. pp. 33–40.

Hamilton, E. (2006) 'Whose story is it anyway?: Narrative accounts of the role of women in founding and establishing family businesses', *International Small Business Journal*, 24 (3): 253–71.

Hamilton, E. (2011) 'Entrepreneurial learning in family business: A situated learning perspective', *Journal of Small Business and Enterprise Development*, 18 (1): 8–26.

Hamilton, J., Coulson, A., Wortley, S., Ingram, D. and Tagg, S. (2002) 'Business finance and security over moveable property'. Edinburgh: Scottish Executive Central Research Unit.

Hampton, A., Cooper, S. and McGowan, P. (2009) 'Female entrepreneurial networks and networking activity in technology-based ventures: An exploratory study', *International Small Business Journal*, 27 (2): 193–214.

Handler, W. C. (1991) 'Succession in family firms: A mutual role adjustment between entrepreneur and next-generation family members', *Entrepreneurship Theory and Practice*, 15 (1): 37–51.

Handy, C. (1993) *Understanding Organisations: How understanding the ways organisations actually work can be used to manage them better.* New York: Oxford University Press.

Hannah, L. (1976) *The Rise of the Corporate Economy* (2nd edn). London: Methuen.

Hansen, D. J., Lumpkin, G. T. and Hills, G. E. (2011) 'A multidimensional examination of a creativity-based opportunity recognition model', *International Journal of Entrepreneurial Behaviour and Research*, 17 (5): 515–33.

Hansford, A., Hasseldine, T. and Haworth, C. (2003) 'Factors affecting the costs of UK VAT compliance for small and medium-size enterprises', *Environment and Planning C: Government and Policy*, 21: 479–92.

Harackiewicz, J. M. and Elliot, A. J. (1993) 'Achievement goals and intrinsic motivation', *Journal of Personality and Social Psychology*, 65 (5): 904–15.

Harbi, S. E. and Anderson, A. R. (2010) 'Institutions and the shaping of different forms of entrepreneurship', *Journal of Socio-Economics*, 39 (3): 436–44.

Harding, R. (2008) 'Entrepreneurship and its role in stimulating sustainable economic development'. Inaugural report to the World Entrepreneurship Summit, 10–11 January. London: Delta Economics.

Harris, R. G. (2001) 'The knowledge-based economy: Intellectual origins and new economic perspectives', *International Journal of Management Reviews*, 3: 21–40.

Harrison, R. T. and Mason, C. M. (1987) 'The regional impact of the small firms loan guarantee scheme', in K. O'Neil, R. Bhambri, T. Faulkner and T. Cannon (eds), *Small Business Development: Some current issues*. Aldershot: Avebury. pp. 121–44.

Harrison, R. T. and Mason, C. M. (1992) 'The roles of investors in entrepreneurial companies: A comparison of informal investors' venture capitalists', in *Frontiers of Entrepreneurship Research 1992*. Wellesley, MA: Babson College.

Harrison, R. T. and Mason, C. M. (1995) 'The role of informal venture capital in financing the growing firm', in R. Buckland and E. W. Davis (eds), *Finance for Growing Enterprises*. London: Routledge.

Harrison, R. T. and Mason, C. M. (1996) *Informal Venture Capital: Evaluating the impact of business introduction services*. Hemel Hempstead: Prentice Hall.

Harrison, R. T. and Mason, C. M. (2000) 'Venture capital market complementarities: The links between business angels and venture capital funds in the UK', *Venture Capital: An International Journal of Entrepreneurial Finance*, 2: 223–42.

Harrison, R. T. and Mason, C. M. (2004) 'A critical incident analysis technique approach to entrepreneurial research: Developing a methodology to analyse the value-added contribution of informal investors'. Paper presented to the Babson-Kauffman Entrepreneurship Research Conference, University of Strathclyde, 3–5 June.

Harrison, R. T., Cooper, S. Y. and Mason, C. M. (2004) 'Entrepreneurial activity and the dynamics of technology-based cluster development: The case of Ottawa', *Urban Studies*, 41: 1045–70.

Harrison, R. T., Jungman, H. and Seppä, M. (2004) 'From capital investors to knowledge investors: The rise of entrepreneurial venture-to-capital', in M. Seppä, Hannula, M., Järvelin, A.-M., Kujala, J., Ruohonen, M. and Tiainen, T. (eds), *Frontiers of e-Business Research*. Tampere, Finland: Tampere University of Technology and University of Tampere.

Harrison, R. T., Mason, C. M. and Girling, P. (2004) 'Financial bootstrapping and venture development in the software industry', *Entrepreneurship and Regional Development*, 16: 307–33.

Hart, D. M. (2003a) *The Emergence of Entrepreneurship Policy: Governance, start-ups and growth in the US economy*. Cambridge: Cambridge University Press.

Hart, D. M. (2003b) 'Entrepreneurship policy: What it is and where it came from', in D. M. Hart (ed.), *The Emergence of Entrepreneurship Policy: Governance, start-ups and growth in the knowledge economy*. Cambridge: Cambridge University Press. pp. 141–55.

Hartog, J., Ferrer-i-Carbonell, A. and Jonker, N. (2002) 'Linking measured risk aversion to individual characteristics', *Kyklos*, 55 (1): 3–26.

Harvey, C., Maclean, M., Gordon, J. and Shaw, E. (2011) 'Andrew Carnegie and the foundations of contemporary entrepreneurial philanthropy', *Business History*, 53: 425–50.

Harvey, D. (2004) 'Keeping it in the family'. London: ACCA.

Harvey, D. (2005) *A Brief History of Neoliberalism*. Oxford: Oxford University Press.

Harvey, M. G., Lusch, R. F. and Cavakapa, B. (1996) 'A marketing mix for the 21st century', *Journal of Marketing Theory and Practice*, 4 (4): 1–15.

Haugh, H. M. (2007) 'Community-led social venture creation', *Entrepreneurship Theory and Practice*, 31 (2): 161–82.

Haugh, H. M. and Pardy, W. (1999) 'Community entrepreneurship in north east Scotland', *International Journal of Entrepreneurial Behaviour and Research*, 5 (4): 163.

Hawkins, P. (1994) 'The changing view of learning', in J. Burgoyne, M. Pedlar and T. Boydell (eds), *Towards the Learning Company: Concepts and Practices*. Maidenhedd: McGraw-Hill. pp. 9–27.

Hay, M., Verdin, P., and Williamson, P. (1993) 'Successful new ventures: Lessons for entrepreneurs and investors', *Journal of Long Range Planning*, 26 (5): 31–34.

Hayek, F. A. (1990) 'Economics and knowledge', in M. Casson (ed.), *Entrepreneurship*. Aldershot: Edward Elgar. pp. 33–80.

Hayes, H. M. (1988) 'Another chance for the marketing concept?', *Business*, January–March: 10–17.

Haynes, G. W. and Haynes, D. C. (1999) 'The debt structure of small businesses owned by women in 1987 and 1993', *Journal of Small Business Management*, 37 (2): 1–19.

Haynie, J. M., Shepherd, D. A. and Patzelt, H. (2011) 'Cognitive adaptability and an entrepreneurial task: The role of metacognitive ability and feedback', *Entrepreneurship Theory and Practice*, 7 September.

Haynie, J. M., Shepherd, D., Mosakowski, E. and Earley, P. C. (2010) 'A situated metacognitive model of the entrepreneurial mindset', *Journal of Business Venturing*, 25 (2): 217–29.

Hayton, J. C., George, G. and Zahra, S. A. (2002) 'National culture and entrepreneurship: A review of behavioural research', *Entrepreneurship Theory and Practice*, 26 (4): 33–52.

Hayton, K. (1995) 'Community involvement in economic regeneration lessons from North East England', *Community Development Journal*, 30 (2): 169–79.

Headd, B. (2003) 'Redefining business success: Distinguishing between closure and failure', *Small Business Economics*, 21 (1): 51.

Heath, C. and Tversky, A. (1991) 'Preference and belief: Ambiguity and competence in choice under uncertainty', *Journal of Risk and Uncertainty*, 4 (1): 5–28.

Hébert, R. F. and Link, A. N. (1988) *The Entrepreneur: Mainstream views and radical critiques*. New York: Praeger.

Hébert, R. F. and Link, A. N. (1989) 'In search of the meaning of entrepreneurship', *Small Business Economics*, 1 (1): 39–49.

Hechavarria, D. M. and Reynolds, P. D. (2009) 'Cultural norms and business start-ups: The impact of national values on opportunity and necessity entrepreneurs', *International Entrepreneurship and Management Journal*, 5 (4): 417–37.

Hellman, P. (1996) 'The internationalization of Finnish financial service companies', *International Business Review*, 3 (2): 191–207.

Henderson, R. and Clark, K. (1990) 'Architectural innovation: The reconfiguration of existing product technologies and the failure of established firms', *Administrative Science Quarterly*, 35 (1): 9–30.

Henrekson, M. (2007) 'Entrepreneurship and institutions', *Comparative Labour Law and Policy Journal*, 28 (3): 717–42.

Henrekson, M. and Sanandaji, T. (2010) 'The interaction of entrepreneurship and institutions'. Stockholm: Research Institute of Industrial Economics.

Herbert, R. F. and Link, A. N. (1988) *The Entrepreneur: Mainstream views and radical critiques* (2nd edn). New York: Praeger.

Hernandez-Canovas, G. and Koetter-Kant, J. (2008) 'Debt maturity and relationship lending: An analysis of European SMEs', *International Small Business Journal*, 26 (5): 595–617.

Heron, L. and Sapienza, H. J. (1992) 'The entrepreneur and the initiation of new venture launch activities', *Entrepreneurship Theory and Practice*, Fall: 49–55.

Herron, L. and Robinson, R. B. J. (1993) 'A structural model of the effects of entrepreneurial characteristics on venture performance', *Journal of Business Venturing*, 8 (3): 281–94.

Hess, M. (2004) ' "Spatial" relationships?: Towards a reconceptualization of embeddedness', *Progress in Human Geography*, 28 (2): 165–86.

Higson, C. (1993) *Business Finance* (2nd edn). Oxford: Butterworth.

Hill, C. J. and Neeley, S. E. (1991) 'Differences in consumer decision processes for professional vs. generic services', *Journal of Services Management*, 2 (1): 17–23.

Hill, J. and McGowan, P. (1997) 'Marketing development through networking: A competency based approach for small firm entrepreneurs', in G. E. Hills, J. J. Giglierano and C. M. Hultman (eds), *Research at the Marketing/Entrepreneurship Interface*. Chicago, IL: University of Illinois at Chicago. pp. 543–61.

Hills, G. E. (1984) 'Market analysis and marketing in new ventures: Venture capitalists' perceptions', in *Frontiers of Entrepreneurship Research 1984*. Wellesley, Babson College.

Hills, G. E. (ed.) (1987) *Research at the Marketing/Entrepreneurship Interface*. Proceedings of UIC Symposium on Marketing and Entrepreneurship. Marietta, GA: United States Association for Small Business and Entrepreneurship.

Hills, G. E. and Hultman, C. (2008) 'History and some theoretical foundations of entrepreneurial marketing'. Paper presented at the 22nd UIC International Research Symposium on Marketing and Entrepreneurship, Stockholm, 14–16 June.

Hills, G. E. and LaForge, R. W. (1992) 'Research at the marketing interface to advance entrepreneurship theory', *Entrepreneurship Theory and Practice*, Spring: 33–59.

Hills, G. E. and Narayana, C. L. (1989) 'Profile characteristics, success factors and marketing in highly successful firms', in *Frontiers of Entrepreneurship 1989*. Wellesley, MA: Babson College.

Hills, G. E. and Shrader, R. C. (1998) 'Successful entrepreneurs' insights into opportunity recognition', *In Frontiers of Entrepreneurship Research 1998*. Wellesley, MA: Babson College.

Hills, G. E., Hultman, C. and Miles, M. (2008) 'The evolution and development of entrepreneurial marketing', *Journal of Small Business Management*, 46 (1): 99–112.

Hills, G. E., Shrader, R. C. and Lumpkin, G. T. (1999) 'Opportunity recognition as a creative process', in *Frontiers of Entrepreneurship Research 1999*. Wellesley, MA: Babson College.

Hiscox (2010) 'Surviving the recession cost entrepreneurs £16bn in personal savings', Hiscox press release, 30 March, London.

Hisrich, R. D. (1989) 'Marketing and entrepreneurship research interface', in G. E. Hills, R. W. LaForge and B. J. Parker (eds), *Research at the Marketing/Entrepreneurship Interface*. Chicago, IL: University of Illinois at Chicago. pp. 3–17.

Hisrich, R. D. and Brush, C. G. (1986) *The Woman Entrepreneur: Starting, financing and managing a successful new business*. Lexington, MA: Lexington Books.

Hisrich, R. D. and Peters, M. P. (1992) *Entrepreneurship: Starting, developing, and managing a new enterprise* (2nd edn). Homewood, IL: BPI/Irwin.

Hisrich, R. D., Langan-Fox, J. and Grant, S. (2007) 'Entrepreneurship research and practice: A call to action for psychology', *American Psychologist*, 62 (6): 575–89.

Hite, J. (2005) 'Evolutionary processes and paths of relationally embedded network ties in emerging entrepreneurial firms', *Entrepreneurship Theory and Practice*, 30 (1): 113–44.

Hite, J. and Hesterly, W. (2001) 'The evolution of firm networks: From emergence to early growth of the firm', *Strategic Management Journal*, 22 (3): 275–86.

HM Treasury (2002) 'Cross-cutting review of services to small businesses'. London: HM Treasury.

HM Treasury (2011) 'Project Merlin: Banks' statement 9 February 2011: Revised'. London: HM Treasury.

HM Treasury and Department for Business, Enterprise and Regulatory Reform (2008) 'Enterprise: Unlocking the UK's talent'. London: HMSO.

HM Treasury and the Department for Business, Innovation and Skills (2010) 'Financing business growth: The government's response to financing a private sector recovery'. London: BIS/HM Treasury.

HM Treasury and the Small Business Service (2003) 'Bridging the finance gap: Next steps in improving access to growth capital for small businesses', December. London: HM Treasury.

Hoang, H. and Antoncic, B. (2003) 'Network-based research in entrepreneurship: A critical review', *Journal of Business Venturing*, 18: 165–87.

Hofer, C. (1975) 'Toward a contingency theory of business strategy', *Academy of Management Journal*, 18: 784–810.

Hofstede, G. (1991) *Cultures and Organizations: Software of the mind*. Maidenhead: McGraw-Hill.

Hogan, R. T. (1991) 'Personality and personality measurement', in M. D. Dunnette and L. M. Hough (eds), *Handbook of Industrial and Organizational Psychology* (vol. 2). Palo Alto, CA: Consulting Psychologists Press. pp. 873–919.

Hogan, R. T., Hogan, J. and Roberts, B. W. (1996) 'Personality measurement and employment decisions: Questions and answers', *American Psychologist*, 51 (5): 469–77.

Hogarth, R. M. (1987) *Judgement and Choice: The psychology of decision* (2nd edn). Chichester: Wiley.

Hogia (2004) Information about the Hogia Group is available online at: www.hogia.com

Hogsved, B.-I. (1996) 'Klyv företagen!: Hogias tillväxtmodell' 'Split the companies!: Hogia's growth model'. Falun, Sweden: Ekerlids Förlag.

Holcombe, R. G. (2007) 'Entrepreneurship and economic growth', in B. Powell (ed.), *Making Poor Nations Rich: Entrepreneurship and the process of economic development*. Palo Alto, CA: Stanford University Press.

Holliday, R. (1995) *Nice Work?: Investigating small firms*. London: Routledge.

Holmquist, C. (2003) 'Is the medium really the message?: Moving perspective from the entrepreneurial actor to the entrepreneurial action', in C. Steyaert and D. Hjorth (eds), *New Movements in Entrepreneurship*. Cheltenham and Northampton, MA: Edward Elgar. pp. 73–85.

Holtz-Eakin, D. (2000) 'Public policy toward entrepreneurship', *Small Business Economics*, 15 (4): 283–91.

Honig, B. and Karlsson, T. (2001) 'Business planning and the nascent entrepreneur: An empirical study of normative behavior', *Journal of Management*, 30 (1): 29–48.

Hoogstra, G. J. and van Dijk, J. (2004) 'Explaining small firm growth: Does location matter?', *Small Business Economics*, 22 (3–4): 179–92.

Hornaday, J. A. (1982) 'Research about living entrepreneurs', in C. A. Kent, D. L. Sexton and K. L. Vesper (eds), *Encyclopedia of Entrepreneurship* (vol. 1). Englewood Cliffs, NJ: Prentice Hall. pp. 281–90.

Hoselitz, B. F. (1960) *Sociological Factors in Economic Development*. Glencoe, IL: Free Press.

House of Commons Business and Enterprise Committee (2009) 'Enterprise Finance Guarantee Scheme: Tenth report of session 2008–9', July. London: TSO.

Howorth, C. and Ali, Z. A. (2001) 'Family business succession in Portugal: An examination of case studies in the furniture industry', *Family Business Review*, 14 (3): 231–44.

Howorth, C., Rose, M. B. and Hamilton, E. (2006) 'Definitions, diversity and development: Key debates in family business research', in M. Casson, B. Yeung, A. Basu and N. Wadeson (eds), *The Oxford Handbook of Entrepreneurship*. Oxford: Oxford University Press. pp. 225–47.

Hsu, D. (2007) 'Experienced entrepreneurial founders, organizational capital and venture capital funding', *Research Policy*, 36: 722–41.

Huerta de Soto, J. (2008) *The Austrian School: Market order and entrepreneurial creativity*. Cheltenham: Edward Elgar.

Huff, A. and Reger, R. (1987) 'A review of strategic process research', *Journal of Management*, 13 (2): 211–36.

Huggins, R. (2000a) *The Business of Networks: Inter-firm interaction, institutional policy and the TEC experiment*. Aldershot: Ashgate.

Huggins, R. (2000b) 'The success and failure of policy-implanted inter-firm network initiatives: Motivations, processes and structure', *Entrepreneurship and Regional Development*, 12 (2): 11–135.

Huggins, R. (2003) 'Creating a UK competitiveness index: Regional and local benchmarking', *Regional Studies*, 37 (1): 89–96.

Huggins, R. (2008) 'The evolution of knowledge clusters: progress and policy', *Economic Development Quarterly*, 22 (4): 277–89.

Huggins, R. (2010) 'Forms of network resource: Knowledge access and the role of inter-firm networks', *International Journal of Management Reviews*, 12: 335–52.

Huggins, R. and Izushi, H. (2007) *Competing for Knowledge: Creating, connecting and growing*. Abingdon: Routledge.

Huggins, R. and Izushi, H. (2008) 'UK competitiveness index 2008'. Cardiff, Wales: Centre for International Competitiveness.

Huggins, R. and Johnston, A. (2009) 'Knowledge networks in an uncompetitive region: SME innovation and growth', *Growth and Change*, 40 (2): 227–59.

Huggins, R. and Thompson, P. (2010) 'UK competitiveness index 2010'. Cardiff, Wales: Centre for International Competitiveness.

Huggins, R. and Williams, N. (2009) 'Enterprise and public policy: A review of Labour government intervention in the United Kingdom: Environment and Planning C', *Government and Policy*, 27 (1): 19–41.

Huggins, R., Johnston, A. and Steffenson, R. (2008) 'Universities, knowledge networks and regional policy', *Cambridge Journal of Regions, Economy and Society*, 1: 321–40.

Hughes, A., Cosh, A., Bullock, A. and Milner, I. (2009) *SME Finance and Innovation in the Current Economic Crisis*. Cambridge: Centre for Business Research.

Hundley, G. (2001) 'Domestic division of labor and self organizationally employed differences in job attitudes and earnings', *Journal of Family and Economics Issues*, 22 (2): 121–39.

Hung, H. (2006) 'Formation and survival of new ventures: A path from interpersonal to interorganizational networks', *International Small Business Journal*, 24 (4): 359–78.

Hyvarinen, L. (1990) 'Innovativeness and its indicators in small and medium-sized industrial enterprises', *International Small Business Journal*, 9 (1): 65–79.

Iacobucci, D. (2002) 'Explaining business groups started by habitual entrepreneurs in the Italian manufacturing sector', *Entrepreneurship and Regional Development*, 14 (1): 31–47.

Iacobucci, D. and Rosa, P. (2005) 'Growth, diversification, and business group formation in entrepreneurial firms', *Small Business Economics*, 25 (1): 65–82.

Iacobucci, D. and Rosa, P. (2010) 'The growth of business groups by habitual entrepreneurs: The role of entrepreneurial teams', *Entrepreneurship, Theory and Practice*, 34 (2): 351–77.

Ibarra, H. (1997) 'Paving an alternative route: Gender differences in managerial networks', *Social Psychology Quarterly*, 60 (1): 91–102.

Ibeh, K., Borchert, O. and Wheeler, C. (2009) 'Micromultinationals: Transcending resource challenges in international business', in K. Ibeh and S. Davies (eds), *Contemporary Challenges to International Business*. Houndmills, Basingstoke: Palgrave Macmillan. pp. 85–105.

Ibeh, K. I. N. (2000) 'Internationalization and the small firm', in S. Carter and D. Jones-Evans (eds), *Enterprise and Small Business*. Harlow: Prentice Hall. pp. 434–52.

Ibeh, K. I. N. (2001) 'On the resource-based, integrative view of small firm internationalization', in J. Taggart, M. M. J. Berry and M. McDermott (eds), *Multinationals in a New Era:*

International strategy and management (vol. 8). Houndmills, Basingstoke: Palgrave Macmillan. pp. 72–87.

Ibeh, K. I. N. (2005) 'Toward greater firm-level international entrepreneurship within the UK agribusiness sector: Resource levers and strategic options', *Management International Review*, 45 (3): 59–81.

Ibeh, K. I. N. (2006) 'Internationalisation and the smaller firm', in S. Carter and D. Jones-Evans (eds), *Enterprise and Small Business*. Harlow: FT Prentice Hall.

Ibeh, K. I. N. and Analogbei, M. (2010) 'SMEs and international entrepreneurship', in S. Nwankwo and A. Gbadamosi (eds), *Entrepreneurship Marketing*. Abingdon: Routledge.

Ibeh, K. I. N. and Kasem, L. (2011) 'The network perspective and the internationalization of small and medium-sized software firms from Syria', *Industrial Marketing Management*, 40 (3): 358–67.

Ibeh, K. I. N., Johnson, J., Dimitratos, P. and Slow, J. (2004) 'Micromultinationals: Some preliminary evidence on an emergent star of the international entrepreneurship field', *Journal of International Entrepreneurship*, 2 (4): 289–303.

Ibeh, K. I. N., Young, S. and Lin, H. C. (2004) 'Information technology and the electronics firms from Taiwan Province of China in the United Kingdom: Emerging trends and implications', *Transnational Corporations Journal*, 13 (3): 21–52.

IFERA (2003) 'Family businesses dominate: International family enterprise research academy (IFERA)', *Family Business Review*, 16 (4): 235–40.

IFF Research Ltd (2010) 'Results from the 2009 finance survey of SMEs'. London: Department for Business, Innovation and Skills.

Ikeda, S. (2008) 'The meaning of "social capital" as it relates to the market process', *The Review of Austrian Economics*, 21 (2/3): 167–82.

Institute of Export (1995) 'Survey of international services provided to exporters'. London: Institute of Export.

International Federation of Accountants and *The Banker* (2009) '*The Banker*/IFAC SME lender survey frequency report'. New York: IFAC and *The Banker*.

Intrum Justitia (2010) 'European payment index 2010'. Stockholm: Intrum Justitia.

IOD (1996) 'Your business matters: Report from the regional conferences'. Report on behalf of IOD, CBI, BCC, TNC, FSB and FPB. London: IOD.

IVA (2008) 'Bankruptcy'. Available online at: www.iva.co.uk/bankruptcy.asp

Izard, C. E. (1984) 'Emotion–cognition relationships and human development', in C. E. Izard, J. Kagan and R. B. Zajonc (eds), *Emotions, Cognition and Behavior*. Cambridge: Cambridge University Press. pp. 17–37.

Izushi, H. (1997) 'Conflict between two industrial networks: Technological adaptation and interfirm relationships in the ceramics industry in Seto, Japan', *Regional Studies*, 31 (2): 117–29.

Jack, S. (2005) 'The role, use and activation of strong and weak network ties: A qualitative analysis', *Journal of Management Studies*, 42 (6): 1233–59.

Jack, S. and Anderson, A. (2002) 'The effects of embeddedness on the entrepreneurial process', *Journal of Business Venturing*, 17 (5): 467–87.

Jack, S., Dodd, S. D. and Anderson, A. R. (2004) 'Social structures and entrepreneurial networks: The strength of strong ties', *The International Journal of Entrepreneurship and Innovation*, 5: 107–20.

Jack, S., Dodd, S. and Anderson, A. (2008) 'Change and the development of entrepreneurial networks over time: A processual perspective', *Entrepreneurship and Regional Development*, 20 (2): 125–59.

Jack, S., Moult, S., Anderson, A. and Dodd, S. (2010) 'An entrepreneurial network evolving: Patterns of change', *International Small Business Journal*, 28 (4): 315–37.

Jackson, G. I. (1981) 'Export from the importer's viewpoint', *European Journal of Marketing*, 15 (3): 3–15.

Jacobs, J. (1961) *The Death and Life of Great American Cities*. New York: Vintage.

Jaffe, A. B., Trajtenberg, M. and Henderson, R. (1993) 'Geographic localization of knowledge spillovers as evidenced by patent citations', *Quarterly Journal of Economics*, 108 (3): 577–98.

Jarillo, J. (1989) 'Entrepreneurship and growth: The strategic use of external resources', *Journal of Business Venturing*, 4 (2): 133–47.

Jarvis, R. (1996) 'Users and uses of unlisted companies' financial statements: A literature review'. London: Institute of Chartered Accountants in England and Wales.

Jarvis, R., Kitching, J., Curran, J. and Lightfoot, G. (1996) 'The financial management of small firms: An alternative perspective', Research Report No. 49, London: ACCA.

Jarvis, R., Lipman, H., Macallan, H. and Berry, A. (1994) 'Small business finance: The benefits and constraints of leasing', Occasional Paper No. 28, Kingston University.

Jelic, R. and Wright, M. (2011) 'Exits, performance, and late stage private equity: The case of UK management buy-outs', *European Financial Management*, 17 (3): 560–93.

Jenei, J. and Kuti, E. (2008) 'The third sector and civil society'' in E. Kuti and S. Osborne (ed.), *The Third Sector in Europe*. New York: Routledge. pp. 9–26.

Jenkins, R. (1984) 'Ethnic minorities in business: A research agenda', in R. Ward and R. Jenkins (eds), *Ethnic Communities in Business*. Cambridge: Cambridge University Press. pp. 231–38.

Jennings, J. E. and McDougald, M. S. (2007) 'Work–family interface experiences and coping strategies: Implications for entrepreneurship research and practice', *Academy of Management Review*, 32 (3): 747–60.

Jenssen, J. and Koenig, H. (2002) 'The effect of social networks on resource access and business start-ups', *European Planning Studies*, 10 (8): 1039–46.

Jo, M. (1992) 'Korean merchants in the black community: Prejudice among the victims of prejudice', *Ethnic and Racial Studies*, 15 (3): 395–411.

Jocumsen, G. (2004) 'How do small business managers make strategic marketing decisions?: A model of process', *European Journal of Marketing*, 38 (5/6): 659–74.

Johannisson, B. (1986) 'Network strategies: Management, technology for entrepreneurship and change', *International Small Business Journal*, 5 (1): 9–30.

Johannisson, B. (1990) 'Community entrepreneurship: Cases and conceptualization', *Entrepreneurship & Regional Development*, 2: 71–88.

Johannisson, B. (2000) 'Networking and entrepreneurial growth', in D. Sexton and H. Landström (eds), *The Blackwell Handbook of Entrepreneurship*. Oxford: Wiley-Blackwell.

Johannisson, B. (2002) 'Energising entrepreneurship: Ideological tensions in the medium-sized family business', in D. Fletcher (ed.), *Understanding the Small Family Business*. Abingdon: Routledge. pp. 47–57.

Johannisson, B. and Huse, M. (2000) 'Recruiting outside board members in the small family business: An ideological challenge', *Entrepreneurship and Regional Development*, 12 (4): 353–78.

Johannisson, B. and Nilsson, A. (1989) 'Community entrepreneurs: Networking for local development', *Entrepreneurship and Regional Development*, 1: 3–19.

Johannisson, B. and Peterson, R. (1984) 'The personal networks of entrepreneurs'. Paper presented at the Third Canadian Conference, International Council for Small Business, Toronto, 23–25 May.

Johannisson, B., Ramirez-Pasillas, M. and Karlsson, G. (2002) 'The institutional embeddedness of local inter-firm networks: A leverage for business creation', *Entrepreneurship and Regional Development*, 14 (4): 297–315.

Johanson, J. and Mattsson, L. G. (1988) 'Internationalisation in industrial systems: A network approach', in N. Hood and J. E. Vahlne (eds), *Strategies in Global Competition*. London: Croom Helm.

Johanson, J. and Vahlne, J. (1977) 'The internationalization process of the firm: A model of knowledge development and increasing foreign market commitments', *Journal of International Business Studies*, 8 (1): 23–32.

Johanson, J. and Vahlne, J. E. (1978) 'A model for the decision making affecting the pattern and pace of internationalization of the firm', in M. Ghertman and J. Leontiades (eds), *European Research in International Business*. New York: Croom Helm. pp. 283–305.

Johanson, J. and Vahlne, J. E. (1990) 'The mechanism of internationalization', *International Marketing Review*, 7 (4): 11–24.

Johanson, J. and Vahlne, J. E. (1992) 'Management of foreign market entry', *Scandinavian International Business Review*, 1 (3): 9–27.

Johanson, J. and Vahlne, J. E. (2009) 'The Uppsala internationalization process model revisited: From liability of foreignness to liability of outsidership', *Journal of International Business Studies*, 40 (9): 1411–31.

Johanson, J. and Wiedersheim-Paul, F. (1975) 'The internationalization of the firm: Four Swedish cases', *The Journal of Management Studies*, 12: 305–22.

Johansson, D. (2007) 'Sweden's slowdown: The impact of interventionism on entrepreneurship', in B. Powell (ed.), *Making Poor Nations Rich: Entrepreneurship and the process of economic development*. Palo Alto, CA: Stanford University Press.

Johns, G. (2006) 'The essential impact of context on organizational behavior', *Academy of Management Review*, 31 (2): 386–408.

Johnson, A. R. and Delmar, F. (2010) 'The psychology of entrepreneurs: A self-regulation perspective', in H. Landström and F. Lohrke (eds), *Historical Foundations of Entrepreneurship Research*. Cheltenham: Edward Elgar.

Johnson, B. R. (1990) 'Toward a multidimensional model of entrepreneurship: The case of achievement motivation and the entrepreneur', *Entrepreneurship Theory and Practice*, 14 (3): 39–54.

Johnson, G. and Scholes, K. (2008) *Exploring Corporate Strategy: Text and cases*. Harlow: Prentice Hall.

Johnstone, H. and Lionais, D. (2004) 'Depleted communities and community business entrepreneurship: Revaluing space through place', *Entrepreneurship and Regional Development*, 16 (3): 217–33.

Johnstone, M. A. (2000) 'Delegation and organisational structure in small businesses: Influences of managers' attachment patterns', *Group Organisation Management*, 25 (1): 4–21.

Jones, D., Keogh, B. and O'Leary, H. (2007) 'Developing the social economy: Critical review of the literature', *Journal of Business Venturing*, 15: 393–410.

Jones, M. V. (1999) 'The internationalization of small high technology firms', *Journal of International Marketing*, 7 (4): 15–41.

Jones, M. V. and Coviello, N. E. (2005) 'Internationalization: Conceptualizing an entrepreneurial process of behavior in time', *Journal of International Business Studies*, 36 (3): 284–303.

Jones, O. and Conway, S. (2004) 'The international reach of entrepreneurial social networks: The case of James Dyson in the UK', in H. Etemad (ed.), *International Entrepreneurship in Small and Medium-sized Enterprises: Orientation, environment and strategy: McGill International Entrepreneurship Series* (vol. 3). Cheltenham: Edward Elgar. pp. 87–106.

Jones, O. and Jayawarna, D. (2010) 'Resourcing new businesses: Social networks, bootstrapping and firm performance', *Venture Capital*, 12 (2): 127–52.

Jones, O., Cardoso, C. and Beckinsale, M. (1997) 'Mature SMEs and technological innovation: Entrepreneurial networks in the UK and Portugal', *International Journal of Innovation Management*, 1 (3): 201–27.

Jones, O., Conway, S. and Steward, F. (2001) 'Introduction: Social interaction and organisational change', in O. Jones, S. Conway and F. Steward (eds), *Social Interaction and Organisational Change: Aston perspectives on innovation networks*. London: Imperial College Press. pp. 1–40.

Jones, R. and Rowley, J. (2011) 'Entrepreneurial marketing in small business: A conceptual exploration', *International Small Business Journal*, 29 (1): 25–36.

Jones, T. (1981) 'Small business development and the Asian community in Britain', *New Community*, 9: 467–77.

Jones, T. (1989) 'Ethnic minority business and the post-Fordist entrepreneurial renaissance'. Paper presented to the conference on Industrial Restructuring and Social Change in Western Europe, University of Durham, 26–28 September.

Jones, T. (1993) *Britain's Ethnic Minorities*. London: Policy Studies Institute.

Jones, T. and McEvoy, D. (1986) 'Ethnic enterprise: The popular image', in J. Curran, J. Stanworth and D. Watkins (eds), *The Survival of the Small Firm*. Aldershot: Gower. pp. 197–219.

Jones, T. and Ram, M. (2003) 'South Asian businesses in retreat?: The case of the United Kingdom', *Journal of Ethnic and Migration Studies*, 29 (3): 485–500.

Jones, T. and Ram, M. (2007) 'Re-embedding the ethnic business agenda', *Work, Employment and Society*, 21 (3): 439–57.

Jones, T. and Ram, M. (2010) 'Ethnic variations on the small firm labour process', *International Small Business Journal*, 28 (2): 163–73.

Jones, T., Barrett, G. and McEvoy, D. (2000) 'Market potential as a decisive influence on the performance of ethnic minority business', in J. Rath (ed.), *Immigrant Businesses: The economic, political and social environment*. Houndmills, Basingstoke: Macmillan.

Jones, T., Cater, J., De Silva, P. and McEvoy, D. (1989) 'Ethnic business and community needs: Report to the Commission for Racial Equality'. Liverpool: Liverpool Polytechnic.

Jones, T., McEvoy, D. and Barrett, G. (1992) *Small Business Initiative: Ethnic minority business component*. Swindon: ESRC.

Jones, T., McEvoy, D. and Barrett, G. (1994a) 'Labour intensive practices in the ethnic minority firm', in J. Atkinson and D. Storey (eds), *Employment: The small firm and the labour market*. London: Routledge. pp. 172–205.

Jones, T., McEvoy, D. and Barrett, G. (1994b) 'Raising capital for the ethnic minority small firm', in A. Hughes and D. Storey (eds), *Finance and the Small Firm*. London: Routledge. pp. 145–81.

Jones, T., Mascarenhas-Keyes and Ram, M. (2011) 'The ethnic entrepreneurial transition: Recent trends in British Indian self-employment', *Journal of Ethnic Migration Studies*, 38 (1): 93–109.

485

Jones, T., Ram, M. and Edwards, P. (2006) 'Shades of grey in the informal economy', *International Journal of Sociology and Social Policy*, 26: 357–73.

Jones-Evans, D. (with Steward, F.) (1992) 'How does previous experience contribute to entrepreneurial success: An examination of technical entrepreneurs as a case study', in J. C. Oliga and T. B. Kim (eds), *Proceedings of the World Conference on Entrepreneurship and Innovative Change, Nanyang Technological University, Singapore, 1991*.

Jones-Evans, D. (1995) 'A typology of technology-based entrepreneurs: A model based on previous occupational background', *International Journal of Entrepreneurial Behaviour and Research*, 1 (1): 26–47.

Jones-Evans, D. (1996) 'Technical entrepreneurship, strategy and experience', *International Small Business Journal*, 14 (3): 13–37.

Jones-Evans, D. and Kirby, D. A. (1995) 'The formation and development of small technical professional service providers in the North East of England: A preliminary study', *Entrepreneurship and Regional Development*, 7 (2): 21–40.

Jones-Evans, D. and Klofsten, M. (1997) 'Universities and local economic development: The case of Linköping', *European Planning Studies*, 5 (1): 77–93.

Jones-Evans, D. and Westhead, P. (1996) 'The high-technology small firms in the UK', *International Journal of Entrepreneurial Behavior and Research*, 2 (1): 15–39.

Joyce, P., Woods, A. and Black, S. (1995) 'Networks and partnerships: Managing change and competition', *International Journal of Innovation Management*, 2: 11–18.

Judge, T. A., and Bono, J. E. (2001) 'Relationship of core self-evaluations traits – self-esteem, generalized self-efficacy, locus of control, and emotional stability – with job satisfaction and job performance: A meta-analysis', *Journal of Applied Psychology*, 86 (1): 80–92.

Julien, P.-A. (2007) *A Theory of Local Entrepreneurship in the Knowledge Economy.* Cheltenham and Northampton, MA: Edward Elgar.

Julien, P.-A., Andriambeloson, E. and Ramangalahy, C. (2004) 'Networks, weak signals and technological innovations among SMEs in the land-based transportation equipment sector', *Entrepreneurship and Regional Development*, 16 (4): 251–70.

Kahneman, D., Slovic, P. and Tversky, A. (1982) *Judgment Under Uncertainty: Heuristics and biases.* Cambridge, MA: Cambridge University Press.

Kaish, S. and Gilad, B. (1991) 'Characteristics of opportunities search of entrepreneurs versus executives: Sources, interests, general alertness', *Journal of Business Venturing*, 6 (1): 45–61.

Kaleka, A. and Katsikeas, C. S. (1995) 'Exporting problems: The relevance of export development', *Journal of Marketing Management*, 11: 499–515.

Kalleberg, A. and Leicht, K. (1991) 'Gender and organisational performance: Determinants of small business survival and success', *Academy of Management Journal*, 34 (1): 136–61.

Kamp, M. (2004) 'Between women and the State: Mahalla committees and social welfare in Uzbekistan', in P. Jones Luong (ed.), *The Transformation of Central Asia: States and societies from Soviet rule to independence.* Ithaca, NY, and London: Cornell Press. pp. 29–58.

Kanfer, R. (1991) 'Motivation theory and industrial and organizational psychology', in M. D. Dunnette and L. M. Hough (eds), *Handbook of Industrial and Organizational Psychology* (vol. 2). Palo Alto, CA: Consulting Psychologists Press. pp. 75–170.

Kanter, R. (1984) *The Change Masters: Innovation and entrepreneurship in the American corporation.* New York: Simon & Schuster.

Kasarda, J. (1989) 'Urban industrial transition and the underclass', *The Annals of the American Academy of Political and Social Science*, 501 (Jan.): 26–47.

Katsikeas, C. S. (1994) 'Perceived export problems and export involvement: The case of Greek exporting manufacturers', *Journal of Global Marketing*, 7 (4): 29–57.

Katz, J. A. (2003) 'The chronology and intellectual trajectory of American entrepreneurship education, (1876–1999), *Journal of Business Venturing*, 18 (2): 283–300.

Katz, J. A. and Gartner, W. B. (1988) 'Properties of emerging organizations', *Academy of Management Review*, 13 (3): 429–41.

Katz, J. A. and Williams, P. (1997) 'Gender self-employment and weak-tie networking through formal organizations', *Entrepreneurship and Regional Development*, 9 (3): 183–98.

Kazanjian, R. K. (1988) 'Relation of dominant problems to stages of growth in technology-based new ventures', *Academy of Management Journal*, 31 (2): 257–79.

Kazuka, M. (1980) 'Why so few black businessmen?: Report on the findings of the Hackney Ethnic Minority Business Project'. London: Commission for Racial Equality, Hackney Business Promotion

Centre, Hackney Council for Racial Equality, Hackney Ethnic Minority Business Project.

Keasey, K. and Watson, R. (1992) 'Investment and financing decisions and the performance of small firms'. Report for the National Westminster Bank, London, September.

Keasey, K. and Watson, R. (1993) *Small Firm Management: Ownership, finance and performance*. Oxford: Blackwell.

Keeble, D. (1993) 'Small firm creation, innovation and growth and the urban–rural shift', in J. Curran and D. Storey (eds), *Small Firms in Urban and Rural Locations*. London: Routledge. pp. 54–78.

Keeble, D. and Wilkinson, F. (2000) 'High-technology SMEs, regional clustering and collective learning: An overview', in D. Keeble and F. Wilkinson (eds), *High-technology Clusters, Networking and Collective Learning in Europe*. Aldershot: Ashgate.

Keeble, D., Tyler, P., Broom, G. and Lewis, J. (1992) 'Business success in the countryside: The performance of rural enterprise'. London: HMSO.

Keefe, L. (2004) 'What is the meaning of "marketing"?', *Marketing News*, 15 September. pp. 17–18.

Keh, H. T., Foo, M. D. and Lim, B. C. (2002) 'Opportunity evaluation under risky conditions: The cognitive processes of entrepreneurs', *Entrepreneurship Theory and Practice*, 27 (2): 125–48.

Kelley, M. and Brooks, H. (1991) 'External learning opportunities and the diffusion of process innovations to small firms: The case of programmable automation', *Technological Forecasting and Social Change*, 39: 103–25.

Kelly, G. A. (1955) *The Psychology of Personal Constructs* (vols 1 and 2). New York: Norton.

Kessler, A. and Frank, H. (2009) 'Nascent entrepreneurship in a longitudinal perspective: The impact of person, environment, resources and the founding process on the decision to start business activities', *International Small Business Journal*, 27 (6): 720–42.

Kesteloot, C. and Mistiaanen, P. (1997) 'From ethnic minority niche to assimilation: Turkish restaurants in Brussels', *Area*, 29 (4): 325–34.

Kets De Vries, M. (1977) 'The entrepreneurial personality: A person at the crossroads', *Journal of Management Studies*, 14 (1): 34–57.

Kets De Vries, M. (1985) 'The dark side of the entrepreneur', *Harvard Business Review*, 63 (6): 160–7.

Keynes, J. M. (1926) *The End of Laissez-faire*. London: L. & V. Woolf.

Khan, G. M. (2004) 'Encouraging entrepreneurship in Brunei Darussalam: Education and training for enterprise development'. Available online at: www.sbaer.uca.edu/research/icsb/1998/115.pdf

Khan, J. H. (2004) 'Determinants of small enterprise development of Bangladesh: Investigation of constraints from institutional perspective'. Stockholm: School of Business, Stockholm University.

Kilby, P. (1971) *Entrepreneurship and Economic Development*. New York: Free Press.

Kim, I. (1981) *New Urban Immigrants: The Korean community in New York*. Princeton, NJ: Princeton University Press.

Kim, M. S. and Hunter, J. E. (1993) 'Attitude–behavior relations: A meta-analysis of attitudinal relevance and topic', *Journal of Communication*, 43 (1): 101–42.

Kingdon, J. W. (2002) *Agendas, Alternatives, and Public Policies* (2nd edn). New York: Longman.

Kinsella, R. and Mulvenna, D. (1993) 'Fast growth firms in Ireland', *Administration*, 41 (1): 3–15.

Kinsella, R., Clarke, W., Coyne, D., Mulvenna, D. and Storey D. J. (1993) 'Fast growth firms and selectivity'. Dublin: Irish Management Institute.

Kirkels, Y. and Duysters, G. (2010) 'Brokerage in SME networks', *Research Policy*, 39: 375–85.

Kirzner, I. M. (1973) *Competition and Entrepreneurship*. Chicago, IL: University of Chicago Press.

Kirzner, I. M. (1979) *Perception, Opportunity, and Profit: Studies in the theory of entrepreneurship*. Chicago, IL: Chicago University Press.

Kirzner, I. M. (1980) 'The primacy of entrepreneurial discovery', in A. Seldon (ed.), *Prime Mover of Progress: The entrepreneur in capitalism and socialism*, Readings No. 23. London: Institute of Economic Affairs. pp. 5–29.

Kirzner, I. M. (1982) 'The theory of entrepreneurship in economic growth', in C. A. Kent, D. L. Sexton and K. H. Vesper (eds), *Encyclopaedia of Entrepreneurship*. Englewood Cliffs, NJ: Prentice Hall. pp. 273–76.

Kirzner, I. M. (1985) *Discovery and the Capitalist Process*. Chicago, IL: Chicago University Press.

Kirzner, I. M. (1990) 'Uncertainty, discovery, and human action: A study of the entrepreneurial profile in the Misesian system', in M. Casson (ed.), *Entrepreneurship*. Elgar Cheltenham: Edward. pp. 81–101.

Kirzner, I. M. (2009) 'The alert and creative entrepreneur: A clarification', *Small Business Economics*, 32: 145–52.

Kisfalvi, V. (2002) 'The entrepreneur's character, life issues and strategy making', *Journal of Business Venturing*, 17 (5): 489–518.

Kistruck, G. M. and Beamish, P. W. (2010) 'The interplay of form, structure, and embeddedness in social intrapreneurship', *Entrepreneurship Theory and Practice*, 34: 735–61.

Kitson, M., Martin, R. and Tyler, P. (2004) 'Regional competitiveness: An elusive yet key concept?', *Regional Studies*, 38 (9): 991–9.

Kitzmann, J. and Schiereck, D. (2005) 'Entrepreneurial discovery and the Demmert/ Klein experiment: Another attempt at creating the proper context', *Review of Austrian Economics*, 18 (2): 169–78.

Klein, P. G. (2008) 'Opportunity discovery, entrepreneurial action, and economic organization', *Strategic Entrepreneurship Journal*, 2 (3): 175–90.

Klein, S. B., Astrachan, J. H. and Smyrnios, K. X. (2005) 'The F-PEC scale of family influence: Construction, validation and further implications for theory', *Entrepreneurship Theory and Practice*, 29: 321–39.

Kleindl, B., Mowen, J. and Chakraborty, G. (1996) 'Innovative market orientation: An alternative strategic orientation', in G. Hills, R. D. Teach and G. M. Guersen, *Research at the Marketing/Entrepreneurship Interface*. Chicago, IL: University of Illinois at Chicago. pp. 211–28.

Klofsten, M. (1994) 'Technology-based firms: Critical aspects of their early development', *Journal of Enterprising Culture*, 2 (1), 535–57.

Klofsten, M. (1995) 'Technology transfer from the university through stimulating small technology-based firms: The case of SMIL'. Report submitted to EU DG XIII/D/4, University of Linköping, Linköping, July.

Klofsten, M. (1997) 'Management of the early development process in technology-based firms', in D. Jones-Evans and M. Klofsten (eds), *Technology, Innovation and Enterprise: The European experience*. Houndmills, Basingstoke: Macmillan. pp. 148–78.

Klofsten, M. (2000) 'Training entrepreneurship at universities: A Swedish case', *Journal of European Industrial Training*, 24 (6): 337–44.

Klofsten, M. (2008) 'Supporting academic enterprise: A case study of an entrepreneurship programme', in R. Oakey, W. During and S. Kanser (eds), *New Technology-based Firms in the New Millennium*, Oxford: Elsevier Science. pp. 53–67.

Klofsten, M., Lindell, P., Olofsson, C. and Wahlbin, C. (1988) 'Internal and external resources in technology-based spin-offs', in

Frontiers of Entrepreneurship Research 1988. Wellesley, MA: Babson College.

Kloosterman, R. (2010) 'Matching opportunities with resources: A framework for analysing (migrant) entrepreneurship from a mixed embeddedness perspective', *Entrepreneurship and Regional Development*, 22 (1): 25–45.

Kloosterman, R. and Rath, J. (2003) 'Introduction', in R. Kloosterman and J. Rath (eds), *Immigrant Entrepreneurs: Venturing abroad in the age of globalization*. Oxford: Berg.

Kloosterman, R. and Rath, J. (eds) (2003) *Immigrant Entrepreneurs: Venturing abroad in the age of globalisation*. Oxford: Berg.

Kloosterman, R. C., and van der Leun, J. and Rath, J. (1998) 'Across the border: Economic opportunities, social capital and informal business activities of immigrants', *Journal of Ethnic and Migration Studies*, 24: 239–58.

Kloosterman, R., van der Leun, J. and Rath, J. (1999) 'Mixed embeddedness: (In)formal economic activities and immigrant businesses in the Netherlands', *International Journal of Urban and Regional Research*, 23 (2): 252–66.

Klyver, K. and Grant, S. (2010) 'Gender differences in entrepreneurial networking and participation', *International Journal of Gender and Entrepreneurship*, 2 (3): 213–27.

Knight, F. (1921) *Risk, Uncertainty and Profit*. New York: Houghton Mifflin.

Knight, G. A. and Cavusgil, S. T. (1996) 'The born global firm: A challenge to traditional internationalization theory', *Advances in International Marketing*, (8): 11–26.

Knight, J., Bell, J. and McNaughton, R. (2003) 'Satisfaction with paying for government export assistance' in C. N. Wheeler, H. Tuselmann and I. Greaves (eds), *International Business*, Harlow: Palgrave Macmillan. pp. 223–42.

Knight, R. M. (1988) 'Spin-off entrepreneurs: how corporations really create entrepreneurs', in *Frontiers of Entrepreneurship Research 1988*. Wellesley, MA: Babson College.

Knott, A. M. and Posen, H. E. (2005) 'Is failure good?' *Strategic Management Journal*, 26 (7): 617–41.

Ko, S. and Butler, J. (2006) 'Prior knowledge, bisociative mode of thinking and entrepreneurial opportunity identification', *International Journal of Entrepreneurship and Small Business*, 3 (1): 3–16.

Kogut, B. and Zander, U. (1992) 'Knowledge of the firm, combinative capabilities, and the replication of technology', *Organization Science*, 3 (3): 383–97.

Kohtamaki, M., Kautonen, T. and Kraus, S. (2010) 'Strategic planning and small business performance: An examination of the mediating role of exploration and exploitation behaviours', *The International Journal of Entrepreneurship and Innovation*, 11 (3): 221–9.

Kolb, D. A. (1984) *Experiential Learning: Experience as the source of learning and development*. Englewood Cliffs, NJ: Prentice Hall.

Koller, R. H. (1988) 'On the source of entrepreneurial ideas' in *Frontiers of Entrepreneurship Research 1988*. Wellesely, MA: Babson College.

Kolvereid, L. (1992) 'Growth aspirations among Norwegian entrepreneurs', *Journal of Business Venturing*, 7 (3): 209–22.

Kolvereid, L. (1996a) 'Organizational employment versus self-employment: Reasons for career choice intentions', *Entrepreneurship Theory and Practice*, 20 (3): 23–31.

Kolvereid, L. (1996b) 'Prediction of employment status choice intentions', *Entrepreneurship Theory and Practice*, 21 (1): 47–57.

Kolvereid, L. and Bullvåg, E. (1993) 'Novices versus experienced founders: An exploratory investigation', in S. Birley, I. MacMillan and S. Subramony (eds), *Entrepreneurship Research: Global perspectives*. Amsterdam: Elsevier Science Publishers. pp. 275–85.

Kolvereid, L. and Bullvåg, E. (1996) 'Growth intentions and actual growth: The impact of entrepreneurial choice', *Journal of Enterprising Culture*, 4 (1): 1–17.

Kolvereid, L. and Isaksen, E. (2006) 'New business start-up and subsequent entry into self-employment', *Journal of Business Venturing*, 21 (6): 866–85.

Komives, J. L. (1974) 'What are entrepreneurs made of?', *Chemtech*, December: 716–21.

Koning, A. (2003) 'Opportunity development: A socio-cognitive perspective', in J. A. Katz and D. A. Shepherd (eds), *Cognitive Approaches to Entrepreneurship Research: Advances in entrepreneurship, from emergence and growth* (vol. 6). Amsterdam: JAI. pp. 265–314.

Koolman, G. (1971) 'Say's conception of the role of the entrepreneur', *Economica*, New Series, 38: 270–86.

Kotler, P. (2003) *Marketing Management*. Upper Saddle River, NJ: Prentice Hall.

Krackhardt, D. and Hanson, J. (1993) 'Informal networks: The companies behind the chart', *Harvard Business Review*, July–August: 104–11.

Krantz, S. (1999) 'Small business', in *Sunday Business Essex*, 11 April.

Kreft, S. F. and Sobel, R. S. (2005) 'Public policy, entrepreneurship, and economic freedom', *Cato Journal*, 25 (3): 595–616.

Kreiner, K. and Schultz, M. (1993) 'Informal collaboration in R&D: The formation of networks across organizations', *Organization Studies*, 14 (2): 189–209.

Krueger, N. F. (1993) 'The impact of prior entrepreneurial exposure on perceptions of new venture feasibility and desirability', *Entrepreneurship Theory and Practice*, 18 (1): 5–21.

Krueger, N. F. (2000) 'The cognitive infrastructure of opportunity emergence', *Entrepreneurship Theory and Practice*, 25 (3): 5–23.

Krueger, N. F. and Brazeal, D. V. (1994) 'Entrepreneurial potential and potential entrepreneurs', *Entrepreneurship Theory and Practice*, 18 (3): 91–104.

Krueger, N. F. and Carsrud, A. L. (1993) 'Entrepreneurial intentions: Applying the theory of planned behaviour', *Entrepreneurship and Regional Development*, 5 (4): 315–30.

Krueger, N. F. and Dickson, P. R. (1993) 'Perceived self-efficacy and perceptions of opportunity and threat', *Psychological Reports*, 72 (3): 1235–40.

Krueger, N. F. and Dickson, P. R. (1994) 'How believing in ourselves increases risk taking: Perceived self-efficacy and opportunity recognition', *Decision Sciences*, 25 (3): 385–400.

Krueger, N. F., Reilly, M. D. and Carsrud, A. L. (2000) 'Competing models of entrepreneurial intentions', *Journal of Business Venturing*, 15: 411–32.

Krugman, P. (2005) 'Second winds for industrial regions?' in D. Coyle, W. Alexander and B. Ashcroft (eds), *New Wealth for Old Nations: Scotland's economic prospects*. Princeton, NJ: Princeton University Press.

Kuczynski, M. and Meek, M. (1972) *Quesnay's Tableau Économique*. London: Royal Economic Society.

Kuhn, T. (1962) *The Structure of Scientific Revolutions*. Chicago, IL: University of Chicago Press.

Lamont, L. M. (1972) 'Entrepreneurship, technology and the university', *R&D Management*, 2 (3): 119–23.

Landström, H. and Johannisson, B. (2001) 'Theoretical foundations of Swedish entrepreneurship and small-business research', *Scandinavian Journal of Management*, 17 (2): 225–48.

Langlois, A. and Razin, E. (1995) 'Self-employment among French-Canadians: The role of the regional milieu', *Ethnic and Racial Studies*, 18 (3): 581–604.

Larson, A. and Starr, J. (1993) 'A network model of organization formation', *Entrepreneurship Theory and Practice*, 17 (2): 5–15.

Larty, J. and Hamilton, E. E. (2009) 'The gendered discourses of entrepreneurship'. Paper presented at the 32nd International Small Business and Entrepreneurship Conference, Liverpool, 3–5 November.

Lavoie, D. (1991) 'The discovery and interpretation of profit opportunities: Culture and the Kirznerian entrepreneur', in B. Berger (ed.), *The Culture of Entrepreneurship*. San Francisco, CA: ICS Press.

Lawless, R. M. and Warren, E. (2005) 'The myth of the disappearing business bankruptcy', *California Law Review*, 93 (3): 745–95.

Lawrence, P. A. and Lee, R. A. (1989) *Insight into Management*. Oxford: Oxford University Press. pp. 73–91.

Lawson, C. and Lorenz, E. (1999) 'Collective learning: Tacit knowledge and regional innovative capacity', *Regional Studies*, 33: 305–17.

Le Breton-Miller, I. and Miller, D. (2006) 'Why do some family businesses out-compete?: Governance, long-term orientations, and sustainable capability', *Entrepreneurship: Theory & Practice*, 30 (6): 731–46.

Le Grand, J. (1991) 'The theory of government failure', *British Journal of Political Science*, 21: 423–42.

Leadbeater, C. (1997) *The Rise of the Social Entrepreneur*. London: Demos.

Leadbeater, C. (2007) 'Social enterprise and social innovation: Strategies for the next ten years. A social enterprise think piece for the Office of Third Sector, November 2007'. London: Cabinet Office of the Third Sector.

Leadbeater, C. and Oakley, K. (1999) *The Independents: Britain's new cultural entrepreneurs*. London: Demos.

Lechner, C. and Dowling, M. (2003) 'Firm networks: External relationships as sources for the growth and competitiveness of entrepreneurial firms', *Entrepreneurship and Regional Development*, 15 (1): 1–26.

Lechner, C., Dowling, M. and Welpe, I. (2006) 'Firm networks and firm development: The role of the relational mix', *Journal of Business Venturing*, 21: 514–40.

Lee, L., Wong, P. K., Foo, M. D. and Leung, A. (2011) 'Entrepreneurial intentions: The influence of organizational and individual factors', *Journal of Business Venturing*, 26 (1): 124–36.

Lee, R. (2009) 'Social capital and business and management: Setting a research agenda', *International Journal of Management Reviews*, 11 (3): 247–74.

Lee, R. and Jones, O. (2008) 'Networks, communication and learning during business start-up: The creation of cognitive social capital', *International Small Business Journal*, 26 (5): 559–94.

Lee, W.-Y. and Brasch, J. J. (1978) 'The adoption of export as an innovation', *Journal of International Business Studies*, 9 (1): 85–93.

Leonard-Barton, D. (1984) 'Interpersonal communication patterns among Swedish and Boston-area entrepreneurs', *Research Policy*, 13 (2): 101–114.

Leonidou, L. C. (1995) 'Empirical research on export barriers: Review, assessment, and synthesis', *Journal of International Marketing*, 3 (1): 29–43.

Levi-Strauss, C. (1966) *The Savage Mind*. Chicago, IL: University of Chicago Press.

Levie, J. and Autio, E. (2008) 'A theoretical grounding and test of the GEM model', *Small Business Economics*, 31 (3): 253–63.

Leys, C. (2001) *Market-driven Politics: Neoliberal democracy and the public interest*. London: Verso.

Li, T. and Florida, R. (2006) 'Talent, technological innovation, and economic growth in China'. Toronto: Joseph L. School of Management, University of Toronto, and the Martin Prosperity Institute. Available online at: www.creativeclass. org/rfcgdb/articles/China%20report.pdf

Liao, J. and Welsch, H. (2005) 'Roles of social capital in venture creation: Key dimensions and research implications', *Journal of Small Business Management*, 43 (4): 345–62.

Liao, J., Welsch, H. and Tan, W. L. (2005) 'Venture gestation paths of nascent entrepreneurs: Exploring the temporal patterns', *The Journal of High Technology Management Research*, 16 (1): 1–22.

Liao, Y. (1992) 'The geography of the Chinese catering trade in Greater Manchester', *Manchester Geographer*, 14: 54–82.

Liberman-Yaconi, L., Hooper, T. and Hutchings, K. (2010) 'Toward a model of understanding strategic decision-making in micro firms: Exploring the Australian information technology sector', *Journal of Small Business Management*, 48 (1): 70–95.

Lichtenstein, B. and Levie, J. (2009) 'Terminal assessment of stages theory: Introducing a dynamic states approach to entrepreneurship',

Entrepreneurship Theory and Practice, 34 (2): 317–50.

Lichtenstein, B. B., Dooley, K. J. and Lumpkin, G. T. (2006) 'Measuring emergence in the dynamics of new venture creation', *Journal of Business Venturing*, 21: 153–75.

Light, I. (1972) *Ethnic Enterprise in America: Business and welfare among Chinese, Japanese and blacks.* Berkeley, CA: University of California Press.

Light, I. (1984) 'Immigrant and ethnic enterprise in North America', *Ethnic and Racial Studies*, 7: 195–216.

Light, I. and Bonacich, E. (1988) *Immigrant Entrepreneurs.* Berkeley, CA: University of California Press.

Light, I. and Rosenstein, C. (1995) *Race, Ethnicity, and Entrepreneurship in Urban America.* New York: Aldine de Gruyter.

Light, I., Sabagh, G. Bozorgmehr, M. and Der-Martirosian C. (1993) 'Internal ethnicity in the ethnic economy', *Ethnic and Racial Studies*, 16 (4): 581–97.

Lim, D. S. K., Morse, E. A., Mitchell, R. K. and Seawright, K. K. (2010) 'Institutional environment and entrepreneurial cognitions: A comparative business systems perspective', *Entrepreneurship Theory and Practice*, 34 (3): 491–516.

Lin, C. and Zhang, J. (2005) 'Changing structures of SME networks: Lessons from the publishing industry in Taiwan', *Long Range Planning*, 38: 145–62.

Lindahl, C. and Skagegård, L.-Å. (1998) *Från Idé till Företag* [*Stay in Place: From idea to firm*] Uppsala: ALMI/Konsultförlaget.

Lindgren, M. and Packendorff, J. (2006) 'Entrepreneurship as boundary work: Deviating from and belonging to community', in C. S. Steyaert and D. Hjort (eds), *Entrepreneurship as Social Change: A third movements in entrepreneurship book.* Cheltenham: Edward Elgar. pp. 210–30.

Lindh de Montoya, M. (2000) 'Entrepreneurship and culture: The case of Freddy, the strawberry man', in R. Sweberg (ed.), *Entrepreneurship: The social science view.* Oxford: Oxford University Press.

Lindholm Dahlstrand, Å. (1999) 'Technology-based SMEs in the Göteborg region: Their origin and interaction with universities and large firms', *Regional Studies*, 33: 379–89.

Lindholm Dahlstrand, Å. and Jacobsson, S. (2003) 'Universities and technology-based entrepreneurship in the Gothenburg region', *Local Economy*, 18 (1): 80–90.

Lindholm Dahlstrand, Å. and Klofsten, M. (2002) 'Growth and innovation support in Swedish science parks and incubators', in R. Oakey, W. During and S. Kauser (eds), *New Technology-based Firms in the New Millennium.* Oxford: Elsevier Science. pp. 31–46.

Lindqvist, M. (1988) 'Internationalization of small technology-based firms: Three illustrative case studies on Swedish firms'. Research Paper 88/15, Stockholm School of Economics.

Litvak, I. A. and Maule, C. J. (1971) 'Canadian entrepreneurship: A study of small newly established firms'. University Grant Program Research Report, Department of Industry, Trade and Commerce, Ottawa, Canada.

Litvak, I. A. and Maule, C. J. (1972) 'Managing the entrepreneurial enterprise', *Business Quarterly*, 37 (2): 42–50.

Ljunggren, E. and Alsos, G. A. (2007) 'Media expressions of entrepreneurs: Presentations and discourses of male and female entrepreneurs in Norway', in N. M. Carter, C. Henry, B. Ó. Cinnéide and K. Johnston (eds), *Female Entrepreneurship: Implications for education, training and policy.* Abingdon: Routledge. pp. 88–109.

Locke, E. A. (1991) 'The motivation sequence, the motivation hub, and the motivation core', *Organizational Behavior and Human Decision Processes*, 50 (2): 288–99.

London Stock Exchange (2011) 'AIM statistics, January 2011'. London: London Stock Exchange.

Long, W. and Graham, J. B. (1988) 'Opportunity identification processes: Revisited', in G. E. Hills, R. W. LaForge and B. J. Parker (eds), *Research at the Marketing/Entrepreneurship Interface.* Chicago, IL: University of Illinois at Chicago.

Long, W. and McMullan, W. E. (1984) 'Mapping the new venture opportunity identification process', in *Frontiers of Entrepreneurship Research 1984.* Wellesley, MA: Babson College.

Lotti, F., Santarelli, E. and Vivarelli, M. (2003) 'Does Gibrat's law hold among young, small firms?', *Journal of Evolutionary Economics*, 14 (3): 213–35.

Lotz, J. (1989) 'Community entrepreneurs', *Community Development Journal*, 24 (1): 62–66.

Low, C. (2006) 'A framework for the governance of social enterprise', *International Journal of Social Economics*, 33: 376–85.

Low, M. B. (2001) 'The adolescence of entrepreneurship research: Specification of purpose', *Entrepreneurship Theory and Practice*, 25 (4): 17–25.

Low, M. B. and MacMillan, I. C. (1988) 'Entrepreneurship: Past research and future challenges', *Journal of Management*, 14 (2): 139–61.

Lucas, R. E. (1988) 'On the mechanics of economic development', *Journal of Monetary Economics*, 22 (1): 3–42.

Luffman, G., Sanderson, S., Lea, E. and Kenny, B. (1991) *Business Policy: An analytical introduction*. Oxford: Blackwell. pp. 3–17.

Lumpkin, G. T., Lichtenstein, B. B. and Shrader, R. C. (2003) 'Organizational learning in the opportunity-recognition process: Implications for corporate venturing'. Academy of Management annual meeting.

Lundstrom, A. and Stevenson, L. (2001) 'Entrepreneurship policy for the future'. Stockholm: Swedish Foundation for Small Business Research.

Luostarinen, R. (1980) *The Internationalization of the Firm*. Helsinki: Helsinki School of Economics.

Luostarinen, R. (1994) *Internationalization of Finnish Firms and their Response to Global Challenges* (3rd edn) Helsinki: UNU/WIDER.

Lybaert, N. (1998) 'The information use in a SME: Its importance and some elements of influence', *Small Business Economics*, 10 (2): 171–91.

Ma Mung, E. (1994) 'L'entreprenariat Ethnique en France', *Sociologie du Travail*, 2: 195–209.

Ma Mung, E. and Guillon, M. (1986) 'Les Commerçants Étrangers dans l'Agglomeration Parisienne', *Revue Européenne des Migrations Internationales*, 2 (3): 105–34.

Ma Mung, E. and Lacroix, T. (2003) 'France: The narrow path', in R. Kloosterman and J. Rath (eds), *Immigrant Entrepreneurship: Venturing abroad in the age of globalisation*. Oxford: Berg.

Ma Mung, E. and Simon, G. (1990) *Commerçants Maghrebins et Asiatiques en France: Agglomeration Parisienne et Villes de l'Est*. Paris: Masson.

MacDonald, R. (1971) 'Schumpeter and Max Weber: Central visions and social theories', in P. Kilby (ed.), *Entrepreneurship and Economic Development*. New York: Free Press. pp. 71–94.

MacKinnon, D., Capman, K. and Cumbers, A. (2004) 'Networking, trust and embeddedness amongst SMEs in the Aberdeen oil complex', *Entrepreneurship and Regional Development*, 16 (2): 87–106.

Macmillan Committee (1931) 'Report of the Committee on Finance and Industry', Cmnd 3897. London: HMSO.

Macrae, D. (1991) 'Characteristics of high and low growth small and medium-sized businesses'.

Paper presented at the 21st European Small Business Seminar, Barcelona, Spain, September.

Madsen, T. K. and Servais, P. (1997) 'The internationalization of born globals: An evolutionary process?', *International Business Review*, 6 (6): 561–83.

Maillat, D. (1998) 'Interactions between urban systems and localized productive systems: An approach to endogenous regional development in terms of innovative milieux', *European Planning Studies*, 6: 117–29.

Mair, J. and Martí, I. (2006) 'Social entrepreneurship research: A source of explanation, prediction, and delight', *Journal of World Business*, 41: 36–44.

Mair, J. and Marti, I. (2009) 'Entrepreneurship in and around institutional voids: A case study from Bangladesh', *Journal of Business Venturing*, 24 (5): 419–35.

Malecki, E. J. (2004) 'Jockeying for position: What it means and why it matters to regional development policy when places compete', *Regional Studies*, 38 (9): 1101–20.

Malecki, E. J. (2007) 'Cities and regions competing in the global economy: Knowledge and local development policies', *Environment and Planning C: Government and Policy*, 25 (5): 638–54.

Mandl, I. (2008) 'Overview of family business relevant issues: Contract No. 30-CE-0164021/00-51 final report'. Vienna: Austrian Institute for SME Research.

Manev, I. M., Gyoshev, B. S. and Manolova, T. S. (2005) 'The role of human and social capital and entrepreneurial orientation for small business performance in a transitional economy', *International Journal of Entrepreneurship and Innovation Management*, 5 (3–4): 298–18.

Manimala, M. (1999) *Entrepreneurial Policies and Strategies: The innovator's choice*. New Delhi: Sage.

Manolova, T. S., Eunni, R. V. and Gyoshev, B. S. (2008) 'Institutional environments for entrepreneurship: Evidence from emerging economies in Eastern Europe', *Entrepreneurship Theory and Practice*, 32 (1): 203–18.

Mansfield, E. (1962) 'Entry, Gibrat's law, innovation, and the growth of firms', *The American Economic Review*, 52 (5): 1023–51.

Marable, M. and Mullings, L. (1994) 'The divided mind of black America: Race, ideology and politics in the post civil rights era', *Race Class*, 36 (1): 61–72.

March, J. G. and Shapira, Z. (1987) 'Managerial perspectives on risk and risk taking', *Management Science*, 33 (11): 1404–18.

Marcucci, P. N. (2001) 'Jobs, gender and small enterprises in Africa and Asia: Lessons drawn from Bangladesh, the Philippines, Tunisia and Zimbabwe'. SEED Working Paper No. 18, WEDGE series.

Markman, G. D., Balkin, D. B. and Baron, R. A. (2002) 'Inventors and new venture formation: The effects of general self-efficacy and regretful thinking', *Entrepreneurship Theory and Practice*, 27 (2): 149–65.

Marlow, S. (1992) 'Take-up of business growth training schemes by ethnic minority-owned small firms', *International Small Business Journal*, 10: 34–46.

Marlow, S. (1997) 'Self-employed women – new opportunities, old challenges?', *Entrepreneurship and Regional Development*, 9 (3): 199–210.

Marlow, S. (2002) 'Self-employed women: A part of or apart from feminist theory?', *Entrepreneurship and Innovation*, 2 (2): 23–37.

Marlow, S. and McAdam, M. (2012) 'Gender and entrepreneurship: Advancing debate and challenging myths: exploring the mystery of the under-performing female entrepreneur', *International Journal of Entrepreneurial Behaviour and Research* (forthcoming).

Marlow, S., Henry, C. and Carter, S. (2009) 'Exploring the impact of gender upon women's business ownership', *International Small Business Journal*, 27 (2): 139–48.

Marriott, N., Collis, J. and Marriott, P. (2006) 'Qualitative review of the accounting and auditing needs of small and medium-sized companies and their stakeholders'. Working paper, January. London: Financial Reporting Council. Available online at: www.frc.org.uk/documents/pagemanager/poba/Case%20studies%20report.pdf

Marshall, J. N., Alderman, N., Wong, C. and Thwaites, W. (1993) 'The impact of government-assisted management training and development on small and medium-sized enterprises in Britain', *Environment and Planning C: Government and Policy*, 11: 331–48.

Martin, J. H., Martin, B. A. and Minnillo, P. R. (2009) 'Implementing a market orientation in small manufacturing firms: From cognitive model to action', *Journal of Small Business Management*, 47 (1): 92–115.

Martin, R. and Osberg, S. (2007) 'Social entrepreneurship: The case for definition', *Stanford Social Innovation Review*, spring: 28–39.

Marvel, M. R. and Lumpkin, G. T. (2007) 'Technology entrepreneurs' human capital and its effects on innovation radicalness', *Entrepreneurship Theory and Practice*, 31 (6): 807–28.

Marvel, M. R., Griffin, A., Hebda, J. and Vojak, B. (2007) 'Examining the technical corporate entrepreneurs' motivation: Voices from the field', *Entrepreneurship Theory and Practice*, 31: 753–68.

Mason, C. and Harrison, R. T. (2010) 'Annual report on the business angel market in the United Kingdom: 2008/09'. London: BIS.

Mason, C., Carter, S. and Tagg, S. (2008) 'The entrepreneur in "risk society": The personal consequences of business failure', Strathclyde Business School: University of Strathclyde. pp. 17.

Mason, C., Kirkbride, J. and Bryde, D. (2007) 'From stakeholders to institutions: The changing face of social enterprise governance theory', *Management Decision*, 45: 284–301.

Mason, C. M. and Harrison, R. T. (1992) 'The supply of equity finance in the UK: A strategy for closing the equity gap', *Entrepreneurship and Regional Development*, 4: 357–80.

Massey, D. (1996) 'Masculinity, dualisms and high technology' in N. Duncan (ed.), *Bodyspace: Destabilizing geographies of gender and sexuality*. London: Routledge. pp. 109–26.

Masters, R. and Meier, R. (1988) 'Sex differences and risk-taking propensity of entrepreneurs', *Journal of Small Business Management*, 26 (1): 31–5.

Mathews, C. H. and Moser, S. B. (1995) 'Family background and gender: Implications for interest in small firm ownership', *Entrepreneurship and Regional Development*, 7 (4): 365–78.

Mathias, P. (1969) *The First Industrial Revolution: An economic history of Britain 1700–1914*. London: Methuen.

Matthews, C. H. and Moser, S. B. (1996) 'A longitudinal investigation of the impact of family background and gender on interest in small firm ownership', *Journal of Small Business Management*, 34 (2): 29–43.

Mayer, M., Heinzel, W. and Muller, R. (1990) 'Performance of new technology-based firms in the federal Republic of Germany at the stage of market entry', *Entrepreneurship and Regional Development*, 2: 125–38.

Mayoux, L. (1995) 'From vicious to virtuous circles?: Gender and micro-enterprise development'. Occasional Paper No. 3, presented at the UN Fourth World Conference on Women, United Nations Research Institute for Social Development, Geneva, May.

McAdam, M. and McAdam, R. (2008) 'High tech start-ups in university science park incubators: The relationship between the start-up's lifecycle progression and use of the incubator's resources', *Technovation*, 28 (5): 277–90.

McClelland, D. C. (1955) 'Measuring motivation in phantasy: The achievement motive', in D. C. McClelland (ed.), *Studies in Motivation*. New York: Appleton-Century-Crofts. pp. 401–13.

McClelland, D. C. (1961) *The Achieving Society*. Princeton, NJ: Van Nostrand.

McClelland, D. C. and Winter, D. G. (1969) *Motivating Economic Achievement*. New York: Free Press.

McCloy, R. A., Campbell, J. P. and Cudeck, R. (1994) 'A confirmatory test of a model of performance determinants', *Journal of Applied Psychology*, 79 (4): 493–505.

McDonald, M. H. B. (1980) *Handbook of Marketing Planning*. Bradford: MCB Publications. p. 2.

McDonald, M. H. B. (2002) *Marketing Plans: How to prepare them how to use them*. London: Butterworth-Heinemann. pp. 1–8.

McDougall, P. P. and Oviatt, B. M. (2000a) 'International entrepreneurship: the intersection of two research paths', *Academy of Management Journal*, 43 (5): 902–6.

McDougall, P. P. and Oviatt, B. M. (2000b) 'International entrepreneurship literature in the 1990s: Directions for future research', in D. L. Sexton and R. W. Smillor (eds), *Entrepreneurship 2000*. Chicago, IL: Upstart Publishing. pp. 291–320.

McDougall, P. P. and Robinson, R. B. (1990) 'New venture strategies: An empirical identification of eight "archetypes" of competitive strategies for entry', *Strategic Management Journal*, 11 (6): 447–67.

McEvoy, D. and Cook, I. G. (1993) 'Transpacific migration: Asians in North America'. Paper presented at the Second British Pacific Rim Seminar, School of Social Science, John Moores University, Liverpool, September.

McGee, J. (1989) 'Barriers to growth: The effects of market structure', in J. Barber, J. S. Metcalfe and M. Porteous (eds) *Barriers to Growth in Small Firms*. London: Routledge. pp. 173–95.

McGee, J., Peterson, M., Mueller, S. L. and Sequeira, J. M. (2009) 'Entrepreneurial self-efficacy: Refining the measure', *Entrepreneurship Theory and Practice*, 33 (4): 965–88.

McGrath, R. G. (undated) 'L'Art d'Entreprendre: Comment la parcimonie peut mener au profit', *Les Echos*. Available online: www.lesechos.fr/formations/entreprendre/articles/article_2_9.htm.

McGrath, R. G. (1999) 'Falling forward: Real options reasoning and entrepreneurial failure', *Academy of Management Review*, 24 (1): 13–30.

McGrath, R. G. (2002) 'Entrepreneurship, small firms and wealth creation: A framework using real options reasoning', in A. Pettigrew, H. Thomas and R. Whittington (eds), *Handbook of Strategy and Management*. London: Sage. pp. 299–325.

McGrath, R. G. and MacMillan, I. C. (2000) *The Entrepreneurial Mindset: Strategies for continuously creating opportunity in an age of uncertainty*. Boston, MA: Harvard Business School Press.

McGrath, R. G., MacMillan, I. C. and Scheinberg, S. (1992) 'Elitists, risk-takers, and rugged individualists?: An exploratory analysis of cultural differences between entrepreneurs and non-entrepreneurs', *Journal of Business Venturing*, 7 (2): 115–35.

McGuinness, N. W. and Little, B. (1981) 'The influence of product characteristics on the export performance of new industrial products', *Journal of Marketing*, 45 (spring): 110–22.

McKechnie, S., Ennew, C. and Read, L. (1998) 'The nature of the banking relationship: A comparison of the experiences of male and female small business owners', *International Small Business Journal*, 16 (3): 39–55.

McMullen, J. S. and Shepherd, D. A. (2006) 'Entrepreneurial action and the role of uncertainty in the theory of the entrepreneur', *Academy of Management Review*, 31: 132–52.

McMullen, J. S., Plummer, L. A. and Acs, Z. J. (2007) 'What is an entrepreneurial opportunity?', *Small Business Economics*, 28 (4): 273–83.

McNaughton, R. (2003) 'The number of export markets that a firm serves: Process models versus born-global phenomenon', *Journal of International Entrepreneurship*, 1 (3): 297–311.

Meadowcroft, J. and Pennington, M. (2009) 'Bonding and bridging: Social capital and the communitarian critique of liberal markets', *The Review of Austrian Economics*, 21 (2/3): 119–33.

Meckstroth, D. D. (2005) '"Creative destruction" closes 35,000 U.S. manufacturing sites'. Arlington, VA: Manufacturing Alliance/MAPI.

Meek, W. R., Pacheco, D. F. and York, J. G. (2010) 'The impact of social norms on entrepreneurial action: Evidence from the environmental entrepreneurship context', *Journal of Business Venturing*, 25: 493–509.

Mellers, B. A., Schwartz, A. and Cooke, A. D. J. (1998) 'Judgement and decision making', *Annual Review of Psychology*, 49: 447–77.

Menger, C. (Dingwall, J. and Hoselitz, B. F. trans.) (1950) *Principles of Economics*. Glencoe, IL: Free Press.

Menzies, T., Brenner, G. and Filion, L. (2003) 'Social capital, networks and ethnic minority entrepreneurs: Transnational entrepreneurship and bootstrap capitalism', in H. Etemad and R. Wright (eds), *Globalization and Entrepreneurship: Policy and strategy perspectives*. Cheltenham: Edward Elgar. pp. 125–51.

Metcalf, H., Modood, T. and Virdee, S. (1996) 'Asian self-employment: The interaction of culture and economics in England'. London: Policy Studies Institute.

Meuleman, M., Lockett, A., Manigart, S. and Wright, M. (2010) 'Partner selection decisions in interfirm collaborations: The paradox of relational embeddedness', *Journal of Management Studies*, 47: 995–1019.

Meyer, M. (2003) 'Academic entrepreneurs or entrepreneurial academics?: Research-based ventures and public support mechanisms', *R&D Management*, 32 (2): 107–15.

Michael, S. C. and Pearce, J. A. (2009) 'The need for innovation as a rationale for government involvement in entrepreneurship', *Entrepreneurship and Regional Development*, 21 (3): 285–302.

Michaelas, N., Chittenden, F. and Poutziouris, P. (1996) 'Determinants of capital structure in small privately held firms'. The Institute of Small Business Affairs Research Series, Monograph 2.

Middlemas, K. (1983) *Industry, Unions and Government: Twenty-one years of NEDC*. Houndmills, Basingstoke: Macmillan.

Miesenbock, K. J. (1988) 'Small business and exporting: A literature review', *International Small Business Journal*, 6 (2): 42–61.

Miles, M. P. and Darroch, J. (2006) 'Large firms, entrepreneurial marketing processes, and the cycle of competitive advantage', *European Journal of Marketing*, 40: 495–501.

Miles, M. P. and Darroch, J. (2008) 'A commentary on current research at the marketing and entrepreneurship interface', *Journal of Small Business Management*, 46 (1): 46–9.

Mill, J. S., (Ashley, W. J., (ed.)) (1909) *Principles of Political Economy*. London: Longman.

Miller, D. (1987) 'Strategy making and structure: Analysis and implications for performance', *Academy of Management Journal*, 30 (1): 7–32.

Miller, D. and Droge, C. (1986) 'Psychological and traditional determinants of structure', *Administrative Science Quarterly*, 31: 539–60.

Miller, D. and Toulouse, J. M. (1986) 'Chief executive personality and corporate strategy and structure in small firms', *Management Science*, 32 (11): 1389–1409.

Miller, T. L. and Wesley, C. L. (2010) 'Assessing mission and resources for social change: An organizational identity perspective on social venture capitalists' decision criteria', *Entrepreneurship Theory and Practice*, 34: 705–33.

Min, P. G. (1991) 'Cultural and economic boundaries of Korean ethnicity: A comparative analysis', *Ethnic and Racial Studies*, 14: 225–38.

Miner, J. B. Smith, N. R. and Bracker, J. (1989) 'Role of entrepreneurial task motivation in the growth of technologically innovative firms', *Journal of Applied Psychology*, 74 (4): 554–60.

Miner, A. S., Bassoff, P. and Moorman, C. (2001) 'Organizational improvisation and learning', *Administrative Science Quarterly*, 46: 304–37.

Miner, J. B., Crane, D. P. and Vandenberg, R. J. (1994) 'Congruence and fit in professional role motivation theory', *Organization Science*, 5 (1): 86–97.

Miner, J. B., Raju, N. S., Stewart, W. H. and Roth, P. L. (2004) 'Risk propensity differences between managers and entrepreneurs and between low-and high-growth entrepreneurs: A reply in a more conservative vein: Commentary', *Journal of Applied Psychology*, 89 (1): 3–21.

Miner, J. B., Smith, N. R. and Bracker, J. S. (1992) 'Predicting firm survival from a knowledge of entrepreneur task motivation', *Entrepreneurship and Regional Development*, 4 (2): 145–54.

Miner J. B., Smith N. R. and Bracker, J. (1994) 'Role of entrepreneurial task motivation in the growth of technologically innovative firms: Interpretations from follow-up data', *Journal of Applied Psychology*, 79 (4): 627–30.

Ministry of Trade and Industry, Finland (2007) *High-growth SME Support Initiatives in Nine Countries: Analysis, categorization, and recommendations*. Helsinki: MTI Publications and Edita Publishing.

Minniti, M. (2005) 'Entrepreneurship and network externalities', *Journal of Economic Behavior and Organization*, 57 (1): 1–27.

Minniti, M. (2008) 'The role of government policy on entrepreneurial activity: Productive, unproductive, or destructive?' *Entrepreneurship Theory and Practice*, 32 (5): 779–90.

Minniti, M. and Bygrave, W. (2001) 'A dynamic model of entrepreneurial learning', *Entrepreneurship Theory and Practice*, 25: 5–16.

Minnitti, M., Arenius, P. and Langowitz, N. (2005) 'Global Entrepreneurship Monitor: 2004 report on women and entrepreneurship'. Wellesley, MA, and London: Centre for Women's

Leadership, Babson College, and London Business School.

Mintzberg, H. (1979) *The Structuring of Organisations*. Englewood Cliffs, NJ: Prentice Hall.

Mintzberg, H. (1994) 'Rethinking strategic planning, Part I: Pitfalls and fallacies', *Long Range Planning*, 27 (3): 12–21.

Mintzberg, H. and Quinn, J. (1991) *The Strategy Process: Concepts, contexts, cases* (2nd edn). Englewood Cliffs, NJ: Prentice Hall.

Mintzberg, H. and Waters, J. (1982) 'Tracking strategy in an entrepreneurial firm', *Administrative Science Quarterly*, 25: 465–99.

Mir, R. and Watson, A. (2000) 'Strategic management and the philosophy of science: The case for a constructivist methodology', *Strategic Management Journal*, 21: 941–53.

Mirchandani, K. (1999) 'Feminist insight on gendered work: New directions in research on women and entrepreneurship', *Gender, Work and Organization*, 6 (4): 224–35.

Mises, L. (1949) *Human Action: A Treatise on Economics*. New Haven, CT: Yale University Press.

Mitchell, F., Reid, G. and Terry, N. (1995) 'Post investment demand for accounting information by venture capitalists', *Accounting and Business Research*, 25 (9): 186–96.

Mitchell, J. (1969) 'The concept and use of social networks', in J. Mitchell (ed.), *Social Networks in Urban Situations*. Manchester: Manchester University Press. pp. 1–50.

Mitchell, R. K., Busenitz, L. W., Bird, B., Gaglio, C. M., McMullen, J. S., Morse, E. A. and Smith, J. B. (2007) 'The central question in entrepreneurial cognition research 2007', *Entrepreneurship Theory and Practice*, 31 (1): 1–27.

Mitchell, R. K., Busenitz, L., Lant, T., McDougall, P. P., Morse, E. A. and Smith, J. B. (2002a) 'Toward a theory of entrepreneurial cognition: Rethinking the people side of entrepreneurship research', *Entrepreneurship Theory and Practice*, 27 (2): 93–104.

Mitchell, R. K., Smith, J. B., Morse, E. A., Seawright, K. W., Peredo, A. M. and McKenzie, B. (2002b) 'Are entrepreneurial cognitions universal?: Assessing entrepreneurial cognitions across cultures', *Entrepreneurship Theory and Practice*, 26 (4): 9–32.

Mitter, S. (1986) 'Industrial restructuring and manufacturing homework', *Capital and Class*, 27: 37–80.

Modigliani, F. and Miller, M. (1958) 'The cost of capital, corporation finance and the theory of investment', *American Economic Review*, 48 (3): 261–97.

Moen, O. (2002) 'The born globals: A new generation of small European exporters', *International Marketing Review*, 19 (2): 156–75.

Mohannak, K. (2007) 'Innovation networks and capability building in Australian high-technology SMEs', *European Journal of Innovation Management*, 10 (2): 236–51.

Moini, A. H. (1997) 'Barriers inhibiting export performance of small and medium-sized manufacturing firms', *Journal of Global Marketing*, 10 (4): 67–93.

Mole, K. (2002a) 'Business advisers' impact on SMEs: An agency theory approach', *International Small Business Journal*, 20 (2): 139–62.

Mole, K. (2002b) 'Street-level technocracy in UK small business support: Business Link, personal business advisers, and the Small Business Service', *Environment and Planning C: Government and Policy*, 20: 179–94.

Mole, K., Hart, M., Roper, S. and Saal, D. (2008) 'Differential gains from Business Link support and advice: A treatment effect approach', *Environment and Planning C: Government and Policy*, 26: 315–34.

Monck, C. S. P., Porter, R. B., Quintas, P., Storey, D. J. and Wynarczyk, P. (1988) *Science Parks and the Growth of High Technology Firms*. London: Croom Helm.

Mondragon (2011) 'Economic data'. Available online at: www.mcc.es/language/en-US/ENG/Economic-Data/Most-relevant-data.aspx

Moran, P. (1999) 'Growth strategies and owner-manager personality: What is the relationship?' Paper presented at the 22nd ISBA National Small Firms Policy and Research Conference, Leeds, November.

Morgan, K. and Nauwelaers, C. (eds) (2003) *Regional Innovation Strategies: The challenge for less-favoured regions*. Abingdon: Routledge.

Morgan, R. E. and Katsikeas, C. S. (1995) 'Determinants of export intention'. Paper presented at the Marketing Education Group Conference, Bradford, 5–7 July.

Morgan, R. E. and Katsikeas, C. S. (1997) 'Export stimuli: Export intention compared with export activity', *International Business Review*, 6 (5): 477–99.

Morris, M. and Lewis, P. S. (1995) 'The determinants of entrepreneurial activity', *European Journal of Marketing*, 29 (7): 31–28.

Morris, M. H., Williams, R. O., Allen, J. A. and Avila, R. A. (1997) 'Correlates of success in family business transitions', *Journal of Business Venturing*, 12: 385–401.

Morris, M., Schindehutte, M. and LaForge, R. (2002) 'Entrepreneurial marketing: A construct for integrating emerging entrepreneurship and marketing perspectives', *Journal of Marketing Theory and Practice*, 10 (4): 1–19.

Morrish, S., Miles, M. P. and Deacon, J. H. (2010) 'Entrepreneurial marketing: Acknowledging the entrepreneur and customer-centric interrelationship', *Journal of Strategic Marketing*, 18 (4): 303–16.

Mort, G. S., Weerawardena, J. and Carnegie, K. (2003) 'Social entrepreneurship: Towards conceptualisation', *International Journal of Nonprofit and Voluntary Sector Marketing*, 8: 76–88.

Mosey, S. and Wright, M. (2007) 'From human capital to social capital: A longitudinal study of technology-based academic entrepreneurs', *Entrepreneurship Theory and Practice*, 31: 909–36.

Moss, T. W., Short, J. C., Payne, G. T. and Lumpkin, G. T. (2010) 'Dual identities in social ventures: An exploratory study', *Entrepreneurship Theory and Practice*, 3 (4): 805–30.

Mowday, R. T. and Sutton, R. I. (1993) 'Organizational behavior: Linking individuals and groups to organizational contexts', *Annual Review of Psychology*, 44: 195–229.

Moyes, A. and Westhead, P. (1990) 'Environment for new firm formation in Great Britain', *Regional Studies*, 24: 123–36.

Mueller, P. (2006) 'Entrepreneurship in the region: Breeding ground for nascent entrepreneurs?', *Small Business Economics*, 27 (1): 41–58.

Mulholland, K. (1996) 'Gender and property relations within entrepreneurial wealthy families', *Gender, Work and Organisation*, 3 (2): 78–102.

Mullins, D. (1979) 'Asian retailing in Croydon', *New Community*, 7: 403–5.

Mullins, J. W. (1996) 'Early growth decisions of entrepreneurs: The influence of competency and prior performance under changing market conditions', *Journal of Business Venturing*, 11 (2): 89–106.

Mullins, J. W. and Forlani, D. (2005) 'Missing the boat or sinking the boat: A study of new venture decision making', *Journal of Business Venturing*, 20 (1): 47–69.

Munari, F. and Toschi, L. (2010) 'Assessing the impact of public venture capital programmes in the United Kingdom: Do regional characteristics matter?' Paper presented to the European Financial Management Symposium, Cirano, Montreal, Canada, April.

Murphy, G. B., Trailer, J. W. and Hill, R. C. (1996) 'Measuring performance in entrepreneurship research', *Journal of Business Research*, 36 (1): 15–23.

Murray, G. (1995) 'Third party equity: The role of the UK venture capital industry', in R. Buckland and E. Davis (eds), *Finance for Growing Firms*. London: Routledge.

Murray, G. C. (1995) 'Evolution and change: An analysis of the first decade of the UK venture capital industry', *Journal of Business Finance and Accounting*, 22 (8): 1077–1106.

Murray, J. A. and O'Gorman, C. (1994) 'Growth strategies for smaller business', *Journal of Strategic Change*, 3: 175–83.

Myers, S. C. (1984) 'The capital structure puzzle', *Journal of Finance*, 39: 575–92.

Nagle, M. (2007) 'Canonical analysis of university presence and industrial comparative advantage', *Economic Development Quarterly*, 21: 325–38.

Nahapiet, J. and Ghosal, S. (1998) 'Social capital, intellectual capital, and the organizational advantage', *Academy of Management Review*, 23 (2): 242–66.

Namiki, N. (1988) 'Export strategy for small business', *Journal of Small Business Management*, 26 (2): 32–7.

Namiki, N. (1994) 'A taxonomic analysis of export marketing strategy: An exploratory study of U.S. exporters of electronic products', *Journal of Global Marketing*, 8 (1): 27–50.

National Audit Office (2011) 'Better regulation and impact assessments'. London: National Audit Office.

National Endowment for Science, Technology and the Arts (2009) 'The vital 6 per cent: Research summary'. October. London: NESTA.

National Women's Business Council (2004) 'Women business owners and their enterprises'. Washington, DC: National Women's Business Council.

Nauwelaers, C. and Wintjes, R. (2003) 'Towards a new paradigm for innovation policy?', in B. Asheim, A. Isaksen, C. Nauwelaers and F. Tödtling (eds), *Regional Innovation Policy for Small–Medium Enterprises*. Cheltenham: Edward Elgar. pp. 193–219.

Neergaard, H. (2005) 'Networking activities in technology-based entrepreneurial teams', *International Small Business Journal*, 23 (3): 257–78.

Neergaard, H., Frederiksen, S. and Marlow, S. (2011) 'The emperor's new clothes: Rendering a feminist theory of entrepreneurship visible'. Paper presented at the ICSB Conference, Stockholm, Sweden, 15–18 June.

Neergaard, H., Shaw, E. and Carter, S. (2005) 'The impact of gender, social capital and networks on business ownership: A research agenda', *International Journal of Entrepreneurial Behaviour and Research*, 11 (5): 338–57.

NESTA (2007) 'Innovative entrepreneurship in the UK'. January. London: NESTA.

Nicholls, A. (2009) '"We do good things, don't we?": Blended value accounting in social entrepreneurship', *Accounting, Organizations and Society*, 34: 755–69.

Nicholls, A. (2010) 'The legitimacy of social entrepreneurship: Reflexive isomorphism in a pre-paradigmatic field', *Entrepreneurship Theory and Practice*, 34: 611–33.

Nicholls, A. and Opal, C. (2005) *Fair Trade: Market-driven ethical consumption*. London: Sage.

Nicholls-Nixon, C. L., Cooper, A. C. and Woo, C. Y. (2000) 'Strategic experimentation: Understanding change and performance in new ventures', *Journal of Business Venturing*, 15: 493–521.

Nicholson, L. and Anderson, A. R. (2005) 'News and nuances of the entrepreneurial myth and metaphor: Linguistic games in entrepreneurial sense-making and sense-giving', *Entrepreneurship Theory and Practice*, 29 (2): 153–72.

Nicolaou, N. and Birley, S. (2003) 'Academic networks in a trichotomous categorisation of university spinouts', *Journal of Business Venturing*, 18: 333–59.

Nicolaou, N. and Shane, S. (2009a) 'Born entrepreneurs?: The genetic foundations of entrepreneurship', *Journal of Business Venturing*, 23: 1–22.

Nicolaou, N. and Shane, S. (2009b) 'Can genetic factors influence the likelihood of engaging in entrepreneurial activity?', *Journal of Business Venturing*, 24 (1): 1–22.

Nicolaou, N., Shane, S., Cherkas, L. and Spector, T. D. (2009) 'Opportunity recognition and the tendency to be an entrepreneur: A bivariate genetics perspective', *Organizational Behavior and Human Decision Processes*, 110 (2): 108–17.

Nonaka, I. and Takeuchi, H. (1995) *The Knowledge-creating Company: How Japanese companies create the dynamics of innovation*. New York: Oxford University Press.

Norburn, D. and Birley, S. (1988) 'The top management team and corporate performance', *Strategic Management Journal*, 9: 225–37.

North, D. C. (1990) *Institutions, Institutional Change, and Economic Performance*. Cambridge: Cambridge University Press.

North, D. C. and Smallbone, D. (1996) 'Small business development in remote rural areas: The example of mature manufacturing firms in Northern England', *Journal of Rural Studies*, 12 (2): 151–67.

North, D. C. and Syrett, S. (2008) *Renewing Neighbourhoods: Work, enterprise and governance*. Bristol: The Policy Press.

North, D. C., Baldock, R. and Ekanem, I. (2010) 'Is there a debt finance gap relating to Scottish SMEs?: A demand-side perspective', *Venture Capital*, 12 (3): 173–92.

Norton, E. and Tenenbaum, B. H. (1992) 'Factors affecting the structure of US venture capital deals', *Journal of Small Business Management*, 30 (3): 20–9.

Norton, E. (1990) 'Similarities and differences in small and large corporation beliefs about capital structure policy', *Small Busness Economics*, 2 (3): 229–45.

Norton, E. (1991a) 'Capital structure and public firms', *Journal of Business Venturing*, 6 (4): 287–303.

Norton, E. (1991b) 'Capital structure and small growth firms', *Journal of Small Business Finance*, 1 (2): 161–77.

Norton, W. I. and Moore, W. T. (2006) 'The influence of entrepreneurial risk assessment on venture launch or growth decisions', *Small Business Economics*, 26 (3): 215–26.

Novy, A. (1990) 'Learning experiences from OECD and EC reviews of local employment initiatives', in W. B. Stöhr (ed.), *Global Challenge and Local Response: Initiatives for economic regeneration in contemporary Europe*. London and New York: Mansell Publishing. pp. 412–37.

Nowikowski, S. (1984) 'Snakes and ladders' in R. Ward and R. Jenkins (eds), *Ethnic Communities in Business*. Cambridge: Cambridge University Press. pp. 149–65.

Nutt, P. C. (1993) 'Flexible decision styles and the choices of top executives', *Journal of Management Studies*, 30 (5): 695–721.

O'Donnell, A., Gilmore, A., Cummins, D. and Carson, D. (2001) 'The network construct in entrepreneurship research: A review and critique', *Management Decision*, 39 (9): 749–60.

O'Dwyer, M., Gilmore, A. and Carson, D. (2009) 'Innovative marketing in SMEs', *European Journal of Marketing*, 43 (1/2): 46–61.

O'Farrell, P. N. O. and Hitchens, D. M. W. N. (1988) 'Alternative theories of small firm growth: A critical review', *Environment and Planning A.* 20: 1365–83.

O'Grady, S. and Lane, H. W. (1996) 'The psychic distance paradox', *Journal of International Business Studies*, 2nd Quarter: 309–33.

Oakey, R. P. (1984) *High Technology Small Firms*. London: Frances Pinter.

Oakey, R. P. (1985) 'British university science parks and high technology small firms: A comment on the potential for sustained economic growth', *International Journal of Small Business*, 4 (1): 58–67.

Oakey, R. P. (1991) 'High technology small firms: Their potential for rapid industrial growth', *International Small Business Journal*, 9: 30–42.

Oakey, R. P. (1995) *High Technology New Firms: Variable barriers to growth*. London: Paul Chapman.

Oakey, R. P. (2003) 'Technical entrepreneurship in high technology small firms: Some observations on the implications for management', *Technovation*, 23: 679–88.

Oakey, R. P. (2008) 'Clustering and the R and D management of high-technology small firms: In theory and practice', *R&D Management*, 37 (3): 237–48.

Oakey, R. P. and Cooper, S. Y. (1991) 'The relationship between product technology and innovation performance in high technology small firms', *Technovation*, 11 (2): 79–92.

Oakey, R. P. and Pearson, A. W. (1995) 'Innovation, technology and regional development', in L. A. Lefebvre and E. Lefebvre (eds), *Management of Technology and Regional Development in a Global Environment*. London: Paul Chapman. pp. 3–12.

OECD (1986) 'Employment creation policies: New roles of cities and towns'. Paris: OECD.

OECD (1997a) *Globalization and Small and Medium Enterprises (SMEs)* (vols 1 and 2). Paris: OECD.

OECD (1997b) 'Information technology outlook 1997'. Paris: OECD.

OECD (2003) 'Entrepreneurship and local economic development: Programme and policy recommendations'. Paris: OECD.

OECD (2006) *The SME Finance Gap: Vol. One: Theory and evidence*. Paris: OECD.

OECD (2007) 'High-growth enterprises and gazelles', Nadim Ahmad and Eric Gonnard, Statistics Directorate, OECD. Paper prepared for the International Consortium on Entrepreneurship (ICE) Meeting, Copenhagen, Denmark, 22–23 February.

OECD (2009) 'Top barriers and drivers to SME internationalization'. Report by the OECD Working Party on SMEs and Entrepreneurship. Paris: OECD. Available online at: www.oecd. org/dataoecd/16/26/43357832.pdf

OECD Eurostat (2007) 'Eurostat–OECD manual on business demography statistics'. Paris: OECD. p. 61.

Ogbor, J. O. (2000) 'Mythicizing and reification in entrepreneurial discourse: Ideology critique of entrepreneurial studies', *Journal of Management Studies*, 35 (5): 605–35.

Ok Lee, D. (1995) 'Koreatown and Korean small firms in Los Angeles: Locating in the ethnic neighbourhoods', *Professional Geographer*, 47: 184–95.

Oldham, G. R. and Cummings, A. (1996) 'Employee creativity: Personal and contextual factors at work', *Academy of Management Journal*, 39: 607–34.

Olson, M. (2007) 'Big bills left on the sidewalk: Why some nations are rich, and others poor', in B. Powell (ed.), *Making Poor Nations Rich: Entrepreneurship and the process of economic development*. Stanford, CA: Stanford University Press. pp. 25–53.

Oman, C. (1984) *New Forms of International Investment in Developing Countries*. Paris: OECD.

Omura, G. S., Calantone, R. J. and Schmidt, J. B. (1993) 'Entrepreneurism as a market satisfying mechanism in the free market system', in G. E. Hills and A. Nohan-Neill (eds), *Research at the Marketing/Entrepreneurship Interface*. Chicago, IL: University of Illinois at Chicago. pp. 161–71.

ONS (2005) 'Labour force survey quarterly survey', April. London: ONS.

Open University Business School (2010) 'The quarterly survey of small business in Britain'. Q4, 26 (4). Milton Keynes: Open University Business School.

Orser, B. J. and Foster, M. K. (1994) 'Lending practices and Canadian women in micro-based businesses', *Women in Management Review*, 9 (5): 11–19.

Osborne, R. L. (1993) 'Why entrepreneurs fail: How to avoid the traps', *Management Decision*, 31 (1): 18–21.

Ostgaard, A. and Birley, S. (1994) 'Personal networks and firm competitive strategy: A strategic or coincidental match?', *Journal of Business Venturing*, 9 (4): 281–305.

Ostgaard, A. and Birley, S. (1996) 'New venture growth and personal networks', *Journal of Business Research*, 36 (1): 37–50.

Oughton, E., Wheelock, J. and Baines, S. (2003) 'Micro-businesses and social inclusion in rural households: A comparative analysis', *Sociologia Ruralis*, 43 (4): 331–48.

Oviatt, B. M. and McDougall, P. P. (1994a) 'Global start-ups: Entrepreneurs on a worldwide stage', *Academy of Management Executive*, 25 (2): 30–43.

Oviatt, B. M. and McDougall, P. P. (1994b) 'Toward a theory of international new ventures', *Journal of International Business Studies*, 25 (1): 45–64.

Oviatt, B. M. and McDougall, P. P. (2005) 'Defining international entrepreneurship and modeling the speed of internationalisation', *Entrepreneurship Theory and Practice*, 29 (September): 537–53.

Owualah, S. (1987) 'Providing the necessary economic infrastructure for small business: Whose responsibility?', *International Small Business Journal*, 6 (1): 10–30.

Ozcan, P. and Eisenhardt, K. M. (2009) 'Origin of alliance portfolios: Entrepreneurs, network strategies, and firm performance', *Academy of Management Journal*, 52 (2): 246–79.

Pache, A.-C. and Santos, F. (2011) 'Inside the hybrid organization: An organizational level view of responses to conflicting institutional demands'. Research Centre ESSEC Working Paper 1101, February. Cergy Pontoise, France: ESSEC Business School.

Pajaczkowska, C. and Young, L. (1992) 'Racism, presentation, psychoanalysis', in J. Donald and A. Rattansi (eds), *Race, Culture & Difference*. London: Sage.

Palich, L. E. and Bagby, D. R. (1995) 'Using cognitive theory to explain entrepreneurial risk-taking: Challenging conventional wisdom', *Journal of Business Venturing*, 10 (6): 425–38.

Paliwoda, S. J., Vissak, T. and Ibeh, K. I. N. (2007) 'Internationalising from the European periphery: Triggers, pressures and trajectories', *Journal of Euromarketing*, 17 (1): 35–48.

Parker, D. (1994) 'Encounters across the counter: Young Chinese people in Britain', *New Community*, 20: 621–34.

Parker, S. (2004) *The Economics of Self-employment and Entrepreneurship*. Cambridge: Cambridge University Press.

Parker, S. (2010) 'Learning and the performance of serial entrepreneurs'. Working Paper, University of Western Ontario, Canada.

Parsa, H. G., Self, J. T., Njite, D. and King, T. (2005) 'Why restaurants fail', *Cornell Hotel and Restaurant Administration Quarterly*, 46 (3): 304–22.

Patel, S. (1988) 'Insurance and ethnic community business', *New Community*, 15: 79–89.

Paton, R. (2003) *Managing and Measuring Social Enterprises*. London: Sage.

Paul, S. and Boden, R. (2008) 'The secret life of UK trade credit supply: Setting a new research agenda', *British Accounting Review*, 40 (3): 272–81.

Paul, S. and Wilson, N. (2006) 'Trade credit supply: An empirical investigation of companies level data', *Journal of Accounting, Business and Management*, 13: 85–113.

Pavord, W. C. and Bogart, R. G. (1975) 'The dynamics of the decision to export', *Akron Business and Economic Review*, 6 (Spring): 6–11.

Peacock, P. (1986) 'The influence of risk-taking as a cognitive judgmental behavior of small business success', in *Frontiers of Entrepreneurship Research 1986*. Wellesley, MA: Babson College.

Pearson, A. W., Carr, J. C. and Shaw, J. C. (2008) 'Toward a theory of familiness: A social capital perspective', *Entrepreneurship: Theory & Practice*, 32 (6): 949–69.

Peattie, K. and Morely, A. (2008) 'Eight paradoxes of the social enterprise research agenda', *Social Enterprise Journal*, 4: 91–107.

Peel, M. J. and Bridge, J. (1998) 'How planning and capital budgeting improve SME performance', *Long Range Planning*, 31 (6, December): 848–56.

Peng, M. W. (2001) 'The resource-based view and international business', *Journal of Management*, 27: 803–29.

Penrose, E. T. (1959) *The Theory of the Growth of the Firm*. Oxford: Blackwell.

Peredo, A. M. (2003) 'Emerging strategies against poverty: The road less traveled', *Journal of Management Inquiry*, 12 (2): 155–66.

Peredo, A. M. (2005) 'Community venture in Agua Dulce: The evolution of civic into economic democracy', *Journal of Applied Behavioral Science*, 41 (4): 458–81.

Peredo, A. M. and Chrisman, J. J. (2006) 'Toward a theory of community-based enterprise', *Academy of Management Review*, 31 (2): 309–28.

Peredo, A. M. and McLean, M. (2006) 'Social entrepreneurship: A critical review of the concept', *Journal of World Business*, 41: 56–65.

Perrini, F. (2006) *The new social entrepreneurship: What awaits social entrepreneurial ventures?* Cheltenham: Edward Elgar.

Perrini, F., Vurro, C. and Costanzo, L. A. (2010) 'A process-based view of social entrepreneurship: From opportunity identification to scaling-up social change in the case of San Patrignano', *Entrepreneurship and Regional Development*, 22 (6): 515–34.

Perry, C., MacArthur, R., Meredith, G. and Cunnington, B. (1986) 'Need for achievement and locus of control of Australian small business owner-managers and super-entrepreneurs', *International Small Business Journal*, 4 (4): 55–64.

Peterson, M. and Roquebert, J. (1993) 'Success patterns of Cuban-American enterprises: Implications for entrepreneurial communities', *Human Relations*, 46 (8): 921–37.

Peterson, R. T. (1988) 'An analysis of new product ideas in small business', *Journal of Small Business Management*, 26: 25–31.

Phan, P. and Siegel, D. S. (2006) 'The effectiveness of university technology transfer: Lessons learned, managerial and policy implications, and the road forward', *Foundations and Trends in Entrepreneurship*, 2 (2): 77–144.

Phan, P., Wright, M., Ucbasaran, D. and Tan, W. (2009) 'Corporate entrepreneurship: Current research and future direction', *Journal of Business Venturing*, 24: 197–205.

Philips, B. and Kirchhoff, B. (1989) 'Formation, growth and survival: Small firm dynamics in the US economy', *Small Business Economics*, 1 (1): 65–74.

Phillips, J. M. and Gully, S. M. (1997) 'Role of goal orientation, ability, need for achievement, and locus of control in the self-efficacy and goal-setting process', *Journal of Applied Psychology*, 82 (5): 792–802.

Phizacklea, A. (1990) *Unpacking The Fashion Industry*. London: Routledge.

Phizacklea, A. and Ram, M. (1996) 'Open for business?: Ethnic entrepreneurship in comparative perspective', *Work, Employment and Society*, 10 (2): 319–39.

Pierrakis, Y. (2010) 'Venture capital: Now and after the dotcom crash'. London: NESTA.

Piore, M. and Sabel, C. (1984) *The Second Industrial Divide*. New York: Basic Books.

Pittaway, L. (2005) 'Philosophies in entrepreneurship: A focus on economic theories', *International Journal of Entrepreneurial Behaviour and Research*, 11 (3): 201–21.

Pittaway, L. and Cope, J. (2007) 'Entrepreneurship education: A systematic review of the evidence', *International Small Business Journal*, 25 (5): 477–506.

Plaschka, G. R. and Welsch, H. P. (1990) 'Emerging structures in entrepreneurship education: Curricula designs and strategies', *Entrepreneurship Theory and Practice*, 14 (3): 55–71.

Plummer, L. A., Haynie, J. M. and Godesiabois, J. (2007) 'An essay on the origins of entrepreneurial opportunity', *Small Business Economics*, 28 (4): 363–79.

Polanyi, K. (1957) *The Great Transformation: The political and economic origins of our time* (9th edn). Boston, MA: Beacon.

Polanyi, M. (1962) *Personal Knowledge: Towards a post-critical philosophy*. Chicago, IL: University of Chicago Press.

Politis, D. and Gabrielsson, J. (2009) 'Entrepreneurs' attitudes towards failure: An experiential learning approach', *International Journal of Entrepreneurial Behaviour and Research*, 5 (4): 364–83.

Porter, M. E. (1980) *Competitive Strategy: Techniques for analyzing industries and competitors*. New York: Free Press. pp. 3–33.

Porter, M. E. (1985) *Competitive Advantage: Creating and sustaining superior performance*. New York: Free Press.

Porter, M. E. (1990) *The Competitive Advantage of Nations*. New York: Free Press.

Porter, M. E. (1995) 'The competitive advantage of the inner city', *Harvard Business Review*, 73: 55–71.

Porter, M. E. (1997) 'New strategies for inner-city economic development', *Economic Development Quarterly*, 11 (1): 11–27.

Porter, M. E. (1998a) *On Competition*. Boston, MA: Harvard Business School.

Porter, M. E. (1998b) 'Clusters and competition: New agendas for companies, governments, and institutions', in M. E. Porter, *On Competition*. Boston, MA: Harvard Business School Press.

Porter, M. E. (2000) 'Location, competition, and economic development: Local clusters in a global economy', *Economic Development Quarterly*, 14 (1): 15–34.

Porter, M. E. (2003) 'The economic performance of regions', *Regional Studies*, 37: 549–78.

Portes, A. (1998) 'Social capital: Its origins and applications in modern sociology', *Annual Review of Sociology*, 24 (1): 1–24.

Portes, A. and Bach, R. L. (1985) *Latin Journey: Cuban and Mexican immigrants in the United States*. Berkeley, CA: University of California Press.

Poutziouris, P., Chittenden, F. and Michaelas, N. (2001) 'Modelling the impact of taxation (direct and compliance costs) on the UK small business economy', in C. Evans, J. Hasseldine and J. Pope (eds), *Tax Compliance Costs: Festschrift for Cedric Sandford*. Sydney, Prospect Media.

Poutziouris, P., Chittenden, F., Watts, T. and Soufani, K. (2003) 'A comparative analysis of the impact of taxation on the SME economy: The case of UK and US – New York State in the year 2000, *Environment and Planning C: Government and Policy*, 21 (4): 493–508.

Powell, B. (2007) *Making Poor Nations Rich: Entrepreneurship and the process of economic development*. Palo Alto, CA: Stanford University Press.

Prahalad, C. K. and Hamel, G. (1990) 'The core competence of the corporation', *Harvard Business Review*, 68 (3): 79–91.

Prais, S. J. (1976) *The Evolution of Giant Firms in Britain*. Cambridge: Cambridge University Press.

Premaratne, S. (2001) 'Networks, resources, and small business growth: The experience in Sri Lanka', *Journal of Small Business Management*, 39 (4): 363–71.

Priest, S. J. (1999) 'Business Link services to small and medium-sized enterprises: Targeting, innovation and charging', *Environment and Planning C: Government and Policy*, 17: 177–94.

Pryke, R. (1981) *The Nationalised Industries*. Oxford: Martin Robertson.

Public Administration Select Committee (2008) 'Public services and the third sector: Rhetoric and reality'. Eleventh Report of Session 2007–08 in the House of Commons. London: HMSO.

Pugliese, E. (1993) 'Restructuring of the labour market and the role of third world migrations in Europe', *Environment and Planning D: Society and Space* (vol. 11) pp. 513–22.

Push (2011) 'The Push national student debt survey'. London: Push. Available online at: www.push.co.uk/document.aspx?id=f98650ae-c830-4a0e-965d-185a173a0f4d

Putnam, R. (1995) 'Bowling alone: America's declining social capital', *Journal of Democracy*, 6 (1): 65–78.

Pyke, E. (1992) *Industrial Development Through Small-firm Cooperation: Theory and practice*. Geneva: International Labour Office.

Quadagno, J. (1987) 'Theories of the welfare state', *Annual Review of Sociology*, 13: 109–28.

Quinn, R. and Cameron, K. (1983) 'Organisational life cycles and shifting criteria of effectiveness', *Management Science*, 29: 33–51.

Racine, W. P. (2010) 'Motivation, conceptualization, and the establishment of a new scientific venture: Entrepreneurship and the environmental professional', *International Journal of Business, Management, and Social Sciences*, 1 (1): 100–12.

Radu, M. and Redien-Collot (2008) 'The social representation of entrepreneurs in the French Press: Desirable and feasible models?', *International Small Business Journal*, 26 (3): 259–98.

Rae, D. (2005) 'Entrepreneurial learning: A narrative-based conceptual model', *International Journal of Entrepreneurial Behaviour and Research*, 12 (3): 323–35.

Ram, M. (1991) 'The dynamics of workplace relations in small firms', *International Small Business Journal*, 12 (3): 42–53.

Ram, M. (1992) 'Coping with racism: Asian employers in the inner city', *Work Employment and Society*, 6: 601–18.

Ram, M. (1994a) 'Unravelling social networks in ethnic minority firms', *International Small Business Journal*, 12 (3): 42–53.

Ram, M. (1994b) *Managing to Survive: Working lives in small firms*. Oxford: Blackwell.

Ram, M. (1997) 'Supporting ethnic minority enterprise: Views from the providers' in M. Ram, D. Deakins and D. Smallbone (eds), *Small firms: Enterprising Futures*. London: Paul Chapman. pp. 148–60.

Ram, M. (1998) 'Enterprise support and ethnic minority firms', *Journal of Ethnic and Migration Studies*, 21 (1): 143–58.

Ram, M. and Deakins, D. (1995) *African-Caribbean Entrepreneurship in Britain*. Birmingham: University of Central England.

Ram, M. and Deakins, D. (1996) 'African-Caribbean entrepreneurship in Britain', *New Community*, 22 (1): 67–84.

Ram, M. and Edwards, P. (2003) 'Praising Caesar not burying him', *Work, Employment and Society*, 17 (4): 719–30.

Ram, M. and Holliday, R. (1993a) 'Keeping it in the family: Family culture in small firms', in F. Chittenden, M. Robertson, and D. Watkins, *Small Firms: Recession and Recovery*. London: Paul Chapman.

Ram, M. and Holliday, R. (1993b) 'Relative merits: Family culture and kinship in small firms', *Sociology*, 2 (4): 629–48.

Ram, M. and Jones, T. (1998) *Ethnic Minorities in Business*. Milton Keynes: Open University Press.

Ram, M. and Smallbone, D. (2002) 'Ethnic minority business support in the era of the small business service', *Environment and Planning C Government and Policy*, 20: pp. 235–49.

Ram, M., Abbas, T., Sanghera, B., Barlow, G. and Jones, T. (2001) '"Apprentice Entrepreneurs"?: Ethnic minority workers in the independent restaurant sector', *Work, Employment and Society*, 15 (2): 353–72.

Ram, M., Edwards, P. and Jones, T. (2002) 'The employment of illegal immigrants in SMEs'. DTI Central Unit Research Report. London: DTI.

Ram, M., Edwards, P., Gilman, M. and Arrowsmith, J. (2001) 'The dynamics of informality: Employment relations in small firms and the effects of regulatory change', *Work, Employment and Society*, 15 (4): 845–61.

Ram, M., Smallbone, D., Deakins, D. and Jones, T. (2003) 'Banking on "break-out": Finance and the development of ethnic minority businesses', *Journal of Ethnic and Migration Studies*, 29 (4): 663–81.

Ram, M., Sanghera, B., Abbas, T. and Jones, T. (2000) 'Ethnic minority business in comparative perspective: The case of the independent restaurant sector', *Journal of Ethnic and Migration Studies*, 26 (3): 405–510.

Ram, M., Theodorakopoulos, N. and Jones, T. (2008) 'Forms of capital, mixed embeddedness and Somali enterprise', *Work, Employment and Society*, 22 (3): 427–46.

Ramos-Rodriguez, A., Medina-Garrido, J., Lorenzo-Gómez, J. and Ruiz-Navarro, J. (2010) 'What you know or who you know?: The role of intellectual and social capital in opportunity recognition', *International Small Business Journal*, 28 (6): 566–82.

Ramsden, M. and Bennett, R. J. (2006) 'The benefits of external support to SMEs: "Hard" versus "soft" outcomes and satisfaction levels', *Journal of Small Business and Enterprise Development*, 12 (2): 227–43.

Rath, J. (ed.) (1998) *Immigrant Businesses on the Urban Fringe: A case for interdisciplinary analysis*. Houndmills, Basingstoke: Macmillan.

Rath, J. (2000) *Immigrant Businesses: The economic, political and social environment*. Houndmills, Basingstoke: Macmillan.

Rauch, A. and Frese, M. (2000) 'Psychological approaches to entrepreneurial success: A general model and an overview of findings', in C. L. Cooper and I. T. Robertson (eds), *International Review of Industrial and Organizational Psychology*: Chichester, NY: Wiley. pp. 101–42.

Rauch, A. and Frese, M. (2007) 'Born to be an entrepreneur?: Revisiting the personality approach to entrepreneurship', in J. R. Baum, M. Frese and R. A. Baron (eds), *The Psychology of Entrepreneurship*. Mahwah, NJ: Erlbaum. pp. 41–65.

Ravasi, D. and Turati, C. (2005) 'Exploring entrepreneurial learning: A comparative study of technology development projects', *Journal of Business Venturing*, 20: 137–64.

Ray, D. M. (1986) 'Perceptions of risk and new enterprise formation in Singapore: An exploratory study', in *Frontiers of Entrepreneurship Research 1986*. Wellesley, MA: Babson College.

Ray, D. M. (1994) 'The role of risk-taking in Singapore', *Journal of Business Venturing*, 9 (2): 157–77.

Razin, E. (1993) 'Immigrant entrepreneurs in Israel, Canada and California', in I. Light and P. Bhachu (eds), *Immigration and Entrepreneurship*. New Brunswick, NJ: Transaction.

Read, S., Sarasvathy, S., Dew, N., Wiltbank, R. and Ohlsson, A. (2011) *Effectual Entrepreneurship*. Abingdon: Routledge.

Read, S., Sarasvathy, S. D., Dew, N. and Wiltbank, R. (2011) 'On the entrepreneurial genesis of new markets: Effectual transformations versus causal search and selection', *Journal of Evolutionary Economics*, 21 (2): 231–53.

Reeves, F. and Ward, R. (1984) 'West Indian business in Britain', in R. Ward and R. Jenkins (eds), *Ethnic Communities in Business*. Cambridge: Cambridge University Press.

Regulatory Policy Commission (2010) 'Reviewing regulation: An independent report on the analysis supporting regulatory proposals December 2009–May 2010'. London: Regulatory Policy Commission.

Rehn, A. and Taalas, S. (2004) 'Znakomstva I Svyazi [acquaintances and connections]: Blat, the Soviet Union, and mundane entrepreneurship', *Entrepreneurship and Regional Development*, 16 (3): 235–50.

Reid, S. D. (1981) 'The decision-maker and export entry and expansion', *Journal of International Business Studies*, 12 (2): 101–12.

Reid, S. D. (1982) 'The impact of size on export behavior in small firms', in M. R. Czinkota and G. Tesar (eds), *Export Management: An international context*. New York: Praeger. pp. 18–38.

Reid, S. D. (1983a) 'Export research in a crisis', in M. R. Czinkota (ed.), *Export Promotion: The public and private sector interaction*. New York: Praeger. pp. 129–53.

Reid, S. D. (1983b) 'Firm internationalization: Transaction cost and strategic choice', *International Marketing Review*, 1 (2): 45–55.

503

Reid, S. D. (1985) 'Exporting: Does sales volume make a difference?: Comment', *Journal of International Business Studies*, summer: 153–5.

Renzulli, L., Aldrich, H. and Moody, J. (2000) 'Family matters: Gender, family, and entrepreneurial outcomes', *Social Forces*, 79 (2): 523–46.

Rerup, C. (2005) 'Learning from past experience: Footnotes on mindfulness and habitual entrepreneurship', *Scandinavian Journal of Management*, 21 (4): 451–72.

Rex, J. (1982) 'West Indian and Asian youth', in E. Cashmore and B. Troyna (eds), *Black Youth in Crisis*. London: Allen & Unwin. pp. 53–71.

Reynolds, P. D. and Miller, B. (1992) 'New firm gestation: Conception, birth and implications for research', *Journal of Business Venturing*, 7: (405–17).

Reynolds, P. D. and White, S. (1997) *The Entrepreneurial Process*. Westport, CT: Quorum.

Reynolds, P. D., Bygrave, W., Autio, E., et al. (2003) 'Global Entrepreneurship Monitor: 2003 Executive Report'. Wellesley, MA, Kansas City, MO, and London: Babson College, Ewing Marion Kauffman Foundation and London Business School.

Reynolds, P. D., Bygrave, W. D., Autio, E., Cox, L. W. and Hay, M. (2002) Global Entrepreneurship Monitor: 2002 Executive Report. Wellesley, MA, Kansas City, MO, and London: Babson College, Ewing Marion Kauffman Foundation and London Business School.

Reynolds, P. D., Camp, S. M., Bygrave, W. D., Autio, E. and Hay, M. (2001) 'Global Entrepreneurship Monitor: 2001 Executive Report'. Wellesley, MA, Kansas City, MO, and London: Babson College, Kauffman Centre for Entrepeneurial Leadership at the Ewing Marion Kauffman Foundation and London Business School.

Reynolds, P. D., Hay, M., Bygrave, W. D., Camp, S. M. and Autio, E. (2000) 'Global Entrepreneurship Monitor: 2000 Executive Report'. Wellesley, MA, Kansas City, MO, and London: Babson College, Kauffman Centre for Entrepeneurial Leadership at the Ewing Marion Kauffman Foundation and London Business School.

Richard, D. (2007) 'Small business and government: Interim report'. London: Conservative Central Office.

Richard, D. (2008) 'Small business and government: The Richard report: Submission to Shadow Cabinet'. London: Conservative Central Office.

Richardson, P., Howarth, R. and Finnegan, G. (2004) 'Jobs, gender and small enterprises in Africa and Asia: Lessons drawn from Bangladesh, the Philippines, Tunisia and Zimbabwe'. SEED Working Paper No. 47, WEDGE Series, 2001. Geneva: ILO.

Ricketts, M. (1987) *The Economics of Business Enterprise: New approaches to the firm*. Brighton: Wheatsheaf. pp. 44–77.

Riddle, D. F. (1986) *Services and Growth: The role of the special service sector in world development*. New York: Praeger.

Riding, A. L. and Swift, C. S. (1990) 'Women business owners and terms of credit: Some empirical findings of the Canadian experience', *Journal of Business Venturing*, 5 (5): 327–40.

Rindova, V., Barry, D. and Ketchen, D. (2009) 'Entrepreneuring as emancipation', *Academy of Management Review*, 34 (3): 477–91.

Roberts, C. and Sian, S. (2006) 'Accounting and financial reporting guidance for small enterprises: A case study of the UK'. Paper presented at the Emerging Issues in International Accounting and Business conference, Padua, 20–22 July.

Roberts, E. B. (1968) 'Entrepreneurship and technology: a basic study of innovators', *Research Management*, 11: 249–66.

Roberts, E. B. (1989) 'Strategic transformation and the success of high technology companies'. MIT Sloan School of Management Working Paper No. 3066-89 Bps. Cambridge, MA: MIT.

Roberts, E. B. (1991) *Entrepreneurs in High Technology: Lessons from MIT and beyond*. Oxford: Oxford University Press.

Roberts, E. B. and Eesley, C. (2009) 'Entrepreneurial impact: The role of MIT'. Kansas City, MO: Ewing Marion Kauffman Foundation.

Roberts, E. B. and Hauptman, O. (1986) 'The process of technology transfer to the biomedical and pharmaceutical start-ups', *Research Policy*, 15 (3): 107–19.

Roberts, E. B. and Wainer, H. A. (1966) 'Some characteristics of technological entrepreneurs'. MIT Sloan School of Management Working Paper No. 195-6. Cambridge, MA: MIT.

Roberts, E. B. and Wainer, H. A. (1968) 'New enterprises on Route 128', *Science Journal*, 412: 78–83.

Robinson, R. and Pearce, J. (1984) 'Research thrusts in small firm strategic planning', *Academy of Management Review*, 9 (1): 128–37.

Robinson, V. and Flintoff, I. (1982) 'Asian retailing in Coventry', *New Community*, 10: 251–58.

Robson Rhodes (1984) 'A study of business financed under the small firms loan guarantee scheme'. London: DTI.

Robson, P. J. A., Akuetteh, C. K., Westhead, P. and Wright, M. (2012a) 'Exporting intensity, human capital and business ownership experience', *International Small Business Journal*.

Robson, P. J. A., Akuetteh, C. K., Westhead, P., and Wright, M. (2012b) 'Innovative opportunity pursuit, human capital and business ownership experience in an emerging region: Evidence from Ghana', *Small Business Economics*.

Roelandt, T. and den Hertog, P. (1998) 'Cluster analysis and cluster-based policy in OECD countries'. Paper presented at the OECD Workshop on Cluster Analysis and Cluster-based Policy, Vienna, May.

Rogers, E. and Kincaid, D. (1981) *Communication Networks*. New York: Free Press.

Rogoff, E. G. and Heck, R. K. Z. (2003) 'Evolving research in entrepreneurship and family business: Recognizing family as the oxygen that feeds the fire of entrepreneurship', *Journal of Business Venturing*, 18 (5): 559–66.

Rogoff, E. G., Lee, M.-S. and Suh, D.-C. (2004) '"Who done it?": Attributions by entrepreneurs and experts of the factors that cause and impede small business success', *Journal of Small Business Management*, 42 (4): 364–76.

Romanelli, E. (1989) 'Environments and strategies of organisation start-up: Effects on early survival', *Administrative Science Quarterly*, 34: 369–87.

Romer, P. M. (1986) 'Increasing returns and long-run growth', *Journal of Political Economy*, 94 (5): 1002–37.

Romer, P. M. (1990) 'Endogenous technological change', *Journal of Political Economy*, 98 (5): 71–102.

Romer, P. M. (2007) 'Economic growth', in D. Henderson (ed.), *The Concise Encyclopedia of Economics*. Indianapolis, IN: Liberty Fund.

Rønning, L. and Kolvereid, L. (2006) 'Income diversification in Norwegian farm households: Reassessing pluriactivity', *International Small Business Journal*, 24 (4): 405–20.

Rønning, L., Ljunggren, E. and Wiklund, J. (2010) 'The community entrepreneur as a facilitator of local economic development', in C. Karlsson, B. Johansson and R. R. Stough (eds), *Entrepreneurship and Development: Local processes and global patterns*. Cheltenham: Edward Elgar.

Ronstadt, R. (1988) 'The corridor principle', *Journal of Business Venturing*, 3 (1): 31–40.

Roomi, M. (2009) 'Impact of social capital development and use in the growth process of women-owned firms', *Journal of Enterprising Culture*, 17 (4): 473–95.

Rosa, P. (1998) 'Entrepreneurial processes of business cluster formation and growth by "habitual" entrepreneurs', *Entrepreneurship Theory and Practice*, 22 (4): 43–61.

Rosa, P. and Hamilton, D. (1994) 'Gender and ownership in UK small firms', *Entrepreneurship Theory and Practice*, 18 (3): 11–25.

Rosa, P., Carter, S. and Hamilton, D. (1996) 'Gender as a determinant of small business performance: Insights from a British study', *Small Business Economics*, 8 (6): 463–78.

Rose, M. B. (2000) *Firms, Networks and Business Values: The British and American cotton industries since 1750*. Cambridge: Cambridge University Press.

Rosenkopf, L. and Nerkar, A. (2001) 'Beyond local search: Boundary-spanning, exploration, and impact in the optical disk industry', *Strategic Management Journal*, 22: 287–306.

Ross, G. C. (1977) 'The determination of financial structure: The incentive signalling approach', *The Bell Journal of Economics and Management Science*, 8 (1): 23–40.

Ross, S. M. (1970) *Applied Probability Models with Optimization Applications*. San Francisco, CA: Holden-Day.

Rothwell, R. (1991) 'External networking and innovation in small and medium-sized manufacturing firms in Europe', *Technovation*, 11 (2): 93–111.

Rothwell, R. and Dodgson, M. (1991) 'External linkages and innovation in small and medium-sized enterprises', *R&D Management*, 21 (2): 125–37.

Rothwell, R. and Zegveld, W. (1982) *Innovation and the Small and Medium-sized Firm*, Boston, MA: Kluwer Nijhoff Publishing.

Rotter, J. B. (1966) 'Generalized expectancies for internal versus external control of reinforcement', *Psychological Monographs: General and Applied*, 80 (1): 1–28.

Rouse, J. and Kitching, J. (2006) 'Do enterprise programmes leave women holding the baby?', *Environment and Planning C: Government and Policy*, 24 (1): 5–19.

Ruda W. (1999) 'Innovative high growth start-ups in Germany: The neuer markt as a possibility for IPOs'. Paper presented at the Thirteenth Research into Entrepreneurship Conference, London, November.

Rumelt, R. P. (1991) 'How much does industry matter?', *Strategic Management Journal*, 12 (3): 167–85.

Salamon, L. and Anheier, H. (1997) 'The civil society sector', *Society*, 34: 60–5.

Salomo, S., Brinckmann, J. and Talke, K. (2008) 'Functional management competence and growth of young technology-based firms', *Creativity and Innovation Management*, 17: 186–203.

Samson, K. J. and Gurdon, M. A. (1990) 'Entrepreneurial scientists: Organisational performance in scientist started high technology firms'. Paper presented at the Tenth Annual Frontiers of Entrepreneurship Research Conference, Babson Centre for Entrepreneurial Studies, Wellesley, MA.

Samuelsson, M. and Davidsson, P. (2009) 'Does venture opportunity variation matter?: Investigating systematic process differences between innovative and imitative new ventures', *Small Business Economics*, 33 (2): 229–55.

Sandberg, W. and Hofer, C. (1987) 'Improving new venture performance: The role of strategy, industry structure, and the entrepreneur', *Journal of Business Venturing*, 2: 5–28.

Sandford, C. (ed.) (1995) *Tax Compliance Costs: Measurement and policy*. Trowbridge: Fiscal Publications.

Sarason, Y., Dean, T. and Dillard, J. F. (2006) 'Entrepreneurship as the nexus of individual and opportunity: A structuration view', *Journal of Business Venturing*, 21: 286–305.

Sarasvathy, S. (2001) 'Causation and effectuation: Toward a theoretical shift from economic inevitability to entrepreneurial contingency', *Academy of Management Review*, 26 (2): 243–63.

Sarasvathy, S. (2008) *Effectuation: Elements of entrepreneurial expertise*. Cheltenham and Northampton, MA: Edward Elgar.

Sarasvathy, S. and Venkataraman, S. (2011) 'Entrepreneurship as method: Open questions for an entrepreneurial future', *Entrepreneurship Theory and Practice*, 35: 113–35.

Sarasvathy, S., Dew, N., Velamuri, R. and Venkataraman, S. (2002) 'A testable typology of entrepreneurial opportunity: Extensions of Shane and Venkataraman (2000)', *Academy of Management Review*, 26 (2): 243–88.

Sarasvathy, S., Dew, N., Velamuri, R. and Venkataraman, S. (2003), 'Three views of entrepreneurial opportunity', in Z. J. Acs and D. B. Audretsch (eds), *Handbook of Entrepreneurship Research*. Dordrecht, NL: Kluwer. pp. 141–60.

Sassen, S. (1991) *The Global City: New York, London, Tokyo*. Princeton, NJ: Princeton University Press.

Sassen, S. (1997) *Globalisation and its Discontents: Collected essays*. New York: New Press.

Sautet, F. and Kirzner, I. (2006) *The Nature and Role of Entrepreneurship in Markets: Implications for policy*. Mercatus Policy Series Policy Primer No. 4. Arlington, VA: George Mason University.

Saxenian, A. (1985) 'Silicon Valley and Route 128: Regional prototypes or historic exceptions?', in M. Castels (ed.), *High Technology, Space and Society*. Beverly Hills, CA: Sage.

Saxenian, A. (1990) 'Regional networks and the resurgence of Silicon Valley', *Californian Management Review*, 33 (1): 89–112.

Saxenian, A. (1996) *Regional Advantage: Culture and competition in Silicon Valley and Route 128*. Cambridge, MA: Harvard University Press.

Saxenian, A. (2005) 'The age of the agile', in S. Passow and M. Runnbeck (eds), *What's Next?: Strategic views on foreign direct investment*. Jönköping, Sweden: ISA and UNCTAD.

Say, J.-B. (Richter, J., trans.) (1821) *A Catechism of Political Economy*. London: Sherwood, Neely and Jones.

Say, J.-B. (Prinsep, C. R. and Biddle, C. C., trans.) (1880) *A Treatise on Political Economy*. Philadelphia, PA: Claxton, Remsen and Haffelfinger.

SBRC, Kingston University (2008) 'Growth challenges for small and medium-sized enterprises: A UK–US comparative study'. Report for HM Treasury and BERR, URN 09/683, December. Small Business Research Centre, Kingston University, Kingston upon Thames, Surrey and Babson College, Wellesley, MA.

Scarman, Lord (1981) 'The Brixton Disorders, 10–12 April 1981'. Cmnd 8427. London: HMSO.

Scase, R. and Goffee, R. (1980) *The Real World of the Small Business Owner*. London: Croom Helm.

Scheré, J. (1982) 'Tolerance of ambiguity as a discriminating variable between entrepreneurs and managers', *Proceedings of the Academy of Management*, 42: 404–8.

Scherer, F. M. (1980) *Industrial Market Structure and Economic Performance*. Chicago, IL: Rand McNally.

Scherer, R. F., Brodzinski, J. D. and Wiebe, F. (1991) 'Examining the relationship between personality and entrepreneurial career preference', *Entrepreneurship and Regional Development*, 3 (2): 195–206.

Schrage, H. (1965) 'The R&D entrepreneur: Profile of success', *Harvard Business Review*, 43 (6): 56–69.

Schreier, J. (1973) 'The female entrepreneur: A pilot study'. Milwaukee, WI: Center for Venture Management.

Schumpeter, J. A. (1934) *The Theory of Economic Development*. Cambridge, MA: Harvard University Press.

Schumpeter, J. A. (1942) *Capitalism, Socialism and Democracy*. London: Routledge.

Schumpeter, J. A. (1947) 'The creative responses in economic history', *The Journal of Economic History*, 7 (2, Nov.): 149–159.

Schumpeter, J. A. (1950) *Capitalism, Socialism and Democracy* (3rd edn). New York: Harper Torchbooks.

Schumpeter, J. A. (1963) *The Theory of Economic Development*. Oxford: Oxford University Press.

Schumpeter, J. A. (1971) 'The fundamental phenomenon of economic development', in P. Kilby (ed.), *Entrepreneurship and Economic Development*. New York: Free Press. pp. 43–70.

Schutgens, V. and Wever, E. (2000) 'Determinants of new firm success', *Papers in Regional Science*, 79: 135–59.

Schwartz, B., Teach, R. D. and Birch, N. J. (2005) 'A longitudinal study of entrepreneurial firms' opportunity recognition and product development management strategies: Implications by firm type', *International Journal of Entrepreneurial Behavior & Research*, 11 (4): 315–29.

Schwartz, E. B. (1976) 'Entrepreneurship: A new female frontier', *Journal of Contemporary Business*, winter: 47–76.

Schwartz, R. G. and Teach, R. D. (2000) 'Research note: Entrepreneurship research: An empirical perspective', *Entrepreneurship Theory and Practice*, 24 (3): 77–81.

Schweitzer, M. E. and Shane, S. A. (2010) 'The effect of falling home prices on business borrowing'. Federal Reserve Bank of Cleveland, 20 December.

Schwenk, C. R. and Shrader, C. B. (1993) 'Effects of formal strategic planning on financial performance in small firms: A meta-analysis', *Entrepreneurship Theory and Practice*, 17 (3): 53–65.

Schwer, R. K. and Yucelt, U. (1984) 'A study of risk-taking propensies among small business entrepreneurs and managers: An empirical evaluation', *American Journal of Small Business*, 8 (3): 31–40.

Scott, A. (1995) 'The geographic foundations of industrial performance', *Competition and Change*, 1 (1): 51–66.

Scott, A. and Storper, M. (2003) 'Regions, globalization, development', *Regional Studies*, 37 (6–7): 549–78.

Scott, J. (1991) *Social Network Analysis: A handbook*. London: Sage.

Scott, M. and Bruce, R. (1987) 'Five stages of growth in small businesses', *Long Range Planning*, 20 (3): 45–52.

Scott, M. and Rosa, P. (1996) 'Has firm-level analysis reached its limits?', *International Small Business Journal*, 14: 81–9.

Scott, M. and Rosa, P. (1997) 'New businesses from old: The role of portfolio entrepreneurs in the start-up and growth of small firms', in M. Ram, D. Deakins and D. Smallbone (eds), *Small Firms: Enterprising futures*. London: Paul Chapman. pp. 33–46.

Scott, T. (1998) 'Two men and a bottle', Inc., 15 May. Available online at: www.inc.com/magazine/19980515/1125.html

Seabright, P. (2004) *The Company of Strangers: A natural history of economic life*. Princeton, NJ: Princeton University Press.

Seelos, C. and Mair, J. (2005) 'Social entrepreneurship: Creating new business models to serve the poor', *Business Horizons*, 48: 241–6.

Seelos, C., Mair, J., Battilana, J., Dacin, M. T. (2010) 'The embeddedness of social entrepreneurship: Understanding variation across geographic communities'. Working Paper WP 858, May, IESE Business School, University of Navarra, Barcelona.

Seifert, C. M., Meyer, D. E., Davidson, N., Patalano, A. L. and Yaniv, I. (1995) 'Demystification of cognitive insight: Opportunistic assimilation and the prepared-mind perspective', in R. J. Stemberg and J. E. Davidson (eds), *The Nature of Insight*. Cambridge, MA: MIT Press. pp. 65–124.

Selsky, J. W. and Smith, A. E. (1994) 'Community entrepreneurship: A framework for social change leadership', *Leadership Quarterly*, 5 (3/4): 277–95.

Sepulveda, L., Syrett, S. and Lyon, F. (2011) 'Population superdiversity and new migrant enterprise: The case of London', *Entrepreneurship & Regional Development*, 23 (7–8): 469–97.

Seringhaus, F. H. R. and Rosson, P. J. (1991) 'Export promotion and public organizations: The state of the art', in F. H. R. Seringhaus and P. J. Rosson (eds), *Export Development and Promotion: The role of public organizations*. Boston, MA: Kluwer. pp. 3–18.

SERT (2008) 'Quarterly survey of small business in Britain'. Small Enterprise Research Team, Milton Keynes, 24 January.

Sexton, D. L. and Bowman, N. (1985) 'The entrepreneur: A capable executive and more', *Journal of Business Venturing*, 1 (1): 129–40.

Sexton, D. L. and Bowman-Upton, N. (1990) 'Female and male entrepreneurs: Psychological characteristics and their role in gender discrimination', *Journal of Business Venturing*, 5 (1): 29–36.

Shackle, G. L. S. (1955) *Uncertainty in Economics and Other Reflections*. Cambridge: Cambridge University Press.

Shane, S. (2000) 'Prior knowledge and the discovery of entrepreneurial opportunities', *Organization Science*, 11 (4): 448–69.

Shane, S. (2003) *A General Theory of Entrepreneurship: The individual–opportunity nexus*. Cheltenham and Northampton, MA: Edward Elgar.

Shane, S. and Cable, D. (2002) 'Network ties, reputation, and the financing of new ventures', *Management Science*, 48 (3): 364–81.

Shane, S. and Eckhardt, J. (2003) 'The individual–opportunity nexus', in Z. J. Acs and D. B. Audretsch (eds) *Handbook of Entrepreneurship Research*. Dordrecht, NL: Kluwer. pp. 161–94.

Shane, S. and Venkataraman, S. (2000) 'The promise of entrepreneurship as a field of research', *Academy of Management Review*, 25 (1): 217–26.

Shane, S. and Venkataraman, S. (2001) 'Entrepreneurship as a field of research: A response to Zahra and Dess, Singh and Erikson', *Academy of Management Review*, 26: 13–18.

Shane, S., Locke, E. and Collins, C. (2003) 'Entrepreneurial motivation', *Human Resource Management Review*, 13: 257–79.

Shane, S., Nicolaou, N., Cherkas, L. and Spector, T. D. (2010) 'Do openness to experience and recognizing opportunities have the same genetic source?', *Human Resource Management*, 49 (2): 291–303.

Shapero, A. (1975) 'The displaced, uncomfortable entrepreneur', *Psychology Today*, November: 83–8.

Sharir, M. and Lerner, M. (2006) 'Gauging the success of social ventures initiated by individual social entrepreneurs', *Journal of World Business*, 41 (1): 6–20.

Sharma, D. (1993) 'Introduction: Industrial networks in marketing', in S. T. Cavusgil and D. Sharma (eds), *Advances in International Marketing* (vol. 5). Greenwich: JAI. pp. 1–9.

Sharma, D. and Johanson, J. (1987) 'Technical consultancy in internationalization', *International Marketing Review*, 4 (4): 20–9.

Sharma, P. (2004) 'An overview of the field of family business studies: Current status and directions for the future', *Family Business Review*, 17 (1): 1–36.

Sharma, P. and Chrisman, J. (1999) 'Toward a reconciliation of the definitional issues in the field of corporate entrepreneurship', *Entrepreneurship: Theory and Practice*, 23 (3): 11–27.

Shaver, K. G. and Scott, L. R. (1991) 'Person, process, choice: The psychology of new venture creation', *Entrepreneurship Theory and Practice*, 16 (2): 23–45.

Shaw, E. (1998) 'Social networks: Their impact on the innovative behaviour of small service firms', *International Journal of Innovation Management*, 2 (2): 201–22.

Shaw, E. (2006) 'Small firm networking: An insight into contents and motivating factors', *International Small Business Journal*, 24 (1): 5–29.

Shaw, E. and Carter, S. (2007) 'Social entrepreneurship: Theoretical antecedents and empirical analysis of entrepreneurial processes and outcomes', *Journal of Small Business and Enterprise Development*, 14: 418–34.

Shaw, E., Lam, W. and Carter, S. (2008) 'The role of entrepreneurial capital in building service reputation', *The Service Industries Journal*, 28 (7): 883–98.

Shepherd, D. A. (1999) 'Venture capitalists' assessment of new venture survival', *Management Science*, 45 (5): 621–32.

Shepherd, D. A. and Wiklund, J. (2009) 'Are we comparing apples with apples or apples with oranges?: Appropriateness of knowledge accumulation across growth studies', *Entrepreneurship Theory and Practice*, 33, 1: 105–23.

Shepherd, D. A. and Cardon, M. S. (2009) 'Negative emotional reactions to project failure and the self-compassion to learn from the experience', *Journal of Management Studies*, 46 (6): 923–49.

Shepherd, D. A. and DeTienne, D. (2005) 'Prior knowledge, potential financial reward, and opportunity identification', *Entrepreneurhip Theory and Practice*, 29 (1): 91–112.

Shepherd, D. A. and Patzelt, H. (2011) 'The new field of sustainable entrepreneurship: Studying entrepreneurial action linking "what is to be sustained" with "what is to be developed"', *Entrepreneurship Theory and Practice*, 35: 137–63.

Shepherd, D. A., Douglas, E. J. and Shanley, M. (2001) 'New venture survival: Ignorance, external shocks, and risk reduction strategies', *Journal of Business Venturing*, 15 (5–6): 393–410.

Shepherd, D. A., McMullen, J. S. and Jennings, P. D. (2007) 'The formation of opportunity beliefs: Overcoming ignorance and reducing doubt', *Strategic Entrepreneurship Journal*, 1: 75–95.

Shepherd, D. A., Wiklund, J. and Haynie, J. M. (2009) 'Moving forward: Balancing the financial and emotional costs of business failure', *Journal of Business Venturing*, 24 (2): 134–48.

Shionoya, Y. (1992) 'Taking Schumpeter's methodology seriously', in F. M. Scherer and M. Pearlman (eds), *Entrepreneurship and Technological Innovation and Economic Growth*. Ann Arbor, MI: The University of Michigan Press, Michigan, pp. 343–62.

Shionoya, Y. (1997) 'Schumpeter and the idea of social science: A metatheoretical study', Cambridge: Cambridge University Press.

Short, J. C., Moss, T. W. and Lumpkin, G. T. (2009) 'Research in social entrepreneurship: Past contributions and future opportunities', *Strategic Entrepreneurship Journal*, 3: 161–94.

Shrader, R. and Siegel, D. (2007) 'Assessing the relationship between human capital and firm performance: Evidence from technology-based new ventures', *Entrepreneurship Theory and Practice*, 31 (6): 893–908.

Siegel, D. S. and Phan, P. (2005) 'Analyzing the effectiveness of university technology transfer: Implications for entrepreneurship education', in G. Liebcap (ed.), *Advances in the Study of Entrepreneurship, Innovation, and Economic Growth* (vol. 16). Amsterdam: Elsevier Science/ JAI Press. pp. 1–38.

Simon, M., Houghton, S. M. and Aquino, K. (2000) 'Cognitive biases, risk perception, and venture formation: How individuals decide to start companies', *Journal of Business Venturing*, 15 (2): 113–34.

Simonton, D. K. (1986) 'Biographical typicality, eminence, and achievement styles', *Journal of Creative Behavior*, 20: 14–22.

Sine, W. D. and David, R. J. (2003) 'Environmental jolts, institutional change, and the creation of entrepreneurial opportunity in the US electric power industry', *Research Policy*, 32: 185–207.

Singh, R. P. (2000) *Entrepreneurial Opportunity Recognition Through Social Networks*. New York: Garland.

Singh, R. P. (2001) 'A comment on developing the field of entrepreneurship through the study of opportunity recognition and exploitation', *Academy of Management Review*, 26 (1): 10–12.

Sjöberg, L. (1993) 'Life-styles and risk perception'. RHIZIKON: Risk Research Report 14, Centre for Risk Research, Stockholm School of Economics.

Slotte-Kock, S. and Coviello, N. (2009) 'Entrepreneurship research on network processes: A review and ways forward', *Entrepreneurship, Theory and Practice*, January: 31–57.

Small Business Council (2004a) 'Small Business Council: Annual report 2004'. London: Small Business Council.

Small Business Council (2004b) 'Evaluation of government employment regulations and their impact on small business'. London: Small Business Council.

Small Business Service (2002a) 'Augmenting productivity in SMEs'. October. London: DTI.

Small Business Service (2002b) 'Small business and government'. London: Small Business Service.

Small Business Service (2003) 'A strategic framework for women's enterprise'. London: DTI.

Small Business Service (2004a) 'A government action plan for small business: Making the UK the best place in the world to start up and grow a business: The evidence case'. London: Small Business Service.

Small Business Service (2004b) 'Household survey of entrepreneurship 2003'. London: Small Business Service.

Smallbone, D. (1990) 'Success and failure in new businesses', *International Small Business Journal*, 8 (2): 34–47.

Smallbone, D. (1997) 'Selective targeting in SME policy: Criteria and implementation issues', in D. Deakins, P. Jennings, C. Mason (eds), *Small Firms: Entrepreneurship in the Nineties*. London: Paul Chapman. pp. 126–40.

Smallbone, D. and Massey, C. (2010) 'Targeting for growth: A critical examination'. Paper presented at the 33rd ISBE National Research and Policy Conference, London, November.

Smallbone, D. and North, D. (1996) 'Survival, growth and age of SMEs: Some implications for regional development', in M. Danson (eds), *Small Firm Formation and Regional Economic Development*. London: Routledge. pp. 36–64.

Smallbone, D. and Welter, F. (2001) 'The distinctiveness of entrepreneurship in transition economies', *Small Business Economics*, 16 (4): 249–62.

Smallbone, D. and Welter, F. (2009) 'Entrepreneurial behaviour in transition environments', in M.-À. Galindo, J. Guzman and D. Ribeiro (eds), *Entrepreneurship and Business in Regional Economics*. New York: Springer. pp. 211–28.

Smallbone, D., Baldock, R. and Burgess, S. (2002) 'Targeted support for high growth start-ups: Some policy issues', *Environment and Planning C: Government and Policy*, 20 (2): 195–209.

Smallbone, D., Berlotti, M. and Ekanem, I. (2005) 'Diversification in ethnic minority business: The case of Asians in London's creative industries', *Journal of Small Business and Enterprise Development*, 12 (1): 41–55.

Smallbone, D. J., Leigh, R. and North, D. (1995) 'The characteristics and strategies of high growth firms', *International Journal of Entrepreneurial Behaviour and Research*, 1 (3): 44–62.

Smallbone, D., North, D. and Kalantaridis, C. (1999) 'Adapting to peripherality: A study of small manufacturing firms in Northern England', *Entrepreneurship and Regional Development*, 11 (2): 109–28.

Smallbone, D., North, D. and Leigh, R. (1993) 'The growth and survival of mature manufacturing SMEs in the 1980s: An urban–rural comparison', in J. Curran and D. Storey and J. Canon (eds), *Small Firms in Urban and Rural Locations*. London: Routledge. pp. 79–131.

Smallbone, D., Piasecki, B., Venesaar, U., Todorov, K. and Labrianidis, L. (1999) 'Internationalisation and SME development in transition economies: An international comparison', *Journal for Small Business and Enterprise Development*, 5 (4): 363–75.

Smallbone, D., Ram, M., Deakins, D. and Baldock, R. (2003) 'Access to finance by ethnic minority businesses in the UK,' *International Small Business Journal*, 21 (3): 291–314.

Smallbone, D., Welter, F., Voytovich, A. and Egorov, I. (2010) 'Government and entrepreneurship in transition economies: The case of small firms in business services in Ukraine', *Service Industries Journal*, 30 (5): 655–70.

Smith, A. (Cannon, E. ed.) (1904) *The Wealth of Nations* (5th edn). London: Methuen & Co.

Smith, B. R., Knapp, J., Barr, T. F., Stevens, C. E. and Cannatelli, B. L. (2010) 'Social enterprises and the timing of conception: Organizational identity tension, management, and marketing', *Journal of Nonprofit and Public Sector Marketing*, 22: 108–34.

Smith, D. A. and Lohrke, F. T. (2008) 'Entrepreneurial network development: Trusting in the process', *Journal of Business Research*, 61: 315–22.

Smith, J. (1999) 'The behaviour and performance of young micro firms: Evidence from businesses in Scotland', *Small Business Economics*, 13: 185–200.

Smith, J. B., Mitchell, J. R. and Mitchell, R. K. (2009) 'Entrepreneurial scripts and the new transaction commitment mindset: Extending the expert information processing theory approach to entrepreneurial cognition research', *Entrepreneurship Theory and Practice*, 33 (4): 815–44.

Smith, M. J. (2010) 'From Big Government to Big Society: Changing the State–society balance', *Parliamentary Affairs*, 63: 818–33.

Smith, N. R. (1967) 'The entrepreneur and his firm: The relationship between type of man and type of company'. Occasional paper, Bureau of Business and Economic Research, Division of Research, Graduate School of Business Administration, Michigan State University, East Lansing, MI.

Smith-Hunter, A., Kapp, J. and Yonkers, V. (2003) 'A psychological model of entrepreneurial behaviour', *Journal of the Academy of Business and Economics*, 2 (2): 180–92.

Snyder, M. and Cantor, N. (1998) 'Understanding personality and social behavior: A functionalist strategy', in D. T. Gilbert, S. T. Fiske and G. Lindzey (eds), *The Handbook of Social Psychology* (vol. 1). Boston, MA: McGraw-Hill. pp. 635–79.

Soar, S. (1991) 'Business development strategies'. Paper presented at the TECS and Ethnic Minorities Conference, Warwick University, Corentry, 22–23 March. Home Office Ethnic Minority Business Initiative.

Sobel, R. S. (2008) 'Testing Baumol: Institutional quality and the productivity of entrepreneurship', *Journal of Business Venturing*, 23 (6): 641–55.

Sobel, R. S., Clark, J. R. and Lee, D. R. (2007) 'Freedom, barriers to entry, entrepreneurship, and economic progress', *The Review of Austrian Economics*, 20 (4): 221–36.

Solemn, O. and Stiener, M. (1989) 'Factors for success in small manufacturing firms – and with special emphasis on growing firms'. Paper presented at the Conference on Small and Medium-sized Enterprises and the Challenges of 1992, Mikkeli, Finland, October.

Solomon, G. T. and Fernald, L. W. (1988) 'Value profiles of male and female entrepreneurs', *International Small Business Journal*, 6 (3): 24–33.

Solow, R. (1956) 'A contribution to the theory of economic growth', *Quarterly Journal of Economics*, 70 (1): 65–94.

Soni, S., Tricker, M. and Ward, R. (1987) 'Ethnic minority business in Leicester'. Birmingham: Aston University.

Spence, J. T. (1985) 'Achievement American style: The rewards and costs of individualism', *American Psychologist*, 40 (12): 1285–95.

Srinavasan, S. (1992) 'The class position of the Asian petite bourgeoisie', *New Community*, 19 (1): 61–74.

Srinivasan, S. (1995) *The South Asian Petty Bourgeosie in Britain: An Oxford case study.* Aldershot: Avebury.

Stacey, R. D. (1990) 'Dynamic strategic management', in M. Armstrong (ed.), *The New Manager's Handbook.* London: Kogan Page. pp. 299–333.

Stacey, R. D. (1996) *Strategic Management & Organisational Dynamics.* London: Pitman.

Stanga, K. G. and Tiller, M. G. (1983) 'Needs of loan officers from large versus small companies', *Accounting and Business Research*, winter: 63–70.

Stanworth, J. and Curran, J. (1976) 'Growth and the small firm: An alternative view', *Journal of Management Studies*, 13: 95–110.

Staring, R. (2000) 'International migration, undocumented immigration and immigrant entrepreneurship', in J. Rath (ed.), *Immigrant Businesses: The economic, political and social environment.* Houndmills, Basingstoke: Macmillan.

Starr, J., and Bygrave, W. (1991) 'The assets and liabilities of prior start-up experience: An exploratory study of multiple venture entrepreneurs', in *Frontiers of Entrepreneurship Research 1991.* Wellesley, MA: Babson College.

Steil, B., Victor, D. G. and Nelson, R. R. (eds) (2001) *Technological Innovation and Economic Performance.* Princeton, NJ: Princeton University Press.

Steiner, M. P. and Solem, O. (1988) 'Factors for success in small manufacturing firms', *Journal of Small Business Management*, 36: 51–56.

Steinmetz, L. L. (1969) 'Critical stages of small business growth', *Business Horizons*, 12 (1): 29–34.

Stephan, U. and Uhlaner, L. (2010) 'Performance-based versus socially supportive culture: A cross-national study of descriptive norms and entrepreneurship', *Journal of International Business Studies*, 41: 1347–64.

Sternberg, R. J. (1997) *Successful Intelligence: How practical and creative intelligence determine success in life.* New York: Plume.

Sternberg, R. J. (2004) 'Successful intelligence as a basis for entrepreneurship', *Journal of Business Venturing*, 19 (2): 189–201.

Stevenson, H. and Gumpert, D. (1985) 'The heart of entrepreneurship', *Harvard Business Review*, 63 (2): 85–94.

Stevenson, H. H. and Jarillo, J. C. (1990) 'A paradigm of entrepreneurship: Entrepreneurial management', *Strategic Management Journal*, 11 (special issue, summer): 17–27.

Stevenson, L. (1983) 'An investigation into the entrepreneurial experience of women'. Paper presented to the ASAC Conference, University of British Columbia, Vancouver.

Stewart Jr, W. H. and Roth, P. L. (2001) 'Risk propensity differences between entrepreneurs and managers: A meta-analytic review', *Journal of Applied Psychology*, 86 (1): 145–153.

Steyaert, C. and J. Katz (2004) 'Reclaiming the space of entrepreneurship in society: Geographical, discursive and social, dimensions', *Entrepreneurship and Regional Development*, 16 (3): 179–96.

Stimpson, D. V., Robinson, P. B., Waranusuntikule, S. and Zheng, R. (1990) 'Attitudinal characteristics of entrepreneurs and non-entrepreneurs in the United States, Korea, Thailand, and the People's Republic of China', *Entrepreneurship and Regional Development*, 2 (1): 49–56.

Stokes, D. (1995) *Small Business Management: An active learning approach* (2nd edn). London: DP Publications.

Stokes, D. (2000) 'Putting entrepreneurship into marketing: The processes of entrepreneurial marketing', *Journal of Research in Marketing and Entrepreneurship*, 2 (1): 1–16, 51–2.

Stokes, D. and Blackburn, R. (2002) 'Learning the hard way: The lessons of owner managers who have closed their businesses', *Journal of Small Business and Enterprise Development*, 9 (1): 17–27.

Stokes, D. and Lomax, W. (2002) 'Taking control of word of mouth marketing: The case of an entrepreneurial hotelier', *Journal of Small Business and Enterprise Development*, 9 (4): 349–57.

Stokes, D. and Wilson, N. (2010) *Small Business Management and Entrepreneurship.* Andover, Hampshire: Cengage Learning EMEA.

Stone, M. and Brush, C. (1996) 'Planning in ambiguous contexts: The dilemma of meeting needs for commitment and demands for legitimacy', *Strategic Management Journal*, 17: 633–52.

Storey, D. J. (1991) 'The birth of new firms: Does unemployment matter?: A review of the evidence', *Small Business Economics*, 3: 167–78.

Storey, D. J. (1994) *Understanding the Small Business Sector.* New York, NY: Routledge.

Storey, D. J. (2003) 'Entrepreneurship, small and medium-sized enterprises and public policies', in

Z. J. Acs and D. B. Audretsch (eds), *Handbook of Entrepreneurship Research: An interdisciplinary survey and introduction*. Dordrecht: Kluwer. pp. 473–511.

Storey, D. J. (2010) 'Optimism and chance: The elephants in the entrepreneurship room'. Paper presented at the 33rd ISBE National Research and Policy Conference, London, November.

Storey, D. J. (2011) 'Optimism and chance: The elephants in the entrepreneurship room', *International Small Business Journal*, 29 (4): 303–21.

Storey, D. J. and Johnson, S. (1987) *Job Generation and Labour Market Change*. Houndmills, Basingstoke: Macmillan.

Storey D. J., Keasey, K., Watson, R. and Wynarczyk, P. (1987) *The Performance of Small Firms: Profits, jobs and failures*. London: Croom Helm.

Storper, M. (1997) *The Regional World: Territorial development in a global economy*. New York: Guilford Press.

Storper, M. and Venables, A. J. (2002) 'Buzz: Face-to-face contact and the urban economy', *Journal of Economic Geography*, 4: 351–70.

Storr, V. H. (2008) 'The market as a social space: On the meaningful extra-economic conversations that can occur in markets', *The Review of Austrian Economics*, 21 (2/3): 135–50.

Stratos Group (1990) *Strategic Orientations of Small European Businesses*. Aldershot: Gower.

Stuart, R. and P. A. Abetti (1988) 'Field study of technical ventures – Part III: The impact of entrepreneurial and management experience on early performance', in *Frontiers of Entrepreneurship Research 1988*. Wellesley, MA: Babson College.

Stuart, T. E., Hoang, H. and Hybels, R. C. (1999) 'Interorganizational endorsements and the performance of entrepreneurial ventures', *Administrative Science Quarterly*, 44: 315–49.

Styles, C. and Ambler, T. (1994) 'Successful export practice: The UK experience', *International Marketing Review*, 11 (6): 24–47.

Styles, C. and Ambler, C. (1997) *First Steps to Export Success*. PAN'AGRA Research Programme, London Business School, Australian Trade Commission and British Overseas Trade Board Secretariat.

Subrahmanya, M. H. B. (2005) 'Technological innovations in Indian small enterprises: dimensions, intensity and implications', *International Journal of Technology Management*, 30 (1/2): 188–204.

Sullivan, D. and Bauerschmidt, A. (1990) 'Incremental internationalization: A test of Johanson and Vahlne's thesis', *Management International Review*, 30 (1): 19–30.

Swedberg, R. (2000) *Entrepreneurship: The social science view*. Oxford: Oxford University Press.

Szarka, J. (1990) 'Networking and small firms', *International Small Business Journal*, 8: 10–22.

Tagiuri, R. and Davis, J. A. (1982) 'Bivalent attributes of the family firm', *Family Business Review*, 9 (2): 199–208.

Tann, J. and Laforet, S. (1998) 'Assessing consultant quality for SMEs: The role of Business Links', *Journal of Small Business and Enterprise Development*, 5 (1): 7–18.

Tapsell, P. and Woods, C. (2010) 'Social entrepreneurship and innovation: Self-organization in an indigenous context', *Entrepreneurship and Regional Development*, 22 (6): 535–55.

Taylor, B., Mathers, J., Atfield, T. and Parry, J. (2011) 'What are the challenges to the Big Society in maintaining lay involvement in health improvement, and how can they be met?', *Journal of Public Health*, 33: 5–10.

Taylor, F. W. (1947) *Scientific Management*. London: Harper & Row.

Taylor, S. and Marlow, S. (2010) 'Engendering entrepreneurship: Why can't a woman be more like a man?'. Paper presented at the American Academy of Management Conference, Montreal, August.

Taylor, S. E. (1998) 'The social being in social psychology', in D. T. Gilbert, S. T. Fiske and G. Lindsey (eds), *The Handbook of Social Psychology* (vol. 1). Boston, MA: McGraw-Hill pp. 58–95.

Teasdale, S. (2010) 'How can social enterprise address disadvantage?: Evidence from an inner city community', *Journal of Nonprofit and Public Sector Marketing*, 22 (2): 89–107.

Teece, D. J., Pisano, G. and Shuen, A. (1997) 'Dynamic capabilities and strategic management', *Strategic Management Journal*, 18 (7): 509–33.

Terziovski, M. (2010) 'Innovation practice and its performance implications in small and medium enterprises (SMEs) in the manufacturing sector: A resource-based view', *Strategic Management Journal*, 31: 892–902.

Tesar, G. and Tarleton, J. S. (1982) 'Comparison of Wisconsin and Virginia small- and medium-sized exporters: Aggressive and passive exporters', in M. R. Czinkota and G. Tesar (eds), *Export Management: An international context*. New York: Praeger. pp. 85–112.

Thomas, L. (2011) 'Managing business growth: The problems with overtrading'. Available online at: http://ezinearticles.com?Managing-Business-Growth---The-Problems-With-Overtrading&id=4491422

Thompson, E. R. (2009) 'Individual entrepreneurial intent: Construct clarification and development of an internationally reliable metric', *Entrepreneurship Theory and Practice*, 33 (3): 669–94.

Thompson, J. L. (2002) 'The world of the social entrepreneur', *International Journal of Public Sector Management*, 15 (2): 412–31.

Thompson, J. L., Lees, A. and Alvy, G. (2000) 'Social entrepreneurship: A new look at the people and the potential', *Management Decision*, 38 (5): 328–38.

Thompson, P., Jones-Evans, D. and Kwong, C. (2009) 'Women and home-based entrepreneurship: Evidence from the United Kingdom', *International Small Business Journal*, 27 (2): 227–37.

Thornton, P. H. and Flynn, K. H. (2005) 'Entrepreneurship, networks, and geographies', in Z. J. Acs and D. B. Audretsch (eds), *Handbook of Entrepreneurship Research* (vol. 1). New York: Springer. pp. 401–33.

Thorpe, R., Holt, R., Macpherson, A. and Pittaway, L. (2005) 'Using knowledge within small and medium-sized firms: A systematic review of the evidence', *International Journal of Management Reviews*, 7: 257–81.

Thurik, A. R., Wennekers, S. and Uhlaner, L. M. (2002) 'Entrepreneurship and economic performance: A macro perspective', *International Journal of Entrepreneurship Education*, 1 (2): 157–79.

Tichy, N., Tushman, N. and Fombrun, C. (1979) 'Social network analysis for organisations', *Academy of Management Review*, 4 (4): 507–19.

Timmons, J. (1994) *New Venture Creation*. Boston, MA: Irwin.

Timmons, J. A., Muzyka, D. F., Stevenson, H. H. and Bygrave, W. D. (1987) 'Opportunity recognition: The core of entrepreneurship', in *Frontiers of Entrepreneurship Research 1987*. Wellesley, MA: Babson College.

Tönnies, F. (C. P. Loomis, trans. and ed.) (1887/1963) *Community and Society [Gemeinschaft und Gesellschaft]*. New York: Harper & Row.

Tötterman, H. and Sten, J. (2005) 'Start-ups: Business incubation and social capital', *International Small Business Journal*, 23 (5): 487–511.

Townsend, D. M., Busenitz, L. W. and Arthurs, J. D. (2010) 'To start or not to start: Outcome and ability expectations in the decision to start a new venture', *Journal of Business Venturing*, 25 (2): 192–202.

Tracey, P., Phillips, N. and Haugh, H. (2005) 'Beyond philanthropy: Community enterprise as a basis for corporate citizenship', *Journal of Business Ethics*, 58 (4): 327–44.

Trettin, L. and F. Welter (2011) 'Challenges for spatially oriented entrepreneurship research', *Entrepreneurship & Regional Development*, 23 (7–8): 575–602.

Trevelyan, R. (2008) 'Optimism, overconfidence and entrepreneurial activity', *Management Decision*, 46 (7): 986–1001.

Tschajanow, W. (1923) *Die Lehre von der bäuerlichen Familienwirtschaft: Versuch einer Theorie der Familienwirtschaft im Landbau [The Theory of Peasant Economy]: Towards a theory of family-farming in the economy*. Berlin: Erstang.

Tsur, Y., Sternberg, M. and Hochman, E. (1990) 'Dynamic modelling of innovation process adoption with risk aversion and learning', *Oxford Economic Papers*, 42 (2): 336–55.

Turnbull, P. W. (1987) 'A challenge to the stages theory of the internationalization process', in P. J. Rosson and S. D. Reid (eds) *Managing Export Entry and Expansion*. New York: Praeger. pp. 18–38.

Turok, I. (2004) 'Cities, regions and competitiveness', *Regional Studies*, 38 (9): 1069–83.

Tuttle, C. A. (1927) 'The function of the entrepreneur', *American Economic Review*, 17: 13–25.

Tybejee, T. T. (1994) 'Internationalization of high tech firms: Initial vs. extended involvement', *Journal of Global Marketing*, 7 (4): 59–81.

Ucbasaran, D., Alsos, G. A., Westhead, P. and Wright, M. (2008a) 'Habitual entrepreneurs', *Foundations and Trends in Entrepreneurship*, 4 (4): 309–449.

Ucbasaran, D., Lockett, A., Wright, M. and Westhead, P. (2003) 'Entrepreneurial founder teams: Factors associated with team member entry and exit', *Entrepreneurship Theory and Practice*, 28 (2): 107–28.

Ucbasaran, D., Westhead, P. and Wright, M. (2001) 'The focus of entrepreneurial research: Contextual and process issues', *Entrepreneurship: Theory and Practice*, 25 (4): 57–80.

Ucbasaran, D., Westhead, P. and Wright, M. (2006a) *Habitual Entrepreneurs*. Cheltenham: Edward Elgar.

Ucbasaran, D., Westhead, P. and Wright, M. (2006b) 'Entrepreneurial entry, exit and re-entry:

513

The extent and nature of opportunity identification'. Max Planck Institute Discussion Paper, No. 0906.

Ucbasaran, D., Westhead, P. and Wright, M. (2008b) 'Opportunity identification and pursuit: Does an entrepreneur's human capital matter?', *Small Business Economics*, 30 (2): 153–73.

Ucbasaran, D., Westhead, P. and Wright, M. (2009) 'The extent and nature of opportunity identification by experienced entrepreneurs', *Journal of Business Venturing*, 24 (2): 99–115.

Ucbasaran, D., Westhead, P., Wright, M. and Flores, M. (2010) 'The nature of entrepreneurial experience, business failure and comparative optimism', *Journal of Business Venturing*, 25 (6): 541–55.

Ucbasaran, D., Wright, M., Westhead, P. and Busenitz, L. W. (2002) 'Using cognitive processes and knowledge structures to distinguish between novice and habitual entrepreneurs'. Unpublished manuscript, University of Nottingham.

Ulijn, J. (2007) *Entrepreneurship, Cooperation and the Firm: The emergence and survival of high-technology ventures in Europe*. Cheltenham: Edward Elgar.

Unger, J. M., Keith, N., Hilling, C., Gielnik, M. M. and Freses, M. (2009) 'Deliberate practice among South African small business owners: Relationships with education, cognitive ability, knowledge and success', *Journal of Occupational and Organisational Psychology*, 82: 21–44.

US Bureau of Labor Statistics (2005) 'Unincorporated self-employed persons in non-agricultural industries by sex, 1976–2002 annual averages'. Current Population Survey. Washington, DC: US Bureau of Labor Statistics.

US Small Business Administration (1996) 'Small business economic indicators: January–December 1995. Washington, DC: US Small Business Administration. Available online at: http://archive.sba.gov/advo/stats/sbei95.pdf

Utsch, A., Rauch, A., Rothfuss, R. and Frese, M. (1999) 'Who becomes a small scale entrepreneur in a post-socialist environment: On the differences between entrepreneurs and managers in East Germany', *Journal of Small Business Management*, 37 (3): 31–42.

Utterback, J. M., Reitberger, G. and Martin, A. (1982) 'Technology and industrial innovation in Sweden', in *Frontiers of Entrepreneurship Research 1982*. Wellesley, MA: Babson College.

Uzzi, B. D. (1996) 'The sources and consequences of embeddedness for the economic performance of organizations: The network effect', *American Sociological Review*, 61: 674–89.

van der Veen, M. and Wakkee, I. A. M. (2004) 'Understanding the entrepreneurial process' in D. S. Watkins (ed.), *Annual Review of Progress in Entrepreneurship Research* (vol. 2). Brussels: European Foundation for Management Development. pp. 114–52.

van der Wees, C. and Romijn, H. (1987) 'Entrepreneurship and small enterprise development for women in developing countries'. Geneva: ILO Management Development Branch.

Varadarajan, P. R. (2003) 'Musings on relevance and rigor of scholarly research in marketing', *Journal of the Academy of Marketing Science*, 31 (4): 368–76.

Varis, M. and Littunen, H. (2010) 'Types of innovation, sources of information and performance in entrepreneurial SMEs', *European Journal of Innovation Management*, 13 (2): 128–54.

Vázquez-Barquero, A. (2007) 'Endogenous development: Analytical and policy issues', in A. J. Scott and G. Garofoli (eds), *Development on the Ground: Clusters, networks and regions in emerging economies*. Abingdon: Routledge. pp. 23–43.

Vega, G. and Kidwell, R. E. (2007) 'Toward a typology of new venture creators: Similarities and contrasts between business and social entrepreneurs', *New England Journal of Entrepreneurship*, 10 (2): 15–28.

Venkataraman, S. (1997) 'The distinctive domain of entrepreneurship research', In J. A. Katz (ed.), *Advances in Entrepreneurship, Firm Emergence, and Growth* (vol. 3). Greenwich, CT: JAI Press. pp. 119–38.

Venkataraman, S. (2002) 'Stakeholder value equilibration and the entrepreneurial process'. *Ethics and Entrepreneurship*, 3: 45–57.

Verheul, I. and Thurik, R. (2000) 'Start-up capital: Differences between male and female entrepreneurs: Does gender matter?' EIM Research Report 9910/E, Erasmus University, Rotterdam.

Verheul, I., Wennekers, S., Audretsch, D. and Thurik, A. R. (2001) 'An eclectic theory of entrepreneurship: Policies, institutions and culture'. Tinbergen Institute Discussion Paper TI 2001–030/3.

Vertovec, S. (2007) 'Superdiversity and its implications', *Ethnic and Racial Studies*, 30 (6): 1024–54.

Vesper, K. (1990) *New Venture Strategies*. Englewood Cliffs, NJ: Prentice Hall.

Vesper, K. H. (1979) 'New venture ideas: Do not overlook the experience factor', *Harvard Business Review*, July–August: 164–70.

Vissak, T., Ibeh, K. I. N. and Paliwoda, S. (2008) 'Internationalising from the European periphery: Triggers, processes, and trajectories', *Journal of Euro Marketing*, 17 (1): 35–48.

Volkmann, C., Wilson, K. E., Mariotti, S., Rabuzzi, D., Vyakarnam, S. and Sepulveda, A. (2009) 'Educating the next wave of entrepreneurs: Unlocking entrepreneurial capabilities to meet the global challenges of the 21st century', World Economic Forum, Geneva.

von Mangoldt, H. (1855) *Die Lehre vom Unternehmergewinn*, [The Theory of Entrepreneurial Profit]. Leipsig: Drud und Verlag von B. G. Teubner.

Wainer, H. A. and Rubin, I. M. (1969) 'Motivation of research and development entrepreneurs: Determinants of company success', *Journal of Applied Psychology*, 53 (3): 178–84.

Waldinger, R. (1995) 'The other side of "embeddedness": A case of the interplay of economy and ethnicity', *Ethnic and Racial Studies*, 18 (3): 555–80.

Waldinger, R., Aldrich, H. and Ward, R. (eds) (1990a) *Ethnic Entrepreneurs*. London: Sage.

Waldinger, R. and Perlmann, J. (1998) 'Second generations: Past, present, future', *Journal of Ethnic and Migration Studies*, 24 (1): 5–24.

Waldinger, R., McEvoy, D. and Aldrich, H. (1990b) 'Spatial dimensions of opportunity structures', in R. Waldinger, H. Aldrich and R. Ward (eds), *Ethnic Entrepreneurs*. London: Sage. pp. 106–30.

Walker, D. (2006) 'Are we backing a Trojan horse?', *The Guardian*, 12 July.

Wallas, G. (1926) *The Art of Thought*. New York: Harcourt-Brace.

Walsh, J. and Dewar, R. (1987) 'Formalisation and the organisational life cycle', *Journal of Management Studies*, 24: 215–231.

Walsh, J. P. (1995) 'Managerial and organizational cognition: Notes from a trip down memory lane', *Organization Science*, 6 (3): 280–321.

Ward, R. (1991) 'Economic development and ethnic business', in J. Curran and R. A. Blackburn (eds), *Paths of Enterprise: The future of the small business*. London: Routledge. pp. 51–67.

Ward, R. and Jenkins, R. (eds) (1984) *Ethnic Communities in Business*. Cambridge: Cambridge University Press.

Ward, T. B. (2004) 'Cognition, creativity, and entrepreneurship', *Journal of Business Venturing*, 19 (2): 173–88.

Warren, L. and Hutchison, W. (2000) 'Success factors for high technology SMEs: A case study from Australia', *Journal of Small Business Management*, 38 (3): 86–91.

Waters, N. (1985) 'The role of local government authorities in economic and employment development'. ILE Notebook. Paris: OECD.

Watkins, D. S. (1973) 'Technical entrepreneurship: a cis-Atlantic view', *R&D Management*, 3 (2): 65–9.

Watkins, J. and Watkins, D. (1984) 'The female entrepreneur: Background and determinants of business choice: some British data', *International Small Business Journal*, 2 (4): 21–31.

Watson, J. (2003) 'Failure rates for female-controlled businesses: Are they any different?', *Journal of Small Business Management*, 41 (3): 262–77.

Watson, J. and Newby, R. (2005) 'Biological sex, stereotypical sex-roles, and SME owner characteristics', *International Journal of Entrepreneurial Behaviour and Research*, 11 (2): pp. 129–43.

Watson, J. and Robinson, S. (2003) 'Adjusting for risk in comparing the performance of male- and female-controlled SMEs', *Journal of Business Venturing*, 18 (6): 773–88.

Webster, F. E. (1992) 'The changing role of marketing in the corporation', *Journal of Marketing*, 56 (40): 1–17.

Weerawardena, J. and Mort, G. S. (2006) 'Investigating social entrepreneurship: A multidimensional model', *Journal of World Business*, 41: 21–35.

Weick, K. E. (1979) *The Social Psychology of Organizing* (2nd edn). Reading, MA: Addison-Wesley.

Weick, K. E. (1995) *Sensemaking in Organizations*. Thousand Oaks, CA: Sage.

Weiner, B. (1985) 'An attributional theory of achievement motivation and emotion', *Psychological Review*, 92 (4): 548–73.

Weiner, B. (1992) *Human Motivation: Metaphors, theories, and research*. Newbury Park, CA: Sage.

Weisberg, R. W. (1999) 'Creativity and knowledge: A challenge to theories', in R. J. Sternberg (ed.), *Handbook of Creativity*. Cambridge: Cambridge University Press. pp. 226–50.

Welch, L. S. and Luostarinen, R. (1988) 'Internationalization: Evolution of a concept', *Journal of General Management*, 14 (2): 34–55.

Welch, L. S., Benito, G., Petersen, B. (2007) *Foreign Operation Methods: Theory, analysis, strategy*. Cheltenham: Edward Elgar.

Welsh, J. A. and White, J. F. (1984) 'A small business is not a little big business', in D. E. Gumpert (ed.), *Growing Concerns: Building and managing the smaller business*. New York: Wiley. pp. 149–67.

Welter, F. (2011) 'Contextualising entrepreneurship: Challenges and ways forward', *Entrepreneurship Theory and Practice*, 35 (1): 165–84.

Welter, F. and Smallbone D. (2008) 'Women's entrepreneurship from an institutional perspective: The case of Uzbekistan', *International Entrepreneurship and Management Journal*, 4: 505–20.

Welter, F. and Smallbone, D. (2009) 'The emergence of entrepreneurial potential in transition environments: A challenge for entrepreneurship theory or a developmental perspective?', in D. Smallbone, H. Landström and D. Jones-Evans (eds), *Entrepreneurship and Growth in Local, Regional and National Economies: Frontiers in European entrepreneurship research*. Cheltenham and Northampton, MA: Edward Elgar. pp. 339–53.

Welter, F. and Smallbone, D. (2011a) 'The embeddedness of women's entrepreneurship in a transition context', in C. G. Brush, A. de Bruin, E. Gatewood and C. Henry (eds), *Women Entrepreneurs and the Global Environment for Growth: A research perspective*. Cheltenham: Edward Elgar.

Welter, F. and Smallbone, D. (2011b) 'Institutional perspectives on entrepreneurial behaviour in challenging environments', *Journal of Small Business Management*, 49 (1): 107–25.

Welter, F., Trettin, L. and Neumann, U. (2008) 'Fostering entrepreneurship in distressed urban neighbourhoods', *International Entrepreneurship and Management Journal*, 4 (2): 109–28.

Wennekers, S. and Thurik, R. (1999) 'Linking entrepreneurship and economic growth', *Small Business Economics*, 13: 27–55.

Werbner, P. (1980) 'From rags to riches: Manchester Pakistanis in the garment trade', *New Community*, 9: 84–95.

Werbner, P. (1984) 'Business on trust: Pakistani entrepreneurship in the Manchester garment trade', in R. Ward and R. Jenkins (eds), *Ethnic Communities in Business*. Cambridge: Cambridge University Press. pp. 166–88.

Werbner, P. (1990) 'Renewing an industrial past: British Pakistani entrepreneurship in Manchester', *Migration*, 8: 17–41.

Werker, C. and Athreye, S. (2004) 'Marshall's disciples: Knowledge and innovation driving regional economic development and growth', *Journal of Evolutionary Economics*, 14 (5): 505–23.

Westerberg, M. (1998) 'Managing in turbulence: An empirical study of small firms operating in a turbulent environment'. Unpublished PhD thesis, Luleå Tekniska Universitet, Luleå, Sweden.

Westhead, P. and Birley, S. (1993) 'Employment growth in new independent owner-managed firms in Great Britain'. University of Warwick, Coventry.

Westhead, P. and Cowling, M. (1998) 'Family firm research: The need for a methodological rethink', *Entrepreneurship Theory and Practice*, 23 (1): 31–56.

Westhead, P. and Howorth, C. (2007) '"Types" of private family firms: An exploratory conceptual and empirical analysis', *Entrepreneurship and Regional Development*, 19 (5): 405–31.

Westhead, P. and Storey, D. J. (1994) 'An assessment of firms located on and off science parks in the United Kingdom'. London: HMSO.

Westhead, P. and Wright, M. (1998a) *Habitual Entrepreneurs and Business Angels*. Leeds: Institute of Small Business Affairs.

Westhead, P. and Wright, M. (1998b) 'Novice, portfolio and serial founders: Are they different?', *Journal of Business Venturing*, 13 (3): 173–204.

Westhead, P. and Wright, M. (1998c) 'Novice, portfolio and serial founders in rural and urban areas', *Entrepreneurship Theory and Practice*, 22 (4): 63–100.

Westhead, P., Ucbasaran, D. and Wright, M. (2003a) 'Differences between private firms owned by novice, serial and portfolio entrepreneurs: Implications for policy-makers and practitioners', *Regional Studies*, 37 (2): 187–200.

Westhead, P., Ucbasaran, D. and Wright, M. (2004) 'Policy toward novice, serial and portfolio entrepreneurs', *Environment and Planning C: Government and Policy*, 22 (6): 779–98.

Westhead, P., Ucbasaran, D. and Wright, M. (2005a) 'Experience and cognition: Do novice, serial and portfolio entrepreneurs differ?', *International Small Business Journal*, 23 (1): 72–98.

Westhead, P., Ucbasaran, D., Wright, M. and Binks, M. (2005b) 'Policy toward novice, serial and portfolio entrepreneurs', *Small Business Economics*, 25 (2): 109–32.

Westhead, P., Ucbasaran, D., Wright, M. and Binks, M. (2005c) 'Novice, serial and portfolio entrepreneur behaviour and contributions', *Small Business Economics*, 25 (2): 109–32.

Westhead, P., Ucbasaran, D., Wright, M. and Martin, F. (2003b) 'Habitual entrepreneurs in Scotland: Characteristics, search processes, learning and performance: Summary report', Glasgow: Scottish Enterprise.

Westlund, H. and Bolton, R. (2003) 'Local social capital and entrepreneurship', *Small Business Economics*, 21 (2): 77–133.

Wheeler, C. N., Ibeh, K. I. N. and Dimitratos, P. (2008) 'UK export performance research 1990–2003: Review and theoretical framework', *International Small Business Journal*, 26 (2): 207–39.

Wheelock, J. and Oughton, E. (1996) 'The household as a focus for research', *Journal of Economic Issues*, 30 (1): 143–59.

Wheelock, J., Oughton, E. and Baines, S. (2003) 'Getting by with a little help from your family: Toward a policy-relevant model of the household', *Feminist Economics*, 9 (1): 19–45.

Wickham, P. (2006) *Strategic Entrepreneurship: A decision-making approach to new venture creation and management* (4th edn). Harlow: Prentice Hall.

Wiedersheim-Paul, F., Olson, H. C. and Welch, L. S. (1978) 'Pre-export activity: The first in internationalization', *Journal of International Business Studies*, 9 (1): 47–58.

Wigren, C. (2003) 'The spirit of Gnosjö: The grand narrative and beyond'. JIBS Dissertation Series No. 17. Jönköping International Business School, Jönköping, Sweden.

Wiklund, J. (1998) 'Small firm growth and performance: Entrepreneurship and beyond'. Unpublished PhD thesis, Internationella Handelshögskolan, Jönköping. Sweden.

Wiklund, J. and Shepherd, D. (2005) 'Entrepreneurial orientation and small business performance: A configurational approach', *Journal of Business Venturing*, 20 (1): 71–91.

Wiklund, J. and Shepherd, D. (2008) 'Portfolio entrepreneurship, habitual and novice founders, new entry and mode of organizing', *Entrepreneurship Theory and Practice*, 32 (4): 701–25.

Wiklund, J., Davidsson, P. and Delmar, F. (2003) 'What do they think and feel about growth?: An expectancy–value approach to small business managers' attitudes toward growth', *Entrepreneurship Theory and Practice*, 27 (3): 247–70.

Wiklund, J., Davidsson, P., Audretsch, D. B. and Karlsson, C. (2011) 'The future of entrepreneurship research', *Entrepreneurship Theory and Practice*, 35, 1–9.

Wiklund, J., Patzelt, H. and Shepherd, D. A. (2009) 'Building and integrative model of small business growth', *Small Business Economics*, 32: 351–74.

Williams, C. (2005) 'The undeclared sector, self-employment and public policy', *International Journal of Entrepreneurial Behaviour and Research*, 11 (4): 244–57.

Williams, C., Round, J. and Rodgers, P. (2007) 'Beyond the formal/informal economy binary hierarchy', *International Journal of Social Economics*, 34 (6): 402–14.

Williamson, O. (1975) *Markets and Hierarchies: Analysis and antitrust implications*. New York: Free Press.

Wilpert, C. (2003) 'Germany: From workers to entrepreneurs', in R. Kloosterman and J. Rath (eds), *Immigrant Entrepreneurship: Venturing abroad in the age of globalisation*. Oxford: Berg.

Wilson Committee (1979) 'The financing of small firms: Interim report of the Committee to Review the Functioning of the Financial Institutions'. Cmnd 7503. London: HMSO.

Wilson, F., Carter, S., Tagg, S., Shaw, E. and Lam, W. (2007) 'Bank loan officers' perceptions of business owners: The role of gender', *British Journal of Management*, 18 (2): 154–71.

Wilson, F., Kickul, J. and Marlino, D. (2007) 'Gender, entrepreneurial self-efficacy, and entrepreneurial career intentions: Implications for entrepreneurship education', *Entrepreneurship Theory and Practice*, 31 (3): 387–406.

Wilson, N. (2008) 'An investigation into payment trends and behaviour in the UK: 1997–2007'. Leeds: Credit Management Research Centre.

Wilson, N. and Summers, B. (2002) 'Trade credit terms offered by small firms: Survey evidence and empirical analysis', *Journal of Business Finance and Accounting*, 29: 317–51.

Wiltbank, R. E. (2009) 'Siding with the angels: Business angel investing – promising outcomes and effective strategies', Research report, May. London: NESTA and British Business Angels Association.

Winborg, J. and Landström, H. (2001) 'Financial bootstrapping in small businesses: Examining small business managers' resource acquisition behaviors', *Journal of Business Venturing*, 16 (3): 235–54.

Winckles, K. (1986) *The Practice of Successful Business Management*. London: Kogan pp. 61.

Withey, J. J. (1980) 'Differences between exporters and non-exporters: Some hypotheses concerning small manufacturing business', *American Journal of Small Business*, 4 (3): 29–37.

Woo, C., Cooper, A., Dunkelberg, W., Daellenbach, U. and Dennis, W. (1989) 'Determinants of growth for small and large entrepreneurial start-ups'. Paper presented at the Ninth Anumal Babson College Entrepreneurship Research Conference, Institute of Entrepreneurial Studies, Saint Louis University, Saint Louis, MO, April.

Woo, C. Y., Folta, T. and Cooper, A. C. (1992) 'Entrepreneurial search: Alternative theories of behavior', in *Frontiers of Entrepreneurship Research 1992*. Wellesley, MA: Babson College.

Wood, R. and Bandura, A. (1989) 'Social cognitive theory of organizational management', *Academy of Management Review*, 14 (3): 361–84.

Woodman, R. W. and Schoenfeldt, L. F. (1989) 'Individual differences in creativity: An interactionist perspective', in J. A. Glover, R. R. Ronning and C. R. Reynolds (eds), *Handbook of Creativity*. New York: Plenum. pp. 77–92.

Woodman, R. W. and Schoenfeldt, L. F. (1990) 'An interactionist model of creative behavior', *Journal of Creative Behavior*, 24: 279–90.

Woodward, M. D. (1997) *Black Entrepreneurs in America: Stories of struggle and success*. New Brunswick, NJ: Rutgers University Press.

World Bank (2000) 'World development report, 2000–2001'. Washington, DC: World Bank.

Wright, M., Robbie, K. and Ennew, C. (1997a) 'Venture capitalists and serial entrepreneurs', *Journal of Business Venturing*, 12 (3): 227–49.

Wright, M., Robbie, K. and Ennew, C. (1997b) 'Serial entrepreneurs', *British Journal of Management*, 8 (3): 251–68.

Wyer, P. and Boocock, G. (1996) 'The internationalisation of small- and medium-sized enterprises: An organisational learning perspective'. Paper presented at the 7th ENDEC World Conference on entrepreneurship, Singapore, 5–7 December.

Wyer, P. and Boocock, G. (1998) 'An alternative framework for considering the internationalisation of SMEs', *Journal of Enterprising Culture*, 6 (3).

Wyer, P. and Mason, J. (1998) 'An organisational learning perspective to enhancing understanding of people management in small businesses', *International Journal of Entrepreneurial Behaviour and Research*, 4 (2): 112–28.

Wyer, P. and Smallbone, D. (1999) 'Export activity in SMEs: A framework for strategic analysis', *Journal of the Academy of Business Administration*, 4 (2): 9–24.

Wyer, P., Donohoe, S. and Matthews, P. (2010) 'Fostering strategic learning capability to enhance creativity in small service businesses', *Service Business: An International Journal*, 4: 9–26.

Wyer, P., Mason, P. and Theodorakopoulos, N. (2000) 'An examination of the concept of the learning organisation within the context of small business development', *International Journal of Entrepreneurial Behaviour and Research*, 6 (4).

Wynarczyk, P., Watson, R., Storey, D. J., Short, H. and Keasey, K. (1993) *Managerial Labour Markets in Small- and Medium-sized Enterprises*. London: Routledge.

Young, S. (1987) 'Business strategy and the internationalisation of business: Recent approaches', *Managerial and Decision Economics*, 8: 31–40.

Young, S. (1990) 'Internationalization: Introduction and overview', *International Marketing Review*, 7 (4): 5–10.

Young, S., Hamill, J., Wheeler, C. and Davis, J. R. (1989) *International Market Entry and Development*. Hemel Hempstead, Hertfordshire: Harvester Wheatsheaf.

Yukl, G. (1989) 'Managerial leadership: A review of theory and research', *Journal of Management*, 15 (2): 251–89.

Yunus, M., Moingeon, B. and Lehmann-Ortega, L. (2010) 'Building social business models: Lessons from the Grameen experience', *Long Range Planning*, 43: 308–25.

Zacharakis, A. L., Meyer, G. D. and DeCastro, J. (1999) 'Differing perceptions of new venture failure: A matched exploratory study of venture capitalists and entrepreneurs', *Journal of Small Business Management*, 37 (3): 1–14.

Zafarullah, M., Ali, M. and Young, S. (1998) 'The internationalization of the small firm in developing countries: Exploratory research from Pakistan', *Journal of Global Marketing*, 11 (3): 21–38.

Zahra, S. A. (2003) 'International expansion of U.S. manufacturing family businesses: The effect of ownership and involvement', *Journal of Business Venturing*, 18 (4): 495–512.

Zahra, S. (2005) 'A theory of international new ventures: A decade of research', *Journal of International Business Studies*, 36 (13): 29–41.

Zahra, S. A. (2007) 'Contextualizing theory building in entrepreneurship research', *Journal of Business Venturing*, 22 (3): 443–52.

Zahra, S. A. and Covin, J. G. (1995) 'Contextual influences on the corporate entrepreneurship-performance relationship: A longitudinal analysis', *Journal of Business Venturing*, 10 (1): 43–58.

Zahra, S. A., Gedajlovic, E., Neubaum, D. O. and Shulman, J. M. (2009) 'A typology of social entrepreneurs: Motives, search processes and ethical challenges', *Journal of Business Venturing*, 24: 519–32.

Zahra, S., Sapienza, H. and Davidsson, P. (2006) 'Entrepreneurship and dynamic capabilities: A review, model and research agenda', *Journal of Management Studies*, 43 (4): 917–55.

Zewde and Associates (2002) 'Jobs, gender and small enterprises in Africa: Women entrepreneurs in Ethiopia'. A preliminary report, Geneva: ILO, IFP/SEED-WEDGE, October.

Zhang, J. (2010) 'The problems of using social networks in entrepreneurial resource acquisition', *International Small Business Journal*, 28 (4): 338–61.

Zhang, Z., Zyphur, M. J., Narayanan, J., Arvey, R. D., Chaturvedi, S., Avolio, B. J., Lichtenstein, P. and Larsson, G. (2009) 'The genetic basis of entrepreneurship: Effects of gender and personality', *Organizational Behavior and Human Decision Processes*, 110 (2): 93–107.

Zhao, H. and Seibert, S. E. (2006) 'The big five personality dimensions and entrepreneurial status: A meta-analytical review', *Journal of Applied Psychology*, 91 (2): 259–71.

Zietsma, C. (1999) 'Opportunity knocks – or does it hide?: An examination of the role of opportunity recognition in entrepreneurship', in *Frontiers of Entrepreneurship Research 1999*. Wellesley, MA: Babson College.

Zimmer, C. and Aldrich, H. (1987) 'Resource mobilization through ethnic networks', *Sociological Perspectives*, 30 (4): 422–45.

Zografos, C. (2007) 'Rurality discourses and the role of the social enterprise in regenerating rural Scotland', *Journal of Rural Studies*, 23 (1): 38–51.

Zontanos, G. and Anderson, A. R. (2004) 'Relationships, marketing and small business: An exploration of links in theory and practice', *Qualitative Market Research: An International Journal*, 7 (3): 228–36.

Zott, C. and Huy, Q. N. (2007) 'How entrepreneurs use symbolic management resources', *Administrative Science Quarterly*, 52 (1): 70–105.

Zukin, S. and DiMaggio, P. (1990) *Structures of Capital: The social organization of the economy*. New York: Cambridge University Press.

Index

3i 63

Aaby, N. 439, 441, 442
Abell, P. 340
Abetti, P. A. 272
ability models of behaviour 170, 175–6
academic entrepreneurs 261, 271, 276–7, 281
ACCION USA 299
achievement, need for 164–5, 166–7, 169
achievement context models of behaviour 170,
    172–5, 176–7
Ackerman, P. L. 158, 161, 164
ACOST 367
Acs, Z. J. 28, 31, 34, 36, 37, 80, 109, 180, 182,
    286, 404, 406
Addis, M. 324, 336
Adler, P. 39, 40
administrative receivership 189
advice and consultancy 65–6, 69, 72–6
AEG 349
affordable loss principle 139–40, 141, 142, 149
African-Americans 202, 203–4
African-Caribbeans 200, 204–6, 207, 208–9, 211,
    212, 213
agency, and context 82–3
agency theory 242, 244
Agilyx 138
agreeableness 159
Ahl, H. 219, 222, 224, 226, 228, 229, 246
AIM Advisers 376
Ajzen, I. 170, 171, 172
Akuetteh, C. K. 262
Al Dajani, H. 219, 223, 224
Albaum, G. 440, 448
Alderman, N. 63
Aldrich, H. E. 18, 38, 81, 83, 84, 85, 108, 109,
    132, 133, 158, 169, 199, 203, 204, 206,
    207, 214, 219, 229, 232, 325, 338, 340,
    351, 353, 356, 358, 360
alertness to entrepreneurial opportunities 126, 127
Alexander, J. 300
Ali, M. 441
Ali, Z. A. 239
Allen, S. 222
Allen, W. D. 84
Allinson, C. W. 127, 373
Almor, T. 388, 399

Alsos, G. A. 229, 252, 255, 257, 259, 260, 261,
    262
Alternative Investment Market (AIM) 62, 365,
    367, 375, 376
Alvarez, S. A. 97, 110, 123, 130, 162
Alvord, S. H. 290
Alvy, G. 293, 303, 306
Amabile, T. M. 125, 126, 131, 174
Ambler, T. 61, 436, 437, 448
AMD 283
Amin, A. 32, 86, 297
Amit, R. 97
Amway 347
Anderson, A. R. 83, 84, 88, 229, 245, 275, 293,
    314, 324, 325, 326, 334, 339, 341, 353
Anderson, B. 295
Anderson, D. E. 32
Anderson, O. 168, 435, 436
Anderson, P. 110
Anderson, Paul Thomas 169
Anderson, S. 368
Andersson, M. 36, 37
angels, business 368, 377, 378–9
Anheier, H. 300
annual reports 383–4
antecedents
    of business failure 183, 186–7
    of social entrepreneurship 295–6
Antoncic, B. 355
Apex 347
Apple 100, 271, 284
Aquino, K. 127, 130, 168
Ardichvili, A. 125
Arenius, P. 220
Arensberg, C. M. 306
Argenti, J. 184
Arkwright, Richard 345
Arnould, O. 449
Arora, V. K. 268
Arrow, K. J. 108, 109, 273
Arrowsmith, J. 210
Arshed, N. 221
Arthurs, J. D. 172, 242
Asante, M. K. 203
Asda 294
Asheim, B. 35
Asset-based Finance Association 380

Association of Chartered and Certified Accountants (ACCA) 367, 369, 370, 373, 375, 379, 380, 381
Association of University Research Parks (AURP) 275
Åstebro 189
Astrachan, J. H. 240, 241, 245
Atari 284
Athayde, R. 169
Atherton, A. 41
Athreye, S. 32, 38
Atler, K. 294
attitude-based models of behaviour 170–2, 176, 177
attitudes towards entrepreneurs 1, 18, 180
attribution theory 184–5
Audit Commission 69
Audretsch, D. B. 2, 28, 29, 30, 32, 33, 36, 37, 38, 41, 109, 293, 338
Auster, E. R. 108, 341, 343, 344
Austin, J. 294, 307, 311, 314, 315
Australia 255, 434
Austria 201, 446
Austrian school, economic theory 13–14, 29, 30
Autio, E. 30, 404
Autio, K. 404
autonomy, desire for 164–5
Axelrod, R. 39
Axelsson, B. 324
Aylward, E. 279

Bach, R. L. 202
Bacq, S. 295
Bagby, D. R. 188, 191
Bagozzi, R. P. 170, 172
Baines, S. 84, 85, 338, 351, 356
Baker, T. 90, 106, 219, 229, 389, 391
Baldock, R. 212, 378, 409
Balkin, D. B. 126
Bamberger 396
Bandura, A. 162, 173, 174, 177
Bangladesh 89, 223, 299
bank finance 61–2, 63, 211–12, 224–5, 226–7, 260, 365–6, 368, 370–3, 383–4
Bank of England 54, 57, 60, 63, 77, 366, 377, 381
Banker, The 371
bankruptcy 189–91, 193
Banks, J. 296
Bannock, G. 50, 51, 52, 56
Bardeen, John 283
Barker, R. G. 108
Barney, J. B. 97, 105, 109, 110, 123, 127, 130, 162, 388
Baron, R. A. 126, 127, 129, 130, 131, 156, 157, 162, 163, 170, 171, 176, 252, 257, 259

Barr, P. S. 130, 166, 170
Barreto, H. 10, 11, 13
Barrett, G. A. 201, 205, 207, 209, 211
barriers to internationalisation 443–5
Barringer, B. R. 405, 406
Barrow, C. 275
Barry, D. 165
Bartelle Columbus Laboratories 270
Barth, F. 304
Barth, H. 401
Basu, A. 205, 207
Basu, D. 206, 210, 211
Bates, T. 79, 203, 204
Bates, V. 376
Bathelt, H. 34, 37, 82
Battelle Columbus Laboratories 275
Batterink, M. H. 325
Battes, T. 84
Battilana, J. 82, 308
Bauerschmidt, A. 436
Baum, J. R. 97, 125, 157, 173, 176
Baumard, P. 182, 183
Baumback, C. 401
Baumol, W. J. 29, 30, 43, 44, 79, 108, 279
Beamish, P. W. 294
Beaver, G. 181, 184, 185
Becker, G. S. 39
Beckinsale, M. 338
Beesley, M. 352
Begg, I. 32
Begley, T. M. 126, 167
behaviour, entrepreneurial 164–78
behaviour models 170–8
behavioural scoring 371
Beldam, Robert 348
Belgium 202
Bell, Alexander Graham 273
Bell, C. 306
Bell, J. 432, 434, 436, 437, 438, 439, 442, 445, 446, 448
Bell Laboratories 283
Belle, A. 227
Bellu, R. R. 165, 167
Benassi, M. 132
Benchmarking Challenge 66
Bengtsson, O. 260
Benito, G. 432
Bennett, J. 89
Bennett, M. 425
Bennett, R. J. 50, 66, 67, 68, 69, 73, 74, 76
Bercovitz, J. 82
Berg, N. G. 82, 86, 221–2
Berlotti, M. 340, 351
Berry, A. 366, 370, 372, 374, 380, 383, 384
Berry, M. 66

Bessant, J. 399
Besser, T. L. 310
Best, M. 274
Better Regulation Executive (BRE) 59, 60
Better Regulation Task Force 54, 60, 61, 69
Bevan, A. A. 371
Beveridge, William 297
Bevin, Ernest 364
Bhave, M. P. 97, 100, 101, 107, 114, 128
Bhide, A. V. 389, 390, 392, 398
Bickenstaffe, Mark 349
Big Society 298
Bilkey, W. J. 436, 443, 445
Bill & Melinda Gates Foundation 291
Binks, M. R. 10, 11, 259, 365, 368, 370, 371, 375
Birch, D. 51, 432
Birch, K. 297
Birch, N. J. 22
Bird, B. J. 22, 173, 176, 226
bird-in-the-hand principle 138–9, 140, 142, 149
Birley, S. 38, 222, 262, 278, 325, 326, 338, 339,
     340, 343, 351, 352, 353, 354, 356, 358,
     360, 395
Bjärsvik, A. 111
Bjenning, B. 111
Black, S. 325
Blackburn, R. 51, 54, 191, 192, 208, 210, 211,
     216
Blair, Tony 297, 298
Blaschke, J. 202, 205
Blundel, R. 344, 351, 356
Boatler, R. 440
Bock, B. B. 85
Boden, R. J. 227, 369
Body Shop 372
Boeing 140, 141
Boeker, W. 398
Bogart, R. G. 443
Boissevain, J. 342, 344
Bolton, R. 32, 39, 40
Bolton Committee/Report 18, 50, 51, 52, 65, 72,
     364, 432
Bonacich, E. 204
Bono, J. E. 159, 173
Bontis, N. 132
Boocock, G. 423
bootstrapping/bricolage 105–6, 140, 182, 293–4,
     353, 355, 381, 389
Borch, O. J. 307, 418
Borchert, O. 431, 434
Bornstein, D. 293
Boschee, J. 291, 292
Bosma, N. 30, 31, 227, 404, 408
Boubakri, H. 201
Bovaird, T. 368

Bowen, H. P. 88
Bower, J. 110
Bowey, J. L. 38, 339, 341
Bowman, N. 157, 165, 168
Bowman-Upton, N. 226
Boxenbaum, E. 82
Boyatzis, R. E. 329
Boyd, D. P. 126, 167
Boyd, N. G. 173
Bracker, J. 167, 390, 392, 423
Braden, P. L. 269, 271, 278
Brandstätter, H. 187
Branson, Richard 140, 141, 153
Brasch, J. J. 436
Brattain, Walter 283
Braund, S. 374
Braunerhjelm, P. 36
Brazeal, D. F. 24, 171
Brearley, S. 10, 22, 157
Breschi, S. 37
Bresnahan, T. 37
Breuner, G. 359
bricolage see bootstrapping/bricolage
Bridge, J. 423
Bridge, S. 28, 29, 30, 31, 41, 43, 44
Brigham, E. 400
Brin, Sergey 291
Brinckmann, J. 99, 280
British Aluminium 347
British Bankers' Association 366, 368, 370
British Business Angels Association (BBAA) 379
British Chamber of Manufacturers 283
British classical school, economic theory 12–13
Brockhaus Sr, R. H. 16, 126, 165, 168, 279
Brodzinski, J. D. 169
Brooks, H. 343
Brooks, M. R. 440
Brown, B. 338, 351, 356
Brown, G. 368
Brown, L. D. 290
Brown, S. 336
Browning Ferris (BFI) 140
Brownlie, D. 319, 336
Bruce, R. 19
Brüderl, J. 40, 83, 351, 353
Brumark case 370, 380
Brunel, Isambard Kingdom 345, 346
Bruni, Gherardi, Poggio 219
Brush, C. G. 221, 224, 226, 313, 392
Bruyat, C. 291
Bryde, D. 290, 295
Buchanan, J. M. 165
Buchholtz, A. K. 126
Buckland, R. 367
Bullock, A. 369, 370

Bullvåg, E. 171, 262
bureaucratic failure 55
Burgess, S. 409
Burrows, R. 204, 209
Burt, R. 40, 132, 344, 353
Burton, B. 376
Busenitz, L. W. 88, 127, 129, 130, 154, 162, 172, 242
business angels 368, 377, 378–9
Business Connect 72
Business Development Service 72
business failure see failure, entrepreneurial
Business Gateway 72
business growth and development 404–29
Business Link 62, 64, 65–6, 68, 69, 70, 72–6, 214, 340
business planning 98–9, 389–92, 415, 422–3
Business Start-up Scheme 62
business start-ups
    community entrepreneurship 313–14
    costs 182
    effectuation 111–17, 136, 144–7
    entrepreneurial process 96–118
    ethnicity 206, 211, 212
    female entrepreneurs 222, 368
    finance 367–8, 375, 377
    government policy 62, 68, 69
    growth and development 409
    habitual entrepreneurs 258, 260, 261, 263, 264
    internationalisation 431
    networks 356
    strategy 389, 392, 401
    technical entrepreneurship 286, 287
business support see support structures
Butler, J. 126, 127, 338, 351, 356
Buttner, E. H. 224
Buzzell, R. D. 395, 398
Bygrave, W. D. 9, 23, 24, 120, 131, 261, 272, 291
Byrne, D. 202

Cabinet Office 60, 66
Cable, D. 133
Cadbury's 246
Cakar, N. D. 427
Calantone, R. J. 328
Calás, M. B. 222, 223, 228, 229
Caliendo, M. 182
Camagni, R. 32, 37
Cambridge Science Park (UK) 275
Cambridge Small Business Research Centre 398, 400
Cameron, David 298
Cameron, K. 393, 401
Cameron, Ross 350
Campbell, D. J. 161

Campbell, J. P. 175
Campi, S. 315
Canada 180, 202, 205, 442, 446
Cannon, M. D. 183, 185, 193
Cannon, T. 221
Cantillon, R. 2, 11, 29
Canton, E. 372
Cantor, N. 157
Capello, R. 34
Capgemini 366, 371
capital structure decision 381–2, 400
Capman, K. 351
Cappelli, P. 79
Caprara, G. V. 157
Caputo, R. K. 84
Carayannis, E. G. 275
Cardon, M. S. 169
Cardoso, C. 338
Cardozo, R. 125
Cardullo, M. 270, 285
Career Development Loans 63
CARF 210
Carland, J. A. 22
Carland, J. W. 19, 22
Carlson, D. S. 420
Carnegie, Andrew 296
Carnegie, K. 292
Carney, M. 247
Carr, J. C. 84
Carree, M. 28, 404
Carroll, G. R. 18, 393
Carson, D. 319, 321, 322, 323, 324, 326, 327, 328, 329, 331, 333, 334, 338, 420
Carsrud, A. L. 126, 157, 162, 169, 171, 172, 173, 340
Carswell, P. 87
Carter, N. M. 96, 97, 100, 102, 120, 126
Carter, S. 84, 85, 107, 181, 185, 219, 221, 222, 224, 225, 226, 255, 262, 265, 291, 292, 307, 312, 313, 314, 330, 351, 358, 359, 368, 411
Cashmore, E. 204
Casson, M. 14, 16, 121, 123, 360, 325, 339, 341
Castells, M. 34, 275
Castilla, E. 342
Cater, J. 203, 207
Cavakapa, B. 323
Cavanagh, R. E. 395
Cavusgil, S. T. 436, 439, 443
CBI 48, 66, 67, 348, 350, 369, 370, 373, 375, 379, 380
CEEDR 425
Celtic FC 296
Cervone, D. 157
Chaffee, E. 393

Chaganti, R. 400
Chaiken, S. 170
Chakraborty, G. 329
chambers of commerce 61, 68, 70, 75, 223, 340
Chandler, A. 28, 113, 438
Chandler, G. N. 24, 100, 113, 128, 129, 175, 259
Chanel, Coco 153
Chaston, I. 340
Chaudhry, S. 441
Chell, E. 10, 12, 17, 22, 127, 157, 338, 351, 356, 409, 410
Chen, C. C. 168, 173
Chen, M. 386
Cherkas, L. 157, 179
China 182
Chinese entrepreneurs 208
Chittenden, F. 50, 61, 382
Cho, A. H. 292, 295
Choo, C. W. 188
Chrisman, J. J. 84, 87, 270, 293, 305, 306, 309, 310, 311, 313, 314
Christensen, C. 110
Chua, J. H. 84
Churchill, N. C. 271, 401, 411, 413
Cialdini, R. B. 98
Ciavarella, M. A. 126, 159
Citron, D. 372
civil society 290, 296, 300
Clark, J. B. 13
Clark, J. R. 29
Clark, K. 110
Clark, T. 75, 436
Clark's shoes 246
Clarke, J. 297
class issues, and ethnic minority businesses 205, 207–8
Cliff, J. E. 84, 85, 226, 232
Clifford, D. K. 395
clusters 35, 275, 276
CNN 141–2
Coalition government 70, 214, 285, 298
Cochran, A. B. 181
Coelho, P. R. P. 191
Coeurderoy, R. 109
cognition 127, 129–30, 156, 162, 170–8, 258–9
cognitive models of entrepreneurial behaviour 170–8
Cohn, T. 390
Coleman, J. S. 224, 225, 314
Coleman, S. 39
collective processes 313–15
Colli, A. 236, 246
Collins, C. J. 164, 166, 167, 278, 406
Collins, J. C. 274
Collins, O. F. 272, 277

Collinson, E. 319, 323, 327, 328, 329, 330, 331, 334
Collinson, S. 351
Collis, J. 383, 384
Colliss, J. 383
Colombelli, A. 376
community 85–7, 204, 210, 306
community enterprises 309–10
community entrepreneurship 303–16
community networks 310–11, 313
community ventures 306–15
Companys, Y. E. 123
comparative optimism 191, 263
competencies 329–30, 442
competition 33–4, 51, 52, 417–18
Competition Commission (CC) 372
competitive advantage 388, 395, 396–9
Concerten Ensemble (Norway) 312–13
conscientiousness 159
Conservative Party 18, 69, 297, 298
Consumer Credit Act 60
contextualising entrepreneurship 78–91, 131–3, 153–4
control, locus of 164–5, 168, 173
control systems 401
Conway, S. 338, 339, 342, 344, 351, 352, 353, 354, 355, 357
Cook, I. G. 203
Cooke, A. D. J. 165
Cooke, P. 32, 35
Cooney, K. 295
Cooney, T. M. 306, 314
Cooper, A. C. 129, 167, 257, 269, 270, 271, 272, 274, 277, 278, 279, 280, 390, 395
Cooper, S. Y. 279, 286, 340, 351
Co-operative Group 296
Cope, J. 22, 23, 131, 277
Copp, C. 351
Corbett, A. C. 126, 127, 132
Cornett, A. P. 35
corporate governance 239, 240, 266, 295, 309, 322–3
corridor principle 261
Cosh, A. 54, 367, 369, 370, 375, 378, 380
cost leadership strategy 396, 397
Costa, C. 271
Costanzo, L. A. 307, 313
Cova, B. 336
Coviello, N. E. 326, 431, 438, 439
Covin, J. G. 270, 324, 327, 394
Cowling, M. 236, 365, 373
craftsman entrepreneur 277–8
Cragg, P. 392
Cramton, C. D. 246
Crane, D. P. 167

Cravens, D. W. 320
crazy quilt principle 140–2, 150
credit card debt 380–1
credit management 379–80
credit scoring 366
Cremer, R. D. 311
Cressy, R. 50
Crick, A. 168, 173
Crick, D. 432, 436, 437, 441, 445, 447
Cromie, S. 28, 221, 319, 323, 334, 338, 339, 358
Cronsell, N. 86
Cross, M. 213
Crossan, M. M. 131, 132
Crowehley, R. 340
Cruickshank, D. 370
Csikszentmihalyi, M. 175
Cudeck, R. 176
culture 38–40, 81, 86, 159, 224, 236, 241–2
    ethnic minority businesses 200, 203, 205, 206,
    207
Cumbers, A. 351
Cumming, D. 43
Cummings, A. 131
Cunnington, B. 167
Curran, J. 51, 54, 204, 207, 208, 209, 210, 211,
    216, 278, 408
Curtis, D. A. 390, 392
customer base, broadening the 426–7
customer concentration 400
Cyert, R. M. 128, 435
Czinkota, M. R. 436, 445, 447
Czuchry, A. 277

D'Cruz, C. 277
Dacin 308
Daft, R. 132
Dahles, H. 292
Dahlqvist, J. 100, 113, 128, 262
Daly, M. 210
Danbolt, J. 371
Daniels, L. 224
Danone 299
Darroch, J. 323, 327, 329, 427
Dart, R. 294
David, R. J. 128
Davidson, W. 399, 400
Davidsson, P. 2, 23, 83, 85, 90, 95, 96, 97, 98,
    100, 101, 107, 111, 113, 114, 116, 122,
    123, 124, 128, 167, 171, 172, 260, 262,
    278, 293, 405, 405, 406
Davies, L. G. 407, 408, 411, 414, 415, 416
Davies, S. 300
Davis, C. D. 326, 327
Davis, E. W. 367
Davis, J. A. 237, 238

Davis, J. H. 243
Davis, J. R. 438
Day, G. 323
de Bruin, A. 87, 304, 305, 311
De Carolis, D. M. 133, 400
De Castro, J. O. 99, 184, 185
De Clercq, D. 88
de Koning, A. 83, 100, 101, 107
De Silva, P. 207
Deacon, J. H. 319
Deakins, D. 84, 199, 206, 207, 209, 210, 211,
    212, 213, 214, 216, 340, 341, 351, 359,
    365
Dean, T. 123
debt gap 364, 375
Deci, E. L. 162, 174
Deeds, D. 400
Deeks, J. 278
Dees, G. 294
Dees, J. G. 290, 291, 292, 293, 295
Defourny, J. 291, 296, 315
Delacroix, J. 393
delegation 271, 413, 414, 420
Delmar, F. 97, 98, 99, 103–4, 113, 116, 156, 157,
    160, 167, 171, 175, 262, 405, 406, 407
Deloitte 294
Demarigny, F. 376
Demmert, H. 126
Demos 298
den Hertog, P. 35
Denmark 180, 446
Department for Business, Enterprise and
    Regulatory Reform 52, 75, 228, 406
Department for Business, Innovation and Skills
    (BIS) 66, 68, 70, 74, 228, 367, 373
Department for Education and Skills 53, 64
Department of Employment 51
Department of Trade and Industry (DTI) 51, 52,
    57, 63, 65, 67, 69, 73, 75, 290
Deprey, B. 434
Deregulation Task Force 59, 60
DeTienne, D. R. 99, 126, 129, 175, 265
development see business growth and development;
    economic growth and development
Dever, J. E. 181, 186, 191, 192
Dew, N. 116, 124, 163, 165, 259
Dewar, R. 401
Dhaliwal, S. 209, 351
Di Domenico, M. 293, 295, 315
Di Pierro, A. 165
Dickson, P. R. 166, 173
differentiation strategy 396–7
Dillard, J. F. 123
DiMaggio, P. 81
Dimitratos, P. 434, 439, 440, 441, 447

Dimov, D. 123, 124, 125, 127, 130, 132
discovery process 96, 99–102, 106–11, 113–17
Discua Cruz, A. 247, 248, 249
Disney 284
displacement theory 17
distal and proximal processes 158, 161, 177
diversity 215
Dobb, M. 13
Dobbs, M. 406, 414
Dodd, S. D. 83, 339, 340, 351, 353, 355, 358
Dodgson, M. 282, 352
Dolinsky, A. 84
Doll, J. 170
Donaldson, L. 243
Donckels 256, 351, 352, 355
Donohoe, S. 424
Dooley, K. J. 123
Douglas, E. J. 188
Doutriaux, J. 269
Dowd, L. 440
Dowling 38, 338, 351, 356
Downing, J. 224
Draheim, K. P. 269
Drakopoulou Dodd, S. 88, 275
Drayton, W. 293
Droge, C. 401
Drucker, P. E. 122, 124, 132, 293, 387
Drury, C. 374
Dubini, P. 133, 340, 351, 353
Dudding, R. 56
Duerr, E. 440
Dun and Bradstreet 185, 409
Dunkelberg, W. C. 167, 278, 279
Dupont, B. 256
Dupuis, A. 87, 304, 305, 311
Durand, R. 109
Durtnell, John and Brian 236
Dutia, D. 399, 400
Dutta, D. K. 131
Duysters, G. 353
Dyck, B. 249
Dyson, James 50, 282, 285, 339, 345–51, 354, 360, 413

e-business/commerce 442
Eagly, A. H. 170
Early Growth Funds (EGFs) 378
EASDAQ 62
East India Company 48
Easton, G. 38, 324, 339, 341
eBay 139, 140
Ebben, J. 397, 398
Eckhardt, J. T. 107, 108, 109, 121, 122, 123, 124, 305
economic growth and development 27–45

community entrepreneurship 304, 305
female entrepreneurs 220
finance 367, 376
government policy 28, 30, 35, 51–2
technical entrepreneurs 282, 285–6
UK 298
economic theory 10–16, 28–31, 297–8
economies of scale 50–1, 411
Edmondson, A. C. 183, 185, 193
education and training 3–4, 18
business growth and development 410
government policy 50, 51, 53, 54, 63, 64–5, 67
networks 353, 355, 359
research on 23
technical entrepreneurship 275–7, 278–9, 286
see also learning
Edwards, P. 210
Eesley, C. 275
Eesley, D. T. 389, 391
effectuation/effectual logic 111–17, 135–51
efficiency, competing on 397–8
Egge, K. A. 167
Egypt 299
Eikenberry, A. M. 300
Eisenhardt, K. M. 325, 394, 396
Ejermo, O. 36
Ekanem, I. 340, 351, 378, 421
Elam, A. 88
Electrolux 110–11, 349
Elfring, T. 353
Elias, J. 294
Elliot, A. J. 175
Ellison, Larry 279
embeddedness
    community entrepreneurship 305, 309, 314
    contextualising entrepreneurship 80–6
    ethnic minority businesses 200, 201, 215
    marketing, entrepreneurial 324–6
Emiel, F. M. 325
Emirbayer, M. 81
emotional stability 158–9
employment 1, 18, 51–2, 313, 405–6
endogenous development 34–6
Energy Savings Trust 294
England 12–13, 62, 68–9, 70–6, 190, 340, 409
Ennew, C. T. 225, 255, 365, 368, 370, 371
Ensley, M. D. 130, 162, 163, 170, 176, 252, 257, 259, 390, 421
Enterprise Agencies 68
Enterprise Allowance Scheme 62
Enterprise Capital Funds (ECFs) 378
Enterprise Finance Guarantee (EFG) 62, 364, 372, 373
Enterprise Initiative 72
enterprise zones 286

entrepreneurial behaviour 164–78
entrepreneurial expertise 136
entrepreneurial failure *see* failure, entrepreneurial
entrepreneurial marketing *see* marketing,
    entrepreneurial
entrepreneurial orientation 393, 394
entrepreneurial process 95–119
entrepreneurial skills, habitual entrepreneurs 259
entrepreneurial transition 215
entrepreneurship
    contextualising 78–91
    dark side 168–9
    domain 2
    ecosystem 274
    government policies 41–4
    vs small business 19–21
    theory, evolution of 9–26
Entrepreneurship Action plan (Wales) 286
environment
    business growth and development 407, 415–16,
        417
    in the entrepreneurial process 116
    internationalisation 442–3
    and strategy 393–4
    technical entrepreneurship 274–5
Epstein, J. A. 175
Equal Opportunities Commission (EOC) 226
equity 374–5
equity gap 364, 378
Erramilli, M. K. 434
Erturk, A. 427
Essie, Tom 349
Estades, J. 356
Estrin, S. 89
Etemad, H. 436, 439
ethics 294
Ethiopia 223
ethnicity 21, 84, 86, 199–217, 359, 440–1
Etzkowitz, H. 35
Eunni, R. V. 88
EUREKA 64
Europe 41, 201, 372
European Commission 41, 53
European Foundation for Entrepreneurial Research
    409
European SMEs Observatory 72
European Union/European Community 49, 53, 60,
    61, 72, 296
European Union Structural Funds 62
European Venture Capital Association 377
exit strategies 191–3
exogenous/external failures 183–6
Experian 367
expertise, entrepreneurial 136
exploitation process 96, 102–11, 113–17

Export Challenge 66
Export Credit Guarantee Scheme 63
exporting 63–4, 262, 395, 399, 400, 433–4,
    435–7, 441–5
external environment *see* environment
external/exogenous failures 183–6
extraversion 158–9

F-PEC scale of family influence 235, 241–2, 245
Fabowale, L. 225
factoring 379–80
Factors and Discounters Association (FDA) 380
Fagenson, E. A. 165
failure, entrepreneurial 180–95
    habitual entrepreneurs 258, 259, 261, 263, 265
    and strategy 392, 393
    technical entrepreneurship 272
Fairchild Semiconductor 283
Fairtrade 294
families 84–5, 201, 205, 208–10, 278, 347, 348,
    350, 352, 358
family businesses/firms/enterprises 21, 232–51,
    266, 389, 391
Fang, S. 341
Faraone, L. 268
Faulkner, S. 366, 370, 383, 384
Fay, M. 224, 225, 226
Fayol, H. 427
FC Barcelona 296
fear of failure 182, 191
Federal Express 115
Feldman, M. P. 37, 38, 82, 286
female entrepreneurs 21, 218–31
    contextualising entrepreneurship 84, 86, 88
    finance 222, 368
    government policy 75
    networks 358–9
    psychology 172
    social capital 84
    technical entrepreneurship 279
feminist analyses 220, 222–31, 225, 226, 230
Fernald, L. W. 222
Fernández Pérez, P. 246
Ferrer-i-Carbonell, A. 188, 189
Fiegenbaum, A. 386
Fielden, S. L. 279
Fiet, J. O. 100, 101, 113, 257
File, K. M. 333
Filion, L. 359
finance 362–85
    business growth and development 419, 420,
        424–5
    Dyson, James 348, 349
    ethnic minority businesses 206, 210, 211–12,
        214

finance (*continued*)
    female entrepreneurs 219, 224–7
    government policy 61–3
    habitual entrepreneurs 260
    internationalisation 445
    networks 348, 349
    strategy 390, 391–2, 399–400
    see also business angels; venture capital
finance gap 364–9
financial reporting 383–4
Finegold, D. 64
Finke, R. A. 125
Finland 255, 446
Finnegan, G. 223
Fiol, C. M. 132
Firnstahl, T. W. 271
First, Tom 102
Fisher, M. 60
Fisher, N. 188
Flamholtz, E. G. 271
Fletcher, D. E. 80, 209
flexibility, competing on 397–8
Flintoff, I. 207
Flores, M. 191
Florida, R. 34, 286
Flynn, K. H. 85
focus strategy 394–6
Folta, T. B. 129, 257
Fombrun, C. 342
Foner, N. 205
Fontes, M. 271
Foo, M. D. 127, 166, 170, 172, 175
Forbes Insights 369, 371, 373, 375, 377, 380, 381
Ford, D. 441, 443
foreign direct investment (FDI) 434, 435, 436
Forlani, D. 166, 188
Fossen, F. M. 182
Foster, M. J. 390
Foster, M. K. 225
France 12–13, 48, 68, 201, 296, 434, 446
franchising 21
Francis, J. 82
Frank, H. 391, 392
Fraser, S. 211, 212, 225
Frazier, E. F. 203, 204
Frederiksen, S. 219
Frederking, L. C. 86
Fredland, J. E. 185
Fredrickson, J. 393
free-riding 50
Freel, M. 338, 351, 357
Freeman, C. 354
Freitag 138
French classical school, economic theory 10–12
Frensch, P. A. 126

Frese, M. 125, 126, 154, 156, 157, 162, 164, 166
Fritsch, M. 32, 338
Fry, F. L. 422
Fry, Jeremy 346, 347, 348, 349
Fryer, P. 205
Fukuyama, F. 39
Fuller, Buckminster 345, 347
Furnham, A. 168
Furr, N. R. 100

Gabrielsson, J. 181
Gaddefors, J. 86
Gaglio, C. M. 127, 130, 340
Galbraith, C. S. 276
Galbraith, J. K. 28
Gammack, Peter 349
García, M. 351, 358, 359
Garcia-Teruel, P. 369
Gargulio, M. 132, 325
Garnier, G. 440, 442, 443
Garofoli, G. 34
Gartner, W. B. 17, 21, 24, 25, 80, 90, 96, 97, 100, 102, 108, 120, 125, 126, 157, 168, 313, 315, 405, 406
Garud, R. 105
Gaskill, L. R. 184, 187
Gates, Bill 157, 279, 291
Gatewood, E. J. 80, 108, 126, 168
Gatewood, R. D. 126
gearing ratio 425
Gedajlovic, E. 90, 247, 293
gender 209, 245–6
    see also female entrepreneurs
Gennaro, E. 449
George, G. 88, 338
Germany 63, 64, 65, 68, 201–2, 235, 446
Gersick, K. E. 239, 240
Ghoshal, S. 325, 341
Gianforte, Greg 140
Gibb, A. 22, 50, 277, 287, 322, 407, 408, 411, 413, 414, 415, 416, 421, 424
Gibson, D. 338
Giddens, Anthony 297
Giglierano, J. J. 166
Gilad, B. 100, 101, 129
Gilbert, B. A. 28, 30, 41
Gilman, M. 210
Gilmore, A. 321, 329, 334, 420
Gilroy, P. 205
Gist, M. E. 173, 174
Giusta, M. D. 325, 339, 341
Gladwell, M. 142
Glaeser, E. L. 32, 33, 34, 39
Global Entrepreneurship Monitor (GEM) 23, 30–1, 88, 220, 368, 404, 408

globalisation 432, 434
Glückler, J. 82
Goff, M. 164
Goffee, R. 17, 221, 272
Golann, B. 426
Gold, S. 351
Goldberg, L. R. 158
Gompers, P. 260
Gonzales, M. 277
Google 100, 138, 291
Gotsis, G. 88
government 46, 76–7
    action for SMEs 49–59, 72–6
    and community entrepreneurship 304, 308,
        311–12
    as economic agent 47
    finance 364, 368–9, 372–3, 376
    habitual entrepreneurs 263–4
    and networks 340
    as regulator 47
    role 46–9
    and social entrepreneurship 290, 294, 297–8
    as strategic planner and promoter 47
    targeting, possibilities for 56–8
government policy
    Business Link 62, 64, 65–6, 68, 69, 70, 72–6
    economic development 28, 30, 35, 51–2
    ethnic minority businesses 213
    internationalisation 432, 445–9
    local 67–72
    national 59–66
    sector 66–7
    support for entrepreneurship 18
    technical entrepreneurship 276, 285–7
    see also public policy; support structures
Graham, J. B. 129
Graham, T. 60, 371
Grameen Bank 289, 299
Granger, B. 207
Granovetter, M. 39, 40, 80, 81, 339
Grant, K. 329, 330, 334
Grant, P. 25, 383
Grant, S. 154, 177, 351, 358, 359
Grant Thornton 380
Gras, D. 301
Grayson, Tim 106
Greece 358, 434
Greene, F. J. 29, 43
Greene, P. G. 168, 173, 224, 227, 313
Greer, M. 227
Gregoire, D. A. 130, 166, 170
Grègoire, O. 315
Greiner, L. E. 18, 19, 271
Greve, A. 132, 340, 351, 352, 358
Grichnik, D. 99

Griffin, A. 270
Grilo, I. 28
Grimes, M. 295
Gromov, G. 283
growth see business growth and development;
    economic growth and development
Guersen, G. 322
Guillon, M. 201
Gulati, R. 325
Gully, S. M. 173
Gump, P. V. 108
Gumpert, D. 386
Gupta, V. K. 172
Gurdon, M. A. 269, 271, 281
Gustafsson, V. 114, 116, 117, 163, 176
Gyoshev, B. S. 83, 88

Haberfellner, R. 201
habitual entrepreneurs 252–67
Haines, G. H. 225
Håkansson, H. 324
Hall, G. R. 188, 400
Hall, P. 34, 275
Hambrick, D. 386
Hamel, G. 388
Hamill, J. 438
Hamilton, D. 185, 222
Hamilton, E. E. 223, 229, 246, 247, 248, 249
Hamilton, J. 419
Hamilton, R. 406, 414
Hampton, A. 340, 351, 352, 353, 354, 356, 358,
    359
Handler, W. 248–9
Handy, C. 427
Hanges, P. J. 164, 166, 167
Hannah, L. 48
Hansen, D. J. 128
Hansford, A. 50
Harackiewicz, J. M. 175
Harbi, S. E. 88
hard capital rationing 364
Harding, R. 30, 31, 227
Haribo 233
Harris, R. G. 34
Harrison, R. T. 279, 365, 378, 379
Hart, D. M. 31, 43, 44, 285, 286
Hart, M. M. 74, 76, 224, 313
Hartog, J. 188, 189
Harvey, C. 296, 297
Harvey, D. 248
Harvey, M. G. 323
Hashai, N. 388, 399
Hasseldine, T. 50
Haugh, H. M. 290, 293, 295, 303, 305, 306, 308,
    309, 311, 314, 315

Hauptmann, O. 280
Hawkins, P. 423
Haworth, C. 50
Haworth, J. 10, 22, 157, 410
Hay, M. 391
Hayek, F. A. 14, 270
Hayes, H. M. 323
Hayes, J. 127, 221
Haynes, D. C. 225
Haynes, G. W. 225
Haynie, J. M. 156, 169
Hayton, J. C. 309, 338
Headd, B. 192
Heath, C. 165
Hebda, J. 270
Hébert, R. F. 10, 11, 29, 122
Hechavarria, D. M. 31, 38
Heck, R. K. Z. 232
Heggestad 164
Heinzel, W. 279
Helliar, C. 376
Hellman, P. 434, 437
Hems, L. 368
Henderson, R. 37, 110
Hennessey, B. A. 174
Henrekson, M. 28, 82, 88
Henry, C. 222
Herbert, T. 24
Hernandez-Canovas, G. 371
Heron, L. 128
Herron, L. 157
Heseltine, Michael 375–6
Hess, M. 82
Hesterly, W. 325, 338, 352, 356
Hettero, M. 271
Hewitt, J. 56
Hewlett-Packard 284
Highlands and Islands 70
Higson, C. 382
Hill, C. J. 75
Hill, J. 319, 334, 338
Hill, K. G. 174
Hill, R. C. 160
Hills, G. E. 128, 129, 319, 320, 321, 322, 324, 326, 327, 328, 329, 330
hire purchase (HP) 373–4
Hiscox 375
Hisrich, R. D. 154, 177, 221, 320, 390
history of thought 9–26
Hite, J. 325, 338, 352, 354, 356
HM Treasury 56, 69, 70, 367, 377
Hoang, H. 133, 355
Hofer, C. W. 120, 291, 387, 393, 396
Hofstede, G. 38
Hogan, J. 158

Hogan, R. T. 158
Hogarth, R. M. 165
Hogia Group 102
Hogsved, B.-I. 101–2
Holcombe, R. G. 33
Holliday, R. 209
Holmquist, C. 89
Holtz-Eakin, D. 28
Honig, B. 83, 96, 97, 98, 260
Hoogstra, G. J. 405
Hooper, T. 422
Hoover 285, 349
Hornaday, J. A. 158
Horwitz, P. S. 279
Hoselitz, B. F. 10
Hoshi Onsen 236
Hotpoint 349
Houghton, S. M. 127, 130, 168
House of Commons Business and Enterprise Committee 373
households 84–5
Howarth, R. 223
Howorth, C. 223, 239, 243, 244, 245, 247, 248
Hoy, F. 22
Hsinchu Science Park (Taiwan) 275
Hsu, D. 260
Huber, G. 132
Huerta de Soto, J. 29
Huff, A. 401
Huggins, R. 32, 33, 34, 35, 37, 38, 39, 40, 41, 43, 326
Hughes, A. 54, 369, 370, 375
Hughes, M. 366, 370, 383, 384
Hulland, J. 132
Hulsink, W. 353
Hultman, C. 326, 327, 329
human capital 258–9, 261, 330
human resources 400, 419–21
Humphreys, L. G. 158, 161
Hundley, G. 227
Hung, H. 353
Hunt, Tony 350
Hunter, J. E. 170
Huse, M. 240, 307, 418
Husqvarna 110
Hussain, G. 210
Hutchings, K. 422
Hutchison, W. 405
Huy, Q. N. 313, 323
Hybels, R. C. 133
Hyvarinen, L. 448

Iacobucci, D. 247, 255, 256
Ibarra, H. 354, 359

Ibeh, K. I. N. 431, 432, 433, 434, 435, 437, 438, 439, 440, 441, 443, 446, 447, 449
Ice Hotel 106
IFF Research Ltd 380
IKEA 111, 233
Ikeda, S. 32, 33, 39, 40
ILO 223
immigration 21, 200–15, 359
imports 63–4
incremental internationalisation 435–7
India 182
indigenous communities 305
indigenous/internal failures 183–6
individual, in the entrepreneurial process 117, 125–7, 407–11
    see also personality
industry structure 393–4, 417–18, 442
informal entrepreneurship 89
information and communications technology 274
information gap 368
information searches 256–7, 265
information systems 401
Ingeus 294
innovation
    community entrepreneurship 306, 310
    economic development 29, 34, 35, 37
    family businesses 246–8, 249
    government policy 64
    habitual entrepreneurs 262, 265
    internationalisation 435–6
    marketing, entrepreneurial 323, 327, 328–30, 335
    networks 346, 351, 352, 354, 356–7
    and risk 189
    social 293, 294, 296, 298, 299, 309
    strategy 398–9
    technical entrepreneurship 270, 273, 280, 282
Innovation Research and Development Grants 64
insolvency 189–91, 193
Institute for One World Health 138
Institute of Directors 54
Institute of Export 57
institutional theory 236
institutions 81, 82–3, 87–90
Intel 284
intelligence, successful 176
interest (emotion) 174–5
internal/indigenous failures 183–6
International Accounting Standards Board (IASB) 383
International Family Enterprise Research Academy (IFERA) 235
International Federation of Accountants 371
internationalisation 399, 430–49
internet 442

Intrum Justitia 369
invoice discounting 380
Iona 347
Ireland, Republic of 394, 446
Isaksen, A. 35
Isaksen, E. J. 257, 263
Italy 68, 235, 255, 296, 358, 434
IVA 189
Ivy, R. 351
Izard, C. E. 175
Izushi, H. 33, 34, 37

Jack, S. 38, 83, 84, 275, 314, 325, 326, 334, 341, 353
Jackson, G. I. 348, 441
Jackson III, W. E. 84
Jacobs, J. 32, 39
Jacobsson, S. 275
Jaffe, A. B. 37
Jansen, E. 259
Janssen, F. 295
Japan 358, 444
Jarillo, J. C. 120, 165, 306, 314, 338, 352, 356
Jarvis, R. 366, 370, 372, 374, 383, 384
Jayawarna, D. 338, 340, 353, 355
Jelic, R. 254
Jenei, J. 300
Jenkins, R. 206
Jennings, J. E. 84
Jennings, P. D. 123
Jenssen, J. 338
Jo, M. 203
job creation 1, 18, 51–2, 313, 405–6
Jobs, Steve 271, 279, 282, 284
Jocumsen, G. 425
Johannisson, B. 85, 87, 240, 303, 304, 305, 306, 308, 310, 311, 313, 314, 326, 338, 340, 354, 355, 356, 360
Johanson, J. 399, 435, 436, 437, 438
Johansson, D. 29
Johns, G. 78, 79
Johnson, A. R. 156, 397, 398
Johnson, B. R. 22, 167
Johnson, G. 414, 415
Johnson, J. 439, 447
Johnson, J. E. 434, 439
Johnson, J. H. 84
Johnson, R. W. 157, 162
Johnson, S. 432
Johnston, A. 37, 38, 39
Johnston, W. J. 436
Johnstone, H. 87, 303, 305, 307, 308, 309, 313
Johnstone, M. A. 420
Jones, D. 291
Jones, F. F. 405, 406

Jones, Gareth 349
Jones, K. 404
Jones, M. V. 431, 439
Jones, O. 39, 325, 338, 339, 340, 341, 342, 353, 355
Jones, R. 319, 326, 327, 336
Jones, T. 84, 199, 201, 203, 205, 206, 207, 209, 210, 211, 212, 213, 215
Jones-Evans, D. 227, 269, 270, 272, 278, 280, 281, 285, 286
Jonker 188, 189
Jordan 224
Joseph Rowntree Foundation 296
Joyce, P. 325
Judd, B. B. 333
Judge, T. A. 195, 173
Julien, P.-A. 81, 291
Jupp, Simeon 349

Kahneman, D. 129
Kaish, S. 100, 101, 129
Kalantaridis, C. 416
Kaleka, A. 443
Kalleberg, A. 395
Kamp, M. 86
Kanfer, R. 161, 164
Kanter, R. 401
Kapp, J. 409
Kapsa, D. 99
Karlsson, C. 2, 37, 293
Karlsson, G. 85
Karlsson, T. 98
Karnini, A. 386
Karnoe, P. 105
Kasarda, J. 204
Kasem, L. 435, 437
Katsikeas, C. S. 443, 448
Katz, J. A. 18, 32, 89, 90, 127, 130, 306, 315, 340, 351
Kauffman Foundation 18
Kawtonen, T. 423
Kazanjian, R. K. 401
Kazuka, M. 204
Keasey, K. 365, 370, 375, 382, 405
Keeble, D. 275, 276
Keefe, L. 327
Keh, H. T. 127, 166, 170, 172
Keilbach, M. 28, 32, 33, 36, 37, 38
Kelley, M. 343
Kelly, G. A. 423
Keogh, B. 291
Kesteloot, C. 202
Ketchen, D. 165
Kets De Vries, M. 17, 169, 401
Keynes, J. M. 53, 364

Khan, G. M. 286
Kickul, J. 174
Kidwell, R. E. 291
Kilby, P. 15, 16
Kim, I. 202
Kim, M. S. 170
Kimball, S. T. 306
Kimmel, S. K. 172
Kincaid, D. 344
King, M. 392
King, T. 184
Kingdon, J. W. 277
Kinsella, R. 390, 394, 398
Kirby, D. A. 286
Kirchhoff, B. 398
Kirk-Dyson 346, 348
Kirkbride, J. 290, 295
Kirkels, Y. 353
Kirkpatrick, S. A. 157
Kirkwood, Lord 348
Kirkwood, Stuart 348
Kirzner, I. M. 13, 14, 16, 22, 29, 30, 33, 37, 38, 100, 122, 126, 130, 294
Kisfalvi, V. 389
Kistruck, G. M. 294
Kitching, J. 227
Kitson, M. 32, 41
Kitzmann, J. 126
Klein, D. B. 126
Klein, P. G. 122, 123
Klein, S. B. 240, 241, 245
Kleindl, B. 329
Klofsten, M. 96, 97, 98, 99, 101, 103–4, 113, 116, 117, 286, 271, 275, 285
Kloosterman, R. 83, 84, 199, 201, 202, 215
Kluver, J. D. 300
Klyver, K. 351, 358, 359
Knight, F. 13–14, 29, 122, 137, 165
Knight, G. A. 439
Knight, J. 448
Knight, Phil 140
Knight, R. M. 269, 271, 280
Knott, A. M. 193
knowledge 34, 35, 36–8, 126–7
knowledge spillovers 36–8
Ko, S. 126, 127
Koenig, H. 338
Koeter-Kant, J. 371
Kogut, B. 109
Kohtamaki, M. 423
Kolb, D. A. 132
Koller, R. H. 128
Kolvereid, L. 171, 257, 260, 262, 263
Komives, J. L. 278
Koolman, G. 11, 13

Korea 64
Korean entrepreneurs 202–3
Kotler, P. 320, 327
Kovner, A. 260
Kraus, S. 423
Kreft, S. F. 30
Kreiner, K. 343
Kritikos, A. S. 182
Krueger, N. F. 126, 133, 169, 171, 172, 173
Krugman, P. 32
Kuczynski, M. 11
Kuhn, T. 300
Kuti, E. 300
Kwon, S. W. 39, 40
Kwong, C. 227

La Valle, I. 227
Labour Force Survey (LFS) 221
Labour Party 18, 48, 61, 69, 297–8
Lacroix, T. 201
Laforet, S. 74
LaForge, R. W. 320, 321, 322, 324, 326, 327, 329
Lam, W. 226, 330
Lambrecht, J. 351, 352, 353, 355
Lamont, L. M. 269, 277
Landström, H. 105, 182, 306, 314
Lane, H. W. 131, 132, 436
Langan-Fox, J. 154, 177
Langlois, A. 202
Langowitz, N. 220
Larson, A. 352, 356
Larty, J. 229
Latin America 305
Lau, C.-M. 88
Laughton, N. 169
Lavoie, D. 38
Lawless, R. M. 190
Lawson, C. 34
Lazier, W. C. 274
Le Breton-Miller, I. 394
Le Grand, J. 55
Leadbeater, C. 289, 290, 292, 298, 315
Learn Direct 63
learning
   from experience 259, 263, 410
   from failure 183
   and opportunities 127, 130–1
   organisational 423–4
   see also education and training
leasing 373, 374
Leca, B. 82
Lechner, C. 38, 338, 351, 356
Lee, D. R. 29
Lee, L. 166, 175
Lee, M.-S. 184

Lee, R. 39, 325, 340, 341
Lee, W.-Y. 436
Lees, A. 293, 303, 306
Lehman-Ortega, L. 299
Lehmann, E. 28, 37
Leicht, K. 395
Leigh, R. 405, 406, 409, 410, 413
lemonade principle 142–3
Leonard-Barton, D. 339, 340, 353, 358, 360
Leonidou, L. C. 441, 443
Lerkx, L. 325
Lerner, J. 260
Lerner, M. 315
Letts, C. W. 290
Leung, A. 166, 175
Levi-Strauss, C. 389
Levie, J. 30, 404, 413
Lewis, P. S. 320, 326, 336, 337
Lewis, V. L. 271, 401, 411, 413
Leydesdorff, L. 35
Leys, C. 298
Li, T. 286
Liao, J. 39, 96, 97–8
Liao, Y. 208
Liberman-Yaconi, L. 422
Lichtenstein, B. B. 123, 128, 413
lifecycle models of business growth 411–13
Light, I. 202, 203, 204, 205, 208
Lim, B. C. 127, 166, 170, 172
Lim, D. S. K. 163, 175
Lin, C. 351
Lin, H. C. 437, 439
Lin, J. 341
Lindahl, Carin 101, 105, 111, 112–13, 115
Lindberg, R. 390
Lindell, P. 271
Lindgren, M. 307
Lindh de Montoya, M. 304
Lindholm Dahlstrand, Å. 275, 276
Link, A. N. 10, 11, 29, 122
Linpak 349
Lionais, D. 87, 303, 305, 307, 308, 309, 313
Liou, N. 219, 229
Lipman, H. 374
Little, B. 442
Littlewood, Joan 347
Littunen, H. 338
Litvak, I. A. 269, 277, 278
Litz, R. 84
Livewire 63
Ljunggren, E. 229, 259, 311
Lloyd, Selwyn 48
loan guarantee schemes 372–3
Local Better Regulation Offices 60
Local Economic Companies 340

Local Enterprise Companies 68
Local Enterprise Partnerships (LEPs) 70, 74, 75, 76, 214
localities *see* regions and localities
Locke, E. A. 97, 125, 157, 164, 166, 167, 171, 173, 406
Lockett, A. 253, 265, 421
locus of control 164–5, 168, 173
Lohrke, F. T. 353
Lomax, W. 333, 334
London Stock Exchange 376
Long, W. 127, 128, 129
Lorenz, E. 34
Lotti, F. 411
Lotz, J. 304, 313
Low, C. 290, 295
Low, M. B. 23, 155
Lubatkin, M. 90
Lucas, R. E. 34
Lucasfilm 284
Lumpkin, G. T. 123, 128, 280, 300, 301, 313
Lundstrom, A. 41, 42, 43
Luostarinen, R. 432
Lusch, R. F. 323
Lyon, D. W. 24, 129
Lyon, F. 215

Ma Mung, E. 201
Macallan, H. 374
MacArthur, R. 167
MacDonald, R. 15
MacKinnon, D. 351
MacMillan, I. C. 155
Macmillan Committee 364
Macrae, D. 395
Madsen, T. K. 436, 437, 438, 439
Maillat, D. 34
Mair, J. 89, 290, 292, 293, 299, 308
Malaysia 255, 434
Malecki, E. J. 32, 34
Malerba, F. 37
Mallory, G. 436
Malmberg, A. 34
management buyins (MBIs) 254, 266, 377
management buyouts (MBOs) 254, 266, 377
management constraints 413, 418–20
managerial skills 259, 262–3, 270–1, 277, 280, 400, 409, 413–15, 421
managers, introducing new 427
Mancuso, P. 401
Mandl, I. 236
Manev, I. M. 83
Mangoldt 13, 14
Manigart, S. 265
Manimala, M. 359

Manning, R. A. 184, 187
Manolava, T. S. 83, 88
Mansfield, E. 181
Marable, M. 204
March, J. G. 128, 188, 435
Marcucci, P. N. 223
market failure 50, 53, 54, 55, 72
market niche strategies 394–6
market structure, and business growth and development 418
marketing mix 321, 333
marketing, entrepreneurial (EM) 319–37
    business growth and development 420, 425–6
    education 3–4
    internationalisation 445
    process 330–3
    and strategy 397, 400
    tools 333–4
Markman, G. D. 126, 156, 176
Marlino, D. 174
Marlow, S. 213, 219, 222, 223, 224, 226, 227, 228, 229, 246
Marriott, N. 383
Marriott, P. 383
Marriotti, Steve 142
Marshall, A. 13
Marshall, J. N. 63
Martí I. 89, 292, 293
Martin, A. 279
Martin, B. A. 418, 426
Martin, F. 255
Martin, J. H. 418, 426
Martin, R. 32, 292
Martinez, M. E. 109
Martinez-Solano, P. 369
Marvel, M. R. 270, 280
Marx, K. 270
Marzena, S. 293
Masakowski, E. 301
Mascarenhas-Keyes 215
Maskell, P. 34
Mason, C. M. 181, 279, 290, 295, 365, 378, 379
Mason, P. 424
Massey, C. 406
Massey, D. 229
Masters, R. 165
Mataira, P. 87
Mathews, C. H. 169
Mathias, P. 345
Matthews, P. 424
Mattson, M. T. 203
Mattsson, L. G. 436, 437
Maule, C. J. 269, 277, 278
Mayer, M. 279
Mayoux, L. 223

McAdam, M. 227, 228, 275
McAdam, R. 275
McClelland, D. C. 16, 126, 154, 166, 167, 277, 359
McCloy, R. A. 175
McClure, J. E. 191
McClurg 291, 292
McCoshan, A. 67, 68
McDonald, M. H. B. 425, 426
McDonald's 111
McDougald, M. S. 84
McDougall, P. P. 28, 393, 396, 431, 439
McEvoy, D. 201, 203, 204, 205, 206, 207, 209
McGee, J. 173
McGowan, P. 319, 334, 338, 340, 351
McGrath, R. G. 97, 101, 165, 188, 261
McGuinness, N. W. 442
McKechnie, S. 225
McLean, M. 291, 293, 294
McMullan, W. E. 127, 128
McMullen, J. S. 80, 120, 123, 124
McNaughton, R. 431, 448
Meadowcroft, J. 39, 40
Meckstroth, D. D. 193
Meek, M. 11
Meek, W. R. 290
Megyesi, M. I. 34
Meier, R. 165
Mellers, B. A. 165
Menger, C. 14
mentoring 264, 275, 359
Menzies, T. 359
Meredith, G. 167
Metcalf, H. 205, 206
Metro 115
Meuleman, M. 265
Meyer, G. D. 184, 185
Meyer, M. 286
mezzanine finance 367, 377
Miccini, A. 61
Michael, S. C. 41
Michaelas, N. 50, 382
Michel, P. 256
microeconomics 13
microfinance 299
Microsoft 100, 284
Middlemas, K. 48, 49
Miesenbock, K. J. 440, 441, 442
Miles, M. P. 319, 323, 324, 327, 427
Mill, J. S. 12
Miller, B. 96
Miller, D. 156, 160, 168, 394, 401
Miller, M. 381
Miller, N. 310
Miller, T. M. 295

Mills, C. 340
Milner, I. 369
Min, P. G. 202, 203
Miner, A. S. 389, 391
Miner, J. B. 165, 167, 423
Ministry of Trade and Industry, Finland 406
Minnillo, P. R. 418, 426
Minniti 33, 38, 40, 43, 44, 131, 220, 368
Mintzberg, H. 388, 391, 393, 401
Mir, R. 130
Mirchandani, K. 225, 226
Mises, L. 14, 122
Mistiaanen, P. 202
MIT 275
MIT Entrepreneurship Center 271
Mitchell, F. 384
Mitchell, J. 344
Mitchell, J. R. 165
Mitchell, R. K. 129, 156, 159, 162, 163, 165, 175
Mitchell, T. R. 173, 174, 393
Mitter, S. 208, 209
Modell, J. 204
Modigliani, F. 381
Modood, T. 205
Moen, O. 418
Mohannak, K. 338, 340, 351, 357
Moingeon, B. 299
Moini, A. H. 444
Mole, K. F. 29, 74, 76
Monck, C. S. P. 275
Mondragon Corporation 296
Moody, J. 84
Moore, D. G. 272, 277
Moore, W. T. 188
Morely, A. 295
Morgan, K. 35
Morgan, R. E. 448
Morris, C. E. 185
Morris, M. H. 248, 320, 324, 326, 329, 334, 335, 336, 337
Morrish, S. 319, 326, 329, 336
Morse, E. A. 163, 175
Mort, G. S. 291, 292
Moser, S. B. 169
Mosey, S. 261, 264
Moss, T. W. 300, 313
motivation 155, 163–4, 166–7, 170
    business growth and development 406–7, 408, 410
    female entrepreneurs 221, 223, 228
    habitual entrepreneurs 255–6, 265
    intrinsic 126, 172, 174–5, 177
    technical entrepreneurs 277–9
Moult, S. 353
Mowday, R. T. 79, 80

Mowen, J. 329
Moyes, A. 67
Mueller, P. 38, 286
Mueller, S. L. 173
Mulgan, Geoff 298
Mulholland, K. 246
Muller, R. 279
Mullings, L. 204
Mullins, D. 207
Mullins, J. W. 166, 188, 389
Mulvenna, D. 394
Munari, F. 378
Munro, H. 438, 439
Murphy, G. B. 160
Murphy, K. M. 39
Murray, G. C. 377
Murray, J. A. 398
Muzyka, D. F. 120
Myers, A. 338, 339
Myers, S. C. 381, 382
Mykhenko, V. 297

Nagle, M. 37
Nahapiet, J. 325, 341
Namiki, N. 439, 444
Nank, R. 300
Nantucket Nectars/Allserve 102, 105, 112, 113, 115
Narayana, C. L. 324
National Audit Office 60, 61
National Economic Development Council (NEDC) 48
National Endowment for Science, Technology and the Arts (NESTA) 287, 367
National Health Service (NHS) 297
National Semiconductor 283
National Women's Business Council 220
nationalisation 48
NatWest 54
Nauwelaers, C. 35
Neeley, S. E. 75
Neergaard, H. 219, 222, 271, 351, 358
Nelson, R. E. 106
Nelson, R. R. 286
neo-Austrian school, economic theory 13–14
neoclassical school, economic theory 13, 29
neoliberalism 297–8
Netherlands 201, 202, 446
network capital 40
Network Challenge 66
networks 338–61
    business growth and development 424
    community 310–11, 313
    contextualising entrepreneurship 83–4
    economic development 37–8, 40

entrepreneurial process 101
ethnicity 205, 359
habitual entrepreneurs 260–1, 265
internationalisation 437–8, 440–1
marketing, entrepreneurial 324–6, 334
and opportunities 132–3
Neubaum, D. O. 293
Neumann, U. 40
New Deal 63
New Labour 298
New Zealand 305, 438, 439
Newbaum, D. 405, 406
Newby, H. 306
Newby, R. 228
Newman, J. 297
NeXT Computers 284
niche strategies 394–6
Nicholls, A. 291, 295, 300
Nicholls-Nixon, C. L. 390
Nicholson, L. 229, 245
Nicolaou, N. 157, 179, 356
Nike 140
Nilsson, A. 304, 305, 306, 310, 313, 314
Njite, D. 184
Nonaka, I. 34
non-predictive control 137
Norburn, D. 278
North, D. C. 39, 87, 378, 405, 406, 409, 410, 411, 413, 416
Northern Ireland 62, 68, 69, 75, 358
Northern Ireland Assembly 69
Norton, E. 382
Norton, W. I. 188
Norway 255, 310–11, 312–13, 358
novice entrepreneurs 253, 255–66
Novy, A. 309
Nowikowski, S. 207
Nucci, A. 227
Nutt, P. C. 188
Nyssens, M. 291, 296

O'Donnell, A. 341, 353
O'Dwyer, M. 321, 322, 329–30, 332
O'Gorman, C. 398
O'Grady, S. 436
O'Leary, H. 291
O'Neill, K. 28
Oakey, R. P. 270, 275, 279, 285, 286
OECD (Organisation for Economic Cooperation and Development) 41, 220, 304, 362, 386, 406, 433, 434, 440, 441, 443, 445, 446, 448
OECD Eurostat 406
Office of Fair Trading 60
Ogbor, J. O. 22, 222

Ok Lee, D. 203
Oldham, G. R. 131
Olm, K. 340
Olofsson, C. 271
Olsen, H. C. 432, 435, 442, 443, 448
Olson, M. 39
Omta, S. W. F. 325
Omura, G. S. 328
ONS 221
Open University 367
openness to experience 159
opportunistic technical entrepreneurs 277, 281
opportunities 120–34
   community entrepreneurship 305–6
   contextual understanding of 80, 83–4
   habitual entrepreneurs 256, 257–8, 259, 264–5
   marketing, entrepreneurial 328–9, 335
opportunity structure 201–4
optimism 164–5, 167–8, 191, 263
organisational culture 419
organisational learning 423–4
organisational structure 427
Orser, B. J. 225
Osberg, S. 292
Osborne, R. L. 184, 193
Ostgaard, A. 38, 325, 326
Oughton, E. 85
overdrafts 370, 371
over-optimism 164–5, 167–8
overtrading 420
Oviatt, B. M. 431, 439
Owen, Robert 296
ownership and management, separation of 381, 382
Owualah, S. 445
Ozcan, P. 325

Pace, D. J. 336
Pache, A.-C. 295
Pacheco, D. F. 290
Packendorff, J. 307
Page, Larry 100
Pajaczkowska, C. 205
Palich, L. E. 188, 191
Paliwoda, S. 437
Pardy, W. 305, 309, 311
Park, D. J. 336
Park, J. 341
Parker, D. 208
Parker, S. 38, 41, 226, 254
Parsa, H. G. 184
Parsons, W. 404
Patel, S. 210
patents 37
Paton, R. 295

Patra, E. 340, 351, 355, 358
Patzelt, H. 156, 290
Paul, S. 369
Pavord, W. C. 443
Payne, D. 68
Payne, G. T. 313
PayPal 100
Peacock, A. 50, 52, 56
Peacock, P. 165
Pearce, C. 421
Pearce, J. A. 41, 392
Pearson, A. W. 84, 279
Pearson, J. 392
Peattie, K. 295
Peel, M. J. 423
Peng, M. W. 438
Pennington, M. 39, 40
Penrose, E. T. 414, 435
perceptions of business failure 186–7
Peredo, A. M. 87, 291, 293, 294, 305, 306, 308, 309, 310, 311, 313, 314, 315
performance
   business growth and development 404–29
   and effectuation 147–50
   family businesses 245
   female-owned firms 227–9
   habitual entrepreneurs 261–3
   and networks 356
   and psychology of the entrepreneur 160–1, 173–4
   social entrepreneurship 295
   and strategy 391, 392, 394
Perkins, R. K. 310
Perlmann, J. 204
Perren, L. 25
Perrini, F. 307, 313
Perry, C. 167
personality 16–17, 21, 22, 125–6, 136, 154–60, 164, 401, 407–11
Peters, M. P. 390
Petersen, B. 432
Petersen, M. 173, 340, 351
Peterson, R. T. 129, 338, 354, 355
Pettersen, L. T. 259
Phan, P. 254, 277
philanthropy 19, 291, 294
Phillips, Andrew 348
Phillips, B. 398
Phillips, J. M. 173
Phillips, N. 306, 308
Phizacklea, A. 200, 209
Pierrakis, Y. 377, 378
Pike, Jeffery 349
pilot in the plane principle 143
Piore, M. 340

Pisano, G. 314
Pittaway, L. 23, 25, 30, 277
Pixar 284
planned behaviour, theory of 171–2
planning, business 98–9, 389–92, 415, 422–3
Plaschka, G. R. 278, 391, 392
Plummer, L. A. 37, 80
Podestà, S. 324, 336
Polanyi, K. 40, 80
Politis, D. 181
Porter, M. E. 32, 34, 35, 275, 394, 397, 417
Portes, A. 39, 202
portfolio entrepreneurs 248, 249, 253–66, 411
Posen, H. E. 193
Poutziouris, P. 50, 382
Powell, B. 28
Power, D. 376
Powers, J. B. 168
Prahalad, C. K. 388
Prais, S. J. 48
Preisendörfer, P. 40, 83, 351, 353
Premaratne, S. 351
Priest, S. J. 74
Prince, R. A. 333
Prince's Youth Business Trust 63
process, entrepreneurial 95–119
producer technical entrepreneurs 281
proximal and distal processes 158, 161, 177
Pryke, R. 48
psychological theory 16–17
psychology of the entrepreneur 152–79, 441
    see also personality
Public Administration Select Committee 300
public community ventures 311
public policy 35, 41–4, 273, 406
    see also government policy
public–private partnerships (PPPs) 298
Pugh, D. S. 436
Pugliese, E. 202
Push 368
Putnam, R. 39, 40
Pyke, E. 340

Quadagno, J. 297
Quesnay 11
Quinn, J. 388
Quinn, R. 393, 401

R. Durtnell & Sons 236
R&D 51, 64
Racine, W. P. 279
Radu, M. 229
Rae, D. 325
Raju, N. S. 165
Ram, D. 206, 209, 210, 215

Ram, M. 85, 200, 208, 209, 210, 212, 213, 265, 351, 411
Ramani, S. 356
Ramirez-Pasillas, M. 85
Ramos-Rodriguez, A. 341
Ramsden, M. 50, 76
Rao, P. 434
Rath, J. 83, 84, 200, 201, 202, 215
Rauch, A. 125, 126, 154, 156, 157, 162, 164, 166
Ravasi, D. 131
Ray, D. M. 168
Ray, S. 125
Razin, E. 202
Read, G. V. 365, 371
Read, L. 225
Read, S. 163, 165
Reagan, Ronald 204
Redien-Collot 229
Reese, P. 351
Reeves, F. 205, 208, 210
Reger, R. 401
Regional Development Agencies (RDAs) 68, 69, 70, 74, 214
Regional Growth Fund 62
Regional Selective Assistance 62
Regional Technology Centres 64
Regional Venture Capital Funds (RVCFs) 378
regions and localities 31–6, 67–72, 85–7, 311–12
regulation 47, 50, 51, 54, 59–61
Regulatory Policy Commission (RPC) 59, 60, 61
Rehn, A. 89, 351
Reid, G. 384
Reid, S. D. 436, 439, 440, 441
Reilly, M. D. 126, 169, 171, 172, 173
Reitberger, G. 279
relationships in small firms 340, 353–4
    see also networks
Renzulli, L. 84, 169, 358
Rerup, C. 252
research/science parks 274–6, 286
research technical entrepreneurs 281
resource-based theory of internationalisation 438–9
Restrictive Practices Act 49
Rex, J. 205
Reynolds, P. D. 28, 30, 31, 38, 95, 96, 102, 120, 368
Ricardo, D. 12
Richard, D. 69, 70, 74
Richardson, P. 223
Ricketts, M. 12, 13
Riddle, D. F. 75
Riding, A. L. 224, 225
Rightnow Technologies 140
Rindova, V. 165

Riordan, C. M. 126
risk 11, 12, 13–14, 16
   and failure 187–9
   finance 365–6, 371, 379
   gender differences in attitudes towards 225–6, 228
   marketing, entrepreneurial 335
   and return, relationship between 365–6
   technical entrepreneurship 274, 277
risktaking propensity 164–6
Robbie, K. 255
Roberts, B. W. 158
Roberts, C. 383
Roberts, E. B. 269, 270, 271–2, 274, 275, 278, 279, 280
Robinson, R. B. J. 157, 392, 393, 396
Robinson, S. 226
Robinson, V. 207
Robson Rhodes 367
Robson, P. J. A. 50, 74, 262, 265
Roddick, Anita and Sam 157
Rodgers, P. 89
Roelandt, T. 35
Roessl, D. 391, 392
Rogers, E. 344
Rogoff, E. G. 184, 232
Rolland, D. 87
Romanelli, E. 393
Romer, P. M. 28, 34
Romijn, H. 221
Rønning, L. 262, 263, 311, 312
Ronstadt, R. 261
Roomi, M. 340, 342
Roper, S. 74, 76
Roquebert, J. 340, 351
Rosa, P. 185, 222, 224, 225, 247, 255, 256, 263, 265, 411
Rose, M. B. 16, 223, 236, 246
Rosen, B. 224, 340
Rosenstein, C. 203, 204
Ross, S. M. 381
Rosson, P. J. 440, 445
Roth, P. L. 126, 165
Rothfuss, R. 126
Rothwell, R. 270, 338, 351, 352
Rotork 346, 347, 349
Rotter, J. B. 16, 168
Round, J. 89
Rouse, J. 227
Route 128 (Massachusetts) 273, 274
Rowley, J. 319, 326, 327, 336
Royal College of Art (RCA) 345, 346, 347, 349, 350
RTZ 348
Rubin, I. M. 270, 280

Rumelt, R. P. 105, 388
Rural Development Commission 68

Saal, D. 74, 76
Sabel, C. 340
Sacerdote, B. 33, 39
Sainsbury's 294
Sakano, T. 340, 351, 358
Salaff, J. 132, 340, 341, 351, 352, 358
Salamon, L. 300
Salomo, S. 280
Samsom, K. J. 269, 271, 281
Samuels, J. 365
Samuelsson, M. 95, 98, 114
Sanandaji, T. 82
Sandberg, W. 393, 396
Sandford, C. 50
Santarelli, E. 411
Santos, F. 295
Saparito, P. 133, 224
Sapienza, H. J. 116, 128
Sarason, Y. 123
Sarasvathy, S. 97, 111, 112, 113, 114, 116, 117, 118, 124, 163, 165, 176, 293, 389
Saren, M. 319, 336
Sassen, S. 200, 204
Sautet, F. 29, 30, 33, 37, 38
Saxenian, A. 38, 276, 325, 340, 351
Say, J.-B. 11–12, 29, 293
SBRC, Kingston University 406
Scarman, Lord 200, 213
Scase, R. 17, 221, 272
Scharfstein, D. 260
Scheré, J. 155
Scherer, F. M. 398
Scherer, R. F. 169
Schiereck, D. 126
Schilling, M. A. 279
Schindehutte, M. 324
Schmidt, J. B. 328
Schmude, J. 32
Schoenfeldt, L. F. 125
Scholes, K. 414, 415
Schoonhoven, C. 394, 396
Schoorman, F. D. 243
Schrage, H. 269, 270, 278, 280
Schreier, J. 219, 221
Schultz, M. 343
Schumpeter, J. A. 15–16, 19, 23, 25, 29, 30, 37, 122, 124, 192, 270, 274, 290, 293, 294
Schutgens, V. 405
Schwartz, A. 165
Schwartz, B. 22
Schwartz, E. B. 219, 221
Schwartz, R. G. 24

Schweitzer, M. E. 381
Schwenk, C. R. 392, 423
Schwer, R. K. 166
science/research parks 274–6, 286
Scotland 62, 68–9, 70–2, 75, 189, 255, 340
Scott, A. 32
Scott, J. 344
Scott, L. R. 17, 22, 126, 129, 162
Scott, M. 19, 411, 424
Scott, Tom 102, 105
Scottish Enterprise 378
Scottish Executive 70
Scottish Parliament 69
Seabright, P. 32, 39, 40
Seaman, S. 420
search for business opportunities 128–9
Sears 138
Seawright, K. K. 163, 175
Sector Skills Councils 65, 67
secured lending 366, 371, 375
Seelos, C. 290, 292, 299, 308
Seibert, S. E. 156, 157, 159
Seifert, C. M. 132
Sekem 299
Selective Finance for Investment 62
Self, J. T. 184
self-efficacy, perceived 172, 173–4, 177
self-employed people
    ethnicity 200, 203–8, 213, 215
    and government policy 48, 49
    habitual entrepreneurs 254
    numbers (1930–2010) 48, 49
    technical entrepreneurship 278, 279, 280
    women 218, 219, 220, 221, 224, 227, 228
self-selected stakeholders 141, 144, 146–7, 150
Selsky, J. W. 305
Senneseth, K. 307, 418
Sepulveda, L. 215
Sequeira, J. M. 173
sequestration 189
serial entrepreneurs 253–66
Seringhaus, F. H. R. 445
SERT 51, 54
Servais, P. 436, 437, 438, 439
Sexton, D. L. 157, 165, 168, 226
Shackle, G. L. S. 123
shadow options 261
Shaikh, M. 277
Shane, S. A. 23, 24, 25, 30, 96, 97, 98, 99, 101,
    103–4, 107, 108, 109, 113, 114, 116, 120,
    121, 122, 123, 124, 126, 133, 157, 159,
    162, 165, 166, 179, 256, 262, 278, 290,
    305, 306, 314, 381, 389, 406, 423
Shanley, M. 188
Shapero, A. 17

Shapira, Z. 188
Sharir, M. 315
Sharma, D. 434
Sharma, P. 242, 245, 270
Shaver, K. G. 17, 22, 80, 108, 126, 129, 162, 168
Shaw, E. 219, 224, 226, 291, 292, 307, 312, 313,
    314, 319, 322, 323, 324, 325, 326, 327,
    328, 329, 330, 331, 333, 334, 338, 315,
    352, 354, 356, 368
Shaw, J. C. 84
Shaw, W. 277
Shell Technology Enterprise Programme 64
Shepherd, D. A. 99, 120, 123, 124, 126, 130, 154,
    156, 157, 166, 169, 170, 181, 188, 261,
    265, 290, 394, 406
Sherer, P. D. 79
Sherman, H. 167
Shionoya, Y. 15
Shockley, William 282, 283–4
Shockley Semiconductor Laboratory 283
Shockley Transistor Company 283
Short, J. C. 300, 313
Shrader, C. B. 392, 423
Shrader, R. C. 128, 129, 389
Shuen, A. 314
Shulman, J. M. 293
Sian, S. 383
Siegel, D. S. 277, 389
Silicon Valley 268, 273, 276, 283, 284, 340
Simon, M. 127, 130, 168
Simonton, D. K. 125
Simpson, J. 380
Sine, W. D. 128
Singh, R. P. 108, 132
Sjöberg, L. 168
Skagegård, L.-Å. 101, 105, 111
Skiippagurra Festival (Norway) 310
Skills for Small Business 65
Skoll, Jeff/Skoll Foundation 291
Slater, S. E. 439, 441, 442
Slevin, D. P. 394
Slotte-Kock, S. 326
Slovic, P. 129
Slow, J. 434, 439, 447
Small Business Act 53
Small Business Administration 72
Small Business Council (SBC) 51, 60, 61
Small Business Initiative 65
Small Business Service 51, 52, 75, 221, 228, 377,
    421
Small Firms Lead Body 65
Small Firms Loan Guarantee Scheme (SFLGS)
    61–2, 364, 372, 373
Small Firms Service 65, 72, 73, 75
Small Firms Training Loans 63

small firms vs entrepreneurship 19–21
Smallbone, D. 57, 82, 83, 86, 88, 89, 206, 212, 213, 214, 340, 351, 359, 405, 406, 409, 410, 411, 413, 416, 418, 420, 421, 425
Smircich, L. 222, 223, 228, 229
Smith, A. E. 12, 305
Smith, B. R. 295
Smith, D. A. 353
Smith, J. B. 165, 391
Smith, K. G. 125, 400
Smith, M. J. 296, 298
Smith, N. R. 156, 165, 167, 270, 272, 277, 278, 423
Smith-Hunter, A. 409
Smyrnios, K. X. 240, 241, 245
Snyder, M. 157
Soar, S. 204
Sobel, R. S. 29, 30, 44
social capital/resources 39–40, 83–4, 247, 260–1, 340–1, 359
social competence 176
social entrepreneurship 289–302, 306, 307, 308
social innovation 293, 294, 296, 298, 299, 309
social marginality theory 17
social networks see networks
sociological theory 16, 17–18
soft capital rationing 364
Solemn, O. 278, 395
Solomon, G. T. 222
Solow, R. 29
Soni, S. 207
Soskice, D. 64
Soufani, K. 50
South Asian entrepreneurs 200, 203–10, 212–15
Soviet Union 86, 89
Spain 68, 296
Specialised Small Business Investment Companies (SSBICs) 204
Spector, T. D. 157, 179
Spence, J. T. 159
Srinivasan, S. 203, 207
Stacey, R. D. 417, 423
stages of development models of internationalisation 435–7
stages of growth models 411–13
Stanford Research Park/Stanford Industrial Park 276
Stanford University 284
Stanga, K. G. 383
Stanworth, C. 207
Stanworth, J. 207, 278, 408
Starbuck, W. H. 182, 183
Starbucks 111, 117
Staring, R. 210
Starr, J. 261, 352, 356

start-ups see business start-ups
Stay In Place 111, 115
Steele, H. 168
Steffenson, R. 37
Steil, B. 286
Steiner, M. P. 278
Steinmetz, L. L. 413
Sten, J. 341
Stephan, U. 340
Stephenson, Robert 345
Sternberg, R. J. 127, 164, 176
Stevenson, H. H. 120, 165, 294, 306, 307, 311, 314, 386
Stevenson, L. 41, 42, 43, 222
Steward, F. 338, 342, 344
stewardship theory 242–3, 247
Stewart Jr, W. H. 126, 165
Steyaert, C. 32, 89, 90, 306
Stiener, M. 395
Stimpson, D. V. 159
Stivers, C. 300
Stokes, D. 191, 192, 322, 323, 327, 332, 333, 334
Stokes, G. S. 126
Stone, M. 392
Stoner, C. R. 422
Storey, D. J. 28, 29, 50, 51, 53, 54, 187, 227, 275, 319, 325, 326, 327, 386, 394, 405, 406, 407, 410, 411, 413, 414, 419, 432
Storper, M. 31, 32, 34
Storr, V. H. 39
Stough, R. 286
Strandstov, J. 440
strategic alliances 325
strategy 386–403, 413, 414–15, 422–3
strategymaking process 389–93
Stratos Group 392
Striegel, W. H. 168
Stuart, R. 272
Stuart, T. E. 133
Styles, C. 436, 437, 448
Subrahmanya, M. H. B. 280
succession 248–9, 391
Sugden, R. 365
Suh, D.-C. 184
Sullivan, D. 436
Summers, B. 369
superdiversity 215
suppliers, as source of finance 369–70
support structures 47–9, 213–14, 223, 264, 265, 274–6, 286–7, 340, 359, 445–9
Surinamese entrepreneurs 202
Sutton, R. I. 79, 80
Swedberg, R. 30
Sweden 255, 358
Swift, C. S. 224

Symantec 100
Syrett, S. 215
Szarka, J. 38
Szerb, L. 34, 180, 182

Taalas, S. 89, 351
Tagg, S. 181
Tagiuri, R. 237, 238
Taiwan 275
Takeuchi, H. 34
Talke, K. 280
Tan, W. L. 96, 97–8, 254
Tann, J. 74
Tanzania 223
Tapsell, P. 306, 307
targeting of government policy 56–9
Tarleton, J. S. 444
taxation 51, 62, 236–7, 264, 374, 381–2
Taylor, B. 296
Taylor, F. W. 427
Taylor, Gill 348
Taylor, S. E. 162, 219, 229
Teach, R. D. 22, 24
Teaching Company Scheme 64
teambuilding and team management 421
Teasdale, S. 303, 308
technical entrepreneurship 268–88
technical skills, habitual entrepreneurs 259
technological competence 356
technology 268–88, 378, 398–9, 401–2
Teece, D. J. 314
Terjesen, S. 88
Terry, N. 384
Terziovski, M. 399
Tesar, G. 436, 444, 445
Tesco 294
Thatcher, Margaret 297
Theodorakopoulos, N. 84, 424
There Will Be Blood 169
Third Sector 290, 296, 298, 300, 312
Third Way 297
Thomas, L. 420
Thompson, E. R. 171, 172
Thompson, J. L. 293, 303, 306, 315
Thompson, P. 33, 227
Thornton, P. H. 85
Thorpe, R. 38
three circles model of family businesses 235–9
three dimensional development model 239–40
Thrift, N. 86
Thunailes, W. 63
Thurik, A. R. 28, 29, 30, 31, 41, 225, 404
Tichy, N. 342, 343, 344
Tidd, J. 399

Tighe, E. M. 174
Tiller, M. G. 383
Timmons, J. A. 120, 391, 393
Tönnies, F. 306
Toschi, L. 378
Tötterman, H. 341
Toulouse, J. M. 156, 160, 168
Townsend, D. M. 172
Tracey, P. 293, 295, 306, 308, 309, 315
Tracy, S. 404
Trade Association Forum 67
trade associations 66
Trade Partners UK 63
Trailer, J. W. 160
training see education and training
Training and Enterprise Councils 68, 69
Trajtenberg, M. 37
Trettin, L. 40, 85
Trevelyan, R. 168
Tricker, M. 207, 368
triple helix approach to economic development 35–6
Truman, C. 222
Tsai, F. 341
Tschajanow, W. 84
Tunisian entrepreneurs 201
Turati, C. 131
Turgot 11, 270
Turkish entrepreneurs 201–2
Turnbull, P. W. 436, 438
Turner, Ted 141–2
Turok, I. 38
Tushman, M. 110
Tushman, N. 342
Tuttle, C. 13
Tversky, A. 129, 165
Tybejee, T. T. 442
Tyler, P. 32

Ucbasaran, D. 25, 129, 130, 191, 252, 253, 254, 255, 257, 258, 259, 261, 262, 263, 265, 306, 421
Uhlaner, L. 340
UK Survey of SME Finances (UKSMEF) 211–12
Ukraine 89
Ulijn, J. 285
uncertainty 11, 12, 13–14, 16, 137, 274, 328, 355, 371
  entrepreneurial process 99, 113, 114, 116–17
unemployed people 53, 63, 205, 207, 304
Unger, J. M. 424
United Kingdom
  community entrepreneurship 304
  ethnic minority businesses 200, 201, 203, 204–15

United Kingdom (*continued*)
   failure, entrepreneurial 185, 189
   family businesses 236
   female entrepreneurs 221, 368
   finance 364–81, 383
   government 48–51, 53, 57, 59–76
   habitual entrepreneurs 255
   internationalisation 446
   inventor-entrepreneurs 345
   size of SME sector 53
   social entrepreneurship 296–9
   strategy 394, 395
   technical entrepreneurship 275, 286, 287
   VAT registrations and gross value added 33
United States of America
   diamond trading in NY 39
   education 18
   entrepreneurial activity 180
   entrepreneurship policy 41
   ethnic minority businesses 201, 202–4, 205
   failure, entrepreneurial 182, 189–91, 193
   female entrepreneurs 220–1, 368
   finance 378, 381
   government policy 72
   habitual entrepreneurs 255
   job creation 18
   networks 358
   philanthropy 19
   R&D 64
   social entrepreneurship 296
   technical entrepreneurship 273, 275, 276, 279
   venture capital 63
universities 275–6, 399
university graduates, and finance 368
university spin-outs 356
Unwalla, D. B. 272, 277
Upton, N. 420
Ursic, M. L. 436
US Bureau of Labor Statistics 221
user technical entrepreneurs 281
Utsch, A. 126
Utterback, J. M. 279
Uzzi, B. D. 325

Vahlne, J. 399, 435, 436, 437, 438
Vaidyanathan, P. 277
Vale, P. 10, 11
Van Auken, H. E. 184, 187
van der Leun, J. 83, 84, 202, 215
van der Veen, M. 100, 102, 107
van der Wees, C. 221
van Dijk, J. 405
van Stel, A. 404
Vandenberg, R. J. 167
Varadarajan, P. R. 319

Varis, M. 338
VAT registration 33
Vázquez-Barquero, A. 34
Vega, G. 291
Velamuri, R. 116, 124
Venables, A. J. 34
Venkataraman, S. 24, 25, 96, 97, 108, 116,
   120, 121, 122, 123, 124, 290, 293,
   305, 308
venture capital 63, 260, 320, 367, 377–8, 379,
   384
venture idea 114–16
Veolia 299
Verdin, P. 391
Verduyn, J. K. 292
Verheul, I. 28, 29, 30, 38, 42, 225
Vertovec, S. 215
Vesper, K. H. 101, 114, 120, 129, 396
Victor, D. G. 286
ViewInn 376
Vila das Canoas (Brazil) 299
Virdee, S. 205
Virgin 140, 141
Vissak, T. 437
Vivarelli, M. 411
Vocational and Technical Entrepreneurship
   Act 286
Vojak, B. 270
Volkmann, C. 28
voluntary sector 312–13, 314
Vozikis, G. S. 173
Vurro, C. 307, 313

Wahlbin, C. 271
Wainer, H. A. 269, 270, 280
Wakkee, I. A. M. 100, 102, 107, 292
Waldinger, R. 199, 202, 204, 206, 213
Wales 62, 68–9, 70–2, 75, 190, 286
Walker, D. 300
Wallas, G. 127, 128
WalMart 233
Walras, L. 13
Walsh, J. P. 132, 401
Warburton 233
Ward, R. 130, 199, 204, 205, 207, 208, 210
Waring, A. 383
Warning, S. 37
Warren, E. 190
Warren, L. 405
Warshaw, P. R. 170
Washington, Booker T. 203
Waters, J. 393
Waterstones 372
Watkins, D. S. 221, 278
Watkins, J. 221

Watson, A. 130
Watson, J. 226, 228
Watson, R. 365, 370, 375, 382, 405
Watt, James 273, 345
Watts, T. 50
WCB 349
Webster, F. E. 320
Wedgwood 282–3
Weerawardena, J. 291, 292
Wei-Skillern, J. 307, 311, 314
Weick, K. E. 130, 131
Weiner, B. 168
Weinzimmer, L. G. 422
Weisberg, R. W. 127, 132
Welch, L. S. 432, 435, 442, 443, 448
Welpe, I. 38
Welsch, H. 39, 96, 97–8
Welsh Assembly 69, 70
Welsh Executive 70
Welsh Hybrid Funds 378
Welter, F. 40, 79, 82, 83, 85, 86, 88, 89, 223
Wennekers, S. 29, 30, 31, 404
Wensley, R. 323
Werbner, P. 200, 207
Werker, C. 32, 38
Wesley, C. L. 295
West, G. P. 22
Westerberg, M. 173, 174
Westhead, P. 25, 67, 129, 130, 191, 237, 243,
    244, 245, 252, 253, 255, 256, 257, 259,
    260, 262, 263, 264, 275, 286, 306, 395,
    421
Westlund, H. 32, 39, 40
Wever, E. 405
Wheeler, C. N. 431, 434, 438, 440, 441
Wheelock, J. 84, 85
White, R. E. 131, 132
White, S. 120
Wickham, P. 360
Wicks, P. J. 68
Wiebe, F. 169
Wiedenmayer, G. 158
Wiedersheim-Paul, F. 432, 435, 442, 443, 448
Wiersema, F. D. 395, 398
Wigren, C. 86
Wiklund, J. 2, 85, 169, 171, 261, 262, 293, 311,
    394, 405, 406, 407
Wilkinson, Chris 350
Wilkinson, F. 275, 276
Willard, G. E. 395
William Grant's 246
Williams, C. 89, 142
Williams, David 349
Williams, L. 224, 225, 226
Williams, N. 38, 41, 43

Williams, P. 340, 351
Williamson, P. 391
Wilpert, C. 201, 202
Wilson Committee 364, 367, 371, 372
Wilson, F. 174, 226
Wilson, N. 369
Wiltbank, R. E. 163, 165, 378, 379
Winborg, J. 105, 182
Wintjes, R. 35
Withey, J. J. 441
WJRJ 142
Wolff, E. N. 279
women see female entrepreneurs
Womenable 220
Wong, C. 63
Wong, P. K. 166, 175
Woo, C. Y. 129, 167, 257, 279, 390, 395, 398
Wood, R. 173
Woodman, R. W. 125
Woodruff, R. B. 320
Woods, A. 325
Woods, C. 306, 307
Woodward, M. D. 211
Woodward, W. 340
word of mouth 323, 333–4, 336
Work Programme 63
workers' cooperatives 296
World Bank 39, 88
Wozniak, Steve 284
Wright, M. 23, 25, 129, 130, 191, 252, 253, 254,
    255, 256, 257, 259, 260, 261, 262, 263,
    264, 265, 306, 421
Wyer, P. 418, 421, 423, 424
Wynarczyk, P. 319, 398, 405

Yasin, M. 277
Yonkers, V. 409
York, J. G. 290
Young S. 432, 434, 436, 437, 438, 439, 446
Young, L. 205
Young, S. 432, 434, 437, 438, 439, 441
Your Business Matters 54
Yucelt, U. 166
Yukl, G. 125
Yunus, Muhammad 289, 299

Zacharakis, A. L. 184, 185
Zafarullah, M. 441
Zahra, S. A. 78, 88, 90, 116, 242, 270, 293, 294,
    338, 431
Zambia 223
Zander, U. 109
Zanussi 349
Zegveld, W. 270
Zewde and Associates 223

Zhang, J. 351
Zhang, Z. 179
Zhao, H. 156, 157, 159
Zietsma, C. 129
Zimmer, C. 18, 38, 129, 325, 338, 340, 351, 356, 360

Zografos, C. 312
Zontanos, G. 324
Zott, C. 97, 313, 323
Zou, S. 439
Zuckerberg, Mark 157
Zukin, S. 81

184737